HOME APPLIANCE REPAIR MANUAL

Popular Mechanics

HOME APPLIANCE REPAIR MANUAL

Hearst Books
New York

Printed in the United States of America
Copyright © 1981 The Hearst Corporation

Published by The Hearst Corporation, New York, New York

Library of Congress Cataloging in Publication Data

Main entry under title:

Popular mechanics home appliance repair manual.

Includes index.

1. Household appliances—Maintenance and repair—Amateurs' manuals. I. Bragdon, Allen. II. Popular mechanics magazine. III. Title: Home appliance repair manual.
TX298.P66 643'.6 80-29670

ISBN O-910990-75-1

Staff and Contributors

Editor-in-Chief, Allen Bragdon
Project Director, Judson Mead
Managing Editor, Katherine Scott

Writers: Introduction—Joseph Foley. Large Appliances—Don Nelson. Small Appliances—Frank Farnham, Lynn Sonberg, Harry Wagner.

Text Editors: Peter Easton, Colin Leinster

Technical Consultants: George McNally, Sven Selander, Milton Wallach

Cover Photography: David Arky

The editors would like to acknowledge with appreciation the technical expertise and thirty years practical experience with the repair of small appliances that Milton Wallach, President, and George McNally, foreman, of Electra-Craft, Inc., New York City, contributed to this book.

Contents

Introduction
How to get the most
out of this book

However sophisticated an appliance might seem, its components are usually simply assembled and its operating principles easy to understand. If you know how it works and follow correct procedures, repairs are easy to make in the vast majority of appliance malfunctions. It is for the home owner who decides to do his or her own repairs—whether to save on repair costs or simply for the satisfaction of doing the job at home—that the *Home Appliance Repair Manual* has been conceived and edited.

There are two main sections in the pages that follow: one covers large appliances, such as refrigerators, ranges, and furnaces, that ordinarily would require a service call to your home when they break down; the other deals with smaller appliances, such as mixers and vacuum cleaners, that would otherwise have to go into the repair shop when they malfunction. The appliance entries in each section are arranged alphabetially. Each begins with a detailed exploded view showing how the parts of the appliance interconnect and operate, and, most important, where the likely sources of trouble lie. These "Troublespots," as we call them, are your visual troubleshooting guide. They tell you where to look in the repair instructions to find out how to deal with the problem. All the repair instructions that follow are illustrated. We photographed the most competent professionals in the business doing the jobs you will be able to do. Wherever a photograph can't show a procedure or component clearly, we have included a detailed drawing.

All appliances, especially large ones, benefit from periodic tune-ups and regular maintenance just as much as any automobile does. The information and step-by-step tune-up and maintenance procedures for large appliances are probably the most important parts of those entries. Even if you never make a large appliance repair yourself, you can save real dollars in repair costs, energy costs, and a long service life for your appliances by following the instructions given in this book.

The section on major appliances describes, for each type, all the procedures you need to know to fix the model you own. The small appliance section gives repair instructions for several different brands of each appliance so that the important variations between brands are clear. If you have one of the models for which specific instructions are given, simply follow those. If you own a model not covered specifically, read the steps for all the different brands and adapt the procedures appropriate for yours.

Before starting any repair, it is important to read the Blue Pages, the section that begins on page 10. This section describes in simple language how electricity works in your home and what you need to know about it to work safely on electrical appliances. Also read Appliance Repair Basics, which starts on page 24. It gives you a lot of useful facts that apply to all appliances—how motors work, where to look for hidden screws, and the like. The Appendix, begining on page 311, describes and shows the tools you need to make successful repairs. It also lists the names, addresses, and telephone numbers of parts suppliers in different regions of the country that can provide hard-to-find parts not always available locally.

Look for These Important Symbols

These little needle-nose pliers identify Bench Tips—shortcuts and tricks that professionals have developed by doing the same repair jobs again and again. The Bench Tips will save time and frustration.

CAUTION We repeat the general rules of appliance repair safety throughout the book. But we mark special cautions as reminders. Don't ignore them! Observing the cautions will make the job go safely and successfully.

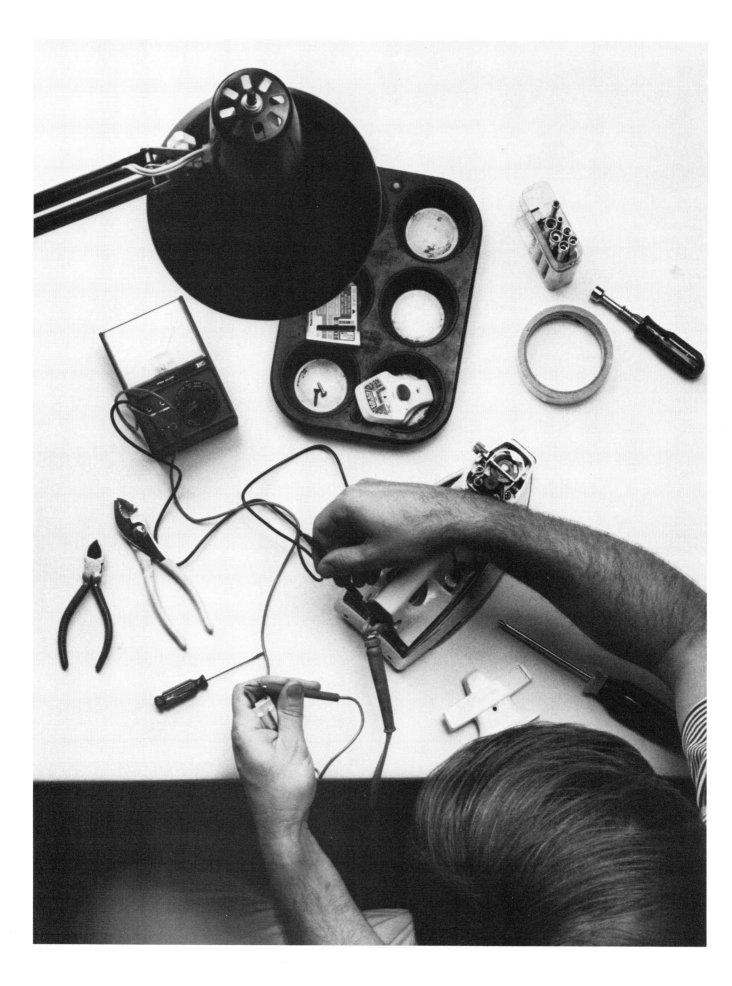

Blue Pages

Everything you need to know about electricity

Basic electricity

To locate trouble in an appliance and to correct the trouble in the most efficient way, it is helpful—not absolutely essential, but helpful—to know something about what electricity is and what some of the most common electrical terms mean. The words and pictures in this section provide a quick review of basic electricity. The electrical terms used in this book are defined in the Glossary found on page 12.

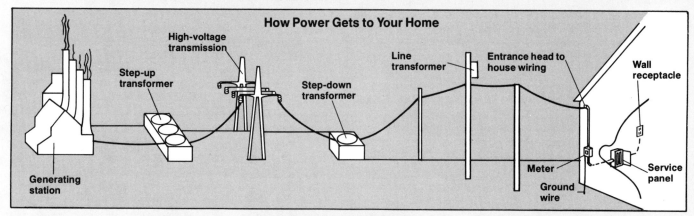

How Power Gets to Your Home

High-voltage transmission · Step-up transformer · Step-down transformer · Line transformer · Entrance head to house wiring · Wall receptacle · Generating station · Meter · Ground wire · Service panel

Generating stations operated by electric utility companies convert either fossil fuel (coal, oil), hydroelectric energy (flowing water), or atomic energy (from nuclear reactors) into electrical energy. This electrical energy is then transmitted by wires to factories, offices, schools, and homes, where it is used.

Unless the power lines in your neighborhood are underground, you have probably noticed that power lines to buildings lead from large canister-shaped devices on utility poles. These devices are called line transformers or pole transformers.

Electricity is transmitted over long distances most efficiently when the voltage is extremely high and the amperage low. The voltage in alternating-current systems is raised or lowered very efficiently by transformers. Applying power to step-up transformers automatically raises the voltage and reduces the amperage. Applying power to step-down transformers reverses the process.

Transformers allow utility companies to get the high voltage levels needed for low-loss cross-country transmission and to reduce voltage when power reaches the consumer.

Utility companies distribute power by raising the voltage to high levels (sometimes as much as 750,000 volts), and then sending it over the high-power lines often seen in rural areas. When these lines reach towns and cities, transformer action is again used to reduce the voltage. The reduction is accomplished in steps as power is distributed, so that the highest practical voltage level can be maintained until the power reaches the consumer. The final voltage reduction takes place on the line transformers mounted on utility poles. Power is carried from these transformers to buildings for use by the consumer.

All matter is composed of atoms. Atoms, in turn, are made up of particles called protons, neutrons, and electrons. One of these particles, the electron, is the source of electrical energy.

Most electrons are bound to a single atom, but some can move from one atom to another. The ones that can move are called free electrons. Copper, steel, and aluminum are called conductors because their atoms have many free electrons and so can conduct electricity efficiently. Wires made of these metals are ideal for transmitting electricity with little loss of power.

Test Your Knowledge of Basic Electricity

If you can score 100 on this quiz, you probably know enough to skip to the *Electrical testers* section of this introduction on page 14.

PART 1
Fill in the blanks in the following statements:

1. Electric current is the free flow of _____ along an electrical conductor.

2. The rate of electron (current) flow is measured in_____.

3. Resistance to the free flow of current in an electrical circuit is measured in _____.

4. The pressure to restore electron balance in a circuit from either a shortage or a surplus to neutral is measured in_____.

5. The work performed by electrical energy is measured in_____.

6. Which of the following are conductors rather than insulators: rubber, copper, plastic, steel, aluminum, paper, wood?_____.

PART 2
Choose the correct word or phrase to complete each statement:

1. The voltage level(s) available in virtually every U.S. household is: (1) 60 and 120; (2) 100 and 150; (3) 200; (4) 120 and 240.

2. The formula for measuring work done by electrical energy is: (1) voltage equals amperage times wattage; (2) wattage equals voltage times amperage; (3) voltage equals wattage divided by amperage; (4) wattage equals voltage divided by amperage.

3. Wire is sometimes coiled around a metal core to: (1) produce heat; (2) increase resistance; (3) create a magnetic field; (4) regulate voltage.

PART 3
Match each wire type with its insulation color (NOTE: More than one insulation color may be used for each type of wire):

hot wire _____

neutral wire _____

grounding wire _____

(1) black; (2) green; (3) gray; (4) red; (5) no insulation; (6) white; (7) blue.

PART 4
The following statements are either true or false:

1. Direct current is required by most kinds of appliances._____

2. The grounding wire in an electrical circuit is the most dangerous as a cause of shock.

3. The neutral wire in an electrical circuit is the main power source_____

4. A high-resistance short circuit makes an appliance operate abnormally without blowing a fuse or tripping a circuit breaker._____

5. The neutral wire in an electrical circuit never causes shock._____

6. An electrical circuit is a combination of source, conductor, load, and switching that enables electrical power to do work._____

Answers to this quiz appear on page 12.

Free Electrons Moving from Atom to Atom

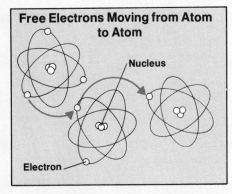

Other materials such as rubber, plastic, paper, and wood are composed of atoms that have almost no free electrons. These materials cannot conduct electricity efficiently, and so they are called insulators.

A wire made of copper or aluminum enclosed in some insulating material provides a safe and efficient way to move electrical energy. These insulated wires are used to carry electricity from the generating plant to the user.

Current Flow between Wires

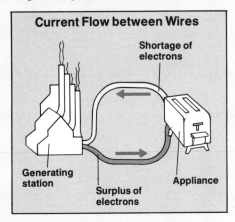

The action of an electrical generator causes all the free electrons in a conductor to move in the same direction. When this happens, a surplus of electrons is created in the atoms of one wire at the output of a generator and a shortage of electrons is created in the atoms of a second output wire from the generator.

When an electrical appliance is connected to the generator wires, electrons move along an electrical path through the appliance in order to restore the natural balance. As long as the generating station is in operation, the electron shortage and surplus in the two wires will be maintained and a force will exist between the two wires to cause an electron to move.

The term current flow describes this electron movement. The rate of the current flow (that is, the number of electrons that pass a point in one second) is measured in units called amperes, commonly shortened to amps.

The force that exists to restore the natural electron balance depends upon how great the difference is between the surplus and the shortage. The larger the difference, the greater the force. This force (or pressure) is called voltage, and the units in which it is measured are volts.

A point that has neither a surplus nor a shortage of electrons is electrically neutral. Electrically neutral points are called ground. Ground means simply the earth or a conductor connected to the earth. The connection can be made via a metal cold-water pipe in your home

(below) or a copper rod driven into the ground near where electrical power enters a house (see drawing, page 18).

The volume of matter represented by the earth is so large that a measurable surplus or shortage of electrons never exists in it. Therefore, earth, or ground, is always electrically neutral. Ground, as well as wires connected to ground, can accept electrons or give them up as necessary to cause electron flow (current flow) between ground and a point at which a shortage or surplus exists.

In home electrical systems, power is distributed to most appliances by two wires. One of the two wires always has either a surplus or a shortage of electrons. This wire is commonly called the hot wire and it almost always has black or red (sometimes blue) insulation. The other wire must always have white or gray insulation and it is called the neutral (or power ground) wire because at some point it is connected to ground.

CAUTION Remember, electrons will flow from *any* ground point to the hot wire when a path exists. When the path is through a human body, shock occurs. To reduce the possibility of shock, some electrical circuits have a third wire called a grounding wire. When a failure occurs in electrical wiring, the grounding wire provides a lower-resistance path to ground than the human body. The grounding wire is usually bare (no insulation), but it may have green (occasionally green and yellow) insulation.

Basement Ground

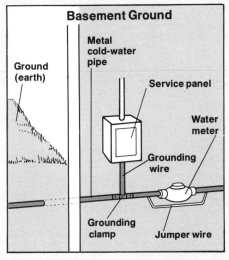

Both the neutral and the grounding wires are connected to ground, but each performs a different job in electrical wiring. The job of the grounding wire is to provide a path to ground for electrical energy when any failure occurs in the house wiring system or in an electrical appliance. Throughout this book the term grounding wire refers to these safety wires. The job of the white or gray neutral wire is to provide the normal path

BENCH TIP

The color of the wire tells you something about the wire in your home electrical system.

Black, red, or blue	hot wire
White or gray	neutral wire
Bare or green	grounding wire

for return current flow to the source when no wiring failure exists. Throughout this book the term hot wire refers to the wire with black, red, or blue insulation. This is the wire that causes current to flow between it and the neutral wire (or the grounding wire if a failure occurs).

Magnetic Field around a Wire

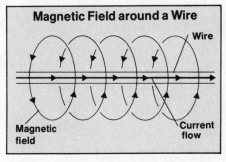

When electricity is generated, the electron imbalance that occurs represents stored energy. If electrons can move between the two points of surplus and shortage, some of the stored energy is released. All materials offer some opposition to this movement of electrons. This opposition is called electrical resistance, and it is measured in units called ohms. When resistance is low, current flow (electron flow) is heavy. When current flow is heavy, electrons tend to bump into each other. When this happens, some of the electron energy is converted to heat. It is this action that makes the wires in room heaters and surface units on electric ranges glow red when the units are turned on.

When current flows through a wire, another phenomenon occurs. A magnetic field is created around the wire.

Magnetic Field in a Motor Winding

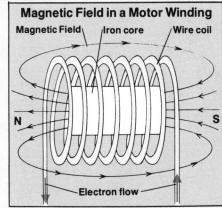

The strength of this field in a single wire is quite small. When many coils of wire are wound around an iron core, however, the magnetic field of each strand adds to the one next to it, and a strong magnetic field is created. It is the attraction and repulsion of the magnetic fields created in this way that makes an electric motor run.

Now, to review for a moment, electricity consists of voltage and current. Voltage can be thought of as pressure, the pressure that exists to restore the natural balance of electrons in atoms. Current can be thought of as the movement of electrons that occurs as a result of the voltage. Both voltage and current flow must be present for electricity to do work.

VOLTS X AMPERES = WATTS

The work done by the combination of voltage and current is found by multiplying the number of volts (pressure) present between two points (wires) by the number of amps of current that flow through the resistance along a path between the two points. The units in which the product of the multiplication is expressed are called watts. In other words, watts equals volts times amps.

Watts represent work performed by electrical energy. Most electrical appliances are rated according to wattage. Nameplates on toasters, vacuum cleaners, and ovens show power consumption in watts. Virtually all households have two voltage levels available: 120 and 240 volts. The nameplate also shows the voltage at which the appliance should be operated. Because wattage is the product of voltage times amperage (current), when you know the voltage you can find the current flow by dividing the wattage by the voltage. A toaster designed to plug into a 120-volt wall receptacle and rated at 1,320 watts has a current flow of 11 amperes (1,320 ÷ 120).

Note that the amount of power consumed by the toaster depends on how long it is used. To calculate power, time as well as voltage must be considered. A 100-watt lamp turned on for an hour uses the same amount of power as a 200-watt lamp turned on for half an hour.

About AC and DC

Electricity can be generated in two quite different forms. One is called alternating current (AC), the other, direct current (DC).

Alternating current is almost universally used for home electric appliances and is, therefore, the form of electricity this book is primarily concerned with. In an AC circuit, the amount of voltage present in the circuit is constantly changing from zero to a peak value and back to zero in one direction and then from zero to a peak value and back to zero in the other direction. The peak voltage is determined by the generating plant. Because voltage is the force, or pressure, that causes current to flow, the current also changes from zero to a peak value to zero and will reverse direction and repeat. The peak amount of current, however, is determined by the load resistance; it can vary as the load resistance varies. Each complete change from zero to maximum to zero in one direction and then zero to maximum to zero in the opposite direction is called 1 hertz (formerly "cycle per second"). The term hertz implies *per second*; therefore, 60 hertz means 60 cycles per second. You may see "cycles per second" marked on older appliances; the abbreviation is "cps."

Direct current in homes is found mostly in the form of electrical energy stored in batteries. The voltage and the direction of application are constant in a DC circuit. The amount of voltage is determined by the type and size of the battery. The direction of current flow is also constant and, as in AC circuits, the amount of current flow will vary if the load resistance varies. Batteries convert chemical energy to electrical energy. Batteries can be either wet as in a car battery or dry as in flashlight and transistor radio batteries. All wet batteries and some dry ones can be recharged from a DC rectifier plugged into an AC source. Unless recharged, the voltage from all batteries will gradually decrease.

Glossary

Alternating current (AC). The voltage and current in this form of electrical energy are constantly changing in amount and are periodically changing in direction of flow. This is the form of electrical power used in almost all home utility systems. (See box, below, left, for details.)

Ampere (amp), aperage. These terms refer to the amount of current flowing in a circuit as a result of the voltage applied and the resistance of the load (an appliance, a motor, or a lamp).

Branch circuit. A circuit wired from the service panel to a part of your home. Every branch circuit has its own circuit breaker or fuse to prevent too much current from flowing into the circuit.

Circuit. A combination of power source, conductors, switching, and load that allows electrical power to do work.

Circuit breaker. A switch that cuts off power to a circuit automatically when current flow is greater than the rating for the circuit breaker. Circuit breakers can also be operated manually so that power can be switched off, for example, for making repairs.

Conductor. Any material (usually metal) that offers low resistance to electrical current and can therefore be used to transmit it.

Direct current (DC). The form of electrical energy stored in batteries. The voltage in a DC circuit remains constant as long as the source (usually a battery) remains charged. (See box at left for details.)

Electron. One of the particles in an atom. Free electrons can move from atom to atom, and this produces an electrical current.

Fuse. A device that safely breaks the flow of current in a circuit when the amperage exceeds the rating of the fuse.

Ground. A path for current flow that leads outside the circuit. It can be provided intentionally as a safety feature of the circuit (see *Grounding wire*, below). A ground can also occur inadvertently if, owing to broken insulation, a bent heating element, or a faulty repair, a part of the circuit within the appliance touches a material—such as the housing of a toaster—that offers a path for some of the current flow. This is also known as a high-resistance short.

Grounding wire. A safety wire, usually bare but sometimes with green (and occasionally green and yellow) insulation, that provides a safe path to ground for hot-wire current in case of circuit failure.

Hertz (Hz). A new term for the older "cycles per second" ("cps"). The number of hertz in an AC power source is the number of times per second the electrical power goes through a complete change in amplitude and direction. Home power is 60 hertz. The term applies to AC only, not DC.

Hot wire. The electric wire that causes current to flow through any path to ground. Any electrical wire can give a shock, but a hot wire is the most dangerous. This wire usually has black or red (occasionally blue) insulation.

Kilowatt-hour (kwh). The unit of measurement for power consumed. One kilowatt-hour is the equivalent of 1,000 watts used for one hour. Electric bills are based on kilowatt-hours.

Load. Any device in an electrical circuit that changes electrical power into another form of energy: light, mechanical movement, heat, etc.

Neutral wire. The electric wire in your home with white or gray insulation. This wire provides the normal return path for current flow to the power source. It is sometimes called the power ground wire.

Ohm. The term for the unit of measure for resistance to the flow of electrical current.

Overload. The result of too many appliances connected to one circuit or of a circuit or appliance failure. Overload may merely result in minor overheating in wires; in more severe cases, the circuit breaker trips or the fuse blows.

Power (electrical). The combination of voltage and current that provides the electrical energy to perform work. The unit of measure for power is the watt (see below).

Resistance. The characteristic of some materials and devices whereby the material opposes current flow. The unit of measure of resistance is the ohm.

Service panel. A panel, containing either circuit breakers or fuses, that distributes power entering your home to the branch circuits.

Source. Any point of origin for power. The service panel or a wall receptacle in your home can be considered a source.

Switch. A device for interrupting and restoring current flow.

Transformer. Transformers are used in AC power systems to raise or lower the voltage.

Volt; voltage. The unit of force that causes current to flow between a hot wire and any point connected to ground is the volt. Most home electrical systems are supplied with either 120 or 240 volts.

Watt; wattage. The electrical power consumed by a load is measured in watts, which are found by multiplying voltage by amperage: i.e, if a 3-amp current is flowing in a 120-volt circuit, 360 watts are being consumed.

Answers to Basic Electricity Quiz on page 10

PART 1	PART 3
1. electrons	Hot wire—(1), (4), (7)
2. amps	Neutral wire—(3), (6)
3. ohms	Grounding wire—(2), (5)
4. volts	
5. watts	
6. copper, steel, aluminum	**PART 4**
	1. False
PART 2	**2.** False
1. (4)	**3.** False
2. (2)	**4.** True
3. (3)	**5.** False
	6. True

Electrical circuits

To get work done with electrical energy (volts and amperes), there must be a continuous path for electron flow between a wire having an electron shortage and a wire having an electron surplus. Electrons will move along this path and provide energy to generate heat or light and to make motors run. The path along which electrons flow is an electrical circuit. Electrical circuits have four parts: a source of power, wires to carry the power where it is needed, some way to control power (stop and start the flow), and an appliance or other device to use the power.

The real source of power is the utility company generator plant. However, for the purposes of appliance repair, the source is considered to be the wall receptacle into which the appliance is plugged.

Conductors. The wires or strips of metal that carry the electrical energy to the place at which work will be done are conductors. Conductors offer only slight resistance to current flow because the atoms in the metals they are made of have lots of free electrons. The external conductors for most appliances are in the cord and plug. Of course, appliances also have internal conductors.

Load. Any device (a lamp, a radio, a washing machine) that uses electrical energy to perform some work is a load. The load (unlike the con-

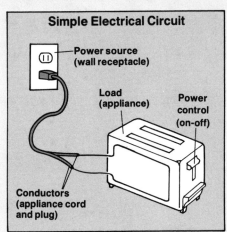

Simple Electrical Circuit

Power source (wall receptacle)

Load (appliance)

Power control (on-off)

Conductors (appliance cord and plug)

ductors) offers considerable resistance to current flow. This high resistance makes it possible for the device to convert electrical energy to another form of energy: light, sound, or mechanical movement. The load resistance determines how much current flows in a circuit. If the resistance in the load increases, the current flowing in the circuit automatically decreases. The watt is a unit of power that indicates the rate at which the load is consuming power. To get the wattage, multiply the voltage applied to a circuit (which is usually constant) by the current in amperes.

Switch. The final necessary element in a circuit is a means of controlling the flow of energy. Control is provided by a switch, which can interrupt and restore current flow as desired by the user. Switches in home appliances control current flow by introducing a high resistance (air gap) in the circuit to stop current flow, and by removing resistance (closing the air gap) to start current flowing again. Some appliances (electric grills, for example) have no separate switch. The appliance is turned on and off by inserting and removing the plug.

Circuit Faults

Short Circuit

Spark

High-resistance Short

Switch

Heating element (hidden)

Spark

Live wire touching frame

Fan assembly

Open Circuit

Broken wire

Now that you know what an electrical circuit is, let's find out about the two most common circuit faults: the short circuit and the open circuit.

A short circuit is a fault that exists when there is a path for current flow other than the normal path through an appliance. For example, in a room heater (above, left), a short circuit could occur if, because of wear or broken insulation, the two conductors in the line cord touched. The resulting high current flow would cause the fuse to blow or the circuit breaker to trip, thus shutting off power to the appliance.

A high-resistance short is another type of short circuit. Typically, this fault occurs inside the appliance itself: through wear or breakage, a part of the circuit touches a metal part, such as the metal housing or a motor part, forming a secondary path for current flow. This type of short is also called a ground, because current is diverted out of the circuit. This ground does not lead to earth, however, but to a metal part of your appliance.

The path may offer enough resistance so that current flow remains low: the fuse will not blow; the circuit breaker will not trip to OFF. The appliance, however, will not operate normally because the secondary path diverts current from the appliance load. If, in the center illustration of the room heater, current is diverted from the heating element to the core of the motor, the heater will operate but will not produce enough heat. If the short is to the housing of the appliance, you may get a shock when you touch it. To test whether a high-

resistance short has occurred, see *Testing for ground*, page 16. You should test an appliance for ground after every repair, and it is a good idea to test any new appliance for ground before plugging it in.

An open circuit is simply a break in the continuous path necessary for current flow (above, right). The effect is usually the same as turning off a switch or pulling a plug. The difference, of course, is that the appliance cannot be turned on again. In an appliance containing both motors and heating elements, breaks may cause only part of the appliance to stop working. Motors contain coils of wire. If a break occurs in these coils, the motor will not run, but heating elements and indicator lights will still function normally.

Electrical testers

Open circuits, short circuits, and high-resistance shorts (grounds) in electrical appliances are generally not visible from outside the unit. Testers must be used to find the source of the trouble. Before using any tester, disconnect the appliance or the part being checked from the supply of electricity. It is not enough to turn the appliance off; the cord must be pulled from the receptacle also.

Continuity refers to the continuous path through which electricity flows without being interrupted. Continuity is mentioned often in this book. When there is an interruption in electron flow, electricity cannot reach the point it is supposed to reach, and the appliance will not work. The job of the home appliance repairman, therefore, is to find the point of interrruption and fix it. The simplest instrument for making continuity tests is called a continuity tester.

Continuity tester

The continuity tester can be a penlike or flashlight-type device. The first has a needle probe at one end and a flexible test lead with an alligator clip at the other; the flashlight device has two alligator clips. The tester generally contains one or two batteries and a low-voltage lamp. (Some testers can be plugged into a wall receptacle for power.) When current flows from the alligator clip to the tip of the probe, the lamp lights. The continuity tester contains its own source of power and is *always* used with the appliance's power turned off at the fuse box or circuit breaker. It is an excellent device for checking repairs before applying power. It is also used to test for ground. You can also test the tester itself; see *Bench Tip* below.

Voltage tester

The voltage tester consists of a plastic holder containing a neon lamp and two probes (test leads) attached to the holder. The neon lamp lights if the test leads touch live power lines or anything connected to those lines. When no voltage is present, the lamp does not light. Since the lamp will also not light when the tester is defective, it is important to test the tester before using it (see *Bench Tip*, below). This tester is useful when you are repairing both small and large appliances; make sure yours can be used to test both 120- and 240-volt lines.

The continuity tester and the voltage tester are "yes-or-no" testers. If the continuity tester lights when the leads are touched to each end of a circuit, there is a low-resistance path for current flow between the points where the test was made. If the tester does not light, there is either a break in the current-flow path or there is a high-resistance path that limits current flow to an amount so small the tester lamp does not light. Also, the voltage tester tells only whether voltage is or is not present at the points tested.

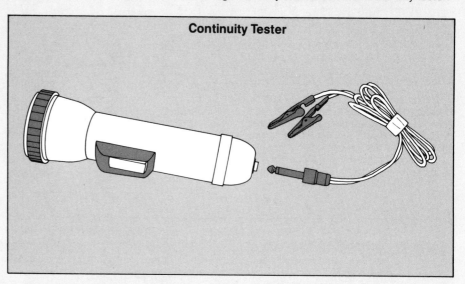

Continuity Tester

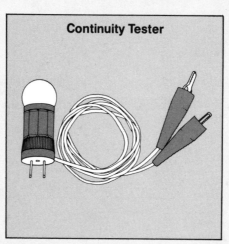

Continuity Tester

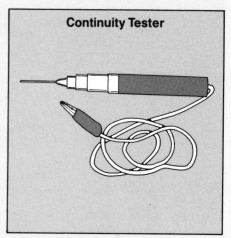

Continuity Tester

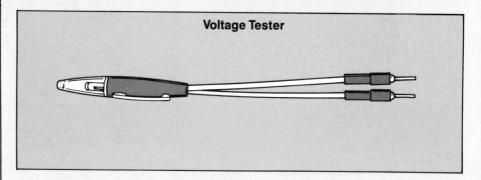

Voltage Tester

 BENCH TIP

Testing the Tester

The continuity tester can easily be checked by touching the tips of the alligator clips or the probes together. If the light goes on, the battery, the bulb, and the tester are all OK. If the light doesn't go on, try changing the bulb. If the light still doesn't go on, replace the battery. If the light still doesn't go on, the wiring in the tester is defective and you should buy a new one. Always test the tester!

The voltage tester can be tested by plugging it into a live receptacle. Touch one probe to the screw on the outside of the cover plate (or the ground slot in a three-slot outlet) and the other to each slot. The bulb should light in one of the two slots.

The multitester or VOM

For more efficient troubleshooting, it is often desirable to know *how much* resistance there is in a current path, or *how much* voltage is present at some point in an appliance, or *how much* current is flowing between two points. For this type of measurement, the best instrument is a multitester called a VOM, or volt-ohm meter. A VOM combines a number of functions in one instrument, usually including an AC/DC voltmeter, ammeter, and ohmmeter. The instruction booklet accompanying a new VOM explains exactly how to use the tester for the various functions it performs. VOM controls are described below.

Volt-ohm Meter (VOM)

Dial and pointer. Test results are shown by needle movement across a dial. The dial contains several scales to show results of resistance tests, voltage tests, and current tests. Note that the resistance scale on most multitesters is the back-off type: that is, the 0 on the resistance scale is opposite the 0 on the voltage and current scales.

Pointer adjustment. A slotted-screw adjustment at the center of the dial allows the meter needle to be set exactly to 0 volts, an adjustment for voltage readings only. Remove the test leads when making this adjustment.

Ohms adjustment. A separate adjustment—usually a small knob—is used to zero the resistance reading. Insert the test leads in the jacks. Set the selector switch to an OHMS position, and touch the tips of the test probes firmly together. Adjust the knob until the meter reads 0 ohms. VOMs contain one or more penlight (type AA) batteries that supply the power for resistance measurement. If the meter cannot be set to 0, the batteries should be replaced. NQTE: Adjust your meter to 0 every time you change the RX setting.

Selector switch. The switch sets the meter to measure either voltage, resistance (ohms), or current (amps). Note that there is more than one switch position (for different ranges of magnitude) for each type of measurement. NOTE: The number of switch positions may vary from VOM to VOM.

For voltage and current measurement, the switch position indicates the amount of voltage or current that causes full-scale deflection in that range. Readings are taken on the scale that applies to the switch setting of the meter needle chosen. To avoid damage to the meter when you are not sure how much voltage is present at a test point, set the selector to the highest voltage available, such as 1,000 volts AC. If only slight movement of the needle occurs, move the switch to the next lower position, such as 250 volts AC. For greatest accuracy, use the meter scale that gives you a reading somewhere near the middle of the scale.

At the settings for resistance (ohm) measurement, numbers must be multiplied by the reading in order to get the correct resistance. The same scale is used for all readings, but the number on the scale is multiplied by the number shown at the switch position. "RX1" means the scale is read directly. "RX10" means scale numbers must be multiplied by 10 to obtain the value of resistance being measured. "RX100" means multiply by 100.

Jack

Test lead

Test lead and jack. Test leads and test jacks are color-coded. The black lead is inserted in the black jack and the red lead in the red jack. Some meters have more than one set of test jacks. Different jacks may be used for different types of measurement.

Test probes. The bare metal needles at the ends of the test probes must be touched to the points at which readings are to be taken. To avoid shock when testing a live circuit, it is best to use alligator clips, which are available as accessories to VOMs. The procedure for testing is as follows: disconnect the appliance (pull out the plug) and attach the alligator clips to the test point in the appliance. When the test probes are in place, plug in and turn on the appliance and note the meter reading without touching the appliance. After the test, remove the wall plug and then disconnect the alligator clips.

How to use a VOM

A VOM is an extremely versatile and useful instrument that can do many jobs. It can, for example, measure current (in milliamps) drawn by a small appliance from a power line, measure the voltage used by an appliance, and check the value of a resistor.

How you check continuity with a VOM depends on what you are testing. If the component you are testing on an appliance does not have resistance (load) built into it—for example, a line cord or a switch—continuity is checked with a VOM (set at RX1) the same as with a continuity tester. If the needle moves to the right, it indicates continuity.

If, however, you are testing a component that has resistance (load) built into it—for example, a circuit containing a heating element or a motor—a simple yes-or-no test for continuity does not tell you enough. You need to know whether the component is offering the right *amount* of resistance. For this you use the ohmmeter function on the VOM (set at RX1 or higher), which indicates the amount of resistance in the component. If the amount meets the manufacturer's specifications, the circuit is in proper working condition. If the resistance is too high or too low, the component is damaged and should be repaired or replaced.

Testing a switch

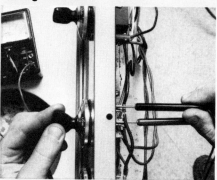

To measure heating element resistance, turn the appliance off and disconnect the element leads. Set the VOM meter at RX1 or higher and touch the probes to the element terminals. Read the resistance on the meter's ohmmeter scale.

Testing a heating element

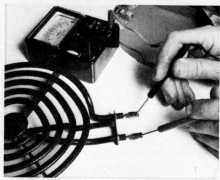

To test switch continuity, turn the appliance off and disconnect the switch leads. Set the VOM at RX1 and touch the probes to the switch terminals. The meter should show continuity at all settings except off.

Testing for Ground

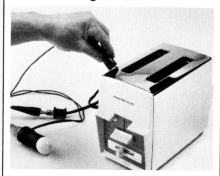

When you have finished reassembling any appliance, before you plug it in test it for ground to make sure there is no short within it. (It is also a good idea to test a new appliance to be sure it's not a lemon!) The test is simple but necessary. It can be made with a continuity tester or a VOM.

If you are using a continuity tester, clip one lead to one of the prongs on the cord plug. Turn the switch to ON. Touch the other lead to various metal parts on the outside of the appliance, including screws and metal trim. If the tester shows continuity at any point, you have a short (ground). Disassemble the appliance and fix the unwanted contact. Then reassemble it and test again for ground.

If you are using a VOM, set it to RX10 or RX1K and follow the same procedure as for the continuity tester. If you have any reading at all on your multitester, however slight, take the appliance apart and find the short. Reassemble it and repeat the test.

Checking Continuity

Most electrical repairs are made to restore continuity to an electrical circuit. A continuity test helps locate the break in the circuit, and enables you to test the success of your repair job—without plugging in your appliance.

To check continuity, let's use the example of a room heater. The illustration at right is a schematic of a simple room heater. The dashed line encloses items inside the heater; the rest of the drawing is the cord and plug.

The test. Any or all segments of an electrical circuit in an appliance can be tested for continuity. Start by attaching the VOM to the prongs of the plugs (points A and B). Turn the appliance switch to ON (unit is unplugged). If the VOM records a reading, there probably is continuity through the whole appliance— "probably," because a short circuit in the line cord can cause the VOM to show continuity. To test the cord, turn the appliance to OFF. If the meter indicates a resistance, the line cord may be shorted. The switch may also be defective. Disconnect a switch lead and test again. If the meter stays where it is, then the line cord is OK.

You can find the point of trouble by probing each segment. For example, place the leads of the VOM across the switch (points C and D). Flip on the switch but do not plug in the heater. If the switch is off, electricity cannot flow and no continuity should show. With the switch on,

This symbol represents the heater on/off switch.

This symbol represents the thermostat that senses the temperature in the room and turns the heater on and off automatically to maintain an even temperature. (Heat controls are described in more detail on page 26.)

This is the symbol for electrical resistance. As used, it represents the heating coils, the wires that glow red when the heater is turned on. Whenever this symbol is used, it identifies concentrated, or "lumped," resistance, that is, any location having more resistance than straight (not coiled) wire.

A
B
C
D
E
F

Room heater schematic

there should be a reading on the meter. If there is not, the switch is defective. Replace it.

Now skip to points D and E, across the thermostat. The thermostat points have to be closed, too. Now skip to points E and F. There should be some resistance.

Lack of continuity indicates a defective thermostat. All segments in an electrical circuit in an appliance can be tested this way to locate breaks in continuity. In this book, you will often be directed to make a continuity test.

Important steps to keep in mind

1. Always, always, unplug an appliance from the wall receptacle before making a continuity test. The purpose of the continuity test is to locate the interruption in the circuit, the path along which electrons flow. To do this, an independent source of electricity (the continuity tester) must be used.

2. The appliance switch must be turned on when testing *most* segments of a circuit.

Two Common Continuity Tests

Testing a cord for continuity

1. Detach one cord lead.

2. Place one tester probe on one prong of the plug.

3. Place the other probe first on one cord lead, then the other. The tester should show continuity on one side only. Continuity on both sides means you have a short circuit in the cord. No continuity means you have an open circuit.

4. Bend the cord back and forth while testing it. If the tester shows intermittent continuity, the cord is defective.

5. Attach one tester probe to the other prong of the plug and repeat the test.

Testing a simple on/off switch for continuity

1. Remove one lead from the switch terminal.

2. Turn the switch to the ON position.

3. Place one tester probe on each terminal. There should be continuity. In the OFF position, there should be no continuity.

Important safety precautions

Remember, you are dealing with electric appliances, and electricity can kill. Read and remember these few precautions. The first is the most important.

1. Never work on an appliance that is plugged in.

2. Have someone around who knows where the service panel is and how to trip the circuit breaker or pull the main fuse block, so that if you make an error, they can cut the power off.

3. Never touch a bare wire without double-checking that the appliance is unplugged. Develop the habit of taping the cord to something so that you see the plug while you work on the unit. The fact that the appliance switch is off (open) does not mean that the appliance is safe. Electricity may find a path to a certain point and that might be the point where you are working.

4. There are times in the course of repairing an appliance when you have to put the plug into the wall and turn on the appliance—when you want to check for voltage, for example. To do this test correctly, follow these steps:

A. Set your VOM for the test you intend to make.

B. Unplug the appliance.

C. Connect the alligator clip lead of the VOM to one of the points where the test is to be made.

D. Now fasten the other alligator clip to the other test point. Keep your free hand away from the appliance.

E. Plug in the appliance and turn the switch to ON.

5. If you must replace a faulty cord, make certain the new cord has conductors of the same gauge as the original. If you are not sure of the gauge, take the old cord with you to the dealer. Undersized cords can cause fire.

6. After you have repaired an appliance, make sure there is no short within it. A short happens when a loose wire comes into contact with part of the housing, deflecting electricity out of the circuit and into the housing or metal parts when the appliance is plugged in and turned on. The user can get a severe shock from touching the housing (see *Testing for ground,* opposite).

7. *Always* check the voltage tester before using it (see page 14).

A word about shock

Electric shock occurs when the human body provides a path along which electric current can flow. When two or more paths are available for the flow of electrical energy, most of the flow will occur along the path that offers the least resistance. The body has many low-resistance paths. If it accidentally becomes part of an electrical circuit, it experiences the heaviest flow of electrical energy—an electric shock.

The way to avoid shock, then, is to avoid contact with the flow of electrical energy: always unplug an appliance before working on it. After you have made your repair, always test for ground before plugging the appliance in again.

The standard means of preventing the possibility of shock are insulating and grounding. By means of insulation, electrical energy is contained in wires, lamps, electrical outlets, and appliances. The energy carrier is enclosed in some material that offers a high resistance to current flow. The rubber or plastic covering on electric wires provides this insulation. Grounding means providing a better path (or lower resistance) to ground for electric energy than the human body. (For a discussion of electrical grounding, see page 11.)

If shock occurs, the victim may not be able to release his or her grip on the hot lead. Turn off the main power immediately if it can be done. If it can't, use a nonconductor such as dry wood or a heavy coat to break the victim's grip on the hot lead; do not touch the victim yourself, or the current will flow through your body too.

When you have broken the victim's grip, call a physician or rescue squad. Keep the victim warm and give artificial respiration by any approved method until help arrives.

Initials for safety

Any discussion of electrical safety would be incomplete without mentioning the Underwriters' Laboratories and the National Electrical Code.

Underwriters' Laboratories (UL) is the most widely used electrical testing laboratory in the United States. Manufacturers submit products for safety tests, and UL issues a report on its findings. Any shortcomings that are uncovered must be corrected by the manufacturer and new samples submitted for testing. Products that perform satisfactorily are listed in UL product directories. Manufacturers whose products are listed in the UL directory are permitted to display the UL symbol on their product.

The UL symbol is your assurance that an appliance meets minimum safety standards. Appliances in a wide range of prices have the UL symbol. Underwriters' Laboratories makes no attempt to judge overall quality, durability, or convenience and is concerned solely with electrical safety standards.

The National Electrical Code (NEC). In 1895, the first nationally recommended electrical code was published. In the years since, this code has developed and changed as technical knowledge and the uses of electricity have increased. It is now called the National Electrical Code (NEC) and is printed and distributed by the National Fire Protection Association; it is everywhere accepted as the basis for safe electrical wiring. The NEC is an advisory document only, but it is meant to be used by lawmakers and regulatory agencies as a basis for local electrical standards and building codes. The NEC becomes law only when it becomes a part of local building codes. Most local codes do, however, refer to the NEC. Whenever applicable, troubleshooting and replacement procedures in this book are in accordance with the NEC.

Power to your appliances

In most houses and apartments, electrical power enters the building on three lines. Two of these are called hot wires because current flows from them to any grounded point. Each carries approximately 120 volts. The third wire is connected to ground and is known as the neutral (or power ground) line. This combination of wires provides two voltage levels for appliances in your home: 120 and 240 volts.

Power enters some small houses and apartments on only two wires, providing only 120 volts. This greatly restricts the use of appliances because of the limited current safely available.

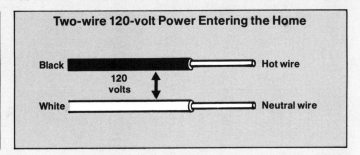

Three-wire 240-volt Power Entering the Home

Red — Hot wire
240 volts
White — Neutral wire
120 volts
120 volts
Black — Hot wire

Two-wire 120-volt Power Entering the Home

Black — Hot wire
120 volts
White — Neutral wire

Electric service to your home

Various devices are used to secure power lines to buildings. The lines must be able to withstand varying weather conditions such as heavy winds or ice. In many cases, the neutral wire doubles as a line support. The wire consists of braided aluminum strands, making it thicker and stronger than the two hot wires. The three wires are then twisted or enclosed in an outer sheath so that the anchoring of the neutral wire to the house provides support for the other two lines. The incoming lines are heavily insulated and sometimes enclosed in a metal conduit, and are then routed to the meter box. Meter boxes are usually mounted on the outside wall of a house, although in some apartment buildings and older houses meters are in the basement.

Reading a Meter

10,000	1,000	100	10	Units
0	3	5	8	7
0	4	5	9	2

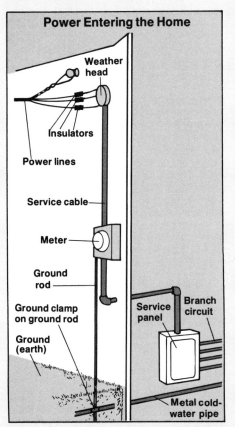

Power Entering the Home

- Weather head
- Insulators
- Power lines
- Service cable
- Meter
- Ground rod
- Ground clamp on ground rod
- Ground (earth)
- Service panel
- Branch circuit
- Metal cold-water pipe

How to read your meter

Utility company bills show the meter readings on which billing is based. If you know how to read your meter, you can check the bill to make certain the reading was accurate.

Meters record power used in units called kilowatt-hours (kwh). Watts are units of power equal to the voltage times the current. A kilowatt-hour represents the use of 1,000 watts for one hour (*kilo* is Greek for 1,000). For example, a washing machine and a refrigerator both running continuously for one hour would consume about one kilowatt of electricity, or 1,000 watts.

The reading on your meter is determined by the positions of pointers on either four or five dials. (While all meters are not the same, most work this way.) Each dial has markings from 0 to 9. The markings on the dials from right to left represent units, tens, hundreds, and so on. The pointer always moves from 0 to 1 to 2 to 3, etc., and back to 0. The pointers on alternate dials move in opposite directions, that is, the numbering of the 10,000-unit dial increases in a clockwise direction, the 1,000-unit dial counterclockwise. The direction of dial rotation is indicated by the way the dials are numbered. Whenever electricity is being used in your home, all the dials move. Each dial moves ten times faster than the dial to its right. Unless power consumption is unusually heavy, movement will be noticeable only on the right-hand dial. To read the meter, start with the dial on the right and note the number the pointer has just passed according to each dial's direction of rotation.

For example, here is a reading of 03587, or 3587 kwh. Meter dials are not precisely marked. The pointer on a dial that may appear to be exactly on a number may actually be slightly above or below it. To decide when a number has been reached or passed, note the pointer on the next dial to the right. If it has not reached 0, the dial you are reading has not reached the nearest number. If the pointer to the right has passed 0, use the next higher number for the dial you are reading.

In the illustration below, the bottom middle dial appears to be on 6, but because the next dial to the right is below 0, the correct reading for the middle dial is actually 5. The full reading is 04592, or 4592 kwh.

Three lines carry power to your home or apartment, going through the meter and then into a service panel that divides the incoming power into circuits. The service panel also contains circuit breakers or fuses to provide protection against overload. The circuit breakers or fuses automatically shut off the power when current flow exceeds a safe level.

All service panels must contain a quick means of shutting off power. Some circuit breaker panels have two main line breakers to produce complete shutoff. Fuse panels often contain a main pullout fuse block that cuts off all incoming power. It is wise to familiarize yourself with the main shutoff on your service panel (the main shutoff may be located outside the house directly under the meter), because in an emergency it is the quickest means of turning off all power.

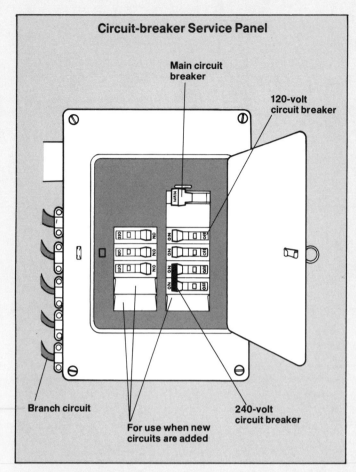

Circuit-breaker Service Panel

Main circuit breaker

120-volt circuit breaker

Branch circuit

For use when new circuits are added

240-volt circuit breaker

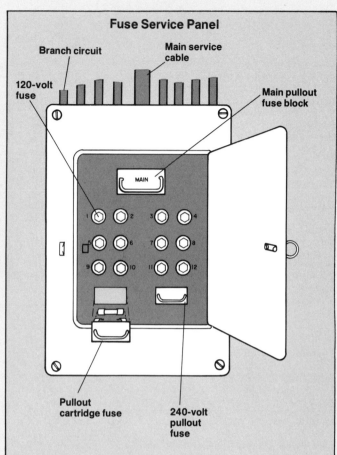

Fuse Service Panel

Branch circuit

Main service cable

120-volt fuse

Main pullout fuse block

Pullout cartridge fuse

240-volt pullout fuse

Household circuits

The service panel is the point at which incoming power is divided into individual circuits. Each circuit is protected by its own circuit breaker or fuse. Modern service installations have any-where from twelve to thirty-two circuits. Four types of individual circuits are used in home power systems:

General-purpose circuits. These 120-volt two- or three-wire (one hot, one neutral, and sometimes one ground) circuits carry power to wall receptacles for general lighting and small appliances. They are usually protected by a 15-amp circuit breaker or fuse.

Appliance circuits. Kitchen and laundry areas, which have greater power needs than other living areas, also have 120-volt two- or three-wire circuits; 20 amps are provided to handle appliance loads.

Individual circuits. Single large appliances such as furnaces and washing machines have individual circuits with a single outlet or recep-tacle. The 120-volt two- or three-wire circuits are usually protected for a 15- or 20-amp load.

Heavy-duty circuits. Large appliances such as central air conditioners, ranges, and clothes driers are more efficiently operated at 240 volts than at 120. A 240-volt circuit may require three wires: two hot and one ground wire. Occasion-ally a 240-volt circuit has a fourth wire (neutral); these circuits are protected by two circuit breakers or fuses joined together by a common connector.

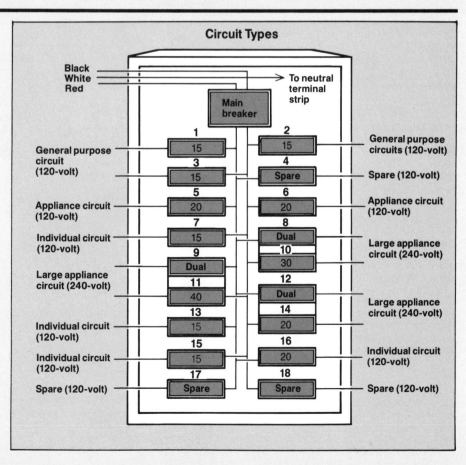

Circuit Types

Black
White
Red

To neutral terminal strip

Main breaker

General purpose circuit (120-volt) — 1 — 15

General purpose circuits (120-volt) — 2 — 15

3 — 15

4 — Spare — Spare (120-volt)

Appliance circuit (120-volt) — 5 — 20

6 — 20 — Appliance circuit (120-volt)

Individual circuit (120-volt) — 7 — 15

8 — Dual

9 — Dual

10 — 30 — Large appliance circuit (240-volt)

Large appliance circuit (240-volt) — 11 — 40

12 — Dual

13 — 15

14 — 20 — Large appliance circuit (240-volt)

Individual circuit (120-volt) — 13 — 15

Individual circuit (120-volt) — 15 — 15

16 — 20 — Individual circuit (120-volt)

Spare (120-volt) — 17 — Spare

18 — Spare — Spare (120-volt)

Circuit breakers

Circuit breakers are toggle or push-button switches that are automatically tripped by an overload but that can also be operated manually. They are available in ratings from 15 to 150 amps, with the rating marked on each circuit breaker. If the current exceeds the rating, the circuit breaker automatically switches to the OFF or TRIP position before any damage can occur. You can also turn off any circuit breaker by hand, to turn off all the power in a particular circuit.

Although circuit breakers are reliable devices and have a long life span, they can become defective. Because replacing them can be hazardous, it is best to have a licensed electrician do the job.

Toggle-switch circuit breakers have either two or three positions. Whether the circuit breaker is at ON or OFF is shown by the position of the toggle: up for ON and down for OFF. Three-position toggles have a center position marked TRIP. For resetting, toggle types must be switched back to the ON position, and three-position types must be moved from the center TRIP position to the OFF position, then back to ON.

Push-button circuit breakers have an on/off indicator. To reset one, simply depress and release the push button and the indicator will change from OFF to ON.

Fuses

All fuses contain a metal strip, enclosed in an insulated housing, that melts when more than a specified amount of current flows through it. The kind of metal and its thickness determine how much current the fuse can carry. When a fuse is removed, all power to the circuit it protects is cut off. **CAUTION** A fuse should *never* be replaced with one rated for higher amperage.

Ordinary plug fuses are screwed into the fuse panel by hand. The metal strip that protects the circuit is visible through a plastic window.

Time-delay fuses look like ordinary plug fuses, but they can carry more than their rated current for a short period. They are useful in circuits powering motor-driven appliances, in which the high current needed only briefly to start the motor would blow other types of fuses.

S-type fuses (also called nontamperable fuses) are time-delay fuses with an added feature — a special separate base that is inserted into the fuse panel socket. The base prevents higher-rated fuses from being screwed into lower-rated sockets. A 20-amp fuse, for example, cannot be screwed into a 15-amp socket.

When a short circuit blows a fuse, the sudden surge of current may cloud the plastic window. When a blown fuse has a clear window, it usually means that current greater than the fuse rating continued to flow long enough to heat the metal strip slowly and eventually to melt it.

Cartridge fuses are used mostly in high-amperage circuits. There are two types: ferrule cartridges, for currents using 10 to 60 amps, have rounded ends that make electrical contact; knife-blade cartridges, for currents above 60 amps, have flat ends to make better electrical contact.

Both types of cartridge fuses make an electri-

cal connection by snapping into spring clips. Because the spring clips are live and exposed, a special tool called a fuse puller must always be used to remove cartridge fuses.

It is impossible to tell from its appearance

whether or not a cartridge fuse has blown. A continuity tester must be used. Connect one lead from the tester to each end of the fuse. If the test lamp lights, the fuse is good; if it does not, the fuse is blown.

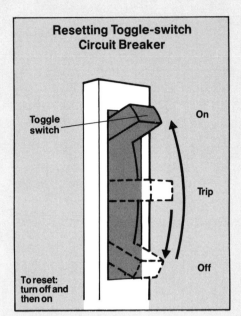

Resetting Toggle-switch Circuit Breaker

Toggle switch

On

Trip

Off

To reset: turn off and then on

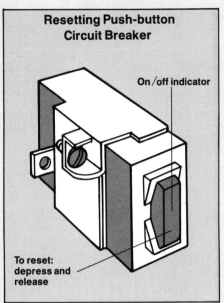

Resetting Push-button Circuit Breaker

On/off indicator

To reset: depress and release

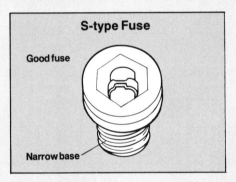

S-type Fuse

Good fuse

Narrow base

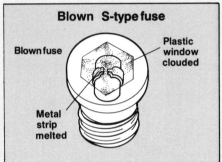

Blown S-type fuse

Blown fuse

Plastic window clouded

Metal strip melted

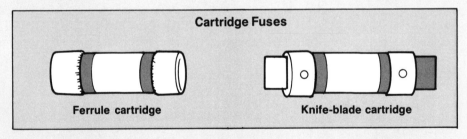

Cartridge Fuses

Ferrule cartridge

Knife-blade cartridge

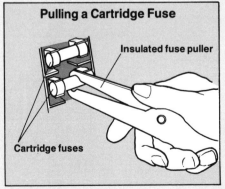

Pulling a Cartridge Fuse

Insulated fuse puller

Cartridge fuses

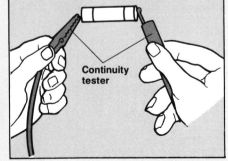

Testing a Cartridge Fuse

Continuity tester

Color coding

Virtually all 120- and 240-volt household circuits are wired in accordance with an industrywide color code, partly mandated by the National Electrical Code and also resulting from industry standardization and long–standing trade practices. The NEC requires that all neutral wires be either white or gray. Grounding wires are usually bare, but they may have green or green and yellow insulation. Grounding wires provide a safe path to ground for electrical power when trouble occurs in the electrical system. They do not *normally* carry current, but if there is a faulty wire in the appliance or in the wall receptacle, leaking current will be carried to ground by this wire.

The following color codes are used for various conductors:

Two-wire 120-volt circuits: black or red (occasionally blue) for hot wire; white or gray for neutral wire.

Three-wire 120-volt circuits: black or red (occasionally blue) for hot wire; white or gray for neutral wire; bare or green (occasionally green and yellow) for grounding wire.

Three-wire 240-volt circuits: black and/or red (occasionally blue) for hot wires; bare or green for grounding wire.

Four-wire 240-volt circuits: black and/or red (occasionally blue) for hot wires; white or gray for neutral wire; bare or green (occasionally green and yellow) for grounding wire.

The terminals on receptacles, switches and most appliances that are directly connected to power lines or ground wires are also color-coded. On a receptacle (right), the hot wires are always connected to the brass or brown terminals. These terminals lead to the narrow plug slots. The neutral wires are connected to the silver or white terminals, which lead to the wide plug slots. Terminals for the grounding wire are colored green.

The NEC requires that the white-insulated (neutral) wire be continuous throughout the electrical system. Whenever you remove a receptacle or switch that is connected to two white wires, you must connect the ends of the white wires with a wire nut. Switches work by interrupting the electrial circuits, and must, therefore, always be connected to the black or red (hot) wires, *with this exception:*

The cabling for residential wiring contains wire conductors with color-coded insulation. Two-wire cable has one black and one white wire. The NEC permits this cabling to be used in switch loop circuits like the one shown at bottom right. This is the only situation in which black and white wires may be joined. Thus, if you find a white-insulated wire connected to a brass switch terminal, do not assume it is a neutral wire.

In a switch loop, the white wire may be hot. Always test before you touch. See *Testing and replacing a switch,* page 23. If you install or repair a switch loop, wrap a piece of black tape around the white wire to show that it is hot when the switch is on.

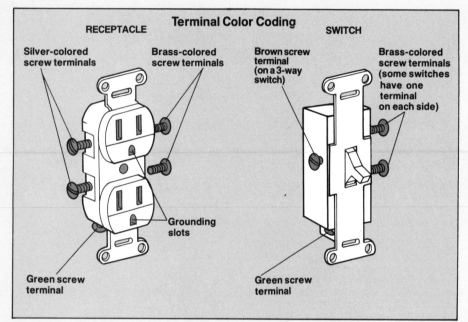

Terminal Color Coding

RECEPTACLE — SWITCH

Silver-colored screw terminals

Brass-colored screw terminals

Brown screw terminal (on a 3-way switch)

Brass-colored screw terminals (some switches have one terminal on each side)

Grounding slots

Green screw terminal

Green screw terminal

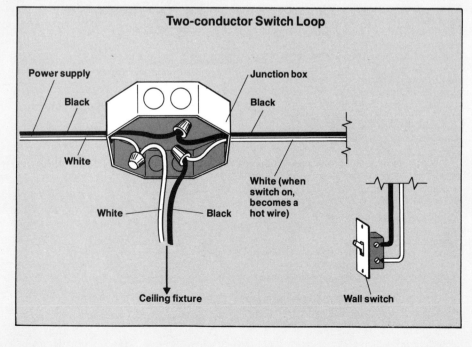

Two-conductor Switch Loop

Power supply

Black

White

White

Black

Junction box

Black

White (when switch on, becomes a hot wire)

Ceiling fixture

Wall switch

Checking the wall receptacle and switch

Appliance troubles often turn out to be caused by defective switches or wall outlets rather than by a defect in the appliance. When an appliance does not work or runs intermittently, and when inspection of its cord and plug shows no faults, check the wall receptacle or outlet. If the receptacle is controlled by a switch, the switch should also be checked. **CAUTION** Do not try to check or work on 240-volt switches or receptacles yourself. Have a licensed electrician do it. It is also wise to leave to an electrician any work on circuits other than switches and receptacles.

The quickest and easiest way to check the receptacle is to manipulate the plug in the receptacle. (If the faceplate of the receptacle is loose, tighten it before you make these tests.) Move the plug from side to side and up and down while pressing it into the receptacle. (You might also separate the prongs of the plug slightly to ensure better contact.) If the appliance runs at all when this is done, the receptacle was not making good electrical contact with the prongs on the plug, and it should be replaced. **CAUTION** Always make the replacement with a receptacle rated for the same amperage.

As an additional check, plug a lamp into the receptacle and then turn it on. If the lamp does not light, the receptacle is electrically dead. If the receptacle is controlled by a switch, turn the switch on and off slowly several times. (If the faceplate on the switch is loose, tighten it first.) If the lamp lights, the switch works only intermittently and should be replaced. **CAUTION** Always make the replacement with a switch rated for the same amperage.

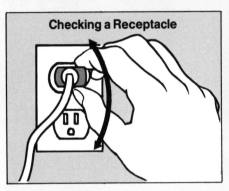

Checking a Receptacle

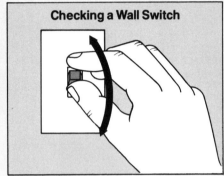

Checking a Wall Switch

Testing and replacing a receptacle

Removing a receptacle. Turn off power to the switch at the service panel. Remove the faceplate. If in doubt as to which circuit breaker or fuse controls the switch, use a flashlight and turn off the main power. Remove the mounting screws at the top and bottom, and pull the receptacle out of the outlet box. Loosen the screw terminals to remove the connecting wires. If the receptacle has push-in connections, insert a small screwdriver in the slot next to the hole where the conductor enters the receptacle. Push in on the screwdriver while pulling out the conductor.

Testing a receptacle. After the receptacle has been removed from its wall box, you should check it with a VOM. With the tester set on RX1, attach one probe to the brass-colored terminal. Touch the other probe to the metal frame of the receptacle. Then touch the probe to the silver-colored terminals. Then touch the probe to the ground terminal (green). All of these tests should show no continuity. If you get a continuity reading at any point, the receptacle is defective.

After completing this series of tests, put one probe of the VOM into one of the plug slots on the receptacle. Put the other probe on the terminal on the same side. The VOM should indicate continuity. Do the same on the other side of the receptacle. If either side shows no continuity, the receptacle is defective.

Installing a new receptacle. If the old receptacle has a green terminal, connect the existing bare or green-insulated wire to the green terminal on the new receptacle. If it does not have a green terminal, a grounding jumper must be added (see opposite page). Connect the black or red wire or wires to the brass-colored terminals and the white or gray wire or wires to the silver-colored terminals. Remount the receptacle in the outlet box and replace the faceplate.

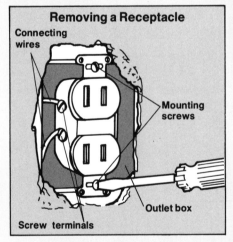

Removing a Receptacle

Connecting wires

Mounting screws

Outlet box

Screw terminals

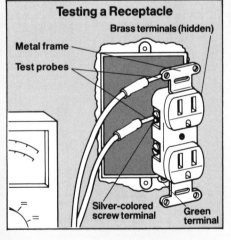

Testing a Receptacle

Brass terminals (hidden)

Metal frame

Test probes

Silver-colored screw terminal

Green terminal

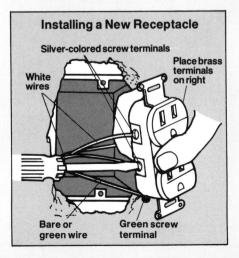

Installing a New Receptacle

Silver-colored screw terminals

Place brass terminals on right

White wires

Bare or green wire

Green screw terminal

Testing and replacing a switch

Removing a switch. Turn off power to the switch at the service panel. Remove the faceplate. If in doubt as to which circuit breaker or fuse controls the switch, use a flashlight and turn off the main power. Remove the mounting screws at the top and bottom of the switch, and pull the switch out of the outlet box. Loosen the brass-colored screw terminals and remove the wire connections. Some switches have push-in connections that you can remove by inserting a small screwdriver in the slot next to the hole where the conductor enters the switch. Push in on the screwdriver as you pull the conductor out. In most cases, both hot wires to the switch will have black or red insulation. CAUTION If you are replacing a loop switch, one of the hot wires may have *white* insulation (see *Color coding*, page 21).

Testing a switch. After the switch has been removed, check it with a continuity tester. Connect the alligator clip to one of the brass-colored terminals and touch the probe to the other. Turn the switch on and off several times, jiggling the toggle. The tester light will respond clearly without flickering to ON and OFF if the switch is good. Now, connect the alligator clip to the switch's mounting bracket or, if there is one, to the green grounding terminal.

Touch the probe first to one then to the other brass-colored terminal, and turn the switch off and on several times. A good switch will not cause the tester to light at all during testing.

Installing a new switch. Newer switches have, in addition to the two brass-colored terminals, a green grounding terminal required by the electrical code for new installations. If the switch being replaced has a green terminal, it is simple enough to connect the bare or the green-insulated wire to the green terminal on the new switch. If the old switch has no green terminal, a jumper must be added (see below). Next, connect the black and red wires (as already noted, one hot wire may be white) to the brass-colored terminals on the switch, and remount the switch in the outlet box. Replace the cover plate, then turn on the power and see if the switch works properly.

Removing a Switch

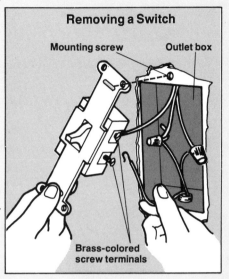

Mounting screw   Outlet box

Brass-colored screw terminals

Testing an Old Switch

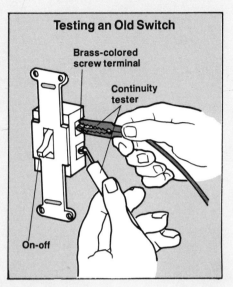

Brass-colored screw terminal

Continuity tester

On-off

Installing a New Switch

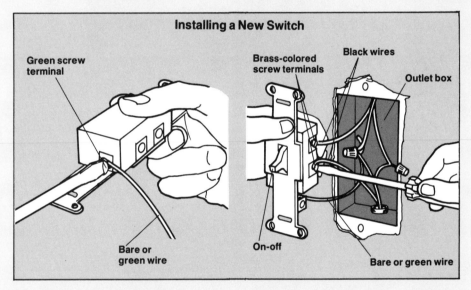

Green screw terminal

Bare or green wire

Brass-colored screw terminals   Black wires

Outlet box

On-off   Bare or green wire

Adding a grounding jumper to a switch or receptacle

If the switch or receptacle you removed does not have a green grounding screw, you will have to add a grounding jumper when you install the new part. The procedure varies according to the type of power cables in the outlet box.

If the cables are the steel-armored (BX) type, connect a jumper of bare or green-insulated wire from a grounding screw in the outlet box to the green screw on the switch or receptacle.

If nonmetallic, plastic-sheathed (Romax) cables are used, the bare grounding wires from all cables entering the box should be joined with one end of a jumper wire by means of a solderless connector (wire nut). The other end of the jumper should be connected to the grounding screw in the box. A second jumper must now be added. Connect one end to the green screw on the switch or receptacle. Remove the wire nut and join the other end of the new jumper to the other grounding wires. Replace the wire nut.

For Steel-sheathed (BX) Power Cables

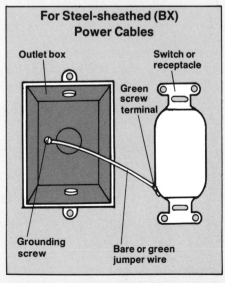

Outlet box   Switch or receptacle

Green screw terminal

Grounding screw   Bare or green jumper wire

For Plastic-sheathed (Romax) Power Cables

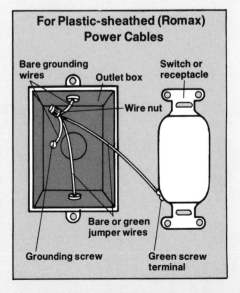

Bare grounding wires   Outlet box   Switch or receptacle

Wire nut

Bare or green jumper wires

Grounding screw   Green screw terminal

Appliance Repair Basics

Virtually all appliances produce heat or mechanical motion or both. The means of producing and controlling heat is similar in all heat-producing appliances. The production of heat and the types of motors used to do the work in appliances are described in the next few pages.

Disassembling an appliance is often difficult because some manufacturers conceal the bolts and screws that hold the appliance together. You will find some tips in this section on how to find concealed parts.

How appliances produce heat

As the Blue Pages explained, what is commonly called current flow is, in fact, the movement of electrons in materials, usually metallic, that are called conductors. No matter how efficient the material may be in conducting current, there is always some opposition to electron movement; this opposition is called electrical resistance. When electron flow is impeded by resistance, some of the electrons' energy is converted to heat. This principle is basic to the design of heating elements in appliances.

How does the heating element get hot? The element is made of a special alloy wire (usually a nickel-chromium alloy called nichrome) that has electrical resistance and is also heat-resistant. Both characteristics are necessary for the heating element to do its job.

The special-alloy wire, generally called resistance wire, has a high melting point, which enables it to withstand the great heat the wire itself produces. The amount of heat depends on how many watts the element consumes. It can be as few as 500 watts or as many as 5,000. In other words, elements differ from one type and size of appliance to another. Those having higher wattage capacity draw more electricity and create more heat than those with low capacity.

To say that a heating element has resistance means that it allows only a certain amount of current to flow through it at one time. Resistance depends on such factors as the type of wire the element is made of, the gauge (size) of the wire, and the number of coils into which the wire is fashioned.

To determine how many watts (and, consequently, how much heat) a heating element can generate, always start with a constant figure. The amount of available voltage (or electrical pressure) at the receptacle is a known factor. In most U.S. homes, for example, the voltage available is 120 and 240.

As stated above, the amount of current that actually flows through a circuit depends on the size and makeup of the wire (that is, on the wire's resistance). The relationship between the current and the wire's resistance is the determining factor in heat output. The heat output in watts is the product of the voltage times the current.

WATTS = VOLTS X AMPS

A heating element that allows 10 amps of current to flow has a wattage of 120 X 10, or 1,200 watts. If another element allows 25 amps to flow, its heat output is 3,000 watts.

Types of heating elements

Enclosed heating coils cannot be repaired. In a few instances spiral wire or flat mica heating elements may be repairable. As a general rule, however, if a VOM resistance test shows high or infinite resistance or if the continuity tester does not show continuity, the complete heating element should be replaced.

Replacement heating coil can be purchased from the manufacturer, appliance parts dealers, or hardware or electrical supply stores. Take the old coil with you, since it is important to buy an element of the same size and gauge. When ordering by mail, be sure to include the appliance model number, serial number, and if possible the element part number.

If either a spiral wire or flat mica heating element is connected electrically to terminal screws and a break occurs near the terminal, repair may be possible. In the case of spiral wire elements, straighten a couple of loops to obtain enough wire to reach the terminal. Clean the wire and the terminal screw by scraping them with a knife or razor blade, being careful not to nick the heating element. Rebend the end of the wire and secure it firmly under the terminal screw.

With flat mica elements, you may have to free one turn of heating wire to get enough slack to reach the terminal screw. Freeing a loop may provide more wire than needed to reach the terminal screw; if so, trim off the excess. If it comes in contact with exposed metal parts of the appliance, someone could get a shock from touching the appliance.

Removal of one turn will not materially affect the heating capability of the unit. Again, clean the wire and terminal screws thoroughly, and be careful not to nick the heating element. Bend the end of the heating wire with needle-nose pliers to fit around the terminal screw.

For information on removal and replacement of the heating element, see instructions for the specific appliance.

Resistance wire is wound on a flat mica insulator. The heating element is close to but does not touch what is being cooked. The spacing of windings can be varied to produce even heat. Breaks can be found by careful inspection. Typical use: toasters.

Band-type elements consist of one or more strands of resistance wire that are bonded to a flexible backing that keeps the wires separated and sandwiched between layers of flexible insulation. Typical use: the main element in slow cookers.

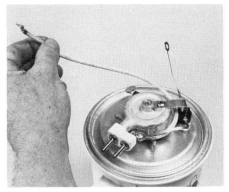

Rope-type elements consist of a resistance wire wrapped in a fiberglass, rope-like insulator. If you suspect a fault in a rope-type element, test it for continuity. Typical use: the warming element in coffee makers.

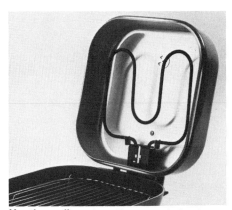

Heating coil, enclosed in a ceramic-lined steel tube, heats food directly. The tube protects the coil from grease. The coil is not visible, so a continuity or resistance check must be made if a coil break is suspected. Typical use: frying pans, broilers.

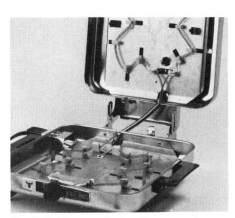

A spiral of heat-producing wire mounted on ceramic standoffs heats a surface that in turn cooks food. Breaks in the wire can usually be found by inspection. Typical use: waffle irons, hot plates.

Controlling heat levels

The heating elements of small appliances can be turned on and off, When an element is on, the heat output is fixed, determined by the size of the element and the material it is made of. How, then, are various levels of heat produced? Two methods are commonly used.

One method simply switches the heating element on and off periodically to produce an average heat output. If the on time is long and the off time brief, average heat output is high. When the reverse is true, average heat output is low. After the unit has been turned on, heat is controlled automatically by means of either a fixed-heat or an adjustable-temperature thermostat.

The second method of heat control involves a tapped heating element. One connection to the element is made through a switch having several positions such as HIGH, MEDIUM, and LOW. Each switch position applies power to a different point on the heating element to produce a different level of heat. Appliances with this type of control may also have an automatic safety switch to prevent overheating.

Thermostats

Bimetallic units. The basic way of controlling heat in a thermostat is by means of a bimetallic unit consisting of two different metals fused together. Both expand when heated, but one expands faster than the other, causing the bimetallic unit to warp or bend. This in turn opens and closes electrical contacts.

Fixed-heat thermostats. These controls, which are used on electric percolators, for example, have a factory-set temperature. The heat control is a circular bimetallic unit. When a certain temperature is reached, the bimetallic disc expands and snaps up, pushing a plunger that opens switch contacts. As the temperature drops, the disc contracts and snaps down, closing the contacts. The correct temperature is maintained by this on-off action.

Repair work is limited to cleaning the switch contacts, if they are accessible. Clean the contacts by pressing them together after inserting a piece of soft cloth or a dollar bill between them. Gently slide the cloth or bill back and forth. If the contacts are inaccessible, the complete thermostat assembly must be replaced when something goes wrong.

Adjustable-heat thermostats. These units are used on appliances that operate at various heat levels—toasters and electric frying pans, for example. They have a temperature-control knob that activates a plunger to apply pressure to one of two electrical contact arms, changing the spacing between them. When the bimetallic unit is heated, it applies pressure to the other contact arm. The less pressure applied by the control knob, the more pressure required by the bimetallic strip to separate the contact arms and switch off current.

Some repair is possible. The control-knob unit is usually accessible with some disassembly. Contacts can be cleaned, as described under fixed-heat thermostats. The most common problem is uneven operation caused by bits of food that become lodged between the contact arms and the knob or plunger. Simply brush or scrape out the food particles and rub the contact points lightly with cloth or paper.

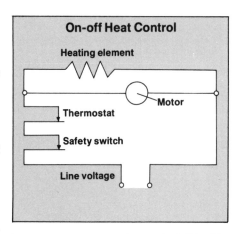

On-off Heat Control

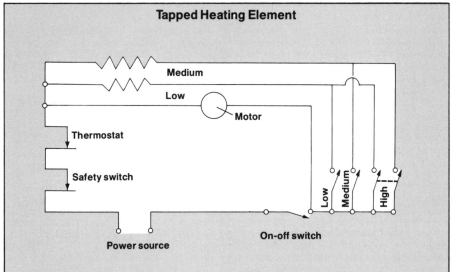

Tapped Heating Element

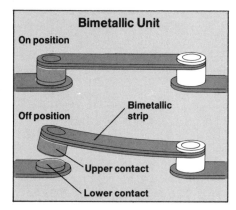

Bimetallic Unit

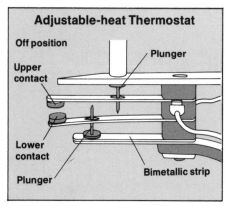

Adjustable-heat Thermostat

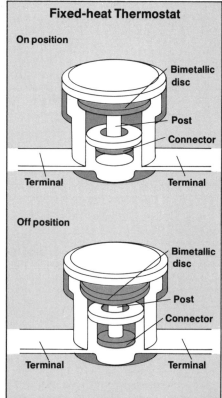

Fixed-heat Thermostat

How motors work

A simple experiment with small permanent magnets shows that opposite poles attract and like poles repel. A magnetic field around each pole exerts force that causes attraction or repulsion.

When current flows through a wire, a circular magnetic field is created around that wire. The strength of the field can be increased by bundling many wires together. The direction of force of the magnetic field depends on the direction of current flow. If the wires are formed into a coil, the magnetic fields create north and south poles similar to a bar magnet. If some coils of wire are wound on a stationary frame, sometimes called a stator, and others are wound on a frame that is free to rotate, also known as a rotor, the magnetic fields can be so arranged that the attraction and repulsion forces will cause the free frame to rotate. This is the principle on which all electric motors operate.

Universal motors

The most widely used motor in appliances is the universal motor. It is called universal not because of its wide use, but because it can run on either AC or DC.

This motor has two important characteristics. First, it provides extremely high starting torque (a force that produces rotation) for its size and weight, and it can attain high speed quickly under a fairly heavy load. Second, it can operate over a wide range of speeds in both small and large appliances. A universal motor may be used in such small appliances as food mixers and blenders.

The rotor of a universal motor is made up of an armature, which is the iron core with coils of wire wrapped around it, and the commutator. The commutator and armature together constitute a single assembly.

The commutator, which is positioned at one end of the armature, consists of a series of copper bars laid out in circular fashion. The commutator is basically a switching mechanism.

Passing right through the middle of the armature and commutator is a shaft that protrudes from both ends. How far the shaft extends from each end varies from appliance to appliance.

One end of the shaft is normally attached to a bearing assembly, enabling the rotor to rotate. In some cases, the shaft has a small fan that cools the interior of the appliance. The other end of the shaft is attached to the appliance's working device. In a food blender, for example, the end of the shaft is attached to the cutting knives. Or the working end of the shaft may be attached to a gear train, which in turn is attached to a working element. This is the case with food mixers and floor polishers.

The stator is the part of the motor in which the rotor is positioned. It is a frame (usually iron) containing coils of wire called field coils. Keep in mind that the rotor is positioned in this way so its movement cannot be impeded.

Essentially, this is what happens: electricity enters one of the field coils through the appliance cord, which is plugged into a wall receptacle. Current passes from the field coil into one of two carbon segments, called brushes, which are positioned directly opposite each other on the commutator. The brushes are held in contact with the commutator by springs.

Current flows through the brush to the one commutator bar the brush is touching, through the armature coil to which the armature is connected, out through another commutator bar that is in contact with the other brush, into another field coil, and back to its source. This means that the brushes and commutator bars act as an automatic switching device that connects and disconnects each coil at exactly the right moment as the armature revolves.

All components of a universal motor are wired together in tandem, and current at every point is the same. This is called a series circuit.

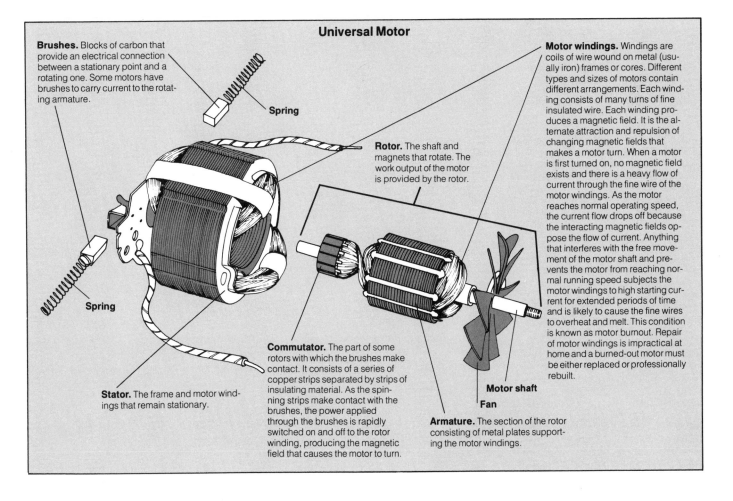

Universal Motor

Brushes. Blocks of carbon that provide an electrical connection between a stationary point and a rotating one. Some motors have brushes to carry current to the rotating armature.

Spring

Rotor. The shaft and magnets that rotate. The work output of the motor is provided by the rotor.

Spring

Stator. The frame and motor windings that remain stationary.

Commutator. The part of some rotors with which the brushes make contact. It consists of a series of copper strips separated by strips of insulating material. As the spinning strips make contact with the brushes, the power applied through the brushes is rapidly switched on and off to the rotor winding, producing the magnetic field that causes the motor to turn.

Motor windings. Windings are coils of wire wound on metal (usually iron) frames or cores. Different types and sizes of motors contain different arrangements. Each winding consists of many turns of fine insulated wire. Each winding produces a magnetic field. It is the alternate attraction and repulsion of changing magnetic fields that makes a motor turn. When a motor is first turned on, no magnetic field exists and there is a heavy flow of current through the fine wire of the motor windings. As the motor reaches normal operating speed, the current flow drops off because the interacting magnetic fields oppose the flow of current. Anything that interferes with the free movement of the motor shaft and prevents the motor from reaching normal running speed subjects the motor windings to high starting current for extended periods of time and is likely to cause the fine wires to overheat and melt. This condition is known as motor burnout. Repair of motor windings is impractical at home and a burned-out motor must be either replaced or professionally rebuilt.

Motor shaft

Fan

Armature. The section of the rotor consisting of metal plates supporting the motor windings.

Shaded-pole motors

One motor widely used in small appliances is known as the shaded-pole motor. It is small (1/100 to 1/20 horsepower) and produces low starting torque. Typically, it is used in such appliances as electric fans and hair driers. Shaded-pole motors operate on AC only.

A shaded-pole motor has no commutator on its rotor and no brushes. Its winding consists of solid copper rings called shades on each pole tip. The rings set up a magnetic field that alternately aids and opposes the main field coil. The effect is a field that produces a turning force and starts the rotor spinning.

Permanent-magnet motors

Small cordless appliances use a motor called a permanent-magnet, or DC, motor. This motor operates in much the same way as a universal motor. There are two basic types. One does not have brushes or a commutator. No power need be applied to the rotor, because, as the name implies, the rotor is made up of permanent magnets. The other type has brushes and a commutator, but the field is a permanent magnet and the rotor is like the one in a universal motor. These motors can be used only in appliances, such as knives and shavers, where low torque is adequate. The fact that permanent-magnet motors operate on 5 to 7 volts makes them suitable for cordless appliances.

Cordless appliances

Cordless appliances contain a battery pack that supplies the energy to drive the permanent-magnet motors. The batteries are usually rechargeable: plugging the battery pack into a wall receptacle recharges the pack. For an AC source (the wall outlet) to recharge a DC source (the battery pack) the AC must first be converted to DC. The device that accomplishes this change is known as a rectifier. A rectifer allows current to flow in only one direction. The AC input is changed at the output to pulses of DC that recharge the battery.

When a cordless appliance fails to operate properly, the cause is probably either the battery pack or the charging rectifier. If, after charging, the appliance runs normally for a short time and then dies, the fault is probably the battery pack. Rechargeable batteries can be recharged just so many times. As they reach the end of their useful life, they can be recharged but they discharge rapidly. Batteries cannot, of course, be repaired. In many appliances the battery pack can be replaced easily.

When batteries show no sign of life after being connected for charging, the cause of trouble may be the charging rectifier. Disassemble the appliance as described in the section on that appliance to gain access to the rectifier.

Rectifiers have two leads. The condition of the rectifier can be checked by measuring the resistance between the leads in each direction. Set the VOM (volt-ohm meter) on the RX1 scale. The resistance should be much higher in one direction than in the other. Actual values depend on the type of rectifier, but the difference between the two readings should be at least 10 to 1—i.e., one should be at least ten times the other. A low reading in both directions or a high reading in both directions indicates the rectifier is defective and should be replaced.

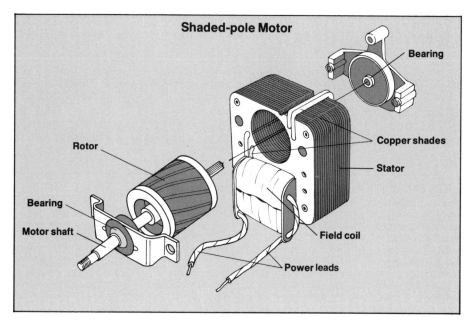

Shaded-pole Motor

Bearing · Copper shades · Stator · Rotor · Bearing · Motor shaft · Field coil · Power leads

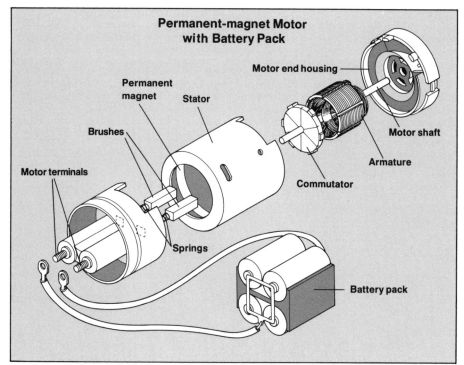

Permanent-magnet Motor with Battery Pack

Motor end housing · Motor shaft · Armature · Commutator · Permanent magnet · Stator · Brushes · Motor terminals · Springs · Battery pack

Motor speed controls

Controlling motor speed is often desirable. Universal motors are especially well suited to this purpose, because speed can be controlled by any one of three devices.

Tapped-field speed controls. When a control has stepped settings such as HIGH, MEDIUM, and LOW, it is likely that a tapped field is used. With a tapped-field speed control, the point at which power is applied to the motor winding can be varied. When only part of the winding is energized, the magnetic field is smaller and the motor speed is reduced. Motor torque remains fairly constant at each tapped setting.

Tapped-field speed controls are relatively trouble-free. If a motor operates at some speeds but not at others, the speed selector switch may be defective and not making contact at those settings. If the motor operates at only one speed, the selector switch is again the likely source of trouble. Switches are usually not repairable.

To replace a switch, make a sketch of the connections to the old switch before you remove it. Note the colors of the wires and terminals they are connected to, or label the wires with masking tape, so when the new switch is installed, the motor will operate in accordance with the marked speed settings.

Solid-state speed controls. These controls are electronic and employ a device called a silicon-controlled rectifier (SCR). The current flow through the rectifier can be controlled by varying a small control voltage, thereby allowing motor speed to be continuously variable over a wide range.

Diodes. A simpler form of solid-state device employs a diode to provide two motor speeds. Current to the motor is switched so that it is connected either directly to the motor or indirectly through the diode. The diode effectively cuts current in half.

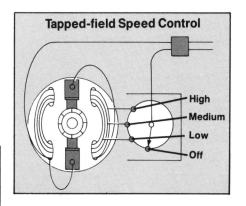

Tapped-field Speed Control

High
Medium
Low
Off

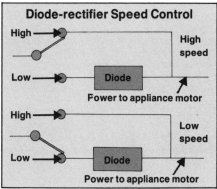

Diode-rectifier Speed Control

High — High speed
Low — Diode — Power to appliance motor
High — Low speed
Low — Diode — Power to appliance motor

The Solid State of the Art

It is characteristic of solid-state devices that when they fail they fail completely. They rarely deteriorate gradually or fail partially. Another characteristic is high reliability, so check other features carefully before deciding that the speed control is at fault.

When solid-state speed controls fail, the complete unit must be replaced.

When a diode-rectifier speed control is defective, the appliance should operate normally at the high setting, but will either not operate at all on a lower setting or will continue to operate at high speed.

Preventing motor breakdowns

Defects in the brushes and commutator of a universal motor can cause the motor to run sluggishly and lose power. Servicing these parts takes a few moments but can restore a motor to almost new.

If a motor is sluggish, check the brush contact by running the appliance in a dimly lighted area. Sparking will be visible through the ventilation openings in the appliance. Small bluish sparks where commutator and brush meet are normal. Light, bright sparks or bright and dim sparks indicate poor brush contact or worn brushes. Disassemble the motor and inspect the brushes and commutator. A good rule of thumb is that brushes should be longer than they are wide. If they aren't, they should be replaced. Check the brush holder and spring to be sure the spring supplies enough pressure to hold the brush firmly against the commutator. If spring tension appears weak, replace both springs.

If brushes are replaced, they may need shaping to fit the curvature of the commutator. You can shape brushes to make good contact in two easy steps. First, wrap a piece of fine-grit sandpaper (rough side out) around the commutator. (Be sure to use sandpaper, not emery cloth, because in emery cloth the abrasive material is a conductor. A short could result, causing the segments of the commutator to arc together.) Then insert the brushes in the holder so they press against the sandpaper. Rotate the commutator back and forth by hand until the brush ends are shaped to fit.

If the copper surfaces are rough, polish them by holding very fine sandpaper against the commutator while turning it. To keep the sandpaper flat against the commutator surface, wrap the sandpaper around a flat stick or use the stick to press it against the commutator.

Excessive brush wear or chipping may be caused by a worn commutator. The commutator consists of copper bars separated by mica insulators, and if the mica projects above the surface of the copper bars, it should be carefully scraped until it is a bit lower than the copper surface.

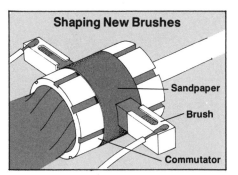

Shaping New Brushes

Sandpaper
Brush
Commutator

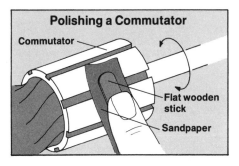

Polishing a Commutator

Commutator
Flat wooden stick
Sandpaper

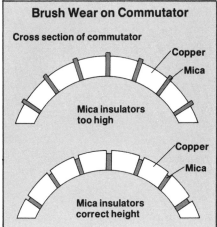

Brush Wear on Commutator

Cross section of commutator

Copper
Mica
Mica insulators too high

Copper
Mica
Mica insulators correct height

Bearings and gears. Because heat can be destructive to any motor, small appliances often have fan blades attached to one end of the motor shaft to force cooling air through the housing. Make sure ventilation openings are not blocked.

Most appliances are not intended for continuous use. Motor bearings can overheat and bind or seize up, causing severe motor damage. Units should be turned off and allowed to cool if the housing gets too hot. When a motor becomes hot even though properly ventilated, it may be overloaded by excessive friction in the bearings or gears.

Lubrication. Motor bearings reduce friction between fixed and moving parts. If bearings become excessively worn or misaligned, the appliance may perform poorly or the motor may burn out. Excessive wear and misalignment are often caused by insufficient lubrication. The problem is avoided on many small motors because of permanently lubricated bearings that are sealed and sufficiently lubricated to last for the life of the motor; no attempt should be made to add more lubricant. In larger motors (⅛ horsepower and up) bearings generally need periodic lubrication.

Lubrication

Both ends of the motor housing should be checked for lubrication points. Look for small holes marked OIL or small metal cups with spring-loaded tops. The type of oil required and the frequency of lubrication are often marked on the motor or elsewhere, or it may be in the appliance manual. If no guide is available, use a light general-purpose oil (SAE 10), adding only a few drops every three or four months. Oil should be used sparingly and only in the bearings.

Oil cups often contain felt wicks to absorb the oil and allow it to flow slowly to the bearings. If these wicks become clogged with dirt, oil will not reach the bearings. To clean a wick, pull it out of the cup with tweezers and dip it in a dry-cleaning solvent. When it is dry, oil it until the wick is saturated, and replace it.

Gears, made of either metal or plastic, convert motion from the motor to the part being driven. Metal gears require heavy lubrication; plastic ones need little or none. If the motor hums but the appliance runs slowly, noisily, or not at all, the gears may be at fault. Gears can jam if they suffer mechanical damage when an appliance is dropped or the motor is severely overloaded. You can repair jammed gears by freeing them; broken or worn gears must be replaced. To free jammed gears, separate them with a wooden or plastic stick. Rotate the gears by hand to check for free movement. If they do not move freely, the gears or the appliance must be replaced. **CAUTION** Gears are sharp, and it is easy to cut yourself.

How to Test a Universal Motor

If the motor in an appliance doesn't run at all, check the appliance circuitry for loose connections and test the line cord, switch, and diode and fuse (if the appliance has them) for continuity. If these tests do not reveal the fault, the problem is most likely in the motor.

On universal motors with brushes, you can make a quick test without disassembling the motor to find the defective component.

To make the quick motor test, simply disconnect one or both of the power leads to the motor and attach VOM probes to the power lead terminals. Set the VOM on either the RX1 or RX10 scale (whichever brings the needle to the middle part of the dial). If the VOM doesn't register at all, the motor has failed the continuity test and its components must be tested individually. If the motor has continuity, turn the rotor slowly by hand and watch the needle on the VOM; it should continue to register roughly in the middle of the scale. If the needle dips suddenly, there is an open winding in the rotor, and the rotor must be replaced. If the needle remains steady (an indication that the motor is OK) but the motor still does not work at all, have the field coil tested at a repair shop. As a last step, remove one VOM probe from the power lead terminals and touch it to the motor shaft. The VOM should show no continuity. If it shows continuity, the motor is grounded and should be serviced at a repair shop or replaced.

If the motor fails the continuity test, disassemble it and examine the brushes for wear (see page 29). If they are OK, test the rotor for continuity by placing one VOM probe on the first copper band and the other probe on each of the other copper bands successively. The VOM should show continuity for each band. If any band fails the test, replace the rotor. If the rotor is OK, make a simple continuity test on the field coil. If the VOM shows no continuity in the field coil, replace the coil. If the coil does have continuity and you have eliminated every other possible source of trouble, have the coil

professionally tested to be sure that none of the windings is defective (something that a continuity test can't show).

In most cases, universal motors can be rebuilt at local shops. Before deciding to have a motor rebuilt, consider the cost of the repair against the cost of replacement, which in some cases may be less.

Motors in large appliances

The basic operating principle behind all electric motors is the same. The forces of attraction and repulsion between a fixed magnetic field and one that can rotate cause the motors to run. The main difference between large- and small-appliance motors is a result of design changes necessitated by the heavier work load carried by larger appliances.

Large-sized universal motors are used in certain large appliances, such as oil burners. In most large appliances, however, one of two types of induction motor is used. Induction motors are well suited to heavy work and are simpler than universal motors: they have no armature, brushes, or commutator. They operate on AC only.

The rotors of induction motors are solid cores that become magnetized by a magnetic field. The stator windings are made up of a number of coils distributed around the stator in such a way that, when energized from an AC source, the magnetic fields of the coils constantly change.

If these magnetic fields were visible, the strength and direction of the magnetic force would appear to move around the stator. In effect, although the stator remains fixed, its magnetic field rotates. The force of this rotating field is transferred to the rotor. This process of transfer of magnetic fields is known as induction.

If the magnetic field induced in the rotor is not aligned with the stator's magnetic field, the rotor will turn as it tries to "catch up" with the stator field. Since the rotor must move its own mass as well as the load it is driving, it cannot catch up, and so the motor runs.

Designers of induction motors must overcome one inherent problem that occurs when the motor is turned on. The rotor is stationary and the magnetic field induced in it is aligned with the stator field; effectively, the rotor remains stationary. Special circuits are therefore added to create an initial magnetic displacement between rotor and stator.

Centrifugal switch. The special circuits that are added are needed only when the motor is started; if they were to remain connected, they would reduce the efficiency of the motor. Induction motors, therefore, have centrifugal switches that cut out the starting circuit when the motor reaches running speed.

Capacitor motors. Two types of starting circuits are used in the induction motors in large appliances, and they give their names to those motors. The motor used most widely in appliances with heavy starting loads, such as washing machines, is a capacitor, or capacitor-start, motor. A large capacitor, easily recognized by the capacitor box mounted on the main motor housing, supplies the initial field displacement that gets the motor going. Capacitor-start motors are highly efficient and draw relatively low starting current. They are available with ratings up to 7½ horsepower.

Capacitors act as temporary storage places for electrical energy. When power is applied to the leads of a capacitor, the capacitor is charged in much the way that a battery is charged. When power is removed and the leads are shorted or reversed, the capacitor discharges. In an AC circuit, this charging and discharging causes a time shift in the buildup of the resulting magnetic field. In capacitor-start motors, the centrifugal switch connects a capacitor across a part of the stator during start-up. The capacitor shifts part of the stator field to get the rotor moving. The centrifugal switch disconnects the capacitor when the motor reaches normal running speed.

Split-phase motors. The second type of motor used in large appliances is a split-phase motor. One winding on a split-phase motor has three electrical connections rather than the customary two. The third tap provides the field displacement necessary to start the motor.

When the motor reaches normal speed, the centrifugal switch opens the connection to the tap. These motors cannot be used to start heavy loads, and they also draw high starting current. They are available with ratings only up to ⅓ horsepower. Split-phase motors look like capacitor-start motors, without the capacitor housing.

Starting circuitry

The problems peculiar to large-appliance motors are those associated with the starting circuitry. Centrifugal switches have a disc that moves back and forth on the motor shaft, on which it is mounted. When the motor is turned off, a spring positions the disc so that it holds a pair of electrical contacts closed. As the motor begins to turn and speed up, a pair of weights moves outward by means of centrifugal force. The weights overcome the spring force and move the disc away from the electrical contacts, allowing them to open.

If switch contacts are clogged or dirty, the switch mechanism will stick and the motor will not start. To clean them, remove one end of the motor housing and run a fine-toothed file between switch contacts to clean them. (This is a temporary repair only. Replace the switch plate as early as possible.) Clean mechanical parts of the switch with a small brush dipped in any household solvent. Dab light oil on sliding surfaces and the pivot point, never on electrical contact points. Hand-operate parts to ensure free movement. Badly bent, pitted contact points or broken switch parts must be replaced.

To check the capacitor on capacitor-start motors, always discharge the capacitor first (see page 42). Then remove the electrical connec-tions, usually push-on types that you can pull off by gripping the end of the connector with pliers.

You will need a VOM to check the capacitor. Set the selector switch to the RX100 resistance scale. Touch the test leads to the capacitor terminals. The needle should swing toward 0 ohms and then gradually drift back to the high-resistance end of the scale. If the needle stays at or near 0, the capacitor is shorted. If the needle stops at the high-resistance reading, the capacitor is open. In either case, the only remedy is to replace the capacitor.

Getting Inside

It's easier than it looks to get inside a large appliance. In general, large appliances consist of metal panels enclosing a frame on which the main parts are mounted. You must remove the front, top, or rear panels (and sometimes side panels, when they are removable) to expose key parts. Rear panels are usually secured with accessible sheet-metal screws. Front and side panels are somewhat more complicated to take off: remove the screws or snap-out spring clips at the bottom edge. Pulling the panel out 2 or 3 inches and pushing it up will free it at the top. Try removing the front panel first to expose the side panel mounting screws. Appliance tops are often secured by hidden spring clips. To release them, slip a putty knife under the edge of the top panel. Push in on the putty knife and pull up on the panel to release it. These clips are usually located about 2 inches from each end.

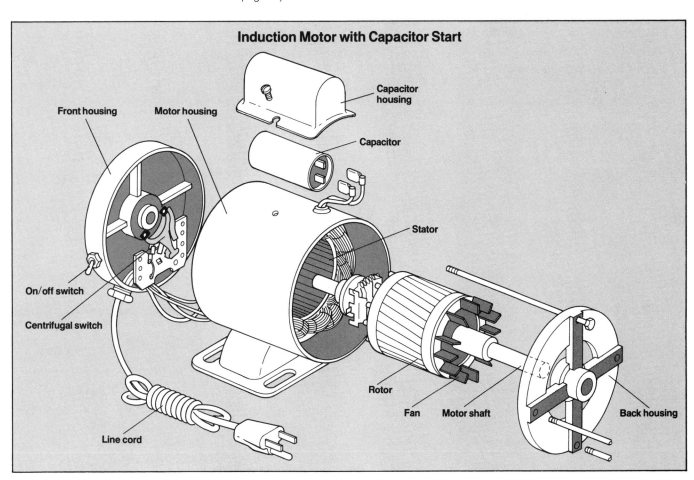

Induction Motor with Capacitor Start

Capacitor housing

Capacitor

Stator

Front housing

Motor housing

On/off switch

Centrifugal switch

Rotor

Fan

Motor shaft

Back housing

Line cord

Basic repair procedures

Testing the cord and plug

Often appliance troubles can be traced to a faulty cord and plug assembly. Inspection is sometimes all that is needed to discover the source of the trouble—whether it is a cracked plug, a loose prong, or a broken wire. In some cases, however, a test must be made to find out whether the cord and plug are at fault. Electrical testers and the tests you can make wth them are discussed in the Blue Pages.

Either a VOM (on resistance range RX1) or a continuity tester can be used. Make certain the appliance is not plugged into the outlet when you are performing these tests. Attach the test leads to the prongs of the plug with alligator clips. If the cord is detachable (with a female receptacle connecting to the appliance), disconnect the cord from the appliance. Make a jumper by stripping both ends of a short length of wire. Insert the stripped ends into the openings of the female receptacle. If the power cord is connected to the appliance internally, turn the appliance switch to OFF and open the unit. Jump the male plug end and, leaving the switch at OFF, measure across both leads of the incoming line cord.

The VOM should read 0 ohms or the continuity tester should light. Twist and bend the cord. If the needle flickers or the light goes out, there is a break in the cord or a loose connection in one of the plugs. With the tester still connected, remove the jumper at the other end, or turn the appliance off. The meter should indicate 0 ohms resistance: the test light on the continuity tester should not light. Again, bend and twist the cord. If the needle moves or the lamp lights, there is a short in the cord or in the plug.

If a cord and plug assembly is defective, you can replace it with a new one; if the trouble can be traced to a plug, the plug can be replaced. **CAUTION** Always replace cords and plugs with ones having the same specifications. A lamp cord used on a room heater, for example, creates a fire hazard.

Replacing a plug

When a plug for a wall outlet is replaced, the connections should be made with a strain-relief knot known as an Underwriters' knot. After looping the leads as shown, pull the knot tight and draw it back into the plug. Make a loop in the bare conductor and route the leads in opposite directions around the prongs.

Put the loop under the screw terminals so that the direction of tightening will be toward the open part of the loop. Do not overlap the wire. No strands of wire should stick out from under the screw head.

The female receptacle on a fully detachable cord and plug for a small appliance can be disassembled and replaced as shown. These plugs are becoming less common: most appliances now come with a built-in cord. If the cord and plug are connected internally to the appliance, refer to the entry on the specific appliance for replacement information.

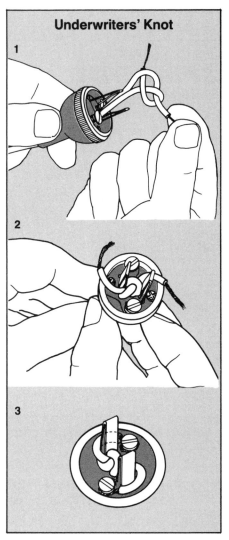

Underwriters' Knot

1

2

3

Making a Loop

Right   Wrong

Right   Wrong

Don't Overlook the Receptacle

When appliances work intermittently or the plug must be manipulated in the receptacle to make the appliance operate, it is natural to suspect the cord and plug. Keep in mind, however, that this type of problem can also be caused by a defective wall receptacle. In a receptacle controlled by a wall switch, a defective switch can cause the same problem. Replacement of wall receptacles and switches is described on pages 22 and 23.

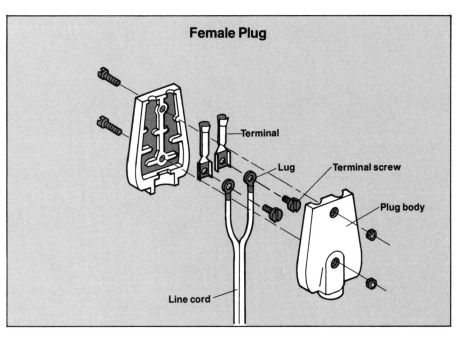

Female Plug

Terminal

Lug   Terminal screw

Plug body

Line cord

Splicing wires

Occasionally it may be necessary to splice wires when repairing appliances. The proper way to make safe, secure splices is to make a mechanical and electrical joint that is strong enough not to pull apart and tight enough to offer no electrical resistance. This is tricky; a continuous run of new wire is always better than any splice.

If you must make a splice, there are various types to choose from. All splices should be soldered and then taped. Splicing, taping and soldering are described below and on page 34.

The Western Union splice has long been used for maximum strength, particularly in dual-conductor cords and cables. To make this splice, begin by cutting one conductor about 2 inches shorter than the other so the completed splices will not be directly opposite each other. Offsetting the splices serves two functions: it keeps them apart from each other, thus preventing a short circuit if the insulating tape tears or works loose, and it also minimizes the unsightly bulge that appears when two splices fall beside each other and each is wrapped with tape.

Strip each conductor or wire of insulation and scrape it clean of dirt and oxidation. Then wrap the bared ends around each other as shown. With light-gauge stranded wire, twist the ends tightly enough with your fingertips; for solid heavy wire, you will need pliers in order to make a tight twist. Solder and then tape the splice.

The pigtail splice makes a good electrical connection and is mechanically strong, but the finished splice is bulky. Strip off at least 1½ inches of insulation from the end of each wire. Twist the wires together tightly, starting at or near the first bit of exposed wire. Trim off sharp points protruding from the end of the twist. Solder the twisted wires at the point where the twist began. Bend the pigtail parallel to one of the conductors and tape the bare splice from the end of the insulation on one side to the beginning of the insulation on the other.

The twist splice makes a good electrical connection, but it is not particularly strong. For light wire, cross about 2 inches of each end of prepared wire. Bend the ends of the wires over each other at right angles and twist them around each other. For heavy-gauge wire, two pairs of pliers are needed to make sure the connection is tight. Use one pair to hold the wires at the beginning of the twist, and the other to twist the wires. Use wire cutters to trim off the excess wire so no sharp ends can penetrate the tape. Solder the wires at the twist and tape them.

Western Union Splice

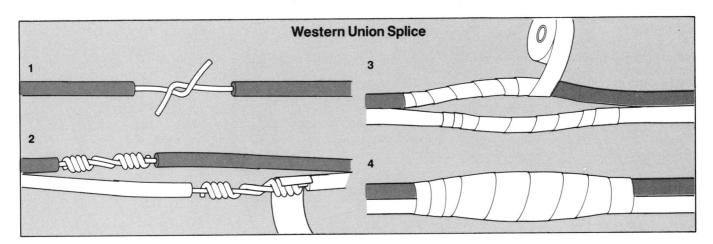

Pigtail Splice

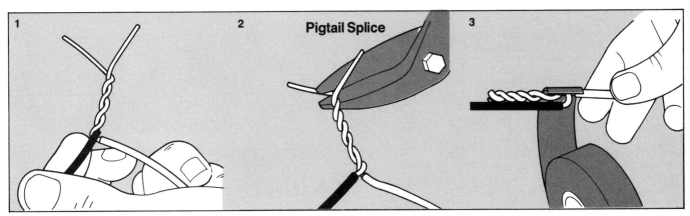

1 Twist splice

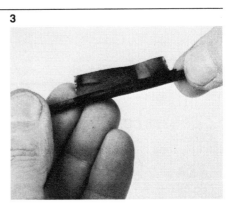

Soldering

To assure a permanent electrical connection always solder splices. A soldering gun with high and low heat settings is the most versatile soldering tool. Low heat (25 to 50 watts) is best for most small appliances. Higher heat levels may damage internal parts, but higher levels can be used on splices not close to internal parts. A low-wattage soldering pencil and a high-wattage soldering iron can be used in place of the dual-heat gun.

Always use solder that is clearly marked as suitable for electrical work: 60/40 rosin-core solder is best. The numbers 60/40 refer to the percentage of tin and lead in the solder. A material called flux, which helps solder to spread and penetrate, must be used on solder joints. Flux also cleans the conductors and prevents tarnish from developing. The rosin in rosin-core solder automatically provides flux. **CAUTION** Never use acid-core solder or acid-core paste, which corrode electrical connections.

Tinning. Before a soldering iron or gun is used, its tip should be coated with a thin, even layer of solder, a process called tinning. First, clean the tip of the iron by sanding or filing it to bare metal. Next, snap off a short length of solder at the end of the spool by bending the short length back and forth a few times. This is done to expose the rosin flux so it will melt onto the tip before the solder does. If you are using a dual-heat soldering gun, set it for low heat. If you are tinning a high-heat iron, hold the solder against the tip before the iron reaches full heat. This will allow the flux to flow before the iron is hot enough to melt the solder. Coat the tip completely with solder and wipe off the excess with a clean cloth or some steel wool.

Soldering a splice. Tin the iron, then hold the wires to be soldered tightly against the iron's tip. Unwind a few inches of solder from the spool and hold the end of the solder against the wire, with the iron touching the other side of the wire. The iron is used to heat the wire so that the wire melts the solder rather than melting the solder directly. To make a good joint, the wire must be hot enough to melt the solder, which should flow down into the wires. After soldering, inspect the joint closely in a good light. The solder should be smooth and a bit shiny; if it is dull and grainy, the chances are that a good joint has not been made. Reheat the joint until the solder flows again. Recheck the joint for mechanical strength after it has cooled.

When taping spliced and soldered joints, use enough tape to make the new insulation about as thick as the original. Use a good brand of plastic electrical tape. Wrap the tape diagonally along the joint, covering about an inch of the old insulation at each end. Plastic tape adheres better if it is kept taut during the wrapping. Make as many turns as necessary to build the tape insulation to the desired thickness. Then cut or tear the tape and press it around itself, finishing it as smoothly as possible.

Solderless connectors

Solderless connectors of several types are used to make electrical connections between the wires inside appliances. Plastic screw-on connectors, called wire nuts, are the most common type and are satisfactory for most uses. They come in size to accomodate different

1 Tinning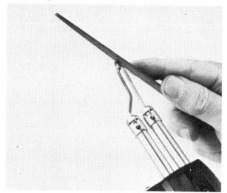

2

1 Soldering a splice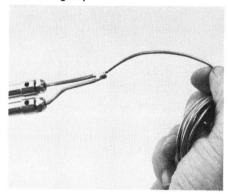

2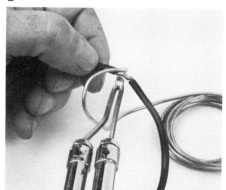

1 Taping a joint

2

1 Solderless connectors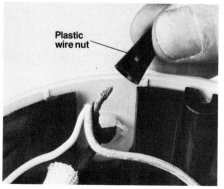

Plastic wire nut

2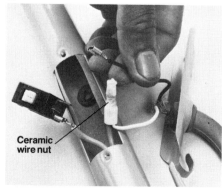

Ceramic wire nut

wire thicknesses and different numbers of wires. If the connection is subject to vibration, as in motor-driven appliances, wrap tape around the wires and the base of the wire nut.

Wire nuts contain a tapered metal insert with spiral grooves that grip the ends of the wires

when you screw on the wire nut. Trim the insulation from the wires so that when the wire nut is screwed down tight no bare wire shows.

Hold the wires together approximately parallel. Twist the wire nut clockwise onto the wires (no. 1, opposite, bottom). Check each wire to

make certain it cannot be pulled free.

In high temperature areas inside appliances such as heaters and irons, ceramic wire nuts (no. 2, opposite, bottom) are used. They are installed in the same way as the plastic type.

Disassembly—locating hidden screws and removing knobs

The objective in do-it-yourself repair should be to inspect the inner workings and repair the appliance or replace parts with as little disassembly as possible. Since many appliances are designed to conceal the method of assembly, some general tips on disassembling will be helpful. (See also page 31.)

Snap-on parts. Look for removable plastic parts on the main housing. Mounting screws are often concealed beneath these parts.

Felt, rubber, or plastic feet. Projections attached to the main housing to protect work surfaces may conceal screws.

Deeply recessed screws. Don't overlook openings in the housing because no screw is visible. Screw heads may be recessed an inch or more, so inspect the housing carefully with a flashlight.

Metal inserts in plastic. The manufacturer's metal nameplate frequently conceals assembly screws on the bottom of an appliance. If the unit otherwise fails to come apart, pry the nameplate off by slipping a knife blade between the edge of the metal piece and the plastic.

Removing knobs. Even after you have located and removed the screws, control knobs may have to be taken off before the panels and trim can be removed. Inspect the knob; loosen any visible setscrews. They may be slotted or have recessed hexagonal-heads. You will need an Allen wrench for the recessed hexagonal-head screws.

If no setscrew is visible, probably the knob can simply be pulled off. If the knob has multiple settings (as opposed to simply ON-OFF) turn it preferably to LOW or HIGH. Make a note of what the setting was. If the part containing the knob's shaft has to be removed, this setting note will help you reassemble the unit properly. Often the shaft has a flat section and the knob has a similar opening. In this case the knob and shaft can be assembled in only one way. In other cases, splined shafts may be used. A spline is a projection on a shaft that holds the knob in place. Your notes will be helpful because knobs and splined shafts are joined in many different positions.

Quick-disconnect spade lugs. They are best removed with needle-nose pliers.

Self-locking terminals. To free the connections to self-locking terminals, insert a straightened paper clip in the opening and pull out the wire. On some self-locking terminals a small screwdriver must be inserted in an adjacent slot.

Foot covering screw

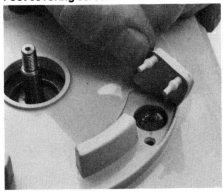

Decal covering screw

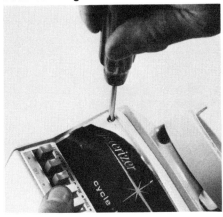

Removing knob

Finding hidden setscrew

Freeing self-locking terminal

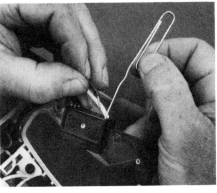

BENCH TIP

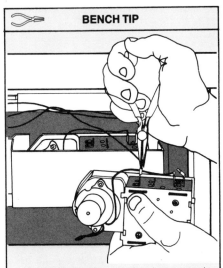

When replacing a part that has several electrical connections, remove the leads from the old part and connect them to the new part one by one. If this is not practical, label them with masking tape or make a careful sketch like this one to show how the connections were made. Be sure to note the colors of the wires and the positions of the parts.

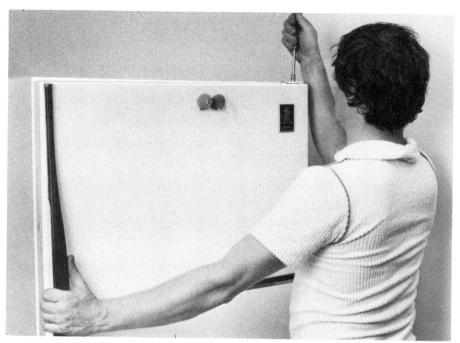

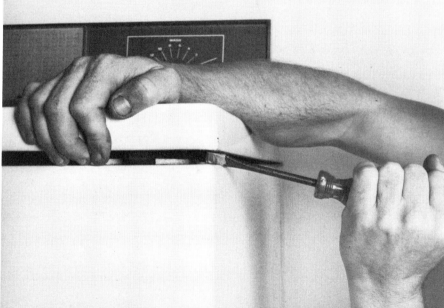

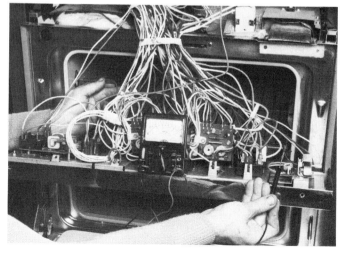

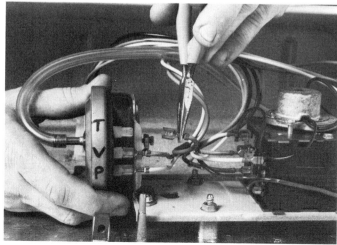

Large Appliances

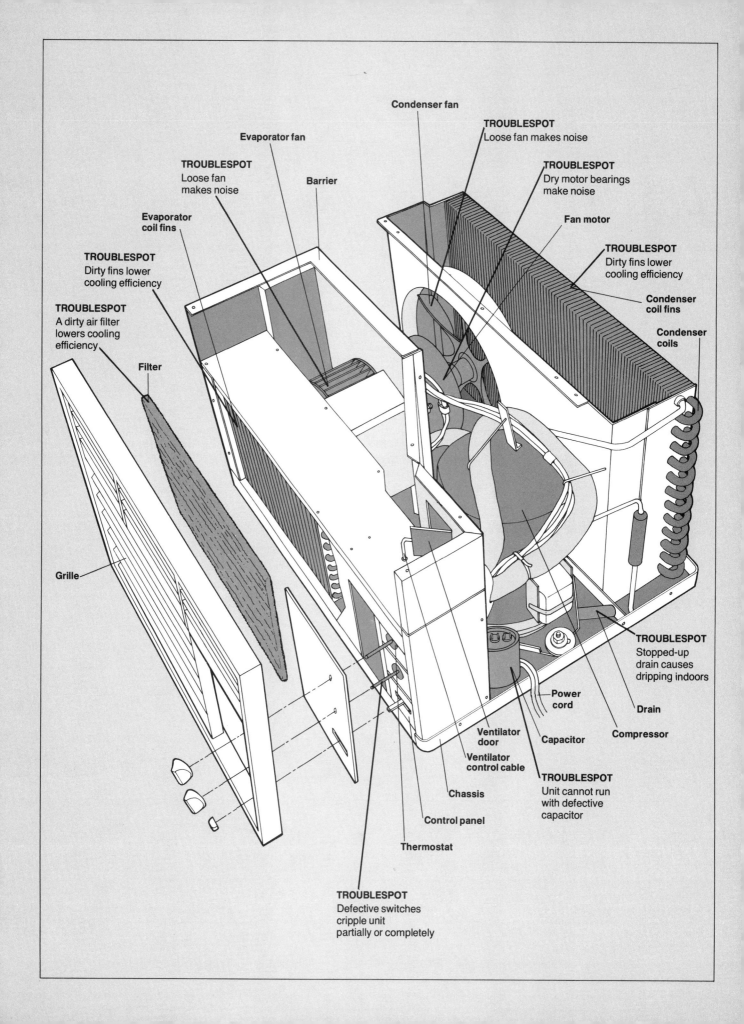

Condenser fan

TROUBLESPOT
Loose fan makes noise

Evaporator fan

TROUBLESPOT
Loose fan
makes noise

Barrier

TROUBLESPOT
Dry motor bearings
make noise

Evaporator
coil fins

Fan motor

TROUBLESPOT
Dirty fins lower
cooling efficiency

TROUBLESPOT
Dirty fins lower
cooling efficiency

TROUBLESPOT
Dirty fins lower
cooling efficiency

Condenser
coil fins

TROUBLESPOT
A dirty air filter
lowers cooling
efficiency

Condenser
coils

Filter

Grille

TROUBLESPOT
Stopped-up
drain causes
dripping indoors

Power
cord

Drain

Ventilator
door

Capacitor

Compressor

Ventilator
control cable

TROUBLESPOT
Unit cannot run
with defective
capacitor

Chassis

Control panel

Thermostat

TROUBLESPOT
Defective switches
cripple unit
partially or completely

Air Conditioners

Air-conditioning units perform three comfort-making jobs in the home: they cool the air, dehumidify it, and filter out floating pollution. The cooling results from the constant circulation of a refrigerant around the unit (see diagram, below left). The refrigerant, usually known by its trade name, Freon, picks up heat inside the house and pumps it outside. Dehumidifying occurs at the same time but for different reasons (see diagram, below right). And the filter just behind the grille cleans the air—at least it does if you keep the filter clean! Other regular maintenance information is given here, as are simple mechanical adjustments. Some uncomplicated electrical tests and replacement procedures are explained step by step.

Anyone familiar with air conditioners knows that a problem can have several causes. Turn first to the troubleshooting chart at the end of the section for help in diagnosing the root of your unit's unhappy symptoms. Even if you would rather not do the repair suggested by the chart, you'll be ahead of the game when you discuss the matter with a repairman.

CAUTION An air conditioner is a complicated, delicate machine. Testing and correcting problems in the cooling system itself requires tools and skills beyond the average homeowner's reach. It is better to let a trained technician handle the compressor and the refrigerant, sealed under pressure in its complicated set of tubing.

TIPS FOR ENERGY EFFICIENCY
Buy an air conditioner with a high Energy Efficiency Rating (EER). Ratings range from 5 to 12. Any rating from 8 to 10 is good.
Buy a unit that fits your needs. The BTU rating of the unit should be appropriate for the size of the space it must cool. Consult your appliance dealer on what unit to buy.
Install a window unit on the shady side of the house. If the unit must be installed on the sunny side, provide a shade for it.
Keep air conditioner grilles and filters clean.
Keep the temperature set as high as possible. In a dehumidified room 78° F. is really not uncomfortable.
Close air ducts and chimney dampers so that cool air is not lost.
Close blinds and window shades when the sun shines in.
Don't make heat while the air conditioner is working. For example, don't run the dishwasher at the same time.

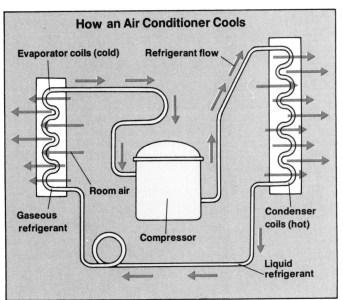

How an Air Conditioner Cools

Evaporator coils (cold) — Refrigerant flow — Room air — Gaseous refrigerant — Compressor — Condenser coils (hot) — Liquid refrigerant

The compressor continually pumps the refrigerant around the sealed cooling system. When pressurized refrigerant reaches the evaporator coils, an expansion valve lets it expand suddenly and change to a gas. It's a law of physics that a liquid changing to a gas absorbs a lot of heat. The squirrel-cage fan blows hot room air across the evaporator coils so the refrigerant has an endless supply of heat to absorb. Then the gaseous refrigerant flows toward the condenser coils, outside the room, where extreme pressure forces it to condense. Another law of physics says that a condensing gas releases a great deal of heat. The bladed fan continually forces a stream of outside air across the condenser coils, from which the air absorbs the unwanted inside heat carried there by the refrigerant.

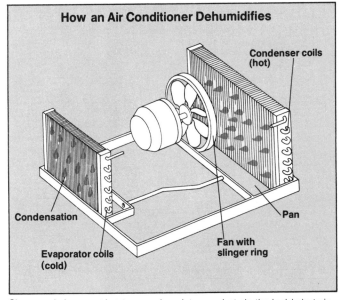

How an Air Conditioner Dehumidifies

Condenser coils (hot) — Condensation — Pan — Evaporator coils (cold) — Fan with slinger ring

Since cool air cannot hold as much moisture as hot air, the inside hot air must drop its moisture as it passes across the cooling evaporator coils. This condensed moisture drains through the unit to the pan under the hot condenser coils. There it evaporates and is blown outside. Many units have a slinger ring around the condenser fan that flips the water out of the pan onto the coils to hasten evaporation.

Getting inside

In most air-conditioning units, all the major components are mounted on a chassis that can be pulled straight out of the unit after the grille is removed. Be prepared to support the chassis on a bench or table close at hand. Some units have no mounting shell but have a removable cover and side panels. Never turn a unit upside down or on its side; something is bound to bend or break.

CAUTION Before starting to work near the wiring or the motor, discharge the capacitor to avoid the risk of shock. (See the box on discharging the capacitor, page 42.)

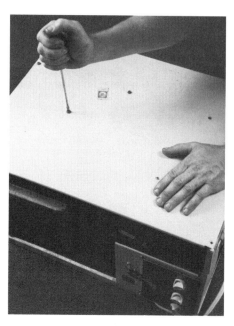

Pull the chassis out after the grille has been removed. Be careful not to damage the fragile aluminum fins or the tubing.

Top and side panels come off when retaining screws are removed. You may need a screwdriver, a Phillips screwdriver, or a hex nut driver.
CAUTION Remove only those screws (if any) that hold the panels.

Regular maintenance

Do all five basic maintenance steps shown here at the beginning of every cooling season. Then clean or replace the air filter every month. Dirty filters cause more unnecessary service calls than any other complaint, and are the easiest to put right. As you work, keep an eye open for loose screws and bolts. Examine wiring for worn spots in the insulation. And at the end of the cooling season, cover the outside of the unit with a plastic sheet or the manufacturer's winter cover. It will prevent rust and save heat, too.

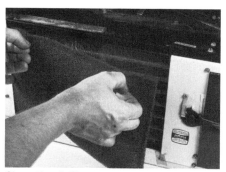

Clean the air filter at the beginning of the cooling season and once a month while the unit is being used. Wash a permanent filter in hot, sudsy water; replace other filters with exact duplicates.

Open clogged drain holes with a piece of stiff wire, so water dripping down on the evaporator side can flow through to the other side of the barrier. Check also for an outside drain hole on the condenser side. Bend the wire so that it can be turned like an auger, as shown above.

Clean condenser fins and surrounding cabinet area with the radiator attachment of a vacuum cleaner. Oily deposits should be removed with a solvent. The air filter should keep dust from accumulating on the evaporator fins, but check them to be sure.

Straighten bent fins on evaporators and condensers; they cut efficiency by blocking airflow and also cause whistling and dripping. Use a pencil, putty knife, or a fin-straightening comb.
CAUTION Work carefully—the fins are fragile.

Lubricate the motor with one or two drops of SAE 10 oil in the oil holes or tubes found at both ends of the motor. Even permanently oiled motors benefit from seasonal oiling of the shaft.

Mechanical adjustments

Strange noises or unusual vibrations coming from the unit may signal the beginning of serious problems. Before sending for the repairman, check the troubleshooting chart on the following pages for possible causes. Often problems can be solved by making the simple mechanical adjustments shown here.

CAUTION Remember to discharge the capacitor first (see page 42).

The basic test (at right) is to hold the two fans, one hand on each fan, and try to turn them in opposite directions. You will discover at once if either fan is loose. Also, turn the fans in the same direction to be sure that they move freely. If the fans are hard to turn, the motor may need lubrication (see opposite page) or realignment.

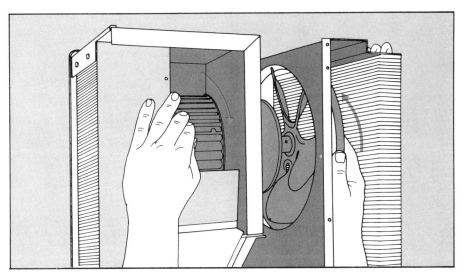

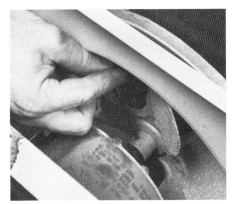

Tighten the bladed fan by turning the setscrew on its hub with a screwdriver or an Allen wrench. If your fan has a rubber hub, replace it when it is hard or cracked. A fan with broken or missing blades should be replaced, because the resulting vibration can damage the motor.

Tighten a squirrel-cage fan on its shaft with a long Allen wrench. To reach the screw on the fan shaft, insert the wrench through the hole in the fan blade.

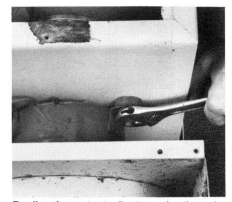

Realign the motor by first loosening the motor mounting nuts. When they are loose, the fans should turn freely. Tighten each nut a couple of turns in sequence around the mounting, testing the fans at each step, until all the nuts are tight.

Hard or cracked compressor mounts magnify the compressor's sound. Replace deteriorated rubber mounts by unscrewing the mounting nuts and lifting the compressor to free the mounts. **CAUTION** Move the compressor as little as possible. A kinked refrigerant tube must be replaced by a repairman.

Silence a rattling exhaust vent by applying a few bits of self-sticking weather stripping around the opening. A thin layer will do the job.

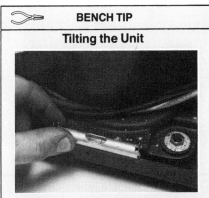

BENCH TIP
Tilting the Unit

To guarantee that the moisture dripping from the evaporator coils will flow through the unit to the outside, set the outside end of the unit about a quarter of an inch lower than the inside end. Use a level laid along the chassis to check this slight tilt. Or pour a little water beneath the evaporator coils and tilt the unit so it gradually flows toward the outside.

Electrical problems

Problems with the thermostat, the capacitor, or the selector switch cause the unit to fail completely or partially; for instance, the compressor may operate, but the fans fail, or the compressor may run continuously. Each electrical component can be tested and replaced if necessary.

CAUTION Before working inside the unit, always discharge the capacitor. (See box at right.)

When replacing any electrical part, always install an exact duplicate of the original. After finishing work and double-checking all wiring, take the added safety precaution of checking the unit for ground (see Blue Pages: *A word about safety*).

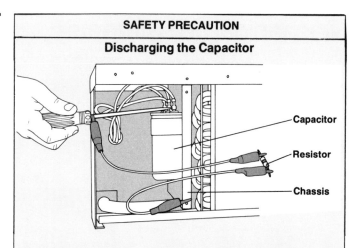

SAFETY PRECAUTION

Discharging the Capacitor

— Capacitor

— Resistor

— Chassis

Before starting to work on the inside of any air-conditioning unit, always discharge the capacitor (there may be two). You can get a severe electrical shock if you touch a charged capacitor. With alligator clips, connect one lead of a 100,000-ohm, 2-watt resistor to the chassis, and the other to the shaft of a screwdriver. (**CAUTION** Hold the screwdriver by its insulated handle.) Then touch the screwdriver tip to each capacitor terminal in turn.

The thermostat

If the compressor runs continuously or not at all, test the thermostat. Unplug the unit, discharge the capacitor (see box above), and pull the knobs off the faceplate to get at the control panel where the thermostat is mounted.

Some older units have a sensing bulb mounted on the evaporator fins and connected to the thermostat by a thin tube; handle it carefully. All newer models have a bimetallic temperature-sensitive switch inside the thermostat. Label the leads to the thermostat and remove them. To prepare the thermostat for testing, disconnect one end of its resistor (if it has one) with a soldering iron.

1 **To test and replace a thermostat,** take out the screws that hold the thermostat to the control panel. Disconnect the leads to the thermostat, marking them so that you can connect the replacement properly. **CAUTION** If your unit has a sensing bulb, disengage it from the unit carefully.

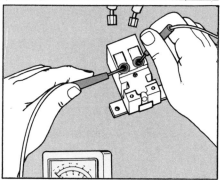

2 Attach probes from a VOM or a continuity tester to the thermostat terminals (see Blue Pages: *Electrical testers*.) With the thermostat in the OFF position, there should be no continuity; at any other setting there should be continuity. After this test, put the thermostat in the freezer for fifteen minutes and test again. The cold thermostat should show no continuity at any setting.

The capacitor

A faulty capacitor will stop the compressor dead, and the fans, too, if they are on the same circuit. Unplug the unit and look for the capacitor behind the grille. If it is not there, take the chassis out to get at the capacitor near the compressor or the fan motor.

CAUTION Discharge the capacitor before working on it. Read the box above.

If the capacitor vent is blown, or the capacitor bulges or leaks oil, replace it.

Test the capacitor with a VOM set at RX1 (see Blue Pages: *Electrical testers*). Disconnect one lead to the capacitor and touch the meter probes to the capacitor terminals. If the needle jumps to HIGH and then returns to 0, the capacitor is OK. If the needle holds at HIGH or does not move, the capacitor is bad. If your capacitor has three terminals, test the terminal at each side with the central terminal.

When replacing a defective capacitor, label the leads as you disconnect the old capacitor so you can connect the new one properly. Pull the leads straight off the terminals. Always use a capacitor of the same peak voltage and rated capacity as the original.

The selector switch

If neither fan nor compressor runs at any selector switch setting, and both thermostat and capacitor test OK (see opposite page), then the switch may be defective. A continuity tester will confirm this (see Blue Pages: *Electrical testers*). If the thermostat is OK and the fans run at one switch setting but not at another, examine all leads connected to the switch. If any terminal appears burned or any insulation on the wires is discolored, replace the switch and repair bad leads. If the compressor runs when the switch is set to COOL but the fans do not, the fan motor is probably bad.

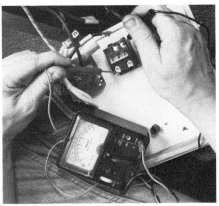

1 **To remove the selector switch,** pry off the control knobs, take off the faceplate, and remove the control panel. Label the switch relative to the faceplate so you can tell OFF from ON. Label the leads before you disconnect them from the switch.

2 Check the switch for continuity at all settings. All settings should show continuity except OFF. If any setting is defective, replace the entire switch.

Central air conditioning

Central air conditioners operate the same way single-room units do, but the components are separated by many feet of piping. The diagram at right shows central air conditioning installed in a home with a forced-air heating system. The evaporator (cooling) coils fit inside the furnace itself, so the furnace blower forces cool, dehumidified air through the same ducts that carry hot air in wintertime. The compressor and condenser coils stand outside the house in a separate cabinet that is connected to the evaporator (called the A-frame in such installations) by insulated tubing. You can't reach the evaporator coils because they're sealed inside the furnace, but don't forget to clean the air filter or replace it regularly. Keep the outside cabinet clean and unobstructed.

If your home has hot water heating, air ducts must be installed for central air conditioning, and the evaporator coils and blower are usually placed together in the attic. In this case, a hose leads the condensed water from the evaporator outside to a drain. Be sure this hose is open and running during the cooling season.

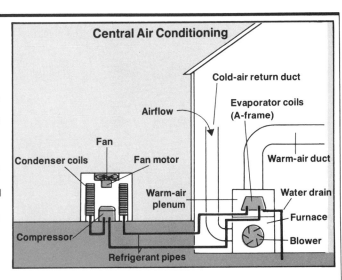

Central Air Conditioning

Cold-air return duct · Airflow · Evaporator coils (A-frame) · Fan · Condenser coils · Fan motor · Warm-air duct · Warm-air plenum · Water drain · Furnace · Compressor · Blower · Refrigerant pipes

Remove any debris

Clean the inside

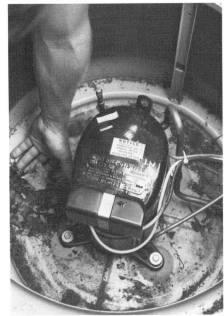

Remove any debris blocking the condenser coils in the outdoor section of the central air conditioning installation so airflow remains unobstructed. Anything on the coils—from leaves to spider webs—cuts down efficiency.

Clean the inside of the outdoor cabinet regularly. Dirt on the compressor makes it work harder and become hotter. See *Mechanical adjustments*, page 41, for procedures to use in checking the fan and fan motor. When the cooling season ends, protect the unit with a heavy plastic cover or a tarp.

Room Air Conditioners Troubleshooting Chart

WHAT'S WRONG	REASONS WHY	WHAT TO DO
Unit does not run at all.	No power reaching unit	Turn off unit; check for blown fuse or tripped circuit breaker; test outlet (see Blue Pages, *Electrical testers*).
	Defective line cord	Test cord and replace if necessary.
	Defective selector switch	Test switch.
	Defective thermostat	Test thermostat.
	Defective capacitor	Test capacitor.
	Low refrigerant level	Call repairman.
	Defective compressor	Call repairman.
Fans run but compressor does not (unit does not cool).	Defective thermostat	Test thermostat.
	Condenser fins clogged with dirt	Clean fins.
	Wrong voltage on line	Check line voltage.
	Defective overload switch	Check switch.
	Defective running capacitor	Check capacitor.
	Defective compressor	Call repairman.
	Defective selector switch	Check switch.
Unit continually blows fuses or trips circuit breaker.	Unit restarted too soon	Wait at least five minutes before restarting.
	Circuit overloaded	Don't run any other appliance on the air-conditioner circuit. Use only the recommended time-delay fuse.
	Short circuit in wiring	Make sure all electrical connections are tight and no exposed wires are touching metal.
	Defective compressor	Call repairman.
	Defective capacitor	Test capacitor.
	Low refrigerant level	Call repairman.
Unit runs but does not cool properly.	Thermostat set wrong	Turn thermostat to cooler setting.
	Filter clogged with dirt	Clean or replace filter.
	Dirty condenser	Vacuum condenser; use solvent to remove oily dirt.
	Unit too small for the job	Ask repairman or appliance dealer for advice. Write Ass'n of Home Appliance Manufacturers (20 N. Wacker Drive, Chicago, Ill. 60606) for a Cooling-Load Estimate Form for a room air conditioner.
	Outside temperature too cool	Don't operate unit when outside temperature falls below 70°F.
	Loose blower fan	Check and adjust fan.
	Air leaks around unit	Seal all joints around unit. Make sure nothing blocks front grille.
	Leaking refrigerant	Put thick soap suds on refrigerant line joints. If bubbles swell, refrigerant is leaking. Call repairman.
	Low refrigerant level	Call repairman.
Compressor turns on and off frequently.	Dirty evaporator	Clean evaporator.
	Dirty condenser	Clean and straighten condenser fins.
	Defective fan motor	Test motor. If motor hums but does not turn, check for obstructions around fan. Lubricate fan motor and fan bearings.
	Dirty filter	Clean or replace filter.
	Low refrigerant level	Call repairman.

Room Air Conditioners Troubleshooting Chart

WHAT'S WRONG	REASONS WHY	WHAT TO DO
Frost forms on evaporator.	Dirty filter	Clean filter and all air-flow areas.
	Outside temperature too low	Don't run unit when outside temperature is below 70°F.
	Leaking refrigerant	Call repairman.
Unit is noisy.	Loose panels, trim, screws, or supports	Tighten all screws and supports; if window rattles, use a wooden wedge to force it tight.
	Loose fan blades	Check and tighten fan screws.
	Worn compressor mounts	Check and replace.
	Dry fan motor bearings	Check and lubricate bearings.
	Tubing rattling	Carefully bend tubing so that it does not touch nearby parts.
	Bent evaporator fins (whistling noises)	Clean and straighten fins.
Water drips from inside unit. (NOTE: outside dripping is normal especially in humid weather.)	Clogged drain	Clean drain.
	Unit not installed correctly	Adjust unit so that outside is 1/4 inch lower than inside.
	Slinger ring needs adjustment	If your unit has a slinger ring, it should run 1/16 inch above the pan for best water pickup.
Unit smells.	Clogged drain holes (musty odor)	Open drain holes and clean pan.
	Dirty evaporator (oil or tobacco odors)	Vacuum fins; spray with deodorizer.

Central Air Conditioning Troubleshooting Chart

Most problems connected with central air conditioning systems are like those described above for room air conditioners. Problems peculiar to central air conditioners are given below. NOTE: Central air conditioning systems installed in forced-air heating systems have the condenser coil (A-frame) mounted inside the furnace – warm air plenum; it should be checked by a serviceman.

WHAT'S WRONG	REASONS WHY	WHAT TO DO
Water leaks into walls or ceiling.	Clogged drain hose from condenser pan (in attic installations)	Make sure hose can empty freely.
Unit cycles on and off.	Leaves and rubbish clogging evaporator unit; fan blocked	Keep evaporator unit clean.
	Hot sun beating on evaporator unit	Make shade for the unit (tree, wall, etc.).
	Insulation has fallen off feed line.	Secure insulation firmly to line; replace worn-out insulation.

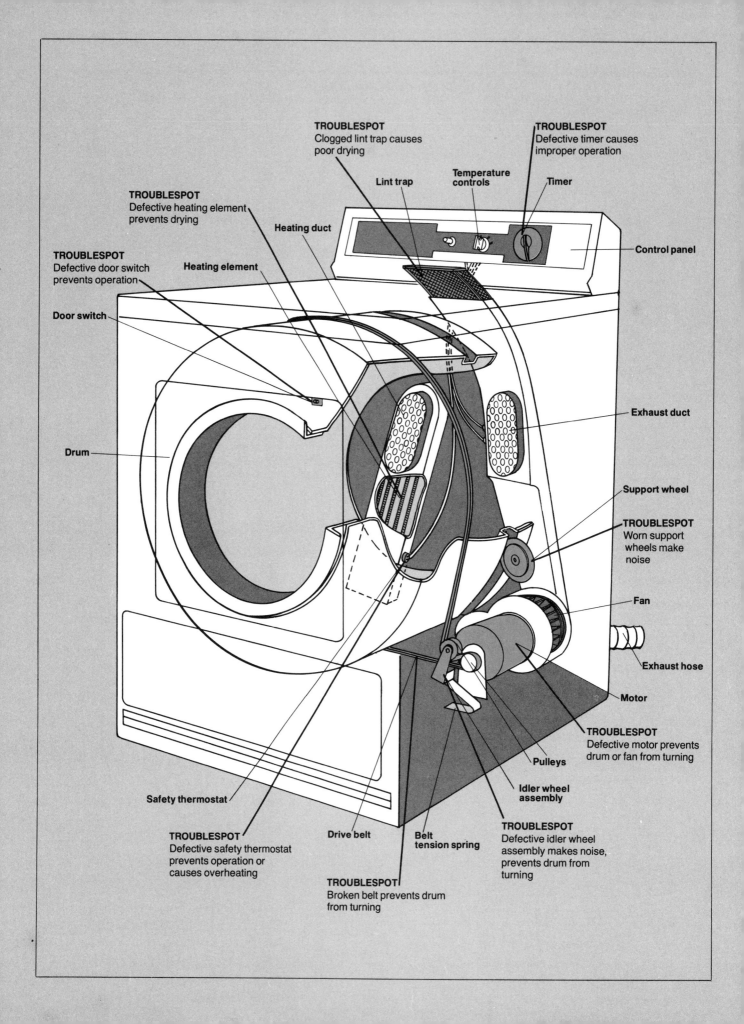

TROUBLESPOT
Clogged lint trap causes
poor drying

TROUBLESPOT
Defective timer causes
improper operation

Lint trap

Temperature
controls

Timer

TROUBLESPOT
Defective heating element
prevents drying

Heating duct

Control panel

TROUBLESPOT
Defective door switch
prevents operation

Heating element

Door switch

Exhaust duct

Drum

Support wheel

TROUBLESPOT
Worn support
wheels make
noise

Fan

Exhaust hose

Motor

TROUBLESPOT
Defective motor prevents
drum or fan from turning

Pulleys

Idler wheel
assembly

Safety thermostat

TROUBLESPOT
Defective safety thermostat
prevents operation or
causes overheating

Drive belt

Belt
tension spring

TROUBLESPOT
Defective idler wheel
assembly makes noise,
prevents drum from
turning

TROUBLESPOT
Broken belt prevents drum
from turning

Clothes Driers
Electric

Clothes driers are generally robust, long-lived machines. Their design and operation are based on simple principles. There is a source of heat, either an electric heating element or a gas burner; there is a motor that turns a drum to tumble the clothes and also turns a fan to circulate the hot air; there are a few controls, either a simple on/off timer or perhaps an elaborate panel offering choices in drying cycles and temperatures. Some safety switches and thermostats complete the electrical setup.

Most owners encounter few problems with the electrical parts of a drier until the appliance begins to wear out, after a long and useful life. Complaints of "poor drying" can usually be traced to clogged lint traps and exhaust systems, so the most important regular maintenance you can do is to keep the unit lint-free.

The most common mechanical problem usually involves a broken drive belt. On some models it may be possible to put a new belt on without taking the drum out, but it's a cumbersome process in any case. Read the suggestions on the next page for the easiest procedure. Take a good look at the diagram that shows how the belt is threaded around the drum, the motor, and the idler wheel, so you can get a new one on right.

A common complaint about driers is "too much noise." The bottom box at right gives hints for solving this problem.

Instructions are given on page 50 for testing the door switch and the centrifugal switch. If you can read your unit's wiring diagram, you can test and replace any other switches your model may have, as well as the timer. You must open up the back to make tests and repairs on the thermostat and the heating element. Before working on an electric drier, carefully read the Blue Pages, which describe electricity and electrical testing, and become thoroughly familiar with your volt-ohm meter (VOM). For information about a gas clothes drier's burner, turn to page 52.

> **CAUTION** Most electric clothes driers operate on 240 volts AC, which is potentially deadly. Always pull the plug or turn the power off at the circuit breaker before starting to work inside the drier, and make sure no one turns the power on while you are working.

TIPS FOR ENERGY EFFICIENCY

Clean the lint trap after each drying.

Clean exhaust vent and hoses regularly.

Use the lowest temperature setting practical or recommended for fabric type.

Dry clothes only to damp-dry condition if you intend to iron them.

Do light drying in one load, heavy drying in another.

Do several loads consecutively to save heat stored up in the drier.

Don't overdry clothes. Natural fibers like wool and cotton need to retain a little moisture to avoid wrinkling.

Install the drier where it can get fresh, dry air.

In summer, vent the drier outside to reduce heat and humidity in the house. In winter, consider venting the drier inside, using a lint filter attachment, to keep heat and humidity levels up.

On a sunny day, try the clothesline.

Reducing Drier Noises

As driers grow older they may develop annoying noises. Here's how to reduce them.

Tighten loose drive belts. There should be about ¼ inch of play in a belt when it's pressed halfway between the pulleys.

Loosen tight belts. Tight belts put a strain on all moving parts, causing wear and noise.

Tighten loose fans, impellers, and pulleys by screwing the shaft setscrews in tight.

Make sure the drier sits level. Use a spirit level to check side to side and front to back.

Sometimes lint or an object becomes wedged between the drum and the cabinet. If the drum binds in any spot, check for an obstruction.

Replace worn support wheels (see page 49).

Cleaning air passages

Regular cleaning of lint traps, air vents, and exhaust hoses is a must: clogged air passages cripple the unit's capacity to dry clothes, thus wasting energy. In many models the lint trap is located on top of the unit, as shown below. For another location, see page 53.

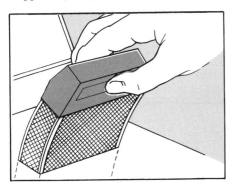

Pull the lint trap out of the drier after every drying session and remove the lint.

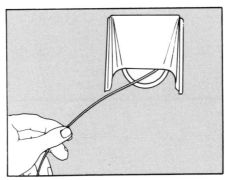

Check the outdoor air vent once a year to make sure there is no obstruction.

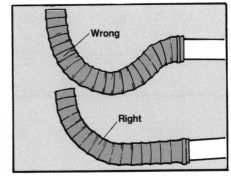

Remove the exhaust hose annually and clean it out. Don't let any dips or kinks develop, as they trap lint. Seal hose joints with duct tape.

Getting inside from the front

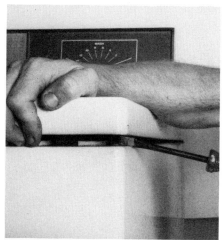

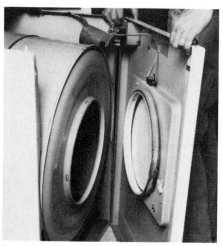

To open the top, pry it up carefully but firmly at the side (near the clips) with a screwdriver.

Wrap the screwdriver end with tape or paper to prevent damage to the finish. When the top pops off the clip, lift it up.

If your unit has screws at the back of the top, remove them, pull the top forward, and then lift it up at the front.

To get the front loose, snap it away from the sides and bottom. Some models may have screws to remove. If there is a front-mounted timer, be careful not to damage the wires attached to it. Label and disconnect them if necessary. On some models, the front panel supports the drum; in such a case, have a block of wood handy to prop up the drum.

To get the drum out, lift it slightly and pull it forward off the support wheels. Reach underneath the drum and slip the drive belt off the idler wheel assembly and motor drive shaft. Lift the drum out of the unit. NOTE: If the drum is supported on a center shaft; open the back of the unit and remove screws or rings holding the drum to the shaft. Then lift the drum out.

Replacing the drive belt

To replace a broken drive belt (or a broken idler wheel assembly), remove the drum as described above and remove the old belt. (In the model shown here, it's easier to install the new belt if you have first tipped the unit on its back.) Put the drum in, slipping it over the support wheels. Rotate the drum slowly to seat the gasket (if there is one). Slip the new belt around the drum, over the idler wheel, and over the motor drive shaft, so that it's in the S-pattern shown at near right. Some models have two drive belts, in the pattern shown below.

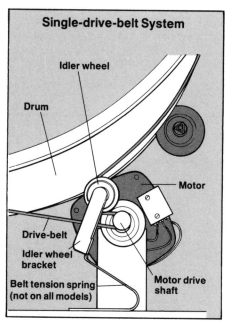

Single-drive-belt System

Idler wheel

Drum

Motor

Drive-belt

Idler wheel bracket

Belt tension spring (not on all models)

Motor drive shaft

Install single drive belts in the S-pattern shown here.

Two-drive-belt systems look like the illustration at right. Remove the belt tension spring and the idler pulley first; then the belts come off easily. Replace both belts together.

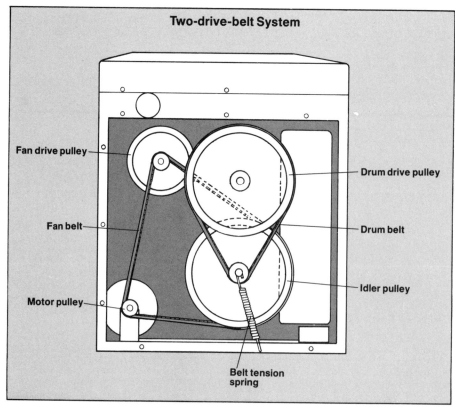

Two-drive-belt System

Fan drive pulley

Fan belt

Motor pulley

Drum drive pulley

Drum belt

Idler pulley

Belt tension spring

Replacing support wheels

Rumbling, bumping noises in the drier can be caused by worn support wheels. Turn the drum by hand and listen closely; if you hear several bumps for each revolution of the drum, the wheels are probably worn out.

To inspect or replace the wheels, turn off the power, lay unit on its back, open the unit from the front and take out the drum (see opposite page). Remove worn wheels and replace them.

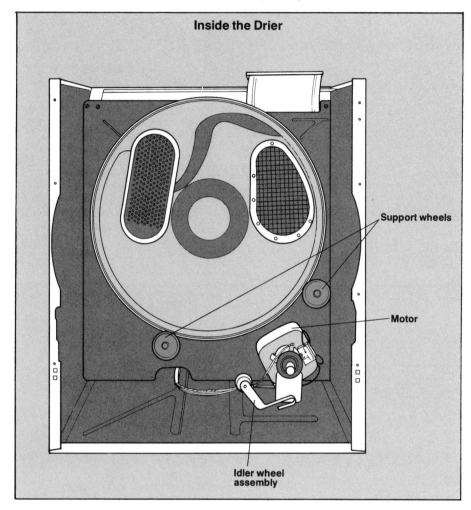

Inside the Drier

Support wheels

Motor

Idler wheel assembly

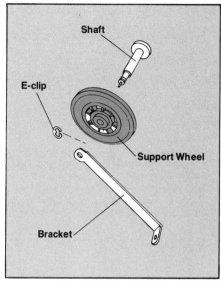

Shaft

E-clip

Support Wheel

Bracket

To remove a support wheel, pry off the retaining clip. Slip the wheel off its shaft and replace it with a new one. Some models may have a bracket screwed to the bottom of the cabinet and the shaft; take the screws out to get the wheel off.

Electrical problems

Some driers, have only a simple timer and one heat level. Others, like the one shown at the right, offer different heat levels and various heating and cooling cycles. In any case, defective timers and switches can be tested for continuity (see Blue Pages: *Electrical testers*) and replaced if defective (see instructions for replacing a timer under *Dishwashers,* page 62). Always install parts identical to those discarded; a nonmatching part can cause electrical failure.

To get inside the control panel, turn off the power, remove the screws that attach the panel to the cabinet and lay the panel down.

To test a push-button on/off switch in the control panel for continuity, pull one power lead off the switch and attach VOM probes to the terminals. There should be continuity with the button pushed in and no continuity with it out. Replace a switch that fails this test.

Door switch

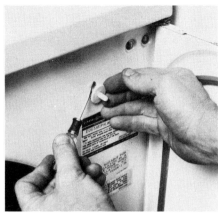

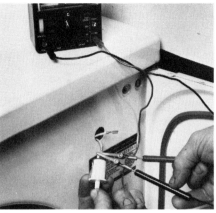

1 **Check the door switch** if there's power to the unit, but it doesn't run. Pry the switch carefully out of the front panel with a screwdriver in order to test it for continuity (see Blue Pages: *Electrical testers*). On some models the switch may be screwed into the panel.

2 Turn off the power, disconnect one power lead to the switch, and attach VOM probes to the switch terminals. There should be continuity when the button is pressed and no continuity otherwise. Replace a switch that fails these tests.

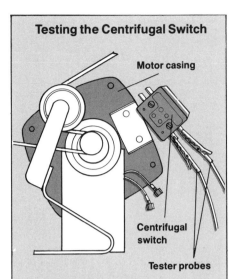

Testing the Centrifugal Switch

Motor casing

Centrifugal switch

Tester probes

Test the centrifugal switch for continuity if the door switch is OK and there's power to the unit but it doesn't run. Check your unit's wiring diagram to locate the connections. If the switch shows no continuity, replace it. This switch is sometimes mounted on the motor casing and sometimes inside the motor.

Getting inside from the back

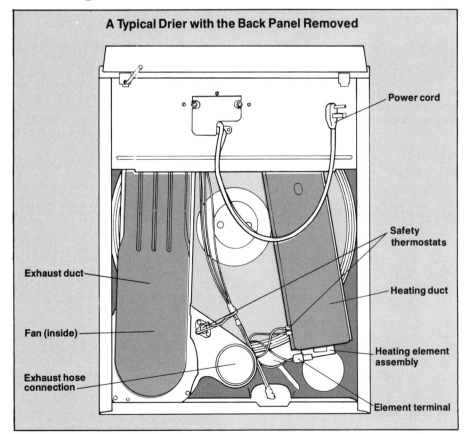

A Typical Drier with the Back Panel Removed

Power cord

Safety thermostats

Heating duct

Heating element assembly

Element terminal

Exhaust duct

Fan (inside)

Exhaust hose connection

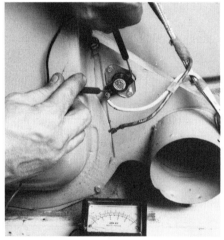

Check the safety thermostat (also called the overheat protector) for resistance if the drier doesn't heat. Turn the power off. Set your VOM at RX1. Disconnect one of the power leads to the thermostat, and attach VOM probes to the terminals. You should read 0 ohms. If the reading is high, the part is defective. Unscrew it from the cabinet and replace it with a duplicate.

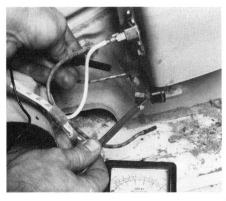

Check the heating element's resistance (right) if the drier heats poorly or not at all. Turn off the power and disconnect the leads to the element. Attach VOM probes to the element terminals. With the meter at RX1, it should read between 8 and 20 ohms resistance. A higher or no reading means a defective element. Then test the element for ground by touching one probe to the heating duct and one to a terminal; if there is low resistance (less than infinity) the element is grounded and defective. Replace it with a duplicate.

Replacing a heating element

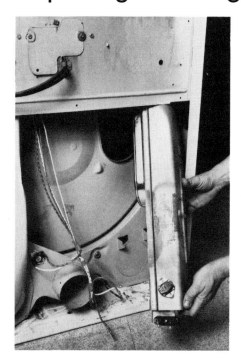

1 To remove a heating element (left), turn off the power and disconnect the power leads to the element. Remove the screws that attach the heating duct to the cabinet and lift it out. You may have to remove the top panels as well as the back to reach all the duct screws.

2 To remove the element from the heating duct, take out the screw that holds the element mounting bracket to the duct. Pull the element out. Element defects are shown at right. When installing an element, be very careful not to bend or stretch the coils; if they touch the heating duct they will ground the element.

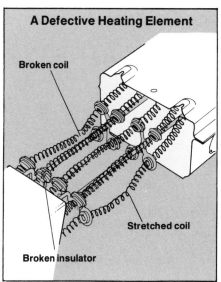

An element assembly with any of these defects must be replaced.

Electric Clothes Driers Troubleshooting Chart		
WHAT'S WRONG	**REASONS WHY**	**WHAT TO DO**
Drier doesn't run at all.	Door open	Shut door tightly.
	No power at outlet	Check fuse box/circuit breaker.
	Loose wiring to motor	Tighten connections.
	Defective door switch	Check switch and replace.
	Defective centrifugal switch	Check switch and replace.
	Defective wiring between outlet and terminal block	Call electrician.
	Defective timer	Check timer and replace.
	Defective motor	Call repairman.
Motor runs, but drum doesn't turn.	Blocked drum	Open unit and check around drum to find obstruction.
	Broken drive belt	Replace belt.
	Broken idler wheel assembly	Check and replace.
	Worn support wheel	Check and replace.
Drum turns, but drier doesn't dry.	Clogged lint trap or exhaust vent	Clean trap and vent.
	Defective safety thermostat	Check and replace.
	Defective heating element	Check and replace.
	Defective timer	Check and replace.
Drier dries poorly or takes too long.	Clogged lint trap or exhaust vent	Clean trap and vent.
	Overloaded drier	Reduce load.
	Clothes too wet	Wring clothes out first.
	Fan loose on shaft	Tighten fan setscrew.
	Worn-out door gasket	Replace gasket (not on all models).
Drier doesn't shut off at end of cycle.	Defective timer	Replace timer.
	Defective dampness-sensor system	If your unit has this type of electronic control, call a repairman.

CLOTHES DRIERS

Gas

Gas clothes driers are virtually the same as electric driers, except that the heat is made by a gas burner. This means that the mechanical and electrical matters (except for the element) discussed in the previous section on electric driers apply to gas driers as well. Read pages 47 to 51 for general information about driers, tips on energy efficiency, cleaning procedures, getting inside the unit, replacing a worn-out drive belt, and checking various switches.

Problems connected with the gas burner should be left to the gas company repairman, with two exceptions. If the pilot light goes out, relight it, following the directions in your owner's manual. If you have a flameless igniter instead of a pilot light, you can test and replace it if the burner fails to light (see the opposite page).

If the drier dries poorly, remove the grille over the burner and check the burner flames. If they are yellow or if there is a roaring sound, the air/gas mixture is incorrect. Call a serviceman to adjust

it. Check the troubleshooting chart on the previous page for solutions to mechanical and electrical problems.

Don't attempt to move the drier; you may rupture a gas line or weaken a gas connection, inviting gas leaks. Call the gas company if the unit has to be moved.

CAUTIONS
If you smell gas around the drier, turn off the gas valve near the burner and call the gas company. Ventilate the room.
Whenever you work inside the unit, turn the gas valve off.
Don't smoke while working inside the unit.
If you can't reach a part you want to work on without moving the unit, call the gas company to help.

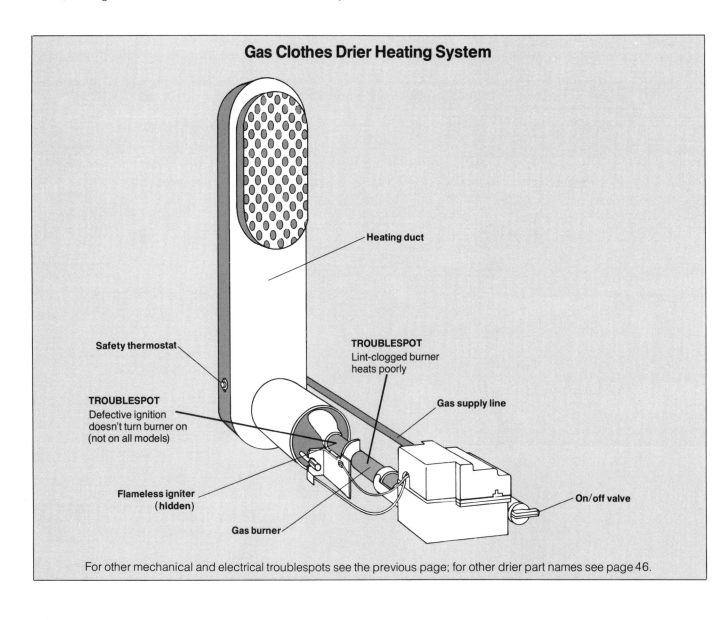

Gas Clothes Drier Heating System

Heating duct

Safety thermostat

TROUBLESPOT
Lint-clogged burner heats poorly

TROUBLESPOT
Defective ignition doesn't turn burner on (not on all models)

Gas supply line

Flameless igniter (hidden)

On/off valve

Gas burner

For other mechanical and electrical troublespots see the previous page; for other drier part names see page 46.

Cleaning air passages

Clean the lint trap after each drying cycle. A lint trap mounted just inside the door is shown at right; another type is shown at the bottom of page 47. Remove the grille over the burner occasionally and check to make sure that lint has not collected around the burner air intake. Also check the exhast hose and vent (see page 47) and make sure there are no obstructions.

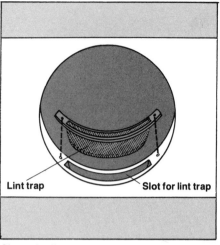

Lint trap   Slot for lint trap

Clean the lint trap after each drying cycle. If you don't keep the lint trap clean, the drier won't dry efficiently.

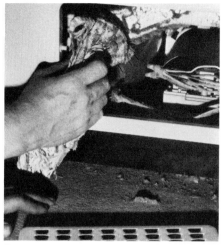

Remove the grille and wipe away any accumulations of lint and dust around the gas burner.

Checking the flameless igniter

If your drier's gas burner doesn't light and you have a flameless igniter (glow coil), first make sure there is electrical power reaching the unit (the drum will turn if there is). Then check the igniter, following this procedure: turn off the power and shut off the gas valve inside the drier. Remove the gas burner and test its igniter for resistance as described here.

After the burner has been reinstalled, check the connection for gas leaks: brush the connection with soapy water; if the bubbles expand, the connection is not tight enough.

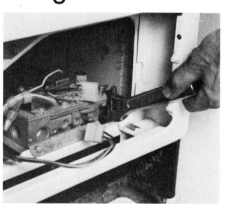

1 **Loosen the nut** that connects the gas line to the burner. Push the gas line gently aside.

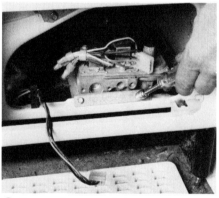

2 Remove the screws that secure the burner mounting bracket to the drier cabinet.

3 Disconnect the wires attached to the burner and lift it carefully out of the drier.

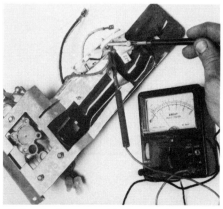

4 Lay the burner upside down and remove one wire to the igniter. Attach VOM probes to the igniter terminals. With the VOM set at RX1, you should read about 100 ohms resistance. If the igniter passes this test, the fault is elsewhere. Call a repairman.

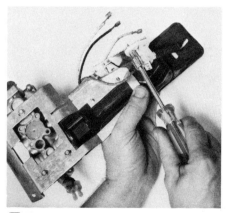

5 If the igniter fails the resistance test, unscrew it from the burner and take it to an appliance dealer for a duplicate to install.

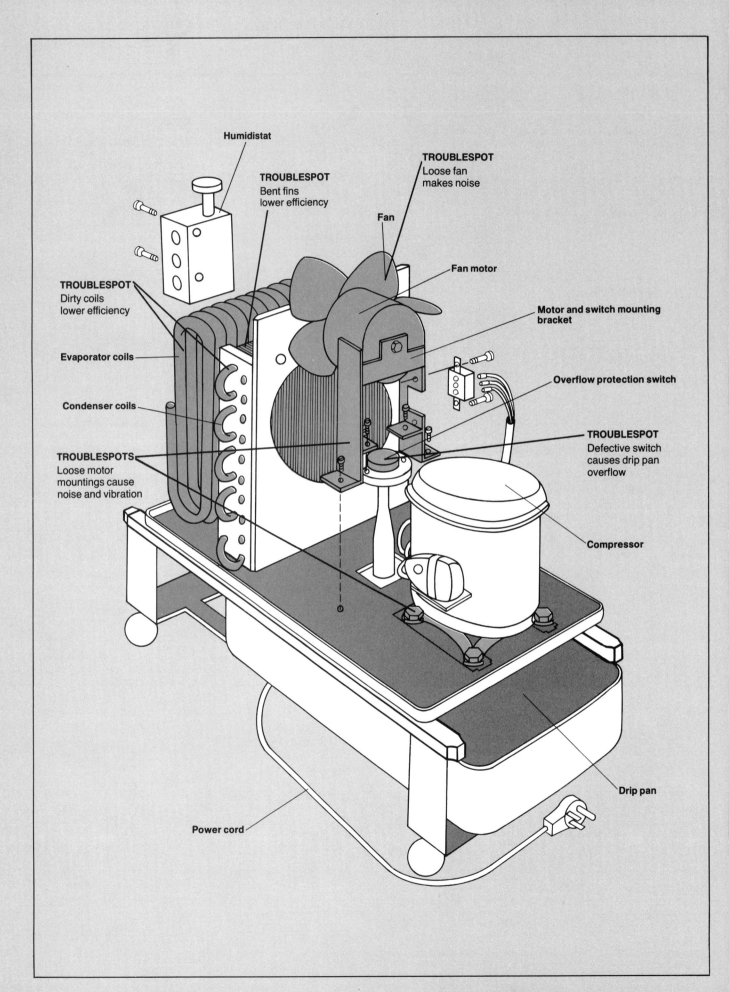

Humidistat

TROUBLESPOT
Bent fins
lower efficiency

TROUBLESPOT
Loose fan
makes noise

Fan

Fan motor

TROUBLESPOT
Dirty coils
lower efficiency

**Motor and switch mounting
bracket**

Evaporator coils

Overflow protection switch

Condenser coils

TROUBLESPOT
Defective switch
causes drip pan
overflow

TROUBLESPOTS
Loose motor
mountings cause
noise and vibration

Compressor

Drip pan

Power cord

Dehumidifiers

High humidity produces not only discomfort but also musty odors, mildewed leather and fabrics, rusting tools, swelling wood (sticking drawers), sweating basement walls, dripping pipes, and peeling paint. Dehumidifiers get rid of these annoyances. A dehumidifier operates on the principle that cold air can't hold as much moisture as hot air. By blowing warm, moist room air across the cold coils of a refrigeration unit, the dehumidifier forces the air to drop its moisture, which collects in a pan beneath the unit. (For more information on the refrigeration cycle, see page 39.) Like air conditioners and refrigerators, dehumidifiers require a trained technician to work on the refrigeration components. But anyone can and should clean a dehumidifier regularly, and make the simple lubrication and bolt-tightening adjustments shown here. You will also find directions here for testing and replacing other components. If your unit doesn't have a safety thermostat to turn it off at low temperatures, read *When to use a dehumidifier,* below.

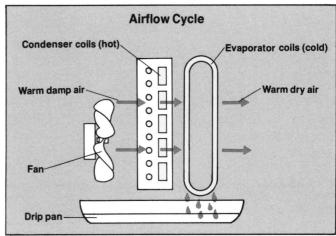

Airflow Cycle

Condenser coils (hot)　　　　　Evaporator coils (cold)

Warm damp air　　　　　Warm dry air

Fan

Drip pan

A dehumidifier has the same components as an air conditioner, running in the same refrigeration cycle. But the components are arranged in different order in a dehumidifier; they take moisture out of the air, like an air conditioner, but don't cool the air. The dehumidifier does not transfer the heat generated in the refrigeration cycle outside the room.

Getting inside

Dehumidifiers are easy to get into since most units have a one-piece cover. Sometimes there is a control switch attached to the cover, as on the model shown here; it must be removed before the cover can be pried off. Before opening the unit, unplug the power, then carefully pull the knobs off the grille.

1 **To get inside the humidifier,** check the grille for screws. If it has no screws, tip out the bottom far enough to get your hands in, then push the bottom back in to snap out the grille. If the grille has screws, remove them and lift it out.

2 If the unit has a humidistat mounted on the cover, remove the mounting screws and lift it away. If there is a grounding wire between the cover and the chassis, disconnect it. Then lift the cover straight up and off.

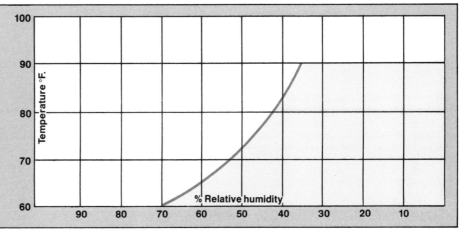

When to Use a Dehumidifier

Dehumidifiers are designed to work in warm, moist air—roughly above 65°F. and 60% relative humidity. The graph, right, gives more detailed limits. Don't run the unit if temperature and humidity fall in the colored area. If you do, the unit may ice up, blocking the refrigerant line and damaging the compressor. To protect against such damage, you can install an inexpensive de-icer thermostat—you will find them at stores that sell refrigerator parts—which will automatically shut down the unit if the line starts to freeze.

% Relative humidity

Regular maintenance

Clean and lubricate the dehumidifier every six months, or more often if its environment is particularly dirty. Dirt and dust on coils, fan, and motor reduce efficiency. Always unplug the unit when working inside, except as noted for cleaning the evaporator coils.

To clean the evaporator coils, remove the cover, plug in the unit, and turn it on. **CAUTION** Touch only the shaft of the switch. After a few moments of operation, the dirt will become soft enough to remove. Unplug the unit and scrape the coils with a wooden stick. Work quickly but don't damage the coils.

Clean the condenser coils and all other areas you can reach with a vacuum cleaner to remove dust and lint. Be very careful not to bend the evaporator coil fins. If there is a drain hole under the evaporator coils, make sure it is unclogged.

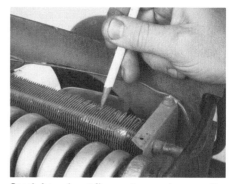

Straighten bent fins on the condenser coils. The easiest tool to use is a lead pencil, but whatever you use, be sure to work gently so as not to damage the fragile coils beneath.

Tighten the fan if it is loose on its shaft. In some models you may have to remove the fan motor from the chassis to work on the fan (see *Getting the motor out,* opposite).

Lubricate the motor with a few drops of light oil in the oil holes at both ends of the motor. If there aren't any holes, put a couple of drops of oil on the motor shaft where it enters the motor casing.

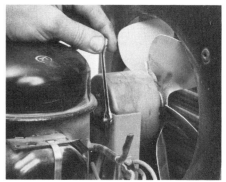

Tighten the motor mounting nuts during the twice-yearly cleaning of the unit, or whenever unusual vibration suggests that they might be loose. After tightening, give the fan a few turns by hand to make sure it doesn't strike anything.

Electrical problems

If the drip pan overflows, suspect a faulty overflow protection switch (if your unit has one) and test it for continuity.

Some models have a simple float switch instead of the electrical type shown here. The float raises a lever that opens a switch to stop the unit. This type should show no continuity when the float is up, continuity when the float is down (see Blue Pages: *Electrical testers*).

If the unit fails to turn on or runs all the time, you have a defective humidistat, which operates like a thermostat but responds to humidity in the air. In extremely humid conditions, the unit may of course run all the time. Before testing either switch, unplug the unit. Disconnect at least one power lead from the switch you are testing.

On the model shown, the motor, fan, and overflow protection switch come out as a single unit when the mounting bracket bolts are removed. Be careful not to damage the condenser coil fins or any tubing while removing the motor.

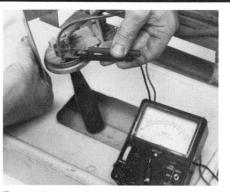

To test the overflow protection switch, attach VOM probes to the switch terminals. With the switch out of water, it should show no continuity. When you lower the switch's flexible tube into water, it should show continuity. If the switch shows continuity out of water, or no continuity in water, replace it.

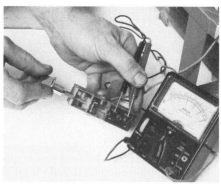

To test the humidistat, attach VOM probes to its terminals. With the humidistat in the OFF position, it should show no continuity. As you turn the humidistat through its range of settings, it should show continuity at some point (this will depend on the humidity when you make the test). If the humidistat shows either continuity or no continuity through the *entire* range, the switch is defective and should be replaced.

Getting the motor out

To remove the motor to replace it or to work on the fan, unplug the unit, open it up, and remove the motor mounting bolts. In the model shown here, you must pry out the rivets that secure the panel surrounding the fan to the chassis. In other models, the panel may be fastened with screws, or there may be no panel at all. Label the motor wires and disconnect them, then lift the motor, fan, and panel out together. In some models you may have to move tubing out of the way—be careful not to kink it. You can now tighten the fan on its shaft, or replace a bent one. The motor can be tested on the workbench by attaching leads from a 110-volt power source to it.

Dehumidifiers Troubleshooting Chart

WHAT'S WRONG	REASONS WHY	WHAT TO DO
Dehumidifier does not run.	No electricity at outlet	Check outlet with a lamp that works.
		Check fuse or circuit breaker.
	Defective cord	Check cord; replace.
	Defective humidistat	Check and replace.
	Defective fan motor	Check and replace.
	Defective overflow switch	Check and replace.
	Defective compressor	Call repairman.
Dehumidifier runs all the time.	Humidistat set too high	Reset humidistat.
	Defective humidistat	Test and replace humidistat.
	Excessive humidity	No problem
Unit blows fuses or trips circuit breaker.	Overloaded circuit	Run dehumidifier on its own circuit.
	Short circuit in cord or plug	Test cord and plug; replace.
	Short circuit in compressor, motor, or fan motor	Test and replace defective parts.
Unit turns on and off frequently.	Dirty coils	Clean coils.
	Fan not running	Check fan motor; replace.
	Low refrigerant level	Call repairman.
	Defective compressor motor	Call repairman.
Unit runs but does not dry air sufficiently.	Unit too small for job	Use in smaller area; buy larger unit.
	Fins clogged by dirt	Clean fins.
	Fan loose on shaft	Tighten fan.
	Fan motor defective	Test and replace fan motor.
	Fan bent or broken	Replace fan.
	Temperature too low	Operate unit above 65°F.
	Defective humidistat	Test and replace humidistat.
	Defective compressor	Call repairman.
Unit is too noisy.	Screws and panels loose	Tighten all screws.
	Fan loose on shaft	Tighten fan.
	Compressor mounts bad	Replace mounts (see *Air Conditioners*).
	Fan motor bearings dry	Lubricate bearings.
Unit frosts up.	Fins clogged with dirt	Clean thoroughly.
	Airflow blocked	Clean inside unit; remove obstructions.
	Air temperature too low	Operate above 65°F.
Unit leaks water.	Pan overflowing	Empty the pan.
	Defective overflow switch	Test and replace switch.
	Defective drain hose	Unkink hose; replace if necessary.

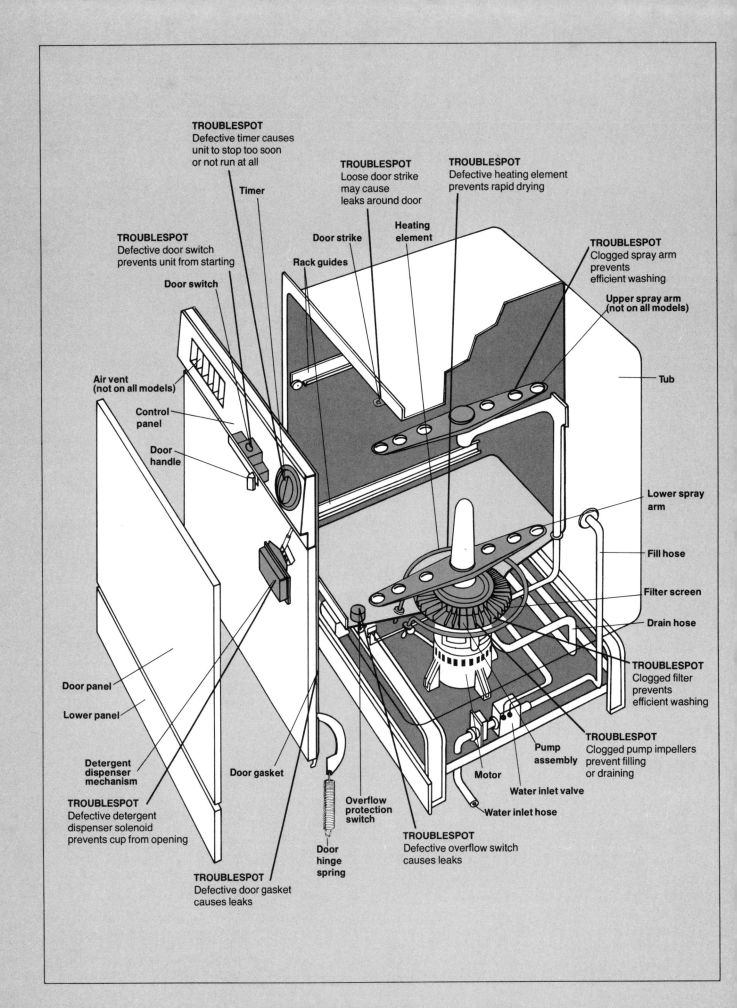

TROUBLESPOT
Defective timer causes unit to stop too soon or not run at all

Timer

TROUBLESPOT
Loose door strike may cause leaks around door

TROUBLESPOT
Defective heating element prevents rapid drying

Door strike

Heating element

TROUBLESPOT
Defective door switch prevents unit from starting

Door switch

Rack guides

TROUBLESPOT
Clogged spray arm prevents efficient washing

Upper spray arm (not on all models)

Air vent (not on all models)

Control panel

Tub

Door handle

Lower spray arm

Fill hose

Filter screen

Drain hose

TROUBLESPOT
Clogged filter prevents efficient washing

Door panel

Lower panel

Detergent dispenser mechanism

Door gasket

TROUBLESPOT
Defective detergent dispenser solenoid prevents cup from opening

Overflow protection switch

Door hinge spring

Pump assembly

Motor

Water inlet valve

Water inlet hose

TROUBLESPOT
Clogged pump impellers prevent filling or draining

TROUBLESPOT
Defective overflow switch causes leaks

TROUBLESPOT
Defective door gasket causes leaks

Dishwashers

An automatic dishwasher is not only an efficient and reliable machine, it is one of the few household appliances that does work more cheaply than you can do it by hand. Running a fully loaded dishwasher through a complete cycle costs less in energy than washing dishes and utensils in two or three batches by hand. But more than any other appliance, a dishwasher won't do its job satisfactorily unless you treat it right. You must prepare dishes properly for washing; you must use the right detergent, and make sure the machine gets water at the right temperature and pressure. In fact, most complaints result from improper use, not machine failure. Read the box at the bottom of this page very carefully.

There is a confusing variety of dishwasher models around. Some are simple, one-cycle models; others are elaborate multi-cycle machines with electronic controls. All of them, however, combine four basic functions (see box, right). The machines pictured here are typical late-model dishwashers. They may not look exactly like yours, but you will find parts on yours that correspond to the ones shown here. One basic tip: never turn a timer dial counterclockwise; it cannot survive such treatment.

CAUTION Electricity and water can be a fatal combination! Turn off the power before you start to work inside the unit. If you have to move the unit, you must also turn off the water and disconnect the plumbing connections. And remember that there's always some water left in the bottom of the unit. Drain it as much as possible before working around the bottom or turning it over.

TIPS FOR ENERGY EFFICIENCY

Operate machine only when it is fully loaded.

Don't use a "rinse and hold" cycle.

Don't use the unit as a plate warmer.

In hot weather, run the dishwasher at night to cut air conditioning expense.

If your operating instructions permit, eliminate the drying cycle. This saves one third of the energy cost. Open the door after the final rinse and let the dishes dry by themselves.

TIPS FOR WASHING EFFICIENCY

Scrape plates well before loading.

Use only fresh dishwasher detergent.

Load dishes carefully. Don't block spray arms or detergent cups; leave space between dishes for circulation.

Clean drains regularly.

Be sure the water temperature is at least 140°F. (see *Water Heaters*).

Make certain the unit sits level and doesn't wobble.

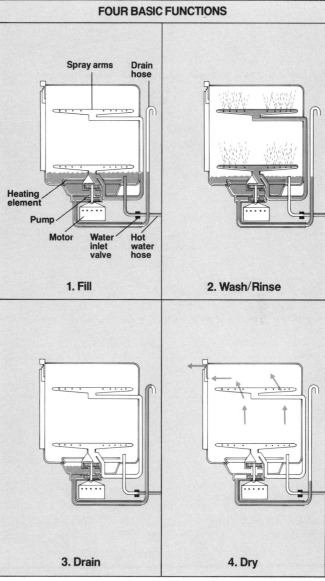

FOUR BASIC FUNCTIONS

1. Fill
2. Wash/Rinse
3. Drain
4. Dry

All dishwashers perform the four functions shown here, in various combinations. (1) When the door is locked, the timer opens the water inlet valve and hot water flows in. When the right level is reached, the timer shuts the water off and the unit is ready to wash or rinse. (2) The timer starts the motor that drives the pump, spraying water through the arms. During the wash cycle, a container opens, adding detergent to the water. (3) When washing or rinsing is finished, the timer starts the motor to pump water out. (4) When the tub is empty, the timer turns on the heating element to dry the load.

Regular cleaning and maintenance

About the only maintenance a dishwasher requires is regular and careful cleaning of drains, filters, and spray arms. Any obstruction of the water's constant flow greatly reduces washing efficiency.

If the rack wheels bind, try a little silicone spray on the axles. If the plastic covering on the racks wears, try a thin application of silicone caulking on the worn spots to stop rust.

To clean the filter and filter trap, lift them out of the dishwasher and scrub with a stiff brush. Some models, like the one shown here, have screens and filters in plain view. Others, like the one on page 62, require some disassembly for access to the filters.

To clear the spray arm holes of food particles or mineral sediment, take the spray arm out of the dishwasher (some simply lift out; others are screwed down at the hub). Ream out the spray holes with a stiff wire, then turn the spray arm over and shake out any debris.

Working on the door

If the door flops down hard, adjust the tension of the door hinge springs by slipping the end into a lower notch. You will have to remove the lower panel to get to the springs (see *Getting inside*, below).

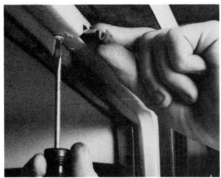

If the door isn't snug when closed, adjust the door strike by loosening the screws and repositioning the strike forward or back as needed. A small adjustment is usually enough. The door shouldn't be too tight: this might damage the gasket.

If you notice leaks around the door, check the gasket. Replace a worn or hardened one. Mark the location of the old gasket before you remove it (or go by the stain on the tub), so you can put the new one in the same position. Some gaskets pop in, some screw in, and others are held in place by clips.

Getting inside

It's fairly simple to remove the three panels on the front of the dishwasher in order to make all the tests and repairs described here. If you have problems with the pump motor or with electrical or plumbing connections, you will probably have to move the unit out to work on it. This process may be complicated, depending on how permanently your unit has been installed. It may be better to call a repairman at this point.

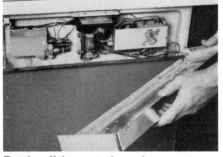

To take off the control panel, remove the screws that hold it in place. (You may have to pry off or unscrew a control dial first.)

To remove the door panel and lower panel, unscrew the door panel from the door. You can now work on the detergent dispenser and the rinse dispenser (if you have one). Remove the lower panel by loosening the screws at the bottom of the panel.

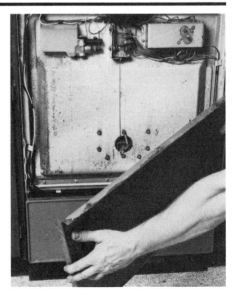

Electrical problems

Door switch

If the dishwasher won't start (and the fuse and power line are OK, and the door is locked), check the door switch.

Turn off the power and remove the top panel. In some models, a broken spring on the switch may prevent proper operation; if the catch on the switch has a broken spring, replace it. In others, an electrical failure may be the cause. Make the continuity test shown here (see Blue Pages: *Electrical testers*). In some models, the door switch is not a part of the door lock, as shown here, but is mounted on a corner or along the side.

1 To test a door switch, turn off the power, mark the wires running to the switch, and remove them from the terminals. Then unscrew the switch from the door and lift it out.

2 Test the door switch for continuity. With the switch button or contact up (door open), there should be no continuity. With the button pressed (door closed), there should be continuity. If the switch fails either test, replace it.

Heating element

Most dishwashers use a heating element to keep the wash water hot and to dry the load after the final rinse. If the unit won't dry dishes (and all other functions seem OK), test the heating element. Turn off the power and remove the bottom panel to reach the power connections to the element.

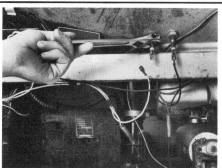

1 To test the heating element, disconnect one lead and attach the clips of a VOM set at RX1 (see Blue Pages: *Electrical testers*). The leads will be directly under the point where the heating rod meets the tub. The element should give a reading of 15 to 30 ohms. Higher readings mean it is defective.

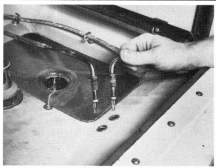

2 Disconnect all wires and retaining nuts from the element (see picture at left), and lift it out of the tub. Always make the replacement with a new element of the same size and electrical rating as the old one.

Other switch controls

Most dishwasher functions are controlled by switches (solenoids and microswitches) commanded by the timer. Two of these—the inlet valve and the drain valve—cannot be reached without moving the unit, a job that usually requires expert help. However, the detergent dispenser solenoid and the overflow protection switch are easy to test (see Blue Pages: *Electrical testers*) and replace through the front of the unit.

If the detergent dispenser fails to open (and it's not clogged with hardened detergent), test the dispenser solenoid as shown here.

If water leaks from the bottom of the door during the first filling, test the overflow protection switch. The switch is attached to the bottom of the tub; it is controlled by a float-type device mounted directly above it in the tub.

To test the detergent dispenser solenoid, clip the leads of a VOM (set at 250 volts AC) onto the solenoid terminals and, with the power on, turn the timer through a full cycle. If there is no continuity at any point, the timer is bad. If there is continuity, but the solenoid fails to click, then the solenoid should be replaced.

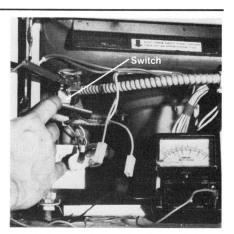

To test the overflow protection switch, turn the power off and disconnect one lead from the switch. It is operated by the float device in the tub. Attach leads from a VOM (set at RX1). There should be no continuity with the float up. If there is, replace the switch with a duplicate.

Timer

The timer controls every operation of the dishwasher except the overflow protection switch. Thus, if the dishwasher fails to run at all, or if it fails to finish its full cycle, the timer may be at fault. To test the timer, you need to be able to read the schematic diagram that comes with the unit and test the timer for continuity in every setting—quite a job! But you can identify the timer as the problem without testing for continuity by making the following checks: check the house circuit fuse, check the door lock and door switch, check that the selector button or dial is correctly set, and check for continuity in the push-button controls if your machine has any (see box, far right). If unit passes all these tests, you can assume the timer is bad. The timer cannot be repaired; it must be replaced with an exact duplicate, as shown here.

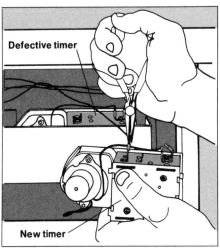

Defective timer

New timer

The easiest way to install a new timer is to hold the new and the old one next to each other in the same orientation and transfer the wires one by one from old to new. Go slowly and carefully—no mistakes allowed! When the wires are all moved, unscrew the old timer and screw in the new one.

Push-button Controls

Some late-model dishwashers have an elaborate push-button control console at the top, while the timer itself is mounted at the very bottom. A bundle of wires connects the two. In this situation, all the push buttons must be tested for continuity before you can assume anything is wrong with the timer.

Pump problems

If the motor hums but doesn't pump water in or out, the impellers (which do the pumping) may be jammed. A complete spray arm assembly from a typical dishwasher is shown disassembled, right; this assembly sits atop the motor, which is at the very bottom of the tub. Since every model is different, yours may not look at all like this one, but you will find parts in your machine doing the same jobs these do.

Whenever you take this assembly apart, lay the parts down carefully in a row, so you can get them back together in the right order.

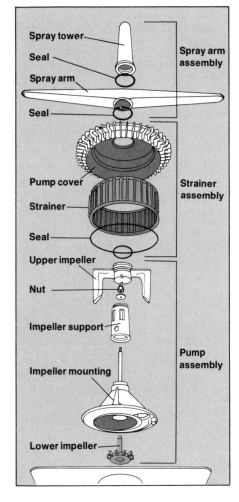

Spray tower
Seal
Spray arm
Seal

Spray arm assembly

Pump cover
Strainer
Seal

Strainer assembly

Upper impeller
Nut
Impeller support
Impeller mounting
Lower impeller

Pump assembly

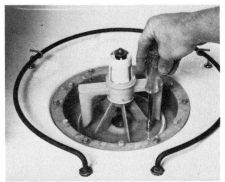

1 **After the spray arm comes off,** the cover can be unscrewed and the strainer (if any) removed for cleaning.

2 With the cover and strainer out of the way, the pump itself (the two impellers) can be unscrewed and taken out piece by piece. The drain pump (lower impeller) is the last part removed here.

Dishwasher Troubleshooting Chart

WHAT'S WRONG	REASONS WHY	WHAT TO DO
Dishwasher won't run at all.	Door not locked	Open the door and lock it again.
	Timer or selector button not properly set	Check timer and button.
	Power not reaching unit	Check fuse box/circuit breaker.
	Defective door switch	Check switch.
	Loose wires	Check all terminals on timer and motor.
	Defective timer	Replace timer.
Dishes don't get clean.	Water not hot enough	Check hot water at the tap; it should be between 140°F. and 160°F. Check hot water heater setting.
	Dishes not correctly prepared for washing	Scrape and rinse dishes before loading.
	Dishes not properly stacked	Dishes must not touch; they should face the direction of the spray.
	Wrong or outdated detergent	Use only fresh dishwasher detergent.
	Detergent dispenser fails to open	Check detergent cup; remove hardened detergent or mineral deposits. Make sure lid is not blocked. Check dispenser solenoid. Timer may be defective.
	Spray arms blocked	Make sure nothing blocks arms.
	No water in tub	See next section.
Dishwasher doesn't fill with water.	Defective water inlet valve or solenoid	Check valve.
	Clogged water filter	Some water inlet valves have filter; check and clean.
	Defective overflow switch	Check switch; if it freezes in FULL position, unit will not fill.
	Defective timer	Replace timer.
Water doesn't shut off.	Water inlet valve stuck open	Check valve.
	Defective timer	Replace timer.
	Defective overflow switch	Check switch; if it freezes in EMPTY position, water will run on and on.
Water doesn't drain out.	Drain hose kinked or clogged	Check drain hose; disconnect it and blow through it to be sure it is open.
	Defective pump motor	Call repairman.
	Defective timer	Replace timer.
Dishes don't dry.	Mineral deposits on heating element	Clean off deposits with vinegar.
	Heating element wire loose	Check electrical connections.
	Heating element burned out	Replace element.
	Defective timer	Replace timer.
Dishwasher leaks water.	Defective gasket	Check gasket and replace.
	Defective overflow switch	Check switch.
	Door hinges broken	Replace hinges.
	Loose heating-element nuts	Tighten nuts that fasten element to the tub.
	Loose hose clamps	Check hose connections (you may have to move the unit).
Dishwasher is noisy.	Spray arm striking dishes	Load the unit properly.
	Defective water inlet valve (a knocking sound while unit is filling).	Replace valve.
	Insufficient water in tub	Don't open other faucets while dishwasher is filling.

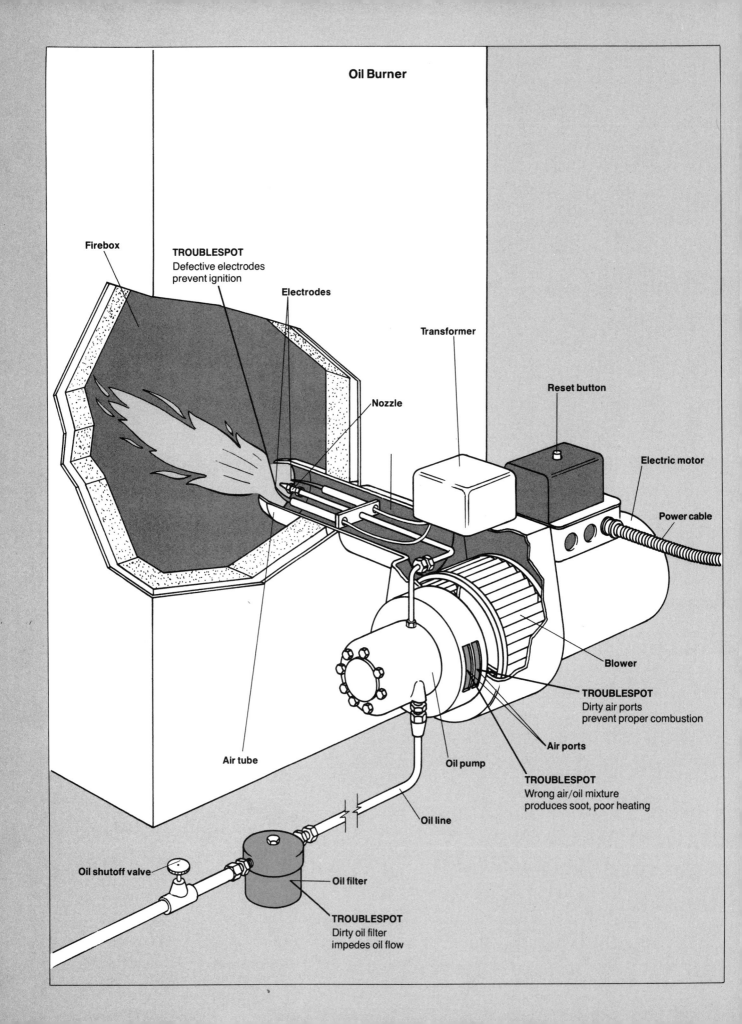

Oil Burner

Firebox

TROUBLESPOT
Defective electrodes
prevent ignition

Electrodes

Transformer

Reset button

Electric motor

Nozzle

Power cable

Blower

TROUBLESPOT
Dirty air ports
prevent proper combustion

Air tube

Air ports

Oil pump

TROUBLESPOT
Wrong air/oil mixture
produces soot, poor heating

Oil line

Oil shutoff valve

Oil filter

TROUBLESPOT
Dirty oil filter
impedes oil flow

Furnaces
Oil burners

A home heating system is easily the most expensive appliance to buy and operate. It's the most complicated, too, with controls, wiring, and pipes or ducts stretching all over the house. There are also numerous options. You can choose gas or oil to make heat for hot-air or hot-water systems.

To sort all this out, we've divided the subject into these separate sections: oil burners, forced-air systems, hot-water systems, furnace control systems, gas burners, and finally, some energy-saving options.

Long ago, when oil was cheap, the oil burner was a very efficient way to say good-bye to shoveling coal. Even today, it's still an efficient way to heat your home (and double as a water heater, too, if you have a hot-water heating system). An oil burner produces a very hot fire by forcing air and heating oil through a nozzle with a blower. This flammable mixture is ignited at the end of the nozzle by a spark that jumps between two electrodes.

A glance at the diagram opposite shows how complicated an oil burner really is; it requires sensitive adjustment to operate properly and safely, and that work is best left to a competent serviceman. You can, however, handle the cleaning jobs described at the bottom of this page. You should also keep alert for the following. (1) Turn the burner off and peer into the furnace through the peephole from time to time to check the firebox for broken bricks. Call the serviceman if you see any. (2) If you find accumulations of soot around the furnace, call a serviceman. (3) If there's a persistent smell of oil around the furnace or coming out the chimney, call the serviceman. (4) Keep the area around the furnace dry. (5) Have leaks in the oil line fixed immediately.

The procedure to follow if there's no heat is detailed at right.

What to do if your oil burner isn't making heat (and power is on).

1. Check the thermostat. Turn it up to maximum and wait thirty seconds. If nothing happens...

2. Check the two furnace switches. There should be one upstairs and one on the furnace. Both should be on red plates. They should be on. If nothing happens...

3. Check the fuse box/circuit breakers. If they're OK...

4. Check the oil tank to be sure there's enough oil. If there is...

5. Push the control panel reset button *once*. If nothing happens...

6. Push the reset button on the oil burner motor *once*. If nothing happens...

7. Push the reset button on the control panel once again, but *no more*.

If the burner starts and then cuts out, you have a problem in the burner or the control panel. Call the furnace man.

If the burner turns on, but the blower (hot-air system) doesn't come on, check the blower motor. If there is a reset button, push it. Check the belt. If it's OK, the problem is in the motor or the wiring to the motor. Call the furnace man.

If the burner turns on, but the circulator pump (hot-water system) doesn't run, listen for a broken coupling (see page 69). If the pump runs but there is no heat, turn your zone valves to manual (if you have them) and call a serviceman. (If one zone valve works and another doesn't, then the fault is in the nonworking thermostat or valve.) If the circulator motor hums or doesn't run at all, the problem is in the motor or motor wiring; that's another problem for the serviceman.

If nothing at all happens when you press the red buttons, call the serviceman. The problem is in the furnace switches or the burner itself.

Regular maintenance

Keep the area around the burner clean, so dirt doesn't obstruct the air ports. Keep the air ports on the burner clean; if the burner doesn't get enough air, it will make soot. You should replace the oil-filter cartridge and gasket twice a year; if dirt clogs the oil line or burner nozzle, the burner could fail to ignite.

To replace an oil filter, shut off the furnace and turn off the valve between filter and tank. Then loosen the nut on top of the filter with a wrench, while holding the filter with your other hand as it drops down. Steady! It's full of oil and gunk. Have an old paint can or other disposable container handy to put the dirty cartridge in. Clean the inside of the filter bowl, then slip the new cartridge and gasket in and put the filter in place, tighten the nut, and turn the valve on. Turn the furnace on.

Clean all air ports on the burner with the radiator attachment on a vacuum cleaner. Do this at least twice a year, and more often if the burner sits in a particularly dusty place. NOTE: Air ports (also called air shutters) are located in different places on different models.

FURNACES
Forced hot-air heating systems

In a forced hot-air heating system, the blower sends air through the heat exchanger that sits on top of the firebox. There, it is heated by the fires from an oil or gas burner. The hot air is forced through the ductwork to the room registers. Cold air returns by another set of ducts through filters to the blower. Although it's much more efficient than the old convection hot-air system, the forced air system remains very simple. There aren't any water pumps, plumbing, valves, or high pressure, and it operates at lower temperatures than do hot-water systems. In addition, you can easily add central air conditioning (see page 43), a humidifier (see page 80), and an electrostatic air cleaner to an existing hot-air system. See pages 70 to 72 for information on temperature controls.

Anyone can handle the basic cleaning and maintenance jobs described on the opposite page, although many people buy a service contract and leave these chores to a professional. Another job you can do (but most people avoid), is cleaning the stack and smoke pipes once a year. Before the heating season starts, number the smoke pipe sections and take them apart carefully. Carry them outside and empty the soot into a box or sack. A long-handled wire brush is a useful tool. Wash your hands thoroughly; most heating oils today contain sulphur, which stains and can burn your hands. Don't get any soot in the house; it makes an enduring mess.

NOTE: It's a good idea to leave the barometric damper on the smokestack alone; let the furnace man set it. If it's out of adjustment, combustion may be inefficient and soot may accumulate.

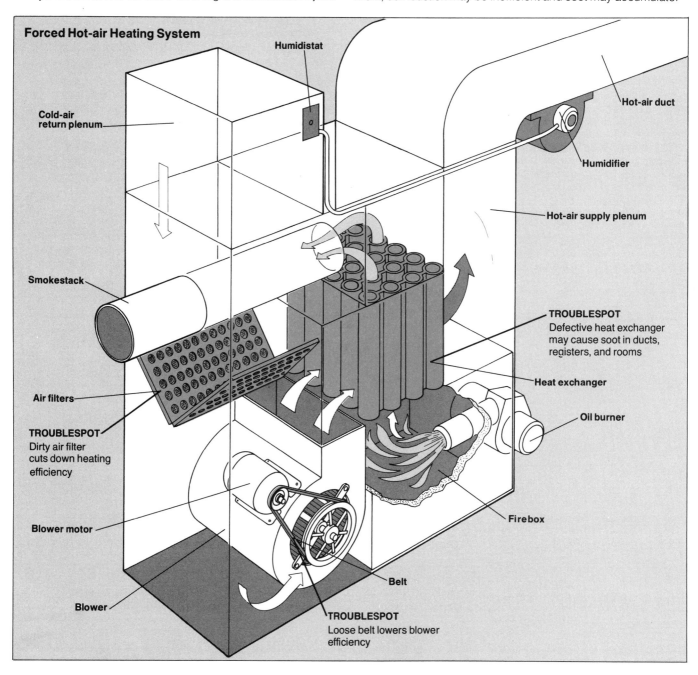

Forced Hot-air Heating System

Humidistat

Hot-air duct

Cold-air return plenum

Humidifier

Hot-air supply plenum

Smokestack

TROUBLESPOT
Defective heat exchanger may cause soot in ducts, registers, and rooms

Heat exchanger

Oil burner

Air filters

TROUBLESPOT
Dirty air filter cuts down heating efficiency

Blower motor

Firebox

Belt

Blower

TROUBLESPOT
Loose belt lowers blower efficiency

Adjusting and maintaining the system

A dirty forced-air system not only circulates dust and dirt all over the house, it also cuts heating efficiency. Change the air filter at the recommended intervals. Once a year, you should also clean the registers (take off the grille and use a vacuum cleaner), and the area in and around the blower, motor, and blower cabinet. If you see soot coming out of the chimney or find it on window panes, make the test described below. Soot in the house may mean a defective heat exchanger in the furnace; call a serviceman to check. Examine the blower drive belt once a year; make the necessary adjustment as shown at far right; replace a worn belt. NOTE: On some newer models, the motor shaft and the blower shaft are connected directly, eliminating pulleys and belt.

Replace the air filter once a month during the heavy heating season. Once every sixty days might be enough during light seasons. Some systems have two filters, as shown above; be sure to replace both. Install filters with the correct side toward the blower, as printed on the filter.

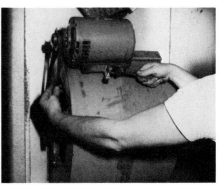

If there is more than half an inch play in the blower drive belt when you press it inward at the middle, adjust the tension by loosening the motor mount and pulling the belt up taut. Then tighten the mounting bolts. Check the belt twice a season and replace it when it becomes worn or cracked.

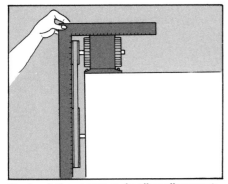

To check the motor and pulley alignment, place a large carpenter's square around the motor, motor pulley, and blower pulley. If the pulleys aren't in a straight line and at right angles to the motor, loosen the inside setscrew on the motor pulley. Adjust it until things are set up square. Then check belt tension and adjust it if necessary.

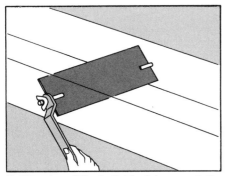

To "fine-tune" the individual dampers in the hot-air ducts, open them all completely. After a day or two of steady heating, walk through all the rooms. If one seems noticeably hotter, close the damper that controls that room about one third. Adjust the dampers until all the rooms are to your liking. NOTE: If you want to shut off the heat in one or more rooms, shut the dampers, not the registers, and take care that the pipes don't freeze.

If you find soot in the house (on window panes), and the filter is OK and the blower area is clean, tape a tissue or white handkerchief over a hot-air register. If soot collects inside, you probably have a defect in the heat exchanger of the furnace (see page 66). Call a serviceman.

Hot-air Furnaces Troubleshooting Chart

WHAT'S WRONG	REASONS WHY	WHAT TO DO
Furnace doesn't heat at all.	No power	Check fuse box/circuit breaker. (See also page 65.)
	Burner problems	See the sections *Oil burners* and *Gas burners*.
	Broken blower belt	Replace belt.
	Faulty blower motor	See Appliance Repair Basics, *How to test a motor*.
Rooms are not warm enough.	Dirty filters	Replace the filters.
	Dirty registers	Clean registers.
	Air leaks in ducts	Seal ducts with duct tape.
	Dirty heat exchanger	Call serviceman to clean.
	Blocked ducts	Remove obstructions.
	Blower belt loose	Tighten belt.
	Blower running slow	Call serviceman to adjust blower speed.
	Register closed	Open register.
	Blocked ducts	Remove obstructions.
	Incorrectly positioned duct damper	Adjust dampers.
Soot collects in house.	Dirty filter	Replace filter.
	Faulty heat exchanger	Call serviceman to check.
	Dirty ducts	Have professional clean them.
The blower makes noises (noticeable when burner is·off).	Loose pulleys	Tighten setscrews.
	Worn blower mounts	Replace mounts.
	Worn belt	Replace belt.
	Belt too tight	Adjust belt tension.
	Blower bearings need oil	Oil bearings.

FURNACES
Hot-water systems

In a hot-water system, the pump sends water into the heat exchanger inside the furnace, where it is heated by the fires of an oil or gas burner. The hot water is pumped through pipes around the house to baseboard heaters or separate convectors, which radiate heat into the room. The water travels back to the furnace via return pipes.

In addition to rather complicated plumbing, this system requires on/off valves controlled by thermostats, regulating valves to control water pressure and temperature, and a high operating temperature. Water must be heated to 180°F. if the convectors are to get hot enough to do their heating job. On the other hand, the heat in a hot-water system is steady; water holds heat a lot longer than air. Thus, less fuel may be consumed. Pipes take much less room than air ducts, and there are no drafts in the rooms.

Some simple maintenance steps and repairs are described on the opposite page. You'll need a plumber for any repairs to the pipes and a serviceman to do any work on the burner, whether it is a gas or oil burner.

Check the troubleshooting chart opposite for steps to take if there's no heat, and also read *Oil burners* or *Gas burners*.

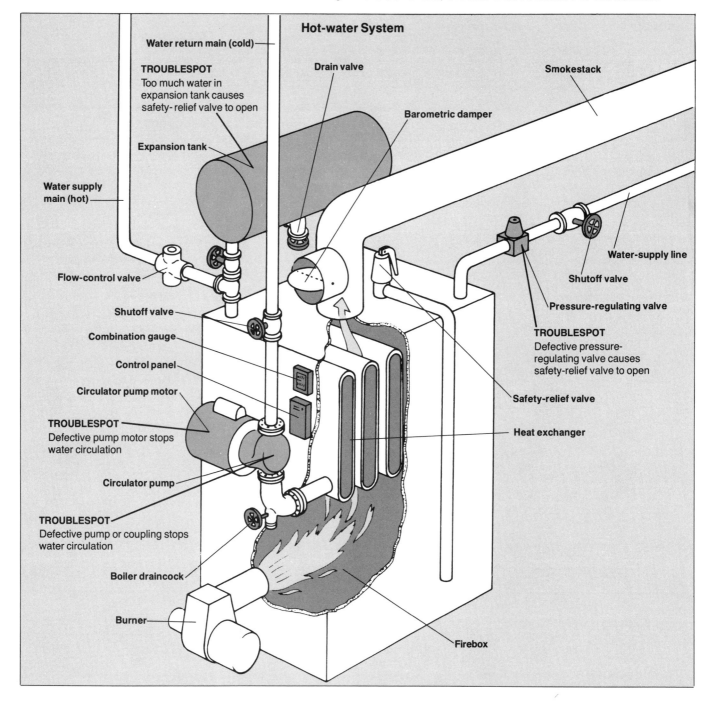

Hot-water System

Water return main (cold)

TROUBLESPOT
Too much water in expansion tank causes safety-relief valve to open

Drain valve

Smokestack

Barometric damper

Expansion tank

Water supply main (hot)

Water-supply line

Flow-control valve

Shutoff valve

Pressure-regulating valve

Shutoff valve

TROUBLESPOT
Defective pressure-regulating valve causes safety-relief valve to open

Combination gauge

Control panel

Circulator pump motor

Safety-relief valve

TROUBLESPOT
Defective pump motor stops water circulation

Heat exchanger

Circulator pump

TROUBLESPOT
Defective pump or coupling stops water circulation

Boiler draincock

Burner

Firebox

Maintenance and repairs

You don't have to do very much to maintain a hot-water heating system, except drain the expansion tank once a year. NOTE: Newer-model expansion tanks (much smaller than the one shown here) contain a rubber diaphragm; they don't need to be drained. You should also listen for a clattering noise in the pump; it signals a broken circulator coupling. Also, watch for a leaking safety-relief valve, which may indicate any number of problems (see box, below).

To drain an (old-type) expansion tank once a year, shut off power to the furnace and let the tank cool. Close the valve between the tank and the furnace and open the draincock in the tank. Have a pail ready to catch the water. When all the water has run out, close the draincock, open the valve, and turn on the furnace. A good time to do this job is just before the heating season.

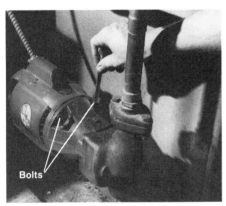

Bolts

1 **To replace a broken circulator pump coupling** (or a burned-out pump motor), first turn off the power to the furnace. Then disconnect the electrical line on the pump. Then use an open-end wrench to remove the nuts that attach the motor to the pump. (To replace a defective pump, you'll have to shut down the whole system, a job best left to an experienced professional repairman.)

2 Loosen the motor end of the circulator coupling with an Allen wrench and then slip it off the motor shaft.

3 Loosen the pump end of the coupling with an Allen wrench inserted through an opening in the pump-mounting flange. Install the replacement coupling by following these steps in reverse order. Be sure you mount the motor with oil ports and connector wires on top.

When a Safety-Relief Valve Lets Go

If the safety-relief valve begins to spit, or a puddle appears beneath the valve drainpipe, turn off the furnace at once! Jot down the boiler temperature and the water pressure reading. Then check the expansion tank. If it's hot all over, it needs to be drained. See the instructions above.

If the expansion tank is OK, there are three possible reasons for a leaky valve. (1) If the water temperature is above the high limit (see *Setting temperature controls,* page 72), then the high-limit control is defective. (2) If the water pressure is below 30 psi (pounds per square inch), then the safety-relief valve is defective. (3) If the water pressure is above 30 psi, the pressure-regulating valve is defective. In *any* of these three cases, call the serviceman. Once you know what is causing the problem, you can intelligently discuss what repairs may be needed.

Hot-water Furnaces Troubleshooting Chart

WHAT'S WRONG	REASONS WHY	WHAT TO DO
Furnace doesn't heat at all.	Power off	Check fuse box/circuit breaker. (See also page 65.)
	No fuel	Call gas company; check oil tank.
	Improperly set thermostat	Adjust thermostat.
	Defective thermostat	Replace thermostat.
	Defective circulator pump	Call serviceman to replace pump.
	Defective motor or coupling	Replace motor or coupling.
	Zone valve problems	See page 65.
Pump makes clattering noise.	Broken circulator coupling	Replace coupling.
Circulator pump leaks.	Seal or impeller defective	Call serviceman to drain system and work on pump.
Safety-relief valve leaks.	Water in expansion tank	Drain tank.
	Valve problems	Call serviceman.

FURNACES
Control systems

No matter what kind of heating system you have—hot-air, hot-water, oil, or gas—they're all operated and controlled by electricity. All these systems require switches, thermostats, heat sensors, and safety circuits, all coordinated to make the system function evenly and continuously, and to produce exactly the heat level you want. Note also that while blowers, pumps, and burners need 120 volts, thermostats run on 24 volts. Thus, you'll always find trans-

formers working somewhere in the circuits to provide the right power for the thermostats.

The diagrams on these pages explain how heating systems are controlled. They are *not* wiring diagrams. (It takes an experienced electrician to handle heating-system wiring competently.) Rather, they outline how the various components are interconnected, both in simple systems and zone systems, and how they affect each other's operation.

Single-thermostat systems

A heating system with only one thermostat is the simplest of systems. Since it has the least amount of wiring and the fewest controls to adjust, there is the least likelihood of things going wrong electrically. On the other hand, it's not possible to vary the temperature in different parts of the house.

How it works. When it gets cold around the thermostat, the thermostat calls the control panel for heat. If the temperature in the furnace is above the blower's low limit (as reported by the temperature sensor) the control panel turns on the blower, forcing hot air out of the plenum, into the ducts, and on to the registers. If the furnace temperature is below the blower's low limit, the control panel turns the burner on first to make enough heat. The blower shuts off when the thermostat's temperature setting is reached. The burner operates only between its own high and low temperature limits.

How it works. When the area around the thermostat gets cold, the thermostat asks the control panel for heat. If the temperature in the furnace is above the cirulator pump's low limit, as reported by the temperature sensor, the control panel turns on the circulator motor. The circulator pump sucks cold water out of the return pipes, forcing hot water out of the furnace toward the convectors or radiators. If the furnace isn't hot enough, the control panel turns on the burner to heat the water in the furnace. The pump shuts off when the thermostat's temperature limit has been reached. The burner operates only within its preset high/low range.

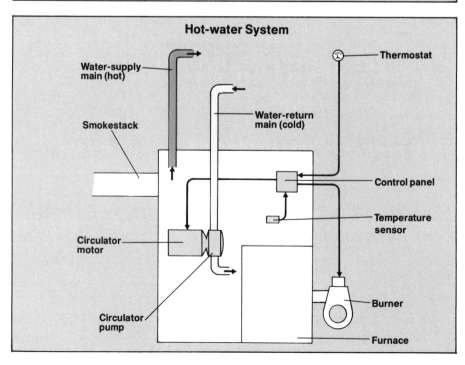

Zone systems

A zone control system divides the house into separate heating areas—upstairs versus downstairs, living quarters versus sleeping quarters—as many divisions as you want. Each area, or zone, has its own thermostat and other controls to bring heat just to that area. The zones can work independently or together, depending on what heat levels you demand from the thermostats.

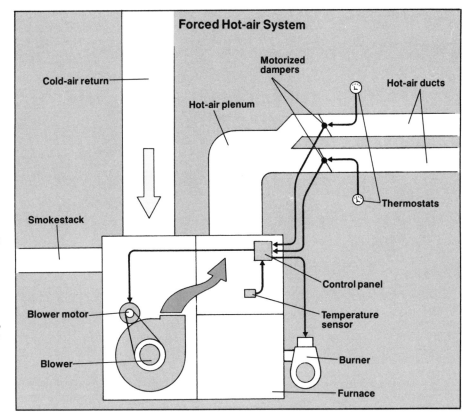

Forced Hot-air System

How it works. When the thermostat calls for heat, it opens the motorized damper in the duct leading to that thermostat's heating area. When the damper is fully open, it signals the control panel. If the furnace is hot enough (as reported to the control panel by the temperature sensor) the control panel turns on the blower, sending hot air through the open duct (but not through the closed ducts). If the furnace isn't hot enough, the control panel turns on the burner to heat the air in the furnace. When the thermostat is satisfied, the damper closes, and the blower is shut off. The burner runs only between its high and low limits. The zones operate independently or together. (Two zones are shown here; more could be installed.)

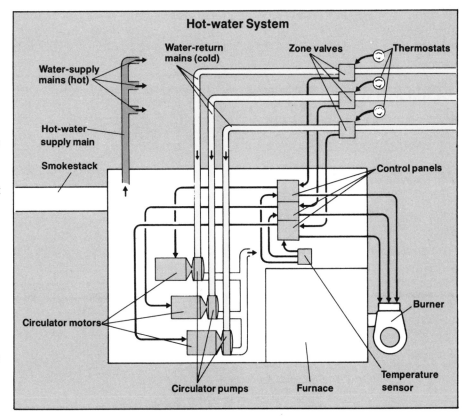

Hot-water System

How it works. When a zone thermostat reaches its cold point, it opens the valve in the supply pipe that brings hot water to that thermostat's zone. The control panel is connected to a temperature sensor in the furnace. If the water is hot enough, when the valve is fully open the control panel for that valve will turn on the zone's circulator motor. If the water isn't hot enough, the control panel turns on the burner to heat the water. The circulator motor drives the pump, pulling cold water out of the zone's pipes and forcing hot water out of the furnace into the zone's convectors. When a thermostat is satisfied, its zone valve closes and the control panel shuts off that pump motor. The burner operates only between its preset high and low temperature settings. Each zone can operate independently, or in any combination with the others. (Three zones are shown here; there could be two or, rarely, four.) It is possible to hook up a multizone hot water system with a single circulator pump for all the zones. It's less expensive, but also less efficient.

Setting temperature controls

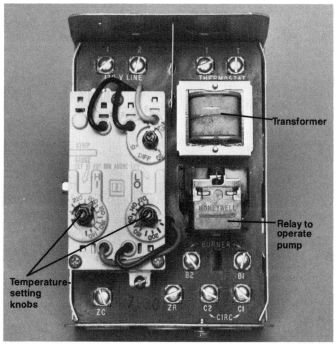

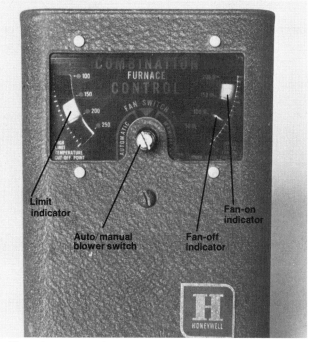

Hot-water systems. The temperature controls for a hot-water system are usually contained in one control panel mounted on the furnace. Behind the panel is a temperature sensor, mounted inside the furnace. The panel is connected to 120-volt power leads. There is a 24-volt transformer for the thermostat circuit. The panel turns the circulator pump and the burner on and off to satisfy the thermostats in the house, within the limits imposed by the high and low settings. For winter house heating, set the low dial at 170°F. and the high dial at 190°F.; set the differential dial at 20°F. This will give an average of 180°F., the temperature necessary for hot-water heating. For summer, if the furnace gives you domestic hot water, set the dials at 120°F. to 140°F. If the furnace makes hot water for a dishwasher in summer, set the dials at 130°F. to 150°F.

Forced hot-air systems. The temperature controls for forced hot-air systems are usually found in two places. One control panel is normally mounted on the burner. It contains the thermostat connection and the 24-volt transformer, and it controls the burner. There is usually a reset button on this panel. There are no temperature dials to set. A second panel, called the combination furnace control, is mounted near the top of the furnace so that its temperature sensor sticks into the hot-air plenum. There are three temperature-setting controls on this panel. The high-limit setting, normally 200°F., is a safety switch that turns the burner off if the temperature in the furnace reaches the high limit. The on/off settings control the blower motor. The ON setting should be about 130°F. and the OFF setting about 100°F. The air coming out of the ducts will be about 90°F. There is usually a separate auto/manual switch to control the blower on this panel.

Checking the stack control

The stack control is a safety device mounted in the smokestack of some furnaces. A metal tube containing a heat-sensing device (a bimetallic element, for example) projects into the smokestack from a control box mounted on it. If the heat in the smokestack reaches a preset upper limit, the stack control will turn off the furnace to prevent overheating. On most models, it is then necessary to push the reset button to start the furnace again. (In newer furnaces, this safety function is handled by a control panel mounted on the furnace itself.) Clean the stack control once a year.

To clean the stack control, turn the furnace off, loosen the mounting screw, and pull the sensor and control box straight out of the smokestack. Handle the control with care; the heatsensing element is delicate. Use a small brush to remove the soot on the outside of the tube. If the tube is clogged with soot, it's a sign of poor furnace combustion, and you should call a serviceman. Clean the stack control just before the heating season starts.

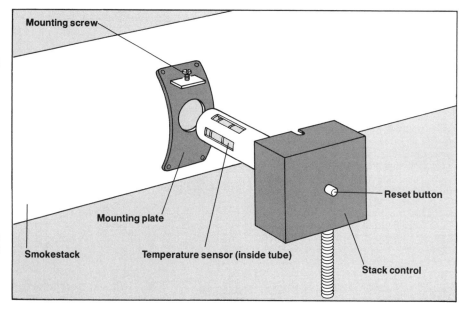

Gas Burner

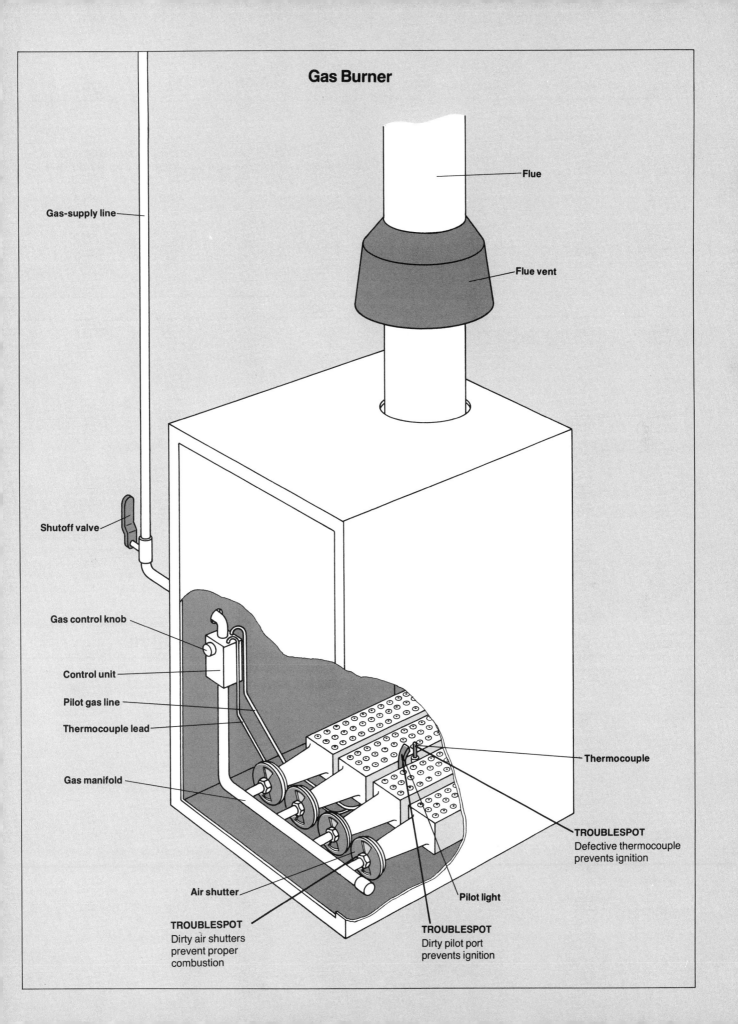

Flue

Flue vent

Gas-supply line

Shutoff valve

Gas control knob

Control unit

Pilot gas line

Thermocouple lead

Gas manifold

Thermocouple

TROUBLESPOT
Defective thermocouple
prevents ignition

Air shutter

Pilot light

TROUBLESPOT
Dirty air shutters
prevent proper
combustion

TROUBLESPOT
Dirty pilot port
prevents ignition

FURNACES
Gas Burners

Gas burners are probably the cleanest and most efficient burners for either hot-air or hot-water home heating systems. They cost less to install, and although gas costs more in some places than oil, more new gas burners are being sold than any other type. They can be made very compact, and a pipeline carrying gas into your home is generally a more reliable source of fuel than a truck that delivers oil.

A gas burner's efficiency depends on the careful adjustment of the air/gas mixture, and it is a job for a gas company serviceman. In fact, there's very little you can or should do to a gas burner. Simple adjustments and cleaning procedures are shown below.

> **If there's no heat from the burner (and the power is on), follow these steps:**
>
> **1.** Check the thermostat. Turn it to maximum. If the burner doesn't light...
>
> **2.** Check the control dial on the burner. It should be on. If it is...
>
> **3.** Check the pilot light; if it's off, relight it (see below). If it doesn't stay lit, call the gas company.
>
> **If you smell gas,** shut off the furnace, close the gas valve, and call the gas company *immediately*.

Maintenance and adjustment

The only regular maintenance required on a gas burner is to clean the air shutters twice a year. If the pilot light goes out, relight it, following the directions given on your model. Two examples are shown below. You can also adjust the temperature setting on most models (see far right).

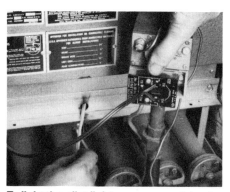

To light the pilot light on some models of gas burner, insert a lighted twist of paper or a long-stemmed match into the burner through a small port while holding the pilot lighting button down. Follow the directions printed on the face of the unit.

To light the pilot light on the type of burner shown here, hold a lighted twist of paper inside a shielded opening at the front of the unit while pressing down the pilot lighting button. The flame actually is drawn down into the unit to reach the pilot. If this method fails, try bending the shield out of the way and inserting the lighted twist into the burner itself. Avert your face.

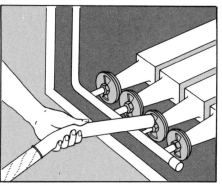

To clean the air shutters and the area around them, use the radiator attachment on a vacuum cleaner. Twice a year is usually enough unless the burner sits in a very dirty environment.

To adjust the maximum temperature setting of the furnace (either hot-air or hot-water system), use a screwdriver to turn the adjusting screw on the control unit. The normal setting is 190°F.

Gas Burners Troubleshooting Chart		
WHAT'S WRONG	**REASONS WHY**	**WHAT TO DO**
Furnace doesn't heat.	Pilot light out	Relight the pilot.
	No gas	Call the gas company.
Pilot light doesn't stay lit.	Dirty pilot port	Clean pilot port if you can reach it; if you can't, call serviceman.
	Defective thermocouple	Call gas company.
	Wrong-sized flame	Call gas company.
You can smell gas.	Pilot out	Relight the pilot light.
	Possible leak	Turn off the gas supply; call the gas company; ventilate the room.

FURNACES
Energy-saving options

Multifurnaces

A multifurnace can heat your home with either of two fuels. The forced hot-air furnace shown here works with an oil burner or a wood fire. Both burner and fire heat a common heat exchanger (see page 66). The furnace can also be set up to use a gas burner or a coal fire. It is also possible to combine a wood- or coal-burning furnace with a preexisting hot-water furnace that is heated by either gas or oil.

In all of these setups, the idea is to save money by burning less expensive fuels, like coal and wood, while holding the gas or oil burner on standby. The burner turns on automatically when the wood fire burns down and the house temperature falls below your thermostat setting.

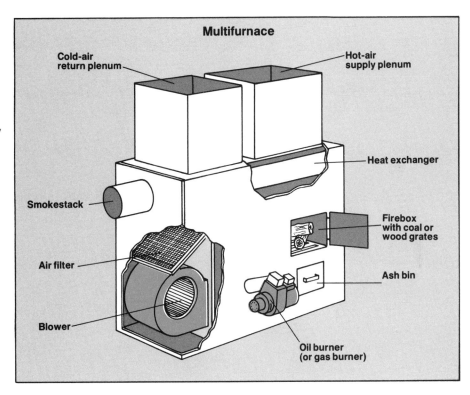

Multifurnace

Cold-air return plenum

Hot-air supply plenum

Heat exchanger

Smokestack

Firebox with coal or wood grates

Air filter

Ash bin

Blower

Oil burner (or gas burner)

Automatic flue dampers

Much of the heat generated in any furnace is simply lost up the chimney. Of course, the chimney has to be open while a burner is on to take waste gases outside. But what about when the burner is off? You can install an automatic flue damper that stays closed while the burner is off, preventing heat in the furnace and surrounding areas from escaping out the smoke-stack. When the thermostat calls for heat, the damper is opened by a small motor and only then does the burner come on. (If the power fails, a strong spring opens the damper.) Believe it or not, there can be a 20% fuel savings on furnaces equipped with this heat miser.

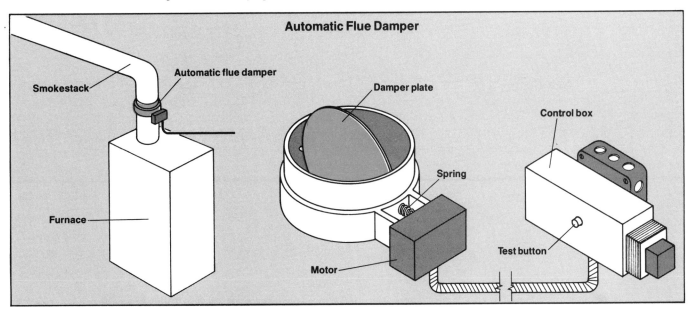

Automatic Flue Damper

Automatic flue damper

Damper plate

Smokestack

Control box

Spring

Furnace

Test button

Motor

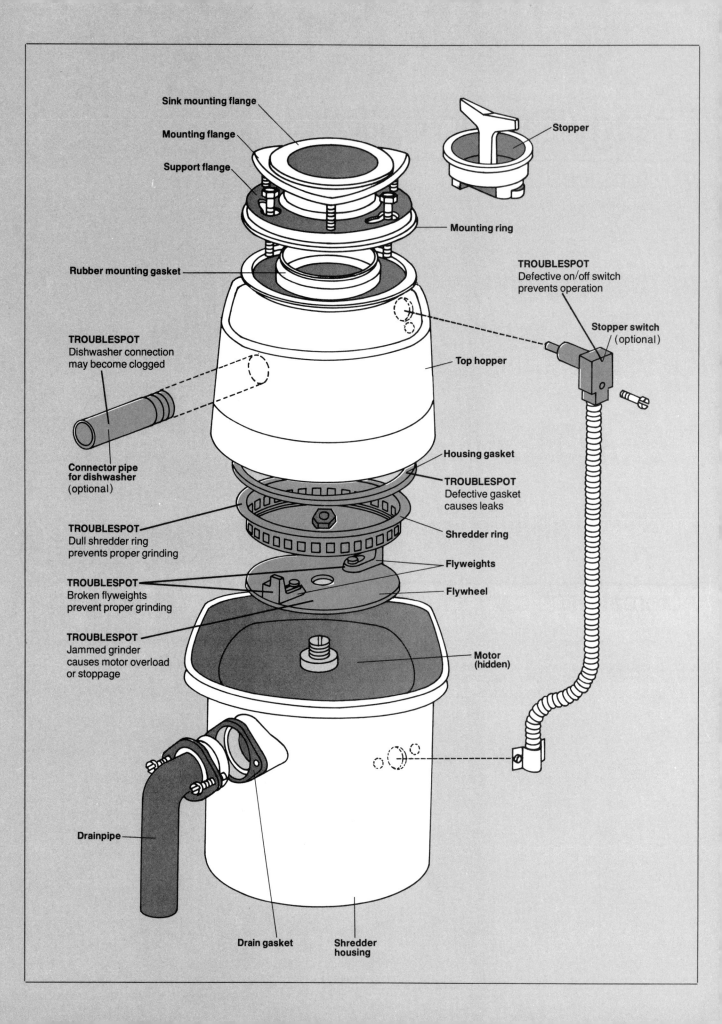

Sink mounting flange

Mounting flange

Support flange

Stopper

Mounting ring

Rubber mounting gasket

TROUBLESPOT
Dishwasher connection
may become clogged

TROUBLESPOT
Defective on/off switch
prevents operation

Stopper switch
(optional)

Top hopper

Connector pipe
for dishwasher
(optional)

Housing gasket

TROUBLESPOT
Defective gasket
causes leaks

TROUBLESPOT
Dull shredder ring
prevents proper grinding

Shredder ring

Flyweights

TROUBLESPOT
Broken flyweights
prevent proper grinding

Flywheel

TROUBLESPOT
Jammed grinder
causes motor overload
or stoppage

Motor
(hidden)

Drainpipe

Drain gasket

Shredder
housing

Garbage Disposers

A garbage disposer—a set of rotary jaws under the sink—turns soft food wastes into a slurry that disappears down the drain. A disposer will give you service for five years or longer, if you don't mistreat it. Read your owner's manual and the suggestions in the box at right to find out what kinds of garbage your unit can take.

There are two kinds of disposers. The continuous-feed type has an on/off switch, mounted on a nearby wall, which, when left on, lets you feed garbage into the unit continuously. The batch-feed type has its switch in the mouth of the unit. You must load the disposer up and put in the stopper. As you turn the stopper in tight, the switch starts the motor. Nothing can be added until that batch has disappeared. Either kind of switch can be tested for continuity and replaced if faulty (see Blue Pages: *Electrical testers*).

There are only a few repairs that can be made inside a disposer. Gaskets, worn-out shredder rings, and broken flyweights (the parts that do the actual grinding) can be replaced as described here. Plumbing connections sometimes leak because they just need tightening. If plumbing connections are worn out, however, you will have to buy a new disposer. The disposer motor is sealed up tight. It usually cannot be repaired, so if it burns out, you must replace the whole unit. Before buying a garbage disposer, consider the following. Disposers are prohibited in many towns, because local authorities don't want the sewer lines clogged with ground-up garbage. If you have a septic tank system, you should check its capacity before installing a disposer. A family of four should have a drainfield of about 750 gallons capacity to handle a disposer's contribution. With eight occupants in the house, a 1,000-gallon capacity is needed.

CAUTION Always turn the power off at the fuse box or circuit breaker before starting to work on the disposer. *Never* put your hand into the unit. Even if the motor doesn't accidentally start up, the shredder ring is sharp enough to cut.

TIPS FOR EFFICIENT OPERATION

Put into the disposer only materials it can handle. Putting glass, bottle caps, rubber, dishrags, silverware, and paper in the unit will only bring you grief. Consult your owner's manual for further details.

Do not pack waste into the unit; just drop it in.

Use lots of cold water when running the disposer.

Never use hot water; it melts grease, which then clogs the drain.

After the unit has finished grinding, run the cold water for twenty or thirty seconds to clear the drain. Don't use chemical cleaners; they may damage the unit.

Never put your hand into the disposer; the machine will shred it just as fast as it shreds the garbage.

If the disposer jams

If the motor hums when you turn it on, but the disposer doesn't grind, the flywheel is probably jammed. If your unit has a reversing switch, try running it backwards for a few seconds to dislodge the obstruction. If you hear metallic noises, a piece of silverware may have fallen in. Try fishing it out with a pair of tongs.

If these procedures don't work turn the power off and use a wooden rod (not your hand) to try to turn the flywheel as shown at right. Use rotary pressure; don't press down. After freeing the flywheel, turn the unit on and put in a handful of ice cubes to help flush it. If you can't free the flywheel, you'll have to open the unit up (see page 78 for instructions); try freeing it from inside, or check if the flyweights are broken.

 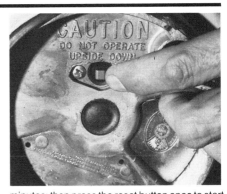

If your unit's motor has an overload protector, the motor will cut out automatically when the unit jams. Some units eventually turn back on automatically. Other units have a reset button, near right. Remove the obstruction. Wait about 15 minutes; then press the reset button once to start the motor again, as shown above. If it doesn't start, the protector switch or the motor may have burned out. Call a repairman if you have to replace the motor, the switch, or the entire unit.

Solving a plumbing problem

If you have a dishwasher installed near your garbage disposer, the drain line from the dishwasher may be connected directly to the hopper of the disposer (see drawing, far right). Waste material from the disposer can back up into the dishwasher line and clog it. You can avoid this problem by connecting the dishwasher drain line (see drawing, near right).

Disconnect the dishwasher drain line from the disposer and plug the hole in the disposer with a cork, sealed with epoxy. Buy a T-elbow connection at a plumbing supply store and install it as shown (near right). Connect the dishwasher drain line to the T-elbow, bypassing the disposer.

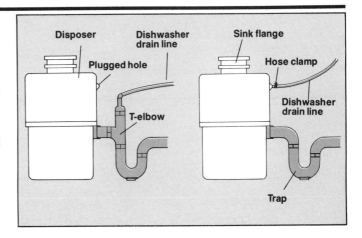

Getting inside

The only repairs you can practically make on a disposer are to replace a worn-out shredder ring, or a flywheel with broken flyweights, or to tighten plumbing connections. Directions for these repairs are given below. Getting into a disposer is a tedious process, complicated by the cramped quarters where it is installed. Be sure to turn off the power before starting to work. Have lots of old newspapers on hand; you will probably find a mess inside the unit. When reassembling the disposer, always install a new housing gasket (see opposite page).

1 **To get inside the unit,** first remove the trap in the drain line from the disposer to the house plumbing system. Use a wrench to loosen the slip nuts.

2 Remove the flexible bottom outer cover (if your unit has one) and the sheet of sound-muffling insulation you may find wrapped around the unit.

3 Loosen the screws or bolts that hold the unit to the support flange. Rotate the unit slightly; the mounting screws will slip out of the flange and the unit will drop down.

4 On this model you must remove the mounting ring to get the top outer cover off. Pull the ring off over the rubber mounting gasket. Then pull off the flexible outer cover (if your unit has one).

5 Remove the screws that secure the top hopper to the shredder housing. On some models that may be a clamp ring (instead of screws) that fits around the hopper and housing. The clamp will be secured with a screw in its edge. You can now remove the top hopper and inspect the shredder ring inside the flywheel.

Replacing the shredder ring and flywheel

If, after some years of service, your disposer begins to take forever to grind the garbage, the shredder ring has probably grown dull or the flyweights have broken. To replace these parts, open the unit up as shown above. A dull shredder ring can then be lifted out and a new one dropped in. Look closely at the flywheel; if the flyweights are broken, the flywheel must be replaced. Look for a nut that holds the flywheel to the motor shaft. If there is one, use method 1 at right to remove the flywheel. If there is no nut, try method 2. Take the defective parts and your model number to the dealer to get duplicates.

METHOD 1: To remove a flywheel secured with a nut, insert a screwdriver into the slot on top of the motor shaft and grip the nut with an adjustable wrench. Hold the shaft rigid and turn the nut counterclockwise. When the nut is off, the wheel can be lifted out.

METHOD 2: To remove a flywheel that has no nut, put a screwdriver into the top slot and hold the shaft rigid. Strike the flyweights sharply with a hammer to move the wheel counterclockwise. The wheel will come loose from the shaft and can be lifted out. Force the new flywheel onto the shaft, applying pressure evenly around it.

Stopping leaks

Leaks from a disposer are a signal that the plumbing connections are not tight enough or that the connections have disintegrated. In the first case, follow the instructions given here for repairing a connection or replacing a gasket. Replace a housing gasket whenever you open the unit for inspection or repairs.

If the connections are worn out, buy a new disposer. The test for any new or repaired connections is simple: plug the disposer mouth and fill the sink with water. Then pull the plug. The pressure built up by that amount of water should reveal any leak.

To remove a housing gasket, just lift it off the rim at the top of the housing. Apply a thin layer of silicone caulk all around the top edge of the new gasket before screwing or clamping the hopper down tight.

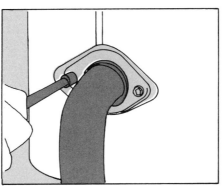

If you notice water leaking from the drain-pipe connection, tighten the screws that secure the flange to the unit. If the gasket breaks or deteriorates, replace it.

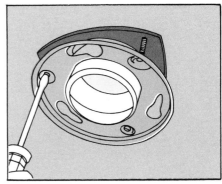

If water leaks from the sink connection, tighten the screws that secure the support flange to the mounting flange. If the leak doesn't stop, try putting a layer of plumber's putty on the top side of the mounting flange.

Garbage Disposers Troubleshooting Chart

WHAT'S WRONG	REASONS WHY	WHAT TO DO
Motor does not turn on.	No power	Check fuse box/circuit breaker. If disposer is plugged into wall outlet check the outlet.
	Defective switch	Check wall switch (for continuous-feed models) and stopper switch (for batch-feed models) for continuity.
	Overload protector switch tripped	Free flywheel if jammed. Press reset button.
	Defective motor	Call repairman.
Motor hums but unit doesn't grind.	Flywheel jammed	Free flywheel.
	Motor bearings frozen	Call repairman; you'll probably have to buy a new unit.
Disposer blows fuses.	Too many appliances on circuit	Install disposer on its own 15-amp circuit.
Disposer doesn't shut off.	Defective switch	Call repairman.
Disposer grinds too slowly.	Not enough water	Use more cold water.
	Improper waste put in unit	Put in only materials allowed by manual.
	Dull shredder ring or broken flyweights	Replace defective parts.
Disposer drains slowly.	Not enough water	Use more cold water.
	Drain line clogged	Flush with hot water to remove grease plug; remove drainpipe and clear. (Don't use harsh chemical agents.)
	Unit not grinding fine enough	Replace dull shredder ring or broken flyweights.
Disposer makes noises.	Metallic object in unit	Fish it out with tongs or forceps.
	Loose mounting screws	Tighten screws.
	Broken flyweight	Replace flywheel.
	Defective motor	Call repairman.
Disposer leaks.	Loose sink connection	Tighten flanges holding gasket or replace gasket.
	Loose drain connection	Tighten drain flanges or replace gasket.
	Defective housing gasket	Replace gasket.

Humidifiers
Hot-air furnace

People, plants, and objects made of porous materials such as wood and leather need a certain amount of moisture in the air. People are generally aware not of any actual amount of moisture in the air, but of the relative humidity level. Since hot air carries much more moisture than cold air, people are comfortable at 75°F. when the relative humidity is about 20%—less comfortable if the relative humidity is 40%. At 70°F. we don't mind 40% relative humidity. And at 65°F. even 55% is pleasant. This means that in hot weather we want to take water out of the air to be comfortable. Air conditioners do this at the same time they cool air. In cold weather, however, we often need to add moisture for comfort indoors. Cold outdoor air seeping into the house may have a relative humidity level of 40% or so, but when the air is heated to 70°F. and expands, that humidity level drops to only 5% or 10% (see chart below). This is much too low for health or comfort. Mucus membranes dry out, causing respiratory ailments; skin becomes dry; carpets generate static electricity when you walk across them; wood and plaster shrink and crack; leather dries out and crumbles; plants die.

Homes in northern states that are heated by forced-air furnaces are particularly liable to low humidity levels in winter and the accompanying problems. A humidifier installed directly in the hot-air supply plenum of your furnace solves these problems easily. Surprisingly, there is no standard type of humidifier. Many mechanical methods can be used to get moisture into the air. Two of the most common types are described here. If you buy a unit with a capacity suited to your home, it will keep the humidity at a pleasant 35% to 40%, regardless of outside temperature.

NOTE: If your home is not well insulated, or if it was built without a vapor barrier, it is pointless to try to humidify the house or even a single room. The moisture will leak through the walls and roof to the outside just as fast as a machine can generate it. Consult a home heating expert for advice in this case.

Both types of furnace humidifier described here require a small flexible tube connection to a cold water supply pipe and a 120-volt AC power connection to operate their motors or pumps. Some units require a 24-volt transformer to provide stepped-down electrical power to operate the motors or pumps.

To operate at top efficiency, all humidifiers need regular—almost constant—cleaning. Evaporating water leaves mineral deposits behind, which clogs the unit, and water always attracts dust, dirt, and airborne bacteria, which can cause unpleasant odors. Be prepared to clean your humidifier monthly during the heating season, and even more often if you use well water.

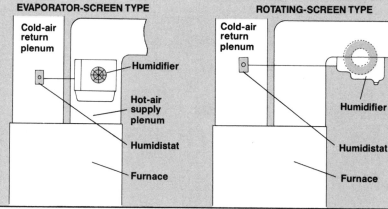

Two Types of Furnace Humidifier

Two types of furnace humidifier are described on the following pages. 1) The evaporating-screen type (see opposite page) is usually mounted on the side of the hot-air supply plenum. 2) The rotating-screen type (see page 82) is usually mounted under a hot-air supply duct, but it can also be mounted on the side of the plenum.

EVAPORATOR-SCREEN TYPE — Cold-air return plenum, Humidifier, Hot-air supply plenum, Humidistat, Furnace

ROTATING-SCREEN TYPE — Cold-air return plenum, Hot-air supply duct, Humidifier, Humidistat, Furnace

TIPS FOR EFFICIENT OPERATION

Buy a unit with sufficient capacity for your needs. Take into consideration the size of the area to be humidified, the type of insulation and tightness of construction of your home, and your own sensitivity to the relative humidity level. Higher relative humidity lets you be more comfortable at lower inside temperatures; this also saves heating costs during the winter.

Keep your unit clean. Accumulations of minerals and scum prevent proper humidifying. Follow the manufacturer's suggestions and those given here. Clean at least twice during the heating season, and more often if you use well water.

If your home water supply has a water softener, the humidifer water supply tube must be connected to the cold-water supply pipe before it reaches the water softener. Softened water contains salts that clog the humidifier.

RELATIVE HUMIDITY LEVELS IN WINTER

OUTDOOR TEMPERATURE	OUTDOOR RELATIVE HUMIDITY	*INDOOR RELATIVE HUMIDITY	**RECOMMENDED INDOOR RELATIVE HUMIDITY
−10°F.	40%	1%	20%
	80	1	
0°	40	3	25
	80	6	
10°	40	5	30
	80	10	
20°	40	7	35
	80	14	
30°	40	9	35
	80	18	

*Without using a humidifier.   **Set your humidifier at this level.

Evaporator-screen furnace humidifiers

An evaporator-screen humidifier is mounted on the side of the hot-air supply plenum of the furnace. A motor-driven pump lifts water from the water pan to the top of a metal mesh or foam rubber screen. As the water slowly trickles down the screen, a fan blows air across the screen, carrying moisture into the plenum. This type of humidifier is controlled by a humidistat mounted in the cold-air return plenum. See page 87 for testing instructions. The fan motor is similar to those used on dehumidifiers (see page 57). The fan operates only when the furnace is on. Oil the motor as your owner's manual recommends. Clean the water pan, evaporator screen, and water inlet valve regularly. When the pan is removed, examine the bottom opening of the pump and clean it if it is clogged.

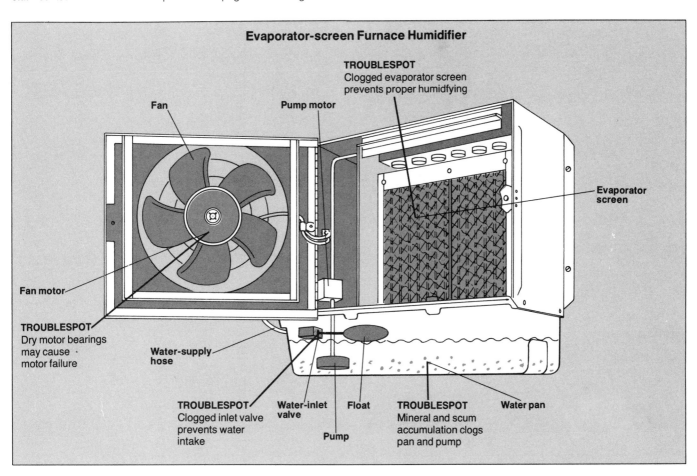

Evaporator-screen Furnace Humidifier

Fan

Pump motor

TROUBLESPOT
Clogged evaporator screen prevents proper humidfying

Evaporator screen

Fan motor

TROUBLESPOT
Dry motor bearings may cause motor failure

Water-supply hose

TROUBLESPOT
Clogged inlet valve prevents water intake

Water-inlet valve

Float

Pump

TROUBLESPOT
Mineral and scum accumulation clogs pan and pump

Water pan

Maintenance

To clean the evaporator screen, loosen the fan mounting screws and swing the fan door open. Lift the screen out. If it's dry, rap it sharply against a hard surface to dislodge mineral accumulations. To remove stubborn accumulations, soak the screen in a solution of 1 cup vinegar to 1 gallon water.

To remove the water pan for cleaning, loosen the mounting screws and lower the pan. Wash it in hot water and detergent.

To clean the water-inlet valve, remove the water pan and insert a thin wire into the valve port. Work the wire back and forth and the float up and down until the port is clear. A small amount of water will spit out as you clean.

Rotating-screen furnace humidifiers

The rotating-screen humidifier is mounted on the underside of the furnace's hot-air supply duct so that its screens project up into the plenum. A motor slowly turns the screens so that they pick up water from the container at the bottom of the unit. As warm air passes over the screens it readily absorbs moisture from them. No fan or pump is needed for this kind of installation. On this model, a humidistat mounted on the cold-air return plenum controls the unit.

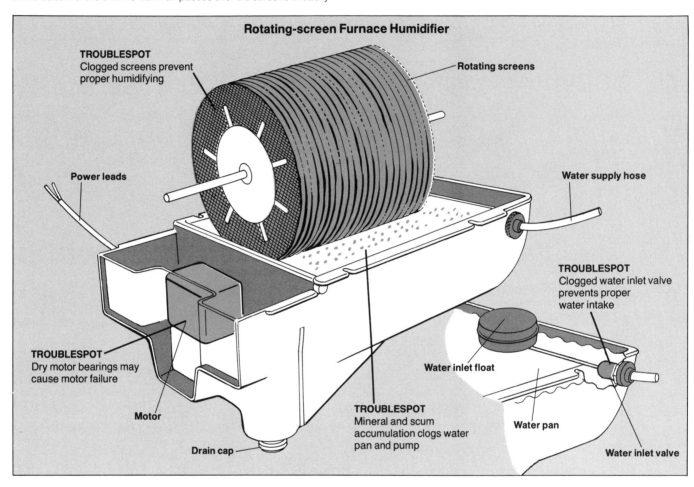

Rotating-screen Furnace Humidifier

TROUBLESPOT Clogged screens prevent proper humidifying

Rotating screens

Power leads

Water supply hose

TROUBLESPOT Clogged water inlet valve prevents proper water intake

TROUBLESPOT Dry motor bearings may cause motor failure

Water inlet float

Motor

TROUBLESPOT Mineral and scum accumulation clogs water pan and pump

Water pan

Drain cap

Water inlet valve

Maintenance

At the end of the heating season, take the unit apart. Clean the screens and the water pan. Check the water inlet valve to be sure it is clear. Oil the motor. Drain the unit during the season whenever there is an accumulation of scum and mineral deposits, and keep the unit dry during the off-season.

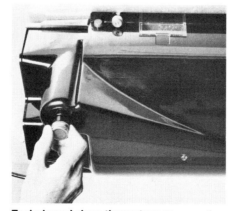

To drain and clean the water pan, open the drain cap. Have a bucket ready to catch the drainage, or connect a garden hose to take the water to a floor drain.

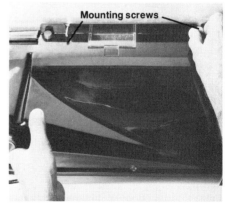

Mounting screws

To remove the unit from the furnace for cleaning or repair, first turn off the power and the water supply. Disconnect the water supply hose. Loosen the mounting screws and lower the water pan while lifting the motor out.

To clean the screens (right), pull the screen shaft carefully out of the motor socket and lift the screens out of the unit. Wash them in hot water and detergent. Remove stubborn deposits by soaking the screens in a solution of 1 cup vinegar to 1 gallon hot water.

To oil the motor (far right), remove the motor cover and locate the motor oil port. It may be on the outside or on the inside of the motor. There may be two ports. Apply a few drops of light oil to each port.

Test the motor if the unit fails to operate and there is power at the unit (right). Turn off the power, disconnect one motor power lead, and connect VOM probes to the motor terminals. You should have between 30 and 100 ohms resistance. Any other reading indicates a defective motor, that should be replaced.

To clean the water inlet valve (far right), loosen the mounting screw and take the float and valve assembly out. Use a thin wire or needle to probe the valve port carefully and clean it out. Work the float arm back and forth and blow through the inlet tube to clean out obstructions.

Humidifiers Troubleshooting Chart

WHAT'S WRONG	*REASONS WHY	WHAT TO DO
Unit doesn't run at all.	No power to unit	Check fuse box/circuit breaker; check power leads to unit.
	Defective humidistat	Test and replace if defective.
	Defective motor	Test motor; replace if defective.
Unit runs all the time.	Unit capacity too small for normal conditions	Buy a larger unit.
	Defective humidistat	Test and replace if defective.
	Humidity level set too high	Adjust controls.
Unit doesn't humidify properly.	Water supply cut off	Check supply hose and pump; clean water pan.
	Clogged float valve	Clean valve.
	Clogged screens, pads, plates, etc.	Clean unit thoroughly.

*If your unit does not have the part mentioned, ignore the entry.

Rotating-drum Room Humidifier

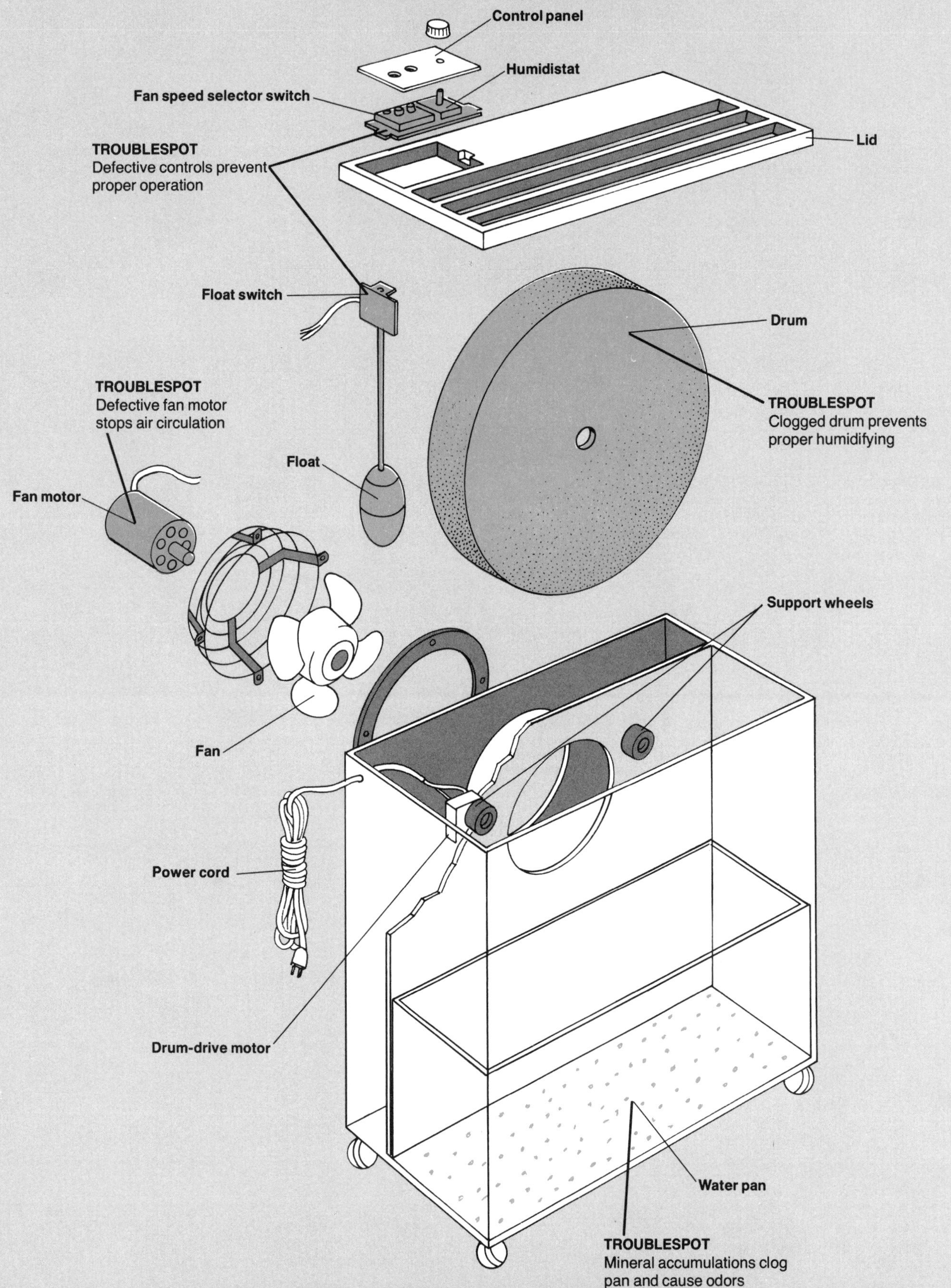

Control panel

Humidistat

Fan speed selector switch

Lid

TROUBLESPOT
Defective controls prevent proper operation

Float switch

Drum

TROUBLESPOT
Defective fan motor stops air circulation

TROUBLESPOT
Clogged drum prevents proper humidifying

Fan motor

Float

Support wheels

Fan

Power cord

Drum-drive motor

Water pan

TROUBLESPOT
Mineral accumulations clog pan and cause odors

HUMIDIFIERS

Room

If your home needs humidifying during the winter season and you don't have a forced-air heating system, use a room humidifier to ease the discomforts of dry air. (See page 80 for information and charts on the need for humidifiers in the home, and for tips on efficient operation.) Room humidifiers are portable cabinet units that use fans to blow dry room air through wet plastic filters. The air picks up moisture from the filters as it circulates through the machine. The units differ in how they wet the filters; three types are described on these pages. Unlike hot-air-furnace-mounted humidifiers, which are hooked up to a water supply pipe, room humidifiers must be filled with water by hand.

Some room humidifiers have very simple controls—just an on/off switch. Others, like the one shown on the opposite page, have a humidistat for automatic operation, fan speed selector switches, and a signal light that indicates when the unit is running out of water.

The main problem encountered with a humidifier is the accumulation of mineral deposits and scum. The deposits clog the unit, preventing efficient humidification and causing unpleasant odors. Clean the unit often to avoid both problems. Check the troubleshooting chart on page 83 for procedures to follow when the unit doesn't run properly.

Rotating-drum room humidifiers

A rotating-drum humidifier has a large plastic-mesh drum that is partially submerged in a pan of water. As the drum slowly turns, it continually picks up water from the pan. A fan blows room air through the drum, evaporating the water and circulating the moisture around the room.

The model shown opposite has several electrical controls, which can be tested when the unit does not run properly. Instructions for finding and solving electrical problems are given on page 86. As with all humidifiers, the most important maintenance requirement is to keep the unit clean.

Maintenance

To clean the water pan, pull it out of the unit and scrub it in hot water and detergent. Stubborn mineral deposits can be removed with a solution of ¼ cup of vinegar to 1 quart of hot water.

To clean the evaporating drum, lift it off the support wheels. Remove the plastic mesh from the metal frame (if instructions in your owner's manual call for it). Use hot water and detergent to remove mineral deposits; soak in a solution of ¼ cup vinegar to 1 quart water in stubborn cases.

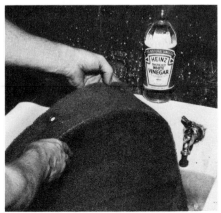

Electrical problems

If the humidifier doesn't run when you turn it on, first check that power is reaching the unit and that there is water in the pan. To find the problem in the electrical circuit, you must do a series of continuity checks (see Blue Pages: *Electrical testers*). Check the float switch; any control switches (they're push buttons on this model); the humidistat, see opposite; and the

motors. The fan motor is like the one found on dehumidifiers (see page 57). The drum-drive motor, shown here, is a combination motor and gearbox. If the motor passes a resistance test (see below) but the unit still doesn't run, something in the gearbox has probably failed. The motor and gearbox assembly will have be replaced.

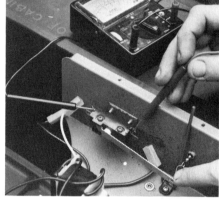

To get inside the unit for tests and repairs, turn off the power and remove the screws that secure the back panel to the cabinet. On the model at right, the panel and fan swing out together. Be careful not to break any electrical connections between the panel and the cabinet.

To test the float switch (far right), turn the power off, disconnect one lead from the switch, and touch VOM probes to the switch terminals. With the float down (no water in pan) the switch should be open and there should be no continuity. With the float up there should be continuity. If the switch fails either test, replace it.

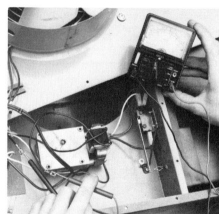

To test the push-button controls (right), read the wiring diagram that comes with the unit to identify the wires and their functions. Turn off the power and test each control for continuity. If there are any faulty controls, the entire control panel will probably have to be replaced.

To test the drum-drive motor (far right), turn the power off, diconnect one lead from the motor, and attach VOM probes to the motor terminals. You should read about 200 ohms resistance. A reading much higher or lower than this means the motor is defective. If the motor runs or hums but the drive shaft doesn't turn, the gearbox is defective. The motor and gearbox assembly must be replaced as a unit.

Roller-belt room humidifiers

A roller-belt humidifier is very similar to the rotating-drum type described on the preceding page, except that a belt of plastic mesh takes the place of the drum. When the unit is running, the belt, which is partially submerged in the water pan, is continuously turned by a small motor. The belt picks up water from the pan. A fan blows dry room air through the belt, carrying moisture into the room. Switches and motors can be tested like those on the rotating-drum humidifier. Clean the water pan and the belt regularly to stop mineral accumulation and to prevent odors.

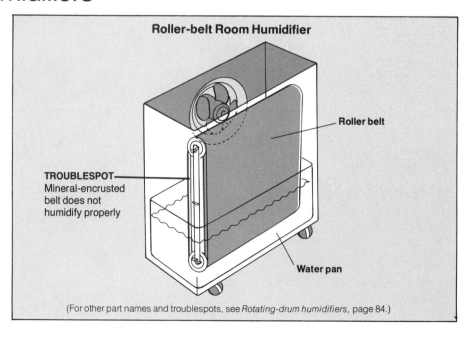

Roller-belt Room Humidifier

Roller belt

TROUBLESPOT
Mineral-encrusted belt does not humidify properly

Water pan

(For other part names and troublespots, see *Rotating-drum humidifiers*, page 84.)

To clean the roller belt, turn off the power, open the lid (or the back panel) of the unit, and lift out the belt and its frame (right). Don't try to take the belt off the frame; wash frame and belt in hot soapy water or soak in a solution of 1 cup vinegar to 1 gallon water.

To test the humidistat for continuity (far right), turn the power off and disconnect one power lead to the humidistat. Clip VOM probes to the power terminals. As you turn the control shaft toward high humidity, at some point the humidistat should click on and show continuity (unless you're in a very humid room). As you turn the shaft toward low humidity, the humidistat should click off and show no continuity (unless you're in a very dry room). If it fails this test, replace it.

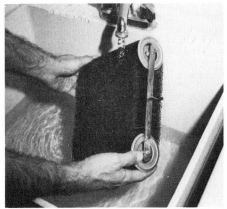

Drip-pad room humidifiers

In a drip-pad humidifier, a plastic-mesh pad sits above a water pan. A pump lifts water from the pan to a drip trough above the pad. Water drips through the trough, soaking the pad. A fan blows room air through the pad to carry moisture into the room. To test the motor and switches, follow directions for the rotating-drum unit described opposite. Test the humidistat as shown above for the roller-belt model. Keep the water pan, fan, drip trough, and pump clean for efficient humidifying.

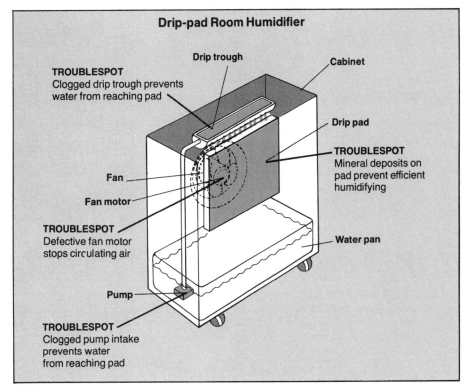

Drip-pad Room Humidifier

Drip trough

Cabinet

TROUBLESPOT
Clogged drip trough prevents water from reaching pad

Drip pad

TROUBLESPOT
Mineral deposits on pad prevent efficient humidifying

Fan

Fan motor

TROUBLESPOT
Defective fan motor stops circulating air

Water pan

Pump

TROUBLESPOT
Clogged pump intake prevents water from reaching pad

Maintenance

To clean the pump, turn off the power, remove the bottom panel of the unit, and take off the C-clamp that holds the two halves of the pump column together (right). You can now clean the inside of the column, the impeller, and the bottom opening.

To clean the drip trough, lift it out of the unit and scrub it with steel wool. Poke a pencil point or thin wire through all the holes in the bottom of the trough (far right).

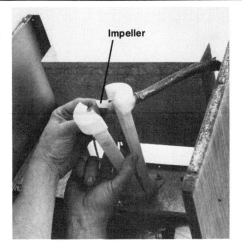

Impeller

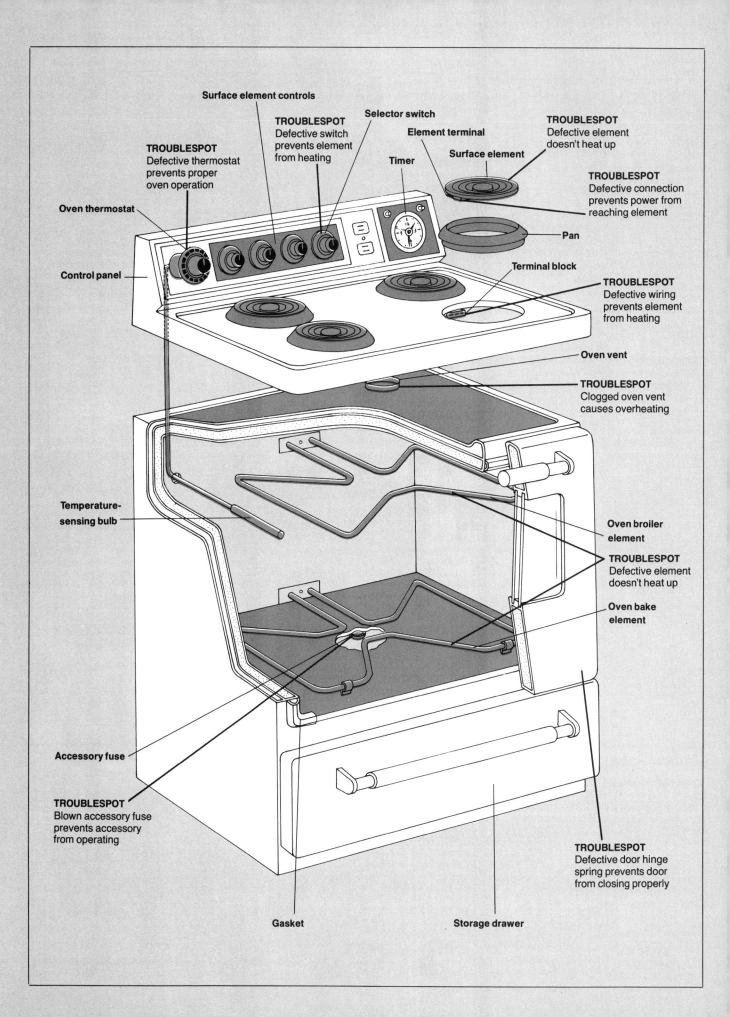

Surface element controls

TROUBLESPOT
Defective switch
prevents element
from heating

Selector switch

Element terminal

TROUBLESPOT
Defective element
doesn't heat up

Timer

Surface element

TROUBLESPOT
Defective thermostat
prevents proper
oven operation

TROUBLESPOT
Defective connection
prevents power from
reaching element

Oven thermostat

Pan

Control panel

Terminal block

TROUBLESPOT
Defective wiring
prevents element
from heating

Oven vent

TROUBLESPOT
Clogged oven vent
causes overheating

Temperature-
sensing bulb

Oven broiler
element

TROUBLESPOT
Defective element
doesn't heat up

Oven bake
element

Accessory fuse

TROUBLESPOT
Blown accessory fuse
prevents accessory
from operating

TROUBLESPOT
Defective door hinge
spring prevents door
from closing properly

Gasket

Storage drawer

Ranges

Electric

An electric range cooks by the heat generated when a high-voltage current passes through metal coils of low resistance, called elements. Basically, a range consists of these elements and the switches to turn them on and off. Thus, there is very little mechanical work involved in maintaining a range, but repairs require a great deal of electrical testing and wiring. Carefully read the Blue Pages, which describe electricity and electrical testing, and become thoroughly familiar with your volt-ohm meter (VOM) before working on a range, and Appliance Repair Basics, which describes different types of heating elements.

Modern ranges have been made more complicated by the many controls added to make things easier for the cook. Selector switches, thermostats, timers, accessory switches and motors, meat temperature controls—all these mean more wiring, more connections, and more things to go wrong. The maze of wires inside an elaborate control panel (see page 92) can look daunting at first, but if you have the patience and aptitude for solving puzzles, you can make the tests and repairs explained here without difficulty. When in doubt, however, call an electrician.

The self-cleaning oven deserves special mention because of the high wattage required to do the pyrolitic (heat) cleaning and the high temperature attained in the oven. Everything about a self-cleaning oven must be heavier and stronger to withstand the 5,000 watts and 1,000°F. heat that do the work. Most important, is the fail-safe door lock: the cleaning cycle will not start if the door is not locked, and the oven door cannot open at high heat.

You can test the cleaning efficiency visually: if there's some gray ash left over, the cleaning cycle was successful. If brown deposits remain, call a repairman.

CAUTION Electric ranges operate on 240 volts AC. This is a lethal dose of current. Make absolutely certain that the power is shut off at the fuse box/circuit breaker before you start any repairs or tests. Take steps to prevent anyone from turning the power on while you're working.

TIPS FOR ENERGY EFFICIENCY

Turn the range off as soon as you're through cooking. In fact, an electric range can be turned off *before* cooking is finished, since it holds heat for some time.

Be sure the pot or pan covers the element. An exposed element wastes energy. A pot too wide for the element may cause uneven cooking.

Pressure cookers save time and energy.

Defrost foods before starting to cook them.

When heating large quantities of water, start with hot water from the tap; it's much cheaper. For long cooking, the oven is more efficient than the burners, since it's insulated and holds heat longer.

Open the oven door as little as possible. Every time you open the door the temperature drops about 50°F. Cook by time and temperature, not by peeking.

Self-cleaning ovens consume large amounts of energy, so wipe up spills when they occur. When self-cleaning is necessary, start immediately after cooking, to save energy.

Adjustments to door and hinge

To work on the door handle or hinges (left), you must remove the door. Grasp it on both sides and pull up firmly. When the door has moved an inch or so, it will fall forward off the top hook of the hinge. Continue pulling and the door will slip off the bottom hook.

To tighten or replace the door handle (below), remove the screws holding the door liner panel. Hold the insulation in the panel as you lift the panel out of the door. The screws holding the door handle will now be accessible.

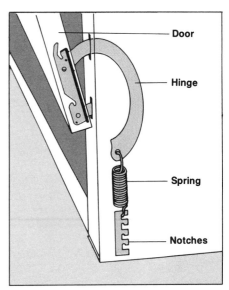

- Door
- Hinge
- Spring
- Notches

To adjust the door spring, remove the door and take out the storage drawer. The notches that hold the end of the spring will be accessible on both sides at the bottom.

Problems with the heating elements

If an element doesn't heat up at any switch setting, it is probably defective. To make sure, turn the power off and remove and test the element, as shown here. If the element is OK, check the switch or the wiring. If none of the elements work at all, check the fuse box/circuit breaker. If that's OK, call an electrician; you may have a problem in the power line that leads to the range.

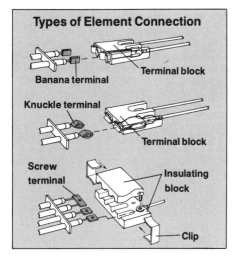

Types of Element Connection

Banana terminal

Terminal block

Knuckle terminal

Terminal block

Screw terminal

Insulating block

Clip

Remove a surface element by pulling it gently out of the terminal block (power is off). If it is screwed on, pull it out as far as you can and remove the screws with your free hand.

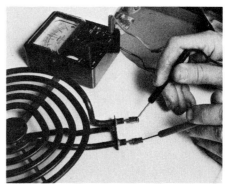

Test a doubtful element for resistance with a VOM, set at RX1. If there is either no resistance or infinite resistance, replace the element. If the element is OK, check the wiring and switches (see below).

Checking the oven elements

1 **To reach the oven element connections,** you'll probably have to unscrew the back panel. It may be possible to remove the elements from inside.

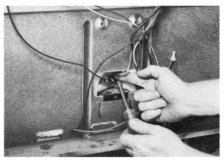

2 Unscrew the wires connected to the terminals of the oven heating elements at the rear of the oven.

3 Pull the element out of the oven. It may be screwed to a mounting bracket. Test an oven element the same way as a surface element (above).

Problems with switches and wiring

If an element does not heat at any switch setting and the resistance in the element itself is OK (see above), the problem is in either the wiring or the switch. To test these parts, remove the panel that covers the back of the switches (power is off). First, check all connections to be sure they're tight and not burned. If they're OK, make the tests described in the Blue Pages under *Electrical testers*. If both the switch and the wiring between the element and the switch are OK, then the problem lies in the wiring between the switch and the fuse box/circuit breaker. Better call an electrician to make the necessary power tests.

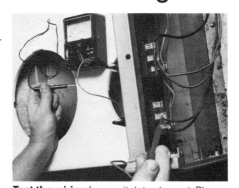

Test the wiring from switch to element. Place one VOM probe on one point in the terminal block and the other on one hot wire terminal on the back of the switch (red and black wires carry power in). Test the other pair of terminals. With the switch off, there should be no continuity in either circuit. With the switch on, there should be continuity in both.

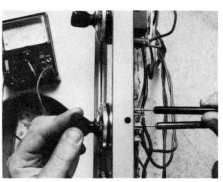

To test a switch, compare it to a working duplicate from your range. Check continuity between all terminals at all switch settings. If the suspected switch does not match the good switch in its responses, replace it with a duplicate.

To work on surface elements, wiring, and terminal blocks, remove the screws that hold the stove top and lift it up. (Elements and reflector pans will have to come out first—see opposite page) When replacing defective wiring, always do one wire at a time, to avoid any wrong connections. Any defective wiring must be replaced with No. 14 solid asbestos-covered wire, marked 105°C. Never use ordinary electrician's tape in a range.

If a terminal block is broken, unscrew it from the bottom side of the stove top, label the wires, unscrew them from the block, and take the block out. (The block is also called *terminal guide* or *porcelain receptacle*). Replace the bad part with a duplicate.

Problems with the oven thermostat

If the oven thermostat works at only one temperature, or doesn't keep the oven at the temperature you set, call a repairman to check the calibration of the thermostat. If the oven doesn't work at all but the top elements work OK, then check the oven elements (see opposite page). If they pass a continuity test, check the wiring from the elements to the thermostat for continuity. Next, test the wiring from the thermostat to the selector switch (if your oven has one). Then check the selector switch itself. If all these parts check OK, then the problem lies in the thermostat itself and its sensing bulb. Replace them as shown below.

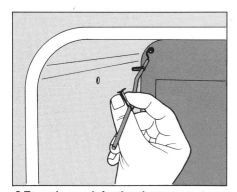
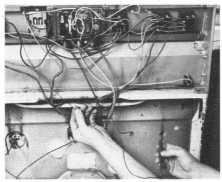

1 **To replace a defective thermostat,** first remove the temperature-sensing bulb from inside the oven by squeezing out the clips that attach the bulb and its tube to the side or back of the oven.

2 Pull the sensing bulb and tube out of the back of the oven. Note how the tube is attached to the oven wall, and how it finds its way from thermostat to oven, so you can install the new one correctly.

3 Label the wires attached to the thermostat with bits of masking tape and remove the wires from the defective part.

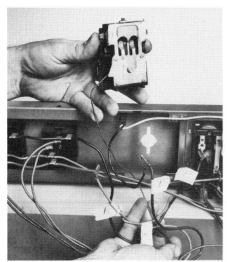

4 Remove the knob from the front of the thermostat and unscrew it from its mounting inside the panel. Replace it with an exact duplicate, installing first the sensing bulb and tube and then the thermostat.

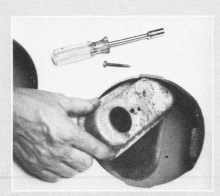

Occasional Problems

If your oven begins to overheat or to burn food, lift out the top elements and reflector pans to locate the oven vent. There is usually a heat deflector that sits above the vent and directs the exhaust out the element hole in the top of the range. Clean this deflector, the space beneath it, and the vent hole.

If your range has an outlet in the control panel for an accessory (such as a coffee pot or waffle iron) there will be a separate fuse somewhere for this independent circuit. On this model it's underneath the oven in the top of the storage drawer. On some models you must lift the stove top (see directions at top this page) to find the fuse underneath at the back. If the fuse blows, replace it with a 15-amp fuse only.

Electric range accessories

Some late-model electric ranges offer a large number of accessories for alternate ways of cooking. By slipping interchangeable parts in and out you can have a broiling grill on top of the range, a motor-driven shish kebab cooker, a deep-fat fryer, a rotisserie, a flat grill, and a ceramic cook top, besides the usual circular elements. There may also be a ventilation system to keep smoke and odors out of the kitchen and a grease collection system to make cleaning up easier. If your range has these parts, be sure to install them according to your instruction manual to prevent electrical problems, and keep them clean to avoid fire hazard from the accumulation of grease.

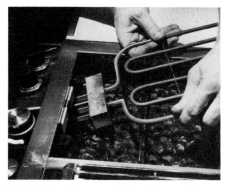

To install and remove interchangeable electric parts, follow the instruction book strictly. Treat the terminals especially carefully so as not to bend them out of shape. Be sure the control panel switches are turned off.

If your range has a ventilation system, there will be a metal air filter somewhere inside. On this model it's just below the ventilation grille. Clean air filters frequently.

If your range has a grease collection system, there will be a grease trap somewhere inside the range. Empty the trap frequently. This model uses a glass jar identical to an ordinary mayonnaise jar.

A range with solid-state components

Some late-model electric ranges that offer elaborate temperature and time controls use solid-state components to conserve space in the control panel. Elaborate controls mean elaborate wiring systems, however, as this model shows. Even if you can't read the wiring diagram, you can, with patience, make the same tests and replacements of elements as on an ordinary range. Just be prepared to spend more time tracing the wiring. You can also test and replace a solid-state component such as the oven's meat temperature control, as shown below.

1 **To get inside the control panel,** you must remove the knob of the oven door lock lever. On this typical model, use a small Allen wrench to press the retaining clip just behind the knob. Press and pull at the same time and the knob will slip off.

2 Remove the screws that attach the control panel to the oven. Then pull the panel straight forward until it clears the door lock lever. Let the panel fall gently down; the wires will support it.

Checking the meat temperature control

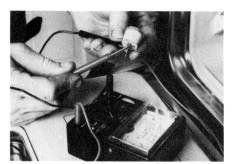

1 **If the meat temperature control doesn't work** but the rest of the oven seems OK, first check the meat probe (the metal rod that you insert into the roast to take its temperature). When cold the probe should show about 100 ohms resistance. When hot (put the probe tip in boiling water) the resistance should be much lower.

2 If the probe is OK, then test the wiring between the probe socket in the oven and the meat temperature control unit in the control panel for continuity. It's mounted right behind the meat temperature dial. If the wiring is OK, the problem is in the control unit, a small solid-state control board in this model.

Solid-state control board

3 To replace a faulty meat temperature control unit, first remove the dial from the front of the panel. Label the wires leading to the unit, disconnect them, unscrew the unit from its mounting, and take it out. Replace it with an exact duplicate.

Solid-state control board

Electric Ranges Troubleshooting Chart

WHAT'S WRONG	REASONS WHY	WHAT TO DO
Nothing works.	No power to range	Check fuse box/circuit breaker. If OK, call electrician.
One top element doesn't heat.	Defective element, wiring, terminal block, or switch	Check each part for continuity and replace if defective.
Top element doesn't cook properly.	Wrong size pot or pan	Use flat-bottomed utensil that just covers element.
	Defective element	Replace element.
Oven doesn't heat.	Defective element, wiring, thermostat, or selector switch	Check each part for continuity and replace if defective.
	Timer not set properly	Reset timer.
	Defective timer	Replace timer.
Top rear element doesn't heat.	Oven in self-cleaning cycle	(Extremely high power requirement during cleaning may prevent top element from working.)
Oven overheats.	Clogged vent	Clean vent.
Oven does not hold set temperature.	Defective door gasket	Replace gasket.
	Thermostat not properly calibrated	Call repairman.
Oven lamp doesn't light.	Bulb burned out	Replace bulb with special oven-type bulb.
	Defective switch or wiring to bulb socket	Test wiring and switch; replace if defective.
Timer doesn't work.	Timer not set properly	Reset; check instructions.
	Timer fuse blown	Check 15-amp fuse in timer circuit.
	Loose connections	Turn power off and check all timer connections for continuity.
	Timer worn out	Replace unit.
Oven door doesn't stay shut.	Defective hinge or spring	Replace defective part.
Condensation forms in oven.	Clogged vent	Clean vent. If there is an air filter, clean or replace it.
	Door not closing properly	Check gasket and door hinge springs.
	Improper preheating	Preheat oven with door ajar.
Accessory receptacle on control panel doesn't work.	Blown fuse	Check 15-amp fuse in accessory circuit.
	Defective wiring	Check wiring and replace.
Oven doesn't self-clean.	Door not locked	Try again.
	Defective door switch, wiring, or thermostat	Call repairman.

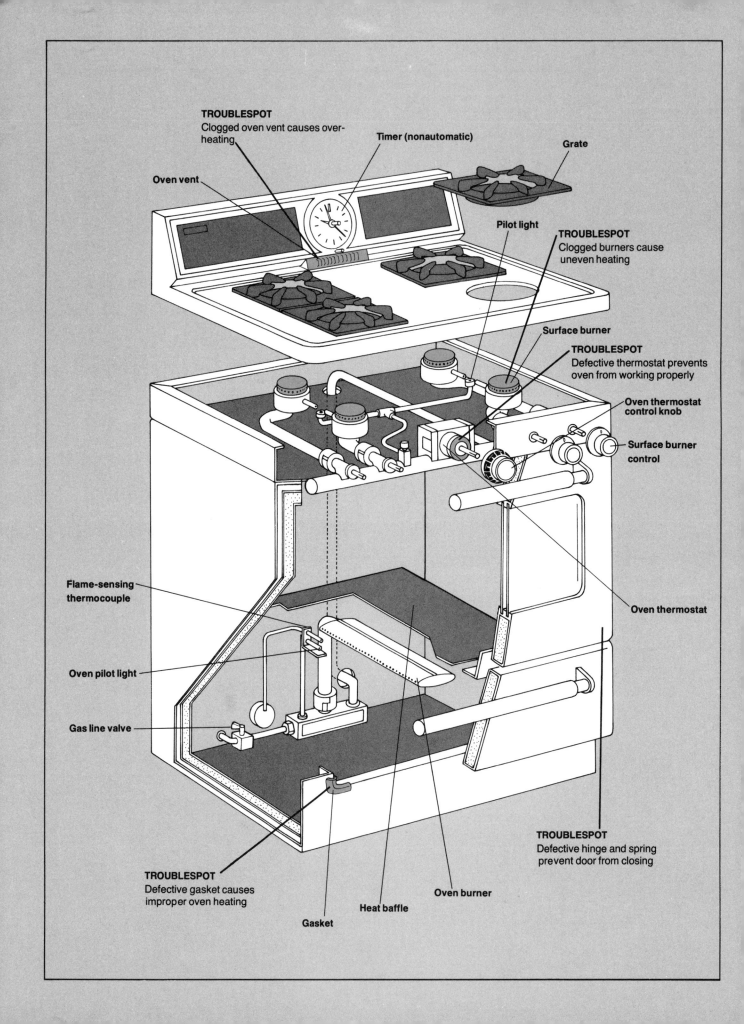

TROUBLESPOT
Clogged oven vent causes over-heating.

Oven vent

Timer (nonautomatic)

Grate

Pilot light

TROUBLESPOT
Clogged burners cause uneven heating

Surface burner

TROUBLESPOT
Defective thermostat prevents oven from working properly

Oven thermostat control knob

Surface burner control

Flame-sensing thermocouple

Oven thermostat

Oven pilot light

Gas line valve

TROUBLESPOT
Defective hinge and spring prevent door from closing

TROUBLESPOT
Defective gasket causes improper oven heating

Heat baffle

Oven burner

Gasket

RANGES
Gas

Gas ranges are probably the simplest large appliances in the home: a few pipes carry gas to the burners, and hand valves turn the gas on and off. The lack of numerous switches and complicated wiring means that there is little to go wrong and little for the owner to work on. In fact, you should not attempt any adjustment of the gas pipes or the gas/air mixture. This means you should never move the range itself or move the air shutters on the burners. These are all jobs for trained personnel from the gas company.

There are a few mechanical problems you can take care of: a sagging door or broken hinge,spring (see page 89); a clogged oven vent (see page 91); or a worn-out door gasket—replace it with a duplicate.

A new feature of gas ranges is pilotless ignition. A red-hot coil ignites the gas instead of the ever burning pilot flame. This adds the complications of electrical components and wiring to the gas range. See page 96 for instructions for testing and replacing an ignition coil.

TIPS FOR ENERGY EFFICIENCY

Turn the range off as soon as you're finished cooking.

Pressure cookers save time and energy.

Defrost foods before starting to cook them.

When heating large quantities of water, start with hot water from the tap.

For long cooking, the oven is more efficient than a burner; it's insulated and holds heat longer.

Open the oven door as little as possible. Every time you open the door the temperature drops about 50°F.

Self-cleaning ovens consume large amounts of energy, so wipe up spills when they occur. If self-cleaning is necessary, start right after cooking to utilize the heat.

Cleaning a Clogged Burner

If the burner flames are uneven, clean the burner ports with a small, stiff wire. If the flames are yellow instead of blue, call the gas company to adjust the air/gas mixture.

Safety Precautions

If you smell a slight odor of gas, check the surface and oven pilot lights. Ventilate the room and relight any pilot that has gone out. If no pilot flames are out, there must be a leak elsewhere in the gas line. Call the gas company.

If there is a heavy, oppressive odor of gas, ventilate the house and call the gas company immediately. Do *not* light any flames and do not turn any electrical switches on *or* off. Never search for a gas leak with an open flame.

Gas ranges are adjusted for either LP or natural gas. If you want to change fuel type, call the gas company.

Relighting an oven pilot light

If the oven doesn't light, check the pilot light. You will probably have to remove the heat baffle, which sits above the burner, to reach the pilot. If the pilot is burning, then there is probably something wrong with the safety thermocouple, which must sense the pilot flame before the gas will come on. The thermostat may also be faulty. Call the gas company to deal with these problems.

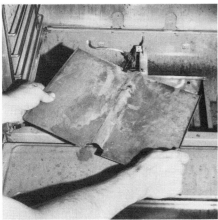

1 **To reach the pilot light to relight it,** first remove the heat baffle that covers the oven burner. You may have to unscrew a wing nut to free the baffle.

2 Clean all the ports in the oven burner with a small, stiff wire while the baffle is off.

3 Relight the oven pilot flame while the oven is turned off. Keep your face out of the oven, just in case.

Checking a pilotless ignition system

Some late-model ranges have eliminated the wasteful pilot light and substituted electric ignition. In this system there is a small coil near each burner that glows instantly when the control knob is turned. The heat from the coil ignites the gas. If none of the pilot coils work, check the fuse box/circuit breaker; if that's OK, call an electrician to check the power cable to the range. If one pilot coil is out (and you have gas), test and replace it as shown here.

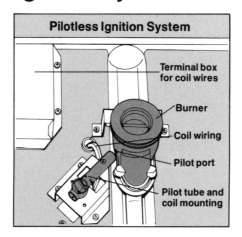

Pilotless Ignition System

Terminal box for coil wires

Burner

Coil wiring

Pilot port

Pilot tube and coil mounting

1 **If a burner doesn't light,** first be sure the pilot port at the side of the burner is open. Use a very thin wire to probe and clear the tiny hole.

2 Test the wiring between the coil and the terminal box for resistance (see Blue Pages: *Electrical testers*). Turn the power OFF. Remove the cover from the terminal box and disconnect at the box one of the two wires leading to the suspect coil. Place the probes on the terminal ends of the two wires. You should read very low resistance, about 1 ohm. If resistance is high, replace the coil.

3 To replace a defective pilot coil, disconnect its wires in the terminal box and unscrew the coil mounting bracket. Pull the coil and wires out of the range and take them to an appliance store for a duplicate.

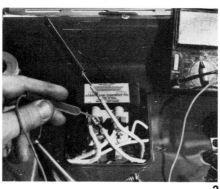

2

3

Gas Ranges Troubleshooting Chart		
WHAT'S WRONG	**REASONS WHY**	**WHAT TO DO**
Surface burner doesn't light.	Pilot light out	Relight pilot; follow instructions for your range.
	Gas supply shut off	Call the gas company.
Pilot flame doesn't stay lit.	Clogged pilot port	Clean port with small wire.
	Drafty location	Prevent drafts around range.
Burner burns erratically.	Clogged burner	Clean burner ports.
	Improper gas/air mixture	Call gas company to adjust.
Oven does not light.	Oven pilot light out	Relight pilot.
	Defective safety thermocouple	Call gas company.
	Gas supply off	Call gas company.
Oven heats poorly.	Improper gas/air mixture	Call gas company.
	Defective thermostat	Call gas company.
Oven bakes unevenly.	Defective door gasket	Replace gasket.
Oven overheats.	Clogged exhaust vent	Clean vent.
	Defective thermostat	Call gas company.
Burners make soot.	Improper gas/air mixture	Call gas company.
Burners are noisy.	Improper gas/air mixture	Call gas company.
Gas odor	Pilot out	Ventilate room; relight pilot.
	Possible leak in gas line	Call gas company to check for possible leak. Ventilate room. Extinguish all flames. Don't fip any electric switch.

Microwave ovens

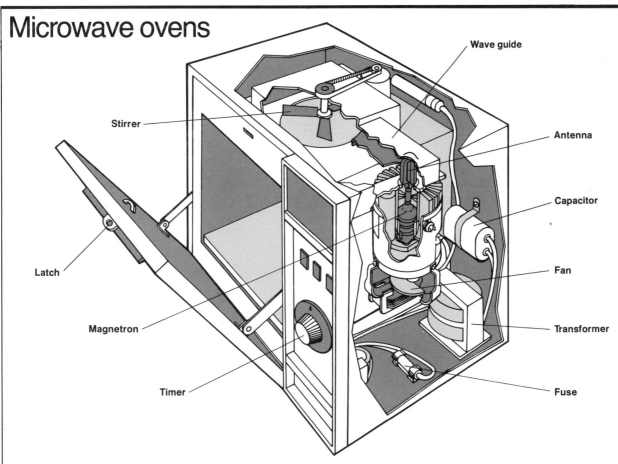

Stirrer

Latch

Magnetron

Timer

Wave guide

Antenna

Capacitor

Fan

Transformer

Fuse

"Cooking with gas" used to be the newest thing. Today, cooking with microwaves is becoming increasingly popular. Microwaves have three important properties: they are reflected by metal; they can pass through glass, paper, plastic, and similar materials; and they are absorbed by foods.

How microwave ovens work
Microwave ovens use a special type of electron tube called a magnetron. The tube is fitted with a magnet whose magnetic field acts on the electron flow to produce electromagnetic radiation in the microwave frequency range.

When the oven is turned on, a step-up transformer raises the normal household power of 120 volts to 4,000 volts. This high voltage is converted to direct current and applied to the magnetron, which then generates the microwaves. The microwaves, fed by an antenna, are then channeled by a metal conduit, called a wave guide, into the oven chamber. A fanlike device, called a stirrer and located at the top of the oven, disperses the microwaves as they leave the wave guide.

The magnetron is cooled by a fan and protected from overheating by a thermostatic switch that cuts off power if the magnetron becomes too hot. A fuse protects the entire oven from damage if there is a sudden surge of current—a short circuit, for example.

Microwave ovens and safety
All microwave ovens made after October 1971 are covered by a radiation safety standard enforced by the Food and Drug Administration. The safety standard limits the amount of radiation leakage allowed for an oven over its lifetime. This limit is far below the level of radiation known to be harmful.

A double interlock system—also required by law—stops the production of microwaves the moment the latch is released or the oven door is opened. In addition, a monitoring system stops oven operation if one or both of the interlocking systems fail. The FDA monitors the manufacture of microwave ovens to assure adherence to these standards.

No documented cases of radiation injury from microwave ovens have been reported. Injuries that have occurred could happen with any oven or cooking surface—burns from heated plates, steam, hot food, and the like.

How food is cooked in microwave ovens
Microwaves cause the water molecules in food to vibrate, producing heat from friction, which cooks the food.

Glass, paper, ceramic, or plastic containers can be used in microwave cooking because the microwaves pass through them. Metal pans or aluminum foil should not be used since they reflect microwaves, causing food to cook unevenly. The instructions that come with each oven tell you what containers to use, and how to test others for possible use in the oven.

Installing the oven
To install a microwave oven, follow these three steps.(1) Remove all packing material from the oven interior. (2) Place the oven where you want it, but be sure to leave 1 inch clearance at the top and rear and 6 inches on the sides to assure proper ventilation. (3) Plug the oven into a standard 120- to 240-volt household outlet. Be sure that the oven is the only appliance on that circuit.

Maintaining the oven
Because of the strict safety standards on microwave ovens, owner service is strongly discouraged, and little disassembly is possible. In fact, manufacturers will usually void their warranties if they see that the oven has been taken apart. Maintenance is thus limited to cleaning.

Clean the oven cavity, door, and seals frequently with water and a mild detergent. A special cleaner is not necessary. Don't use a scouring pad, steel wool, or other abrasives. To remove odors in the oven, boil a solution of a cup of water and several tablespoons of lemon juice in the oven for five to seven minutes.

Recommendations for Operating a Microwave Oven
Examine a new oven for evidence of shipping damage.

Follow the manufacturer's instruction manual for operating procedures and safety precautions.

Never operate an oven if the door does not close firmly or if the door is bent, warped, or damaged.

Never insert objects through the door grille or around the door seal.

Never turn on the oven when it is empty.

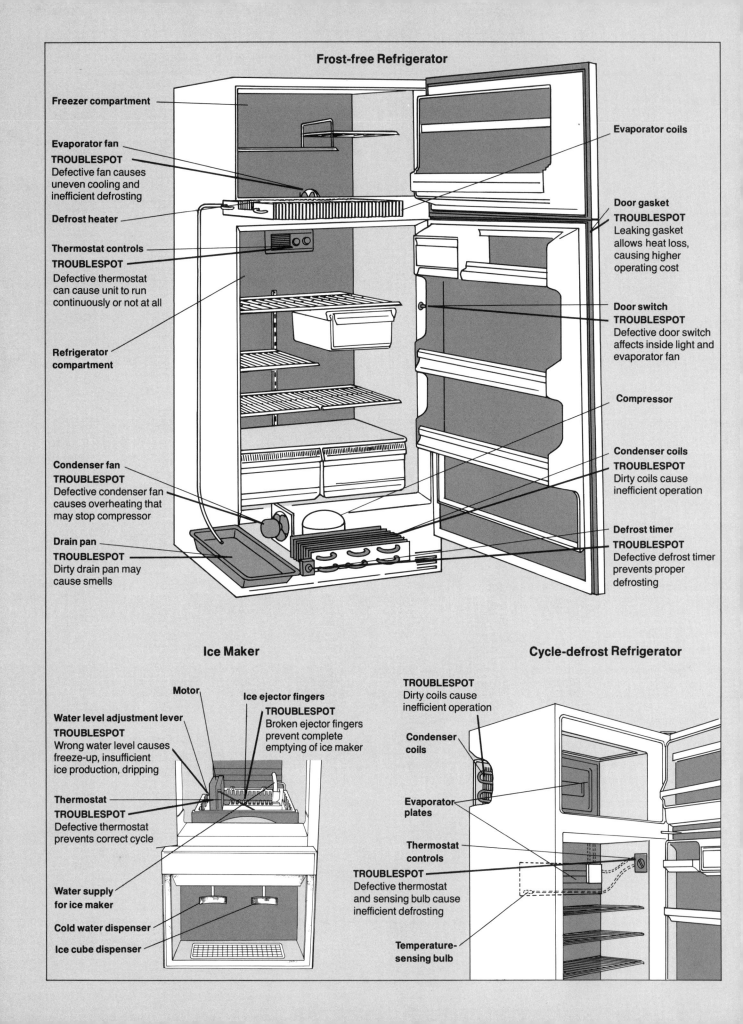

Frost-free Refrigerator

Freezer compartment

Evaporator coils

Evaporator fan
TROUBLESPOT
Defective fan causes uneven cooling and inefficient defrosting

Defrost heater

Door gasket
TROUBLESPOT
Leaking gasket allows heat loss, causing higher operating cost

Thermostat controls
TROUBLESPOT
Defective thermostat can cause unit to run continuously or not at all

Door switch
TROUBLESPOT
Defective door switch affects inside light and evaporator fan

Refrigerator compartment

Compressor

Condenser fan
TROUBLESPOT
Defective condenser fan causes overheating that may stop compressor

Condenser coils
TROUBLESPOT
Dirty coils cause inefficient operation

Drain pan
TROUBLESPOT
Dirty drain pan may cause smells

Defrost timer
TROUBLESPOT
Defective defrost timer prevents proper defrosting

Ice Maker

Motor

Ice ejector fingers
TROUBLESPOT
Broken ejector fingers prevent complete emptying of ice maker

Water level adjustment lever
TROUBLESPOT
Wrong water level causes freeze-up, insufficient ice production, dripping

Thermostat
TROUBLESPOT
Defective thermostat prevents correct cycle

Water supply for ice maker

Cold water dispenser

Ice cube dispenser

Cycle-defrost Refrigerator

TROUBLESPOT
Dirty coils cause inefficient operation

Condenser coils

Evaporator plates

Thermostat controls
TROUBLESPOT
Defective thermostat and sensing bulb cause inefficient defrosting

Temperature-sensing bulb

Refrigerator-freezers

A refrigerator is an expensive necessity. Its purchase price represents only about one fifth of its ten-year cost, the rest being the cost of electricity to run it. Thus, sensible operating practices that can improve efficiency are important (see box below). Regular cleaning procedures (see below) also help the unit to run more easily and cheaply. A refrigerator uses the same kind of cooling components as an air conditioner. They are described on page 39. As with the air conditioner, you should leave all repairs to the pressurized refrigerant system to a trained service person. Take care when you are working around a refrigerator not to bend or break any of the refrigeration lines.

There is always some moisture in the air in the refrigerator. Since cold air can't carry much moisture, it collects as frost on the evaporator coils, the coldest surface. The refrigerator has to have a way of getting rid of the frost that accumulates inside. On manual-defrost models, you have to turn the unit completely off and let the ice melt away. Several years ago, cycle-defrost units were developed in which the frost accumulates on evaporator plates in plain sight inside the unit. Every so often a timer turns on a heater that melts the frost, which drains down and out the bottom into a drain pan. In the latest frost-free models the place where the frost accumulates—the evaporator coils—is hidden so you never see any frost. Again, a timer turns on a heater occasionally to melt the frost.

The refrigerator-freezer combination is used by almost everyone today. Separate freezer units, however, are really just like refrigerators in terms of basic components and functions, except that the whole machine runs at near-zero temperatures, not just a section. The mechanical and electrical problems found in freezers and refrigerators are virtually identical, even if the components are arranged somewhat differently.

If your refrigerator develops any suspicious symptoms, turn first to the troubleshooting chart at the end of this section. You can eliminate the possible causes of your trouble one by one until you find the culprit. Very often a simple adjustment—such as cleaning the coils—will take care of the problem.

NOTE: There are probably hundreds of models of refrigerators. Our pictures show typical late-model frost-free units. Some of the components in your refrigerator may be in a different place, but they're doing the same jobs and are repaired the same way.

Basic maintenance

Refrigerators require a minimum of regular maintenance, but a thorough cleaning and disinfecting once a year, inside and underneath, makes the unit run more efficiently and prevents bad odors. The coils underneath are not easy to reach, and to get to those in back you must move the unit (see page 104). But the effort is worth it: dirty coils can make a unit run continuously or stop altogether. The drip pan should be cleaned more often, perhaps once a month in hot weather.

 Don't put the pan in the dishwasher; it may bend out of shape.

Clean the drip pan in soapy water to prevent bad odors. To get at the pan, snap out the bottom grille. ⟳ If the pan rattles while the refrigerator is in operation, move it slightly so it's not touching the unit at the sides. If that doesn't help, try putting a flat stone in it.

Clean the coils underneath with the crevice attachment on your vacuum cleaner. On older models, the coils hang on the back of the unit. To do an honest job on many late models, you have to lay the unit on its side (see page 104).

Adjust the front feet of the unit so that it sits level from side to side, and tilts backward just enough so that the doors will close slowly by themselves. A crowbar on a piece of two-by-four gives the necessary lift. Older units may have four adjustable feet; on later models only the two in front are adjustable.

Clear the drain holes with a screwdriver or a piece of wire. You'll find a drain at the bottom of both refrigerator and freezer compartments. (On late models, the freezer drain cannot be reached without extensive dismantling.) After you have opened the drain, force water through the passage with a baster or syringe.

💧 TIPS FOR EFFICIENT OPERATION

Do not open the door any more often than necessary.

Clean the coils regularly.

Check the gasket for tightness.

Keep liquids and damp foods sealed up, especially in frost-free units.

Never put hot food into the unit.

Place containers to allow air circulation.

Never block circulation vents in a frost-free unit.

Set the thermostat so the unit runs at 5°F. in the freezer and 35°–40°F. in the refrigerator.

Mechanical problems

To adjust a sagging door, hold it steady with one hand while you loosen the hinge screws with the other. Lift the door to the proper position and tighten the screws. To adjust the bottom door you may have to open or sometimes even remove the top door.

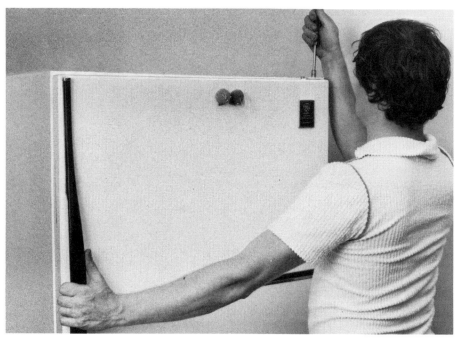

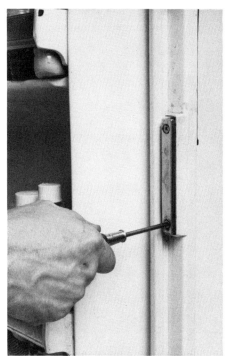

To adjust a loose magnetic catch, screw the door magnet all the way down, until there is space between door and body. Then loosen the door magnet little by little until it just touches the body.

1 To replace a damaged door handle, first pry out the metal or plastic insert that most models have covering the screws. Some models have a small movable socket at the bottom of the handle into which the insert fits and which can be forced down with a screwdriver.

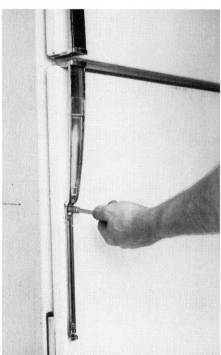

2 Unscrew the damaged handle from the unit body and replace it with a duplicate.

Replacing a defective gasket

A worn or hardened gasket leaves gaps between the door and the body of the refrigerator. This allows warm air and moisture into the unit, forcing it to work harder and longer, making it frost up. If a test shows gaps, make sure the door is not just sagging or warped (opposite). Before you start, be sure you have an exact duplicate of your old gasket.

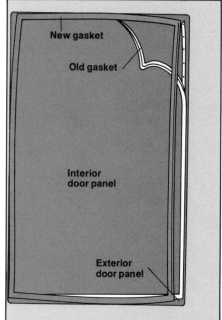

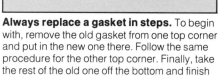

Always replace a gasket in steps. To begin with, remove the old gasket from one top corner and put in the new one there. Follow the same procedure for the other top corner. Finally, take the rest of the old one off the bottom and finish installing the new one.

If you take the entire gasket off in one piece, on most models the door panel comes off, the insulation falls out, and the door sags out of shape (it may even kink). Getting it all back together is a real problem.

When you have finished installing a new gasket, examine the door carefully to make sure the door has not slumped out of shape. If it has, loosen the retaining screws, press the door (not the door panel) up into true shape, and tighten the screws. You may have to loosen and tighten them several times.

To test a gasket, try to push a crisp bill under the gasket all the way around with the door closed. If the bill slides under, the gasket is defective. Another test is to shut the door on a bill; there should be moderate resistance when you pull it out.

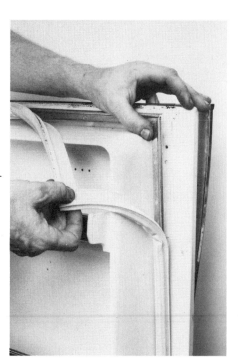

2 Pull the gasket off the retaining strips, going only halfway across the top and about halfway down one side.

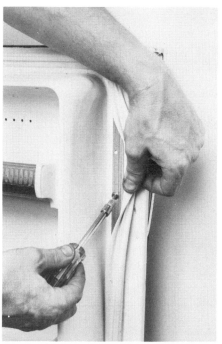

1 To replace the gasket, loosen the retaining screws under the gasket around one corner of the door. If you can get the gasket off the retaining metal strips without removing the screws entirely, so much the better. If not, you may have to take both screws and strips out entirely.

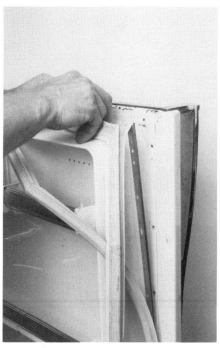

3 Slip the new gasket over the retaining strips while the old gasket hangs out of the way, and put the screws back in halfway. Proceed with the other corner, then the bottom. After the new gasket is in, hold the door up square and tighten the screws all around.

Electrical problems

Fixing a door switch

If a bad door switch leaves the inside light burning, the resulting heat may force the unit to run continuously. On frost-free models, the same switch may control the evaporator fan, shutting it off when the door is open; on other models (like the one shown here) there are two identical-looking switches, one for the light and the other for the fan. If the evaporator fan switch fails, the freezer will frost up.

If the light does not turn off when you depress the switch button with your finger, or if it does not turn on when you open the door (and you've made sure the bulb is good), unplug the unit and proceed as shown here. If the evaporator fan doesn't work (see *Checking the evaporator fan*, opposite, to tell whether it's operating) check its switch as shown here.

1 **To test a door switch** it is usually necessary to pry off the side panel. (The switch pulls forward out of the panel, but the wires are often too short to let the switch drop completely out of the hole.) Hold the wall insulation in place with masking tape.

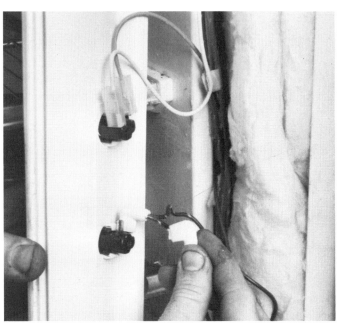

2 Unclip the leads from the switch. Pull the leads straight off so as not to bend the terminals.

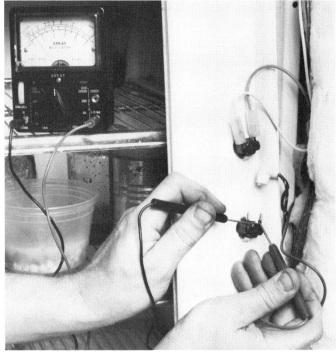

3 Test the switch for continuity (see Blue Pages: *Electrical testers*). On the light switch there should be continuity with the button out, and no continuity with the button pushed in. (The results for the fan switch should be exactly the opposite.) If the switch is defective, replace it .

Testing the thermostat

If the refrigerator won't maintain the right temperature (and you've made sure the coils are clean and the door gasket is tight), check the thermostat or "temperature control." In a frost-free unit, this control is easy to get at. In a cycle-defrost refrigerator, it's more complicated, since there is a sensing bulb that must be removed from behind the compartment liner. When replacing the new bulb, be careful not to kink the tubing; place the new bulb exactly where the old one was. **CAUTION** Turn off the power before starting to work.

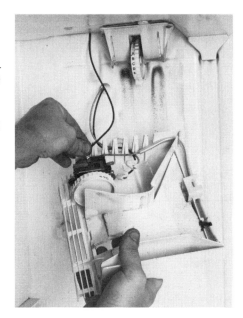

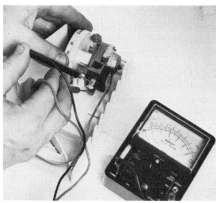

1 **To reach and test the thermostat,** unscrew the cover or pry it off. On some models, first pry off the control knob and then take out retaining screws to get to the thermostat. Label and disconnect the wires. (Be sure that the power is off!)

2 Test the thermostat for continuity (see Blue Pages: *Electrical testers*). At OFF, there should be no continuity. As you turn the shaft to ON it should start to show continuity at some point (depending on how much it has warmed up) and continue to show continuity through the coldest setting. If it's defective, replace it with a duplicate.

Checking the evaporator fan

If you find frost in the freezer of your frost-free refrigerator, and if you're sure the air circulation vents aren't blocked and there are no open food containers in the unit, the evaporator fan may have failed. Open the refrigerator door and listen for the compressor. When it's running, press any buttons on the door jamb. The fan should go on and there should be a draft through the air ducts. If this does not happen, unplug the unit and check the evaporator fan door switch (see opposite page). If the door switch is OK, unscrew the bottom plate or other covers in the freezer; lift them and any insulation out to expose the fan. Check the blades first; they may be blocked. If they turn freely, turn the power off, then check the motor as shown here.

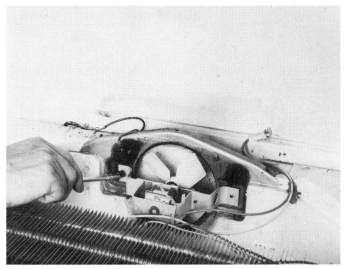

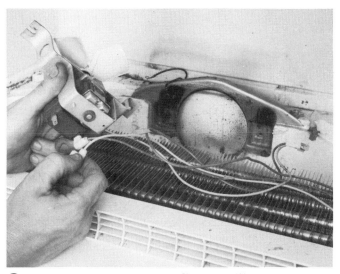

1 **To test the evaporator fan motor,** unscrew the fan mounting and lift the fan and motor out. (If you can reach the motor terminals without removing the fan, make the test with the motor in place). Lay a towel over the sharp evaporator fins to avoid cutting yourself or damaging the fins.

2 Disconnect the leads and attach VOM probes. With the meter set at RX1, you should read between 50 and 200 ohms resistance. A higher or no reading means a defective motor. Save the fan blades and mounting and replace the motor.

Getting into the unit from the back

Moving the refrigerator out of its usual spot takes some muscle, but it's the only way to check the condenser fan, the water connections to the cold water dispenser and ice maker, and (on some models) the defrost timer. It's also the only way to clean the condenser coils properly, and if you want your unit to operate efficiently you should make the extra effort.

To get inside the back, unplug the power cord from the outlet and take out the screws that hold the rear cover. You may have to disconnect the power cord from the cover.

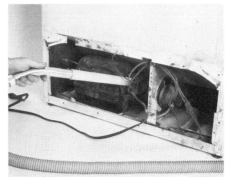

Clean the condenser coils and as much of the bottom compartment as you can reach with the radiator attachment on a vacuum cleaner.

Checking the condenser fan

If your frost-free refrigerator runs all the time or cools poorly (and you've kept the coils clean), check the condenser fan. It should run when the compressor does. With the back of the refrigerator off, plug in the unit and watch to see whether the fan turns. If it doesn't, unplug the unit and make sure the blades are not obstructed or bent, then make the following test. **CAUTION** Be sure the refrigerator is unplugged.

1 **To check and adjust the condenser fan and motor,** remove the assembly by taking out the screws that hold the mounting bracket in place.

2 If the fan blades are loose, tighten the nut (or screw) that holds them in place. If the blades are bent or broken, replace them.

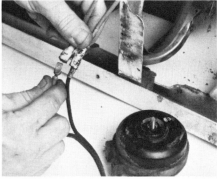

3 If the fan blades are tight, test the motor. Disconnect the motor leads and attach VOM probes to the terminals. With the meter set at RX1, it should read between 50 and 200 ohms resistance. If the reading is higher, the motor is defective and should be replaced.

A Difficult Cleaning Job

Many late-model refrigerators must be laid on their sides for proper cleaning of the condenser coils; the coils are mounted on the bottom and there's no other way to get at them.

Reaching under from the front will not do the job. Be sure to empty the unit before you turn it over! Put down a rug or old blanket to avoid scratches. Once a year should be often enough for this job, and the extra effort will be repaid in lower operating costs and less strain on the compressor.

Replacing a defective defrost timer

When a frost-free refrigerator starts frosting up (and the evaporator fan is OK), the defrost timer may have failed. (The timer turns on the heater in the evaporator coils to melt the frost accumulated there.) On most units, the timer is at the bottom in front. On some, it's mounted at the bottom in the rear.

Remove the timer bracket from the refrigerator, then take the timer off the bracket and take the cover off the timer so that you can see into the gears. With the power on, turn the thermostat to the coldest setting. Don't touch the timer. You should see at least one gear turning. If not, turn the power off, disconnect the leads, and make the test in step 3. If the gears *are* turning, turn the power off, disconnect the leads and, as shown in step 4, make these tests. NOTE: The circuit schematic, usually pasted on the back of the refrigerator, explains which terminal is which. If you can't read it, stop and call a repairman. (1) Between the motor terminal and the common there should be between 500 and 3,000 ohms resistance. (2) Between the heating terminal and the common there should be continuity for only about 10 degrees of the circle as you turn the timer adjustment dial completely around. The timer clicks at this point. (3) Between the cooling terminal and the common there should be continuity for the remaining 350 degrees of the circle. If the timer fails *any* of these tests, replace it.

1 **To test the defrost timer,** unscrew the bracket attaching it to the refrigerator and lift off the bracket and timer.

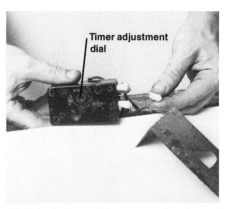

Timer adjustment dial

2 Take the timer off the mounting bracket and disconnect the power leads. (Label them first, for identification.)

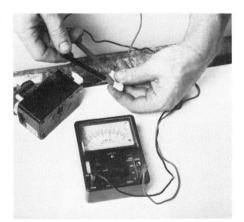

3 Attach VOM probes to the power leads (see Blue Pages: *Electrical testers*), turn the thermostat all the way up, and turn the power on. You should read about 120 volts. If you don't, the problem is elsewhere.

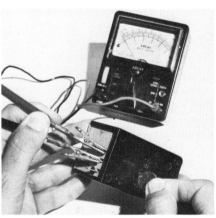

4 Use a VOM to make the three electrical checks listed at the left. All the leads must be disconnected for these tests.

Checking the cold water dispenser

Refrigerators that have a cold water dispenser mounted on the front have a water supply pipe coming into the unit at the bottom rear. The pipe is connected there to a solenoid-operated valve. (There may be a second valve for an ice maker.)

If you're not getting cold water, first check the valve. Unplug the unit and pull the refrigerator out carefully. Remove the rear panel, and unscrew the valve mounting bracket to get the valve out. Disconnect the cold water line (on the refrigerator side of the valve).

Put a pan under the valve. Plug in the unit, being careful to keep any wires away from the pan and water. Then press the dispenser lever. The solenoid should click and water should flow out of the valve. If it doesn't, the solenoid is defective and the valve can't function. If it *does*, the problem is in the unit itself. Check the cold water line on the unit for kinks or blockage.

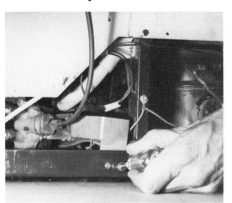

1 **To check and replace the solenoid water valves,** unscrew the valve mounting bracket from the body of the refrigerator and carefully pull the valves out of the unit. Be sure not to break any wire connections.

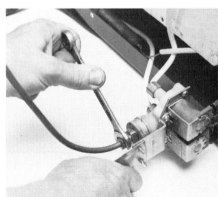

2 If the solenoid valve is bad, unplug the refrigerator, turn off the water supply, and disconnect the valve with a wrench, taking care not to bend any copper tubing. Disconnect the refrigerator tubes and power leads, and replace the entire valve assembly.

Ice makers

Automatic ice makers use the cold in the freezer compartment to freeze ice in a tray. The ice is then momentarily heated to loosen it so that rotating fingers, driven by a small motor, can eject it from the ice maker. Some units dump the ice into a container in the freezer from which you pick the ice out by hand. Others, like the model shown here, dispense the ice through the front. (This requires a second motor hidden below the freezer.) If the ice maker unit doesn't make ice, check the water supply solenoid valve to be sure water is flowing into the unit. If ice covers the ice ejector fingers, adjust the water level adjustment screw (see box below) before starting any repair.

Getting inside

1 **To get inside a dispensing ice maker,** remove the bottom plate in the freezer unit. The plate usually lifts out; there may be screws to remove in some models. (A nondispensing unit will be visible inside the freezer.)

2 Take out the ice container (in dispensing units), to clean it or to remove ice that has frozen solid inside, by disengaging a retaining lever on the side and then lifting the container up out of the freezer.

A Common Problem

If the ice maker freezes solid or if water runs into the ice container or down into the compartment below, reduce the water flow by moving the adjustment lever on the ice maker. (This model has a lever and a screw for finer adjustment.) Water should just fill the individual ice slots in the ice maker, and go no higher.

Repairing an ice maker

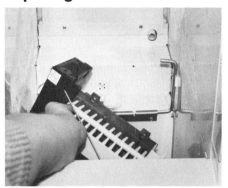

To get the ice maker out of the freezer, take out the ice container (see step 2, above), take off the water supply pipe, remove retaining screws, unplug the unit and lift off the long thin arm that hangs down in front (it operates the on/off switch). Then you can lift the ice maker out.

To replace broken ice ejector fingers, take out retaining screws and clips on the end of the ice maker opposite the motor, and lift the broken parts out for replacement.

Checking the thermostat

If the ice doesn't eject (and the ice maker isn't overfilling) the thermostat that controls the heating cycle may be defective.

To get to the thermostat, unscrew the retaining nuts from the back of the motor housing. Lift the cover off, taking care not to break any connections (the motor will come away attached to the cover).

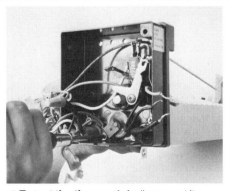

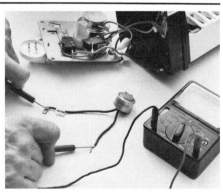

1 **To test the thermostat,** disconnect its leads and remove it from the motor housing. Put the thermostat in the freezer for at least half an hour; it must be well below freezing to test. (The one shown must be below 18° F.)

2 Quickly attach probes from a VOM or continuity tester to the thermostat leads. The thermostat should show continuity; as it warms up, it should show no continuity. If the thermostat shows no continuity when cold, or does show continuity when warm, replace it.

Refrigerator-freezers Troubleshooting Chart

WHAT'S WRONG	REASONS WHY	WHAT TO DO
Refrigerator does not run; no sound can be heard; light is out.	No power at outlet	Check fuse box/circuit breaker. Check outlet with VOM or a lamp. If refrigerator blows fuses, put it on its own circuit.
	Defective power cord	Test cord; replace if defective.
Refrigerator does not run; light is on; occasional clicking may be heard.	Dirty condenser coils	Clean coils.
	Defective condenser fan (frost-free type)	Check fan.
	Incorrect voltage	Check voltage with VOM; call power company if not between 105 and 125 volts.
	Defective thermostat	Test thermostat; replace if defective.
	Defective compressor	Call repairman.
Refrigerator cycles on/off.	Incorrect voltage	Run unit on its own circuit; check voltage at outlet (see above).
	Defective compressor	Call repairman.
	Refrigerant leak	Call repairman.
	Dirty condenser coils	Clean coils.
Refrigerator cools poorly or runs all the time.	Thermostat set wrong	Adjust the thermostat.
	Dirty condenser coils	Clean coils.
	Defective door gasket	Check gasket.
	Sagging door	Straighten door.
	Heavy frost accumulation	Defrost unit more often; if frost-free type, see under "Refrigerator frosts up rapidly...."
	Door open too much	Open door as little as possible.
	Hot, humid weather	If unit runs continuously but cools well, there is no problem.
	Light on inside	Check door switch.
	Wet insulation in door and sides	Open unit on a dry day and let it dry out; repair or replace cracked door jambs and panels.
	Room too warm	Move to a cooler place, or air-condition room.
	Defective evaporator fan	Check fan.
	Defective condenser fan	Check fan.
	Defective defrost timer	Check timer.
	Refrigerant leak	Call repairman.
Refrigerator frosts up rapidly or does not defrost at all.	Door open too much	Open door as little as possible.
	Sagging door	Straighten door.
	Defective door gasket	Test and replace.
	Foods uncovered	Cover or seal all foods, especially liquids.
	Clogged drains	Open and clean drains.
	Defective defrost timer, heater, or thermostat	Check timer, heater, or thermostat.
Refrigerator makes noise.	Unit is not level.	Adjust unit.
	Rattling drain pan	Move pan so it doesn't touch sides.
	Hard or broken compressor mounts	Replace rubber mounts (see p. 41, under *Air Conditioners*).
	Obstructed fan blades	Check evaporator and compressor fans.
Refrigerator smells bad.	Clogged drains	Open and flush drains.
	Dirty drain pan	Clean and disinfect pan.
Water leaking underneath or inside unit.	Broken drain hose or drain pan	Replace broken parts.
	Clogged drains or full pan	Open drains.

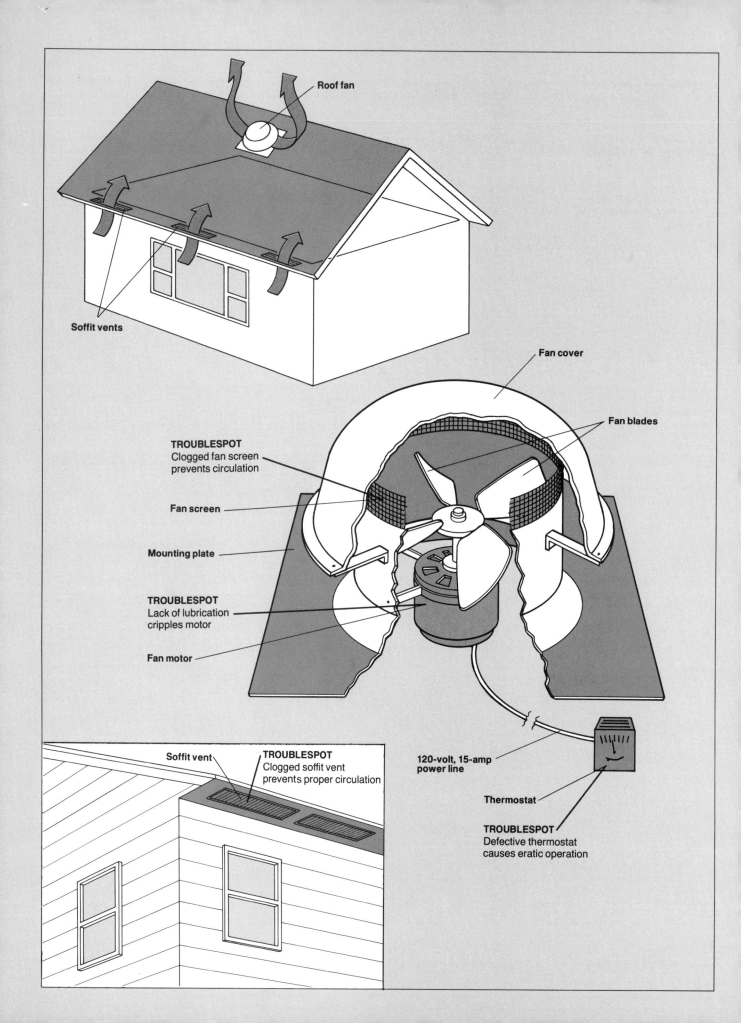

Roof fan

Soffit vents

Fan cover

Fan blades

TROUBLESPOT
Clogged fan screen
prevents circulation

Fan screen

Mounting plate

TROUBLESPOT
Lack of lubrication
cripples motor

Fan motor

Soffit vent

TROUBLESPOT
Clogged soffit vent
prevents proper circulation

120-volt, 15-amp
power line

Thermostat

TROUBLESPOT
Defective thermostat
causes eratic operation

Roof and Attic Fans

Roof fans

In these days of widespread refrigerated air conditioning, it's easy to forget that simply moving the air around you makes you more comfortable, no matter what the temperature. The secret is that moving air increases evaporation of perspiration, which makes you feel cooler.

So fans can reduce the need for air conditioning dramatically. In many situations, a properly installed fan can eliminate the need for air conditioners altogether. This saves roughly 90% of the energy costs of cooling.

Two ways to use fans for energy savings are described here. A fan installed in the roof (opposite) exhausts very hot air from the attic, thus lightening the burden on an air conditioner working downstairs. An attic fan, sometimes called a "whole-house" fan, ventilates the entire house (following pages), saving cooling costs at night and often during the day as well.

Roof fans cut home air conditioning costs by moving hot air out of the attic. During hot summer days the temperature in the attic can reach 130° F. or even higher, depending on where you live. Even with heavy insulation on the attic floor, heat is bound to radiate into the rooms below, making the air conditioner's work much harder. Lowering the attic temperature can reduce the load on the air conditioner by as much as 50%.

A roof fan is installed as close as practical to the highest and hottest point, the ridge line. A thermostat turns the fan on automatically whenever the temperature reaches a preset level, usually 100°F. Since they have to change only the air in the attic, roof fans need a capacity of only 1,000 cubic feet per minute. A 14- or 16-inch fan driven by a small motor—usually 1/10 horsepower — can handle the job adequately. This size motor can be connected directly to the normal 15-amp house electrical circuit.

Since these fans exhaust directly through the roof, they must be enclosed by weatherproof housings.

Maintenance and repair

At the start of hot weather, clean the fan blades thoroughly and check that they turn freely. Make sure the screen is unobstructed. You may have to climb up on the roof to dislodge leaves or birds' nests. If the motor has oil ports, put a few drops of machine oil in each. Make sure the soffit vents are unobstructed, both outside and inside the attic. Listen occasionally on hot days to verify that the fan is operating. Since it's automatic, it's easily forgotten. If it fails to operate, you can check the thermostat as described at far right. If the motor seems at fault, remove the blades, take the motor out of its mounting, and test it (see Appliance Repair Basics: *How to Test a Universal Motor*). If defective take it to a repair shop or replace it. **CAUTION** Disconnect the fan before doing any maintenance.

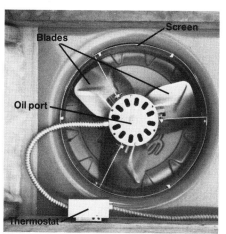

To ensure efficient operation, keep the fan blades and the screen clean; lubricate the motor annually if it has oil ports. Keep the attic area near the fan open for good air circulation.

To test the thermostat, turn the power off and attach VOM clips to the two leads from the thermostat to the motor. Turn the power on, and turn the thermostat control button all the way up and down. You should get a reading of 120 volts AC at the top of the thermostat's scale and no voltage at the bottom. If the thermostat fails this test, replace it. If it is OK, but the motor does not turn on, the problem is in the motor or the wiring from the thermostat to the motor. **CAUTION** This is a power-on test, so be very careful.

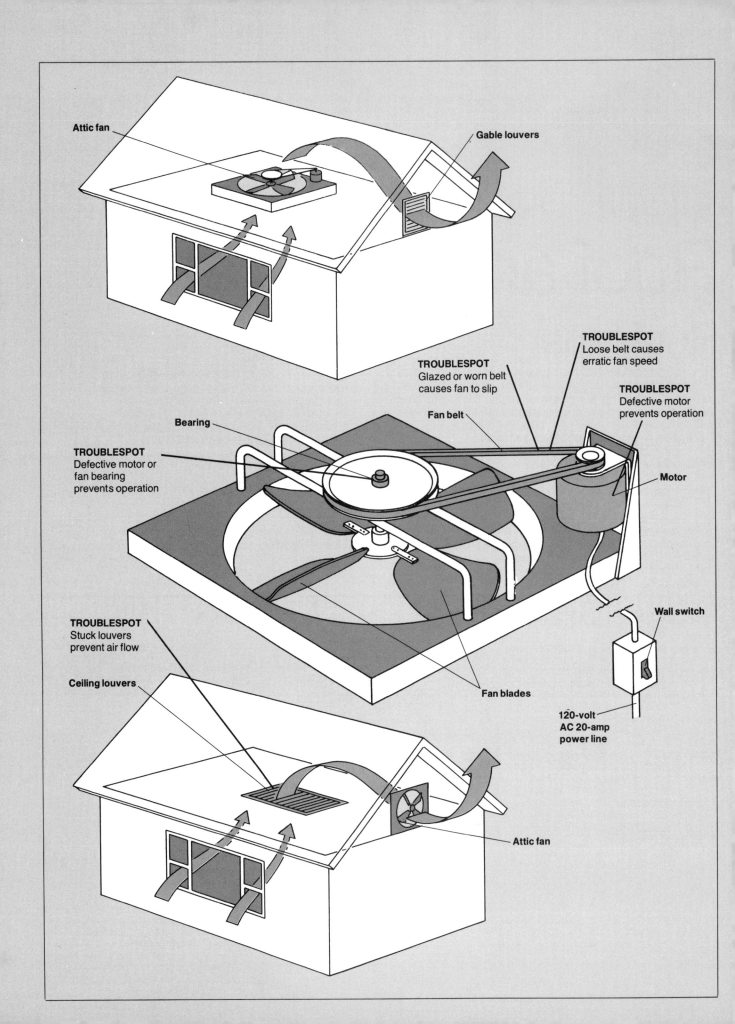

Attic fan

Gable louvers

TROUBLESPOT
Loose belt causes
erratic fan speed

TROUBLESPOT
Glazed or worn belt
causes fan to slip

TROUBLESPOT
Defective motor
prevents operation

Fan belt

Bearing

TROUBLESPOT
Defective motor or
fan bearing
prevents operation

Motor

Wall switch

TROUBLESPOT
Stuck louvers
prevent air flow

Fan blades

Ceiling louvers

**120-volt
AC 20-amp
power line**

Attic fan

ROOF AND ATTIC FANS
Attic fans

Attic fans cool the entire house by drawing air in at lower levels and exhausting it through the attic. This works effectively at night when cooler outdoor air can be drawn in through the windows to replace hot, stale indoor air. If the outdoor temperature is not too high, say, up to 80°F., cooling by attic fan can replace air conditioning altogether, at a considerable energy saving.

To be effective, an attic fan must move at least 5,000 cubic feet of air a minute through an average house. This requires a 24-inch fan, which needs a ⅓- or ½-horsepower motor to drive it. To guarantee an adequate electricity supply, an attic fan should be connected to its own individual 20-amp circuit.

In many installations the fan is mounted horizontally on the floor of the attic just above a set of louvers (opposite, top). Air is exhausted through gable louvers. Alternately, the fan can be mounted vertically in the gable itself just in front of the louvers (opposite, bottom). In this setup, another set of louvers is mounted in the attic floor, normally in a central hallway. In all these cases the louvers are normally spring-loaded; that is, when the fan is on, the airflow forces the louvers open; when the fan stops, the springs hold the louvers closed. If passive louvers are installed (those that are always open) you will want to seal them during the heating season to avoid heat loss.

Maintenance and adjustment

At the beginning of the cooling season, make sure the fan blades are clean and the louvers (both ceiling and gable, if you have two sets) are clean and move freely. Apply a drop of oil to each pivot point in the louvers. Oil the motor bearings (if there are oil ports) and the pulley bearings. Check the drive belt; replace it if its sides are glazed (shiny, smooth, and slippery), or if there are cracks or fraying. Check drive-belt tension and adjust as necessary (see right). Spin the blades; they should turn easily and quietly. If there is noise or resistance, you may have bearing problems; call a serviceman. **CAUTION** Never touch the belt while the fan is running.

To adjust drive-belt tension, turn the power off, loosen the motor-mounting bolts, and push the motor away from the fan shaft to take up the slack in the belt. Then tighten the bolts. The belt should deflect about ½ inch when pressed inward at its middle.

To remove a drive belt, turn the power off and press down on the belt near the motor pulley. Turn the blades slowly and the belt will slip off. To put a new belt on, slip one end around the fan pulley and press the other end into one side of the motor pulley. Turn the blades slowly while pressing the belt into the pulley, and it will slip on. NOTE: You will probably have to readjust the drive-belt tension.

Roof and Attic Fans Troubleshooting Chart		
WHAT'S WRONG	REASONS WHY	WHAT TO DO
Motor doesn't run.	No power	Check fuse box/circuit breaker.
	Faulty switch	Check switch; replace.
	Shaft bearings seized up	Lubricate or replace bearings.
	Defective motor	Take motor to repair shop or replace it.
Motor runs but no air circulates.	Broken belt	Replace belt with a duplicate.
	Louvers stuck shut	Lubricate louver pivot points.
Air circulates poorly.	Glazed belt	Replace belt with a duplicate.
	Loose drive belt	Adjust motor mount to tighten drive belt.
	Fan too small for the job	Buy a larger fan.
	Louvers partially closed or blocked	Lubricate louver pivot points; remove obstructions.

One family's investment in solar heating. The house shown here was designed to make both passive and active solar heating principles work for the occupants. The house faces south with generous areas of glass open to catch the sun. A greenhouse absorbs solar warmth at a high level of efficiency. At night or in warm weather, the greenhouse can be closed with insulating blinds. The house is especially well insulated from roof to basement. The interior of the house uses an open design, so that heat trapped by the greenhouse naturally circulates and rises through all the rooms. Most of the roof is a solar hot-air heat collector, which sends its heat through ducts to a storage pit in the basement. From there a small electric fan forces it throughout the house as needed. Just underneath the deck are two solar hot-water collector panels that collect heat to provide domestic hot water. These solar heating systems are described and illustrated on the following pages.

Solar Heating Systems

Someone has calculated that every three weeks the sun beams to earth as much energy as is locked up in all the known coal, oil, and gas reserves in the world. Surely this mind-boggling quantity of free energy could satisfy all our domestic heating needs many times over. That is, it could if the sun always shone on our house and if we had the technology at hand to capture it. But our industrialized society has been committed over the centuries to building self-contained, totally isolated miniclimates in homes and other buildings; we've tried to shut out all the surrounding weather and create our own. When fuels were cheap, perhaps it didn't matter. Today, however, attitudes are changing.

Not all Americans have tried to shut out the sun's free gift of heat. Centuries ago, the pueblo builders in the Southwest knew how to make the most of solar energy (see below). Not until the last ten years or so have many others begun to think seriously about building homes that take advantage of the sun's energy, and finding the best means to collect and store it. These new solar design concepts may bring about some radical changes in how our homes look, as the following pages show. On the other hand, many "solar-smart" techniques are not radical at all. If you orient your house toward the sun, you may save up to 30% of your heating bill. If you insulate your house effectively, you may save another 30%. Such "passive" solar heating techniques could save enormous amounts of fuel and slash heating bills, but old building habits are hard to change, and economic interests in conventional construction methods are deeply entrenched.

Some Americans have been going even further and building "active" solar heating systems. They're called active because they include the installation of special heat collecting and storing devices, as well as plumbing, pumps, fans, and controls to circulate the heat. Some people are adding solar water heaters to existing homes, especially in the sunbelt states. Others are designing their new homes to be solar efficient from the ground up, like the one shown on the opposite page, which uses solar heat to provide both hot water and space heating.

Solar technology is a new field, still in its expanding stages. Solar heating is not for everyone, and not for every part of the country. The information on the following pages gives some of the basic ideas and devices current in solar heating practice. If you're interested in adding solar heating, you should visit solar supply stores, talk to solar architects, read books on solar construction, and visit solar homes in your neighborhood. You'll find an endless variety of installations that are custom designed to fit individual families' needs and resources. Before you can answer the question "Is solar heating for me?" you need answers to technical and economic questions that only experts can supply.

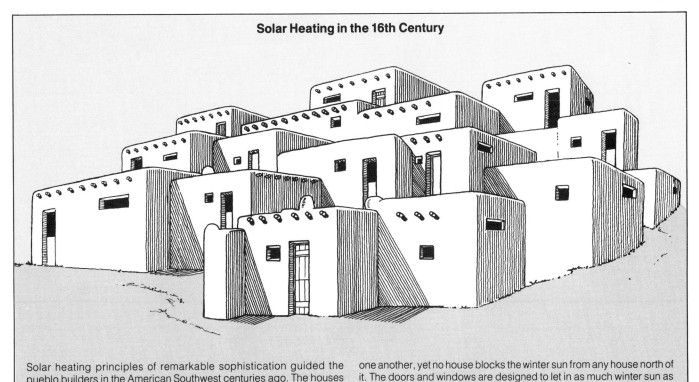

Solar Heating in the 16th Century

Solar heating principles of remarkable sophistication guided the pueblo builders in the American Southwest centuries ago. The houses all face south to let in as much winter sun heat as possible. The thick adobe walls absorb heat during the day and release it slowly during the cold nights. The houses are clustered together, providing shelter for one another, yet no house blocks the winter sun from any house north of it. The doors and windows are designed to let in as much winter sun as possible, at the same time sheltering the interiors from direct sunlight during the summer months.

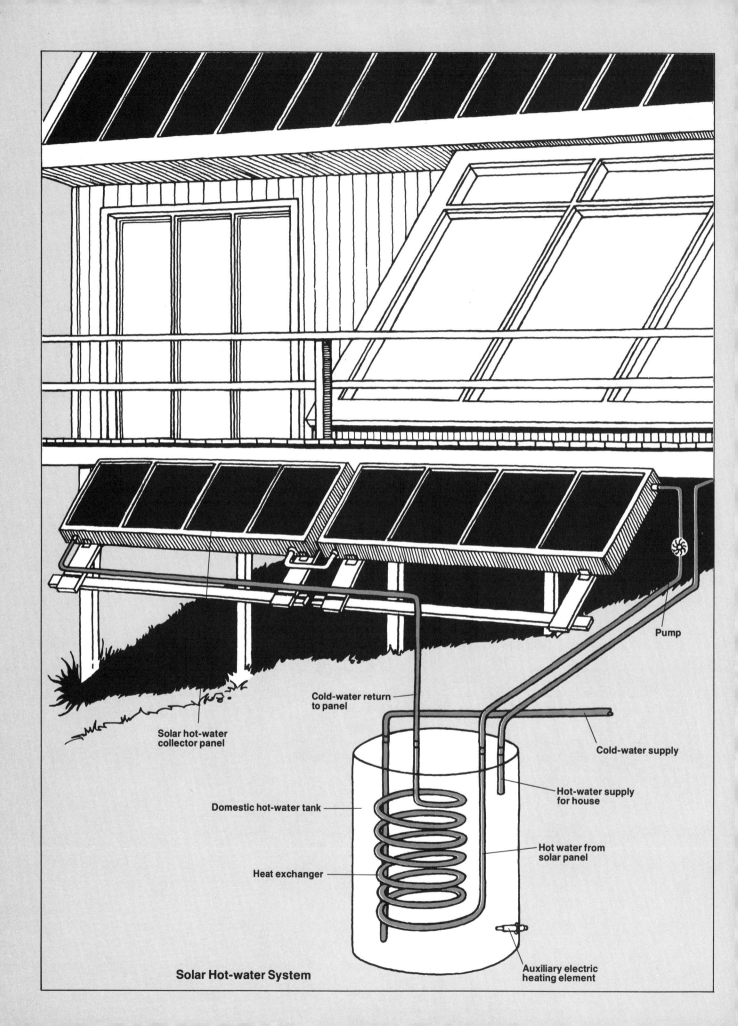

Pump

Cold-water return
to panel

Cold-water supply

Solar hot-water
collector panel

Hot-water supply
for house

Domestic hot-water tank

Hot water from
solar panel

Heat exchanger

Auxiliary electric
heating element

Solar Hot-water System

Solar hot-water systems

The energy-efficient house shown on page 112 uses a solar hot-water system to heat water for domestic use. Two solar heat-collecting panels are mounted at the front of the deck, facing south. They are elevated so that the noon rays of the winter sun strike them at right angles, in order to raise the temperature inside the panels to the highest possible level. The water in the panels (the panels themselves are described below) absorbs the sun's heat and is pumped down into the hot-water storage tank in the basement. The hot water from the panels passes through a heat exchanger inside the tank, heating the domestic water that surrounds the

exchanger. A thermostat controls the pump so that only hot water is drawn down from the panel to the tank.

Since the house is located in a region of winter freezing, the water in the panels contains antifreeze so that there is no danger of damage to panels or plumbing on cold nights. This also means that the panel water must be isolated in a closed loop that prevents any mixing of panel water with domestic water in the storage tank. (An alternate drain-down system is described at the bottom of the page.) Hot water is drawn out of the storage tank as needed for bathing and washing. An electric heating element in the tank provides auxiliary heating when the sun is hidden for long periods.

Hot-water collector panels

The sun's rays penetrate the glass cover of the collector panel and are trapped inside, creating a kind of greenhouse heating effect. Nearly 60% of the sun's heat is absorbed directly by the black absorber plate inside the panel. The plate can be aluminum, steel, copper, or plastic. Water running through the plate absorbs the heat and is pumped through the plumbing

connections to the storage tank. In the parabolic collectors (below, right), the inside mirror surface focuses the sun's rays on the liquid-filled center tube. In some commercial applications, small motors drive banks of parabolic collectors so that they follow the sun across the sky for the most efficient heat collecting.

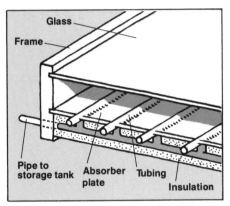

Water flowing through the tubes in the absorber plate absorbs the heat of the sun's rays that strike the plate.

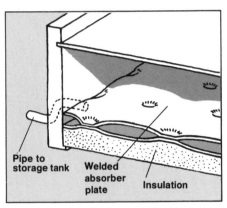

Water flows through the spaces inside the spot-welded absorber plate, picking up heat from the sun-warmed panel.

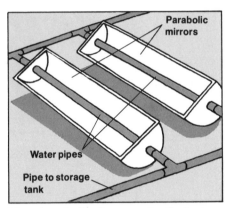

The mirror inside the curved collector focuses the sun's heat on the pipe in the center, raising the temperature of the water flowing through the pipe.

A drain-down water-heating system

In a drain-down solar water-heating system, the hot water from the collecting panels passes directly into the storage tank from which domestic hot water is drawn. The plumbing system for the panels is "open," i.e., not kept separate in a heat exchanger as in the system shown on the opposite page. This is a more efficient way of heating water for domestic use than the closed-loop system. In regions where there is danger of freezing, an automatic system drains the panels of water when the temperature falls near freezing.

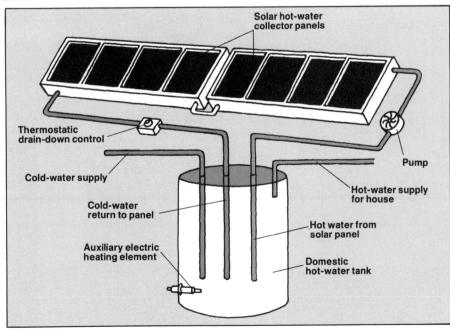

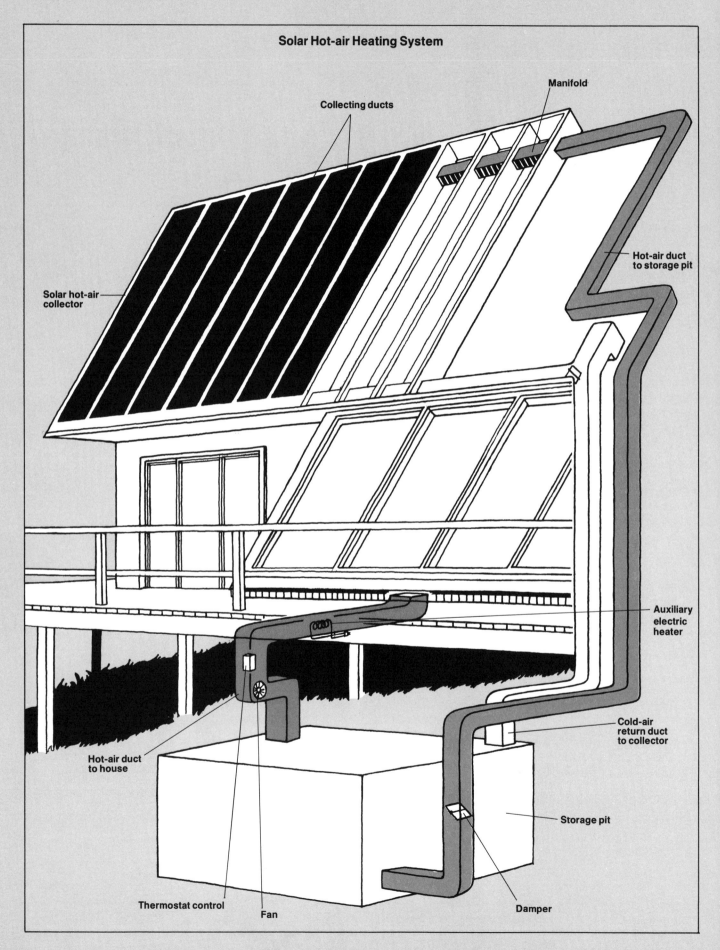

Solar Hot-air Heating System

Manifold

Collecting ducts

Hot-air duct to storage pit

Solar hot-air collector

Auxiliary electric heater

Cold-air return duct to collector

Hot-air duct to house

Storage pit

Thermostat control

Fan

Damper

Solar hot-air heating system

The solar energy house on page 112 uses a solar hot-air system to satisfy space-heating requirements. Nearly the entire roof is covered with solar hot-air collecting ducts. The roof faces south and is elevated so that the rays of the winter sun strike the roof at right angles at noon; this raises the temperature inside the collecting ducts as high as possible. The hot air rises to the top of the collecting ducts and is drawn by fan down into the storage pit in the basement. The pit (described at the bottom of the page) holds the heat for distribution around the house when the thermostat calls for heat. Cold air from the house returns to the bottom of the collecting ducts on the roof to be reheated. Heat stored in the pit is withdrawn during the night hours as needed. An electric heater provides auxiliary heat during cloudy periods.

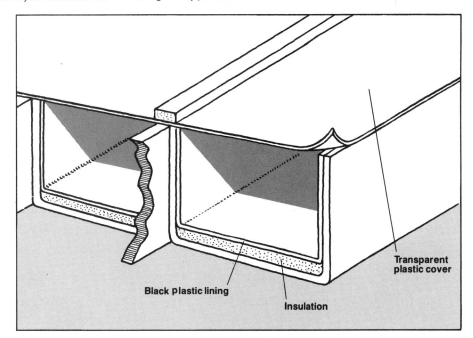

A single hot-air collecting duct can be about 1½ feet wide and 1 foot deep; the duct in this installation is about 18 feet tall. The duct is covered with a sheet of transparent plastic, which traps the sun's heat inside. The duct is lined with black plastic sheeting, which absorbs the heat. A layer of insulation on the bottom prevents heat loss. House air passing through the collecting duct is heated directly by the sun and by radiation from the surfaces of the duct.

Black plastic lining

Insulation

Transparent plastic cover

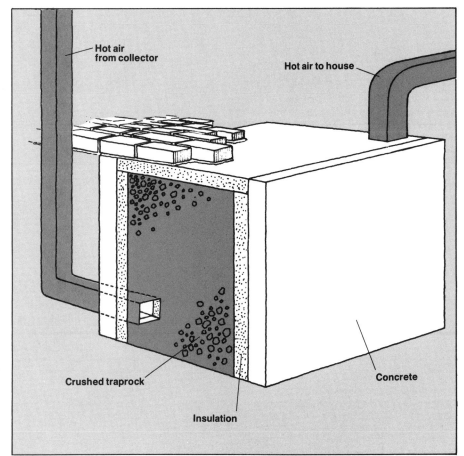

The hot-air storage pit in the basement of the house is a massive concrete chamber with additional thick insulation on sides and top. In this installation, it occupies about 150 cubic feet. The pit is filled with traprock (the kind used as railroad ballast), which readily absorbs the heat from the air that is drawn down from the collecting ducts on the roof and forced through the pit by the fan. Even on a cold night there is normally enough heat trapped in the rock to keep the house comfortable.

Hot air from collector

Hot air to house

Crushed traprock

Insulation

Concrete

How a solar heating system copes with weather changes

An active solar heating system is designed to collect solar heat when the sun is shining and store it for use at night or other times when the sun is hidden. The system also distributes this heat around the house and includes an auxiliary heating source that takes over when the solar heat-storage device is exhausted.

The solar hot-air system described on the previous pages automatically shifts from direct sun heat to stored heat to auxiliary heat, so that the demands of the home thermostat are constantly satisfied. These three phases of operation are described below.

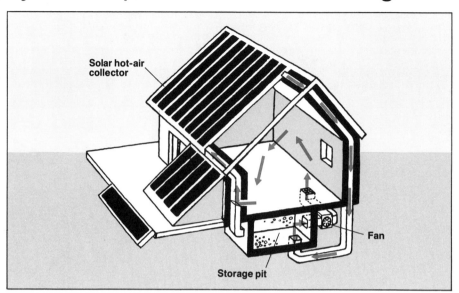

When the sun is shining, hot air from the collector flows into the storage pit. If the thermostat calls for heat, the fan draws hot air from storage and circulates it throughout the house. Cool air returns to the collector to be reheated.

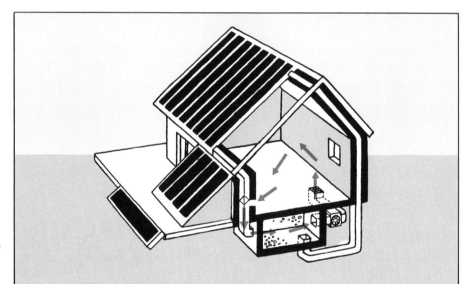

During the night, the air ducts to and from the collector are shut off, and hot air from the storage pit circulates around the house. During cold spells, a wood fire may be lit in a wood stove to supplement the solar heat.

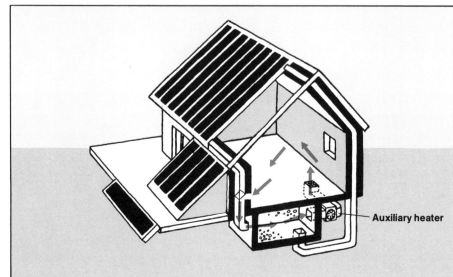

When the sun is hidden for long spells, or during severe cold weather, both collector and storage pit are shut off. The auxiliary heater in the duct is turned on automatically to provide the necessary heat as demanded by the thermostat. A fire in a wood stove also adds warmth.

Making the most of your solar heating potential

Should you invest in solar heating? The answer to this question depends on many factors. Do you live in a region that gets sufficient sunshine to run a solar heating system efficiently? Is your house shaded by trees, buildings, or hills that could seriously cut the amount of sunlight reaching your collectors? What are your heating needs? How big is your family? Are you building a new house that can be solar-efficient from the ground up, or are you trying to adapt solar heating to an older, less efficient house? How much money are you willing to invest? Can you get financing in your locality for solar technology? What are the building requirements in your town? To answer these and many other questions you need the help of skilled solar consultants and solar architects. Some of the factors to be considered and some solar-efficient design concepts are described on this and the following pages.

As you ponder the various questions, don't forget to take a long view of costs. Initial costs for solar technology currently are higher than for conventional technology, but the cost of the fuel—the sun's heat—is and always will be zero.

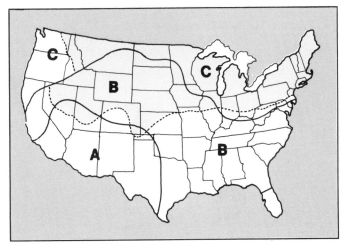

Regions vary not only in the amount of sun they receive but also in the heating demands imposed by climate. Region A on the map at right has excellent sunshine, perhaps 70% or more of the possible sunshine. Region B has good sunshine, perhaps 50% to 60%. Region C has only fair sunshine, from 40% to 50%. The shaded area has a high heat demand during the heating season. Other areas have moderate or low heating demands. These are approximate areas and figures; you should get basic information from your local weather bureau to use as a starting point in calculating your solar heating potential.

You may live in a sunny region, but can the sun reach your house easily? Examine the microclimate surrounding your home. Is the sun blocked by trees, by other buildings, or by a hill? Any of these obstructions could prevent sufficient sun from reaching your solar heat collectors to make them economically justifiable. A tree can be cut down, but other permanent sun shades must be carefully considered in evaluating any possible solar heating investment.

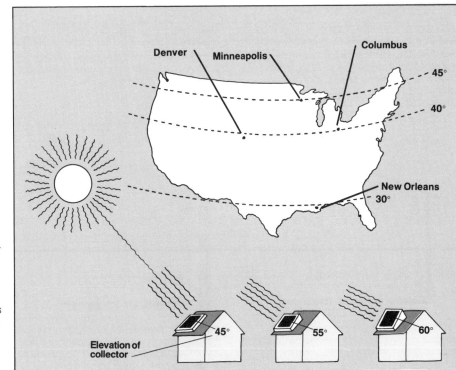

For highest heat collecting efficiency, solar collectors must face straight south, and must be elevated so that the rays of the winter sun strike them at right angles at noon. A rule of thumb says, add 15 degrees to your latitude to determine the proper elevation for a solar collector. As the map at right indicates, in a southern city like New Orleans, a collector should be at a 45-degree angle of elevation. In Denver or Columbus, Ohio, a 55-degree elevation would be about right. In Minneapolis, about 60 degrees.

Designs for passive solar heating

You can take advantage of the sun's free energy without installing any active collecting machinery at all. All the passive designs and devices on this page catch and conserve the sun's heat without plumbing, pumps, fans, drains, or special duct work. Adapted singly or in combination, these solar-oriented concepts will make new houses energy efficient. In any construction plans, remember to include adequate insulation of roof and walls to stop heat loss. Use thermopane or double glazing in all windows. Rebuilding an existing house along these lines may be too costly, but some remodeling for greater efficiency is usually possible, as described on the opposite page.

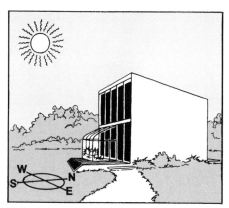

Build the house so it faces the sun. Let the long side and the windows face south to catch all the heat available during the heating season in your locality.

Provide overhangs or other shading devices to keep hot summer sun out of east, south, and west windows.

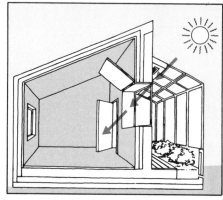

Build a greenhouse on the south side of the house; it will catch an enormous amount of the sun's heat during the day and radiate it into the house at night.

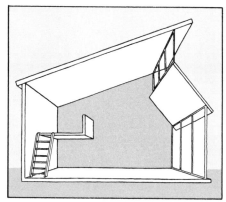

Design an open interior for your house, so that heat from the ground floor and greenhouse rises throughout the house, heating upstairs rooms.

Build a berm—an insulating bank of earth—around your house on the cool side to hold heat inside and block cold northern winds.

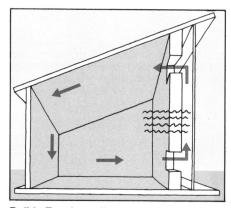

Build a Trombe wall—a massive stone or concrete heat-storage wall—on the south side of your house, to provide winter heating by convection during the day and by radiation at night.

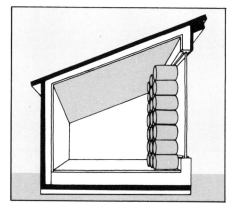

Set up a wall of water-filled steel drums or tubes to soak up the sun's heat during the day and to radiate it into the home during the night.

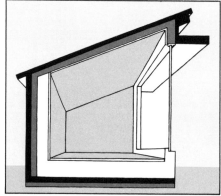

Surround the house with thick walls and floors of concrete, stone, masonry, or adobe to catch and store sun heat directly during the day and to radiate it throughout the house at night.

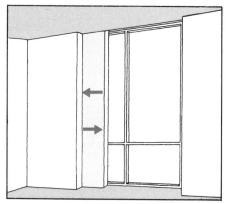

Cover windows with insulating panels or shades to keep heat in when the sun is not shining, or to block out the sun when it is too hot.

Adapting older homes for solar efficiency

Passive solar heaters

Rebuilding older homes to incorporate the passive solar heating devices described on the opposite page is often uneconomical. The house may not be oriented toward the south, there may be too much shade, or the house may lose too much heat through loose construction. There may simply be too little sun during the heating season. But many homes can profit by the addition of a greenhouse or a window-box collector to help meet space-heating requirements on sunny winter days.

Build a greenhouse on the southern wall of the house if you get a lot of sun there. Provide doors or windows into the house so that heat can flow in during the day and night cold can be kept out.

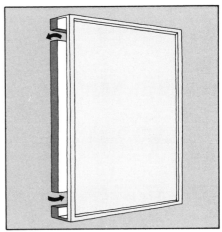

Install window-box collectors on sunny eastern, southern, or western walls to absorb sun heat, which is carried into the house by convection or driven inside by a small fan.

Active solar collectors

Solar hot-water heat collectors can be added to any home that has a place to mount collectors at right angles to the sun, has a place to install a storage device, and, of course, gets enough sun to run the collecting system economically. In sunny southern states, solar heaters can supply all the domestic hot water needed. Even in northern states, they can fill most of the domestic hot water needs. Heating water for a swimming pool is a job well suited to a solar heater in most localities.

If the roof faces south, the solar collectors can be mounted at the right elevation on the roof and the storage tank installed directly below, in the basement.

If the roof is unsuitable for solar collectors, they can be mounted on a rack or shed oriented properly, with the storage tank installed inside or nearby.

In some localities, solar hot-water collectors may be connected to hot-air space-heating systems to provide heating on sunny days. The same collectors may also be part of the domestic hot-water supply system.

Solar heaters for swimming pools can be mounted near the pool or on a nearby roof. An auxiliary heater for cloudy days is usually part of the system.

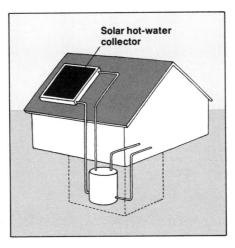
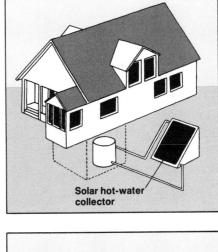
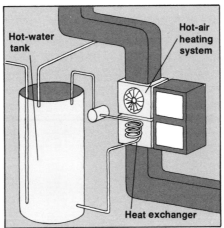

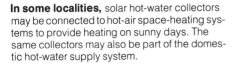

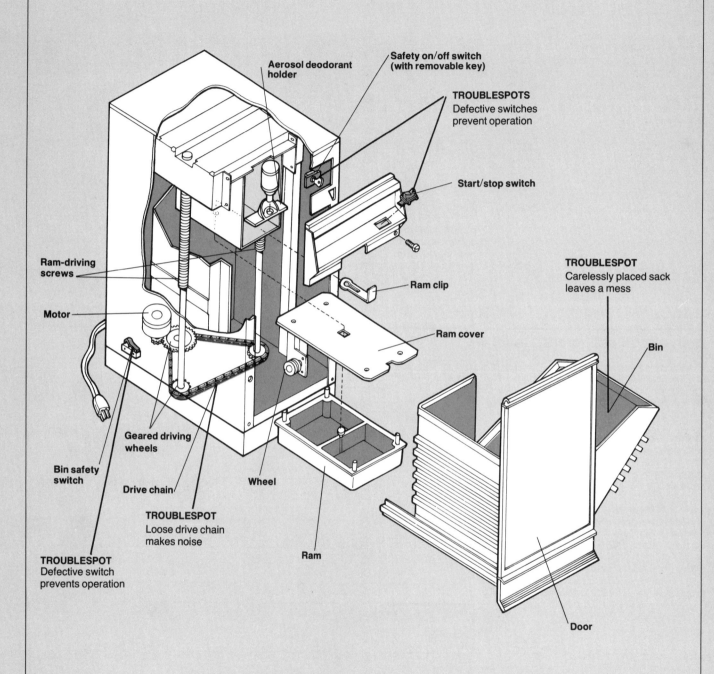

Aerosol deodorant holder

Safety on/off switch (with removable key)

TROUBLESPOTS
Defective switches prevent operation

Start/stop switch

Ram clip

Ram cover

TROUBLESPOT
Carelessly placed sack leaves a mess

Bin

Ram-driving screws

Motor

Geared driving wheels

Bin safety switch

Drive chain

Wheel

TROUBLESPOT
Loose drive chain makes noise

Ram

TROUBLESPOT
Defective switch prevents operation

Door

Trash Compactors

A trash compactor reduces unmanageable amounts of dry garbage and trash to neat, convenient packages by applying a surprising amount of brute force. For example, two full 20-gallon garbage bags subjected to 2,000 pounds pressure are compacted into one 9 x 17 x 18-inch package. The compacting ram that delivers this force is driven by reducing gears, which deliver great power, and by ram driving screws. Since such machinery can be dangerous, compactors have numerous fail-safe switches: the compactor will not operate if the door is open, if the unit is not level, if the safety lock is off, and so on. Some manufacturers build their units so you can't get access to the works. In such cases, all you can do is clean the unit regularly and follow the operating tips on the following page. For those who *can* get inside their compactors, directions for lubrication, adjusting the belts and gears, and checking switches are also given.

Basic maintenance

Install the trash sack so that it fits neatly into its bin, the top folded flat around the rim of the bin and the edges held firmly in the clips. A sloppily installed bag means a mess in the compactor. Clean the bin every month or so with warm water and detergent, and dry thoroughly to prevent odors and rust. If the bin does rust, sand and repaint it.

Lubricate the bin latch mechanism. Apply white grease (not oil) to all parts that turn or rub against one another. If a finger full of grease bothers you, use a cotton-tipped swab.

To lubricate inside, unplug the unit first. Lift the door and bin assembly off its track. Be careful, the door is heavy! In most units the door comes out easily in any position; in some units it must be pulled forward first.

Lubricate all the wheels on the door and inside the unit that supports the door. If the wheels run on ball bearings, use a few drops of light oil on each. If they are nylon wheels without ball bearings, squirt a little silicone lubricant onto each wheel shaft.

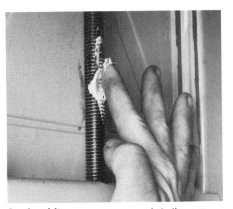

Apply white grease generously to the ram-driving screws, both at the base and along the threaded parts. Then put the door back in, close it securely, plug the unit in, and run the ram up and down for a cycle or two. Check that the grease is spread all over the threaded parts of the screws.

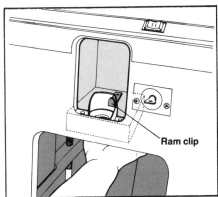

Ram clip

Take the ram out every month or so to clean it and its rubber cover pad with soap and water. Unplug the unit. To get the ram out, pull the clip that lies above the ram in the center of the unit. (It's directly behind the aerosol can holder in this model.) Support the ram with your other hand as it drops out of the clip.

<table>
<tr><td>Tips for Safe and Efficient Operation</td></tr>
</table>

Tips for Safe and Efficient Operation

Run the unit on its own circuit.

Make sure the unit sits level.

Make sure the unit doesn't wobble.

Don't load above the sack level.

Put in only dry trash.

Lay bottles flat in the middle of the sack, preferably inside another container such as a milk carton.

Never put aerosol cans in the compactor.

Never allow children to play with the unit.

Clean ram and bin regularly.

Getting inside

Many trash compactors are designed to discourage owners from working on the inside mechanism. A unit carelessly repaired could become dangerous because of its great power. But the faceplates of most models can be removed to allow testing and replacement of switches.

To remove the faceplate, take the screws out and (in this model) knock the plate sharply upward with the heel of your hand to dislodge it. On other models, the plate may fall forward when all screws are removed.

Switch problems

Different models have different combinations of switches, but start/stop, safety on/off, the door latch switches, and the top-limit switch (stops the ram at the top of its run) appear on all models. If any of these switches fails a continuity test, take the defective switch to an appliance store and replace.

To test and replace the start/stop switch, first unplug the unit and take the door out (see preceding page). Before removing the switch, label it to identify the START and STOP positions so you can tell which is which when the switch is dangling outside the panel. Then remove the faceplate (see above).

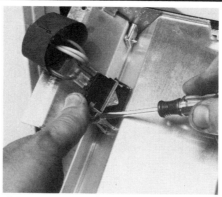

1 To test the start/stop switch for continuity, detach the switch from the faceplate. On this typical model, it is a rocker-type switch clipped to the faceplate. To release it, insert a screwdriver carefully under the clip, spread the clip, and angle the switch out.

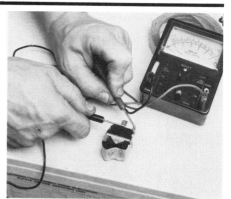

2 Before detaching any wires, label them to correspond to the switch terminals they connect to. There are usually helpful letters or numbers next to the terminals on the back of the switch. (The wires can always be put back right if you can read the schematic electrical diagram pasted somewhere on the unit, but careful labeling saves a lot of time.) Test the switch with a VOM (see Blue Pages: *Electrical testers*). START should show continuity; STOP should show no continuity. All the other switches on the unit can be tested in the same way.

Working on the drive mechanism

Repairing the motor drive assembly is impossible in many units because the manufacturer has deliberately sealed it up. But it is sometimes possible to get inside if you're willing to do a little more work. You can get inside the unit shown here, for example, through the bottom. First, unplug the unit. Take the door out (see preceding page), and lay the unit on its side. Remove the bottom panel screws and take the panel off.

Lubricate the sprocket (or pulley) wheels with white lubricant. Put a little on the plastic gears, too. Adjust the tension if the drive chain is loose and replace gears if the teeth are worn or missing. On most models, the permanently sealed motor cannot be reached without totally dismantling the unit. If you suspect a defective motor, call a repairman.

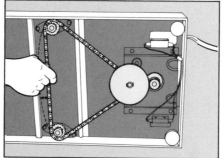

1 Test the drive chain (or drive belt) for proper tension by pushing it sideways. If there is more than ½ inch play, the chain is too loose. A loose chain can cause noisy, rough operation.

2 To tighten the drive chain (or drive belt), loosen the four motor mount bolts (the four *outer* bolts on this model) and move the motor mount until there is no more than ½ inch play in the chain. Tighten the bolts carefully. The motor bolts (the four *inner* bolts here) should also be kept tight.

Trash Compactors Troubleshooting Chart

WHAT'S WRONG	REASONS WHY	WHAT TO DO
Compactor doesn't go on.	No power at outlet	Check fuse box/circuit breaker.
	Defective cord	Test cord and replace.
	Safety lock is off.	Turn it on.
	Drawer not closed	Remove obstructions.
	Motor overloaded with ram down	Pull wall plug and wait 10 minutes for motor to cool. Check drive chain or drive belt; look for broken gears and worn ram screws.
	Defective switch	Check start/stop switch, safety switch, overload switch. Check your owner's manual for the switches on your unit.
	Loose electrical connection	Check all wires and connections.
Unit starts but blows fuse or trips circuit breaker.	Too many appliances on circuit	Run unit on its own circuit.
	Short circuit in cord or plug	Test plug and cord for continuity (see Blue Pages: *Electrical testers*).
	Short circuit in switch	Test switches for continuity.
	Short circuit in motor	Call repairman.
Motor runs but trash is not compacted.	Loose or broken drive chain (belt)	Check chain; adjust and replace.
	Loose gears or pulleys	Check; tighten and replace.
	Ram seized up	Ram screws need lubrication; if screws are stripped, replace them.
Unit is too noisy.	Drive chain (belt) too loose	Tighten chain.
	Unit needs lubrication	Lubricate.
	Loose parts	Tighten every bolt and screw in sight.
Unit smells bad.	Aerosol can (or other deodorant supply) empty	Put in a new can.
	Aerosol nozzle clogged	Ream out with thin wire.
Unit won't stop running.	Defective top-limit switch	Pull plug; check switch for continuity.
	Defective start/stop switch	Check and replace.
Unit makes a mess.	Bag not in proper position	Check bag and clips that hold it.
Drawer won't open.	Ram stalled part way down	Make sure unit is plugged in. Check that door is completely closed. Unplug, look for broken belt, chain or pulleys, or drive screws.
	Motor overloaded	(See above, "Compactor doesn't go on.")

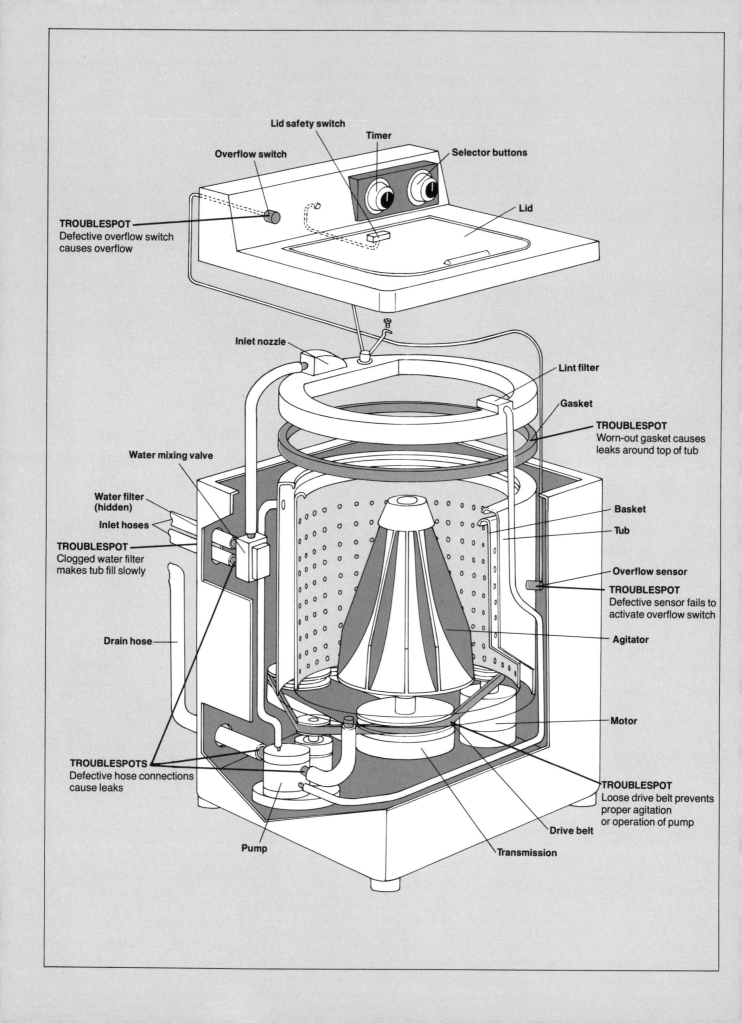

Lid safety switch

Timer

Overflow switch

Selector buttons

Lid

TROUBLESPOT
Defective overflow switch
causes overflow

Inlet nozzle

Lint filter

Gasket

TROUBLESPOT
Worn-out gasket causes
leaks around top of tub

Water mixing valve

Water filter
(hidden)

Inlet hoses

Basket

Tub

TROUBLESPOT
Clogged water filter
makes tub fill slowly

Overflow sensor

TROUBLESPOT
Defective sensor fails to
activate overflow switch

Drain hose

Agitator

Motor

TROUBLESPOTS
Defective hose connections
cause leaks

TROUBLESPOT
Loose drive belt prevents
proper agitation
or operation of pump

Drive belt

Pump

Transmission

Washing Machines

Washing machines are ruggedly built to withstand the violent back-and-forth motion of agitating a heavy load and the high-speed spinning that follows. Modern washing machines have a combination of valves, switches, and temperature sensors to give you options in water temperature and quantity, and in wash cycles. The timer controls all these operations. With all this convenience, little maintenance is required—just clean the lint and water filters regularly and check the drive belt occasionally.

The electrical problems that may occur involve a defective overflow switch (see next page), and faulty overload and lid safety switches. Standard continuity tests can be used to test the latter (see Blue Pages: *Electrical testers*). The solenoids in the mixing valves can be tested the same way you test those found on refrigerators (see page 105). The washing machine timer can be treated the same way as the dishwasher timer (see page 62).

Mechanical problems eventually do crop up. (1) A hose may spring a leak. Instructions for handling this situation are given on the next page. (2) The drive belt can break. On most models it is very difficult to replace a belt without complicated disassembly, and you had better call a repairman. On a few models, drive belt replacement is easy: when you tip the unit on its side and open up the bottom, the belt and its pulleys are all out in the open. (3) The pump wears out. Replacing the pump is a job for an experienced repairman. (4) The motor wears out. By this time the unit has come to the end of its useful life; rather than replace the motor, buy a new washing machine.

> **CAUTION** Electricity and water can be a lethal combination. Always pull the cord from the wall receptacle before making any tests or repairs inside the machine. Never work on an electrical appliance while standing on a wet floor. After completing repairs, check all electrical connections to make sure they're tight. Take special care that the grounding wires are correctly and tightly connected.

Easy maintenance

To clean the water filters (near right), close the water faucets or valves, pull the unit away from the wall, and disconnect the hoses. Have a pan handy to catch the runout. Take out the fine-mesh filters just inside the connections on the machine and the other end of the hoses, and clean them thoroughly. Do this every two months if you have a well and twice a year if you're on city water. When the machine is back in place, be sure the hoses are not kinked. ⟞⟝ If a hose must be bent to make a connection, install a right-angle hose.

To tighten a loose drive belt (far right), unplug the unit and pull it away from the wall to reach the motor mounting. There may be a panel to remove. Loosen one motor mounting bolt, pull the motor against the belt, and tighten the bolt again. There should be no more than ½ inch play when you push against the belt. If you can rotate any pulley against the belt, it should be tightened. Examine the belt for signs of wear. A worn belt usually should be replaced by a repairman.

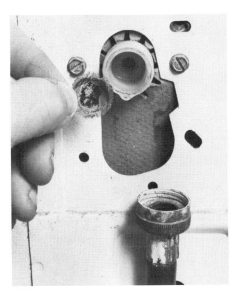

Getting inside from the top

To get the top panel off, first check to see whether your unit uses clips in front to hold the top, like the top-loading model shown here, or has screws at the back. If you can slip a credit card all around under the top except at two points in front, you have clips. If you can see hinges at the back of the top, there will be screws.

To lift a clip-held top, pry the top up carefully but firmly at the side (not at the clips) with a screwdriver. ⟞⟝ Wrap the screwdriver end with tape or paper to prevent damage to the finish. When the top pops off the clip, lift it up.

If your unit has screws at the back of the top, remove them, pull the top forward, and then lift it up at the front.

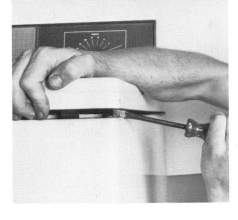

> ⓢ **TIPS FOR ENERGY EFFICIENCY**
>
> Wash when you have a full load, but don't overload.
>
> Don't use too much soap.
>
> If you have a "gentle wash" cycle, switch to "fast spin" for drying; it saves drying time.
>
> Use the cold water cycle whenever possible; hot water is expensive.
>
> ⓢ **TIPS FOR EFFICIENT OPERATION**
>
> Make sure the unit sits level and doesn't wobble and that the load is evenly distributed in the basket.
>
> Make sure the hot water is at least 140°F.
>
> Check the lint filter regularly; keep it clean.
>
> Always turn the water supply faucets or valves off after washing; if a water mixing valve fails, it could cause a flood.

Water leaks

If you discover water leaking out of your washing machine while it's filling, STOP! Don't touch the machine. First turn off the electricity. Then examine the unit. If the water is running over the top of the tub, the overflow switch has failed. See the instructions at the bottom of this page. If the tub is not overflowing, then the water inlet hoses or valves at the back of the unit may be defective. If the unit leaks after filling, then an inside hose or hose connection has failed, the gasket is worn out (see below), or the pump has sprung a leak (call a repairman). You'll have to open the top, peer in at the back or lay the unit on its side to check all these possibilities. When you must empty the tub or disconnect a hose, remember that there's always some water left in the hoses and pump even after the tub is empty. Have a pan ready to catch the runout, unless the unit is near a floor drain.

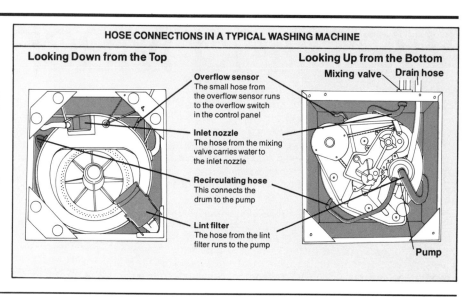

HOSE CONNECTIONS IN A TYPICAL WASHING MACHINE

Looking Down from the Top

Looking Up from the Bottom

Mixing valve   Drain hose

Overflow sensor
The small hose from the overflow sensor runs to the overflow switch in the control panel

Inlet nozzle
The hose from the mixing valve carries water to the inlet nozzle

Recirculating hose
This connects the drum to the pump

Lint filter
The hose from the lint filter runs to the pump

Pump

Replacing hoses and gaskets

Replace any hose that leaks from a crack or puncture. If the leak seems to be at the connection, try moving the clamp to a slightly different position on the hose. Be sure the clamp grips both hose and pipe end. The best tool to use is hose-clamp pliers, because it's made for the job. If you use regular pliers, watch your fingers! This tool easily slips off the springy clamp. To replace a worn-out gasket, just lift it off the tub rim and slip a duplicate on. (On some models you'll have to remove the splash guard that sits just above the gasket.)

To remove a defective hose or to adjust a hose clamp, use hose-clamp pliers to squeeze the clamp open.

In place of the common pinch clamps, you can also use screw-type clamps. They are more easily adapted to different-sized connections.

Testing and replacing an overflow switch

When the water in the tub rises above the level of the overflow sensor, it creates air pressure in the air tube that connects the sensor with the overflow switch in the control panel. This pressure turns the switch off and stops the water flow.

If the tub overfills, the problem may be a defect in the tubing, in the switch, or in the sensor. First, turn off the power. Make sure the air tube is securely in place at both the switch and the sensor. If it slips off too easily, clip ½ inch off the end of the hose and press it on firmly. Test the switch mechanically by detaching the tube at the sensor and blowing through the tube into the switch. You should hear a click as the switch is activated to turn off. If you do not hear a click, test for continuity across the two terminals that are closed under normal circumstances (see Blue Pages: *Electrical testers*). Check your wiring diagram to identify the terminals. There should be no continuity while you are blowing into the tube. If the switch itself is OK, check the sensor in the tub. Attach the tube at the sensor and detach it from the switch. Fill the tub with water and blow through the hose into the sensor. You should feel solid pressure.

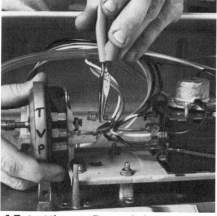

1 **To test the overflow switch,** first label the wires or the terminals by color or number. Then remove the push-on connectors carefully.

2 Blow through the air hose into the overflow switch; there should be no continuity between the normally closed terminals.

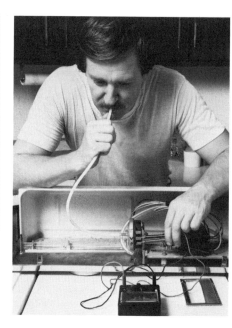

Washing Machines Troubleshooting Chart

WHAT'S WRONG	REASONS WHY	WHAT TO DO
Washing machine doesn't run at all.	No power at outlet	Check fuse box/circuit breaker.
	Safety switch tripped	Make sure lid is closed; distribute clothes evenly in basket.
Machine doesn't fill with water.	Filters clogged	Check inlet hose filters and clean.
	Hoses kinked	Straighten water supply hoses.
	Timer not set	Turn timer slightly; push buttons firmly.
Water doesn't shut off.	Overflow switch hose disconnected	Replace hose.
	Defective overflow switch	Check and replace switch.
	Defective timer	Replace timer or call repairman.
	Defective mixing valve	Replace valve.
Tub fills but motor doesn't run.	Lid safety switch tripped	Make sure lid is closed; test switch.
	Tub overloaded	Reduce load; wait 15 minutes for motor to reset.
	Motor defective	Call repairman. (You may hear humming sound.)
	Defective timer	Replace timer.
Motor runs but machine doesn't agitate or spin.	Drive belt loose or broken	Tighten or replace belt.
	Defective gears or transmission	Call repairman.
Machine vibrates or walks across floor.	Machine or load not level	Adjust feet or distribute load evenly.
Machine leaks.	Loose hose connections	Check and tighten connections.
	Defective hoses	Replace hoses.
	Defective gasket	Check gasket and replace.
	Defective mixing valve	Check valve; replace if cracked.
	Defective pump	Call repairman.
	Defective overflow switch or sensor	Check and replace.
Machine doesn't drain.	Drain hose kinked	Straighten hose.
	Drain hose too high	Hose should empty no more than 4 feet above floor.
	Defective timer	Replace timer or call repairman.
	Drain pump jammed	Call repairman.
Water isn't hot enough.	Water heater set too low	Set water heater thermostat at 140°-160°F.
	Water supply hoses misconnected	Reverse the hoses.
	Defective mixing valve	Replace valve.
	Defective timer	Replace timer or call repairman.

Electric Water Heater

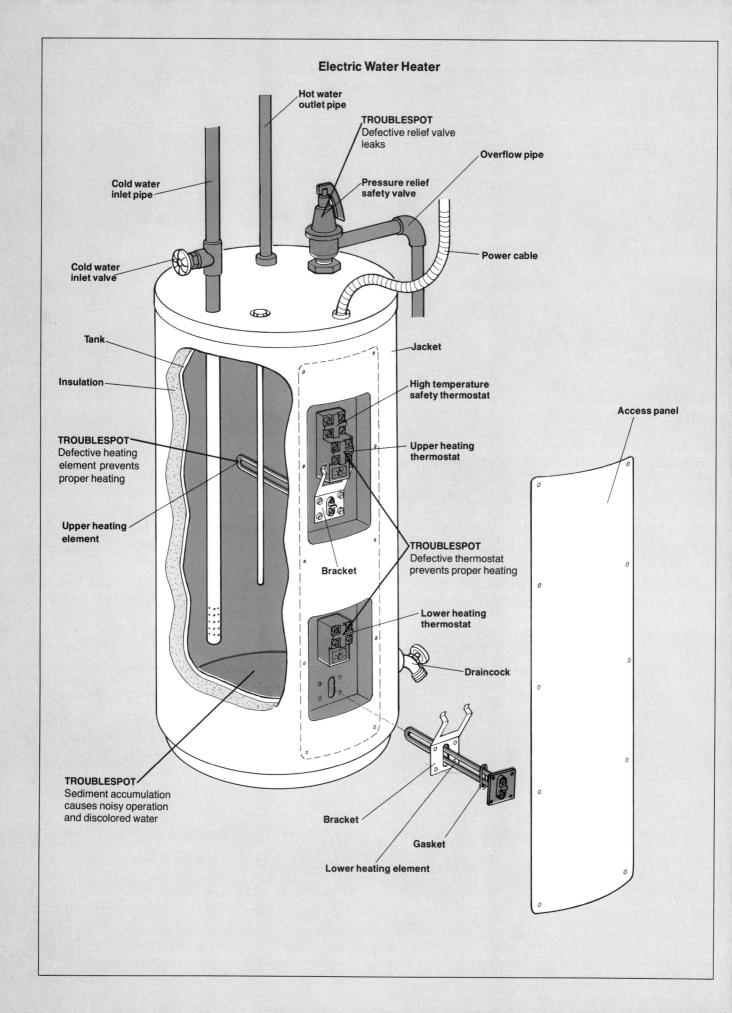

Hot water outlet pipe

TROUBLESPOT
Defective relief valve leaks

Overflow pipe

Cold water inlet pipe

Pressure relief safety valve

Power cable

Cold water inlet valve

Tank

Jacket

Insulation

High temperature safety thermostat

Access panel

TROUBLESPOT
Defective heating element prevents proper heating

Upper heating thermostat

Upper heating element

TROUBLESPOT
Defective thermostat prevents proper heating

Bracket

Lower heating thermostat

Draincock

TROUBLESPOT
Sediment accumulation causes noisy operation and discolored water

Bracket

Gasket

Lower heating element

Water Heaters

Electric

In most homes water heaters are the forgotten appliances. These simple, long-lived devices carry on their job of providing hot water automatically without anyone paying them any attention, sometimes for five or ten years at a stretch. In fact, most complaints about water heaters have nothing to do with any mechanical failure, but rather with the user's misunderstanding about how much hot water there is in the tank and how long it takes the heater to replenish the supply. For example, if you have a 40-gallon tank, there will be about 30 gallons of really hot water at the top of the tank ready to be drawn out. This is about the amount it takes for a good bath. And if your unit requires another forty-five minutes or an hour to heat another 30 gallons (its "recovery rate"), you can see how you can easily run out of hot water. If this happens often in your home, perhaps you need a larger tank, or a heater with a faster recovery rate. The capacity and recovery rate are shown on the nameplate of the heater.

Eventually, any hot water tank will wear out and begin to leak because of rust and corrosion inside. When this happens, get a new water heater. There isn't any practical way to repair a leaky tank. Make sure, though, that the puddle under the heater is not from a leaking safety valve(see page 133)or water pipe connection. Besides replacing a failed safety valve, you can also test and replace defective thermostats and heating elements in an electric water heater. Instructions are given on the following pages. And be sure to take the following paragraph to heart.

> **CAUTION** Water and electricity are a lethal combination, especially the 240 volts that power most electric water heaters. Always turn off the power at the fuse box/circuit breaker before starting any tests or repairs. Always drain the tank before replacing elements or thermostats. Never go into a flooded basement if electrical appliances are on. Never touch an operating appliance while standing in water or on a damp floor.

TIPS FOR ENERGY EFFICIENCY

If the water heater is intended to supply only one bath or shower, set both thermostats at 130°F. If the heater supplies two baths or dishwasher, too, set both thermostats at 140°F. For every increase of 10° above 140°F. the cost goes up 3%.

Locate the heater near the points of use if possible.

Use the smallest pipe to carry hot water; this lowers both heat loss and the amount of hot water trapped in the pipe.

Insulate the hot water pipe from the heater to the points of use.

A quick shower uses much less hot water than a bath. For a long soak, however, a bath is more economical. Test your own consumption: the next time you take a bath, put a piece of tape at the high water mark (when you're not lying in the tub). Then the next time you shower, leave the plug in and see if the water rises to the tape mark.

Draining the tank

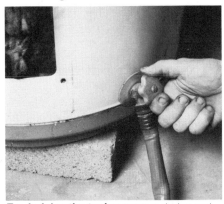

Try draining the tank to remove sludge and rust scale if your hot water runs cloudy or rusty, or if your heater makes rumbling noises. Turn off the power at the fuse box/circuit breaker, close the cold water inlet valve, and open the draincock at the bottom of the tank. (If the tank is not near a floor drain, connect a hose to the draincock; the end of the hose must be lower than the draincock.) Then, open a hot water faucet upstairs to let air into the heater. When the tank is empty, close the draincock and let in a little cold water for a final flush. Drain. Close the draincock, leaving the upstairs hot water faucet open. Open the cold water supply valve. When water runs out of the upstairs faucet, close the tap. You can now turn the power back on.

Getting inside

To gain access to thermostats or heating elements, turn off the power at the fuse box/circuit breaker and remove the access panel by taking out the screws that hold it to the jacket. You will find insulation covering the thermostats and elements; push it to the side, or take it out if it's a separate piece. When closing up the heater, always replace the insulation just as you found it before you put the access panel back.

Adjusting the thermostats

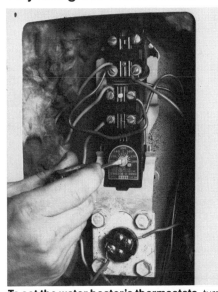

To set the water heater's thermostats, turn the small pointer at the bottom of the thermostat to the desired temperature. Some pointers can be turned by hand; others require a small screwdriver. If you want your hot water to come out about 140°F., set both thermostats at 140°F.

Checking thermostats and heating elements

If the thermostats are correctly set, the fuse box/circuit breaker is OK, and there's still no hot or only lukewarm water, make the following tests to locate the difficulty. (Turn the power off!) (1) Test the heating elements. (If your heater suddenly takes a lot longer to heat water, it may mean that one of the elements has failed.) (2) Test the heating thermostats. (3) Test the safety thermostat at the top of the upper thermostat. (4) Test the power coming into the unit.

CAUTION The last test is a power on test. If you haven't found the trouble through the first three tests and don't want to make this test, call an electrician.

To replace a defective heating element, see the instructions given on the opposite page.

To replace a defective thermostat, be sure the power is off. Label the wires connected to the defective part and disconnect them. Lift the bracket and remove the thermostat. Install an exact duplicate. Replace the insulation and the access panel before turning the power on.

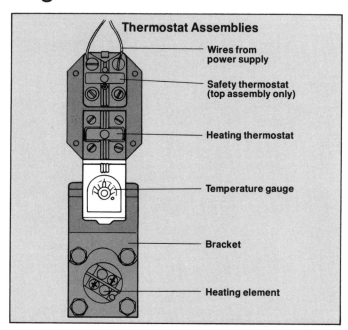

Thermostat Assemblies

- Wires from power supply
- Safety thermostat (top assembly only)
- Heating thermostat
- Temperature gauge
- Bracket
- Heating element

To test either heating element, turn the power off, and disconnect one wire leading to the element. Attach VOM clips to the two external element terminals to test resistance. With the VOM set at RX1, you should read about 10 ohms. A much higher reading or no reading means a defective element. To replace it, see the opposite page.

To test either heating thermostat, turn the power off and disconnect one of the two wires from its terminal on the left side of the thermostat or from the heating element. Make a continuity test between the two left terminals (see Blue Pages: *Electrical testers*). If the water in the tank is cold, there should be continuity at any temperature setting of the thermostat. If the water is hot, the thermostat should click at some point as you turn the temperature-setting shaft higher. At that point the continuity should drop to zero. Test the two terminals on the right side in the same manner. Put the other thermostat through the same procedure. If either thermostat fails either test, replace it.

To test the safety thermostat, turn the power off and remove the wires from one of the two terminals on the left side of the thermostat. Test for continuity between the terminals (see Blue Pages: *Electrical testers*); there should be continuity. Test the two terminals on the right in the same manner. If the thermostat fails either test, replace it with a duplicate.

To test the power reaching the heater, turn the power off and attach VOM clips to the two topmost terminals on the safety thermostat. Set the meter to read at least 250 volts AC. Then turn the power on. **CAUTION** Do not touch any part of the heater or the clips. You should read within 10% of the required voltage indicated on the identification plate of the heater (120 or 240 volts). If you don't, turn the power off, remove the VOM clips, and call the power company.

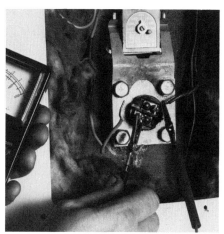

Testing a heating element

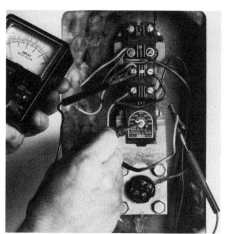

Testing a heating thermostat

Testing the safety thermostat

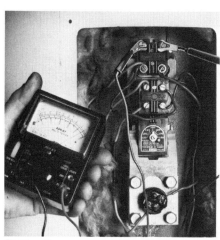

Testing the power reaching the heater

Replacing a heating element

If either heating element fails the tests described opposite, here's how to replace it. First, turn the power off and drain the tank (page 133).
Then remove the two wires connecting the element to its thermostat: using a socket wrench, loosen the four bolts holding the element in place. The bolts and the bracket come off (there may also be a gasket). Then pull the bad element out of the tank. Before installing the new element, ream out the

hole and clean all scale away. Dry the surfaces of the hole and apply a coat of gasket cement to the mounting surfaces on element and tank. Put the new element (and gasket) and bracket back in place; put the bolts in and screw them in *tight*. Replace the insulation and access panel before turning the power on.

Loosen the bolts with a socket wrench.

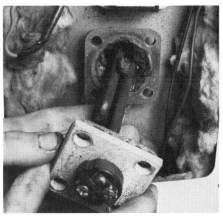

Pull the defective element out of the tank.

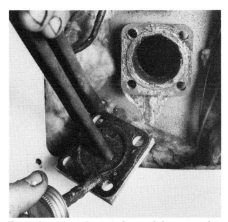

Coat the mounting surface of the new element with gasket cement before installing it.

Checking the safety valve

If the safety valve starts steaming or dripping, turn the power off at once. Your thermostat may be defective, causing overheating, or the safety valve itself may be defective. Take the temperature of the hot water upstairs by putting a candy or meat thermometer into a pan of running hot water. If the water is near normal—140°F.—the thermostat is OK, and the safety valve is defective. It must be replaced as described here. If you have a well,

check the water pressure; high pressure may have blown the safety valve. Call the plumber.

If the hot water temperature is well above your thermostat setting, the thermostat is defective and must be replaced. See page 132 for directions.

NOTE: Never "test" the safety valve by lifting the metal lever to let it blow off. The valve seldom will reseat itself correctly.

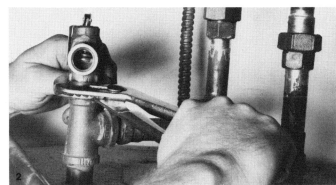

1 **To replace a defective safety valve,** first turn off the power and the cold water supply. Open a hot water faucet upstairs and partially drain the tank to relieve the pressure (see page 131). Then unscrew the overflow pipe (if your valve has one) with a wrench.

2 After the pressure has been relieved, unscrew the safety valve from the pipe on top of the heater with a wrench.

3 Before screwing on the new safety valve, wrap two turns of Teflon thread-seal tape clockwise around the threads of the valve. Install the valve, attach the overflow pipe, and open the cold water inlet valve. When water runs out of the faucet upstairs, close the tap. You can now turn the power back on.

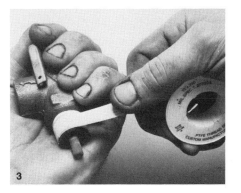

Electric Water Heaters Troubleshooting Chart

WHAT'S WRONG	REASONS WHY	WHAT TO DO
No hot water	No power at heater	Check fuse box/circuit breaker.
		If heater repeatedly blows fuses, call electrician.
	Safety thermostat has cut out	Push reset button (if you have one).
		Test heating thermostats and elements.
	Defective heating thermostats	Test thermostats and replace.
	Defective heating elements	Test elements and replace them.
	Rust, scale, or sediment accumulation in tank or pipes	Drain and flush out tank and pipes.
Not enough hot water	Thermostat set wrong	Reset thermostat to higher temperature.
	Tank too small	Install larger heater.
	Heat lost in pipes	Locate heater near point of use if possible; insulate hot water pipes.
	Defective heating element	Test and replace element.
	Leaking hot water faucets	Repair or replace faucets.
Water is too hot.	Thermostat set wrong	Reset thermostat to lower temperature.
	Not enough insulation around thermostats	Pack insulation tightly around thermostats.
	Defective elements	Test and replace elements.
	Defective thermostats	Test and replace thermostats.
Heater leaks water.	Defective gasket or seal on heating element	Check and replace.
	Defective safety valve	Check and replace valve.
	Tank rusted through	Buy a new heater.
	Leaky plumbing connection	Call a plumber if not covered in this article.
Heater is noisy.	Rust, scale, or sediment accumulation in tank	Drain and flush out tank.
	Scale-encrusted elements	Remove elements, soak in vinegar, scrape off scale.
Hot water is rusty or discolored.	Rust or sediment accumulation in tank	Drain tank.
	Scale-encrusted elements	(See under "Heater is noisy," above.)
	Corroded water pipes	Call a plumber to replace pipes.

Gas Water Heater

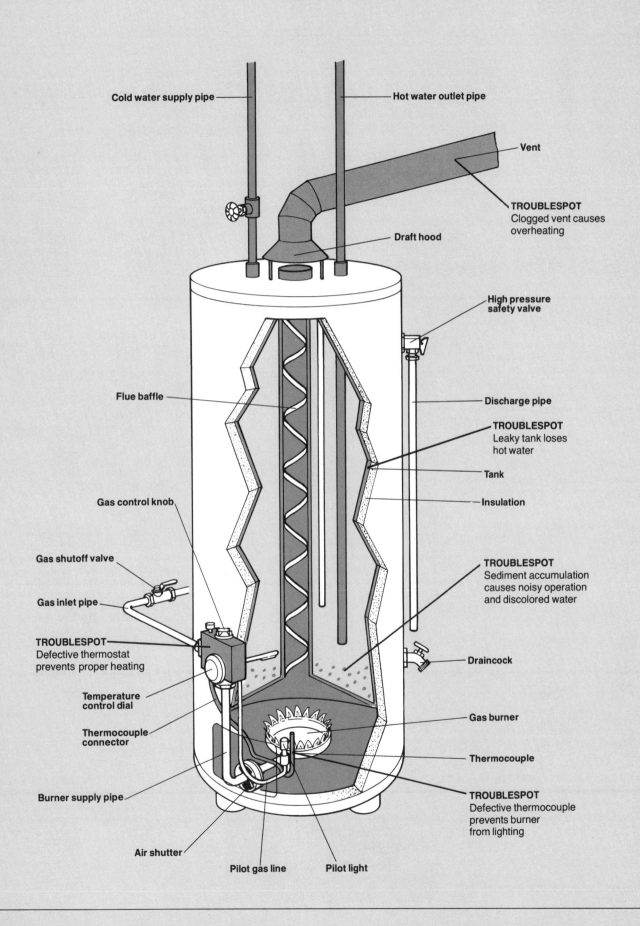

Cold water supply pipe

Hot water outlet pipe

Vent

TROUBLESPOT
Clogged vent causes overheating

Draft hood

High pressure safety valve

Flue baffle

Discharge pipe

TROUBLESPOT
Leaky tank loses hot water

Tank

Insulation

Gas control knob

TROUBLESPOT
Sediment accumulation causes noisy operation and discolored water

Gas shutoff valve

Gas inlet pipe

TROUBLESPOT
Defective thermostat prevents proper heating

Temperature control dial

Draincock

Thermocouple connector

Gas burner

Thermocouple

Burner supply pipe

TROUBLESPOT
Defective thermocouple prevents burner from lighting

Air shutter

Pilot gas line

Pilot light

WATER HEATERS

Gas

Gas water heaters are efficient, long-lasting appliances that require a minimum of attention from the user. Care must be taken, however, to install the heater correctly. You should allow 3 feet of open space all around the heater for proper ventilation and fire safety. The vent pipe must rise at least ¼ inch for every foot it travels horizontally. Observe these precautions:

1. If you find soot around the vent or the top of the tank, call the gas company. Don't try to make any adjustments.

2. If the burner flame burns yellow, call the gas company. Don't attempt any adjustments.

3. Gas heaters are adjusted for either LP or natural gas. If you want to change from one to the other, you must call the gas company to regulate the heater or install another model.

4. If you need to drain the tank to remove sediment, or if you are shutting the house up for the winter, turn the gas control knob off. Then follow the procedure given on page 130 for draining the tank of an electric heater. Don't turn the gas back on or light the pilot light until the tank is full of water.

Any repair or adjustment of the gas lines, gas controls, or the burner is a job for the gas company. You can, however, replace a defective thermocouple. This is a heat-sensing safety device that prevents gas from flowing to the burner if the pilot light has gone out. Instructions for replacing a thermocouple are given on page 137. You can also replace a defective safety valve. See directions in *Electric Water Heaters,* page 133.

Read the introductory paragraphs on page 130 for other pertinent information about water heaters. The *Tips for energy efficiency* for electric units apply equally to gas units (see box, page 130).

Regular maintenance

1. Every six months, inspect the exhaust vent to make sure it's unobstructed. The vent pipe should rise at least ¼ inch per foot.

2. Every six months remove the covers of the burner unit and inspect for dust and dirt. See directions below. Be sure the air shutter openings are unobstructed. Use a small, soft brush to clean them.

3. To adjust the temperature of the hot water, turn the control dial to the desired setting.

4. To relight the pilot light, carefully follow the directions printed on your heater. See also the directions on the next page.

CAUTION If you smell gas, ventilate the room thoroughly before lighting a flame. Never "test" for a leak with a lighted match. Call the gas company.

To check the vent, remove the draft hood while the heater is on. You should feel a strong flow of hot air. If you do not, check the vent pipe and the chimney to see if they are obstructed. If there is still no draft, call the gas company.

To adjust the temperature of the hot water, set the control dial at the desired level. This typical model shows WARM, NORMAL and HOT, instead of specific temperatures. WARM is probably about 120°F., NORMAL about 140°F., HOT about 160°F. Test the temperature with a candy or meat thermometer in a pan of hot running water upstairs, and adjust the dial.

Getting inside

To clean the air shutter openings or check the thermocouple, remove the covers that protect the burner unit. On this model, both the outer and inner covers simply lift out.

CAUTION Be careful not to bend or kink any tubing, especially the soft copper kind. If a tube gets bent, call the gas company to fix it. Don't attempt to adjust the air shutter; that's a job for the gas company, too.

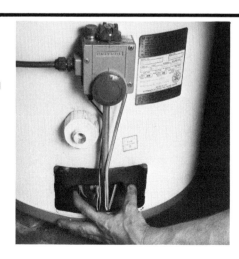

To get inside the bottom of the heater, lift off the protective covers.

Problems inside the heater

You can relight the pilot light or replace a defective thermocouple in a gas heater. Instructions for these two jobs are given here. All other repairs to the gas mechanism of the heater should be left to the gas company. Don't attempt to adjust the air shutters or the burner; an improper adjustment can cause an explosion. If you replace the thermocouple, test the pilot gas line for leaks, using soapy water.

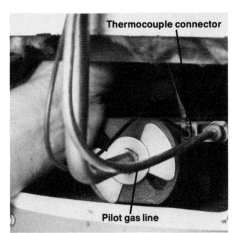

Thermocouple connector

Pilot gas line

To relight the pilot light, follow the directions for your heater; they normally appear on the control unit. On this model, you press a button while touching a flame to the pilot. Use a twist of lighted paper about 6 to 8 inches long, so you don't have to cram your hand inside.

1 **If the burner won't start,** but the pilot light can be lit, then the thermocouple may have failed. Turn the gas control knob off. Use a small screwdriver to remove the screw that holds the pilot and thermocouple mounting bracket inside the heater.

2 Pull the mounting bracket out of the heater. You may have to disconnect the pilot gas line with a wrench. Then pull the thermocouple out of the bracket and disconnect it from the control unit. Take it to your appliance dealer to get an exact duplicate to install.

Gas Water Heaters Troubleshooting Chart

WHAT'S WRONG	REASONS WHY	WHAT TO DO
No hot water	Pilot light out	Relight pilot.
	Pilot won't stay lit.	Make sure gas controls are fully on.
		Check the thermocouple; it must be firmly connected to the gas control unit and positioned near the pilot flame.
	Burner clogged	Call the gas company.
	Defective thermocouple	Replace thermocouple.
	No gas	Call the gas company.
Not enough hot water	Thermostat not properly set	Reset thermostat higher.
	Defective thermostat	Call the gas company.
	Exposed hot water pipes	Insulate hot water pipes.
	Tank too small	Install larger unit.
	Burner clogged	Call gas company.
	Sediment in tank	Drain tank; shut off gas first.
	Leaky hot water faucets	Repair or replace faucets.
Operation is noisy.	Scale and sediment in tank	Drain tank; shut off gas first.
Water is too hot.	Thermostat not properly set	Reset thermostat lower.
	Defective thermostat	Call gas company.
	Blocked vent	Check vent and clear.
Water leaks from heater.	Draincock leaking	Close tightly or replace.
	Safety valve leaking	Check water temperature; too-high temperature may indicate faulty thermostat.
		Replace safety valve if defective.
	Hole in tank	Buy a new water heater.
	Leaky plumbing connection	Call a plumber if not covered in this article.

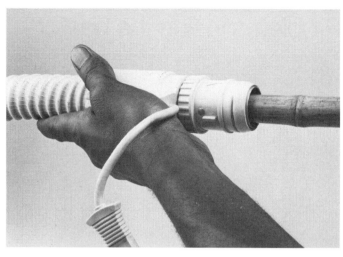

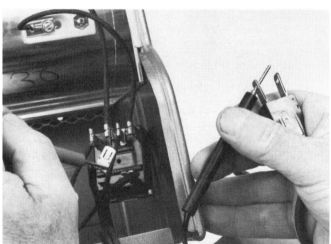

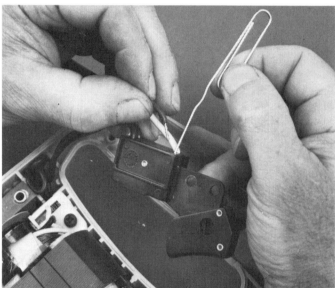

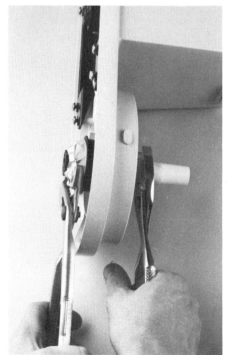

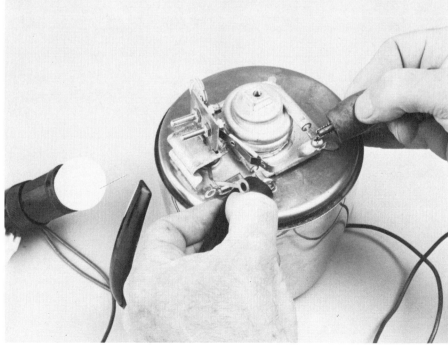

Small Appliances

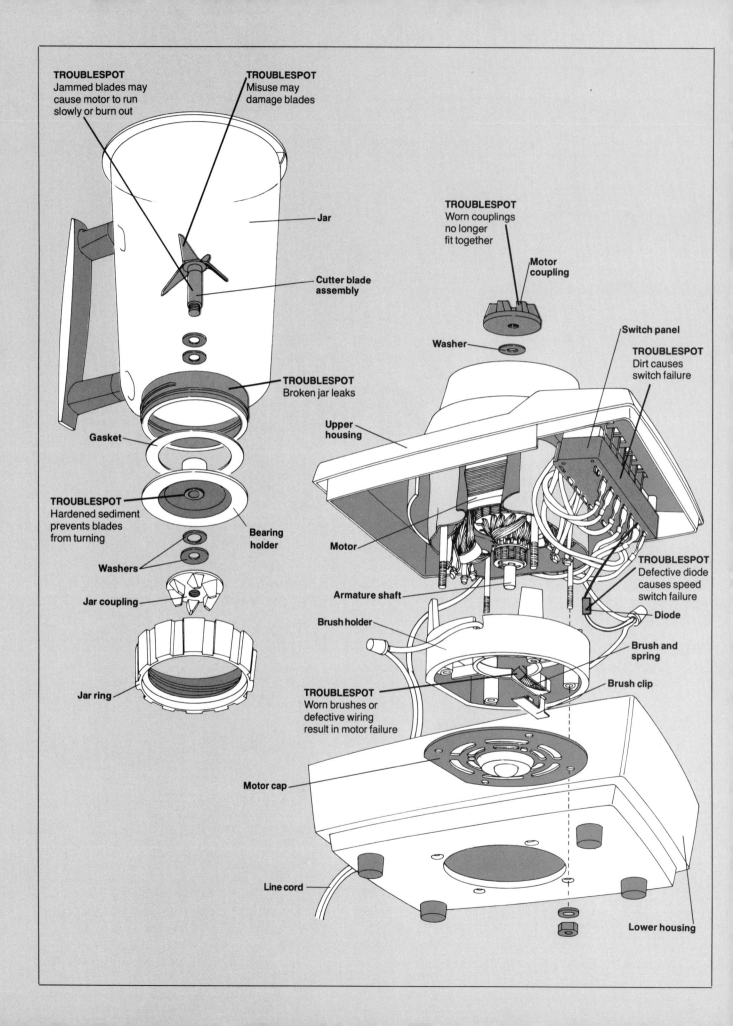

TROUBLESPOT
Jammed blades may
cause motor to run
slowly or burn out

TROUBLESPOT
Misuse may
damage blades

TROUBLESPOT
Worn couplings
no longer
fit together

Motor
coupling

Washer

Switch panel

TROUBLESPOT
Dirt causes
switch failure

Jar

Cutter blade
assembly

Upper
housing

TROUBLESPOT
Broken jar leaks

Gasket

TROUBLESPOT
Hardened sediment
prevents blades
from turning

Bearing
holder

Motor

TROUBLESPOT
Defective diode
causes speed
switch failure

Diode

Armature shaft

Washers

Brush and
spring

Jar coupling

Brush holder

Brush clip

TROUBLESPOT
Worn brushes or
defective wiring
result in motor failure

Jar ring

Motor cap

Line cord

Lower housing

Blenders

The basic design of a blender is simplicity itself: the armature shaft of a small motor is coupled directly to a set of small, sharp blades that stick up through the bottom of a glass jar. When the motor runs, the blades spin at very high speeds, making them an ideal tool for mixing all sorts of liquids. Not being geared for power, however, a blender is not well suited for heavy grinding. Some owner's manuals claim their blenders can chop, crack, knead, and grind almost anything. Perhaps they can, but the strains imposed may lead to early breakdowns. Thus, Rule One for extending the life of your blender is: Use it for liquid mixing and other light work, and leave the heavy work to another appliance.

Since motor, shaft, and blades sit under the liquid load, leakage down into the mechanism is unavoidable as the unit ages. If the food that leaks into the blade assembly is allowed to harden, the shaft may seize up tight in its bearing, causing damage to glass jar and motor. This is, in fact, the most common problem that afflicts blenders and is the simplest to avoid. Rule Two: Clean the blender after every use (see *Tips for Efficient Operation,* at right).

As a blender grows older, electrical problems may appear, even in a carefully used unit. Instructions for testing and replacing switches and motor parts are given on the following pages. But Rule Three will be given here: If the motor hums but does not turn, or if it emits a burning smell, shut it off at once, before any damage is done. Then read pages 142 to 145 for the proper steps to take. The illustrations accompanying this article show several of the most common models. The procedures given for cleaning and repairing them can be applied to other models as well.

NOTE: Blenders vary considerably from brand to brand, and even models bearing the same brand name are not identical. The most obvious point of difference is the couplings, where the motor and blades are joined. Directions for inspecting and repairing couplings and blade assemblies are given below and on the next page.

TIPS FOR EFFICIENT OPERATION

Always be sure the jar is properly seated before starting the motor.

Never lift the jar off until the motor has stopped.

Clean the blender after each use. Cover the blades with water and add a little detergent; put the jar in place, cover it, and run the motor for about ten seconds. Empty the jar, rinse it, half-fill it with clear water, and run again for ten seconds. Empty the jar and run for another ten seconds to dry out the blade assembly. Dry the jar, especially around the bottom. Clean the housing with a damp sponge. The glass jar can go in the dishwasher, but *not* the blade assembly or the housing.

Every month or so, remove the cutter blade assembly (see instructions below and on the next page), wash it in warm soapy water, and dry it thoroughly. Don't use abrasive powders or metal cleaning pads.

Don't let the jar stand full for any length of time.

Don't put ice cubes into the jar without adding at least a cup of water. If the motor gives off an odor or stalls at any time, shut it off immediately or you may burn it out. Try lightening the load. If that doesn't help, check the blades for binding (see below), or check the motor (see page 144).

CAUTION Keep hands out of the jar while the motor is running, and always handle the jar with care. The blades are sharp!

Problems with the blades

If the blades don't turn and the load isn't too heavy (the motor may hum or smell), the blade shaft and bearing may be seized up with hardened food. Make the test shown at far right. To remove the blade assembly for cleaning, follow the directions shown here for the two models that fasten directly to the glass bottom. Other models that fasten with a jar ring are shown at the top of the next page. Notice that these blade assemblies

connect with the motor in different ways. Some models use a toothed coupling (next page); others have serrated sockets for the motor stud (below, left). In some cases, when the blade shaft is seized up, the motor will turn the whole blade assembly and socket together, cracking or chipping the jar bottom. A damaged jar will have to be replaced. Regular cleaning (see *Tips,* above) can prevent this problem.

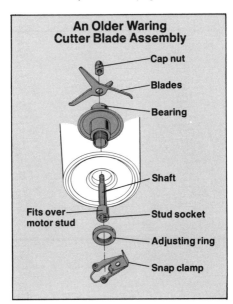

An Older Waring Cutter Blade Assembly

- Cap nut
- Blades
- Bearing
- Shaft
- Fits over motor stud
- Stud socket
- Adjusting ring
- Snap clamp

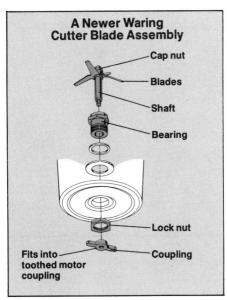

A Newer Waring Cutter Blade Assembly

- Cap nut
- Blades
- Shaft
- Bearing
- Lock nut
- Coupling
- Fits into toothed motor coupling

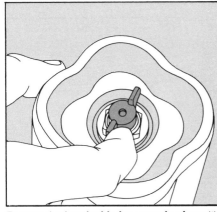

To test whether the blades are seized up with hardened food, turn the blender off and turn the jar coupling by hand. If the blades don't move easily, take the assembly apart (instructions, left, and next page, top) and clean it thoroughly. Clean the inside of the bearing with a roll of fine emery cloth. Don't apply any lubrication when you put the assembly back together.

If the blades turn easily, the jar coupling may be damaged (see next page), the motor coupling may be damaged (see page 143), or you may have electrical problems (see page 142).

To remove the older Waring cutter blade assembly, pull the clamp down and lift the assembly out of the jar.

To remove the newer Waring cutter blade assembly, hold the blades with needle-nose pliers and take off the coupling with a wrench. Then remove the lock nut and take the assembly out of the jar.

Problems with the blades, continued

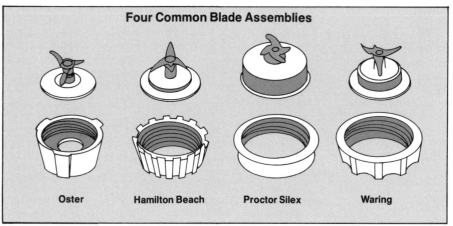

Four Common Blade Assemblies

Oster   Hamilton Beach   Proctor Silex   Waring

Couplings

Worn   New

Worn couplings prevent the blades from turning properly. The damage shown here can be caused by not seating the jar properly, by taking the jar off while the motor is running, or by trying to blend too heavy a load. A cutting blade assembly with a worn coupling should be replaced. Check the motor coupling or stud for damage at the same time (see instructions on the opposite page).

These four cutter blade assemblies are fastened to the jar with jar rings. To remove the assemblies for cleaning or replacement, first unscrew the ring. Then grip the blades with taped pliers and grip the jar coupling (on the Hamilton Beach, for example) with other pliers. Turn the coupling counterclockwise to get it off. Lift the blade assembly out of the jar. These assemblies are held together by a top rivet, so the blades cannot be removed separately like those shown on the preceding page. Each assembly must be replaced as a unit.

Getting inside

To work on the motor

To open up the housing to work on the motor or the switches, you must remove the lower housing (right) and separate the switch panel from the upper housing (see below). On most models, the lower housing is secured with screws or hex nuts and can be taken off. If the lower housing is secured by rivets, the unit cannot be repaired by the user.

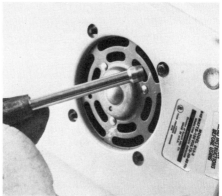

To remove the lower housing from a Hamilton Beach or newer Waring, remove the four hex nuts with a nut driver. The lower housing separates from the upper housing, freeing the motor cap.

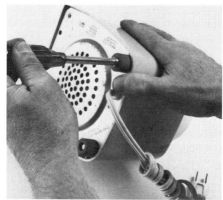

To remove the base plate from an Oster or an older Waring, remove the hex nuts inside the rubber feet with a nut driver. The base plate and cord will come out of the housing.

To work on the switch

To separate the switch panel from the housing, you must usually peel back a decorative decal. Underneath are the screws that secure the switches to the upper housing. It may be possible to replace the decal with five-minute epoxy or a similar adhesive. But if it's too bent out of shape, you can order another one from an appliance parts dealer.

Another way to get at the screws is to rub the upper corners of the decal with one finger to locate the screw holes. Cut a small hole in the decal at each screw. You can repair the cuts with silicone rubber cement.

1 **To separate the switches from the upper housing on the Hamilton Beach,** first pry off the high/low switch cap, using a small screwdriver; pry evenly from both sides. Then use a single-edge razor blade to lift a corner of the decal and pull it off.

2 With the decal off, you can remove the Phillips mounting screws and pull the switch assembly out of the housing.

1 **To separate the switches from the upper housing on the Oster** and similar models, slip a single-edge razor under a corner of the decal and peel the decal off the front of the unit.

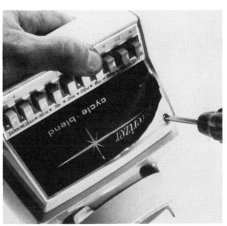

2 Remove the Phillips screws hidden beneath the decal on the top of the housing.

3 Remove the base plate (opposite page) and remove the screws found inside under the switches. Housing and switches can now be separated.

Motor coupling problems

Different blenders use different means to connect the top of the motor armature shaft (where the turning power is) to the cutter blade assembly in the jar bottom. Some, like the Hamilton Beach, use a toothed coupling. Others, like the Waring, use a square stud. The Proctor Silex uses a spoked-wheel coupling. If the coupling is broken or worn, remove it, following the instructions given here, and replace it with a duplicate.

When you all use any kind of pliers in these repairs, tape either the pliers or what they are gripping to protect the surface.

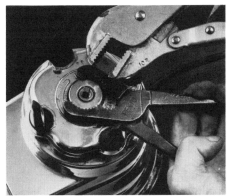

1 **To remove the stud from an older Waring,** grip the collar around the stud with a wrench or pliers. Then grip the stud with a vise-grip and turn it counterclockwise to get it out. Gas pliers, shown above, are just right for this job.

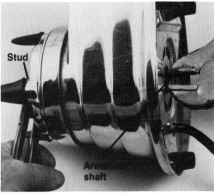

2 On some older models, you must remove the base plate and grip the bottom of the armature shaft with a pair of pliers. Then grip the stud with a wrench and turn it counterclockwise to get it out.

To remove the stud from an Oster, remove the base plate and the fan (see bottom of page 145 for instructions). Then grip the bottom of the armature shaft with pliers and the stud with a wrench. Turn the stud counterclockwise to remove it.

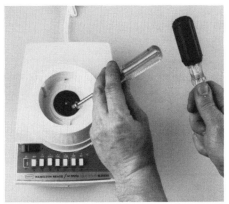

To remove the motor coupling from the Hamilton Beach, place a nut driver at the rim of the coupling and rap it lightly. Try to turn the coupling clockwise to unscrew it from the shaft. If this doesn't work, remove the lower housing (see opposite page) and grip the armature shaft from the bottom while turning the coupling with pliers.

To remove the coupling from a Proctor Silex, grip the coupling with pliers to keep it from turning. Then turn the slotted motor shaft with a screwdriver to free the coupling.

Switch problems

If the blender doesn't run at all, and the fuse box/circuit breaker is OK, start troubleshooting by making the switch tests described here (see Blue Pages: *Electrical testers*). If the buttons stick, spilled food may have hardened inside the switch panel. Remove the switches from the upper housing as described on pages 142 and 143 and clean them. You may have to use a small screwdriver to scrape off dirt, or a cotton swab or toothbrush dipped in hot water to loosen the obstructions.

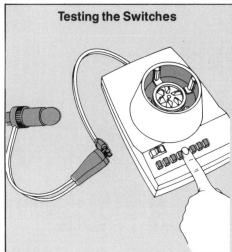

Testing the Switches

To test the switches, attach tester probes to each prong on the blender's plug. Set the high/low switch on HIGH and push each function button in turn. If the tester doesn't show continuity for all, there are three possible reasons: (1) The blender cord is defective (see Appliance Repair Basics: *Testing the cord and plug* for cord testing and replacement). (2) The high/low switch is bad. Remove the switch panel (see pages 142 and 143) and follow the instructions below. (3) The motor may be defective. Remove upper and lower housings (see page 142), then follow the instructions at the bottom of this page. If the tester lights for only a few buttons, the motor field coil may be defective (see instructions for testing and replacing it below and opposite), or the switches may be bad; they must be replaced as a complete unit (see below).

To test the high/low switch for continuity, remove one wire from one switch terminal and attach tester probes to the two switch terminals. The tester should light at HIGH but not at LOW. If it fails either test, replace the switch.

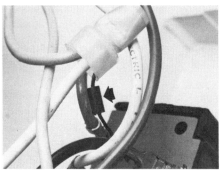

If the high/low switch is OK, but you don't get low speed, then the diode is defective. (The diode partially blocks power to get low speeds.) Replace it. (The diode is usually connected to the circuit with wire nuts.)

To replace a defective switch unit, hold the new duplicate part next to the old one still in the blender. Transfer the wires from the terminals on the old switch to the new switch one at a time.

Motor problems

If the blender doesn't run (and you've checked out the fuse box/circuit breaker, the cord, and the switches), the fault lies in the motor. Try the two tests described below. If the motor runs but you hear crackling noises and blue flames can be seen through the holes in the bottom of the housing, then the motor is defective and both field coil and armature must be replaced. At this point, you must weigh the cost of replacement (and the age of the unit) against the cost of a new blender. Instructions for replacing motor parts are given on the opposite page.

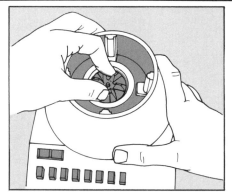

If the motor hums but doesn't run, turn if off, unplug the unit, and try to turn the coupling by hand. If it turns easily, the problem is in the cord, switches or motor. If the coupling turns with difficulty or doesn't turn at all, either the bearings have seized up or the motor brushes are bound against the commutator. Instructions for replacing the brushes and for cleaning the bearings are given opposite and on page 141. Instructions for getting inside the unit are given on page 142.

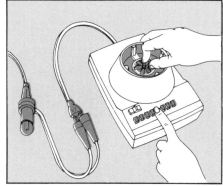

If the motor doesn't run at all and the switches are OK, determine whether the armature is faulty. Attach tester probes to the blender cord. Then turn the blender to ON, push down one of the function buttons, and turn the motor coupling by hand. If the tester shows intermittent continuity, the armature is defective and should be replaced. If the light stays on, cord and switch are OK, but a motor field coil could be bad. Examine the field coils (see instructions opposite). If one is burned, replace it. If not, it is difficult to test; you must take the unit to a repairman or replace the field coil.

Hamilton Beach

1 To repair the Hamilton Beach motor, first remove the lower housing (see page 142) and the motor cap. Then carefully pry off the two spring clips that hold the brushes in place. Lift gently with two fingers; the clips are brittle metal. The brushes may jump out of the holders.

2 Lift the brush-holder assembly off the four studs. Replace worn brushes, springs, and attached wires together as a set. With the holder off, you can now get at the field coil and armature.

To remove the field coil, take out the four hex nuts that hold it to the upper housing. The wiring of the field coil should be shiny; it is often a bright copper or green color, and is usually covered with clear lacquer. If it is dark, discolored or smells bad, it is probably defective and should be replaced. Unless you are skilled at rewiring, take the unit to a repair shop.

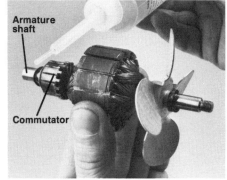

To get the armature out, remove the motor coupling from the top end of the armature shaft (see page 143). Then lift the armature and fan assembly out of the housing.

If you cannot turn the motor freely by hand, check the commutator for discoloration and the shaft ends for gritty sediment. Remove these with fine emery cloth. (Clean the bearing at the same time; see next step). When putting an old armature back or installing a new one, apply a little light oil to both ends of the armature shaft.

To clean both upper and lower bearings, insert a roll of fine emery cloth into the bearing and rotate gently. Shake out or vacuum up any loose filings, then clean the bearing out with an oiled cotton swab.

Oster

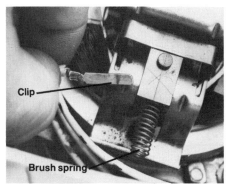

To repair an Oster blender's motor, first remove the bottom plate (see page 142). Then take the fan blade off the armature shaft. To do this, hold the fan blades steady and turn the hex nut counterclockwise with an adjustable wrench.

To get the brushes out, straighten the end of the clip that holds them in place. Pull the clip out as shown, and the brush spring will pop out. Then pull the spring and brush out of the holder. (The brush connecting wire is attached to the clip.)

To remove the bearing retainer, take out the two screws that attach it to the field mounting. Then remove the motor coupling from the other end of the armature shaft (see page 143). The armature can now be lifted out. You can check the armature, field coil, and bearings as described above for the Hamilton Beach.

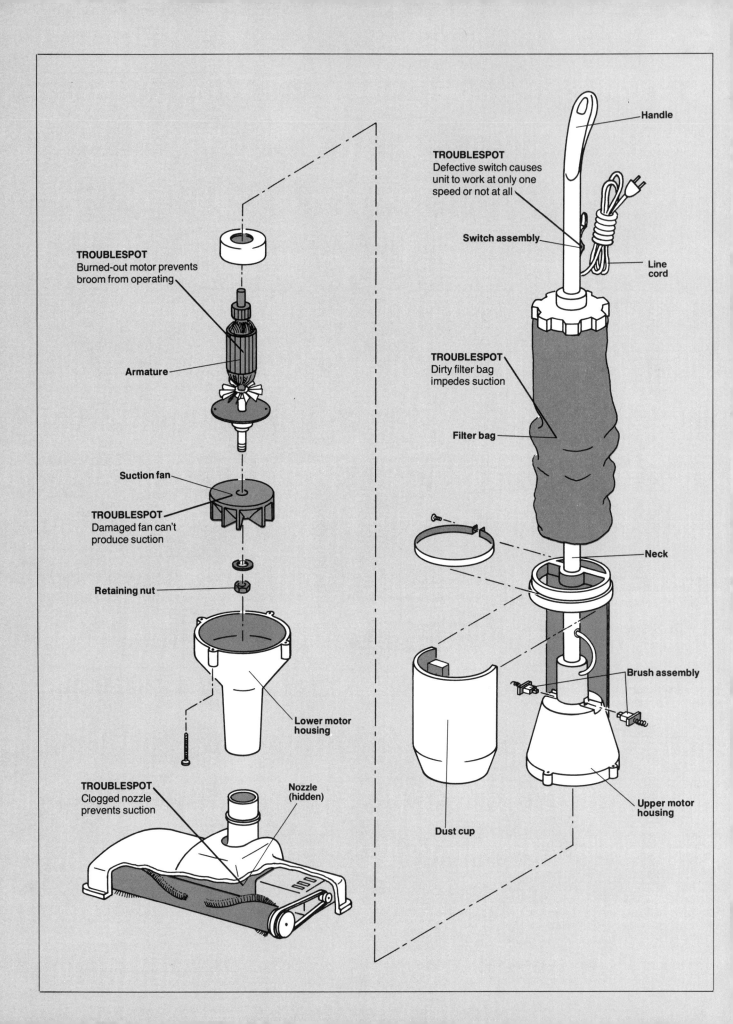

TROUBLESPOT
Burned-out motor prevents broom from operating

Armature

Suction fan

TROUBLESPOT
Damaged fan can't produce suction

Retaining nut

Lower motor housing

TROUBLESPOT
Clogged nozzle prevents suction

Nozzle (hidden)

TROUBLESPOT
Defective switch causes unit to work at only one speed or not at all

Handle

Switch assembly

Line cord

TROUBLESPOT
Dirty filter bag impedes suction

Filter bag

Neck

Brush assembly

Dust cup

Upper motor housing

Brooms

The electric broom operates on the same principle as the vacuum cleaner, only it is lighter and more maneuverable—and less expensive. A small universal motor with a fan mounted on its armature provides suction to pick up dirt. Air and dirt are sucked into a container, where the dirt is trapped and the air is forced out. This container may be a porous disposable dust bag or a cloth filter bag with a dust cup.

Two-speed brooms have a diode on the switch to cut down current flow at the lower setting. Some deluxe models are equipped with a motorized nozzle (see Vacuum Cleaners: *Motorized nozzles*, page 290). Instructions for caring for and repairing an electric broom are demonstrated here on the Hoover (two-speed, with disposable dust bag), the Bissell (disposable dust bag), and the Regina (cloth filter bag, dust cup, and motorized nozzle).

An electric broom's cleaning power depends on strong suction. If the broom runs but doesn't pick up anything, it has impaired suction. Change the disposable bag (shake out and clean a cloth filter bag) and empty the dirt cup. Check the nozzle and the neck

for clogging. If there is a ball of dust or debris in the neck, clean it with a bent wire clothes hanger. If your broom has an adjusting knob on the nozzle, you can remove it to get a dirt clog out.

It is important to keep the filters clean; if the collected debris is not filtered efficiently, it may penetrate the motor assembly, jam the motor's bearings, and cause the motor to overheat and eventually burn out. If your broom uses disposable bags, you may need added filtration to protect the motor. Cut the foam part of an air conditioner filter to fit over the bulkhead between the bag compartment and the motor housing. Then no dust will get through.

Avoid using the broom to pick up fine dirt such as plaster dust or ashes, as such dust will pass easily through the filter and into the motor. On the other hand, avoid picking up small objects such as pebbles or nails; they can destroy the fan, and cause the motor to burn out. The Regina is especially vulnerable to damage from such objects.

Always unplug the broom before changing disposable bags or filters, clearing blockages, or doing any repair work.

Replacing the cord and switch

If the broom doesn't run when you turn it on, test the cord for continuity. If the cord is OK test the switch (see Blue Pages: *Electrical testers*). If a two-speed broom runs at the same speed at both switch positions, you may have a defective diode on the switch. On the Hoover model shown in this article, if this is the case you must replace the whole switch if you want to use the low speed.

The cord leads must be removed at the switch, which may be attached either to the handle (Bissell and Regina) or to the motor housing (Hoover). In the Bissell and the Regina, the switch and switchplate are one assembly. If you have another model, adapt the procedures shown here for gaining access to and replacing a cord or switch.

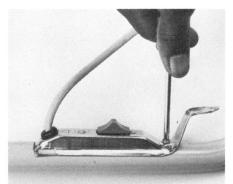

1 To test and replace the Bissell or Regina cord and the switch, first remove the screw attaching the switch assembly to the handle. Detach a cord lead from the switch and test the cord for continuity. If it's OK, remove one lead of the diode and test the switch for continuity. Replace a faulty cord or switch.

2 To replace the cord, disconnect the other cord lead. Squeeze the strain relief with pliers and pull the cord out. Replace the cord. To replace the switch assembly, remove the cord and disconnect the other switch lead. Replace the switch assembly, using a wire nut to reattach the lead.

1 To test and replace the Hoover cord and switch, you must open the motor housing. First remove the broom handle. Turn the corrugated plastic collar until the handle is released; pull out the handle and lay it aside.

2 Remove the three screws from the upper motor housing and lift the housing off. Disconnect a cord lead and test the cord for continuity. To replace a defective cord, remove the other cord lead, squeeze out the strain relief with pliers, pull out the cord, and replace it.

3 To test and replace a defective switch, unsolder a lead and one end of the diode. Test the switch for continuity; if it is defective, remove all the leads and replace the switch assembly.

Fan problems

If the broom motor runs but there is no suction, or if suction is not strong enough (and you've checked the nozzle and neck for clogs), check the suction fan for damage. Another warning that the fan is causing problems is a motor that runs more noisily than usual. A wobbling or nicked fan can eventually cause the motor to burn or wear out.

To inspect and replace the fan you must separate the motor housing from the bag compartment and get inside the motor housing from below. The Hoover fan is force-fitted to the armature; if the fan is defective, you must replace the fan-armature assembly.

1 To replace a defective Bissell fan, release the side clasps and separate the motor and the bag compartment. Lift the rubber gasket from around the bulkhead, and then lift out the bulkhead. The fan is directly behind it. The fan may have sharp edges.

2 Hold the fan steady with one hand while you unscrew the fan's retaining nut with a nut driver. Remove the nut, a washer, and the fan, but do not remove the washer under the fan, which should remain on the armature shaft. Install a new fan.

1 To replace a defective Regina fan, first remove the dust cup and the nozzle. Unscrew the four screws that hold the upper and lower motor housings together. Remove the upper housing and set it aside.

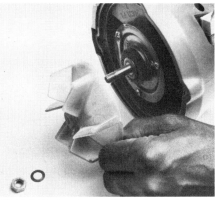

2 Hold the fan steady with one hand while you remove the fan nut with a nut driver. Remove the nut, a washer, and the fan, and install a duplicate fan.

1 To replace a defective Hoover fan, release the side clasps (on some models there is also a hinge pin to remove) and separate the bag compartment and the motor. Remove the handle (see *Replacing the cord and switch*, preceding page). Remove the screw in each clasp. This releases the bulkhead.

2 Remove the bulkhead and then the rubber gasket, and lift out the fan-motor assembly. The motor is still attached to the housing by the cord and switch leads.

3 Pry open the two metal spring clips that hold the fan housing to the motor assembly.

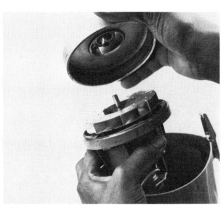

4 If the suction fan is damaged, lift off the top of the fan housing and remove the fan-armature assembly. To install a new assembly, release the brush assemblies at their terminals and pull them far enough out of their housings to permit removal of the armature.

Testing and replacing the motor

If the motor doesn't run at all and the cord and switch are OK, you will have to check the motor. There may be a loose connection, the brushes may be worn out, or the motor itself may be defective (see Appliance Repair Basics: *Universal motors* and *How to test a motor*). First, check the wires and terminal connecting the switch and motor.

If they are OK, set your VOM at RX1 and test the motor's continuity at the brush terminals. If you get no continuity, examine the brushes for wear or damage. (A motor that sends out visible blue sparks and seems to be laboring may have defective brushes.) If the brushes are OK, test the armature (rotor) for defective wiring by placing one VOM probe on one commutator bar and touching the other probe to the other commutator bars in turn. You should get the same reading each time. If you get either no resistance or infinite resistance, replace the armature. If your test on the brush terminals showed no continuity, and yet there is nothing apparently wrong with the brushes or armature, the problem may be in the field coil. Remove the field coil and have it tested at a repair shop.

To check the motor brushes on most brooms, remove the motor for access to the brushes. On the Regina (right), remove the brush covers and the field terminal clip. If either brush is damaged or is shorter than it is wide, replace both brushes. If the brushes are OK, test the armature.

1 **To test and replace the Regina motor,** first remove the three motor-mounting screws (far right).

2 Grasp the motor-mounting plate and pull the armature out of the field coil. Test the armature's continuity. If the armature is defective, replace it. If the armature is OK, have the field coil tested.

3 To replace the field coil, loosen the two screws holding it to the upper motor housing and remove it. Disconnect all the leads to the switch and cord and install a new field coil.

To test and replace the Bissell motor assembly, remove the four motor-mounting hex screws and lift out the motor assembly. You now have access to the brush terminals. Defective brushes can be replaced. If there is anything wrong with the armature or the field coil, the whole motor assembly must be replaced. Disconnect all leads and install a duplicate.

Replacing the Regina cloth filter bag

The Regina electric broom has a nondisposable cloth filter bag. You can change it, however, if it becomes damaged or simply too dirty. The bag is held taut by a spring, and to remove or attach a new bag you must push down the spring and create slack in the bag.

1 **To replace a Regina filter bag,** unscrew the outer ring on top of the filter bag. When this ring is free, push the inner ring and the bag down the handle until the bag is slack, and clamp it in place with a taped vise grip. Unscrew the retaining screw from the metal retaining ring at the bottom of the bag and release the ring.

2 Pull the bag free from the bottom of the broom. You can now release the vise grip and pull the bag up over the handle and off the broom. To install a new bag, clamp its inner ring as before and secure the bag with the metal retaining ring.

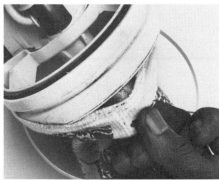

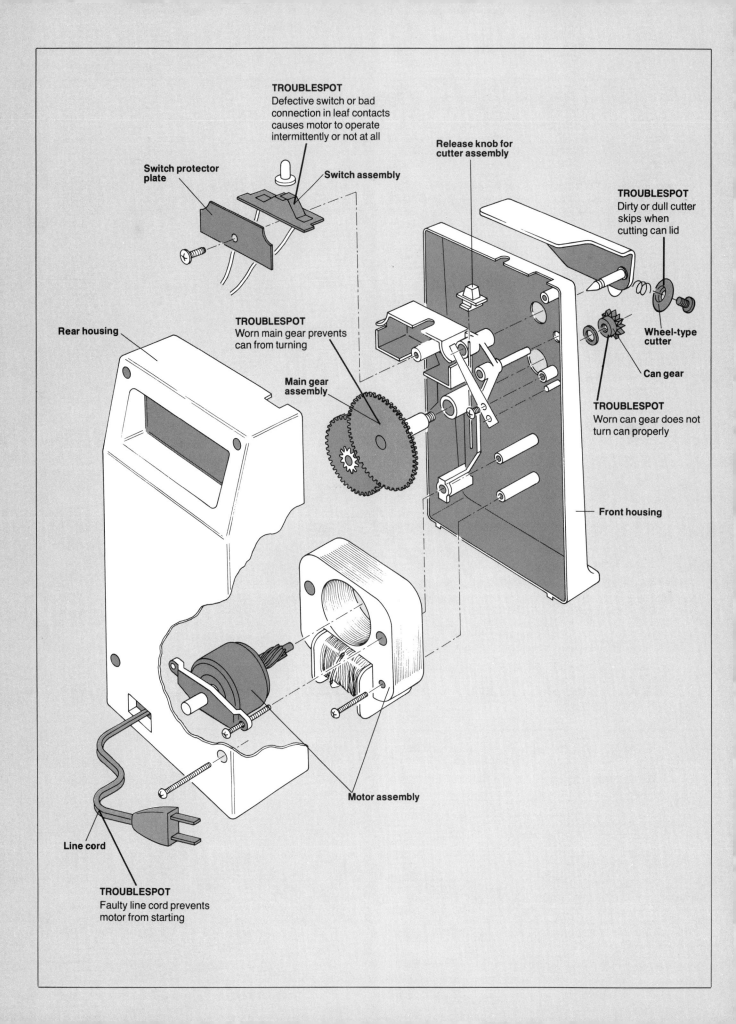

TROUBLESPOT Defective switch or bad connection in leaf contacts causes motor to operate intermittently or not at all

Switch protector plate

Switch assembly

Release knob for cutter assembly

TROUBLESPOT Dirty or dull cutter skips when cutting can lid

Rear housing

TROUBLESPOT Worn main gear prevents can from turning

Main gear assembly

Wheel-type cutter

Can gear

TROUBLESPOT Worn can gear does not turn can properly

Front housing

Motor assembly

Line cord

TROUBLESPOT Faulty line cord prevents motor from starting

Can Openers

Can openers use a simple electric motor and a system of reduction gears to turn a can gear (also called a feeder gear), which in turn rotates the can. As the can turns, its lid is pressed against a sharp cutting blade that cuts the lid cleanly. The cutter may be either a wheel type or blade type (see below). Because the motor is very simple, there isn't much that can go wrong with it. If it should burn out, however, it must be replaced. There is nothing to repair on it. Replacing the can opener makes more sense.

Most of the problems with can openers come from not keeping the cutting unit clean. A dirty cutting unit will lead to skipping: The cutter skips over and does not cut some part of the can lid. Proper maintenance of the cutter is the first step in keeping your electric can opener in good working order. The cutter cannot be sharpened; it must be replaced when it becomes dull.

There are two ways to clean the cutter: either remove it and wash it in soapy water, or use a stiff brush to clean away accumulated matter on it or on the can gear. Do this frequently to prevent food that has splashed on the cutter from hardening and thus becoming fairly difficult to remove. Under no condition should any part of the can opener other than the cutting unit be immersed in water.

Other problems that can arise with can openers involve the gear assemblies. On both the can gear and the inside gears, teeth may be worn, broken, or missing. Worn or defective gears can be replaced.

If the motor fails to work when the machine is turned on, the problem is probably in the line cord or in the switch. Both of these can be checked for continuity (see Blue Pages: *Electric testers*). Can opener switches generally have leaf contacts; you can check the switch to make sure that the leaf contacts make proper contact when the switch button is pressed.

Many can openers have a grindstone attachment for knife sharpening. The grindstone can usually be replaced if it grows smooth or worn from prolonged use.

The steps for the maintenance and repair of can openers are demostrated on Rival, Sunbeam, Oster, Hamilton Beach, Montgomery Ward, Dazey, and Farberware can openers.

Replacing cutters

Keeping the cutter clean on your can opener is essential. Food often spurts out of cans when they are opened and gets on the cutter and on the can gear. This spillage collects and clogs the cutter, causing it to labor and putting a strain on the motor. Nevertheless, both wheel and blade cutters do become dull after prolonged use, and must be replaced.

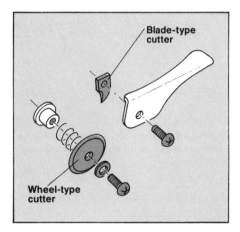

1 **To take off the Rival and other wheel-type cutters,** remove the center retaining screw with a screwdriver.

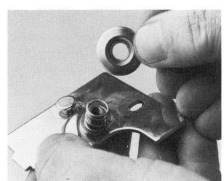

2 Take the cutter off the shaft, along with its accompanying screw. You can easily obtain a replacement cutter.

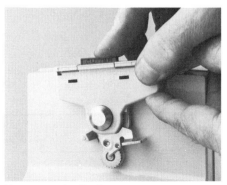

To remove the Sunbeam cutter, simply press down the button on top of the blade assembly and lift off the assembly. If the cutter is defective, you must replace the whole assembly.

To remove the Oster and other blade-type cutters, unscrew the center screw. Be sure to install the replacement in the proper direction.

Getting inside

To diagnose and correct problems other than those with the cutter, you will have to get inside the can opener. With the housing apart, you will be able to get at the line cord leads, switch, and gears. On this page we demostrate how to get inside the Rival, Hamilton Beach, and Montgomery Ward can openers. If you have a different make, adapt the instructions given here for the model that most closely resembles yours.

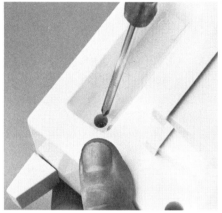

1 **To get inside the Rival,** remove the screws on the top rear of the housing. Different models have different numbers of screws. All are easily accessible. Tape the switch button as shown on the Montgomery Ward, below right.

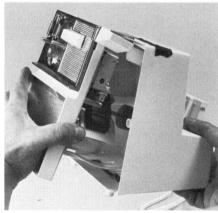

2 Tilt the unit a bit and pull off the front housing. This exposes the motor assembly, the gear, the switch assembly, and the grindstone —all the repairable parts.

To get inside the Hamilton Beach, remove the four recessed screws in the back of the unit.

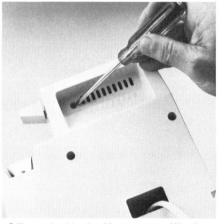

1 **To get inside the Montgomery Ward,** remove the four recessed Phillips screws in the back of the unit.

2 Tape the switch button as shown so it won't fall into the machine before you open the housing. It is also easier to reassemble the housing with the switch button in place.

3 Find and remove the Phillips screw that holds the protective housing covering the grindstone.

4 Pull away the plastic plate on the front of the housing that was released when you took out one of the rear screws.

5 Pull away the front part of the can opener's housing, which contains the motor and gear assemblies.

Mechanical problems

Replacing the can gear

If the can gear rotates cans slowly or not at all, but the motor runs, or if the opener makes an excessive amount of noise as the can rotates, examine the can gear for wear. The can gear is the gear that rotates the can so that the cutter can go all around the lid to cut it open. If the can gear becomes so worn that it doesn't grasp the can tightly enough to rotate it properly, it must be replaced. You can unscrew the can gear from the shaft, but this requires that you hold the shaft steady from the inside. There are several ways to do this. Repairs are shown here on the Dazey, Oster, and Rival machines.

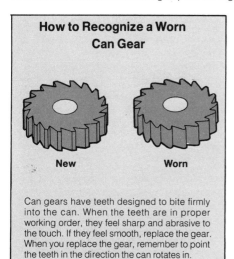

How to Recognize a Worn Can Gear

New   Worn

Can gears have teeth designed to bite firmly into the can. When the teeth are in proper working order, they feel sharp and abrasive to the touch. If they feel smooth, replace the gear. When you replace the gear, remember to point the teeth in the direction the can rotates in.

1 To remove the Dazey can gear, hold the machine so that the main drive gear and shaft are facing toward you. Grip the main-gear shaft with an adjustable wrench. Holding the wrench, stand the unit back up.

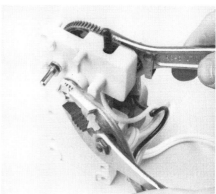

2 Hold the main gear firmly with an adjustable wrench, and remove the can gear by unscrewing it from the shaft with pliers. Replace the worn can gear with a new one.

1 To remove the Oster can gear, first loosen the main gear as shown here, by using a screwdriver to remove the retaining C-clip holding the gear.

2 Remove the main gear and use a pair of pliers to take firm hold of the shaft.

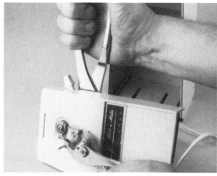

3 Use a pair of pliers to unscrew the can gear while you hold the shaft steady with another pair of pliers. Replace the gear if it is defective.

1 To remove the Rival can gear, you don't need to take off the main gear. Insert the square end of a nut driver handle into the square hole on the main gear, thus getting a grip on the gear and its shaft.

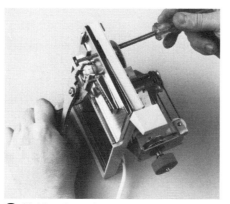

2 Holding the main gear and the shaft steady with the nut driver handle, use pliers to unscrew the can gear from the shaft. Replace it with a new one, screwing it on with pliers.

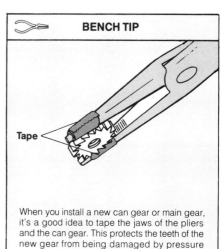

BENCH TIP

Tape

When you install a new can gear or main gear, it's a good idea to tape the jaws of the pliers and the can gear. This protects the teeth of the new gear from being damaged by pressure from the pliers.

Replacing the inside gears

If the can opener rotates cans slowly or not at all, or if the unit makes excessive noise when working and the can gear is OK, the problem is probably in one of the inside gears. The same problem of broken or worn teeth that affects the can gear may affect the other gears. In most cases, the gears lift out easily once the can gear has been loosened (see preceding page). The Sunbeam, however, is a little different. Directions for removing the Sunbeam main gear are given at far right.

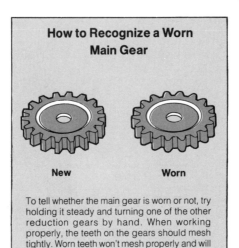

How to Recognize a Worn Main Gear

New   **Worn**

To tell whether the main gear is worn or not, try holding it steady and turning one of the other reduction gears by hand. When working properly, the teeth on the gears should mesh tightly. Worn teeth won't mesh properly and will slip under pressure.

To remove the Sunbeam main gear, loosen the Phillips screw holding it in place. On this model, the can gear pulls out separately from the main gear.

Checking the cord and switch

If the unit doesn't work at all, or if the motor starts and stops, the problem is very likely in the line cord or switch. Check both of these for continuity (see Blue Pages: *Electrical testers*). Checking the line cord is quite simple. Remove the wire nut attaching the line cord to the motor lead, disconnect the other cord lead, and do a continuity check on the cord. The switches on can openers also must be checked for continuity and, since they are generally leaf switches, you must inspect them to see that the proper contact is made when the switch button is pressed.

1 **To check the cord and switch on the Dazey,** remove the plate (shown here) that covers the switch assembly. To remove the plate, first remove the main gear and then loosen the Phillips screw that holds the plate.

2 Do a continuity check on the line cord. If the cord is OK, check the leaf contact for continuity; press the switch button several times to see that the leaf contact is making proper contact. The entire switch board is replaceable.

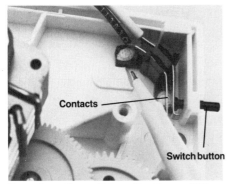

To replace the switch on the General Electric, lay the leaf contacts of the new switch in the grooves in the plastic switch block. If necessary, bend the leaf contacts so that a firm contact is made between them when the switch button is pressed. However, there should be a gap between them when the switch is open.

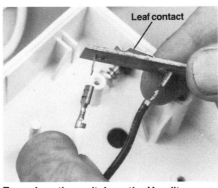

To replace the switch on the Hamilton Beach, lift out the defective switch board, disconnect its leads and attach them to the new switch board. Adjust the leaf contact so that it makes a firm contact when the switch button is pressed.

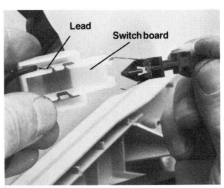

To replace the switch on the Sunbeam, lift out the switch board and cut the leads at the old switch. Attach the new switch, using wire nuts..

Knife sharpeners

Many electric can openers have a built-in knife sharpener made up of a grindstone attached to the motor shaft. The knife is sharpened when it is inserted through the slots in the can opener housing. Grindstones can be worn out through prolonged or improper use and thus fail to shar- pen properly. A grindstone also won't sharpen properly if it is loose. Check the screw or C-clip that holds the stone to its shaft, to make sure it is tight. If the stone is worn, replace it. Secure the new grindstone tightly so it doesn't wobble.

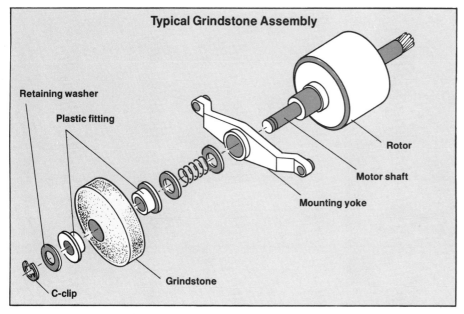

Typical Grindstone Assembly

Retaining washer

Plastic fitting

C-clip

Grindstone

Rotor

Motor shaft

Mounting yoke

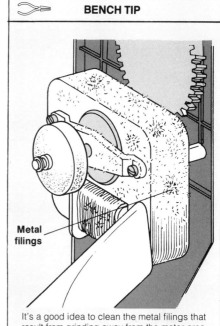

BENCH TIP

Metal filings

It's a good idea to clean the metal filings that result from grinding away from the motor area. These filings are drawn by the electric motor's magnetic properties and may enter the motor, causing a short. Use a vacuum cleaner or magnet to clean out the filings.

1 **To remove the Farberware grindstone** (right), get a firm grip on the motor shaft with a pair of taped pliers. Remove the nut holding the grindstone with a nut driver or wrench. Remove the grindstone and replace it with a new one.

2 Note the permanent washer on the shaft behind the grindstone. When you install the new grindstone, remember to put the large washer (far right) next to the grindstone; then install the locking washer (small washer shown at far right), and finally, the nut. Be sure to fasten tightly so the grindstone doesn't wobble.

BENCH TIP

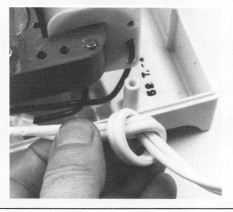

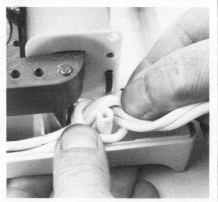

1 If there is no strain relief on the line cord, a sudden pull on the cord can loosen its connection to the switch or motor. To prevent this, knot the cord as shown here when you are checking or replacing it.

2 Place the knot around the rear screw housing. The screw housing then functions as a kind of capstan to prevent any strain or pull on the cord from affecting the cord's terminal in the switch.

Grinding type

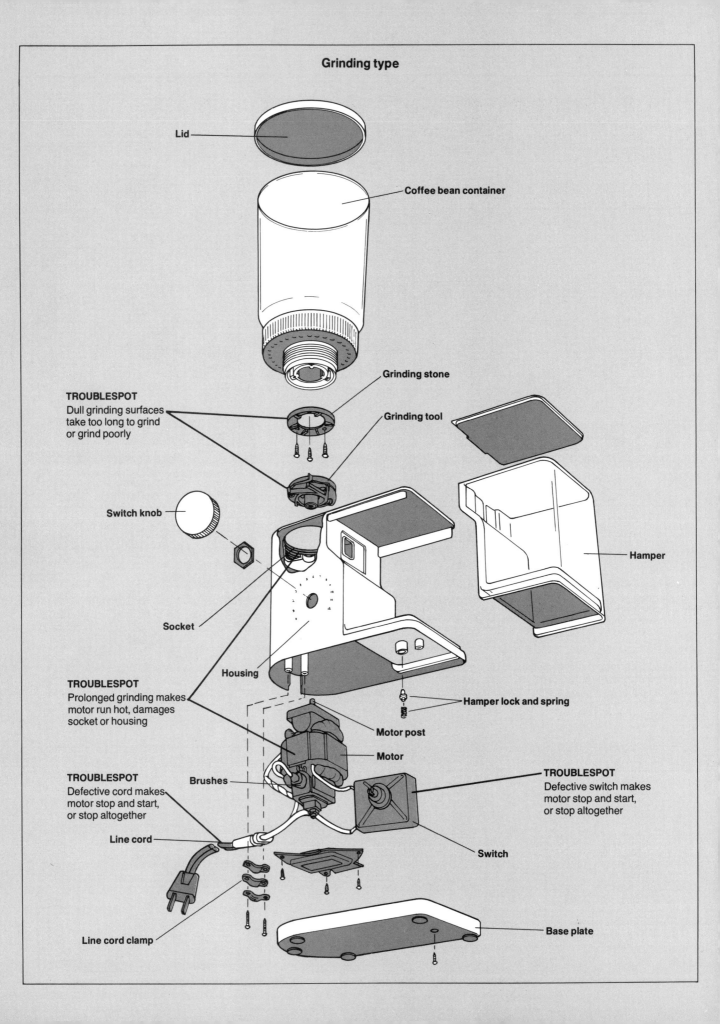

Lid

Coffee bean container

Grinding stone

Grinding tool

TROUBLESPOT
Dull grinding surfaces
take too long to grind
or grind poorly

Switch knob

Hamper

Socket

TROUBLESPOT
Prolonged grinding makes
motor run hot, damages
socket or housing

Housing

Hamper lock and spring

Motor post

Motor

TROUBLESPOT
Defective switch makes
motor stop and start,
or stop altogether

Brushes

TROUBLESPOT
Defective cord makes
motor stop and start,
or stop altogether

Line cord

Switch

Line cord clamp

Base plate

Cutting type

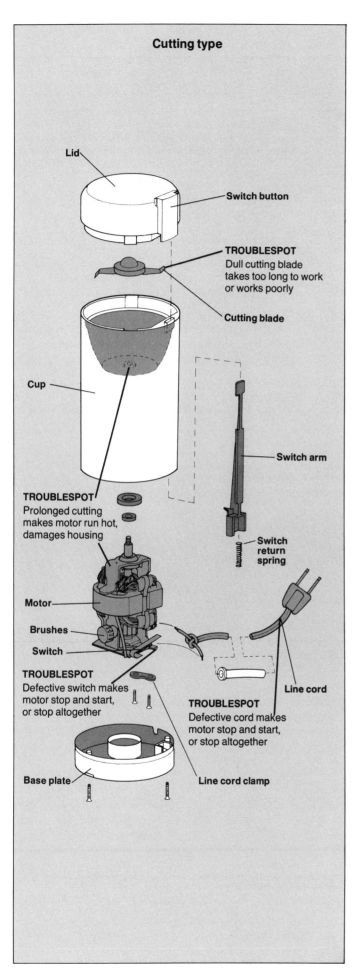

Lid

Switch button

TROUBLESPOT
Dull cutting blade
takes too long to work
or works poorly

Cutting blade

Cup

Switch arm

TROUBLESPOT
Prolonged cutting
makes motor run hot,
damages housing

Switch
return
spring

Motor

Brushes

Switch

Line cord

TROUBLESPOT
Defective switch makes
motor stop and start,
or stop altogether

TROUBLESPOT
Defective cord makes
motor stop and start,
or stop altogether

Base plate

Line cord clamp

Coffee Grinders

Counter-top coffee grinders that prepare roasted beans for brewing in a few seconds come in two different types: those that grind and those that cut. The grinding type, like the one diagrammed on the opposite page, uses a set of grinding wheels. The upper wheel, called the grinding stone, is attached to the base of the removable bean container and remains stationary. The lower one, called the grinding tool, is attached to the motor in the housing and spins when the appliance is turned on. The beans are pulverized as they pass between the two grinding surfaces and fall into a removable hamper at the bottom, ready for the pot. The fineness of the grind is determined by the amount of space between the tool and the stone; you adjust this space by rotating the base of the bean container. Since the container holds more beans than will be ground at once, the amount of coffee ground is determined by how long the machine runs. On the type shown opposite, a timer switch takes the guesswork out of this procedure by shutting off the motor automatically when the desired quantity of coffee has been ground. On other models the user shuts off the motor with a simple on/off snap switch.

The cutting type of coffee grinder, like the one diagrammed on this page, has a rotating cutting blade at the base of the metal bean cup. The blade is driven by a motor mounted beneath the cup. With the lid in place, you depress the switch for as long as you wish to grind the beans, up to a maximum of 30 seconds. The longer the grinding time, the finer the coffee.

Both types of grinders suffer from the same problem: when the cutting blade or grinding mechanism grows dull, the user fails to replace it. Instead, he tries to compensate for poorly ground coffee with longer grinding cycles. This makes the motor overheat, which may damage the motor, the switch, the line cord, and even the housing. An additional problem crops up in the cutting type. Since it can be used to grind nuts, seeds, and beans other than coffee, its blade may be damaged if you load it with something too hard.

To show you how to fix any of these problems, we have chosen three typical late-model grinders as demonstrators. The grinding type is illustrated on the following pages by a Braun model with a timer switch and a Braun model with a snap switch. The cutting type is represented by a Waring model.

> Avoid repeated opening and closing of the Waring model base. Its threaded plastic screw holes wear easily and eventually fail to hold the screws. If this happens, tape the base tightly in position, put a drop of silicone adhesive into the holes, and replace the screws. As the glue dries around the screws, new threads will form where the old ones had worn away.

Getting inside

All the coffee grinders shown here have a flat top they can stand on while you remove the base plate to get inside.

To open the grinding types (represented here by the two Braun models), first detach their upper containers by turning them counterclockwise all the way to the last brew-selection setting. Beyond that position the container bases are threaded and can be unscrewed.

To open the cutting type (represented here by the Waring model), first remove the lid and turn the machine upside down.

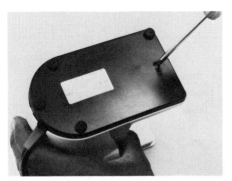

Timer-switch grinding model. The base plate is held in place by a single screw. The rubber feet are only for traction and do not conceal additional screws.

Snap-switch grinding model. The base plate has one visible screw plus several others hidden under the thick rubber cushion around the rim. Gently peel the cushion off for easy access to the screws.

Cutting model. Loosen the screws that hold the base plate; as you do, a spring underneath may push the plate up slightly. The spring will not pop out; when you remove the base screws, it remains in position inside the housing.

Replacing the cord

If you flip the switch and the coffee grinder doesn't go on, or if it stops and starts erratically, first check the line cord for continuity (see Blue Pages: *Electrical testers*).

To get inside a grinder, first remove the upper container and the base plate, following the directions given above for your model.

To test the cord on a timer-switch grinding model, remove only the base. To replace the cord, you must remove the motor also.

1 Timer-switch grinding model. Remove the screws holding the metal line cord clamp and the two fiber clamps underneath it.

2 Insert a narrow flat-blade screwdriver through the front of the housing and under the grinding tool.

3 Pry from below while rotating the grinding tool until it moves up far enough to be grasped from the top and removed.

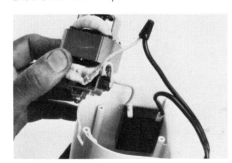

4 Lift the motor out. One cord wire is attached to the motor lead by a wire nut. The other is soldered to the switch. If the cord wire is broken at the switch, resolder it. If not, undo the wire nut and cut the cord wire a few inches from the switch. Connect the new cord with wire nuts.

Snap-switch grinding model. Both cord wires are attached by screw-type connectors to the mounting plate on top of the motor. They are easy to see and require no soldering. Just screw the new connectors in place.

Cutting model. Remove the screws holding the line cord clamps. The cord ends are soldered to connectors in the mounting plate. Melt the soldered connections and remove the bad cord. Tie an Underwriters' knot in the new cord and solder the ends in place.

Switch problems

If the grinder won't run when the switch is on or runs erratically, and the cord is OK, the problem may be in the switch or motor. You can check the brushes and replace them if necessary (see Appliance Repair Basics: *Preventing motor breakdowns*). For all models shown here, you'll have to remove the motors to check the switches. You can test both Braun model switches for continuity (the Braun with the timer switch is a special case—see box, right) and, if they're defective, replace them. On the Waring model, the switch is an exposed copper blade that cannot be tested as the others. It can be cleaned and adjusted if necessary.

Testing the Braun Timer Switch

To test the timer switch, turn the switch all the way to its last setting and test across the switch terminals for continuity as the switch runs all the way down. (see Blue Pages: *Electrical testers*). There should be continuity all the time the switch is running. If there is none, or if it flickers on and off, the switch is faulty and must be replaced.

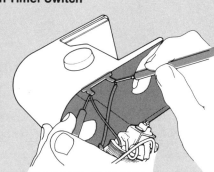

Replacing the grinding model's timer switch

1 **To remove the timer switch,** pry off the knob with a flat-blade screwdriver. The switch won't drop out; it's held in place by a nut.

2 Unscrew the nut and remove the switch. Connect the new switch, using push-on leads (far right) or wire nuts.

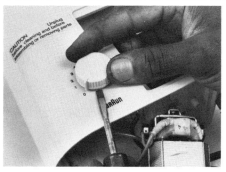

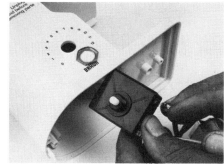

Testing and replacing the grinding model's snap switch

1 **To remove the switch,** unscrew the retaining clip attaching the switch to the housing.

2 Lift out the motor with the switch attached and test across the switch terminals for continuity. If the switch is defective, clip or unsolder the wires off near the switch. If the new switch has leads, either solder them in place or use wire nuts.

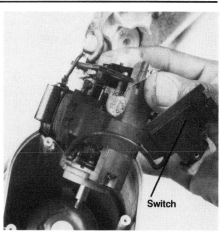

Switch

Inspecting the cutting model's switch

1 **To check the switch contacts** for dirt you must remove the motor from the housing. Follow the directions on page 161 for removing the cutting blade, and the motor will come free. Inspect the switch contacts. If they are not shiny and smooth, clean them with fine sandpaper.

2 Lift out the plastic arm that rests at the side of the housing. The button on top of the grinder pushes against this arm, which in turn presses the two switch points together. Replace the plastic arm if it's broken; free it up if it's stuck. Clean out any accumulated coffee grounds.

Switch contacts

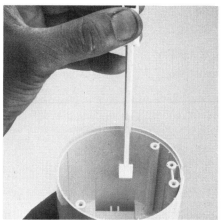

Replacing dull grinders and cutting blades

If it seems to be taking longer and longer to grind the coffee fine enough, that's a sign that the cutting blade or the grinding mechanism has grown dull. If a cutting blade is damaged or dull, as in the Waring model on the opposite page, you can tell it at a glance. But a dull grinding tool or grinding stone doesn't always look or feel much different from a sharp one. Let the grinding time be your guide. Replace both grinding tool and grinding stone when they seem to have served their term.

Directions for replacing both grinding tool and grinding stone on the snap-switch model are given on these pages.

Directions for replacing the timer-switch grinding model's grinding stone are given on the next page. To replace the grinding tool, follow the first three steps shown on page 158 for replacing the timer-switch cord.

Directions for replacing the cutting blade on a cutting model are given on the opposite page.

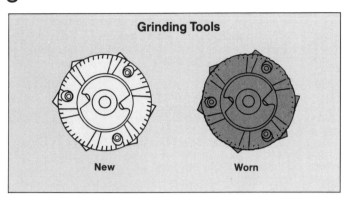

Grinding Tools

New   Worn

Replacing the snap-switch model's grinding tool

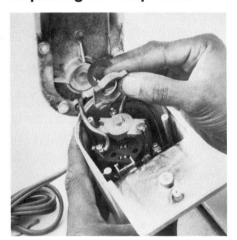

1 **With the base plate off,** remove the gasket and rubber cushion.

2 Insert a screwdriver into one of the holes in the motor plate and hold it against the rotor so that the rotor is prevented from turning.

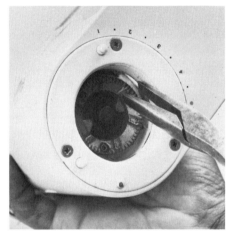

3 Reach into the top of the grinder with a pair of needle-nose pliers and grip the grinding tool on one side.

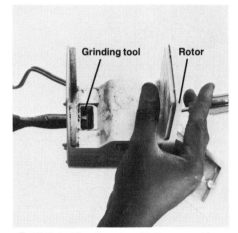

Grinding tool   Rotor

4 While holding the rotor with the screwdriver, rotate the grinding tool with the pliers until it loosens; then unscrew it the rest of the way by hand. Screw the new grinding tool on tight with the same tools.

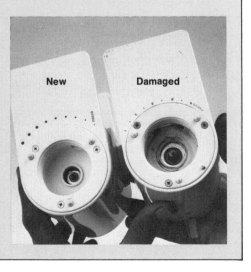

Replacing a Damaged Grinder Housing

If a Braun grinder is forced to work beyond its 30-second time limit over and over again, the excess heat thus generated may damage the plastic housing, as in the one shown above (such misuse may also damage the motor, switch, or cord). If the housing is damaged, remove all its contents and replace it with a duplicate part. Directions for removing the grinding tool, switch, and motor are given on these pages.

New   Damaged

Replacing the grinding stone

1 **To remove the grinding stone,** turn the bean container upside down and remove the three screws holding the stone. You'll need a screwdriver with a very narrow head because the screws are recessed.

2 Pry evenly around the underside of the rim of the stone with a screwdriver to pop it out of its socket. Don't be afraid to apply pressure. Install the new grinding stone by pressing it firmly into the socket and screwing it down.

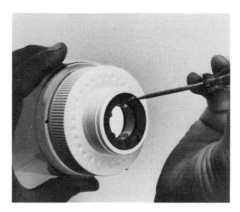

Replacing the cutting blade

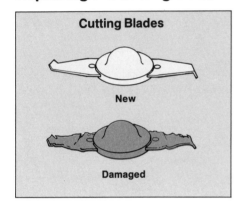

Cutting Blades

New

Damaged

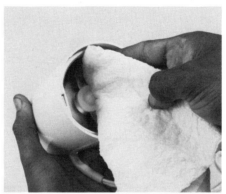
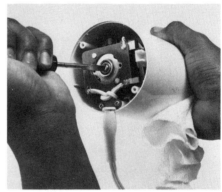

1 **To replace the cutting blade,** reach into the cup with a cloth and grip the blade. The cloth will protect your fingers against the sharp blade and will help you to hold it immobile.

2 Turn the slotted end of the motor armature with a screwdriver while holding the blade stationary. The blade will loosen and can then be unscrewed. Screw the new blade on, using the screwdriver and cloth.

BENCH TIP

A Better Grip

If you can't get a firm enough grip on the cutting blade to turn it by hand, enlist the aid of your workshop vise. Lock a screwdriver with a sturdy handle into the vise, blade up. Hold the slotted end of the motor post firmly against the tip of the screwdriver. Then reach into the top of the grinder with pliers. Insert the tips into the two holes in the blade and turn the pliers to loosen the blade.

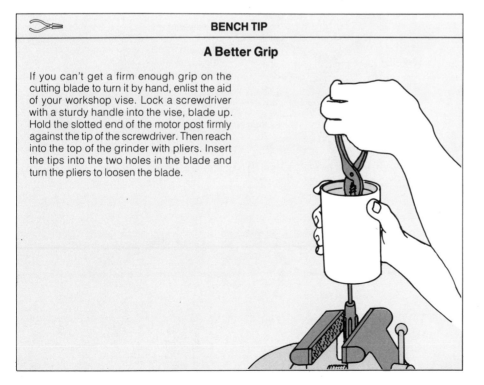

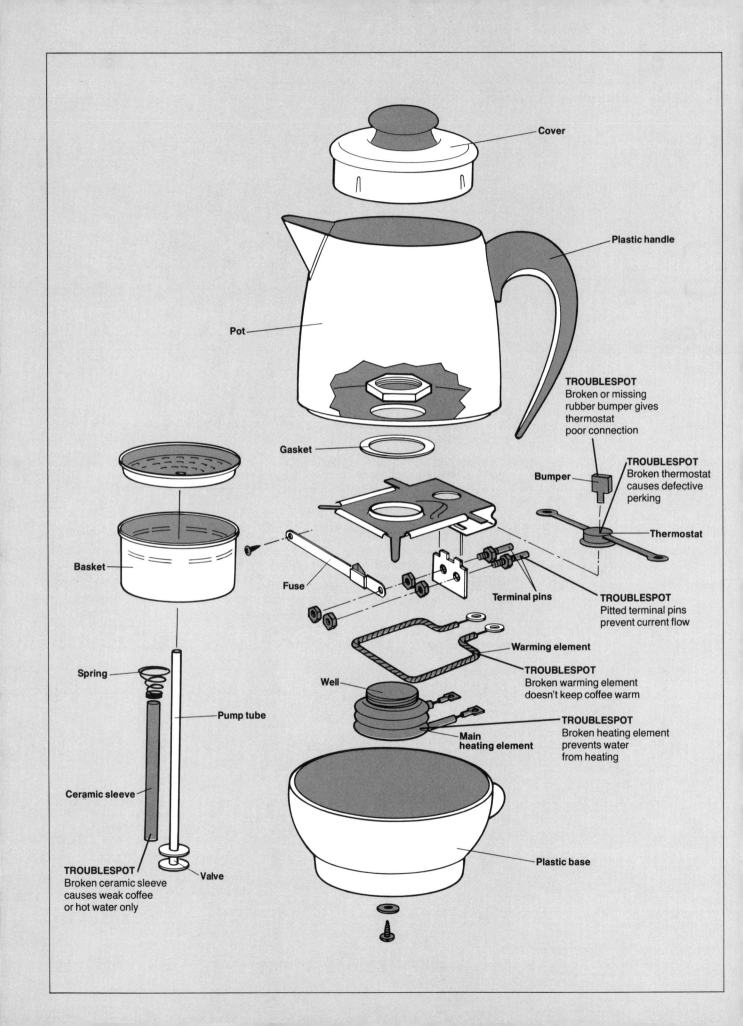

Cover

Plastic handle

Pot

TROUBLESPOT
Broken or missing
rubber bumper gives
thermostat
poor connection

Gasket

Bumper

TROUBLESPOT
Broken thermostat
causes defective
perking

Thermostat

Basket

Fuse

Terminal pins

TROUBLESPOT
Pitted terminal pins
prevent current flow

Warming element

Spring

Well

TROUBLESPOT
Broken warming element
doesn't keep coffee warm

Pump tube

Main
heating element

TROUBLESPOT
Broken heating element
prevents water
from heating

Ceramic sleeve

Plastic base

TROUBLESPOT
Broken ceramic sleeve
causes weak coffee
or hot water only

Valve

Coffee Makers
Percolators

All coffee makers brew coffee by means of an element that heats water, which then drips through a basket containing coffee grounds. Percolators recirculate the water so that it passes through the grounds repeatedly. (Drip-type coffee makers are discussed on pages 170 through 175.)

When the percolator is plugged in or switched on, the cold water in the pot is fed into a small well in the bottom of the pot by a valve. As the water in the well is heated to boiling by the brewing element, steam forces the valve up against the plates above it, shutting off the supply of water from the pot. The boiling water in the well is forced up the pump tube and spurts out against the top of the unit, where it is deflected down on the grounds in the basket. It percolates through the grounds and drips back into the pot as coffee.

As the hot water spurts up the pump tube, the steam closing the valve escapes, the valve falls, and water from the pot again enters the well to be heated to boiling. The cycle continues until the coffee reaches the desired strength. At that time, a thermostat switches most of the current from the main heating element to the warming element, and the coffee is kept at a constant temperature.

To obtain the best results from your coffee maker, follow the manufacturer's directions for the amount of coffee grounds to use for the amount of coffee desired; keep the insides of the unit spotlessly clean; and always start brewing with cold water. Generally, percolators do not give much trouble, but there are several kinds of repairs that you can make.

If your unit does not work at all; that is, if the main heating element does not get hot, check the cord, the terminal pins, the fuse, the switch (if there is one), the thermostat, and the main element to determine where the current is blocked. If the element heats up but the unit does not percolate, check the pump tube and valve for clogging. If the water heats and perks but the coffee in the pot cools rapidly, the thermostat or the warming element is defective. (In some models, an indicator light tells whether the warming element is working or not.) Some units are immersible because the electrical elements are sealed. In this case, defective elements and thermostats must be repaired by the manufacturer. Percolator urns have spigots that may become damaged, and these can be replaced (see page 166).

External repairs

There are a few common problems with percolators that can be corrected without disassembling the pot. If the water isn't heating at all, check the detachable cord for continuity (see Blue Pages: *Electrical testers*). If the cord is OK, look for pitting or damage on the cord terminal pins; if the pins are damaged, see *Terminal pins and fuse* on the next page. If the problem is weak coffee, or plain hot water that hasn't brewed at all, check the ceramic sleeve that fits over the perking tube or pump. If the pot's plastic handle is cracked or broken, it can be replaced.

If the percolator makes weak coffee or produces only hot water, check the ceramic sleeve that fits over the perking tube (also called the pump). If it is cracked or broken, replace it.

1 **If the plastic handle is cracked,** you can replace it. To remove the old handle, loosen the recessed screw.

2 If the threaded handle mounting on the pot has become loose and water leaks out, take the pot to a professional repair center so the handle mounting can be soldered on again.

Getting inside

All percolators have a plastic base that encloses the electrical parts. This base is attached to the pot by one or more screws or nuts located on the bottom of the pot. You can remove the base by removing the screws or nuts. Before you do this, check the cord and plug for continuity to make sure the problem isn't there.

To open a percolator base, loosen the screw at the center of the base plate. Remove the plate so you can have access to the electrical parts.

Immersible Pots

If you have an automatic coffee maker, do not attempt to open the base to make your own repairs. This pot is immersible, so the base has gaskets and seals to make it watertight. If these seals are broken, the pot is no longer watertight. This pot *cannot* be repaired by either the home mechanic or a service center; it must be returned to the manufacturer.

Electrical problems

Terminal pins and fuse

If your coffee maker doesn't work at all, first check the cord for continuity (see Blue Pages: *Electrical testers*). If the cord is in working order, then check the terminal pins. Pitted pins should be replaced (see right) because they inhibit the flow of current. If the pins are not pitted, make a continuity check of the fuse. It is located just behind the terminal pins. If there is no continuity, take out the screws holding the fuse in place and install a duplicate.

To replace corroded or pitted terminal pins, release the nuts on the ends of the pins behind the terminal block.

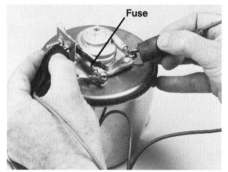

To test the fuse for continuity, attach the tester leads to both sides of the fuse. If there is no continuity, the fuse must be replaced.

Replacing the thermostat

If the pot doesn't work, and the cord, pins, and fuse are OK, check the thermostat for continuity. Remove the thermostat leads (see below) and set the pot's selector arm at STRONG. Attach tester probes to the thermostat leads; the thermostat should show continuity. If it doesn't, replace it.

If the coffeepot does not stop perking when the coffee has brewed, it probably means that the thermostat is not functioning properly. Fill the pot with water, turn it on, and use a candy thermometer to measure the temperature of the water when the pot shuts off. The proper reading is between 190°F. and 200°F. If the reading is significantly lower or higher, or if the pot fails to shut off at all, replace the thermostat.

1 To replace the thermostat, use a nut driver to remove the nuts that attach the thermostat lead to the terminal block. Remove the other lead with a Phillips screwdriver.

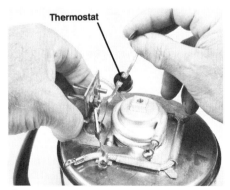

2 Carefully pull out the thermostat. Place the new one in the same position and attach leads to the terminal block.

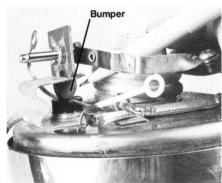

Replace the rubber bumper above the thermostat if it is deteriorated. A corroded bumper can prevent the thermostat from working properly.

Replacing the warming element

If the coffee does not stay warm after it is perked, or if the pot starts perking again after the coffee is brewed, you have a problem with the warming element. In the latter case, the coffee starts cooling down; when it gets cold enough, the thermostat activates the heating element to start the brewing cycle. Disconnect one lead of the warming element and test the element for continuity. If it is defective, replace it, following the steps below.

1 **To replace the warming element,** which is a cordlike device, detach the leads, gently lift its soft metal bracket with a screwdriver, and remove the old element.

2 Insert the new warming element in the same position, and bend the soft metal brackets back in place. Attach the warming element leads to the terminal block.

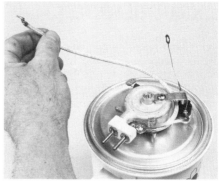

In some coffeepots, such as the Regal Poly Perk, the warming element is not under a bracket but is wrapped around the heating element. To replace it, detach the leads, unwind the element, and wind the new one on. Attach the leads to the terminal block.

Replacing the heating element

If the water in the coffeepot does not heat up, and the cord, terminal pins, fuse, and thermostat are all OK, and there are no loose connections, the heating element is probably defective. To be sure, check the element for continuity as shown below. If the element is defective, replace it with a duplicate. You will need a socket wrench to remove the nut at the bottom of the well inside the pot; this nut holds the element in place.

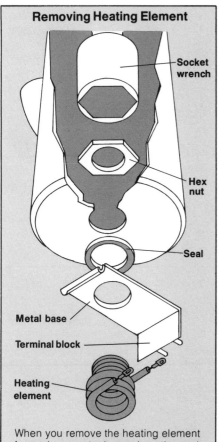

Removing Heating Element

- Socket wrench
- Hex nut
- Seal
- Metal base
- Terminal block
- Heating element

When you remove the heating element for replacement, also replace the seal. Check the metal base and hex nut for corrosion and replace them if necessary.

To test the element for continuity, remove one thermostat lead from the element terminal and touch tester probes to both element terminals (see Blue Pages: *Electrical testers*). If the element doesn't show continuity, replace it.

To remove the heating element, disconnect all the leads from its terminals and use a socket wrench to release the nut surrounding the well in the bottom of the pot.

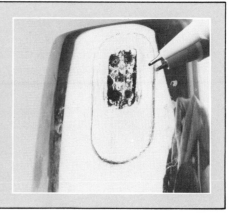

Leaky Handle

If water leaks out of the pot from the handle, the threaded handle mounting may be corroded. Do not attempt to repair this yourself, take the coffeepot to a service center to have the handle mounting soldered on again.

COFFEE MAKERS
Percolator urns

External repairs

Percolator urns work the same as smaller percolator pots, except that the coffee is emptied from the urn through a spigot rather than poured out through a spout. Coffee urns also have a safety thermostat. As with percolator pots, there are a few things that can be checked and corrected without disassembling the urn. Major repairs to the spigot (below) require taking apart the spigot assembly but do not require getting inside the base of the urn. You must open the base of the urn to work on the switch, the thermostats, or the elements.

On some coffee makers, the pump tube has a small hole in the bottom end (like the West Bend shown). If water is not rising up the pump tube, check whether the hole is clogged and clear it.

1 If coffee at either end of the glass tube leaks, check the tube for cracks. If it is broken, replace it by unscrewing the cap at the top and pulling out the tube.

2 If the glass tube is OK, check the rubber at the bottom of the tube and in the cap. If either is worn or deteriorated, replace it.

Spigot problems

If water leaks from the top mount of the spigot, remove the screw and check the rubber washer. If it is worn, it should be replaced. If water leaks from the spigot, check the spigot and the valve seat washer (see also *External repairs*, above). If the washer is deteriorated, it should be replaced. If the faucet is cracked, the entire spigot assembly should be replaced.

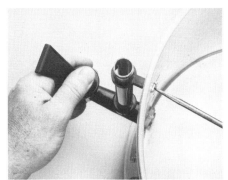

1 To inspect the rubber washer on the top mount of the spigot, unscrew the top mount screw, which is on the inside of the urn.

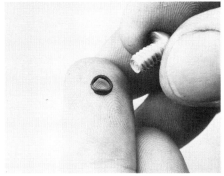

2 If the O-ring washer that surrounds the screw is deteriorated (like the one shown here), water will leak from the top mount. The O-ring washer must be replaced.

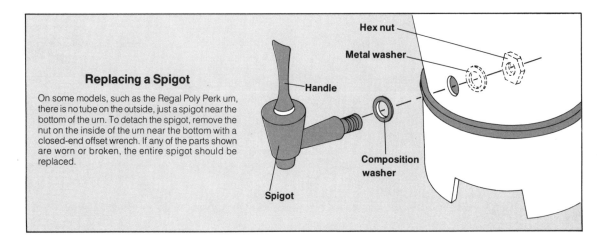

Replacing a Spigot

On some models, such as the Regal Poly Perk urn, there is no tube on the outside, just a spigot near the bottom of the urn. To detach the spigot, remove the nut on the inside of the urn near the bottom with a closed-end offset wrench. If any of the parts shown are worn or broken, the entire spigot should be replaced.

Hex nut

Metal washer

Handle

Composition washer

Spigot

1 **To remove the spigot handle,** grip it tightly with pliers and unscrew it. Wrap the handle with cloth or tape to prevent the pliers from damaging it.

2 If the spigot leaks because threads are cracked or broken, the entire spigot assembly will have to be replaced (see directions below).

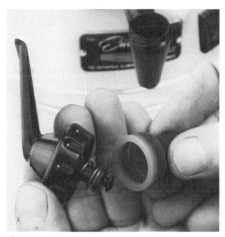

3 If the valve seat washer (also called the rubber cup seal) is deteriorated, coffee will drip from the spigot. Replace the seal.

1 **To detach the spigot from the coffee urn,** wrap a cloth around the spigot and hold it firmly with offset pliers (right).

2 While holding the spigot in place, remove the nut on the inside of the urn, using an offset box wrench (far right).

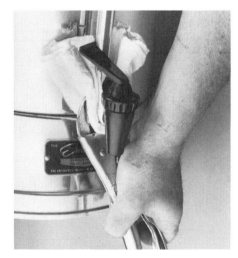

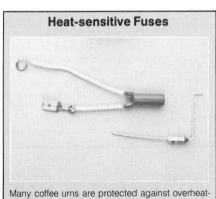

Getting inside

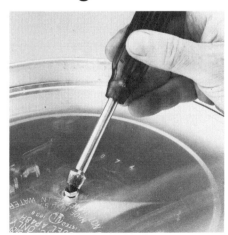

1 **To open the base of the urn,** release the nut in the center of the bottom plate with a nut driver or socket wrench.

2 Pry out the bottom plate by inserting a screwdriver under the edge of the plate and lifting it out.

Heat-sensitive Fuses

Many coffee urns are protected against overheating by heat-sensitive fuses. If the urn gets too hot, the fuse melts, cutting power to the elements. Whenever you have a problem that requires checking the cord and switch for continuity, check the heat-sensitive fuse also. The two shown above are common types used in appliances that heat.

Electrical problems

Replacing the switch

If the urn does not work at all, first check the cord for continuity (see Blue Pages: *Electrical testers*). The urn shown has three leads from the power cord, and all three should be tested. If the cord is OK, check the switch for continuity; if it is defective, replace it. If the indicator light is burned out, it can be replaced by adapting the instructions below for replacing the switch.

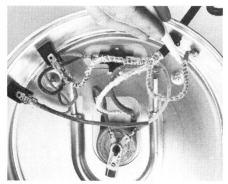

To test the cord, detach all three leads and test each one. If the cord is defective, replace it with a cord with the same rating and insulation.

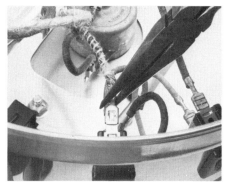

1 **To replace a defective switch,** first label the wires, then pull off the leads with needle-nose pliers.

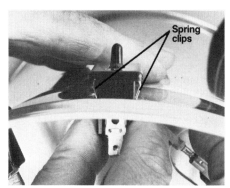

2 Push in the spring clips on both sides of the switch; push the switch out. Break the clips if the switch is stuck. Install a replacement.

Replacing the warming element thermostat

If an urn fails to keep coffee warm after the brewing cycle, the problem may be in the warming element thermostat. Check for loose connections between the warming element and its thermostat, and test the warming element for continuity (see opposite page). If the element is OK, the thermostat must be defective. Remove the thermostat from the bottom of the urn as shown at right, disconnect one of the leads, and test the thermostat for continuity (see Blue Pages: *Electrical Testers)*. If the thermostat is defective, replace it with a duplicate.

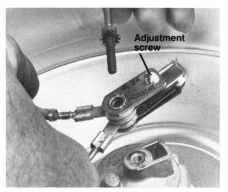

The warming element thermostat on some models, like the Enterprise, above, has a preset adjustment screw, sealed with plastic. Don't attempt to adjust this screw. If the thermostat doesn't keep coffee warm enough (and the heating element is OK), replace it.

Replacing the main element thermostat

A defective main element thermostat can prevent the water in an urn from heating at all or cut off power to the main element too soon, preventing the water from reaching proper brewing temperature or completing the brewing cycle. Also, a defective thermostat may fail to shut off the element when brewing is finished.

If you have any of these problems—and the cord and switch are OK—check the main heating element for continuity (see opposite page). If the element is OK, the thermostat must be defective.

1 **To replace the thermostat,** remove the leads on either side. Slip a screwdriver under the bracket that holds the thermostat in place.

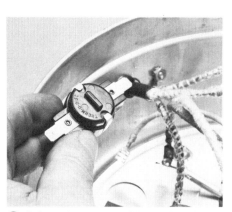

2 Release the pressure of the bracket with the screwdriver and slide out the thermostat. Replace it with a duplicate.

Replacing the heating element

If the water does not heat, remove one lead from the heating element and test the element for continuity (see Blue Pages: *Electrical testers*). If the element shows no continuity, it must be replaced with a duplicate. To do this on an urn where the main element is below the well, you will need a socket wrench with T-bar extension for leverage to loosen the nut. You may find it difficult to maneuver the wrench and hold the urn at the same time, so have someone hold the urn as you loosen the nut.

On some models, the main heating element protrudes above the bottom of the urn. To replace this type of element, you will need a deep-well socket.

1 **To remove the main element,** have someone hold the urn as you fit a socket wrench over the nut and turn the bar to release the nut.

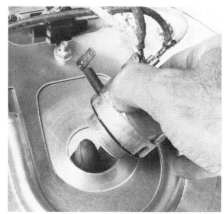

2 With the nut released, you can remove the main element from the underside of the urn. To replace it, insert the new element in the hole and attach the nut from the inside, using the socket wrench and bar.

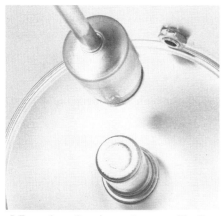

1 **To replace the element on urns like the West Bend,** you must first remove the pump tube. Underneath it is the main element, which protrudes into the pot.

2 Use a deep-well socket to replace this type of element. Turn the pot upside down and remove the nut holding the element in place.

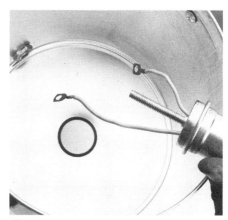

3 From the inside, you can simply lift out the heating element. To replace it, insert the gasket and the new element from the inside of the pot and replace the nut.

Replacing the warming element

If the coffee urn perks but doesn't keep the coffee warm afterwards, the problem is either in the warming element or the thermostat. To check the element for continuity, remove one lead and touch the tester probes to the element terminals. No continuity indicates a defective element.

1 **To replace a defective warming element,** turn the urn upside down, remove the nuts from the base, and lift off the base.

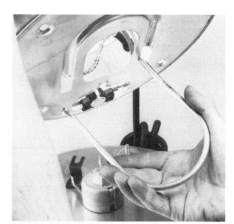

2 Remove the defective element and install a replacement.

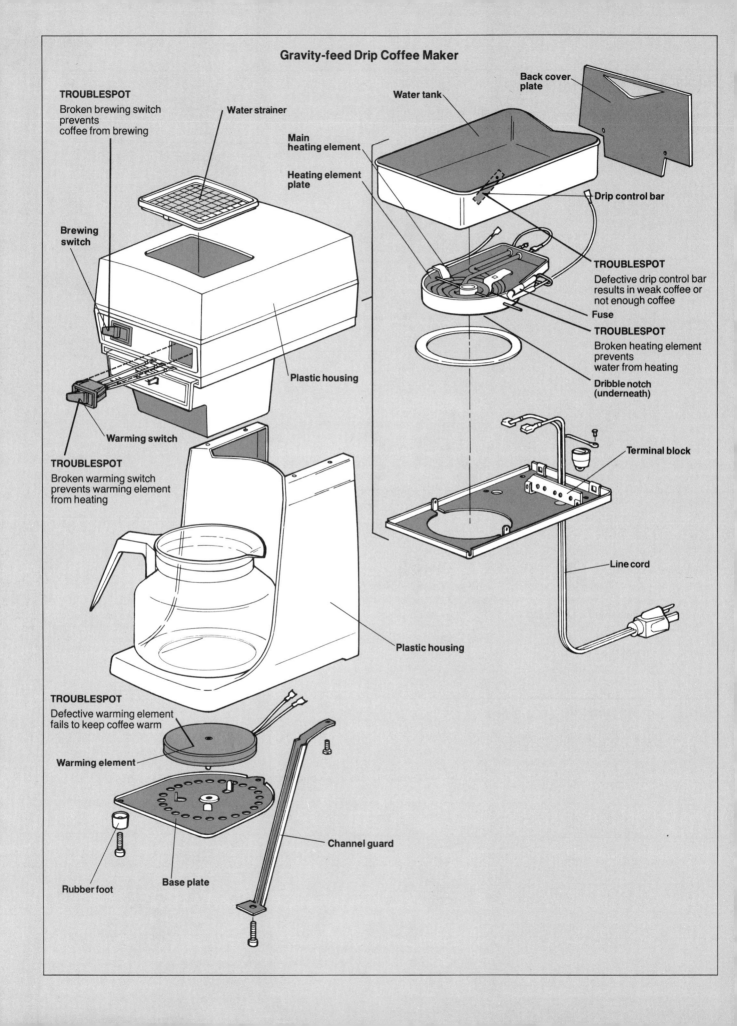

Gravity-feed Drip Coffee Maker

Water tank

Back cover plate

TROUBLESPOT
Broken brewing switch prevents coffee from brewing

Water strainer

Main heating element

Heating element plate

Drip control bar

Brewing switch

TROUBLESPOT
Defective drip control bar results in weak coffee or not enough coffee

Fuse

TROUBLESPOT
Broken heating element prevents water from heating

Dribble notch (underneath)

Plastic housing

Warming switch

TROUBLESPOT
Broken warming switch prevents warming element from heating

Terminal block

Line cord

Plastic housing

TROUBLESPOT
Defective warming element fails to keep coffee warm

Warming element

Channel guard

Rubber foot

Base plate

COFFEE MAKERS
Gravity-feed drip coffee makers

Drip coffee makers brew coffee by dripping near-boiling water slowly through coffee grounds. In contrast to percolators, which circulate the water through the grounds continuously until the coffee has become strong enough, drip makers circulate water through the grounds only once. Some coffee connoisseurs say that this process makes a better cup of coffee.

Drip coffee makers consist of a plastic housing that holds a water tank, a heating element, a warming element, a basket for coffee grounds, and a separate coffee pot. In addition to an on/off switch, some models have a switch for activating the element that keeps the coffee warm after it stops brewing.

There are two basic types of drip coffee maker: the gravity-feed type and the pump-feed type. The gravity-feed type has the tank and the main heating element above the pot. Heated water drips onto the grounds and into the pot by gravity alone. On the pump type, the water reservoir and heating element are at the bottom of the unit, and the heated water is pumped to the top of the unit to drip through the grounds. In both types, a thermostat controls both the main heating element and the warming element, which is always located immediately below the coffee pot. There is a button to activate the brewing cycle. On some models the warming element goes on automatically when the coffee is brewed, and other models have an on/off switch controlling the warmer.

Getting inside

If your coffee maker doesn't work properly, you must open up the housing to make tests and repairs on the electrical components. First, unplug the unit and remove the water strainer. Remove the back panel to gain access to the terminal block, the main heating element, and the switches. The base plate must be removed for access to the warming element.

If the unit makes coffee but doesn't keep it warm, the problem is in the warming element or the warmer switch. Directions are given for testing and replacing both components. If the unit doesn't work at all, test the cord and the brewing switch for continuity (see Blue Pages: *Electrical testers*). In many models, the thermostat, fuse, and main element are all in one assembly. If any part of the assembly is faulty, the whole assembly must be replaced.

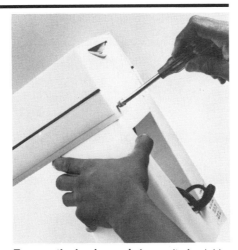

To open the back panel of a gravity-feed drip coffee maker, unscrew the back cover plate using a nut driver to release the two nuts. Unscrew the channel guard that covers the warmer element leads, and disconnect those leads before you remove the terminal block and the element assembly.

Electrical problems

Testing the warming element

If the coffee maker makes coffee but the coffee doesn't stay warm, the problem is in either the warming element or the warmer switch (if your unit has one). Check the element for continuity first, because it is easier to get at than the switch (see Blue Pages: *Electrical testers*). If the element is defective, replace it with a duplicate. If it is OK, test the switch. A defective switch can also be replaced (see next page).

Before you do any continuity tests, make sure the problem isn't caused by a loose connection.

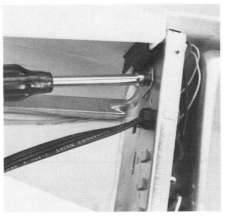

1 **To test the warming element,** remove the back panel and the base plate. Unscrew the top and bottom screws of the channel guard, which covers the warming element leads. Disconnect the element leads at the terminal block.

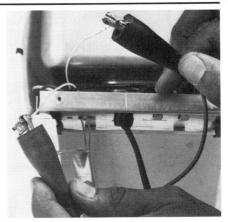

2 Test the leads of the warming element for continuity (see Blue Pages: *Electrical testers*). If there is no continuity, you will have to replace the warming element (see next page).

Replacing the warming element

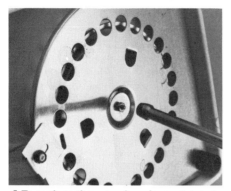

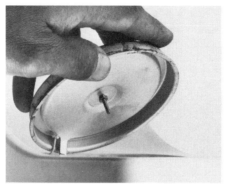

1 **To replace the warming element,** turn the unit on its side and loosen the nut in the center of the bottom plate.

2 Lift off the plate on which the coffee pot sits, pulling out the leads of the warming element as you remove the disc.

3 Loosen the nut in the center of the plate and remove the top piece. The warming element is the ropelike part that lies inside the plate.

Testing and replacing the warming switch

If the coffee doesn't stay warm, and the element is OK, the problem is the switch. To gain access to the switch and the terminal block, you must remove the metal plate that holds the water tank and the heating element.

If you must replace the warmer switch, and the replacement comes without leads, you will have to use the leads from the old switch. Instructions are given for installing a new switch, with and without its own leads.

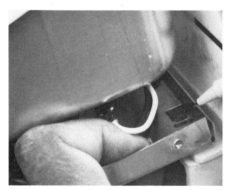

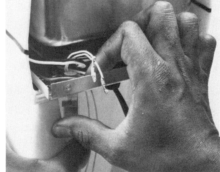

1 **To remove the heating element and water tank,** first remove the plate holding the heating element in place. The warming switch and terminal block are also mounted on this plate. The plate is secured by a latch on either side. With a screwdriver, lift up the latch as you pull out the plate slightly.

2 When both latches are released, you can slide the plate, the heating element, and the water tank out together.

3 The water tank sits on top of the element. When you lift it off, you have access to the warmer switch.

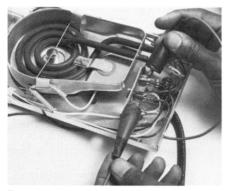

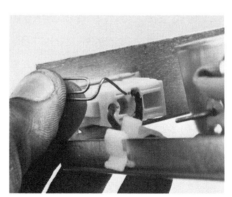

To test the warmer switch for continuity, (see Blue Pages: *Electrical testers*), set it in the ON position. On the Mr. Coffee unit shown here, the test is made on the black and white switch leads. Detach either lead at the terminal block, and touch the tester probes to both leads. If there is no continuity, replace the switch.

To install a switch with its own leads, disconnect one switch lead at the terminal block. Attach the new switch by connecting its lead to the same terminal on the block. Then remove the other switch lead and attach the new one.

To install a new switch using the old leads, label and remove the leads from the old switch by inserting one end of a paper clip into the tiny holes next to the leads and pulling the lead out. Remove the switch by pressing on the spring clips on either side of it. Then install the new switch and attach the leads.

Main heating element

If your coffee maker does not work at all, and there is nothing wrong with the house circuit or the cord, the problem may be in the brewing switch or the heating unit. The brewing switch can be tested and replaced the same way as the warming switch (opposite page).

The heating unit consists of the fuse, thermostat, and heating element, which in many coffee makers are all part of one assembly. If any part is defective, the whole assembly must be replaced. In some models, the parts can be replaced separately. Directions are given here for testing and replacing a heating element assembly. You can test the element assembly without removing the element from the support plate.

To check the heating element assembly (if the brewing switch is OK), disconnect one lead from the fuse (it's located under the insulating sleeve) and test for continuity; then do the same for the element. If either shows no continuity, replace the whole assembly.

1 To replace the heating element assembly, disconnect the leads, then straighten the ends of the thin metal retaining rod, which runs across the center of the unit and attaches it to the support plate.

2 With pliers, pull the retaining rod from the center until one of the ends is free of the hole in the housing.

3 Lift the heating element out by sliding the other end of the rod from its hole. Insert the new element, bend the ends of the rod to hold it in place, and attach the leads.

Checking element assembly

Lead
Fuse

1 Replacing element assembly

2

3

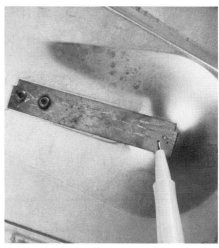

Water flow problems

If you are getting weak coffee, or less coffee than the amount of water you put in, there is something wrong with the drip control. The drip control is a bimetallic bar with a small hole in it, located on the bottom of the water tank. It works the same way as a bimetallic thermostat: when the water is hot enough, the bar bends to let water drip through at the correct rate. Weak coffee results when water drips too fast, and not enough coffee results when the water drips too slowly. The hole can become clogged and requires periodic cleaning. You should also clean the small hole in the bottom of the water tank just above the drip control bar.

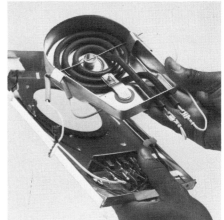

Drip Control Bar

Water tank

Drip control bar

If the drip control bar breaks or is corroded beyond cleaning, or it lets too much water run through, the whole water tank will have to be replaced.

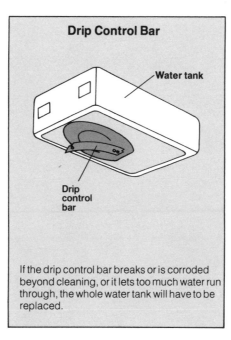

If water is not flowing or is flowing too slowly, check to see that the tiny hole in the center of the metal bar is clear. If it is clogged, clean it out with a thin wire. You may not have to open the unit to see the clogged hole; it should be visible from the top of the coffee maker.

Pump-feed Drip Coffee Maker

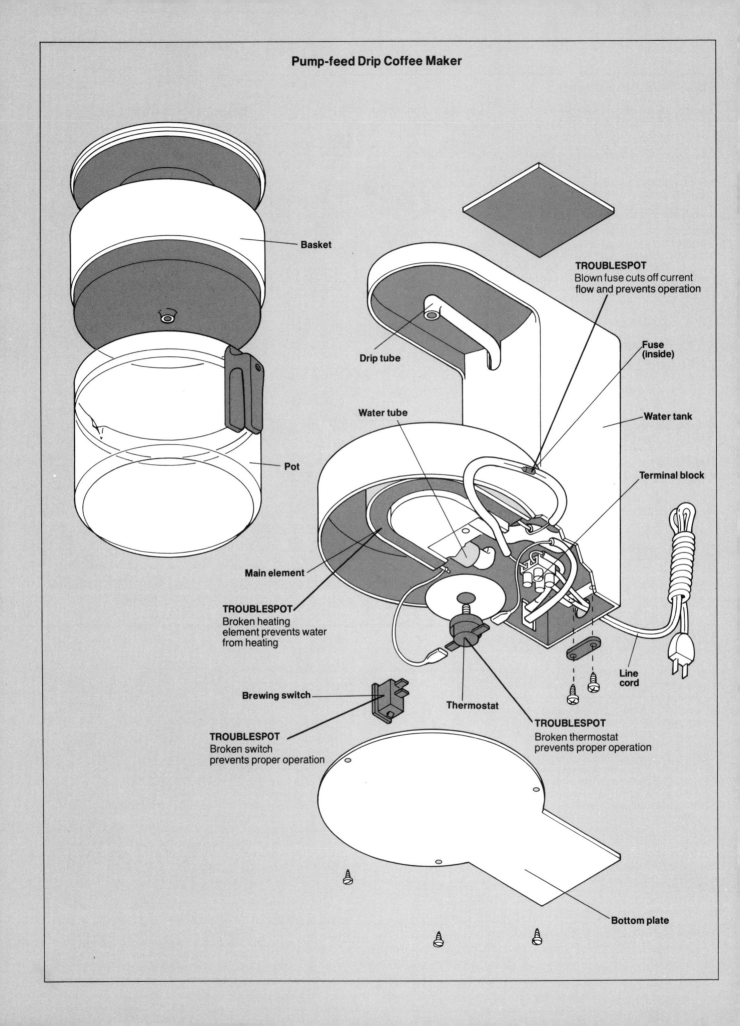

Basket

Drip tube

Water tube

Main element

TROUBLESPOT
Broken heating element prevents water from heating

Pot

Brewing switch

TROUBLESPOT
Broken switch prevents proper operation

Thermostat

TROUBLESPOT
Broken thermostat prevents proper operation

TROUBLESPOT
Blown fuse cuts off current flow and prevents operation

Fuse (inside)

Water tank

Terminal block

Line cord

Bottom plate

COFFEE MAKERS
Pump-feed drip coffee makers

Getting inside

In pump-feed drip coffee makers, heated water is pumped to the top and out over the coffee grounds. The water tank is at the back of the unit, and the warming and heating elements are in the base. To get access to the electrical components and the pump valve, simply remove the bottom plate. The steps for opening the unit and making electrical repairs are demonstrated here on a Krups coffee maker.

CAUTION Do not work on units that are sealed and labeled to be serviced only at the factory.

To open the housing, remove the three screws in the bottom plate with a Phillips screwdriver and lift off the plate.

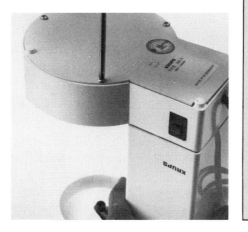

Cleaning the Water Tube

If your coffee has a mineral taste, minerals from the water have accumulated in the water tube. To clean it, remove the thermostat and insulated mica plate, and unscrew the top plate. Scrape out mineral scale.

Electrical problems

Replacing thermostat, switch, or fuse

If the coffee maker doesn't work at all and the cord is OK, the problem could be in the thermostat, the switch, or the fuse. First, test the thermostat for continuity (see Blue Pages: *Electrical testers*). If it needs to be replaced, follow the directions at right. Next, test the switch. Take off the lead to the heating element. Clip one tester probe to the thermostat lead that goes to the switch. Attach the other tester probe to the power lead from the switch at the terminal block. You should get continuity at the ON position. Replace a faulty switch with a duplicate. If the switch is OK, test the fuse. If there is no continuity, replace it, following the directions at right.

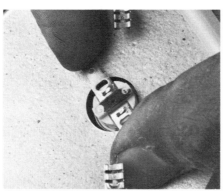

To replace the thermostat, label the leads for identification and remove the thermostat by turning it counterclockwise. Attach the new thermostat by turning it clockwise.

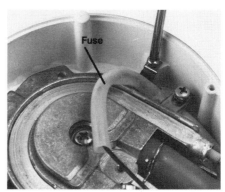

To replace the fuse, take off the thermostat and remove the insulated mica plate underneath. Unscrew the screws holding the fuse leads and install a duplicate.

Replacing the main element

If the coffee maker doesn't work at all and the cord, thermostat, fuse, and switch are OK, the problem is probably in the heating element. Test it for continuity to make sure (see Blue Pages: *Electrical testers*). Disconnect the element leads. Set your VOM at RX1 and place the tester probes on the element terminals. A reading of 20 to 40 ohms is OK. To replace a defective element, remove it from the base, following the directions below.

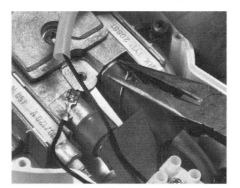

1 To replace the main element, use a pair of pliers to release the clamps that attach it to the water tube. This may require some force, but work carefully. The clamps are bare wires wrapped around the rubber sleeves.

2 Push the rubber sleeves off both ends of the water tube with a pair of pliers.

3 Remove the screws at the sides that hold the element inside the unit and lift it out. Insert the new element, screw it tight, and attach the rubber sleeves, clamps, and leads.

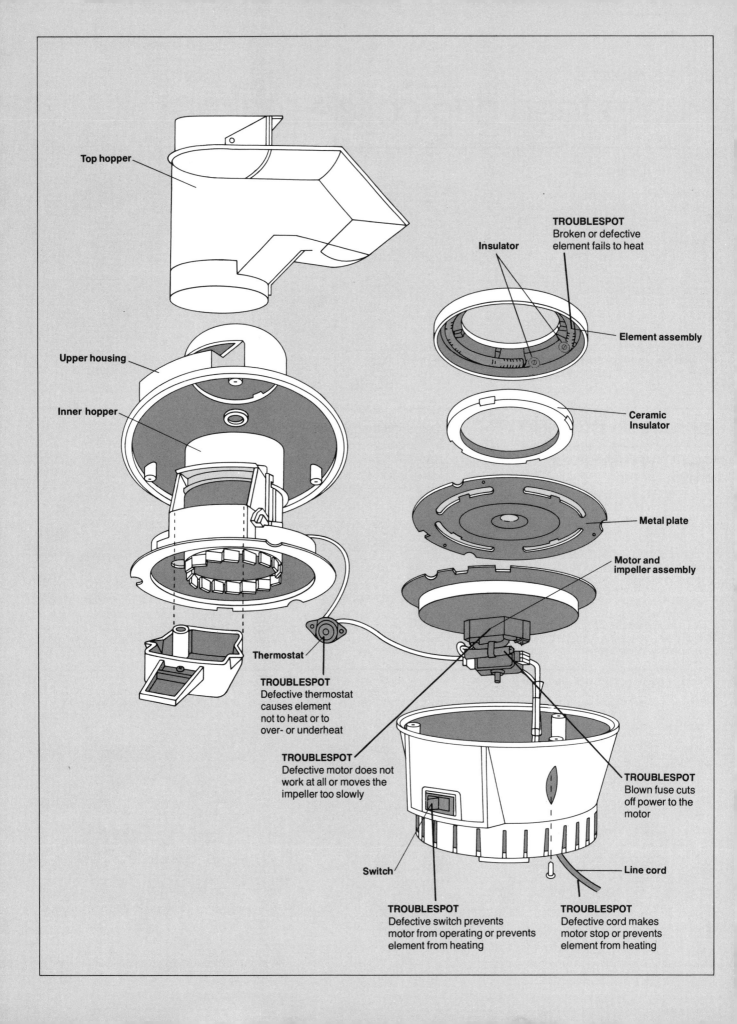

Top hopper

Upper housing

Inner hopper

Thermostat

TROUBLESPOT
Defective thermostat
causes element
not to heat or to
over- or underheat

TROUBLESPOT
Defective motor does not
work at all or moves the
impeller too slowly

Switch

TROUBLESPOT
Defective switch prevents
motor from operating or prevents
element from heating

Insulator

TROUBLESPOT
Broken or defective
element fails to heat

Element assembly

Ceramic
Insulator

Metal plate

Motor and
impeller assembly

TROUBLESPOT
Blown fuse cuts
off power to the
motor

Line cord

TROUBLESPOT
Defective cord makes
motor stop or prevents
element from heating

Corn Poppers

Corn poppers work simply: hot air is supplied by a heating element and blown by a motor-driven fan (the impeller) into the hopper, which contains the popcorn. Most models are equipped with an on/off switch or a thermostat, or both, to regulate the heat level and cooking time. If your popper burns the corn, takes too long, or turns off before the corn has popped, most probably the thermostat is at fault; it must be replaced. Other problems are more difficult to diagnose.

If the unit is completely dead—that is, if neither the element nor the motor works—you will have to perform a series of continuity checks to locate the problem (see Blue Pages: *Electrical testers*).

If the motor and impeller work (you can hear this), but the element doesn't heat up, check for loose element connections; then check the element for continuity. If the element glows and you cannot hear the impeller rotating, the problem is probably in the motor. Although the motor can be replaced, the price of a new motor may be almost equal to the price of a new corn popper.

Problems with the cord, switch, fuse, element, and the thermostat usually can be fixed, either by repair or replacement. The steps to be followed are demonstrated on three late-model corn poppers: the Wear-Ever, the Presto, and the Hamilton Beach.

Getting inside

To open up the three types of corn popper shown here, separate the base from the top housing by removing the screws. With the popper disassembled, you can inspect and test the cord, and the switch, fuse, and thermostat, if your model has any of these. If the problem is in the impeller, the motor, or the heating element, you may have to disassemble the unit further.

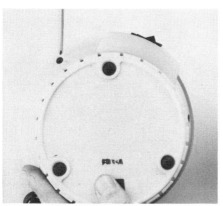

1 **To get inside the Wear-Ever,** turn the machine upside down and remove the three Phillips screws on the upper sides of the base. This will free the top housing.

2 Return the popper to an upright position. Lift off the top housing in order to expose the inner hopper.

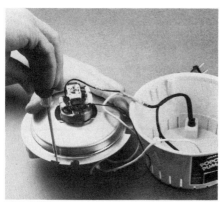

3 Remove the two side pieces that hold the inner hopper in place. (Note the position of these pieces for later reassembly.) Lift out the inner hopper.

4 Pull out housing containing the motor and element assembly from the base, exposing the cord and switch connections.

5 Remove the three screws on the operating unit that hold it together. The operating assembly consists of motor, impeller, and heating element.

Getting inside

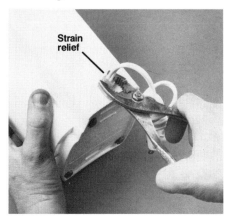

1 **To get inside the Presto,** grasp the cord with a pair of pliers. Pinch the strain relief tightly and pull out.

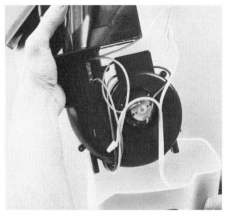

2 Remove the two Phillips screws from the base plate and then pull out the operating unit as shown. You now have access to the cord connections.

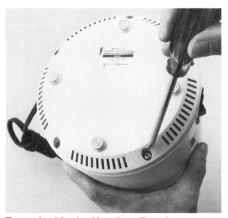

To get inside the Hamilton Beach, remove the five Phillips screws on the base plate and take it off. You now have access to the cord, switch, and fuse.

Electrical problems

Checking the cord and switch

If your corn popper does not work at all, first check the cord for continuity. If it passes the test, examine the switch (if your unit has one) and check it for continuity (see Blue Pages: *Electrical testers*). If either switch or cord fails the continuity test, replace it with a duplicate.

If the element on your corn popper heats up but the impeller does not work, the problem is in the motor. On the Presto, however, which has a DC motor, the problem may be in the rectifier.

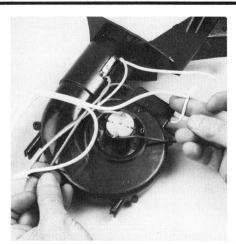

To check the Presto cord (there is no switch), disconnect the cord leads and test the cord for continuity. If the cord is bad, replace it.

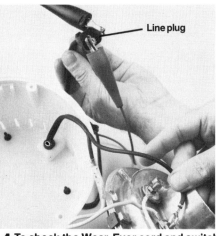

1 **To check the Wear-Ever cord and switch,** disconnect the cord's push-on leads from the switch and test the cord for continuity. If the cord shows no continuity, replace it.

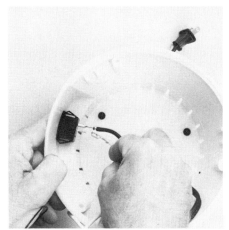

2 If the cord is OK, check the switch for continuity. Leave one cord lead disconnected and attach VOM probes to the switch's terminals. If the switch is faulty, replace it with a duplicate.

1 **To check the Hamilton Beach cord,** disconnect a lead and make a continuity test. If there is no continuity, replace the cord with a duplicate.

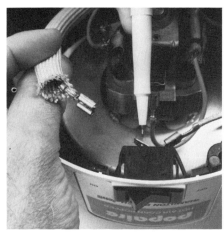

2 If the cord is OK, test the switch for continuity. If it is defective, replace it. Using a screwdriver, push in on the switch retaining clips and push out of the housing.

Checking the fuse

If both the cord and the switch have checked out OK, or if you have replaced those parts and the unit still doesn't work, the trouble may be with the fuse. Your next step depends on the make of your popper. On the Presto the fuse is part of the element assembly, and you will have to replace the element assembly if the fuse has blown. On some Hamilton Beach models (such as the one shown on this page), the fuse is replaceable; on others it may be part of the heating element, which can be replaced.

1 To check the fuse on the Presto model shown here, remove the Phillips screw from the bottom of the housing that covers the motor.

2 Remove the two screws from either side of the top of the housing. They are recessed and difficult to get at.

3 Remove the screws from the top of the housing. The housing will now come apart and you can pull out the sleeve containing the heating element.

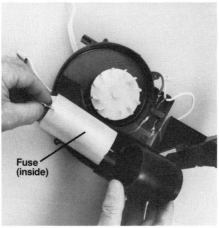

Fuse (inside)

4 Pull the element out of its sleeve and look for a blown fuse (it may have melted completely). If the fuse is blown, replace the heating element.

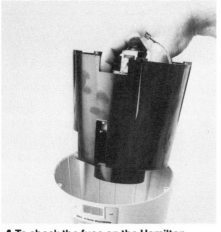

1 To check the fuse on the Hamilton Beach, first remove the strain relief that holds the cord in place and remove the cord; next remove the switch. Pull out the inner housing that contains the operating assembly.

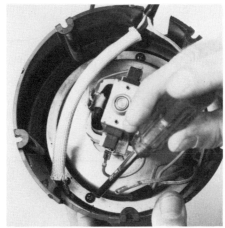

2 Remove the three screws and nuts that attach the operating assembly to the inner housing.

3 Pull the motor/element assembly out of the inner housing. This will expose the motor fuse and the thermostat.

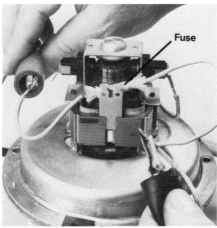

Fuse

4 Take the fuse out of the bracket that secures it. Test it for continuity if it is not obviously blown (see Blue Pages: *Electrical testers*). Replace the fuse if defective.

Checking the thermostat

If, after these checks, the unit still does not work at all, owners of Wear-Ever and Hamilton Beach poppers should next check the thermostat for continuity, and replace it if it is defective. (A defective thermostat is also the cause of over- or undercooking.)

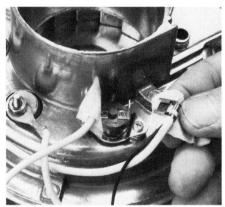

1 **To test the thermostat for continuity,** take off the wires at the thermostat that lead from the heating element contacts. These leads and their protective coverings slip off the terminals easily.

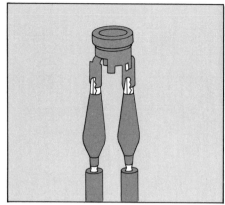

2 Place VOM clips on the thermostat terminals and test for continuity. If there is none, replace the thermostat. Remember, however, that a thermostat that is over- or underheating will pass the continuity test. If your unit is burning the corn or not heating it enough to make it pop, replace the thermostat in any case.

Checking the element

If the cord, switch, fuse, and thermostat are all OK, but the corn popper doesn't heat, the element is probably defective. First, inspect it for any breaks. If a break is close to a terminal—that is, not more than a coil or two away—cut away the broken part, straighten out a few loops of the element, and rejoin the wire to the terminal (see Appliance Repair Basics, *Types of heating elements*). If the break in the wire is farther away from the terminal than this, you must replace the element. Always clean the terminals before installing a new or repaired element, since the buildup of dirt may have caused the problem in the first place and it impairs current flow.

CAUTION When you replace the heating element on either the Hamilton Beach or the Wearever, be sure to reinstall the silicon rubber insulators on both sides of the heating element terminals.

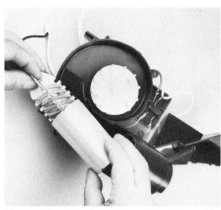

To examine the element on a Presto, pull it out of the sleeve that holds it. (There are no screws. The element is held in place by the frame it is wound on.)

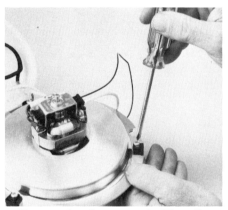

1 **To get at the element on the Wear-Ever,** remove the Phillips screws that hold the metal housing together around the element and motor assembly. Open the housing.

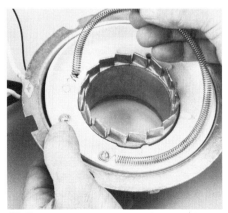

2 Remove the metal plate and ceramic insulators from the element, which is a spiral type. Inspect and test it, and repair or replace it.

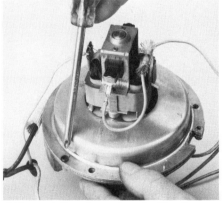

1 **To reach the element on the Hamilton Beach,** unscrew the three Phillips screws that hold the housing together. Take the housing apart.

2 Remove the metal plate, and then the circular ceramic protector that covers the element. (Like the Wear-Ever element, it is a spiral type.) Repair a broken element if possible, or replace the element assembly.

Electric Knives

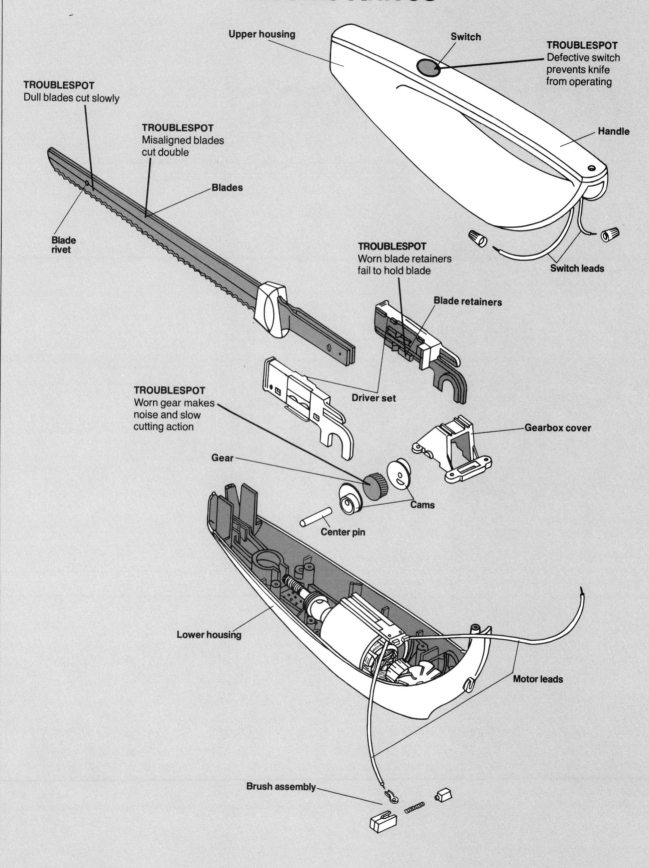

Upper housing

Switch

TROUBLESPOT
Defective switch prevents knife from operating

Handle

TROUBLESPOT
Dull blades cut slowly

TROUBLESPOT
Misaligned blades cut double

Blades

Blade rivet

TROUBLESPOT
Worn blade retainers fail to hold blade

Switch leads

Blade retainers

Driver set

TROUBLESPOT
Worn gear makes noise and slow cutting action

Gearbox cover

Gear

Cams

Center pin

Lower housing

Motor leads

Brush assembly

Electric Knives

Electric knives have two serrated blades that lie flat against each other and cut with a double sawing action. This sawing action is produced by a small motor driving a gear train that rotates two cams; the cams push one blade forward while pulling the other back, then pull the first blade back while pushing the other forward. An electric knife need only be guided; it should not be forced down or pulled back and forth to assist cutting. Forcing the knife will cause the blades to separate slightly and cut double.

Most problems with electric knives can be repaired, but when the blades become dull or damaged they must always be replaced.

CAUTION Always unplug the knife before removing or inserting the blades.

Getting inside

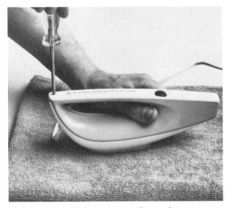

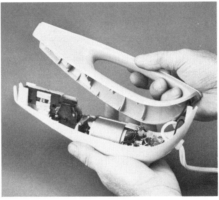

1 Remove all the screws from the upper and lower housing of the knife. Some models have two screws on the lower housing and one on the upper housing; others have only screws on the lower housing.

2 The upper and lower housings separate easily when the screws are removed.

BLADE MAINTENANCE

Before using the knife, be sure that the blade tips are fastened by the blade rivet, and that they are securely latched in the knife.

After removing the blades for washing, slide them apart at the tip; never pull them apart, or the blade rivet may snap off.

Wash and dry the blades as you would any knife. Apply a little vegetable oil to the blades when dry so they will work together easily.

CAUTION The blades are not meant to cut frozen food or bones. Cutting such hard substances will distort and dull the blades.

Electrical problems

If the knife fails to operate when switched on, there is a problem with either the cord, the switch, or the motor.

To identify the fault on models like the Hamilton Beach shown here, open the knife and remove the wire nuts from the switch leads. Test both the switch and the cord for continuity (see Blue Pages: *Electrical testers*). If the cord is defective, replace it. If the switch is defective, replace the entire upper housing. NOTE: You have nothing to lose by trying to pry the nameplate off the handle to gain access to the switch for replacement, although you may break it in the process. Use glue to reassemble the switch handle.

In models with a two-speed switch, the switch can be removed and replaced as a separate unit.

If both the cord and the switch are in working order, but the motor still does not operate, the problem lies in the motor, for which no repairs other than replacing the brushes are practical.

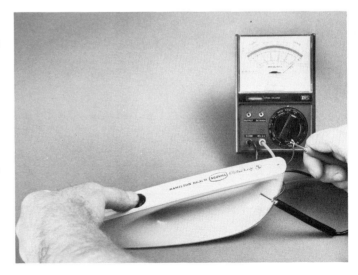

Securing loose blades

The blades are held in the knife by two small metal retainers in the driver set. When the retainers are worn, the blades will not snap securely into place and cutting action is slowed; when the retainers break down completely the knife will fail to hold the blades at all. The blade retainers are replaced by installing a new driver set.

Different models have slightly different mechanical configurations, but the basic parts are the same and all can be repaired by adapting the steps shown here for working on the Hamilton Beach.

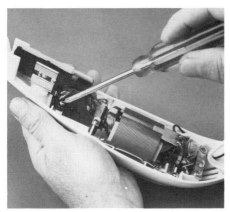

1 **To inspect and replace the blade retainers,** remove the four screws from the driver set mount.

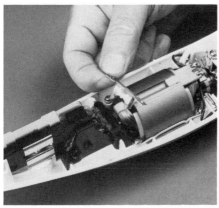

2 Remove the metal clip at the back of the gearbox cover. The assembly can be lifted from the housing without removing the clip, but setting it aside first leaves one less part to juggle when disassembling the driver set.

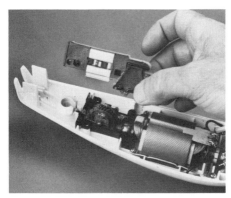

3 Lift the driver set and gearbox cover from the lower housing. If you dislodge the main gear from the housing when you lift the cover, simply set it back in.

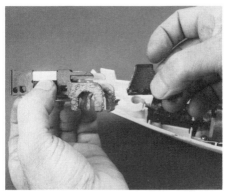

4 Pull the driver set from the gearbox cover and set the cover aside. Separate the two parts of the driver set.

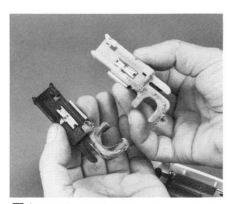

5 Inspect the metal retainer on each half of the driver set for breaks or excessive wear. If you find damage on either one, replace the driver set.

Replacing the main gear

Excessive rattling from inside the knife is an indication that the main gear is breaking down. As the gear deteriorates, cutting action will slow down; when it fails completely, the blades will stop moving.

The main gear is an assembly of four parts: the gear itself, a cam on either side, and a pin through the center holding the unit together. When the gear must be replaced, remove the pin from the old one and save it: a new gear will come with new cams, but not a new pin.

To gain access to the main gear follow the first three steps for *Securing loose blades*, above.

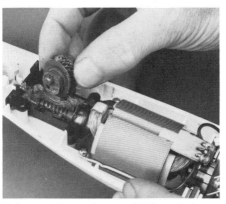

To inspect the main gear, lift it from the housing, wipe off the lubricant, and look for wear or damage. If the gear is damaged, remove the center pin and set it aside for use in the replacement. Order a new gear and cam set.

To replace the gear, push the pin through the center and seat the cams on either end. Lubricate the gear lightly with petroleum jelly and set it back in the housing.

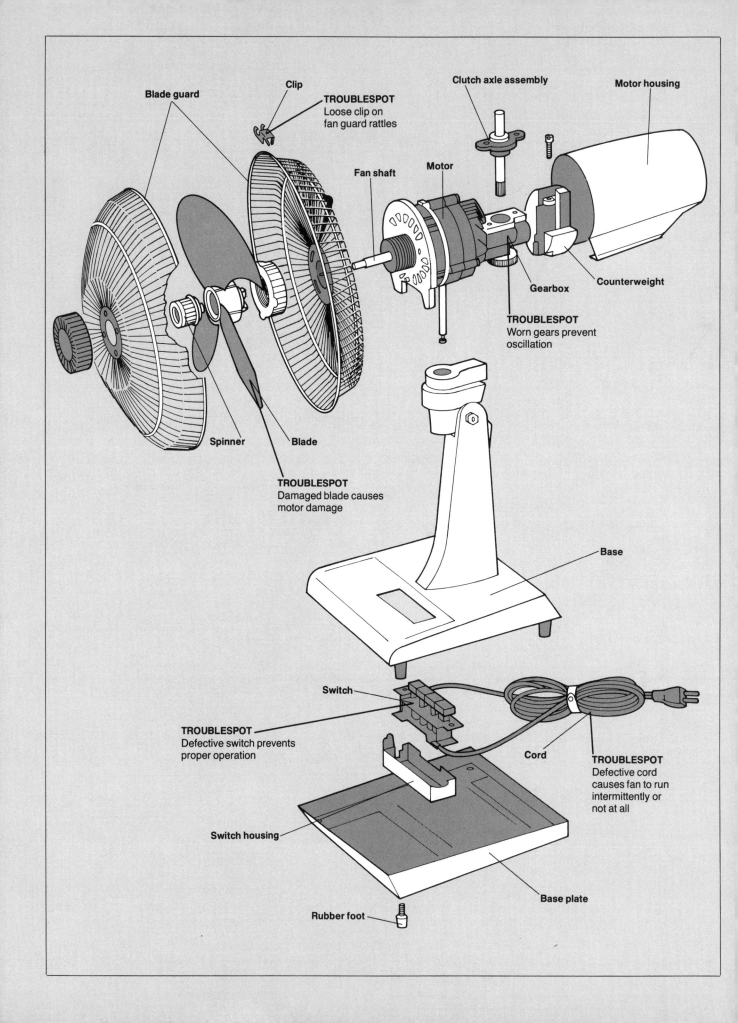

Blade guard

Clip

TROUBLESPOT
Loose clip on
fan guard rattles

Clutch axle assembly

Motor housing

Fan shaft

Motor

Gearbox

Counterweight

TROUBLESPOT
Worn gears prevent
oscillation

Spinner

Blade

TROUBLESPOT
Damaged blade causes
motor damage

Base

Switch

TROUBLESPOT
Defective switch prevents
proper operation

Cord

TROUBLESPOT
Defective cord
causes fan to run
intermittently or
not at all

Switch housing

Base plate

Rubber foot

Fans

Electric fans produce drafts of air that speed the evaporation of moisture on your skin, thereby cooling you. They do not reduce humidity as air conditioners do, but they are much less expensive to run. Three types of fans are covered here: oscillating fans, box fans, and personal fans. Oscillating fans are mounted on pedestals and can be set to swivel to and fro, producing a swirl of cooling air. Box fans remain stationary and are usually set in a window to draw cooler outdoor air into a stuffy room. Personal fans are tabletop fans that produce a mild short-range draft.

Whichever model you have, you should follow the same basic maintenance procedures to keep it in good condition. The blades and grille should be kept clean of any dust buildup. You can vacuum them or clean them with soap and water. Always unplug a fan before cleaning it; if you use water, dry the appliance thoroughly afterward. Whether or not to oil a fan depends on the model: some manufacturers recommend a drop of light machine oil on the motor shaft once a season, others suggest no oil at all. Be sure to follow the manufacturer's instructions provided with your model.

Fans should run almost silently. If a fan is noisy, you may be able to correct the problem without opening it up (see below for oscillating fans and page 188 for box fans). To solve other problems, however, you will have to open the housing. Steps for electrical and mechanical repairs are demonstrated here on Edison, Lasko, and Panasonic oscillating fans, and on the Edison box fan. Repairing small personal fans is demonstrated on the Salton.

> **CAUTION** When you open up an oscillating fan's housing, the first thing you should do is discharge the capacitor (if the fan has one) to avoid shock (see page 187).

Oscillating fans

External adjustments

Noises such as clattering or rattling can often be corrected by tightening loose screws around the blade guard or by bending the clasps on the guard so that they grip more tightly. A loose decal is another possible noisemaker; simply glue it back in place. A damaged blade is a more serious source of noise: Never try to repair a metal or plastic blade that is bent, chipped, or warped. Unless the blades are perfectly balanced, the motor of your fan can burn out. Instead, replace a damaged blade.

CAUTION Always unplug the unit before making any external adjustments.

To gain access to the blades (for cleaning or removal), first pry open the clips that hold the two halves of the blade guard together. Remove the front half.

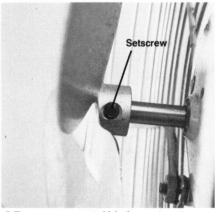

1 **To remove a metal blade,** such as the one on the Edison oscillating fan shown here, locate the setscrew in the hub of the blade, which fastens it to the motor shaft.

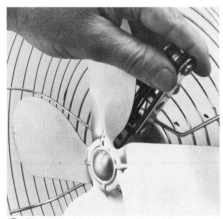

2 Reach past the blades with an Allen wrench and loosen the setscrew. (You may have to try different wrench sizes until you find one that fits properly.) Remove the damaged blade.

3 When you put in a new blade, be sure to position it so that the setscrew is seated against the flat part of the motor shaft.

To replace damaged plastic blades, unscrew the plastic fastener, called the spinner, that holds the blades to the motor shaft. If it won't unscrew, use multiple-joint pliers to force it off. Put on a new spinner with the new blades.

Testing and replacing the cord and switch

If your fan doesn't work at all or operates only in fits and starts, it may have a defective cord or switch. To test or replace the cord and switch, you must get into the fan-motor housing (Edison) or the base (Lasko and Panasonic). Test the cord for continuity and replace it if it is defective. If it is OK, test the switch (see Blue Pages: *Electrical testers*). To test a multiple-position switch (Lasko, Panasonic), place one tester probe on the single cord terminal. Depress one of the ON positions and place the second tester probe on the corresponding switch terminal. Test each switch position this way. If you don't get continuity each time, replace the switch. If you do get continuity at each setting, the problem may be in the motor (see Appliance Repair Basics: *How to Test a Universal Motor*).

1 To test and replace the Edison cord and switch, first remove the Phillips screws on both sides of the fan-motor housing that hold the front and rear of the housing together. Remove the rear housing; the switch is attached to it.

2 Cut the leads at the crimp-on connectors and test the cord and switch for continuity. If the cord doesn't show continuity, connect the new leads with wire nuts. If the switch is defective, unscrew the nut and remove the switch. Connect the new switch leads with wire nuts.

1 To test and replace the Panasonic cord and switch, turn the fan on its side and remove the four screws inside the rubber feet. This frees the base so you can remove it.

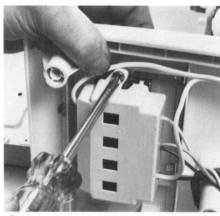

2 Take out the two screws that secure the switch housing to the upper part of the base.

3 Pull off the switch housing and then pull the switch out. You can now test the switch and cord for continuity and replace them if need be.

1 To test and replace the Lasko cord and switch, remove the four screws that attach the base plate to the base. This also loosens the switch housing, which is held by two of the screws. (The two slotted holes are for mounting the fan on a wall.)

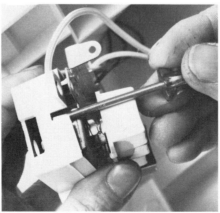

2 Pry open the switch housing with a screwdriver. You can now test the switch and the cord and replace them if necessary.

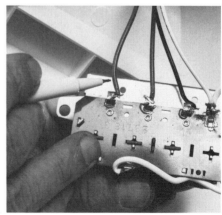

3 To put in a new switch, first cut the wires off the old switch, leaving a little wire attached for a color code. Then solder the wires to the new switch, following the same color coding as on the old switch.

Checking the Panasonic and Lasko gears

If your fan does not swivel back and forth at all or does so only in jerks, one or more of the gears may be stripped. One way to check it is to turn off the fan, set the oscillator control at ON, and try to swivel the fan by hand. It shouldn't move. If it moves, a gear may be stripped. To inspect the gears, you must open the motor housing. On some fans, if a gear is stripped you must replace the whole motor assembly. On others, individual gears can be replaced. Check with your repair shop or the manufacturer.

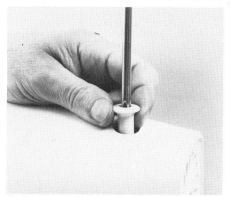

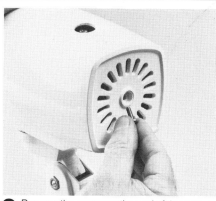

1 To remove the Panasonic or Lasko motor housing, first remove the oscillating control button. On the Panasonic (shown here) it is screwed on; on the Lasko, you can just pull it off.

2 Remove the screw on the end of the motor housing and take the housing off.

1 To gain access to the Panasonic gears, (right), remove the screw that secures the counterweight to the rear of the motor mount and take off the counterweight.

2 Remove the remaining screw from the gearbox cover. Lift out the clutch axle assembly and inspect its teeth for wear. Take out the round plastic gear (far right). Check the worm gear on the motor shaft. If this part is worn or damaged, take the fan to a repair shop.

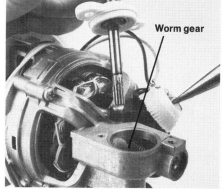

Worm gear

1 To gain access to the Lasko gear assembly, first remove the two screws (right) that secure the gearbox cover (which holds the clutch axle).

2 Remove the clutch axle assembly. Two ball bearings and a spring, which hold the axle in the correct position, will come out of the gearbox with the axle (far right). Examine the clutch axle, the round gear, and the worm gear for damage. If any part is worn or broken, you must replace the whole gear assembly.

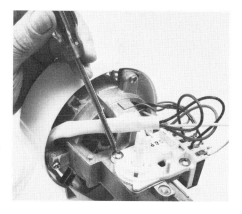

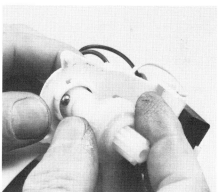

Discharging and Testing the Capacitor

The capacitor stores electricity so it can give a short surge of power when the fan is turned on. To avoid electric shock, you must discharge the capacitor as soon as you have removed the motor housing. A defective capacitor will prevent the fan from turning, although the motor may hum.

To discharge the capacitor, see the instructions on page 42. Test the capacitor with a VOM set at RX1 (see Blue Pages: *Electrical testers*). Disconnect one lead to the capacitor and touch the meter probes to the capacitor terminals. If the needle jumps to HIGH and then returns to 0, the capacitor is OK. If the needle holds at HIGH or does not move, the capacitor is bad. If your capacitor has three terminals, test the terminal at each side with the central terminal.

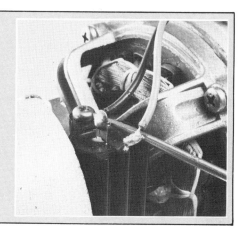

Checking the Edison gears

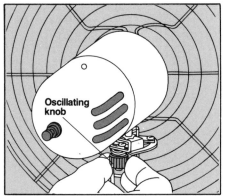

1 To correct faulty oscillation on a fan, make sure the oscillation mechanism is functioning properly. Tighten the oscillation knob if it is loose. Check the oscillating locking screw, by removing the oscillating knob and swinging away the oscillating arm attached to the neck of the fan.

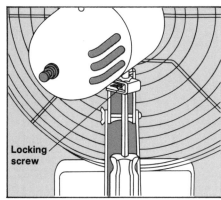

2 Tighten the oscillating locking screw; it protrudes from the bottom of the gearbox. If this doesn't solve the problem, check the gears. Remove the motor housing (see *Testing and replacing the cord and switch,* page 186, and *Checking the Panasonic and Lasko gears,* page 187).

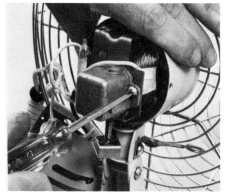

3 Unscrew the two Phillips screws that attach the gearbox to the motor mount. Remove gearbox.

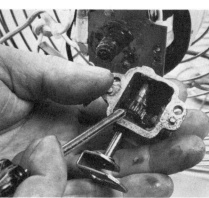

4 Examine the teeth of the round gear for damage, and check the motor shaft, which works as a worm gear. If the round gear is worn or broken, replace the gear and gearbox as an assembly. If the worm gear is damaged, take the fan to a repair shop.

Cutoff fuse

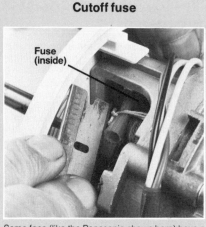

Some fans (like the Panasonic shown here) have a cutoff fuse to cut off current if the motor overloads, thus protecting it from burning out. If the motor doesn't run and the switch and cord are OK, check the cutoff fuse. On the Panasonic it is located in a fiberglass sleeve next to the field coil. Cut the tie holding the sleeve and pull out the sleeve and fuse.

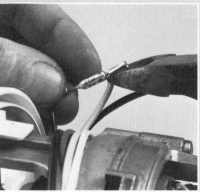

Push the sleeve away and, if the fuse isn't obviously damaged, test it for continuity by first removing the lead on one side and then touching tester probes to the two leads (see Blue Pages: *Electrical testers*). If the fuse is defective, install a new one with solder or crimp-on connectors. First, however, remedy the cause of the motor overload—for example, jammed gears or a damaged blade.

Box fans

Box fans are more simply constructed than oscillating fans, since they do not have the oscillating gear mechanism. Problems with the cord and switch can be easily fixed at home. If your fan doesn't run and the line cord and switch are OK, either replace the motor or purchase a new fan, whichever is less expensive.

Box fans are somewhat more susceptible than oscillating fans to developing rattling noises. Try tightening the screws that secure the grille to the housing, and gluing or taping down loose decals. If a damaged or warped blade is causing the noise, do not attempt to repair it. Instead, replace it as shown here.

Steps for repairing a cord or switch and replacing the blades are demonstrated on an Edison 20-inch fan.

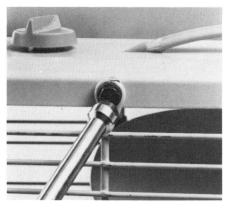

1 To remove a damaged fan blade, first unscrew the hex nuts that secure the grille to the housing. (On some makes, the grille is held by spring clasps and can be pulled off.)

2 With plastic blades, you may have to cut the blade unit off the motor shaft. With metal blades, remove the decal (above), unscrew the setscrew. If there is no screw, pull the blades off.

Replacing the switch and cord

If your box fan doesn't run at all, first unplug it and remove the grille and check for any loose connections in the switch. Then test the cord for continuity (see Blue Pages: *Electrical testers*) and replace it if it is defective. If the fan runs irregularly, test the switch. On some fans you must remove the switch housing to check for loose connections and test the cord and switch. Test for ground after completing any repair (see Blue Pages: *Testing for Ground*).

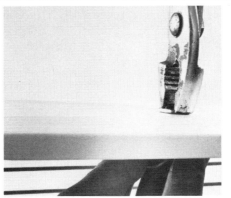

1 To test and replace an Edison switch, first lift off the fan-control knob. Unscrew the locking nut that holds the switch to the top of the housing. Pull out the switch.

2 Before replacing a defective switch, label the leads for later identification. If the switch has spring-loaded terminals, free the leads by inserting a paper clip and depressing the spring. To remove a defective cord, use pliers to squeeze out the strain relief. Remove the cord leads from the switch and put in a new cord.

Personal fans

Small fans, such as the Salton personal fan shown here, are designed to provide a breeze over a small area. A personal fan requires little maintenance: unplug it, and clean off dust with a small, soft, dry brush. If the fan doesn't run, open it up as shown at right, and check for loose leads. Then test the cord and the switch for continuity (See Blue Pages: *Electrical Testers*). Repairs on cord, switch, and blades can be done at home, as described here. If your fan has a defective motor, it probably would be less expensive to buy a new fan.

1 To get inside a Salton personal fan, first remove the two screws from the front of the motor mount. Then remove the screws from the angled stand and take it off.

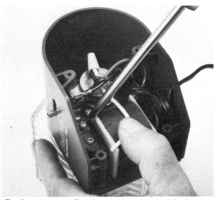

2 Remove the Phillips screw that holds the switch assembly in the motor housing. motor housing wide enough to lift it out of the motor housing.

3 Spread the sides of the motor housing wide enough to lift the switch assembly out. You can now test the cord and switch for continuity. To replace a defective cord or switch, label the leads so you can connect them correctly later. Disconnect them, remove the defective part, and install a duplicate.

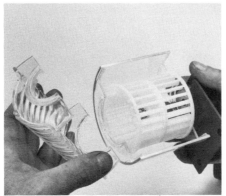

1 To replace a damaged blade, first remove the hood; it consists of two guards, one vented and one solid. Pull them free one at a time by twisting them off carefully. You can now inspect and replace the blades.

2 The blade on the Salton fan has two parts. Remove the front half first, by taking off the clip that secures the hub to the motor shaft. Remove the other half by pulling the clip from the hub. The two halves of the blade are not identical. If you are replacing only one, be sure you order the correct part.

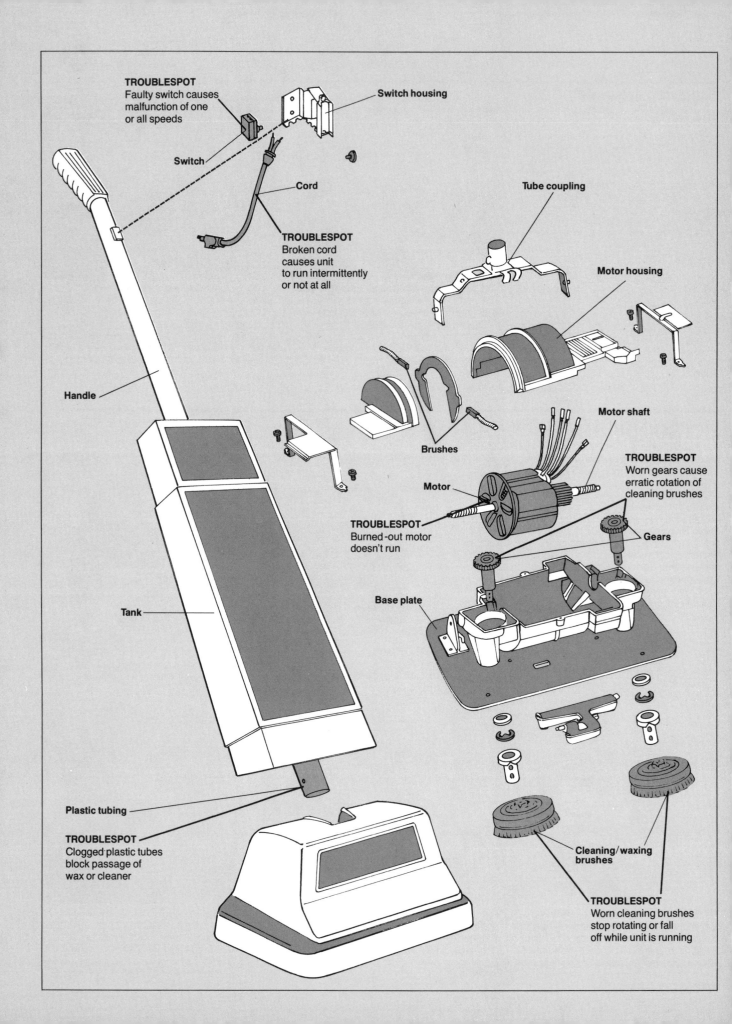

TROUBLESPOT
Faulty switch causes malfunction of one or all speeds

Switch housing

Switch

Cord

TROUBLESPOT
Broken cord causes unit to run intermittently or not at all

Tube coupling

Motor housing

Handle

Brushes

Motor shaft

TROUBLESPOT
Worn gears cause erratic rotation of cleaning brushes

Motor

TROUBLESPOT
Burned-out motor doesn't run

Gears

Base plate

Tank

Plastic tubing

TROUBLESPOT
Clogged plastic tubes block passage of wax or cleaner

Cleaning/waxing brushes

TROUBLESPOT
Worn cleaning brushes stop rotating or fall off while unit is running

Floor Polishers

Floor polishers look like upright vacuum cleaners, but the resemblance is superficial. Mechanically, the machine is more like a food mixer: a similar gear system drives two rotary brushes in opposing directions (see also Mixers: *Problems with the gears,* page 238). Floor polishers also can shampoo rugs. A tank attached to the handle holds the polish or shampoo, whioh the operator dispenses by moving a lever. The rotary brushes on the machine's base spread the liquid, while buffing and beating the floor or rug.

If your polisher isn't working, the most likely cause is a defective cord or on/off switch (see below). The cause could also be worn-out motor brushes. These can be inspected and replaced; get at the motor by following the steps for *Getting inside*. Polishing brushes (the ones that actually do the cleaning) should be snapped securely on their drive shafts. Worn-out polishing brushes must be replaced. You can check the cord and switch, and re-

place brushes without opening the housing. If your problem is with the gears or motor, you will have to get inside the appliance (next page).

	MAINTENANCE

It is important to keep your floor polisher clean. After every use, empty out any unused wax or shampoo from the tank. This will prevent the dispensing tubes between the tank and the base plate from getting clogged.

If the tubes do get clogged, empty the tank and refill it with hot water; the buildup will loosen and flow out.

At regular intervals, you also should detach the brushes and remove any dirt and debris from the shafts.

Cord and switch problems

If your polisher doesn't run at all, you may have a problem with either the cord or the switch; if it runs at only one or two of the multiple speed settings, you have a problem with the switch. To check the cord and switch, remove the switch from the handle of the polisher and open it up (below).

After opening the motor switch, check for loose connections. If all the leads are secure, detach one of the cord leads and test the cord for continuity (see Blue Pages: *Electrical testers*). Directions are given for

replacing a defective cord. If the cord is OK, test the switch for continuity by placing one probe of the VOM in the cord-lead terminal and the other in one of the other terminals. Try all positions of the switch except OFF; you should get continuity at one of the switch positons. Make the same test for the other terminals one at a time. If the switch doesn't show continuity in any one of the positions, it is defective and should be replaced.

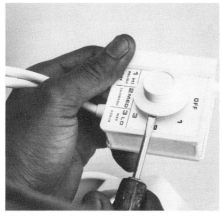

1 To test and replace either the cord or switch, first undo the screw that attaches the switch to the handle. Use a screwdriver to pry gently all around the switch knob until you can pull it off.

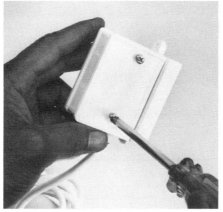

2 Remove the two Phillips screws from the bottom of the switch housing. Take off the housing cover and pull out the switch. Detach the cord leads; you can now inspect and test the cord and switch. If the switch proves defective, replace it with a duplicate.

3 If the cord is defective, replace it. One cord lead is fastened by a wire nut; the other is held inside the switch by a jawed clamp.
As shown here, a small nail is useful for opening the clamp and pulling out this lead.

Getting inside

If you have a problem with the motor or gears, you will have to remove the motor housing to make any repairs. The motor shaft has a worm gear on either end, driving two vertically set gears, one on either side of the motor. They in turn are attached to the shafts to which the brushes are fixed.

1 To remove the motor housing, first lift the handle and the tank off the base. Then remove the switch (see previous page). Using a nut driver or socket wrench, remove the two hex screws that fasten the tank support to the base.

2 Tip the base upward for easy access and pull off the brush heads. Remove the four hex screws that attach the outer housing to the base plate. Put the appliance back in its normal upright position.

3 At this stage, the tube coupling alone holds the tank support to the base. Using a screwdriver, maneuver the coupling back and forth until you can pull it out. This will release the tank support.

4 Lift off the tank support and work the tube coupling down through the upper housing of the base. When the coupling is completely through, lift off the housing. Then, as shown, remove the screws on the motor housing to get to the motor.

1 Removing the motor housing

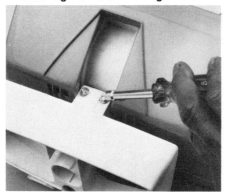

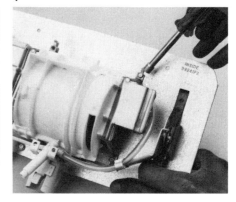

Gear and motor replacement

If the polisher doesn't run and you've checked the cord and switch, examine the two leads attached to the motor for loose connections. Then test the motor for continuity (see Blue Pages: *Electrical testers* and Appliance Repair Basics: *Preventing motor breakdowns*). A burned-out motor can be replaced, but you should check the cost.

If the polishing brushes are in good condition and are securely snapped in place but still do not turn properly, the gears may be at fault. Inspect them for damage. Worn or defective vertical gears alone are not expensive to replace. Often, however, there is corresponding damage to the worm gear. When this has happened, you will have to put in a new motor assembly or replace the entire machine.

1 To replace either of the vertical gears, turn the base upside down. You will see a plastic cap covering the end of the gear shaft and a metal pin running through the shaft at right angles. First, push the pin out using pliers.

2 After removing the pin, you will see a plastic sleeve lining the empty pin slot. Pull it out.

3 There is a spring-loaded ball within the gear shaft that locks the plastic cap in place. Push in on the ball with a screwdriver, and then pull off the cap.

4 Place the unit on its side and pull the base plate away from the motor assembly. Remove the C-clip from the vertical gear shaft behind the plate. Next, push the entire gear through the motor housing. Install a new gear.

1 Replacing vertical gears

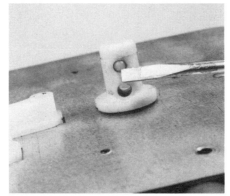

Working with Rivets

Rivets are frequently used in appliances to fasten together various electrical components or sheet metal assemblies. Generally any component that has been riveted in place is designed to have a long service life, but such components do sometimes fail and require replacement. The following sequence of steps shows how to remove rivets and how to replace them with either nuts and screws or with new rivets.

1 **To remove a rivet,** use a ⅛-inch drill bit to drill the rivet out of the face of the component (right). Take special care not to damage any internal parts when the drill bit goes through the rivet.

2 Lift away the riveted component (far right), labeling and disconnecting any leads. Use a small brush or vacuum cleaner to remove any metal shavings that may have fallen into the appliance as you drilled out the rivet.

Using screws to replace rivets

Once the rivets have been drilled out and the replacement part is ready for installation, you can use a nut, lockwasher, and screw instead of a rivet to make the attachment. You will, of course, have to find a screw that fits the rivet hole (generally you can use a No. 4 machine screw). Always use a lockwasher with the screw and nut when replacing a rivet so that when the appliance is in operation, vibration does not shake the nut loose.

1 **To replace a rivet with a screw,** insert the screw through the rivet hole, install a lockwasher and nut on the other side, and tighten the screw.

2 The finished job, with screws replacing rivets, will look like this.

Using a pop-rivet gun

Instead of nuts and screws, you can use a pop-rivet gun to fix new rivets when you remove old ones. A pop-rivet gun is a tool that holds a replacement rivet, and compresses it so that its head flattens out and makes a secure fastening.

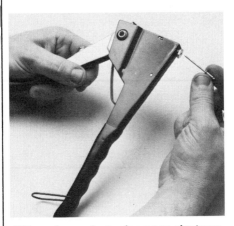  

1 **To replace a rivet using a pop-rivet gun,** insert a new rivet by its shank into the rivet gun, then insert the rivet's head into the hole from which the old rivet was removed.

2 Hold the pop-rivet gun flat against the component to be fastened and squeeze the handles of the gun until the rivet head flattens and the shank breaks free of its rivet.

3 The finished job, with new rivets, will look like this.

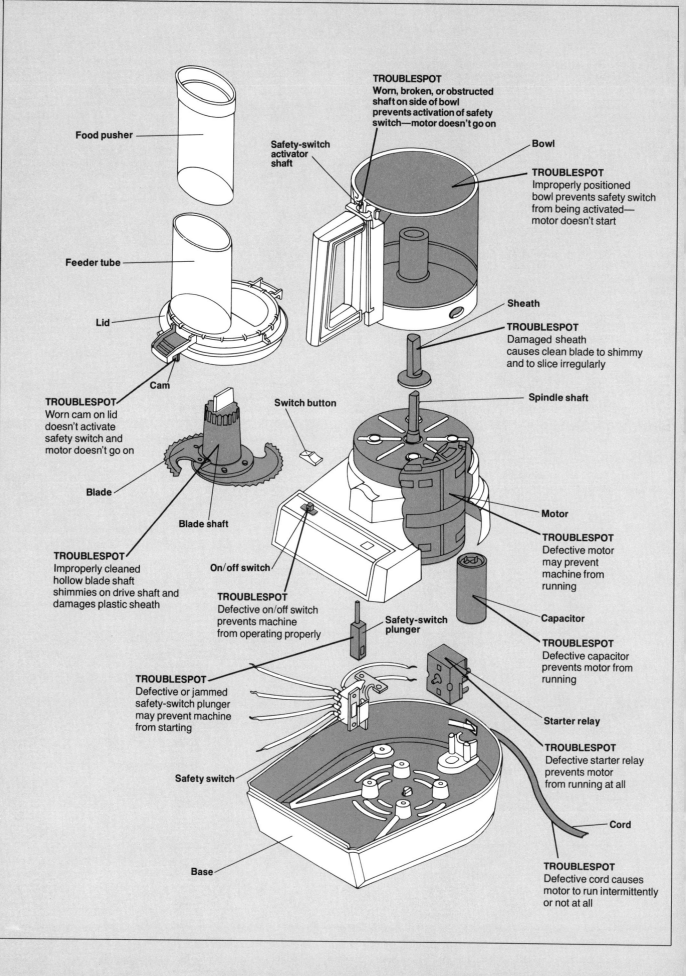

Food pusher

Feeder tube

Lid

Cam

Safety-switch activator shaft

TROUBLESPOT
Worn, broken, or obstructed shaft on side of bowl prevents activation of safety switch—motor doesn't go on

Bowl

TROUBLESPOT
Improperly positioned bowl prevents safety switch from being activated— motor doesn't start

Sheath

TROUBLESPOT
Damaged sheath causes clean blade to shimmy and to slice irregularly

Spindle shaft

TROUBLESPOT
Worn cam on lid doesn't activate safety switch and motor doesn't go on

Switch button

Blade

Blade shaft

Motor

TROUBLESPOT
Defective motor may prevent machine from running

On/off switch

TROUBLESPOT
Improperly cleaned hollow blade shaft shimmies on drive shaft and damages plastic sheath

TROUBLESPOT
Defective on/off switch prevents machine from operating properly

Safety-switch plunger

Capacitor

TROUBLESPOT
Defective capacitor prevents motor from running

TROUBLESPOT
Defective or jammed safety-switch plunger may prevent machine from starting

Starter relay

TROUBLESPOT
Defective starter relay prevents motor from running at all

Safety switch

Cord

Base

TROUBLESPOT
Defective cord causes motor to run intermittently or not at all

Food Processors

The food processor is a highly sophisticated version of the blender. It is characterized chiefly by the variety of blades that can be interchanged to suit the task at hand.

There are two basic types: direct-driven and belt-driven models. On direct-drives, the bowl holding the blades and food to be processed is mounted on top of the appliance. As the name of this type implies, the blades are connected directly to the drive shaft. On belt-drives, the bowl is positioned to one side of the motor; the blades are fitted to a spindle shaft that is driven by a belt.

Since the blades are sharp and dangerous, federal laws require that all processors be equipped with a safety mechanism ensuring that the processor cannot start until both the bowl and its cover are securely in place. In addition, other safety mechanisms switch off a processor if the blades can't handle the job and jam. Usually, stoppage is caused by overloading; the motor will run again once the bowl is cleaned out and loaded properly. If it doesn't, there may be a problem with the starter relay (see page 198). An exception is the model made by American, which is equipped with a reset switch (see box, page 196).

Problems with various safety mechanisms and other components of a food processor can usually be solved at home, provided the motor is working. If you have problems with the motor, see Appliance Repair Basics: *Preventing motor breakdowns.*

MAINTENANCE

It is essential to keep your processor clean, particularly the blade assembly. As a result of faulty or inadequate maintenance, this area is the chief source of problems on food processors. On all models, whether direct- or belt-driven, the blade is attached to a hollow plastic shaft. This fits over the plastic-sheathed metal shaft that turns it. Any obstruction within this connection can cause the blades to shimmy, resulting in permanent damage to the sheath (see below). Clean both shafts regularly. Use a percolator brush to clean inside the sheath.

The blades themselves should be washed after every use. If your machine has metal blades—some are plastic—dry them promptly to prevent rust. (Always hold a blade by its shaft to avoid cutting yourself.) Keep the housing dry. If spillage seeps inside, it can ruin the motor.

External repairs

Blade shafts and sheaths

If the blades on your processor shimmy, rattle badly, and don't cut properly, turn off the unit immediately. The problem is caused by food buildup on the blade shaft, or inside the plastic sheath that fits over the drive shaft (on direct-drive models) or spindle shaft (on belt-drive models). Clean both the blade shaft and sheath. If the shimmy has caused damage to the sheath, you will have to replace it. On belt-drive models, you may have to replace both the sheath and the spindle shaft. Never try to repair a damaged sheath—this could damage the blade shaft.

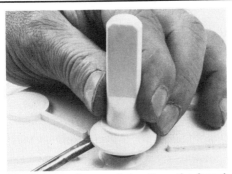

To replace a damaged sheath on the American, pry it up evenly with a screwdriver. Clean the spindle shaft underneath with a plastic scouring pad and slip on the new sheath.

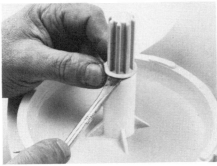

On the Farberware, the sheath is harder to remove. First, try to loosen it with a screwdriver. If that doesn't work, cut it free. On other makes, don't try to remove it—you may ruin your machine.

Safety-switch activators

If your processor doesn't start, first check to see that the bowl and lid are fitted together securely. The machine won't run unless the fit is accurate. On all makes, this proper fitting activates a safety interlock switch that completes the power circuit in the machine. How this is done varies from one model to the next. On all belt-drives and on some direct-drives, a tooth or cam on the lid makes direct contact with a plunger that trips the switch. On other direct-drives (American, Sunbeam, and Cuisinart) there is an intermediary part between the lid and the plunger—a shaft that runs down the side of the processor to the housing. When the bowl and lid are fitted, the cam pushes down the shaft. The bottom of the shaft then hits the plunger, which in turn triggers the switch. If your problem is not a broken cam or jammed shaft, you must get inside the machine (see following pages) and check the switch itself. It is important to keep the safety-switch activator shaft clean. If food particles jam it, the bowl may have to be replaced.

To check the activator on American, Cuisinart, and Sunbeam processors, inspect the cam on the lid. If the part is worn or broken, replace the lid. Next, push down on the shaft that runs down the side of the bowl and pushes the plunger that pushes the safety switch. If the shaft doesn't move freely, replace the bowl.

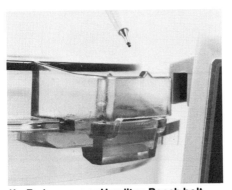

If a Farberware or Hamilton Beach belt-drive processor doesn't start, examine the tooth on the side of the lid that activates the plunger and switch. If the tooth is worn or has snapped off, you must replace the lid.

Getting inside

To get inside American, Farberware, Hamilton Beach, and Sunbeam models, remove the recessed screws in the base and take off the housing (right). **CAUTION** The American and Sunbeam both have a capacitor, which stores electricity in order to give a short surge of power when the processor is switched on. Before doing anything else, discharge the capacitor to avoid shock (see box, page 42)

To take off the housing on Cuisinart and Moulinex processors, tip back the machine and remove the recessed screws in the front of the base (far right). **CAUTION** The Cuisinart also has a capacitor, which must be discharged (see box, page 42).

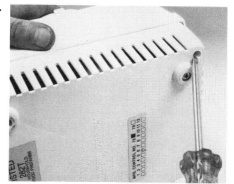

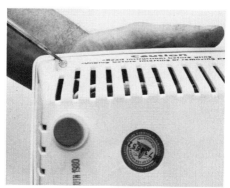

Electrical problems

On/off switch

If your processor doesn't start (and if the safety-switch activator is OK), first check the cord (see box, below, right). If that is OK, the problem may be with the on/off switch. Test it for continuity (see Blue Pages: *Electrical testers*). The Cuisinart runs on two positions: PULSE, which turns itself off when the switch is released, and ON, which stays on until the machine is switched off. Test this switch as described. On Cuisinart, Hamilton Beach, and Moulinex models, the switch can be replaced at home. To replace a defective Sunbeam switch, you must remove rivets (see page 193) or go to a repair shop. American and Farberware processors switch on automatically when the safety switch is activated. If you have a starting problem with either of these models, you should follow the directions in *Safety interlock switches*, opposite.

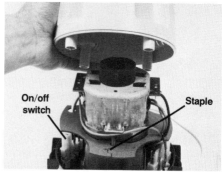

To replace the Moulinex on/off switch, unscrew the two Phillips screws that attach the switch to the housing. Pull out the switch and take off its plastic and rubber cap. Disconnect the two leads one by one and connect the leads to a new switch. Replace the cap, screw the switch back in place, and restaple the cover. **CAUTION** Do not confuse the on/off switch (two leads) with the almost identical safety-interlock switch, on the opposite side of the bowl (four leads).

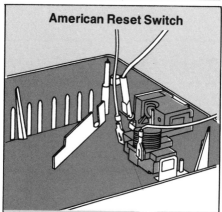

American Reset Switch

If motor overload causes current to be cut off to the motor of an American processor, you must press the reset switch to start it again. If the appliance doesn't start up again, the reset switch may be defective. Test it for continuity (see Blue Pages: *Electrical testers*). If it is defective, unscrew the switch from the housing. Take out the lead wires, label them, and replace the switch.

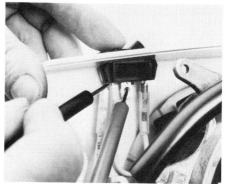

To test the Cuisinart switch for continuity, label and remove the leads. Place one probe on the middle or common terminal, as shown. Put the other probe on either of the other terminals and switch back and forth from PULSE to ON. Now place the second probe on the third terminal and repeat the test. You should get continuity both times. If the switch is defective, squeeze the switch through the housing, and replace it.

To replace the Hamilton Beach switch, you must first remove the motor (see page 198); the switch is tucked away inside the motor housing. Next, pull off the switch button from the housing. Using a razor blade, peel off the decal that covers the two screws holding the switch in place and undo the screws. You can now push the switch through into the housing and remove it.

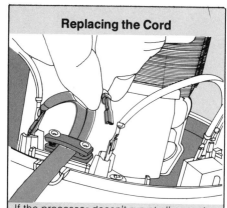

Replacing the Cord

If the processor doesn't run at all or cycles on/off, it may have a defective cord. Open the housing and examine the cord terminals for loose connections. If these look OK, test the cord for continuity (see Blue Pages: *Electrical testers*). If the cord is defective, detach it from the terminals and replace it.

Safety interlock switch

If your processor still doesn't start and there is nothing wrong with the external safety mechanism, the cord, and the on/off switch, your problem may be with the safety interlock switch. This is the mechanism that prevents a machine from starting until the bowl and cover are firmly secured. On most models, this switch is a separate component you can see within the housing. On processors equipped with a shaft-plunger safety mechanism (American, Sunbeam, and Cuisinart), you can test the switch without opening the housing, as shown here. The safety system on Moulinex processors varies, depending on which of the different bowls and attachments you are using.

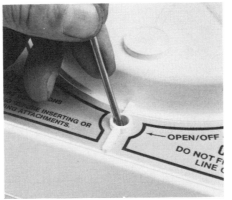

1 To test a shaft-plunger safety mechanism on an American, remove the bowl, plug in the machine, and insert a screwdriver into the hole where the bowl's shaft normally would run down to the plunger and switch. You should be able to hear the motor and see the sheath turn. If not, either the plunger, switch, or motor is defective.

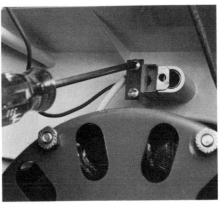

2 To inspect plunger and switch, first unplug the machine, then remove the two Phillips screws that secure the switch unit to the housing. Pull out the switch. The plunger should fall out. If it doesn't, push it free with a screwdriver.

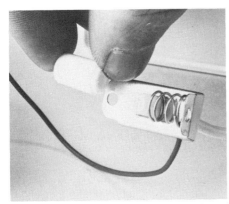

3 Make sure that the plunger is free of dirt and food particles. If it moves up and down freely, check the switch for continuity (see Blue Pages: *Electrical testers*). You should get continuity when the plunger is depressed.

1 To test the safety mechanism on the Cuisinart, you must first detach the combined plunger-safety switch unit from the housing. Unscrew the screws from the underside of the upper housing and pull out the unit until you can see it clearly.

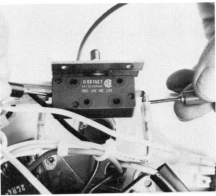

2 Check that the plunger is clean and moves easily. Then test the switch for continuity. Remember to depress the plunger while performing the continuity test. With a Cuisinart, you will have to pull the switch away from the housing, as shown here, to reach the leads.

1 To test the plunger and switch on the Farberware and Hamilton Beach, you must first take the motor out (see page 198). The plunger-switch housing is located close to the top of the motor. Undo the screws that hold the housing in place.

2 Pull the plunger-switch housing away from the motor housing to gain access to the terminals. Remove a lead and test the switch for continuity (see Blue Pages: *Electrical testers*). If it fails the continuity test, replace it.

To replace the plunger-switch unit, unscrew the two Phillips screws that hold the plunger and switch inside the switch housing. Remove the unit and install a new one.

Safety interlock switch (continued)

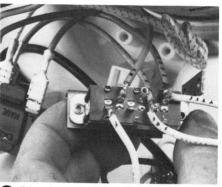

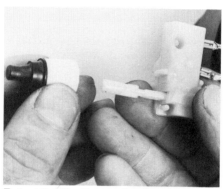

1 **To test the safety switch on a Sunbeam,** remove the metal bracket that attaches the plunger and switch to the upper housing (held by two screws). Pull out the switch and check the plunger. If it doesn't move freely, replace it.

2 If the plunger is OK, mark the leads on the switch and mark the position of the switch, unsolder all the leads and test the switch for continuity (see Blue Pages: *Electrical testers*). If the switch is defective, replace it.

To test the Moulinex safety interlock switch, follow the procedure for getting at the on/off switch (see page 196). They look similar, but the safety switch has four leads, not two.

Capacitor Test	Starter Relay	Rectifiers
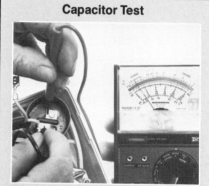		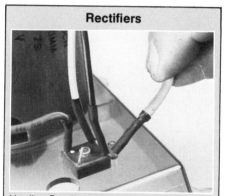

Discharge the capacitor first (see box, page 42). Then disconnect one lead. Set the VOM at RX100 and touch the terminals with the probes. The needle should jump to 0 and then move to infinite resistance. Move the probes to the opposite terminals and repeat the test. If the needle doesn't move at all or stays at 0, the capacitor is defective and must be replaced.

All processors with capacitors are designed to stop if the blades become blocked. A starter relay cuts off the current. Unplug the unit and clear the blockage. All processors except the American, which has a reset switch (page 196), should run again when the blockage is cleared. If they don't, the starter relay (shown here) may be at fault. Take the processor to a repair shop.

Hamilton Beach processors are equipped with a rectifier, shown here, that converts the electric current from AC to DC. If your processor doesn't start, and the cord, switches, and motor are all OK, use a VOM set for DC voltage to test across the leads from the rectifier to the motor (this is a power-on test). If no voltage registers, the rectifier is defective.

Mechanical problems

Checking and replacing the belt

If you own a belt-driven processor, such as the Farberware or Hamilton Beach, and the blade turns irregularly, your problem is either with the belt itself or the gears. First check the belt for signs of wear or cracks. You may have to replace it. If the belt is loose, check the motor mount and adjust it as described at far right. Steps for examining and replacing damaged gears are demonstrated on the Hamilton Beach processor (opposite page), but they can be adapted to any belt-driven model.

1 **To check or replace the Hamilton Beach belt,** first remove the lower housing (see *Getting inside,* page 196). Remove the six screws that attach the motor mount to the base of the processor.

2 Shift the loosened motor mount toward the larger of the two gears. This will create slack in the belt. Take the belt off and examine it. If it shows signs of damage or wear, put in a new one. Push the motor mount back to the left to take up the slack. Screw the motor back in place.

Checking and replacing the gears

If the belt is in good condition but the blade still turns irregularly, you will have to inspect the gears. Both the Farberware and Hamilton Beach models have two gears, a small one with sixteen teeth over the drive shaft and a large one with thirty-two teeth at the base of the spindle shaft where the blades are mounted. Before you can inspect the gears, you must first take off the belt, as shown on the opposite page.

1 **To inspect or replace the gears,** lift the drive belt off the larger of the two gears. Check the gear for worn or damaged teeth. If there are signs of damage, remove the gear.

2 To remove a thirty-two-tooth gear, first tape the gear and blade shaft to prevent damage. Grip the shaft at its thickest part with ordinary pliers. Hold the gear with multiple-joint pliers, and turn counterclockwise.

3 It may take considerable strength to free the gear. Once the bond is broken, however, it will unscrew easily. Still holding the shaft with the pliers, spin the gear off by hand.

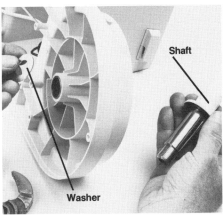

Shaft

Washer

4 Before you replace the large gear, check the plastic spindle shaft for damage. If it is chipped or split, you should replace it. Remove it from the bowl base. Save the space washer from the bottom of the old shaft for the new shaft.

5 Screw the replacement gear onto the shaft and replace the drive belt. Maintain belt tension with one hand while you tighten the motor mount screws.

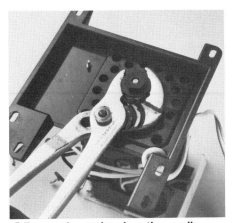

1 **To examine and replace the smaller, sixteen-tooth gear,** turn the motor unit on its side. If the gear is damaged you should replace it. To remove it, first grip the space washer with multiple-joint pliers.

2 Grip the top of the gear with a wrench and turn the gear clockwise as you hold on to the space washer with the pliers. When the bond breaks, the gear will turn freely.

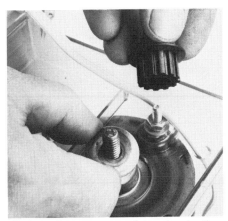

3 Spin off the gear, removing and saving the washer. Screw on the replacement gear, put back the belt, and screw on the motor mount. Make sure the belt and gears turn together before reassembling the processor.

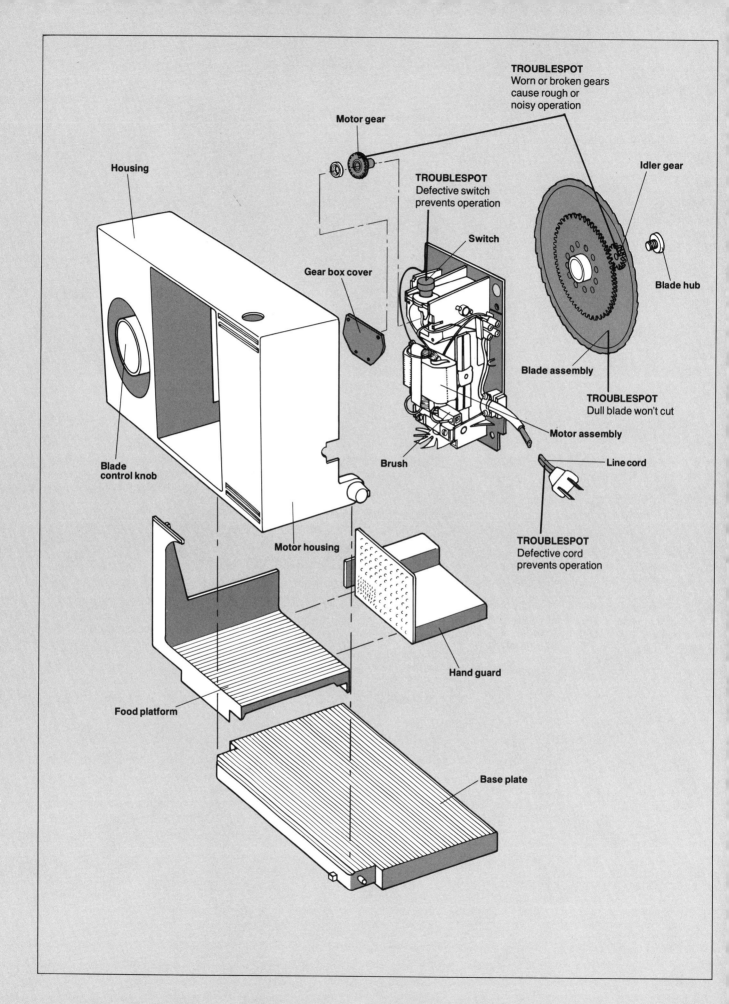

Housing

Motor gear

TROUBLESPOT
Worn or broken gears
cause rough or
noisy operation

Idler gear

TROUBLESPOT
Defective switch
prevents operation

Switch

Gear box cover

Blade hub

Blade assembly

TROUBLESPOT
Dull blade won't cut

Motor assembly

**Blade
control knob**

Brush

Line cord

TROUBLESPOT
Defective cord
prevents operation

Motor housing

Hand guard

Food platform

Base plate

Food Slicers

A food slicer is designed to cut meats, vegetables, cheeses, and breads into slices of variable thickness. A knob adjusts the position of the blade to control the thickness of the slice. A small motor inside the housing turns gears that rotate a very sharp, thin serrated circular blade. Trying to cut bones, food covered with aluminum foil, frozen foods, or fruit with large seeds will easily dull or damage the blade. If what you're slicing makes the motor jump or labor heavily, stop at once and use a knife to finish the job. Food that does not slice cleanly should be chilled, but not frozen, until it can be sliced evenly.

As with most small appliances, if the machine makes excessive noise while operating, the problem is most likely mechanical. You should check the gears that drive the cutting blade. If the appliance does not work at all, the problem is probably electrical. First, inspect the wires from the switch to the motor for loose connections. Then, check the cord and the switch for continuity (see Blue Pages: *Electrical testers*), and replace them with duplicates if they are faulty. On certain slicers (the Krups, for instance), check the motor brushes to see that they are making proper contact with the commutator.

All parts of the slicer except the motor assembly should be washed in soapy water. Be very careful handling the blade. It's sharp! After washing the blade, apply a little petroleum jelly to the gear on the back to maintain easy operation.

The steps for repairing a food slicer are demonstrated on four late-model machines: Krups, Rival, Waring, and Oster.

External repairs

The most common problem with a food slicer is a dull blade. The blade cannot be sharpened at home and should be replaced when it wears out. Fortunately, most models are constructed so that you can remove a defective blade and replace it without having to open up the housing.

In addition, on some models the idler gear can be replaced without taking the slicer apart.

 If the plastic housing of the food slicer cracks, repair it with five-minute epoxy.

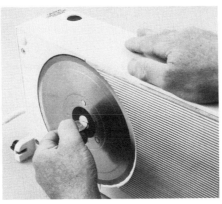

**1** **To check and replace the blade,** remove it by unscrewing the hub. Some models have a thumbscrew. The blade on the Krups model, shown here, can be loosened with a coin.

2 If the blade seems to be sharp but cuts slowly or is slipping, check the gear on the back of the blade. If any teeth are missing or chipped the blade should be replaced.

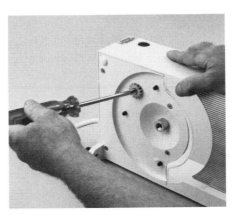

1 **To check the Krups or Rival idler gear,** remove the blade and look for damage on the small gear that protrudes through the housing and drives the blade gear. If there are missing or broken teeth, remove the screw at the center of the idler gear.

2 Lift off the damaged idler gear and replace it with a duplicate.

Getting inside

To deal with problems affecting the switch, the motor, and in some cases, the gears, you'll have to get inside the motor housing. On the Waring, Oster, and Krups slicers, remove the hand guard, food platform, base plate, and cutting blade; on the Krups, also remove the idler gear. Follow the instructions below to complete the disassembly.

To get inside the Krups and Oster models, remove the four Phillips screws from the front of the housing, directly behind the blade.

To get inside the Waring, remove the four recessed Phillips screws from the rear of the motor housing.

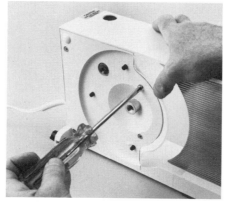

Krups, Oster

Waring

1 **To get inside the Rival model,** remove the motor setscrew with a screwdriver. Lift the motor up and slide it out of the blade housing.

2 Remove the three Phillips screws from the face of the motor housing and lift off the faceplate. NOTE: One screw is shorter than the other two.

1. Rival

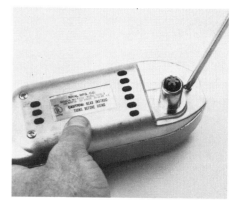

2. Rival

Replacing the switch

If the slicer doesn't run at all when you turn it on, first test the line cord for continuity and replace it if it's faulty (see Blue Pages: *Electrical testers*). If the cord is OK, then test the switch. Disconnect one lead to the switch and touch the probes of a continuity tester to the switch terminals. If the switch fails the test, follow these directions for replacing it. Instructions for other models are given below.

To replace the Krups switch, lift the switch off the end of the motor/switch assembly. Remove the push-on connectors and install a duplicate.

To replace the Waring switch, lift it out of the motor housing. Unsolder or cut the wires at the switch and replace the switch. Resolder or use wire nuts.

1 **To replace the Rival switch,** unscrew the two Phillips screws holding the switch.

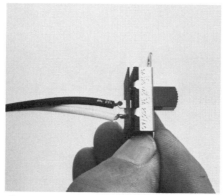

2 Pull the switch out, noting which terminals the leads are soldered to. Cut the leads close to the switch. Solder the leads to the correct terminals on the new switch.

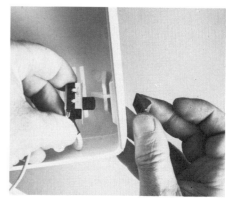

To replace the Oster switch, pry off the switch knob and lift out the switch. Remove the push-on connectors and attach them to the new switch. Snap the switch knob back into place.

Replacing the gears

If the blade doesn't turn smoothly, or if you hear grinding noises coming from inside the housing, check the gears. The idler gear can be checked without going inside the motor housing; see page 201. Instructions for checking the other gears are given here. If you find that any gear teeth are broken or missing, replace the damaged part with a duplicate.

To check the Rival gears, remove the housing. Push the gear shaft from the blade side with one finger so that you can grab the gear wheel with the other and pull it completely out.

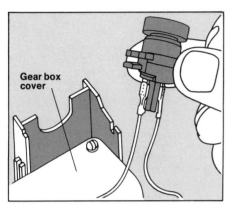

1 **To check the Krups gears,** lift the switch out of the housing so you can remove the four screws from the gearbox cover. Lift the cover off to gain access to the gears.

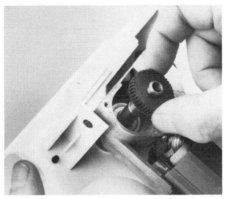

2 Push the gear shaft from the front of the housing with your left hand. Pull the gear out with your right hand, as shown here.

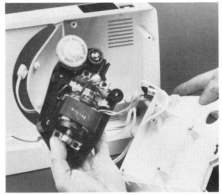

1 **To check the Oster gears,** lift the switch knob off the top of the switch. Pull the switch out of its seat so that you can lift out the motor and gear assembly. Remove the four recessed Phillips screws from behind the blade. Then turn the motor housing over to get at the gears.

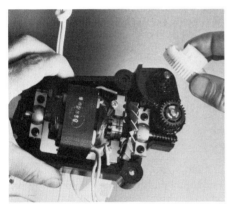

2 Check the gears for wear. If the large white plastic gear is worn, simply lift it out for replacement.

3 If the small black gear is worn, use a screwdriver to pry off the C-clip that attaches it to the shaft. The gear will then lift off. Be careful not to lose the C-clip! Hold your finger against it when you remove it.

1 **To replace a damaged Waring motor gear,** remove the idler gear by holding the large motor gear immobile with one hand while rotating the idler gear clockwise with the other hand.

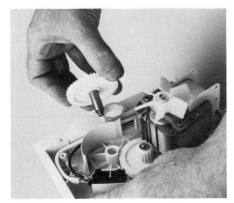

2 Lift out the motor gear; install the new gear, screwing the idler gear back on as directed in the first step.

Motor Problems

If the slicer fails to work at all when you turn on the switch and you have checked both the cord and the switch, then the trouble lies in the motor. In most cases, repairing or replacing parts of the motor is a job for a qualified appliance repairman. But you can check the brushes on the Krups, Oster, and Rival.

To check the brushes on a Krups motor, release the brushes by bending in the spurs on the brush terminal. Pull up on the brush terminal, as shown, and slip the brush assembly out of the housing. If either one is scorched, pitted, or chipped, replace the pair.

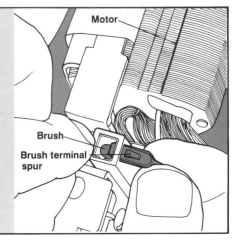

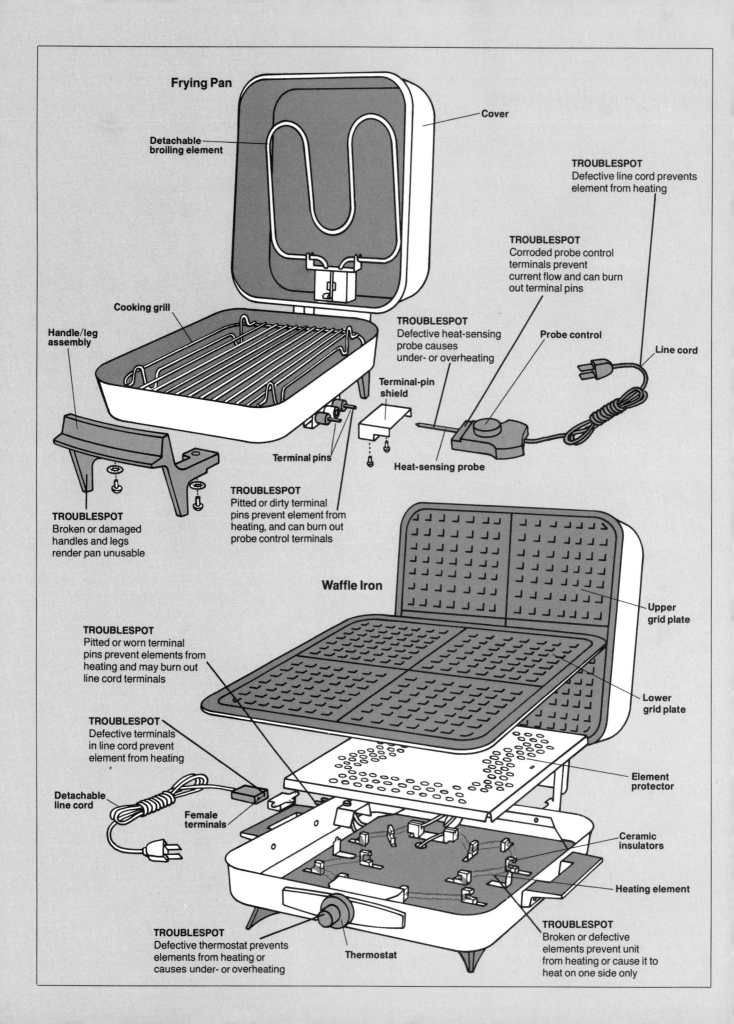

Frying Pan

Cover

Detachable broiling element

TROUBLESPOT
Defective line cord prevents element from heating

TROUBLESPOT
Corroded probe control terminals prevent current flow and can burn out terminal pins

Cooking grill

TROUBLESPOT
Defective heat-sensing probe causes under- or overheating

Probe control

Line cord

Handle/leg assembly

Terminal-pin shield

Heat-sensing probe

Terminal pins

TROUBLESPOT
Broken or damaged handles and legs render pan unusable

TROUBLESPOT
Pitted or dirty terminal pins prevent element from heating, and can burn out probe control terminals

Upper grid plate

Waffle Iron

TROUBLESPOT
Pitted or worn terminal pins prevent elements from heating and may burn out line cord terminals

Lower grid plate

TROUBLESPOT
Defective terminals in line cord prevent element from heating

Element protector

Detachable line cord

Female terminals

Ceramic insulators

Heating element

TROUBLESPOT
Defective thermostat prevents elements from heating or causes under- or overheating

Thermostat

TROUBLESPOT
Broken or defective elements prevent unit from heating or cause it to heat on one side only

Frying Pans and Waffle Irons

Frying pans

The electric frying pans and cookers discussed here are those that use a detachable thermostat control. They have a heating element sealed into the bottom of the pan, which allows the pan to be immersed. If this element is defective, it cannot be repaired or replaced. In addition, some models have an element in the cover of the appliance that can be used for broiling. This element is detachable and can be replaced.

The adjustable thermostat control for the appliance is in a housing on the line cord called the probe control. The probe control has female terminals that fit over the terminal pins in the fry pan. The terminal pins for the broiler element are attached to the upper heating element and protrude from the cover. The probe control holds a heat-sensing probe that touches the side of the pan, monitors the heat and signals the thermostat to keep the pan at the selected temperature.

If the pan does not work, check the terminal pins and then the cord and thermostat. In addition, you can make certain mechanical repairs, such as replacing pan handles and legs. Repairs are demonstrated here on the Farberware frying pan and the Therm-o-Ware broiler-skillet.

CAUTION Be sure to test an electric frying pan for ground after any repair (see Blue Pages, *Testing for Ground*).

Replacing handles and legs

Occasionally it is necessary to replace damaged cover handles, bottom handle and leg assemblies, or separate legs. The steps to do this are usually described in the manufacturer's brochure and require simply unscrewing the damaged part and replacing it with a new one.

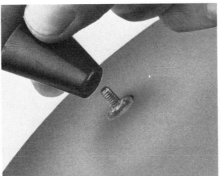

To replace the Farberwear cover knob, simply unscrew the knob from the cover and replace it with a new one. The handle on the Farberwear pan cannot be replaced.

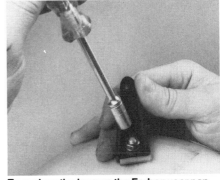

To replace the legs on the Farberwear pan, use a nut driver (shown above) or a wrench to remove the nut on the inside of the leg. Take the leg, washer and metal brace off together and attach a new leg.

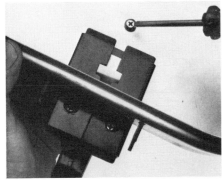

1 **To replace the handles on the Therm-o-Ware broiler-skillet,** first loosen the Phillips screw on the inside of the cover.

2 Remove the two Phillips screws that secure the handle to the side of the cover. Lift off the handle.

3 To remove the pan's leg and handle assembly, remove the two screws attaching the assembly to the bottom.

Checking the terminal pins

If the frying pan doesn't work at all, first check the line cord (see Waffle irons: *Checking the cord*). If the line cord is OK, the cause of the problem may be poor contact between the terminal pins and the female terminals in the probe control. The pins can easily become worn, pitted, and dirty because the probe control is constantly being plugged into and pulled off them. Damaged terminal pins will often damage plug terminals and vice versa, so inspect both. To clean terminal pins, see Bench Tip, page 208.

When the pins are clean, test them for continuity. No continuity means the problem could be in the pins or in the heating element. If your unit has replaceable pins, take them out and place your tester probes on the element terminals. If the element is defective or if your appliance's terminal pins are not replaceable, the whole pan, the top element, or the whole top element assembly will have to be replaced.

1 **To test and replace Farberware terminal pins,** first do a continuity check, attaching tester probes as shown. If you get no continuity, examine the pins visually and replace any defective ones.

2 To inspect the pins, loosen the two Phillips screws that secure the terminal housing and remove the cover.

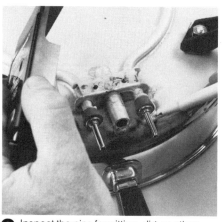

3 Inspect the pins for pitting, dirt, or other signs of wear or burning that could cause a defective connection.

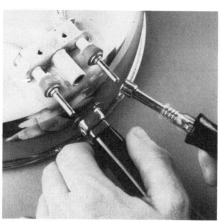

4 Unscrew one or both terminal pins if they are corroded or badly pitted, using a nut driver. If only one pin is replaced, be sure to clean the other one.

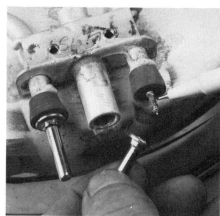

5 After the terminal pin has been removed, screw on the replacement. Always test for ground after repairing or replacing a pin (see Blue pages: *Testing for Ground*).

Checking the probe control and thermostat

If the frying pan doesn't heat, and you haven't discovered any defect in the terminal pins and element (or if you found corroded or pitted terminal pins and replaced them), check the probe control female terminals.

A defective thermostat may cut out all current, or it may cause improper heating. Test the accuracy of the thermostat and heat-sensing probe as follows: set your thermostat at 225°F. and put some water in the frying pan. When the water boils, turn the control toward 200°F. The current should cut out and the water should soon stop boiling. If the water continues to boil, the thermostat is not cutting off current properly.

1 **Visually inspect the female terminals** in the probe. If they are damaged, as is the case here, the probe must be replaced.

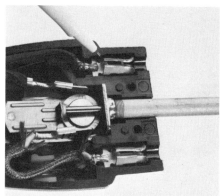

2 To open the probe housing, remove the four Phillips screws. Inspect the female terminals. If they are dirty, spray them with electrical-contact cleaner. If they are damaged, replace the probe.

FRYING PANS AND WAFFLE IRONS

Waffle irons

Waffle irons cook waffles from above and below by means of hot metal plates. Both the top and base of the appliance hold a metal grid plate with the familiar waffle pattern, which is heated by a heating element. Some waffle irons have a built-in cord, and some have a detachable cord with a female plug. A thermostat controls heat at the cooking surface and in many cases also functions as an on/off switch.

If the waffle iron does not work at all, no current is getting through to the elements. Unless your appliance has a detachable line cord, you will have to open the housing to test the cord and other electrical components. If your unit has a detachable cord, test it first, and if it is OK, inspect the terminal pins for dirt, pitting, or other damage, and replace them if necessary as described here. Do a continuity check on the terminal pins, the thermostat, and the elements.

If the unit under- or overheats, there is a good chance that the thermostat is defective. If one element fails to heat, check that element for loose connections and breaks, test it for continuity, and replace it if defective. You may be able to repair a broken element.

The steps for repairing a waffle iron are demonstrated on a Black Angus model, which has a detachable cord and a temperature-control knob. These instructions can be adapted for any waffle iron that has replaceable parts. If the parts aren't replaceable, about all you can do is test a detachable line cord for continuity. An additional continuity test on the terminals (or on the prongs of a built-in line cord) will let you know whether there is a break in the appliance's circuit.

Checking the cord

If the waffle iron is not working at all, the first check to make is a continuity test on the line cord (see Blue Pages: *Electrical testers*). If the cord is defective, it should be replaced, not repaired. Make sure the new cord has an identical rating. Line cords to appliances that heat carry a large load of current and should always be in perfect condition. **CAUTION** Unplug the appliance before doing any work.

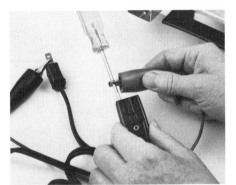

To test a detachable line cord, pull it off the waffle iron and use a screwdriver (as shown) or other conductor to connect the test probe to the female terminal. If the cord is defective, replace it with one of the same rating.

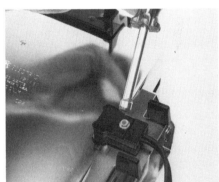

To test a nondetachable line cord, remove the cover of the terminal block where the cord enters the waffle iron. This exposes the cord leads. Detach one lead and test the cord. Replace a defective cord with one that has the same rating.

Testing and replacing the terminal pins

If your waffle iron doesn't work at all and the line cord tests OK, check the terminal pins (if your unit has them). You must first remove the bottom grid plate. Examine the pins visually for pitting and other obvious damage.

In some models, the pins are replaceable as a unit—in the Black Angus, each pin can even be replaced separately. If the pins aren't replaceable, a defect means you will have to replace your whole waffle iron.

1 **To inspect and replace the terminal pins in the Black Angus,** remove the inner terminal-pin shield (the protective metal housing inside the appliance). **CAUTION** Leave the outer shield in place. It has been removed here only to show the pins.

2 To remove a defective pin, unscrew the hex nuts that hold the pins on the inside, saving the washer. Carefully install a new pin. Clean the remaining pin thoroughly so it will make good contact with the cord terminal. **CAUTION** It is absolutely essential to check for ground after replacing one or both terminal pins (see *Checking for Ground,* next page).

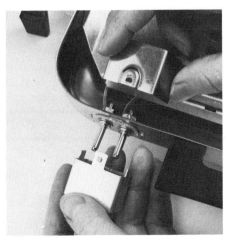

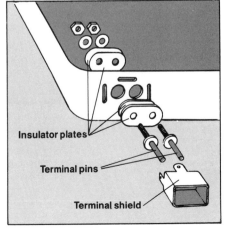

Insulator plates

Terminal pins

Terminal shield

Checking for ground

It is very important to check for ground after making any electrical repair on a waffle iron or frying pan, and especially after replacing one or both terminal pins (see Blue Pages: *Electrical circuits*). If a pin touches the side of the pan inadvertently, you could get a nasty shock when you turn the appliance on.

To test the waffle iron for ground, touch one tester probe to one terminal pin and the other probe to the waffle iron's metal housing. If the tester shows continuity, you have a high-resistance short (ground). Examine the insulator plates to make sure they're properly positioned. Test for ground again.

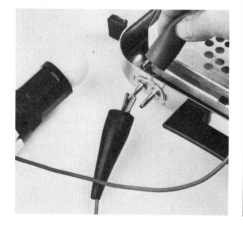

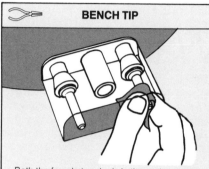

BENCH TIP

Both the female terminals in the probe control and the terminal pins of waffle irons and frying pans must be kept clean to ensure a good electrical contact. Clean the female terminals occasionally with electrical contact cleaner. Use metal polish to clean the terminal pins. Buff them with fine emergy cloth (above) if the polish doesn't do the job.

Checking and repairing the elements

If one element doesn't work, you must remove the grid plate and the element protector to test and inspect the element. If the waffle iron doesn't heat up at all, there is a slight possibility that both elements might have burned out simultaneously, but a faulty line cord, terminal pins, or thermostat are most likely explanations for an appliance that doesn't work at all.

Test the element for continuity (see Blue Pages: *Electrical testers*), and if there is no continuity, check for loose terminals and breaks. If a break is close to a terminal, you may be able to repair it. Follow the directions given here. Most waffle iron elements are replaceable.

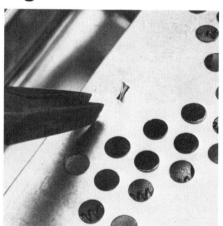

1 **To test, replace, or repair an element,** first remove the grid plate and the metal element protector. Straighten the tabs that secure the element protector to the element tray.

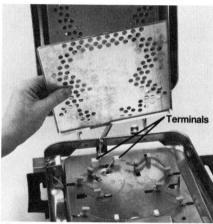

Terminals

2 Disconnect the line cord and test the element's continuity by placing tester probes on the terminals. If you do not get continuity, check to see that the connections are tight and then look for any breaks.

3 Inspect the terminals' ceramic insulators and check the insulated wire for fraying, pinching, or breaks near the spring that protects the leads to the top element.

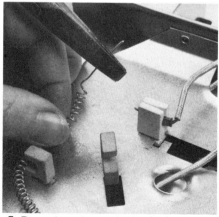

4 To repair an element that has broken at the connection, first free it gently from the supports. Then straighten out two or three turns of the coil, using flat-nosed pliers. Straighten just enough to fit through the porcelain insulator and make a splice.

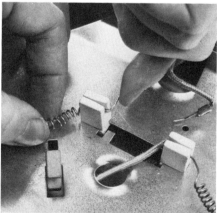

5 Remove the terminal lead from the insulator. Place the straight end of the element wire in the insulator slot, and bend the free end, as shown above. *(Continued on the following page)*.

6 Cut off the old crimp-on connector and make a new splice, using a new crimp-on connector.

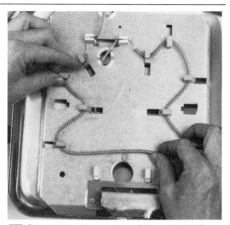

7 Stretch the element carefully so that it fits around the supports. Do not stretch the wire more than ½ inch (see box, right). Be sure to put the element back in its original position.

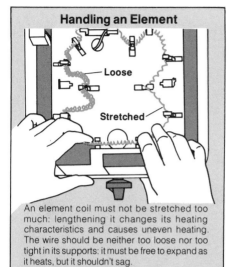

Handling an Element

An element coil must not be stretched too much: lengthening it changes its heating characteristics and causes uneven heating. The wire should be neither too loose nor too tight in its supports: it must be free to expand as it heats, but it shouldn't sag.

Testing and replacing the thermostat

If the waffle iron doesn't work properly, and there is nothing wrong with the cord and the terminal pins, check the thermostat. A defective thermostat may prevent current from reaching either element. You should also suspect a defective thermostat if one or both elements are either under- or overheating. To gain access to the thermostat, you must remove the grid plate and the element protector (see *Checking and repairing the elements*, opposite). Before testing the thermostat for continuity, check the contacts for dirt, corrosion, or lack of tension.

1 To test and replace the Black Angus thermostat, first pry off the thermostat knob with a screwdriver.

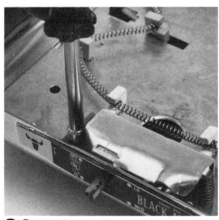

2 Remove the metal thermostat cover with a nut driver by unscrewing the hex nuts that attach it to the housing.

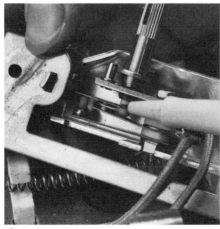

3 To check the contact points, turn the thermostat shaft to an ON setting to see if this pushes the contacts together. The contacts should separate when you turn the shaft to OFF. Try sanding any dirt or corrosion away with fine emery cloth. (This is a temporary repair only.)

4 Disconnect one lead and test the thermostat for continuity (see Blue Pages: *Electrical testers*). To replace the thermostat, unscrew the nut holding the unit, remove the leads, and lift out the thermostat. Label the leads before removing them, for later identification.

5 Connect the leads to the new thermostat in the same way as on the old thermostat, and install the thermostat in the unit.

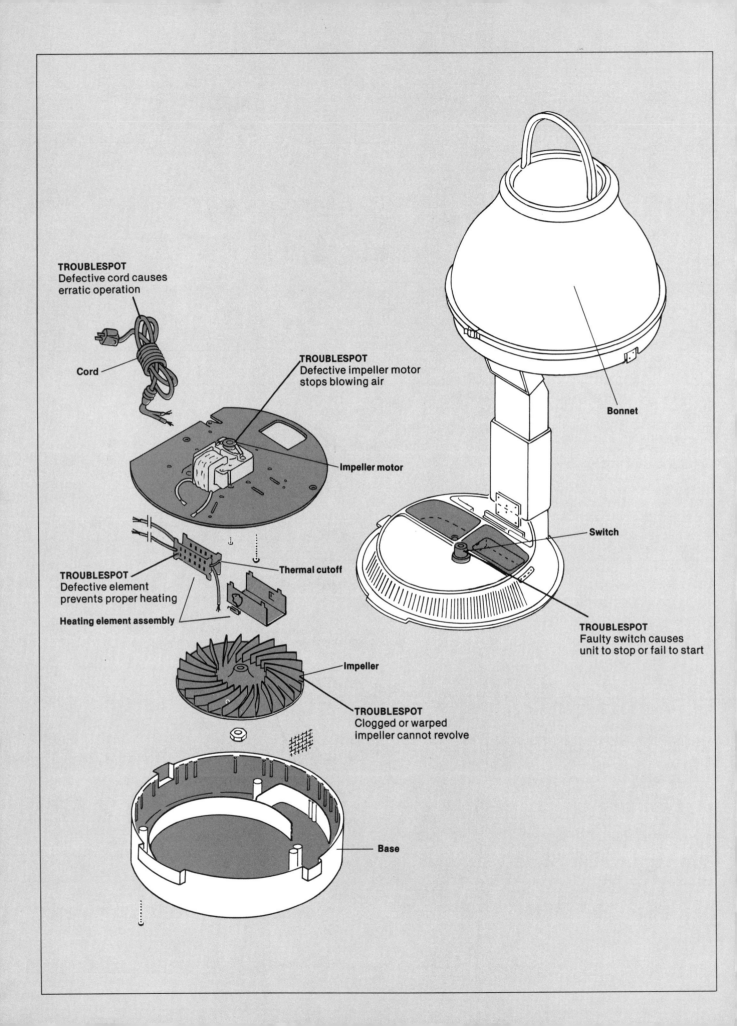

TROUBLESPOT
Defective cord causes
erratic operation

Cord

TROUBLESPOT
Defective impeller motor
stops blowing air

Impeller motor

TROUBLESPOT
Defective element
prevents proper heating

Thermal cutoff

Heating element assembly

Impeller

TROUBLESPOT
Clogged or warped
impeller cannot revolve

Base

Bonnet

Switch

TROUBLESPOT
Faulty switch causes
unit to stop or fail to start

Hair Driers

There are two basic types of hair driers: those with bonnets (hard or soft) and hand-held models. In both types, a hot draft of air is produced in the same way: it is blown by a fan, the impeller, over a wire coil, the heating element. These components are contained in the housing, along with the switch mechanism, the motor that drives the impeller, and the thermal cutoff. The thermal cutoff is a type of fuse that turns off the appliance if it overheats. Any problem—a drier that won't start, that heats but doesn't blow, or that blows but doesn't heat—can be diagnosed only by taking the housing apart. If the motor is burned out, the appliance must be replaced. Other repairs usually can be done at home.

Extreme caution is necessary when you are handling driers. On all types the heating element is a live uninsulated wire, which means that there is always a danger of shock. Never use a drier while you are bathing. If, somehow, the drier should drop into the water, be sure to pull the plug from the wall outlet (with hands dry) before you touch either the appliance or the equally dangerous water.

For general maintenance, keep air intake vents free of dust, hair, and other debris that can foul the impeller if they enter the housing. Directions for cleaning the impeller are given below. Do not oil your drier.

Getting inside

Hard-bonnet models

On this type of drier, the housing that contains the components doubles as the base and rests on a table. The hot air is driven up a connecting neck into its bonnet, under which you sit, much as in a beauty salon. The neck is elbowed so that the bonnet can be folded into the base for convenient carrying and storage. On some hard-bonnet models, after opening the housing you will find that the switch is riveted in place. If your drier doesn't start, the switch is probably defective. If it is riveted, see *Working with Rivets,* page 193. Most switches, however, can be replaced, as can defective cords, impellers, and heating elements. Directions for these repairs are given.

1 **To remove the housing,** fold the bonnet into the base and turn the closed unit upside down (right). Remove all the screws from the base. Place it on a pillow to prevent it from rolling.

2 After lifting off the housing, you'll see the impeller and heating element (far right). Clean out any debris with a soft brush.

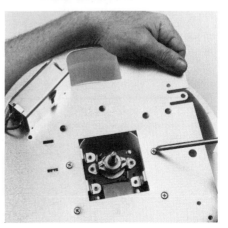

3 To remove the impeller for cleaning or replacement, hold the hub nut with a combination wrench or an adjustable wrench. Put a screwdriver in the slotted fan-motor shaft (right) and turn it until the nut comes off and frees the impeller.

4 To inspect a motor that doesn't run, remove the motor mount. On the Sunbeam model, four Phillips screws hold it in place (far right). Look for any loose connections and tighten them. A burned-out motor, which makes the drier irreparable, may smell and may be covered with carbon.

Soft-bonnet models

On this type of drier, hot air is produced in a base similar to that used on hard-bonnet models. The air is blown through a flexible plastic hose into a bonnet that resembles a shower cap. A faulty bonnet (one that is ripped, for example) can be replaced without opening the housing. The hose, on the other hand, can be replaced only by taking the housing apart. The housing must be opened to replace the cord. A feature of some soft-bonnet models is that the impeller *and* switch are riveted or welded in place; in such cases, see *Working with Rivets,* page 193, or take the drier to a repair shop.

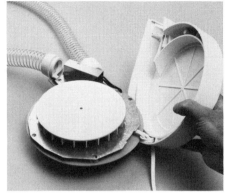

1 To open the housing, remove all of the screws, top and bottom. If the housing halves won't separate after you've removed the screws, look for any obstruction that might be holding them together.

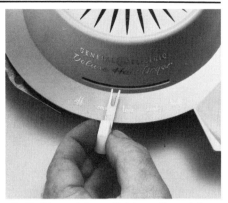

2 On this model, a switch lever through the upper half of the housing is attached to the mounting plate fixed to the bottom half of the housing. Pull it out to free the two halves of the housing.

Electrical problems

Cord and switch

If the drier doesn't work at all, first test the cord and on/off switch for continuity (see Blue Pages: *Electrical testers*). On most models they can be replaced, though on some models this repair must be made in a repair shop. The directions for cord and switch replacements are given here.

To replace the cord, first open up the housing. Follow the wire leads inside the housing to the two terminals, one on the switch, the other fastened by a wire nut to the element and the motor. Mark where they're connected for identification later, then unsolder or cut them. Using pliers, pull out the strain relief that holds the cord inside the appliance. Replace the cord.

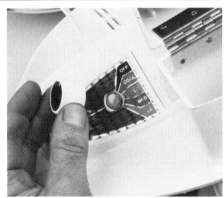

To replace a defective switch, pull off the switch knob and remove the hex nut that holds it in place. Label the switch leads for later identification and remove the wire nuts from the leads. Put in a new switch.

Heating element assembly

If the impeller is blowing but the air is cold, first make sure the selector is turned to HOT. Then check inside for any loose wires. If all wire connections are tight, and the heating element still doesn't get hot, either the element or the thermostat is defective, or the thermal cutoff (a heat-sensitive fuse) has blown. Test all of these parts for continuity (see Blue Pages : *Electrical testers*). If any of them fail the test, the entire assembly must be replaced.

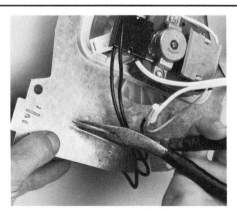

1 To remove a faulty heating element, unscrew the mounting plate to which it is attached and gently untwist the tabs that, on most models, hold the element in place.

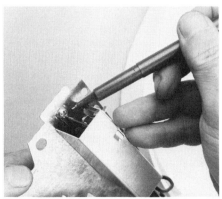

2 On some models, the element is also attached to the base with screws. Remove them. Label the three leads for later identification: one to the cord, one to the motor, and one to the thermal cutoff. Cut the leads and replace the element, using wire nuts.

Hand-held driers

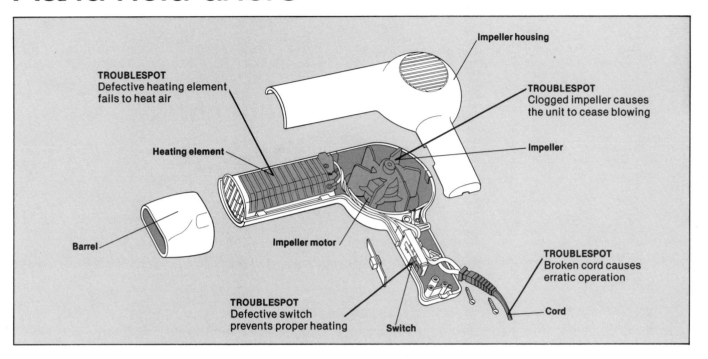

Impeller housing

TROUBLESPOT
Defective heating element
fails to heat air

TROUBLESPOT
Clogged impeller causes
the unit to cease blowing

Heating element

Impeller

Barrel

Impeller motor

TROUBLESPOT
Broken cord causes
erratic operation

Cord

TROUBLESPOT
Defective switch
prevents proper heating

Switch

Getting inside

For all their convenience, hand-held driers are difficult to repair at home. (Maintenance such as the removal of dust, hair, or debris is therefore especially advisable.) In fact, if the heating element, impeller, or switch becomes defective, you will probably have to replace the drier. A problem that can be solved at home is the common tendency for a hand drier to operate properly in certain positions and then to run in fits and starts as you move it around. Usually a defective cord or a loose connection is the cause of this problem. You'll have to get into the housing to fix it or to replace the cord.

1 **To open the housing,** remove all the screws. ⟋⟍ The handle of some driers has a decorative adhesive strip. It covers a screw head and must be peeled back.

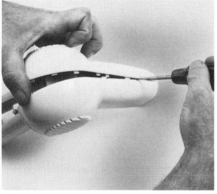

2 Interlocking tabs inside the housing will still hold the two halves of the appliance together. Separate them with a screwdriver.

3 On some models, the housing also is held together by the barrel. Unscrew it. If the barrel is also attached to the body by interlocking tabs, work the barrel back and forth until it comes free.

4 Next, look for any remaining tabs holding the housing together. Carefully insert a screwdriver between the two halves and pry them gently apart.

5 To clean the drier, lift off the impeller housing. Remove all hair from the fan and the heating coil. To replace a defective cord, cut it at least 1 inch from the soldered connection. Attach the new cord with small wire nuts, or resolder.

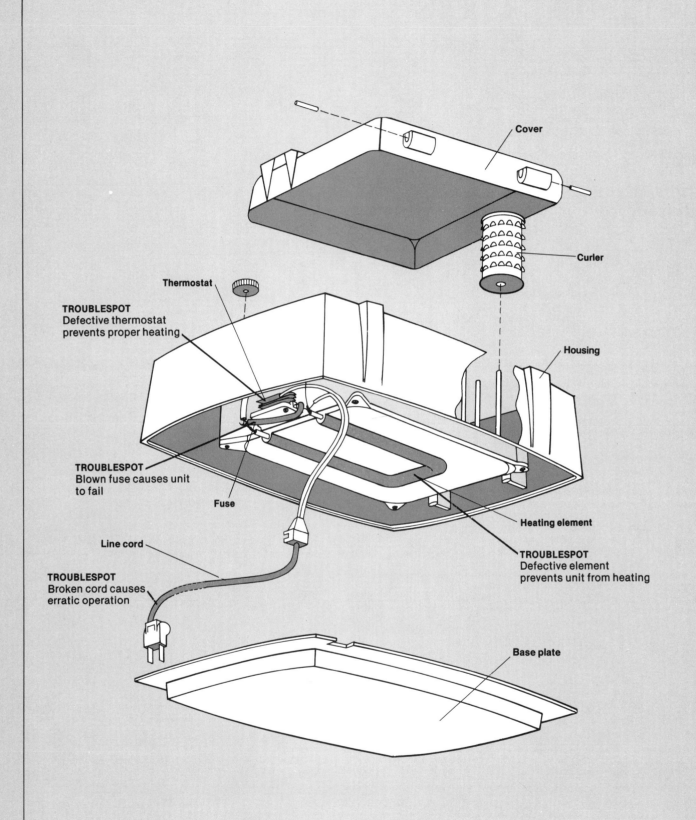

Cover

Curler

Thermostat

TROUBLESPOT
Defective thermostat
prevents proper heating

Housing

TROUBLESPOT
Blown fuse causes unit
to fail

Fuse

Heating element

TROUBLESPOT
Defective element
prevents unit from heating

Line cord

TROUBLESPOT
Broken cord causes
erratic operation

Base plate

Hair Setters

There are many makes and models of electric hair setters or hair curlers. All of them work the same way: plastic curlers sit on heating rods and are then removed and used for hair setting when they are hot. Some units, like the model pictured here, use steam to heat the rollers. A thermostat regulates the temperature within the unit.

As with all electric appliances that are likely to be used near water, it's essential to guard against possible shock. Dry your hands before touching the appliance and never touch a hair setter while bathing. With a new appliance that is likely to be used near water, it is a good idea to make sure that it's properly grounded. In addition, *always* check for a ground after making a repair (see Blue Pages: *Testing for ground*). Setters where the rollers are heated by steam are perfectly safe, provided the user pours in the water only up to the marked line and heeds all other instructions of the manufacturer.

Getting inside

As with hair driers, the heating mechanism of hair setters is contained within a housing that must be taken apart to investigate any problems. If the hair setter doesn't heat, first test the cord for continuity. Then check the fuse and the thermostat (see Blue Pages: *Electrical testers*). Directions are given below for replacing a defective cord, fuse, or thermostat. If the heating element is defective—a rare occurrence—it is best to replace the hair setter. The cost of repair is likely to approach the cost of a new one.

1 **To remove the base plate,** unplug the appliance and remove the curlers from the heating compartment. With steam models, empty any water in the unit and wipe it dry. Close the cover over the compartment, turn the unit over, and remove all the screws from the base plate.

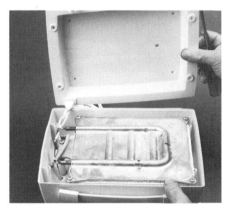

2 With the unit still upside down, lift off the lower housing. On the GE model shown here, the plastic carrying handle is held in place by double prongs on either side of the base plate. When you reassemble the unit, make sure the prongs fit snugly into the handle retainer slots that extend inside the base.

Electrical problems

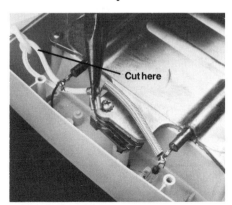

To replace a defective cord, first pull off the cord lead that is attached to the thermostat. Cut the other lead midway between the loop in the cord and the heating element that it connects to. Using a push-on lead, attach the new cord to the thermostat; attach it to the element with a wire nut.

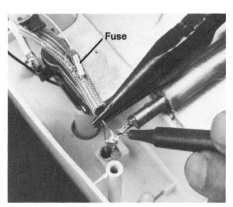

To replace a defective fuse, first remove it by melting the solder on the leads. When soldering on the new fuse, hold the leads with pliers as shown to deflect the heat. If you expose the fuse to the heat, it will blow.

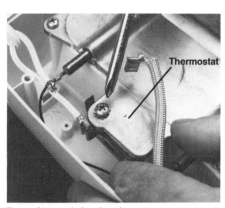

To replace a defective thermostat, label and detach the leads from the thermostat, pull off the heat control knob, and remove the screw holding the thermostat in place. Put in a new thermostat and connect the leads.

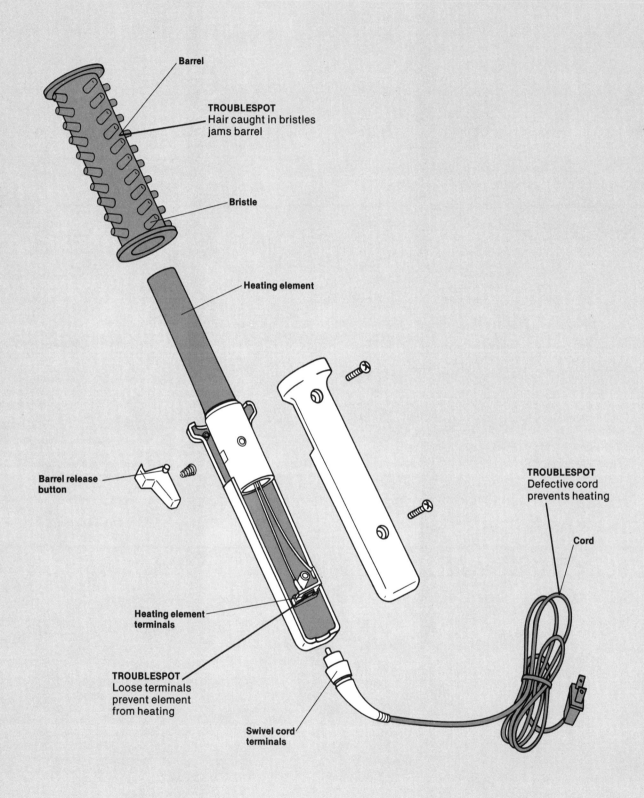

Barrel

TROUBLESPOT
Hair caught in bristles
jams barrel

Bristle

Heating element

**Barrel release
button**

TROUBLESPOT
Defective cord
prevents heating

Cord

**Heating element
terminals**

TROUBLESPOT
Loose terminals
prevent element
from heating

**Swivel cord
terminals**

Hair Stylers

The hair styler, also known as a curling iron or curling wand, is a relatively simple unit that is heated by a heating element inside its barrel. Some models are also equipped with bristles, and these models are called electric brushes. Maintenance is easy: a styler should be kept clean. A rag works well on the handle; the bristles of an electric brush can be cleaned with a comb and toothbrush. Stylers should never be washed: as with hair driers and setters, water presents the constant hazard of electric shock. **CAUTION** Keep the hot barrel away from your skin. It generates enough heat to cause a bad burn. Some models are equipped with an insulated tip, which decreases the burn hazard.

Getting inside

If the styler doesn't heat up, you have to get inside to find the problem. Occasionally, models with bristles that are designed to rotate jam. You must get inside in order to remove hair and other debris that caused the blockage, and also to check the cord.

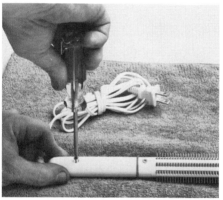

1 **To get inside,** remove the Phillips screws from the handle (most models have only two screws). ⟳ The screws are apt to be hard to turn without damaging the screw heads, so be sure to use a screwdriver that exactly fits the head, and turn the screws slowly but firmly while bearing down. Do this with the styler flat on a carpet or folded towel.

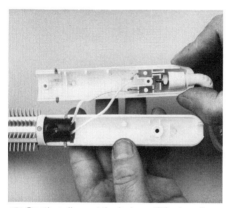

2 Gently pull apart the halves of the handle, taking care not to break any wire connections. If the handle does not come apart easily, you may have to pry it open with a flat-blade screwdriver.

Electrical problems

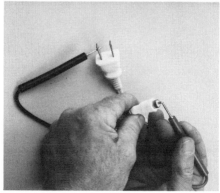

1 **If the unit does not heat up,** check the cord first. Look for signs of burning and wear, and then test it for continuity (see Blue Pages: *Electrical testers*).

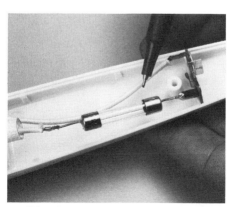

2 If the element doesn't heat up, check the fuse (if the drier has one). It is located between the heating element and the swivel cord terminals. If it has blown, put in a new one, using solderless connectors.

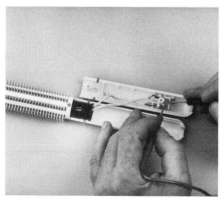

3 Examine the heating element terminals to make sure that they make proper contact with the cord. Test them for continuity. If the terminal circuit is defective or the element itself is broken, the appliance must be replaced.

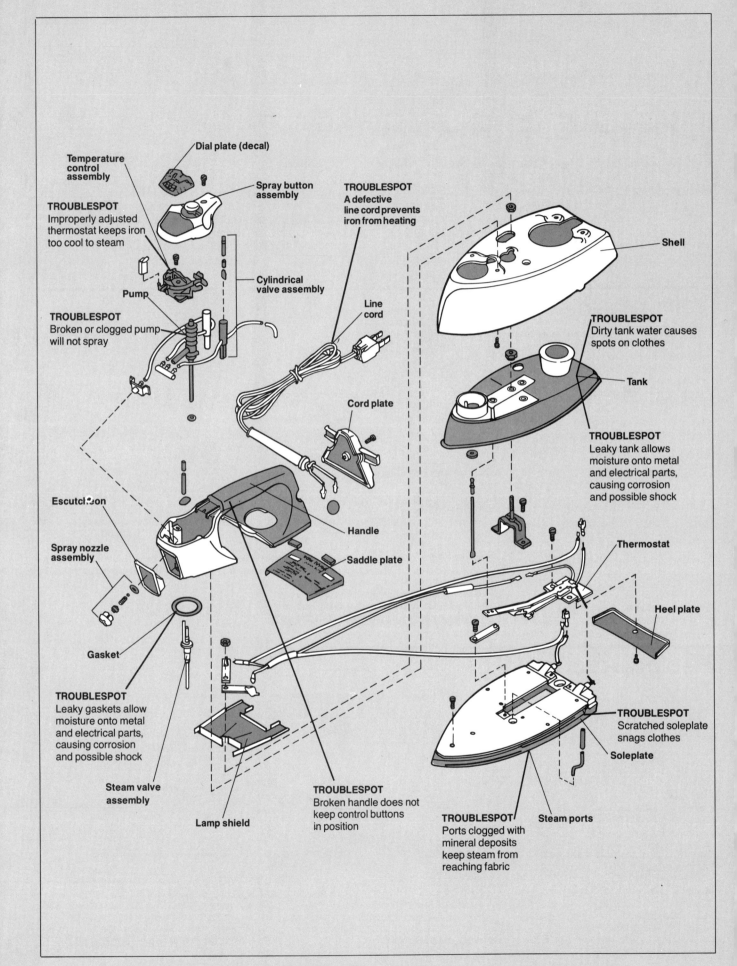

Dial plate (decal)

Temperature
control
assembly

Spray button
assembly

TROUBLESPOT
A defective
line cord prevents
iron from heating

Shell

TROUBLESPOT
Improperly adjusted
thermostat keeps iron
too cool to steam

Cylindrical
valve assembly

Pump

Line
cord

TROUBLESPOT
Dirty tank water causes
spots on clothes

TROUBLESPOT
Broken or clogged pump
will not spray

Cord plate

Tank

TROUBLESPOT
Leaky tank allows
moisture onto metal
and electrical parts,
causing corrosion
and possible shock

Escutcheon

Thermostat

Handle

Spray nozzle
assembly

Saddle plate

Heel plate

Gasket

TROUBLESPOT
Leaky gaskets allow
moisture onto metal
and electrical parts,
causing corrosion
and possible shock

TROUBLESPOT
Scratched soleplate
snags clothes

Soleplate

Steam valve
assembly

TROUBLESPOT
Broken handle does not
keep control buttons
in position

Lamp shield

Steam ports

TROUBLESPOT
Ports clogged with
mineral deposits
keep steam from
reaching fabric

Irons

The most frequently encountered problems with steam irons are caused by the buildup of mineral deposits that prevent the steam from getting through the ports on the bottom of the iron; frayed or broken cords; and by broken handles resulting when the iron accidentally slides off the ironing board and onto the floor, a common occurrence even among careful users.

Clogged steam ports can be cleaned easily and further build-up prevented by regular maintenance of the soleplate. Likewise, broken cords can be replaced with relative ease. But a broken handle on a steam iron is a more complicated problem. Inside the handle is an intricate arrangement of wires, valves, and tubes that make up the steam and spray system. When the handle breaks, these parts lose their support and become misaligned. Knobs and buttons may fail to stay in position, and gaskets may leak, allowing water to get into the rest of the iron and corrode the metal parts or short out the cord, thermostat, or heating element.

Removing the broken handle to replace it or to inspect the iron for other disorders is relatively easy. Putting it back again, however, is an entirely different matter, as anyone who has tried

unsuccessfully can testify! When you lift off the handle on some irons, parts seem to tumble out in all directions before you have a chance to see where they came from. This is the point at which most people give up and buy a new iron. But if you follow the steps given here, you can do the job: the only secret to successful iron repair is observing the correct order for reassembly. Before disassembling your iron, read both the sections *Getting inside* and *Reassembly* for your iron model (pages 222 through 227). Have a receptacle handy for placing small parts, screws, etc., as you remove them.

General instructions for iron repairs are given on the first three pages of this section, followed by specific directions for disassembling and reassembling the four most widely used irons: General Electric, Hamilton Beach, Sunbeam, and Sears.

Iron Care Tips

Empty the water in your iron after each use. Allowing water to remain in the tank allows sediment buildup and could cause corrosion.

Unplug the cord when the iron is unattended, even if you plan to return to it shortly. Otherwise, an accidental jarring could send it crashing to the floor. This could result in a strain to the cord or, worse, the control knob could turn on and the iron could heat up on the floor, furniture, or in the laundry basket.

Allow the iron to cool completely before putting it away. Its storage area should be in a dry location and away from liquids that could accidentally spill on or into the iron.

Avoid ironing over zippers, buttons, or sharp ornamental items on clothing that could scratch the soleplate and cause snagging. If a scratch occurs, buff the plate lightly with steel wool until the scratch disappears. Then test by ironing over a piece of scrap cloth to be sure that the soleplate no longer snags.

MAINTENANCE

Regular attention to the three areas where cleaning is important will greatly affect your iron's performance for the better.

The ports: For best results, use distilled water in your steam iron. Clean the steam ports on the bottom of the iron if they show any sign of sediment or mineral buildup. Use a small round brush of the type used to clean electric shavers, or use a piece of thin wire or a straightened paper clip.

The steam channels: Flush the residual sediment, dust, or lint particles out of the interior steam channels with a solution of vinegar and water in equal parts. Commercial solutions for dissolving mineral buildup are also available. Turn the iron to the lowest steam setting, place it flat on a wire pastry rack with an old towel underneath, and lock the steam button into place. Allow a full tank of the solution to steam through until the sediment has all disappeared (in about 30 minutes). Then flush the tank once with clear water to remove any vinegar smell.

The soleplate: Remove starch buildup or residue from scorched synthetic fabrics by scrubbing the soleplate gently with ammonia or liquid household cleaner. On polished aluminum soleplates, you may use fine steel wool if necessary, and on soleplates with nonstick coatings, use a plastic scouring pad.

Electrical problems

Checking and replacing the cord

If the iron fails to heat at all, the first thing to check is the cord. A faulty cord can be replaced if you adapt these directions for getting the old one out. If your iron has a cord that can be moved from one side of the iron to the other (a reversible cord), see the top of the next page.

Unlike old-fashioned irons that had terminal pins at the back onto which a detachable cord was plugged, today's models (with a few exceptions) have cords that connect inside the appliance. The terminals can be reached for inspection by removing a plastic cord plate, usually held in place by a single screw.

Some irons have a built-in heat-sensitive fuse that opens the circuit to prevent dangerous overheating when the thermostat fails. If the line cord is OK, but the iron doesn't heat, check to see if the fuse has blown. If it has, take the iron to a repair shop.

To test and replace the cord, remove the cord plate and disconnect the cord. Test the cord for continuity (see Blue Pages: *Electrical testers*) and replace it if it is faulty. If the cord is attached to the terminals with ring connectors that must be unscrewed, tilt the iron and make the last few turns by hand so the screws don't fall into the body of the iron.

If the cord sleeve is worn, replace it; add one if your iron doesn't have this feature. You can buy one at any electrical supply store. The cord sleeve gives protection against fraying and breaking where the cord enters the iron.

Reversible cords

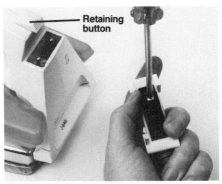

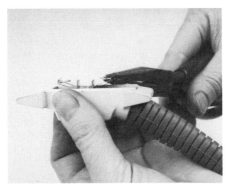

To test the cord or reverse its direction on models that offer this feature, unscrew the reversible cord plate and lift it out. To test the cord, detach it and test it for continuity (see Blue Pages: *Electrical testers*). To change sides, simply turn the cord plate around and reconnect. On irons with non-plug-in reversible cords, simply unscrew and remove the cord plate to test the cord.

1 To test the cord in clip-on connector plates, release the cord plate by pulling back on the retaining button at the back of the handle. Turn the plate over and remove the plastic cover on the bottom. Test the cord for continuity (see Blue Pages: *Electrical testers*).

2 Check the copper blades that come in contact with the iron's terminals. If the blades are bent, straighten them with needle-nose pliers; if they are broken, replace the push-on cord plate.

Testing and adjusting the thermostat

If the iron doesn't heat on some settings or fails to heat at all (and the cord is OK) the thermostat has probably failed or needs adjustment.

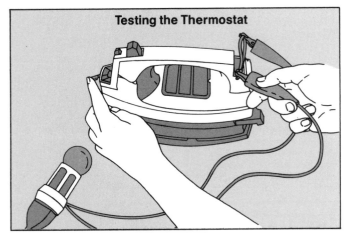

Testing the Thermostat

To test and adjust the thermostat, set the temperature control knob in the OFF position, and clip continuity tester leads to the iron's element terminals (see Blue Pages: *Electrical testers*). You can also make this test by attaching the continuity tester to the line cord prongs. Move the knob to the first temperature setting; if the tester fails to show continuity, the thermostat needs adjustment. This is accomplished by turning a screw, which is easy to reach on most irons (see below).

If the thermostat shows no continuity at the first setting, try the rest of the settings. No continuity at any setting indicates a faulty thermostat or heating element. The iron must be disassembled to reach them (see the directions for disassembly and reassembly on the following pages).

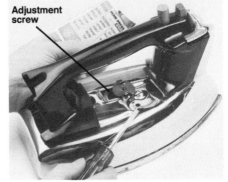

On the GE, the adjustment screw is located under the saddle plate, which can be pried off the iron with a flat-blade screwdriver. Set the thermostat at the lowest temperature and adjust the screw until you get continuity.

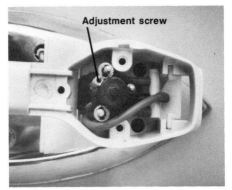

On the Hamilton Beach, the adjustment screw is on top of the temperature control shaft. Remove the plastic dial plate and you will see it at the very back of the opening. The top of the shaft is slotted so it can be turned with a screwdriver.

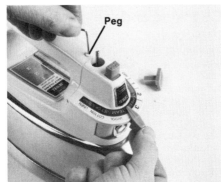

On the Sunbeam and Sears, set the temperature control straight ahead. Turn the spray button to the side and push the peg out of the rivet (the peg can be shaken out of the front of the iron). Reach through the rivet with an Allen wrench and turn the thermostat control rod, then check the adjustment as described above. Replace the peg in the rivet.

Checking for leaks

If the iron starts to drip from around the top of the soleplate, there is a good possibility that the tank has sprung a leak. The likelihood is even greater if the iron has been dropped recently. Disassemble it to check (see *Getting inside*, pages 222 through 227, for your model). All iron tanks are fairly similar, and the source of the leak will be apparent as you look at the tank. While checking the tank, it is a wise precaution to check the large gasket around the tank's fill port for signs of wear: looseness, brittleness, or breaks in the rubber. Look all the way around the seams where the tank's parts are clamped together. If there are breaks, clean the area around the break and run a bead of silicone adhesive around the seam to reseal it. If the tank has a large break or is corroded, replace it. Worn or leaky gaskets should be replaced. Good ones can be anchored in place with a little silicone adhesive, if necessary, to help keep them properly seated while you reassemble the iron.

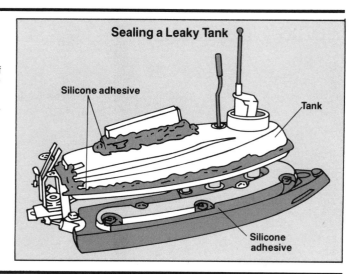

Sealing a Leaky Tank

Silicone adhesive

Tank

Silicone adhesive

Checking the pump

Steam iron pumps fail for a variety of reasons: rubber parts may corrode, water passages may become clogged with mineral sediment, or a spring may even lose its tension, causing the pump shaft to move with less than adequate force. If your iron suffers from any of these symptoms, disassemble it to check (see *Getting inside*, pages 222 through 227, for your model). All pumps are replaced as an assembly.

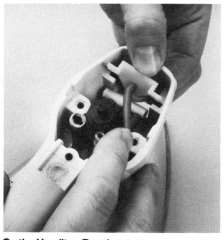

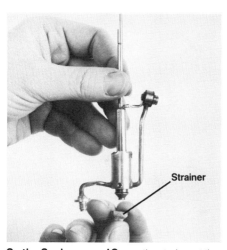

Strainer

On the GE put the pump tube into a container of water and press the lever a few times. Look closely to see if water squirts out. If it does, the diaphragm is faulty and the pump must be replaced. Use a paper clip to clean out clogged tubes.

On the Hamilton Beach, take the spray assembly out and look for any breaks in the rubber parts. The pump cannot be tested outside the handle. Rinse any tube sections that seem clogged and make sure that they fit firmly onto their fittings when reassembled. If tubes are broken, replace them.

On the Sunbeam and Sears the strainer at the base of the intake may accumulate enough sediment from the tank to keep water from getting through adequately. Pull the strainer off and rinse it thoroughly. If it is too corroded to serve its function, replace it.

Testing the Iron for Ground

Before plugging in an iron that has been disassembled and reassembled, always test to be sure that no electrical part has accidentally come in contact with other metal parts of the iron (see Blue Pages: *Testing for ground*). First, place the temperature dial at the center position to ensure that the thermostat points are in contact. Clip one lead from the continuity tester to one of the cord terminals in the iron or to one side of the cord plug. Touch the other clip to the exposed metal parts of the iron. If the continuity light goes on, you have a short within the iron. Take the iron apart again to see where the electrical circuit is touching the rest of the iron. Test each terminal or each side of the cord plug independently, using this method.

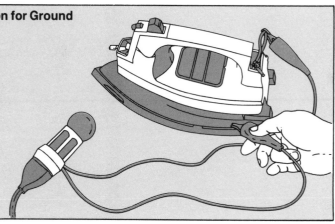

Getting inside: GE

Locking nut

1 **To disassemble the GE iron,** pry off the saddle plate with a flat-blade screwdriver and loosen the locking nut underneath. Sometimes this nut is a conventional hex nut, sometimes a disc-shaped retainer.

2 Remove the nut or retainer along with the clip underneath it. This clip holds the water level indicator plate under the glass water level tube. When the clip is loose, the plate will slip free.

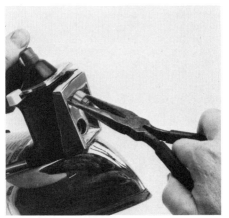

3 Unscrew the nut holding the pump nozzle in place and pry off the metal escutcheon through which the nozzle protrudes.

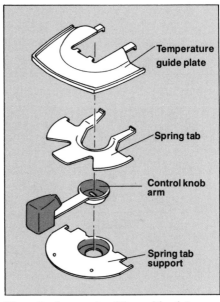

Temperature guide plate

Spring tab

Control knob arm

Spring tab support

Place the four parts of the guide plate assembly in front of you in the proper order, making note of the arrangement of the parts before you disassemble them.

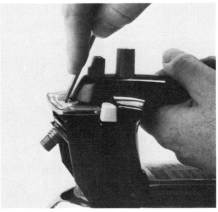

4 Press down on the temperature guide plate assembly and slide it out. Use a screwdriver, if necessary, to pry it out from the center point. See the box, at left, for arranging the parts of the assembly.

Pump

Water level tube

5 Lift away the handle and shell; the spray button (in left hand) will probably fall out. From this point you can either replace the handle or work on the tank and pump. The glass water-level tube can also be removed so you can examine for leaks.

6 The pump and the steam valve button lift directly out of the tank without further disassembly. The thermostat control rod (shown here standing straight up in the tank) should be left in place.

7 To remove the handle from the shell for replacement, turn the shell over and remove the screws on the underside that secure the handle. The metal shell itself never needs replacement.

Reassembly: GE

1 **To reassemble the GE iron,** put the tank back in place (if you have removed it) and insert the pump in the front opening in the tank dome, leading the thermostat control rod between the arms of the pump's spray lever. Replace the glass water level tube.

2 Place the stem of the steam button in the tube at the back of the tank dome behind the pump.

3 Connect the handle assembly to the shell. Then, working from the front so you can watch the parts, lower the handle over the rest of the iron, guiding it from underneath with your other hand if necessary.

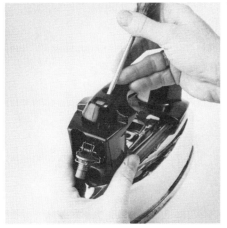

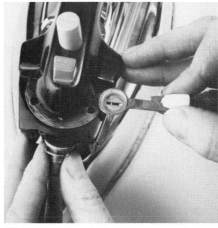

4 When the steam button is as close to the hole as it will go, reach through from the hole behind it with a screwdriver to ease it into place.

5 Hold the spray nozzle with one hand and with the other snap the spray button onto the pump lever. In a good light, you can see this maneuver through the front of the iron.

6 Now, return to the four-part temperature guide plate assembly (see box, preceding page) and place the spring tab support in the slot from which it came. Then slide the control knob arm over it and slip its slotted end over the end of the thermostat control rod inside the iron.

7 Before putting the spring tab in place, bend its tips a little to ensure adequate tension (right). Then place it in the slot with its edges up.

8 Put the temperature plate over the first three pieces of the temperature guide plate assembly (far right) and snap it into place. Replace the front escutcheon and spray nozzle, replace the clip for the water level indicator plate and the retaining nut, and snap on the saddle plate. Reattach the cord, and test the iron for ground (see box, page 221).

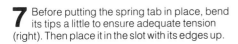

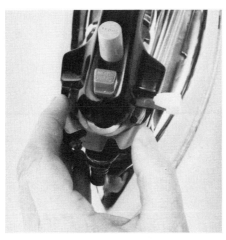

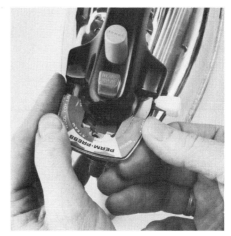

Getting inside: Hamilton Beach

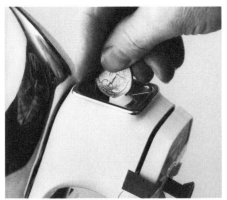

1 **To get inside the Hamilton Beach,** leave the cord in place, rest the iron on its heel, and remove the slotted plastic nut holding the spray nozzle. A coin is the best tool for this job.

2 Carefully lift out in order: the plastic nut, the escutcheon, the spray nozzle, the spring, and the little plastic bearing below the spring. Tilt the iron over to dump the bearing out. Put the iron down flat and remove the heel rest and cord.

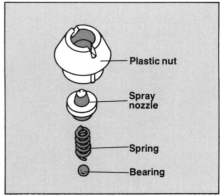

3 Put the spray nozzle assembly in a coffee cup or other safe container. Be careful not to let the plastic bearing roll away—the iron will not spray without it.

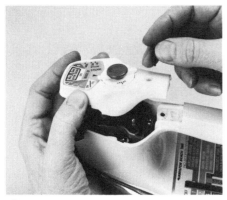

4 Remove the screw holding the spray button assembly at the front of the iron's handle. This piece will include the dial panel and the spray button. Lift off the section and set it aside.

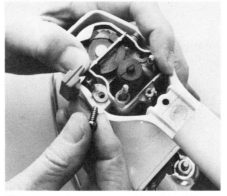

5 Take out the screws on either side of the temperature control assembly that you see in the top of the handle. The assembly rests on pins that are spring-loaded, so you may want to press down on the assembly to ease tension on the screws as you remove them.

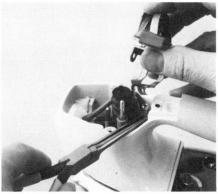

6 Lift the assembly up and disconnect it at the back by snapping it out of the top of the temperature control rod. What you now see underneath is the pump assembly. Lift the plastic spray valve out of the slots that hold it in position at the front of the handle.

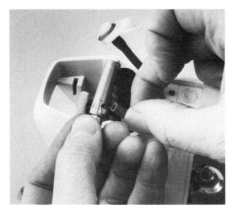

7 Disconnect the tube leading to the left side of the plastic connector. Slip the tube backward through the cylindrical valve at the left of the pump. The pump assembly can be removed from the handle cavity for inspection or replacement.

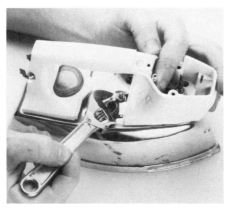

8 Pry off the saddle plate with a screwdriver and remove the water level indicator by pressing together the angled ends that hold it on its shaft. Mark the position of the water-level indicator on the shell before removing it. Then remove the nut that attaches the shell to the bottom of the iron.

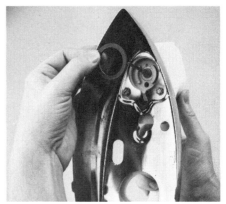

9 If the handle itself is broken and needs replacing, turn it over and remove the hex screws attaching it to the metal shell. Examine the rubber gasket that rests on the underside of the opening at the front of the shell for damage.

Reassembly: Hamilton Beach

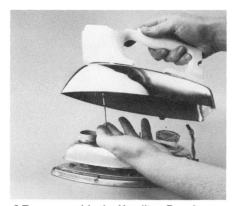

1 **To reassemble the Hamilton Beach,** connect the handle and shell and place them back over the rest of the iron, guiding the temperature control rod up into the rearmost hole in the handle cavity. Make sure that you haven't forgotten the gasket under the shell (see step 9 of disassembly).

2 Lead the heating element wires up through the hole at the back of the shell. As they emerge you may have to give a gentle tug from the outside to bring them fully into position for reconnecting. Then replace the nut on the top of the shell and tighten it firmly.

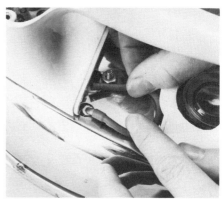

3 Insert one end of the metal right angle tube into the tank and connect the long rubber tube to the other end. Feed the tube into the handle cavity and place the water level indicator back in position.

4 Guide the pump tube through the center opening and insert the right cylinder valve in its socket next to the pump.

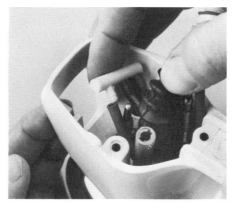

5 Lead the tube from the steam chamber through the hole in the left cylinder valve and insert the valve in its socket on the left side of the pump. Connect the end of the tube to the plastic connector in front of the pump.

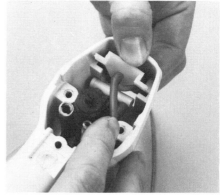

6 Place the spray assembly in the slots at the front of the handle. Put the blades, springs, and pins back in each of the cylindrical valves on either side of the pump (see exploded drawing of valve parts on page 218).

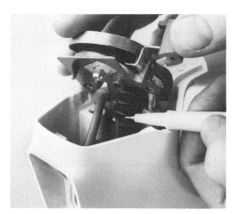

7 Snap the back of the temperature control assembly into the top of the temperature control rod. As you lower the front of the assembly into the handle, guide the steam valve into the opening in the underside of the frame.

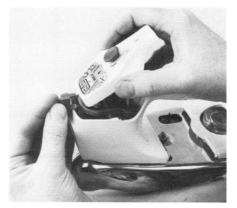

8 Replace the screws on the sides of the temperature control assembly and replace the spray button assembly on top of the handle. Connect the power cord and heel plate.

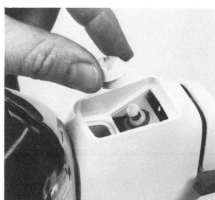

9 Stand the iron on its heel and put the bearing, spring, and spray nozzle back into the valve—it is easiest to drop them in with needlenose pliers. Replace the escutcheon and secure the whole assembly with the slotted plastic nut. Test the iron for ground (see box, page 221).

Getting inside: Sunbeam and Sears

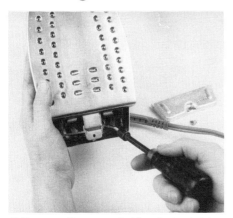

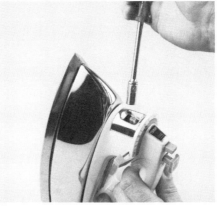

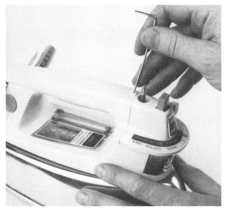

1 **Remove the screw** holding the heel plate and lift the plate free. Reach into the iron and remove the two screws extending up into the handle. On these two brands, removing the cord first is not the most convenient move.

2 Rest the iron on its heel and unscrew the spray nozzle, using a nut driver. Remove the nozzle carefully, then remove the white plastic spray plug and the spring with the ball valve. Put these parts together in a container for safekeeping.

3 Rest the iron flat again and pull off the spray button on the handle top. Just behind it is a small plastic rivet with a peg in its center. Push the peg down into the iron, using an Allen wrench. Then pry the rest of the rivet up and out, using a flat-blade screwdriver.

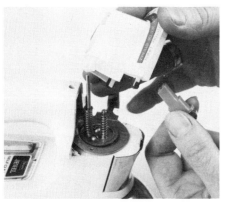

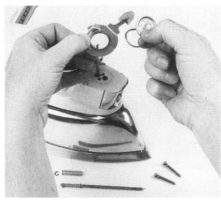

4 Remove the temperature dial assembly by moving it forward and up, so that it clears the pump shaft. The steam button will drop out. Set the assembly and button aside, along with the two metal spring clamps from the back of the plate (if they fall off).

5 Pull out the needle valve assembly (at the front of the exposed handle area) together with its spring, E-clip, and washer. Remove the E-clip and spring from the pump. Then remove the two long screws holding the temperature-control assembly in place. Lift off the three-part assembly.

6 If either the cord or the handle needs replacing, remove them at this point by disconnecting the cord terminals from their pins. The indicator light lifts off as a part of the cord assembly.

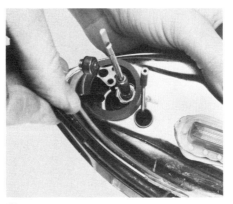

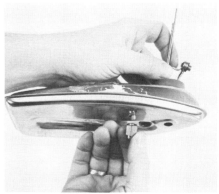

7 Remove the clamp supporting the pump and nozzle assembly by pressing in on its sides and lifting up and out. Then lift off the iron's shell to expose the tank and soleplate assembly. The pump will remain connected at this point to the inside of the tank.

8 To separate the tank and pump assembly from the soleplate, loosen the steam valve nut inside the tank, using an Allen wrench. The tank will lift off the soleplate; the tank may be inspected and, if necessary, sealed against leaks. Don't lose the washers.

9 To remove the pump and nozzle assembly from the tank, unscrew the steam jet assembly from under the bottom of the tank and slip the pump assembly forward through the fill port.

Reassembly: Sunbeam and Sears

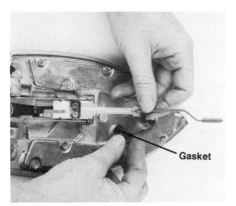

1 **Make sure that the temperature control shaft** is in place on the thermostat lever, with its top end angling sharply toward the center. Check that the steam jet gasket is seated on the soleplate.

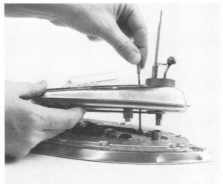

2 Place the pump assembly back in the tank and secure it. Then place the pump and tank on the soleplate, leading the temperature control shaft through the opening in the tank. Tighten the steam valve nut (remember to insert all the washers).

3 Reinstall the clamp over the tank port and reseat the gasket over the port's lip. Then reattach the shell.

4 Connect the cord terminals, positioning the indicator light on top of the shell, and guiding the pump shaft and temperature control shaft through their respective holes in the front of the handle.

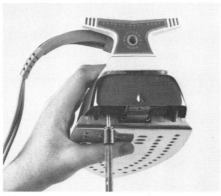

5 Holding the iron tightly together, turn it over and retighten the screws that extend into the handle. It is easiest to put the screws on the driver and reach *up* into the iron.

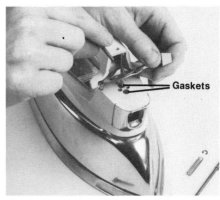

6 Make sure that the rubber pump and needle valve gaskets are in place. Put the temperature control assembly over the pump shaft. Screw the assembly into place and install the pump shaft spring with the E-clip. When that is done, push the needle valve assembly back into its hole.

7 Put the steam button into the dial assembly and guide the assembly into its original position. Use a screwdriver blade to depress the needle valve assembly from the front while you are lowering the dial assembly and button with the other hand.

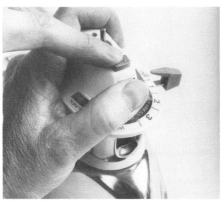

8 When the dial assembly is in place, hold it firmly on the handle and press the steam button. If the button locks into place, the assembly is correctly situated over the shaft; if it doesn't, you must raise the dial assembly again and adjust it.

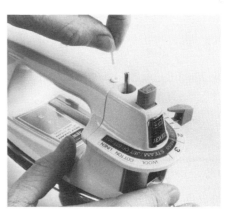

9 Push the rivet into the handle and the peg into its hole. Replace the spray button and test the iron for ground (see box, page 221).

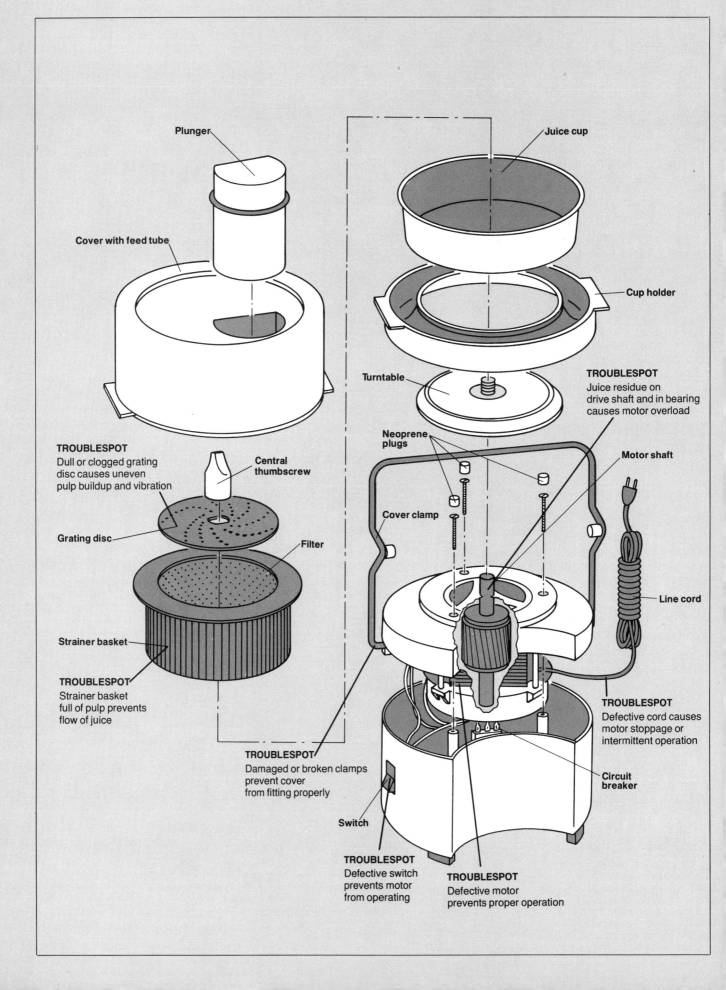

Plunger

Cover with feed tube

Juice cup

Cup holder

TROUBLESPOT
Dull or clogged grating disc causes uneven pulp buildup and vibration

Central thumbscrew

Turntable

TROUBLESPOT
Juice residue on drive shaft and in bearing causes motor overload

Grating disc

Filter

Neoprene plugs

Motor shaft

Cover clamp

Strainer basket

Line cord

TROUBLESPOT
Strainer basket full of pulp prevents flow of juice

TROUBLESPOT
Defective cord causes motor stoppage or intermittent operation

Circuit breaker

TROUBLESPOT
Damaged or broken clamps prevent cover from fitting properly

Switch

TROUBLESPOT
Defective switch prevents motor from operating

TROUBLESPOT
Defective motor prevents proper operation

Juice Extractors

A juice extractor is an ingenious but straightforward mechanism. It uses a grating disc inside a strainer compartment, both sitting on a motor shaft, which spins them at high speed. Fruits or vegetables are fed onto the disc through an opening in the unit's cover; their fibrous parts are shredded, releasing juice and pulp, which are then flung against the sides of the strainer by centrifugal force. The strainer holds the pulp while the juice spins through and collects in a bowl or cup. Strainer filters—for added straining efficiency and easy cleaning up—are available on most juice extractors.

A citrus juicer, a near relative of the juice extractor, works slightly differently, shredding the pulp of thick-skinned citrus fruits with a vertical agitator. Citrus juicers are described on page 233.

MAINTENANCE
Don't use force when feeding fruits and vegetables onto the grating disc; gentle pressure is enough. If you force material onto the disc you risk straining the motor.
Clean the disc and strainer frequently when juicing fibrous vegetables. If pulp accumulates unevenly on the strainer sides it may throw the spinning parts out of balance, causing the machine to vibrate and overheat.
Wash the parts of the juice extractor by hand—never in the dishwasher. Use a stiff brush to loosen accumulated pulp.
To get rid of mineral stains on the disc and strainer, soak them overnight in cold water to which you've added a little mild detergent. After soaking, the stains will come off with a stiff brush.

External repairs

Some common problems with juice extractors—dull grating discs, a damaged housing clamp, or clogged or damaged strainer filters (if the model has them)—can be fixed without opening the housing. Also, if your juice extractor is vibrating more than it should, you can make a simple check of the motor without disassembling the appliance.

If the disc is clean but juices inefficiently, it is probably dull. Another indication that the disc is dull is uneven distribution of pulp on the strainer.

If the motor begins to vibrate and labor excessively, clean the strainer and disc and then run the unit empty. If the vibration continues, check the motor shaft as explained below.

To replace a dull disc or to remove it for cleaning, take off the cover and loosen the central thumbscrew on the disc. If you can't do this easily by hand, wrap a piece of cloth around the screw and use pliers.

To remove the strainer filter for replacement or cleaning, take off the cover and look for the pull tab. Grip the tab and pull out the filter.

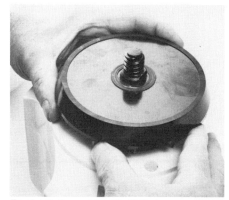

To check the motor shaft, first remove the disc and strainer. Move the turntable up and down. If it doesn't move, the motor is probably jammed. On the other hand, if there is a great deal of play, the motor mounts may be loose. In either case you have to open the housing to correct the problem.

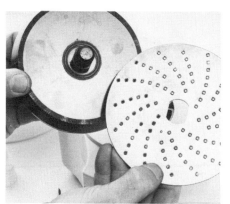

The disc and shaft of some juicers are shaped to fit together in only one position. A circular gouge on either the turntable or the bottom of the bowl indicates that you are setting the disc incorrectly. Reset the disc.

To replace the clamps that hold the cover tightly shut on some machines, locate the screw that attaches the metal or plastic arm of the clamp to the housing. Remove the screw, pull off the damaged clamp, and replace it.

Getting inside

If you have problems with the switch or cord on a juice extractor, you must open the lower base to make repairs.

On the Acme, Oster, and Waring juicers, the base can be opened without removing the turntable; on the Braun the turntable must be removed to get into the base.

If you have problems with the motor in most models, you can get at it through the top by taking off the turntable. The Acme juicer is an exception: the turntable cannot be removed:

To gain access to the Acme, Oster, or Waring base, take off the cover, the disc, the strainer, and the juice cup or bowl. Turn the unit upside down; remove from the base all the screws you can find and lift it off.

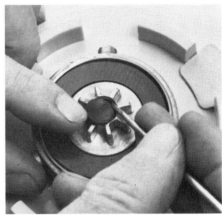

1 **To remove the Oster turntable** so the motor assembly can be taken out, use a screwdriver to pry out the rubber plug from the center of the turntable, where it covers a screw-in collar.

2 Fit a hefty flat screwdriver into the slot on the collar and turn. gently. Remove the collar and lift off the turntable. To avoid damage to the collar, you should allow no play between the blade and the slot: the screwdriver must be just the right size.

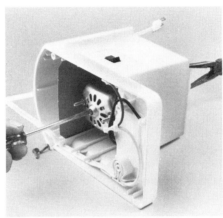

1 **To remove the Waring turntable,** place the unit on its side and fit a screwdriver into the slot on the end of the motor shaft. Grip the turntable with pliers to hold it stationary while you turn the motor shaft with the screwdriver.

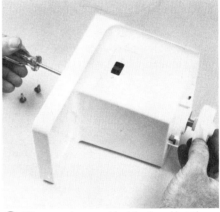

2 When you hear and feel the bond break, spin the turntable off by hand; you don't need pliers for this.

1 **To open the base of the Braun juicer,** find the slotted setscrew, which is recessed inside a hole in the side of the turntable. After loosening this screw, you can remove the turntable by lifting it straight up.

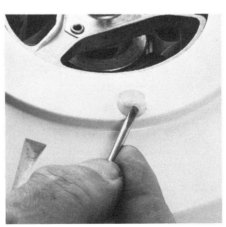

2 The turntable covers three neoprene plugs on top of the base. Pry them up and off with a screwdriver. This reveals three screws underneath. Remove the three screws.

3 Using a screwdriver, gently pry apart the upper and lower portions of the housing. Care must be taken to avoid chipping the paint. As soon as there is some space between the two portions, you should be able to lift the upper housing off, with the motor attached.

Cord and switch problems

If the motor doesn't run at all, or runs intermittently, it's likely that the cord, switch, or motor is at fault. Test all three for continuity (see Blue Pages: *Electrical testers*) and replace if defective.

On two-speed models, if the motor doesn't operate on one setting, or operates at the same speed on both settings, you have a defective diode.

The diode is the device that cuts the power in half when the motor is set on the lower speed. You can have a repairman replace only the diode, or you can replace the switch and diode as a unit yourself, which in most cases turns out to be less expensive.

To test a cord, detach one of the leads (to either the motor or the switch) and check both sides of the cord for continuity. If there is no continuity on either side, replace the cord, using wire nuts if needed.

To test and replace the switch on the Acme, detach one lead from the switch and test for continuity across the switch's terminals. If the switch is defective, label the leads for identification, disconnect both leads, lift the switch out of the housing, and replace it.

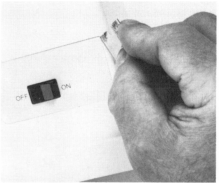

To test and replace the Waring's switch, detach one lead from the switch; test for continuity across the terminals. To remove a defective switch, peel back the decal around the switch and remove the two screws underneath.

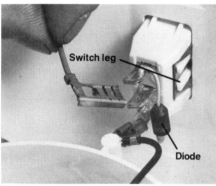

To remove a defective Braun two-speed switch, detach the leads and the diode, squeeze in the switch legs, and push the switch out of the housing. Replace it with a duplicate.

(labels: Switch leg, Diode)

1 To remove a defective Oster two-speed switch, gently pry off the switch knob while rotating the switch.

2 Using needle-nose pliers or a socket wrench, remove the hex nut holding the switch. Pull the switch out, detach and label the leads, and replace the switch, using the old diode.

Braun Reset Button

A special safety feature unique to the Braun juicer is a heat sensor attached to the field coil of the motor. If the motor overheats, the heat sensor trips a bimetallic circuit breaker, cutting off current to the motor. Current will not flow again until the reset button has been pushed. If the motor doesn't restart, you will have to open the base (see *Getting inside*, opposite) and test the circuit breaker for continuity.

To replace a defective circuit breaker, label the three leads for identification, pull them off, and remove the two screws that hold it in place. Pull out the circuit breaker and install a new one.

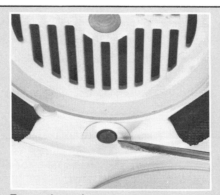

To reactivate the motor, remove the cause of the overheating and wait for the motor to cool. Press the reset button on the base of the unit and switch the appliance on.

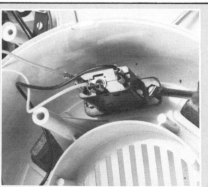

To test the circuit breaker for continuity, hold one tester probe on the common terminal (the one in the middle) and test each of the other two terminals. The switch should show continuity on both sides.

Motor problems

If the motor is straining—it may whine or vibrate when you turn it on, or give off a burned smell—the drive shaft may be obstructed. If the motor hums but the grating disc doesn't move, the drive shaft is jammed. In either case, turn off the juice extractor immediately. After waiting for it to cool, check the motor bearing for juice residue or other debris and clean it out.

Directions are given here for getting access to the Braun, Oster, and Acme motors; access to the Waring motor is through the base (see *Getting inside,* page 230).

If the motor is apparently burned out (if the switch, cord, and all connections test OK, but the unit doesn't run), it is probably best to take the entire unit to a repair shop for service or replace it.

1 To remove the Braun motor, first take off the turntable (see *Getting inside*), and undo the screws on the base. Remove the base, freeing the field coil and the rotor.

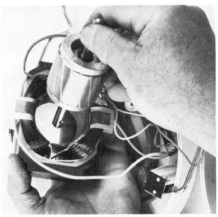

2 Pull out the motor by the field coil and remove the rotor to check for damage or blockage. If you are replacing the motor yourself, first label and remove the leads from the motor to the terminal block.

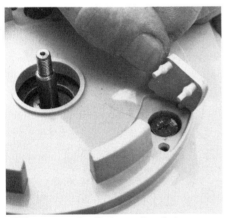

1 To remove the Oster motor, first remove the base and the turntable (see *Getting inside*), then pry off the rubber shock absorbers from the top of the base. Remove the screws underneath, which will release the motor from the top of the base.

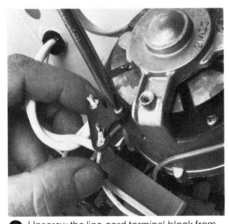

2 Unscrew the line-cord terminal block from the motor housing, using a Phillips screwdriver. Lift out the motor for inspection.
➤ If you have to replace the motor, cut the leads close to the old motor. This will leave plenty of wire for attaching the new motor.

1 To remove the field coil on the Acme, loosen the two screws on the metal bracket in its base. Remove the motor leads and rock the field coil back and forth to pull it out. The rotor and turntable cannot be removed without professional help.

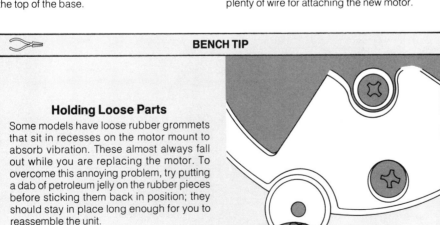

BENCH TIP

Holding Loose Parts

Some models have loose rubber grommets that sit in recesses on the motor mount to absorb vibration. These almost always fall out while you are replacing the motor. To overcome this annoying problem, try putting a dab of petroleum jelly on the rubber pieces before sticking them back in position; they should stay in place long enough for you to reassemble the unit.

Petroleum jelly   Rubber grommet

2 The cap of the motor bearing may fall off when you remove the field coil. When you reassemble the unit, make sure that the cap is back in the position indicated by the pen.

Citrus juicers

The citrus juicer is a less powerful version of the juice extractor, and it operates somewhat differently. It has a vertical reamer, that extracts juice from the flesh of thick-skinned fruit; some models have a simple gear system attached to the drive shaft in order to slow down the rotary speed that is transferred to the reamer; and the switch is activated by pressure on the reamer and bowl.

When a juicer is operating inefficiently or not at all, there's a chance that a thorough cleaning of the external shaft area may solve the problem. Juice or pulp residue can prevent the shaft from activating the switch or interfere with the proper fit between shaft and reamer.

To inspect, repair, or replace the switch, cord, gears, or motor, you must open the housing. The repairs described are demonstrated on a Braun.

Getting inside

 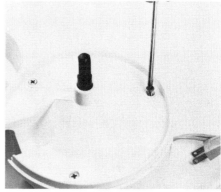

1 **To open up the housing,** lift out the reamer, the strainer bowl, and the small black collar on the shaft. The fit between the collar and the shaft is tight, so you'll have to use some force to twist and pull it off.

2 Remove the three Phillips screws that are recessed in the top housing. Pull up on the shaft, removing the internal parts—the gears, the switch, and the motor—all of which are attached to the upper housing.

Cord and switch problems

Citrus juicers have no external switch. The machine turns on when you push a piece of fruit against the reamer. If the unit doesn't run at all or runs intermittently, first check the cord for continuity (see Blue Pages: *Electrical*

testers). If the cord is OK, test the switch for continuity. If the switch is OK, the problem is probably a defective switch activator or motor. Examine the activator to see if it is pushing down on the switch.

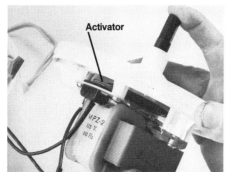 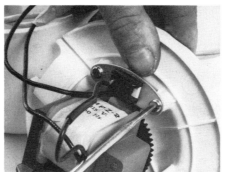 

1 **To check the action of the switch,** push down on the shaft. Look closely to see if the activator is making contact with the switch. Hold the shaft down with your finger and check the switch for continuity.

2 If the switch is defective, take out the two screws on the switch bracket and pull out the switch. Remove the tape from the wire nuts on the switch leads, remove the leads, and replace the switch.

3 If the switch activator fails to activate the switch because it is bent, you can bend it back into proper shape. To gain access to the activator, follow the steps for *Gear replacement*, below.

Gear replacement

If the motor is running properly, but the reamer doesn't ream the fruit efficiently or works only intermittently, probably the gear system is defective. Examine the gears for broken or worn teeth and replace any gears that are damaged.

If the motor has burned out and must be replaced, you can follow these steps to get it out of the juicer. If you remove the motor, be sure to leave enough wire to reconnect a new one. However, you may want to buy a new juicer, depending on the price of a replacement motor.

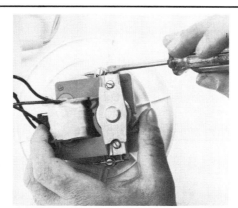 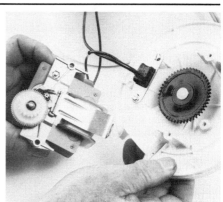

1 **To remove the gears,** the switch activator, and the motor, first take out the screws on the motor mount, one on each side of the motor. Lift the motor from the housing.

2 Lift out the gears and examine them for damage. You can also lift out the switch activator to bend it back into shape, or to replace it.

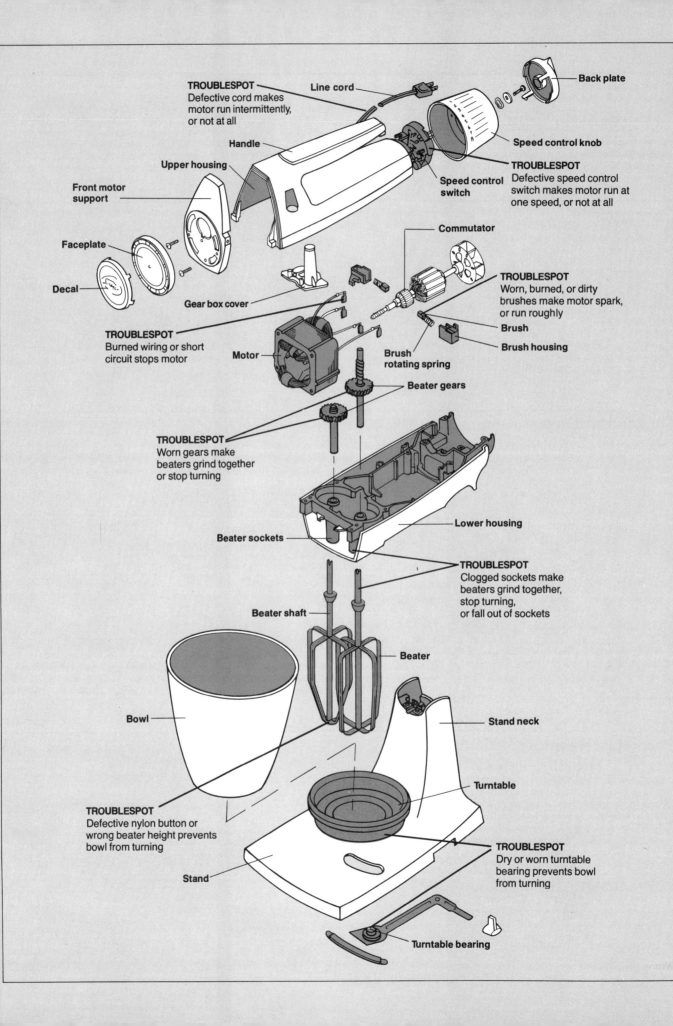

TROUBLESPOT Defective cord makes motor run intermittently, or not at all

Line cord

Back plate

Handle

Speed control knob

Upper housing

TROUBLESPOT Defective speed control switch makes motor run at one speed, or not at all

Front motor support

Speed control switch

Faceplate

Commutator

Decal

TROUBLESPOT Worn, burned, or dirty brushes make motor spark, or run roughly

Gear box cover

Brush

TROUBLESPOT Burned wiring or short circuit stops motor

Brush rotating spring

Brush housing

Motor

Beater gears

TROUBLESPOT Worn gears make beaters grind together or stop turning

Lower housing

Beater sockets

TROUBLESPOT Clogged sockets make beaters grind together, stop turning, or fall out of sockets

Beater shaft

Beater

Bowl

Stand neck

Turntable

TROUBLESPOT Defective nylon button or wrong beater height prevents bowl from turning

Stand

TROUBLESPOT Dry or worn turntable bearing prevents bowl from turning

Turntable bearing

Mixers

A mixer, whether it's a hand-held or a stand model, is basically a housing containing a motor. The motor runs a set of gears that turn two shafts. Beaters attached to these shafts spin when you turn on a switch that controls the motor. Some models have a variable-speed control switch that lets you adjust beater speed.

Hand-held mixers have enough power to whip cream, beat eggs, and in general mix liquids. Stand mixers have a much more powerful motor that can beat bread dough and mash potatoes. Some stand mixers also have attachments for grinding meat, or for blending, shredding, slicing, and juicing other foods.

Most user problems with mixers are caused by putting the beaters into the housing incorrectly, not keeping the mixer clean, or by trying to mix foods too heavy for the motor to handle. The right way to install the beaters is explained at the bottom of this page. Read the box at right for other tips on how to keep your mixer running efficiently.

Many mixer models are constructed so that most repairs are impossible except by a trained technician. The repairs and adjustments anyone can make are described on the following pages. The instructions are specially tailored to the popular models shown in the illustrations, but they can be used as guides to most other models as well.

Adjustments on the outside of the mixer are explained first. Then, the ways to get inside different models are given in detail. Once inside, you can replace the gears on most models. Electrical repairs, however, are more limited, but step-by-step instructions are given for those that are practical for the user.

 TIPS FOR EFFICIENT OPERATION

When you finish working, unplug the mixer and clean it with a damp sponge before the food hardens. Dry the unit with a soft cloth. Try a little full-strength detergent on stubborn spots, then wipe with a sponge.

Detach the beaters, scrape them with a rubber spatula, and wash them with the flatware. Don't bang the beaters against the bowl or sink to clean them. If you bend them out of shape, they'll never spin properly.

To clean the turntable on a stand model, lift it out of its socket and wash it with the dishes.

Don't try to mix anything too heavy for the motor. Read your instruction booklet. While you're mixing, if the motor begins to growl, the beaters slow down, or the housing gets warm, stop the mixer! You will damage the beater sockets, strip the gears, or burn out the motor if you persist. Either dilute the mixture or finish mixing by hand.

Inserting the beaters correctly

You will ruin the beater sockets if you force the beaters into the housing. If the beaters are inserted incorrectly, they will grind together and may strip the gears. Here's the right way to put them in: insert each beater gently into its socket and rotate it slowly until it slips all the way in and locks in place. If you feel resistance, keep turning; you'll feel the beater catch in the socket when you do it correctly. If the beaters snap into their sockets securely, but are incorrectly positioned as in the picture at the left, you have a problem with the mixer's gears.

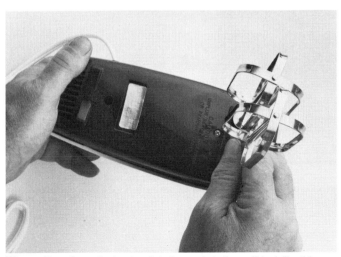

Wrong. If you force the beaters into the sockets they will look like this; they'll grind against each other and damage the gear mechanism.

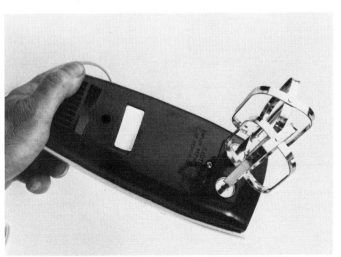

Right. When the beaters are inserted correctly they look like this; they'll turn freely without touching.

External mechanical adjustments

Checking the beater sockets

If the beaters don't snap into place easily, or if they grind together while mixing, check the beater sockets. If they are clogged with bits of food, clean them thoroughly. If the sockets have been damaged, the beater gears must be replaced. See instructions on the next page.

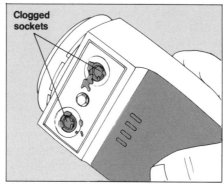

Clean clogged sockets thoroughly with a toothpick.

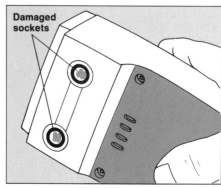

A beater gear with a damaged socket must be replaced.

Setting the right beater height

Most stand mixers, like the Sunbeam, Hamilton Beach, and GE models, turn the bowl automatically while mixing. (The Waring bowl must be turned by hand.) If the bowl doesn't turn, first look at the bottom of the beaters. If one of them has a nylon button attached, that beater should be closest to the side of the bowl. Then check the beater height. Beaters with a nylon button should just touch the bottom of the bowl. Beaters without a button should just clear the bottom.

To adjust beater height, tilt the mixer housing backward on the stand and look for an adjustment screw. On the Sunbeam and Hamilton Beach it's on the underside of the housing; on the GE it's on the top of the stand neck. Turn this screw and check the beater height until you find the right setting.

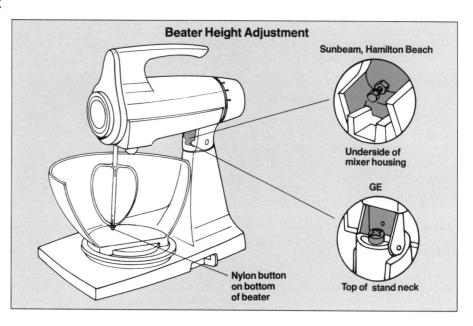

Beater Height Adjustment

Sunbeam, Hamilton Beach

Underside of mixer housing

GE

Nylon button on bottom of beater

Top of stand neck

Checking the turntable

If the bowl doesn't turn (and you've set the beaters at the right height), check the turntable. Take the bowl off and rotate the turntable by hand. If it binds, lift the turntable off the stand and clean out the socket. If there is a bearing in the socket, apply a couple drops of light oil (if there is no bearing, put a dab of petroleum jelly in the hole). Try the turntable again; if it still won't turn freely, you have a bad bearing that must be replaced.

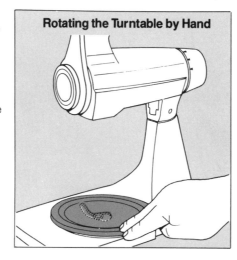

Rotating the Turntable by Hand

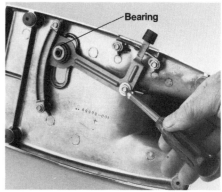

Bearing

If a lubricated turntable won't rotate easily, turn the stand over and take out the screws that hold the bearing assembly. Lift out the bearing and if possible relubricate it; if not, replace it.

Getting inside

To check the gears or the switch you must get inside the mixer housing. The specific techniques for getting into five typical models are shown on this page. Although other models may require somewhat different techniques, these will be helpful guides.

As you remove the parts one by one, lay them out in order on the workbench so you can get them back in properly.

1 **Sunbeam Senior.** Pry off the back plate of the speed control knob with a screwdriver.

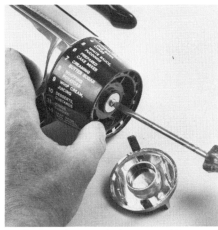

2 Remove the screw in the center of the speed control knob and take the knob off.

3 Remove two screws, one on each side, at the back of the housing.

4 Rotate the handle as if ejecting the beaters and remove the two recessed screws at the front of the housing.

5 Remove the decal from the front of the housing with a single-edge razor blade.

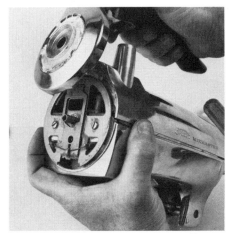

6 Remove the screw under the decal. The faceplate and a spring will come off. Then lift off the handle. The upper housing can now be lifted off, and you're inside.

GE, Waring. Unscrew the recessed Phillips screws on the bottom of the lower housing and separate the upper housing from the lower.

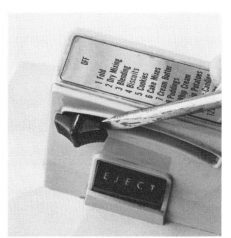

Sunbeam Vista, Hamilton Beach. After removing the housing screws, pry off the speed control knob with a screwdriver and lift the housing off.

Problems with the gears

If the beaters refuse to turn or if they grind together while turning (and the motor runs properly and the beaters seem to fit snugly in their sockets), check the gears. After getting inside the housing (see previous page), first look for a C-clip holding the gears (box, far right). Then follow the directions for your model.

If you find a cracked gear, or a gear with missing or worn teeth, replace both gears.

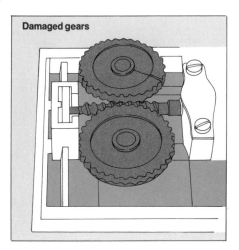

Damaged gears

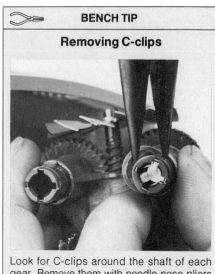

BENCH TIP

Removing C-clips

Look for C-clips around the shaft of each gear. Remove them with needle-nose pliers to free the gears.

Removing the gears

Sunbeam Senior. Unscrew the four screws holding the gearbox assembly (see arrows). Lift off the gearbox cover and pry up the gears.

Sunbeam Vista. Pry out the gears with a screwdriver.

Half gear

Hamilton Beach. Unscrew and remove the half gear from the top of the governor assembly. Remove the two side mounting screws on the governor assembly and take the assembly out. Pry out the gears with a screwdriver.

Replacing the gears

1 **To replace the gears in any model,** seat one gear completely and insert the second without seating it. Then insert both beaters into the sockets.

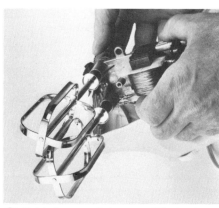

2 Rotate the unseated gear until the beaters look like this. Then seat the gear. If there were C-clips on the gear shafts, replace them.

3 After the gears are installed, dab some white grease on them.

Electrical problems

Problems with the switch

If the mixer doesn't run when the variable speed control switch is turned on (and the motor doesn't hum), check the cord for continuity (see Blue Pages: *Electrical testers*). If it's OK, then the switch is bad. If the mixer runs at only one speed, the switch is defective. You can replace the switch on some models. Others must be taken to a repair shop.

1 Sunbeam Senior. After taking off the speed control knob, remove the three screws holding the speed control switch.

2 Remove the push-on connectors with needle-nose pliers, take out the switch, and replace it with a duplicate.

1 Waring. After prying off the speed control knob and beater release button, remove the three screws that hold the motor and beater gear assembly in place. Lift out the assembly, then the switch, and reattach the speed control knob.

2 Place one probe of a VOM on the power cord lead. With the other probe check each of the motor wires starting with the one closest to the knob. Turn the knob to the next setting for each wire. Each should read 0 ohms.

Contacts

1 GE. The problem may be a faulty contact, which you can repair or a faulty capacitor, which you can replace. Remove the white plastic cam that sits at the front of the housing and check the contacts underneath. They should touch. If they don't, bend up the bottom contact switch.

Capacitor

2 If the contacts are OK, check the capacitor at the back. **CAUTION** Discharge the capacitor first (see page 42). Test the capacitor (see Blue Pages: *Electrical Testers*) and replace it if necessary.

Problems with the motor

If the motor doesn't run (and the cord and switch are OK) or if the motor sparks excessively, check the motor brushes. If they are so worn that they do not fit snugly against the commutator, they must be replaced. No further repairs on mixer motors are practical.

Sunbeam Senior, Sunbeam Vista. Remove the screws holding the brush housing and lift the housing off. Pull out the brushes and replace.

Brush and brush housing

Retaining strip

Hamilton Beach, GE. Remove the screws holding the retaining strip. Take the strip off and the brush housings will come off easily.

Waring. Lift the retaining spring with a screwdriver. The brushes will then slide out.

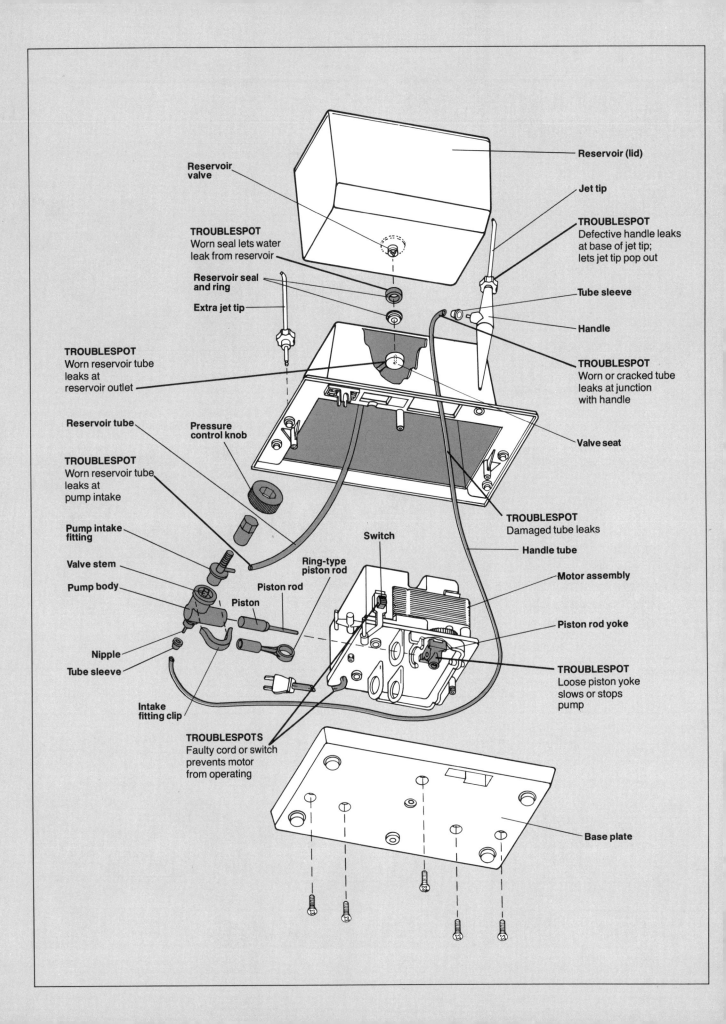

Reservoir (lid)

Reservoir valve

Jet tip

TROUBLESPOT
Defective handle leaks at base of jet tip; lets jet tip pop out

TROUBLESPOT
Worn seal lets water leak from reservoir

Reservoir seal and ring

Extra jet tip

Tube sleeve

Handle

TROUBLESPOT
Worn reservoir tube leaks at reservoir outlet

TROUBLESPOT
Worn or cracked tube leaks at junction with handle

Valve seat

Reservoir tube

Pressure control knob

TROUBLESPOT
Worn reservoir tube leaks at pump intake

TROUBLESPOT
Damaged tube leaks

Handle tube

Pump intake fitting

Switch

Ring-type piston rod

Motor assembly

Valve stem

Piston rod

Pump body

Piston

Piston rod yoke

Nipple

TROUBLESPOT
Loose piston yoke slows or stops pump

Tube sleeve

Intake fitting clip

TROUBLESPOTS
Faulty cord or switch prevents motor from operating

Base plate

Oral Irrigators

An oral irrigator is actually a powerful little pump. It consists of a boxlike cover that lifts off and, flipped upside down, plugs into the valve seat on top of the lower housing to serve as a reservoir. A motor-driven pump draws water from the reservoir and ejects it under high pressure through the jet tip.

The most common problems with oral irrigators are leaks (from either external or internal tubing) and weak pumping action, which has several causes. Leaks and pump problems can be remedied at home. The motor, however, is a sealed unit; consequently, motor problems must be serviced at a repair shop.

The model shown in the following repair instructions is a Water Pik, the most widely distributed brand of oral irrigator. Other brands have the same basic components and operating principles—although they are put together differently—and they can be repaired by adaptation of the instructions given on these pages.

MAINTENANCE
Keep the jet tips clear by washing them occasionally in warm soapy water and reaming them if necessary with a thin wire or fine-bristled brush.
Never run saltwater through the system. Sediment will accumulate and cause malfunctioning.
Don't place the appliance near radiators or heaters. High temperatures cause the flexible plastic parts to become brittle or to bend.
If storing in a location subject to freezing temperatures, run the appliance until no water comes through the jet tip. Shake water out of the tubes and wipe the machine dry.
When securing tubes to their fittings, never use glue. Bits of the substance can get into the works and cause a breakdown. And the solvents in some glues will melt plastic parts.

External leaks

The three most common leaks on an oral irrigator—at the reservoir seal, and at the top and side of the handle—can all be remedied without going inside the appliance. The leaks are easy to spot: water running from under the reservoir atop the pump housing indicates that the reservoir seal has failed; water dripping from the base of the jet tip indicates a defect in the handle; and water leaking from the junction of the tube and the handle means a cracked or loose-fitting tube. A defective reservoir seal or handle must be replaced. A cracked tube can be repaired.

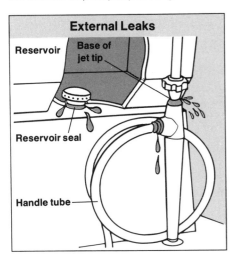

External Leaks

Reservoir

Base of jet tip

Reservoir seal

Handle tube

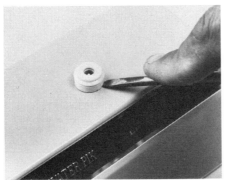

1 **To replace a defective reservoir seal,** pry the seal up gently around the edge with a flat-blade screwdriver until you free it from the valve socket.

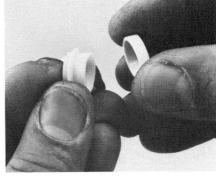

2 Separate the soft plastic seal from its rigid outer ring and save the ring to use on the new seal. Put the replacement seal in the ring and press the assembly into place on the valve socket.

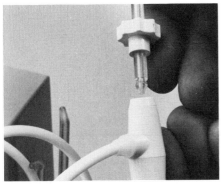

Replace the handle when the problem is leaks around the jet tip base. Snap out the jet tip and save it. If the tubing between the handle and the pump is in good condition, salvage it, following the procedure given in the next step.

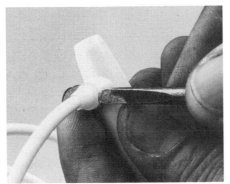

1 **To replace or repair a faulty tube,** pry the sleeve loose at the junction with the handle and slide it down the tube. The tube should pull away from the nipple on the handle—if it sticks, pry it off gently, taking care not to cut the nipple.

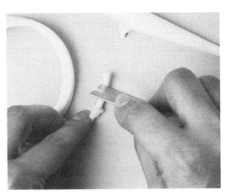

2 Trim off the worn end of the tube, making a flat cut that will fit back on the handle. Reattach the tube to the nipple and slide the tube sleeve back in place.

Getting inside

To inspect the Water Pik for any malfunctions other than exterior leaks, you have to get inside the base, which houses the motor and pump. Before starting any repair procedures that involve the base, unplug the appliance and set aside the reservoir and accessories.

There may be residual water in the base, which will spill out when you open it, so work on a few sheets of newspaper or paper toweling.

1 To get inside the Water Pik base, turn it upside down and remove all the screws from the base plate.

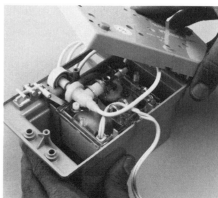

2 Lift off the base plate. The motor and pump assembly can be lifted out of the base without further disassembly.

Internal leaks

Water seeping from the bottom of the Water Pik indicates a leak from either the handle tube or the reservoir tube.

To find and correct the leak, open the base and check the junction of the handle tube with the pump. If it is loose or defective, repair the tube using the procedure shown for external leaks. If the handle tube and its connections are sound, the leak is from the reservoir tube.

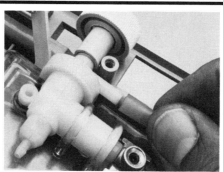

1 To check and repair the reservoir tube, inspect it at the pump end for loose fit or deterioration. To inspect the rest of the tube, disconnect it from the pump and lift the motor and pump assembly out of the base. Check the junction of the tube with the reservoir valve seal.

2 If either end of the reservoir tube is loose or worn, cut away the damaged portion and fit the tube back on the junction. If you have to cut away so much of the tube that it will no longer reach from the reservoir valve to the pump, or if the tube is leaking anywhere between the ends, replace it with a piece of surgical tubing of the same dimensions.

Motor and gear problems

The Water Pik's motor and switch are arranged in such a way that, in order to test the switch and cord, you must break down the motor assembly as shown in the steps at right.

If the motor runs and there is no pumping action, the problem is likely to be a clogged or defective pump, but the gears that drive the pump should be checked first.

To check the gears, open the base, leaving the motor and pump assembly in place. Turn the switch on and plug in the cord.

CAUTION Do not plug the cord in first; you risk shock if you touch any part of the open housing.

Look to see whether the gears are turning; if they are not, open the motor housing to inspect and replace the gears.

1 To inspect and replace the gears, remove the pump assembly (see steps for removing pump in *Pump problems*, opposite) and lift the motor out of the base. Turn the motor over and remove the screws from its housing. Hold the whole assembly together with your hands and turn it back gear side up.

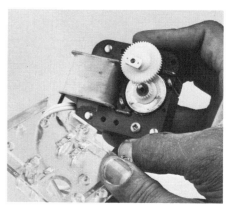

2 Lift the plastic cover off the gears. The larger gear can be slipped off its post and replaced if damaged. If the smaller gear is damaged, pull out the motor armature and replace it.

Pump problems

If the pumping action is weak or fails entirely, check the tubes for leaks (lowered pressure will weaken the pumping action), and check the gears. If there are no leaks and the gears are working properly, the problem is in the pump.

The pump slows or fails either because the piston is not working, or because the pump is clogged.

To check the piston action, perform the same procedure described for checking the gears (see *Motor and gear problems*). Watch to see that the piston is moving back and forth. If it is slipping or not moving at all, tighten the setscrew in the piston yoke. If the piston is not the problem, disassemble the pump and clean it. Replace the entire pump assembly if you find any broken parts.

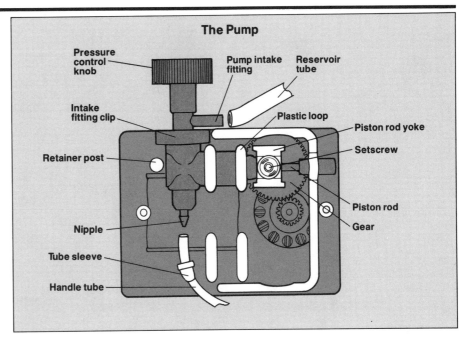

The Pump

Pressure control knob · Pump intake fitting · Reservoir tube · Intake fitting clip · Plastic loop · Piston rod yoke · Setscrew · Retainer post · Piston rod · Gear · Nipple · Tube sleeve · Handle tube

To tighten a loose piston rod yoke, loosen (but do not remove) the setscrew on the piston rod yoke with an Allen wrench. Push the piston all the way into the pump, move the yoke as far toward the piston as it will go, and then tighten the setscrew.

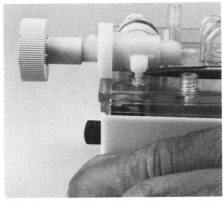

1 To disassemble and clean the pump, disconnect both tubes from the pump and loosen the piston rod yoke. Pry up the plastic retainer post in the motor plate. The pump is now free of the housing.

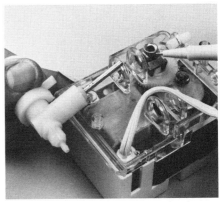

2 Slide the pump out of the plastic loops, leaving the piston rod yoke in place. Remove the pressure control knob.

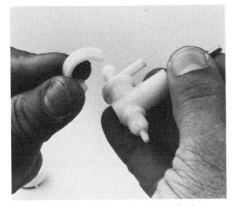

3 Snap out the C-shaped plastic clip that holds the upper and lower parts of the pump together, and twist the two sections of the pump apart, taking care not to lose the spring and valve stem. Put the spring and valve stem in a cup for safekeeping; if the spring gets lost, search for it with a magnet.

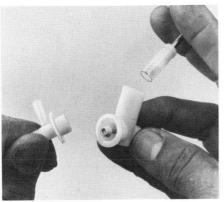

4 Clean inside each section, scraping away any sediment with a toothpick. Lubricate the piston with petroleum jelly, or with Water Pik's own brand of lubricant. Reassemble and install the clean pump, but leave off the pressure control knob until you reset the pressure control as shown in the box, right.

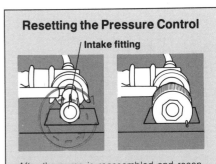

Resetting the Pressure Control

Intake fitting

After the pump is reassembled and reconnected, the pressure control must be reset before you close up the base.

To reset the pressure control, orient the housing so the pressure control faces you. Turn the intake fitting all the way to the right until it stops (but don't tighten it), then turn it one revolution to the left. Now replace the pressure control knob on the intake fitting, so that when the knob slips into the slot, the stopping peg rests on the housing to the right.

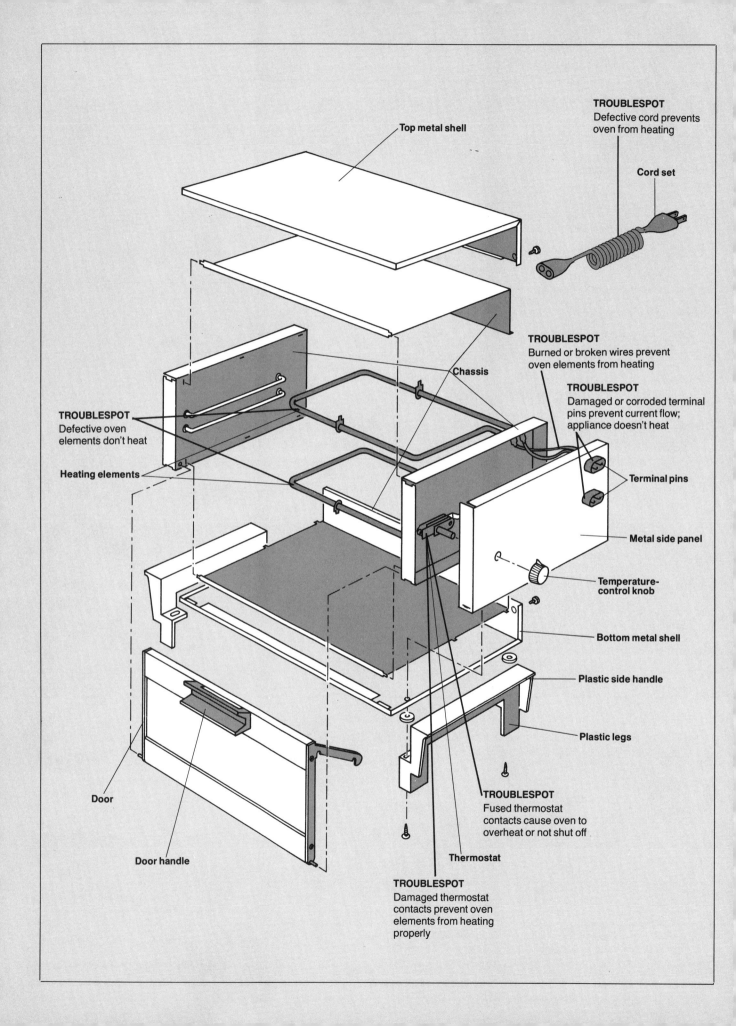

Top metal shell

TROUBLESPOT
Defective cord prevents
oven from heating

Cord set

Chassis

TROUBLESPOT
Burned or broken wires prevent
oven elements from heating

TROUBLESPOT
Damaged or corroded terminal
pins prevent current flow;
appliance doesn't heat

TROUBLESPOT
Defective oven
elements don't heat

Heating elements

Terminal pins

Metal side panel

**Temperature-
control knob**

Bottom metal shell

Plastic side handle

Plastic legs

Door

Door handle

TROUBLESPOT
Fused thermostat
contacts cause oven to
overheat or not shut off

Thermostat

TROUBLESPOT
Damaged thermostat
contacts prevent oven
elements from heating
properly

Ovens
Broiler

Broiler ovens are counter-top appliances that can be used for baking and broiling. They are designed to perform the functions of the oven in a range while using relatively less energy and needing less room. Many models are available, all with different combinations of elements and controls. While one of the models shown here has one heating element, generally two or more heating elements are used separately or together to broil or bake. Most models have an on/off switch, a thermostat, and a temperature-control dial. The thermostat controls the temperature by opening and closing the circuit. The electrical connections are located in one or both of the side panels.

The most common problems encountered with broiler ovens are defective cords and cord connections and burned wires inside the ovens. Cords, thermostats, switches, and heating elements can be replaced if they are defective, as can corroded, bent, or broken terminal pins on most ovens that have detachable cords. If the pins are faulty, the cord can't plug into the cord receptacle securely.

MAINTENANCE TIPS

Grease and food spills can damage your broiler oven. They coat reflective metal surfaces, and this impairs heating efficiency. Always clean the appliance after each use, so spills don't bake on. Use nonabrasive cleaners to avoid dulling the shiny metal surfaces. If you have a self-cleaning broiler oven, follow the manufacturer's suggestions for cleaning. The surfaces of these ovens are coated with a catalytic material that causes grease and spills to oxidize immediately. This surface could be damaged by the wrong cleaner.

A dirty oven can prevent proper heating, so if your oven doesn't heat properly, give it a thorough cleaning before you look for any problems in the electrical circuit.

CAUTION Be sure to unplug the unit before working on it. When working on a broiler oven you must excerise extreme caution. These appliances draw a very high electrical current. In addition, and unlike most small appliances, almost all models are encased in metal, which increases the hazard of shock. Checking for ground after any repair is therefore essential (see Blue Pages: *Testing for ground*).

Getting inside

In order to do any checks and repairs on the electrical components of a broiler oven (except checking a detachable cord), you must open up the oven's metal housing. This gives you access to a permanently attached cord, the terminal pins (in ovens with detachable cords), and the heating elements. All of these components can be replaced if they are defective. The Presto element must be unriveted to be replaced (see *Working with rivets,* page 193).

Unplug the unit before starting to take it apart. Take out any removable trays and racks. Then, remove all control knobs. If they don't come off easily, look for a setscrew in the plastic knob.

If you have to remove any decals, put them on a smooth, clean surface such as glass or Formica, so the stickum doesn't get dirty.

To get inside the Toastmaster, first unplug the unit and remove the temperature-control knob. Take the door off and pull out the rack and tray. Remove the Phillips screws from the interior side walls of the oven. You can now pull off the plastic side panels.

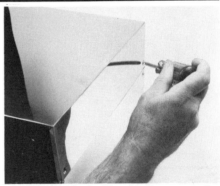

1 **To get inside the Munsey,** first remove the detachable cord, the door, and the rack and tray. Remove the four screws from the back of the oven.

2 Pull the metal shell that forms the upper housing toward you and lift it up. It will remain attached to the chassis at the front. Now push the shell toward the front to release its metal lip and tabs from notches in the chassis front.

3 Turn the oven upside down, and remove the Phillips screw from each plastic leg. This releases two fiber washers, two metal safety legs, and the two plastic side panels. You can now remove the bottom half of the metal shell as you did the top half.

4 Pull the right metal side panel away from the chassis. You now have access to the leads that connect the line cord terminal pins, the thermostat, and the element terminals.

1 **To open the housing of the Presto,** unplug the oven, remove the rack and tray and the cord, and pull off the temperature-control knob. Underneath is a round metal plate, which covers the thermostat. The screws in this plate partially secure one of the black plastic handles to the metal frame. Remove the screws.

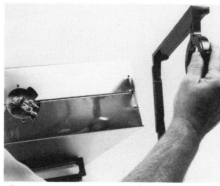

2 The handle is also attached to the chassis by two screws near the back of the oven. Remove these screws and lift off this handle.

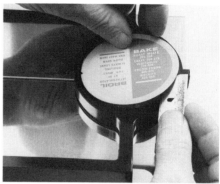

3 Remove the screws from the plastic handle on the other side of the oven. Using a single-edge razor blade, pry up the decal and lift it off gently. If the stickum is no longer good, order a new decal from the manufacturer.

4 A bracket underneath the decal attaches the handle to the chassis with two Phillips screws. Remove the screws and lift off the bracket and the plastic handle.

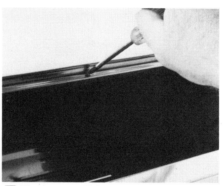

5 There are two Phillips screws at the front of the oven in the center, one on the top and one on the bottom of the shiny metal shell. Remove these screws. Now remove the two screws on the back of the oven.

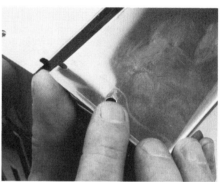

6 Pull the upper part of the metal shell toward the rear of the oven and tilt it upward. You may have to work it back and forth to free it from the chassis at the front. Turn the oven upside down and remove the bottom part of the shell the same way.

Electrical problems

Replacing the cord and switch

If your broiler oven doesn't heat up at all, open up the housing and test the cord and switch for continuity (see Blue Pages: *Electrical testers*). Of course, if your oven has a detachable line cord (like the Presto and the Munsey), you can test the line cord without removing the housing. Be sure your replacement cord has the same rating. To remove the Toastmaster cord, squeeze the strain relief out with pliers.

If the oven doesn't work at one thermostat setting, or if the oven operates the same for all settings, the chances are good that the thermostat is defective.

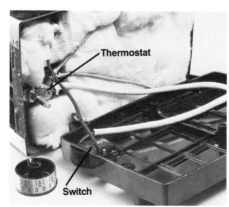

To test the Toastmaster cord, first remove the right side panel (see *Getting inside,* page 245). Follow the cord leads to the switch and thermostat. Unscrew the thermostat lead and test the cord for continuity. Replace it if it is defective. If the cord is OK, test the switch.

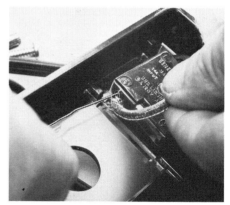

To test and replace the Toastmaster switch, detach each lead by inserting a paper clip wire as shown to release the spring holding the lead. Test for continuity. To replace the switch, detach all the leads and remove the switch from the side panel by pulling off the switch knob and undoing the hex nut from the metal shaft. Install a new switch.

Replacing the thermostat

If the broiler oven doesn't heat at all, and the line cord and the switch are OK, the problem may be in the thermostat. A defective thermostat can also cause a broiler oven to under- or overheat. In the Presto, where there is no separate on/off switch, a malfunctioning thermostat can cause the oven to stay on when you have turned the control to OFF (see box below). If you think something is wrong with the thermostat, first examine it for fused or burned contacts and loose leads, and then test it for continuity (see Blue Pages: *Electrical testers*). You needn't remove it for these tests. Defective thermostats can be replaced.

One type of heat control found in broiler ovens (such as the Presto) uses a thermostat but no separate on/off switch. Turning the temperature dial to any ON setting closes the thermostat contacts and allows current to flow. When the oven reaches the desired temperature, the contacts open and the current is cut off.

Another type of heat control uses a thermostat plus a separate on/off switch (as in the Toastmaster). When the switch is on, the thermostat turns the current on or off to maintain the desired temperature. To turn the unit completely off, flip the switch to OFF. Some models like the Munsey are turned off by pulling the plug out.

To replace a damaged or defective Toastmaster thermostat, first remove the slotted screw from the inside right wall of the oven (right). Removing this screw releases the thermostat from the outside of the chassis. Pull the thermostat out, label and detach the leads, and install a new thermostat.

To replace the thermostat on the Presto and Munsey, first label and detach the leads to the thermostat (push-on connectors on the Munsey; screwed-on on the Presto, far right). Then remove the Phillips screw that attaches the thermostat to the chassis. Pull the thermostat out and install a duplicate.

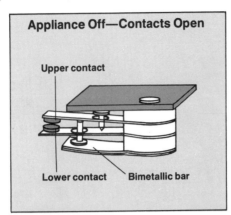

Appliance Off—Contacts Open

Upper contact

Lower contact   Bimetallic bar

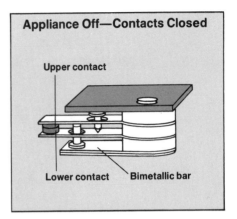

Appliance Off—Contacts Closed

Upper contact

Lower contact   Bimetallic bar

Replacing a heating element

If the oven doesn't heat up at all, first check to see whether the cord, the switch, or the thermostat is at fault. If they are all OK, test the elements for resistance with a VOM (see Blue Pages: *Electrical testers*).

In an oven with more than one element, if just one element doesn't heat up at a setting where it should be working, most likely that element is defective, and not the switch, cord, or thermostat. The Toastmaster has four elements, two in the top and two in the bottom assembly. If one element is defective, the whole assembly (top or bottom) must be replaced. The Munsey has two elements. (Directions are included here for replacing the terminal pins on the Munsey.)

If, after testing the elements, you still can't locate the problem, take your broiler oven to a repair shop.

1 **To replace either the upper or lower element assembly on the Toastmaster,** remove the screw from the element bracket located on the left side of the chassis. Each element assembly has its own bracket.

2 The leads from the thermostat to all the elements are on the right side panel. Label and unscrew both element leads from the thermostat to the element assembly you are replacing. Release the two leads from the switch by inserting a paper clip wire into the terminal (see *Replacing the cord and switch,* opposite). Pull out the element assembly and replace it.

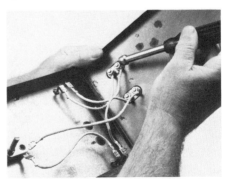

To replace a defective top or bottom element in the Munsey, first detach the leads from the element terminals on the right side of the chassis. Each element is held in place by three brackets. Straighten the tabs that attach the brackets to the chassis. (The new element comes with its own brackets.) Pull the element out and install a duplicate. To replace defective Munsey terminal pins, use a nut driver to remove the hex nuts holding the pins.

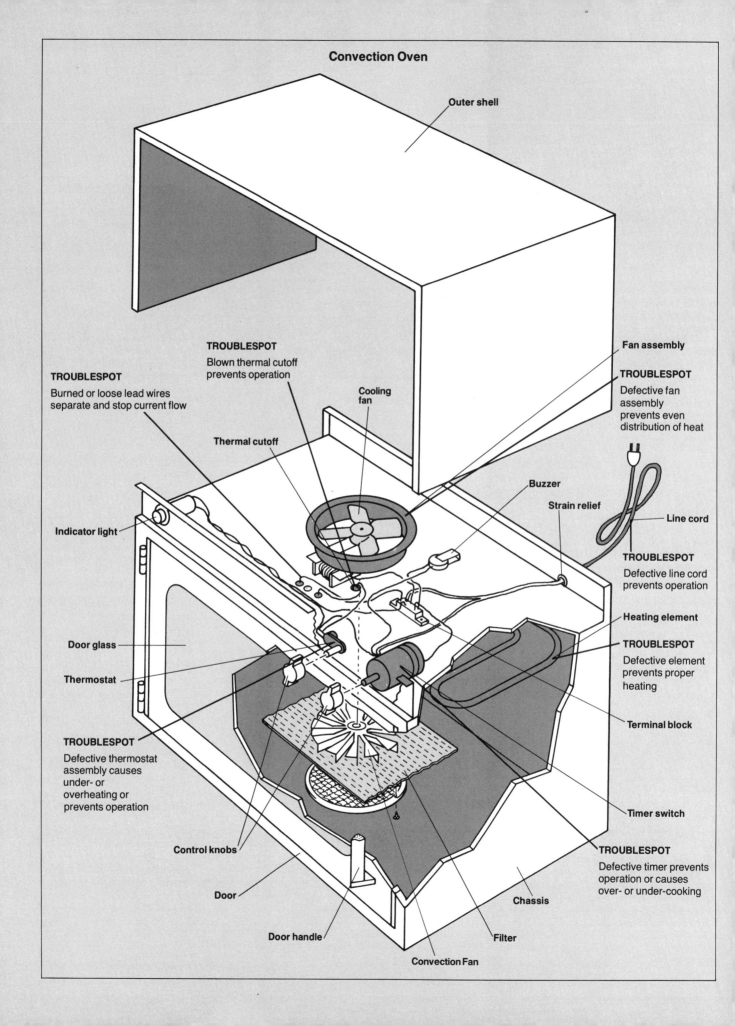

Convection Oven

Outer shell

Fan assembly

TROUBLESPOT
Blown thermal cutoff prevents operation

Cooling fan

TROUBLESPOT
Burned or loose lead wires separate and stop current flow

TROUBLESPOT
Defective fan assembly prevents even distribution of heat

Thermal cutoff

Buzzer

Strain relief

Indicator light

Line cord

TROUBLESPOT
Defective line cord prevents operation

Heating element

TROUBLESPOT
Defective element prevents proper heating

Door glass

Thermostat

Terminal block

TROUBLESPOT
Defective thermostat assembly causes under- or overheating or prevents operation

Timer switch

Control knobs

TROUBLESPOT
Defective timer prevents operation or causes over- or under-cooking

Chassis

Door

Door handle

Filter

Convection Fan

OVENS

Convection

Except for one distinguishing feature—a fan—convection ovens operate much like traditional built-in ovens or portable broiler ovens. In all three types, current flows through an insulated resistance wire (the heating element), creating heat for baking and broiling. In addition, the convection oven's fan circulates hot air within the oven. This has the advantage of cooking food more quickly, more evenly, and with less energy consumed.

Apart from the heating element(s) and the fan, the other main components of convection ovens are electrical controls: the on/off/timer switch, the thermostat assembly, and the thermal cutoff, a safety device to prevent overheating.

The repair instructions are demonstrated here on two typical models, the Farberware and the Toastmaster. In the Farberware, the convection fan is mounted on the top of the unit; in the Toastmaster it is on the side. If you own a different model, read through all the instructions and adapt the steps to your own oven.

CAUTION Convection ovens require a great deal of current. If you plug another appliance into the same circuit, you are likely to overload the circuit and trip a circuit breaker or blow a fuse. Always unplug the oven before starting to work on it. After making

any electrical repair, always test the appliance to make sure that it is properly grounded (see Blue Pages: *Testing for ground*).

MAINTENANCE AND SAFETY
Many convection ovens are self-cleaning: the oven walls are coated with a catalyst that oxidizes spatters when the oven is on. If additional cleaning is needed, follow the manufacturer's instructions. Avoid oven cleaners, steel wool, and other abrasive materials, which could impair the self-cleaning action.
Some models, such as the Farberware, have filters in front of the fan to protect both you and the fan from spatters. The filter should be removed periodically for cleaning, but be sure to put it back before using the oven again. If you open the oven door when the fan is spinning and the filter is not in place, you risk being burned by spattering grease.
The outside metal surfaces should remain relatively cool (on the Farberware, a cooling fan helps cool down the outside surfaces). Make certain that you don't block the heat exhaust vents on the side panels as well as the top exhaust louvers. Avoid touching any glass surfaces when the oven is on—they get very hot.

Getting inside

The metal surfaces of all models and the Farberware's filter and element baffle can be cleaned without removing the oven housing. However, you have to get inside the appliance to diagnose and correct problems with the fan, the cord, the on/off/timer switch, the thermostat assembly, the thermal cutoff, and the buzzer (if the unit has these). All electrical components of the Farberware can be replaced. On the Toastmaster, everything except the elements can be replaced.

Before you dismantle the oven, take out any removable racks and trays.

1 **To get inside the Farberware oven,** first lift the door off its hinges. Remove the filter (right) by unscrewing the two thumb nuts that hold it to the element baffle. Use a screwdriver to remove the four screws that hold the element baffle to the oven roof. Take out the filter and the baffle.

2 There are four screws on the outer shell on each side, where it meets the side panels. Remove the screws from both sides (far right). Once you have loosened the screw head a bit, insert your fingernail beneath it to make unscrewing easier.

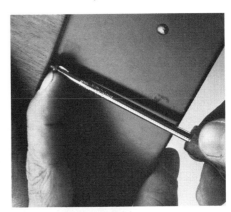

3 Using a Phillips screwdriver, unscrew the screws on the front top rim of the outer shell, which attach it to the chassis (right).

4 On the back panel, at the extreme right and left edges, there are three screws aligned vertically (far right). Remove these six screws. Next, remove the five screws aligned horizontally along the top edge of the back panel. This releases the outer shell. Grasp the shell at both sides and pull it apart, so that you can lift the shell clear of the chassis.

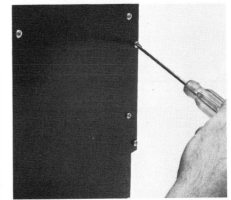

1 **To remove the outer shell of the Toast-master,** take off the door by lifting it off its hinges. Remove the screws all around the edges of the back plate, but leave all the other screws alone. Pull off the back plate. The cord is attached to it; be careful not to damage its leads.

2 Remove the two Phillips screws on the front edge of each side of the outer shell.

3 Using a Phillips screwdriver, remove the three screws along the top front edge.

4 Grasp the sides of the outer shell and pull them apart enough so that the shell clears the chassis as you lift it off. All the internal parts except the elements are now accessible on the right side panel.

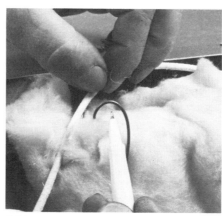

5 It may be easier to work on the electrical component and connections if you remove the insulation. To do this, first remove the fan housing (see *Fan problems*, opposite). Remove the fiberglass insulation gingerly, to avoid bending any leads or damaging the capillary tube. Wear gloves, or wash your hands thoroughly after handling this insulation.

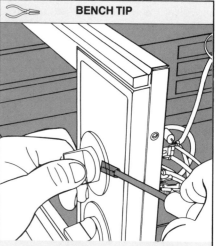

BENCH TIP

Pry off the control knobs with a screwdriver whose tip has been wrapped in masking tape. This way you won't damage the panel around the knobs. Turn the knobs as you pry them off, to avoid bending the shafts.

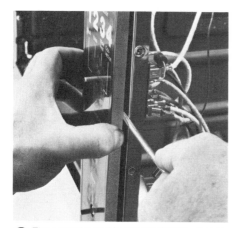

6 The control panel is attached to the chassis by four metal tabs located on the chassis behind the front panel. They are difficult to see, but they must be gently straightened with pliers in order to get the panel off. Then use a taped screwdriver to pry the panel off.

7 Lift the control panel away from the oven, and lay it face down on a paper towel to avoid nicks and scratches.

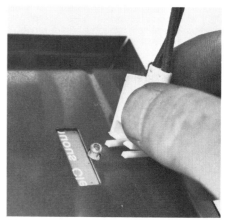

8 To free the control panel completely, pull straight down on the indicator light to get it off the pin that secures it to the panel.

Fan problems

If the fan stops turning, a convection oven works just like an ordinary broiler or toaster oven, and you lose the advantage of the convection. Generally, you can tell if the fan has stopped, because you no longer hear the whirring sound it makes when it is going.

If the oven is heating properly but the fan has stopped (and the selector dial is turned to "convection" on the Toastmaster), first take off the outer shell (and the fan housing in the Toastmaster) and make sure that the fan is firmly attached to its shaft. Next, follow the leads from the fan motor to their terminal points and check whether there is a loose connection or a burned-off lead wire.

If the connections are sound, test the fan motor for continuity (see Blue Pages: *Electrical testers*). Replace it if it is defective. Find out from the manufacturer whether the fan and fan motor can be replaced separately. On the Farberware, the motor and cooling fan are one assembly; you must remove the convection fan in order to remove the motor assembly.

1 **To test and replace the Farberware fan motor,** remove one motor lead, place tester probes on the motor lead terminals, and check for continuity (right). If the motor is defective, you must first remove the fan (see next step). Then, take out the four screws in the motor mount (two parallel silvery bars beneath the white cooling fan). Detach the motor leads and remove the fan motor assembly. Install a new motor assembly if needed.

2 To remove the Farberware fan, loosen the setscrew from the fan's hub (far right), and pull the fan from the drive shaft. You can now remove the fan motor assembly, as described in the previous step. An undamaged convection fan can be reused.

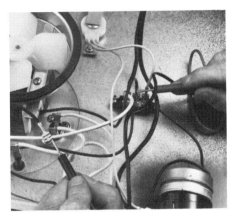

1 **To remove the fan motor housing on the Toastmaster,** unscrew the six screws from the right side panel on the inside of the oven. This releases the fan motor housing from the chassis. Mark all leads for later identification.

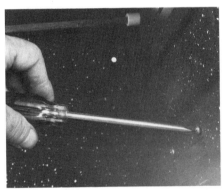

2 Lift out the fan housing and remove the fiberglass insulation from the outside panel of the chassis, to get more room to work (see *Getting inside,* page 249). Wear gloves, or wash your hands thoroughly after handling this insulation.

3 Remove the fan from the fan motor housing by using pliers to straighten the tabs (see arrows, step 2) that stick out along the curved edge of one side panel of the fan housing. Gently pry open the panel with a screwdriver.

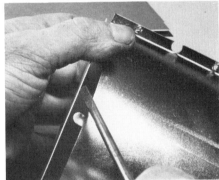

4 Straighten all the tabs around the base of the fan motor housing, and continue pulling open the side panel, until you can pull out the fan blade, the fan housing, and the fan motor.

5 If the fan blade is damaged, remove the nut, pull the blade off the shaft, and replace it. If the fan is OK, detach one motor lead and test the motor for continuity (see Blue Pages: *Electrical testers*). If it is defective, replace the fan and motor assembly.

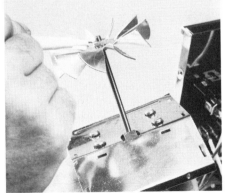

Replacing the Door Glass

On certain models, it is possible to replace a broken pane of glass in the oven door. Simply lift the door off its hinges and locate the screws that hold the two sides of the door together. Remove them, replacing the broken pane only with glass recommended by the manufacturer. Do *not* use ordinary window glass. It may be easier and more economical simply to replace the door.

Testing the thermostat

The thermostat assembly on Toastmaster and Farberware convection ovens consists of a heat-sensing bulb containing a heat-sensitive gas, a capillary tube, and a thermostat. When the oven temperature rises slightly above the desired setting, pressure from the heat-sensor bulb signals the thermostat contacts to open, breaking the circuit. Opening and closing the circuit in response to the gas pressure, the thermostat maintains the desired temperature. Use an oven thermometer to check for a possibly defective thermostat. Try different temperature settings and open the oven door occasionally to check that the oven returns to the proper temperature.

If the oven doesn't heat up at all, if the temperature stays the same regardless of the temperature setting, or if the oven overheats, the thermostat may be at fault. (On the Toastmaster, the selector switch—marked 1-2-3-4—may also be defective. See box, opposite.)

First, see if the cord is OK (see *Replacing the cord*, opposite). If it is, check the thermostat for continuity. If it shows continuity, remove and test the heat-sensor bulb and the capillary tube as described here. If any part of the assembly fails the test, replace the whole thermostat assembly.

To test the Farberware thermostat, disconnect one lead and touch tester probes to both thermostat terminals. When cold, the thermostat should show continuity through all settings; if it doesn't, replace the thermostat.

To remove the Farberware thermostat assembly, carefully bend open the curved supports on the bracket that holds the heat-sensing bulb to the inside of the oven roof. Gently pull up on the capillary tube from above, guiding the bulb out through the hole in the oven roof. Pull off the temperature-control knob and remove the hex nut that holds the thermostat assembly.

1 **To test and remove the Toastmaster thermostat assembly,** first attach tester probes as described above. If the thermostat is defective you must replace the whole assembly. Label the leads for later identification and remove them. Remove the hex nut, and pull the thermostat out of the chassis from behind.

2 To remove the capillary tube, straighten the tabs of the capillary tube protector on the outside of the chassis top. Pull the protector away from the oven roof inside, and gently pull on the capillary tubing from outside, guiding the bulb through the hole in the side of the oven. The assembly is now free.

Replacing the timer switch

If the oven doesn't go on, and there's nothing wrong with the cord (see *Replacing the cord,* opposite) or the thermostat, the timer switch may be defective. An oven that doesn't go off when it should is another indication that this switch may be faulty. Test it for continuity (see Blue Pages: *Electrical testers*). If the timer keeps inaccurate time or fails the continuity test, replace it as described here.

Place second probe here

To test and replace the Farberware or Toastmaster timer switch, detach one lead and place tester probes as shown. Turn the switch to ON. If you get no continuity, replace the timer. Label the leads for later identification, and detach them from the timer terminals. Remove the control knob and unscrew the hex nut. Remove the timer, and install a duplicate.

Replacing the cord

If the oven doesn't run at all when you plug it in and turn it on, check the cord. Look for burned or frayed cord insulation, a damaged plug, and faulty connections inside the housing. Reattach any loose leads. If you find nothing obviously wrong, test the cord for continuity (see Blue Pages: *Electrical testers*). If you must replace the cord, take the old cord to the electrical supply store to be sure you get a cord with the same rating (load capacity).

To test and replace a defective cord, detach one lead and place the tester probes as shown. Bend and twist the cord to see whether continuity is maintained. If the cord is defective, detach the other lead and, using pliers, squeeze together the strain relief as you pull the cord out of the housing.

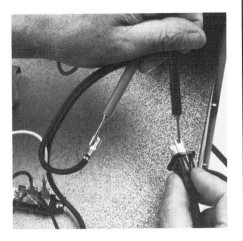

Replacing the Buzzer

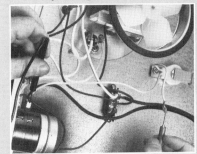

On most broiler ovens, a buzzer sounds when the oven is turned off by the automatic timer. If the timer is operative but the buzzer doesn't sound, examine the buzzer contacts for any loose leads or other damage. If there is no apparent damage, test the buzzer for continuity as shown above. If it is defective, label and detach the leads and remove the nut that attaches the buzzer to the chassis. Install a new buzzer.

Replacing an element

If the oven doesn't heat at all and the cord, timer switch, and thermostat assembly are all OK, the elements may be defective. Examine the element leads for loose or burned connectors, then test the element for continuity (see Blue Pages: *Electrical testers*).

On the Farberware, you can replace a defective element yourself. The element is held in place with speed nuts, which are special locking nuts. Have new speed nuts on hand, in case you damage the old ones while removing them. A defective Toastmaster element should be repaired in a repair shop.

On the Toastmaster model, a faulty selector (1-2-3-4) switch could also account for an element that doesn't work (see box, far right, bottom).

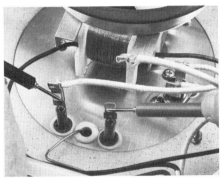

To test and replace the Farberware element, remove one lead and test the element (as shown). If the element is defective, remove the two speed nuts that hold the element to the top of the housing. Reach inside the oven and gently pry open the clasps that support the element. Remove the element and install a new one.

Indicator Light

If the indicator light doesn't go on when the oven is turned on, unplug the oven and follow the leads to their terminals and check for a loose connection. If the light still doesn't work with the connectors firmly in place, it must be replaced. Detach the leads, and push the light out through the front of the oven. On the Farberware, squeeze the pin on the sides of the light (shown here) so it can pass through the front housing. Install a new indicator light.

Thermal cutoff

A thermal cutoff is a safety device that operates like a circuit breaker, cutting off the current if the oven overheats for any reason. It is wired between the thermostat and the element. When the oven cools down, the thermal cutoff will once again let current through. However, you would be wise to find the cause of the overheating and remedy it before using the oven again. If you can't diagnose the problem, take the oven to a repair shop.

To test the thermal cutoff for continuity, remove one lead and place tester probes as shown. You should have continuity. To remove a defective thermal cutoff, follow the leads to their terminal points and detach them. Use a Phillips screwdriver to remove the two mounting screws. Pull off the thermal cutoff and install a duplicate.

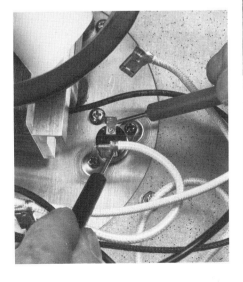

Selector Switch

Some convection ovens have a selector switch for various oven functions. If the oven doesn't work at one or more of the switch's settings, or if the oven runs the same on all settings, this switch may be at fault. The problem, however, may also be the fan motor, the elements, or the thermostat assembly. If all of these components test out OK, test the selector switch and diode. Replace either if necessary.

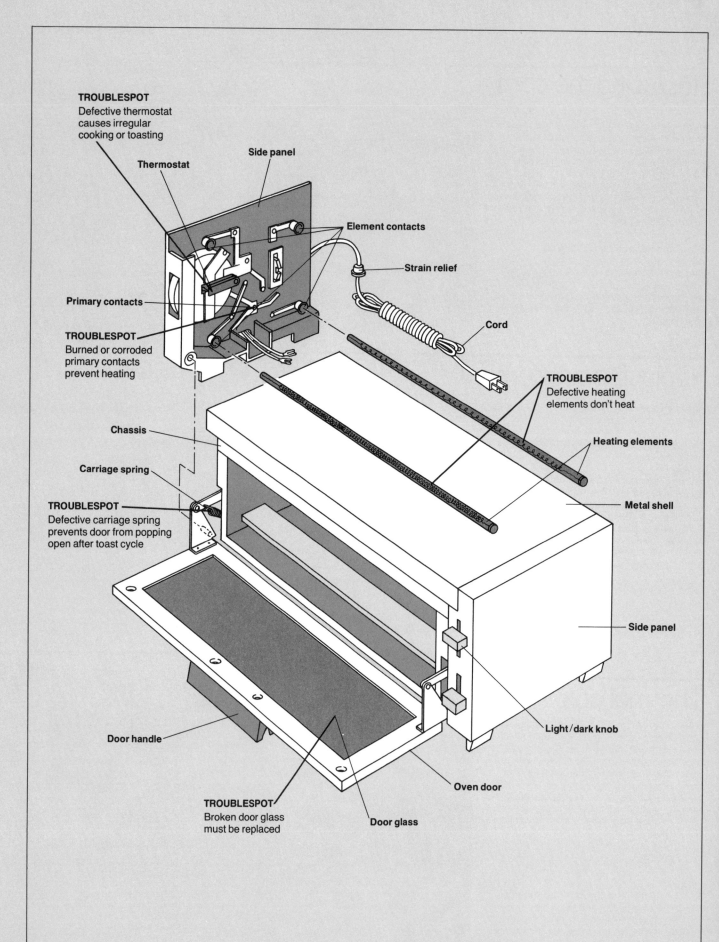

TROUBLESPOT
Defective thermostat causes irregular cooking or toasting

Thermostat

Side panel

Element contacts

Strain relief

Primary contacts

Cord

TROUBLESPOT
Burned or corroded primary contacts prevent heating

TROUBLESPOT
Defective heating elements don't heat

Chassis

Heating elements

Carriage spring

Metal shell

TROUBLESPOT
Defective carriage spring prevents door from popping open after toast cycle

Side panel

Light/dark knob

Door handle

Oven door

TROUBLESPOT
Broken door glass must be replaced

Door glass

OVENS
Toaster

As the name implies, toaster ovens can be used to make toast, but you can also use them to toast rolls and muffins that are too large for a regular toaster, to bake small casseroles, heat up frozen foods and pastries, or top-brown sandwiches and other items. Do not broil meat in your toaster oven unless it is a self-cleaning model. In the Toastmaster, for example, interior metal surfaces are treated so that splatters are oxidized and disappear.

Toaster ovens have heating elements attached near the top and bottom surfaces. Toast and Bake settings determine which elements heat up. A thermostat maintains temperature for Bake, and turns the heat off after a toast cycle. On some models, (*not* the one *opposite*), the door pops up after toasting.

Ordinarily, a toaster oven should be cleaned after every use. Unplug it and wipe up any drips or spills while it is cooling. Never use spray-on cleaners of any kind, as this could cause electrical problems. After cleaning, run a short toast cycle to dry the oven

thoroughly. Follow the manufacturer's instructions for the care of self-cleaning ovens.

On many makes of toaster oven, the parts are riveted or welded in place (see *Working with rivets,* page 193). Steps for repairing toaster ovens are demonstrated here on the Proctor Silex and Toastmaster. These steps are easily adapted to other toaster ovens that have replaceable parts. Unplug the oven and remove any movable racks or trays before you start working on it.

Always test a toaster oven for ground after you have taken it apart to make an electrical repair (see Blue Pages: *Testing for ground*).

> **CAUTION** Unplug a toaster oven before doing any tests or repairs. Also, another appliance running on the same circuit while the oven is in operation, may blow a fuse or trip a circuit breaker.

Problems with the door

A toaster oven door can generally be repaired at home. If the door doesn't open at the end of the toasting cycle, the problem may be in the door latch or the carriage spring. In order for the door to open, the latch must release, and the spring must pull the door up. If the spring is defective, the door will not rise. If the latch is damaged or obstructed, it may not release at all.

The carriage spring is replaceable on the Proctor Silex but not on the

Toastmaster. The latch, on the other hand, is accessible on the Toast-master but not on the Proctor Silex. Examine the latch as described. If you can't fix the latch, take the oven to an authorized service center.

A broken or cracked door glass can be replaced on both the Proctor Silex and the Toastmaster. Order the replacement glass from the manufacturer, specifying the make and model number of the oven.

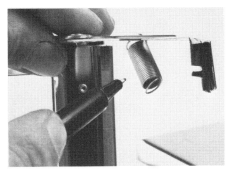

To replace the Proctor Silex carriage spring, remove the left side panel (see *Getting inside,* below). Unhook the spring from the side of the oven chassis and the door, and lift it out.

To gain access to the Toastmaster door latch, remove the right side panel (see below). The latch is just behind the "bake" knob. Remove any obstructions, file off metal burrs, and straighten any bends in the metal. If the door still doesn't open, take the unit to a repair shop.

To replace the door glass on the Toastmaster and Proctor Silex, remove the screws that hold together the handle, door frame, and glass. On the Toastmaster, use a screwdriver that fits the screw slot tightly so as not to strip the screw. Lift out the old glass and replace it.

Getting inside

To make any electrical repairs on a toaster oven, you must remove one or both of the side panels. On both the Toastmaster and the Proctor Silex, remove both panels to check the contacts and to test and replace the elements. On the Toastmaster, remove the right panel to check and replace the cord or the diode. On the Proctor Silex, remove the left panel to check and replace the cord.

NOTE: Before taking off the right panel on the Proctor Silex toaster oven, get a replacement light/dark toaster control knob. The knob is likely to break when you pry it off. Also, be especially careful when removing either side panel from the Proctor Silex, because the glass-enclosed heating elements inside are freed once the panels are removed and may slide out and break if the oven is tilted.

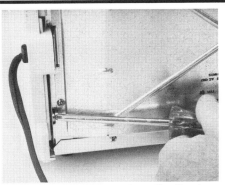

To remove the side panels on the Proctor Silex, remove the two Phillips screws at the bottom of each side panel, attaching it to the base. There are two screws on either side of the back of the oven at the top. Remove the outside screw on each side and pull off the panels.

To remove the side panels on the Toastmaster, tilt the oven onto its back. There is a hex nut on either side, next to each leg. Remove them, using a nut driver. You can now pull off the panels.

Electrical problems

Replacing the cord

If the oven doesn't work at all, first test the cord for continuity (see Blue Pages: *Electrical testers*), and replace it with a duplicate if it is defective. Take the old cord with you when you buy the new cord, to be sure the rating is the same.

To test or replace the Proctor Silex cord, remove the left side panel; on the Toastmaster, you must remove the right side panel to gain access to the cord terminals.

1 **To replace the cord on the Toastmaster and the Proctor Silex,** first pull off the cord connectors. If the connection is soldered, cut or unsolder the cord leads.

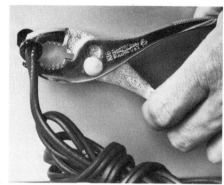

2 Use pliers to squeeze together the strain relief, which will enable you to pull the cord out through the hole in the side panel. Reattach the new cord by soldering, or use crimp-on connectors.

Checking and cleaning contacts

If the oven doesn't work at all and the cord is OK, the problem could be a loose or broken connection, or a faulty contact.

Unplug the oven. Open both side panels and look first for loose connections or broken wires. Push loose connectors back in position, or reattach any broken wire with noninsulated crimp-on connectors wrapped in insulation if you're absolutely sure you know where it belongs. (If you don't, take the oven to a repair shop.)

If there are no loose connections, check the primary contacts for dirt or corrosion (on the left side in the Proctor Silex and the right side in the Toastmaster). Next, check the element contacts on the Proctor Silex. You can clean pitted contacts yourself, using metal polish or fine emery cloth (this is only a temporary measure). If any contacts are burned, worn, or don't meet properly, take the oven to a repair shop.

If the appliance heats but the temperature remains the same regardless of the setting, you may have a defective thermostat. On the Proctor Silex it is on the left side; on the Toastmaster it is on the right side.

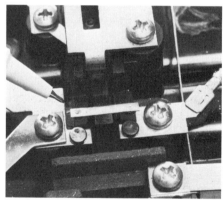

To check the primary contacts on the Proctor Silex, look on the left side. Check for burn damage, and press the contacts together with your fingers to check for loss of spring tension. If the contacts can't touch or don't separate when released, take the unit to a repairman.

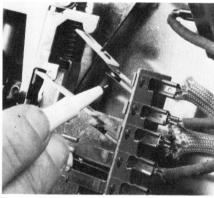

To check the primary contacts on the Toastmaster, look on the right panel. When you close the oven door, the contact should be pressed closed by the upside-down L-bracket (as shown). Clean the contacts if necessary, and check the spring tension as described in the preceding step.

To check the element contacts on the Proctor Silex, examine the small cups on the inside of each side panel (right), which serve as element terminals. Clean the cups if necessary (this is a temporary repair); if they are burned or damaged, take the oven to a repair shop.

To check the thermostat contacts on the Proctor Silex oven, look just behind the temperature-control knob (far right) on the left side. (The Toastmaster thermostat is on the right side, at the end of the arm attached to the temperature-control knob.) Clean the contacts if necessary, and examine for damage.

Replacing the diode

Some toaster ovens contain a diode to cut down the amount of current reaching the top element when the oven is on the BAKE setting. If food is burning on top, or if both elements glow equally red when the controls are set on the BAKE setting, the problem is in the diode. You know you have diode problems if you can see that the diode has charred its insulating sleeve or burned a hole in it—in this case the top element will not work at all. The Toastmaster diode is on the right side, near the bottom. You can get a replacement diode from the manufacturer or an authorized dealer. Include the make and the model and serial number of your oven when ordering, to make sure you get the right replacement diode.

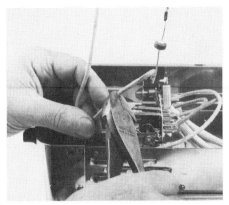

1 To replace the diode on the Toastmaster, first remove the right side panel. Slip the insulating sleeve away from the diode and cut away the diode and its crimp-on connectors.

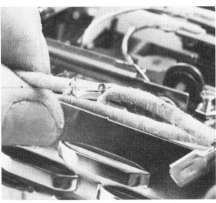

2 To install a new diode, slip the insulating sleeve over it. If the insulation is damaged, replace it with new heat-resistant insulation. Reattach the diode leads and wrap the connections with insulating material.

Replacing an element

If neither element heats at all, first check the cord connections and test the cord for continuity (see opposite). Then check the contacts. If all of these are OK, test the elements for continuity. If the cord, the connections, the contacts, and the elements are all OK, you may have a defective on /off switch, in which case you must take the appliance to a repair shop.

If only one element heats when both should be on (for example on toast setting), first check for loose wires and connections, and poor contacts. If the top element is dead, check the diode. If nothing is wrong with the connections and contacts or diode, test the suspect element for continuity. You don't have to remove the elements; just touch the tester probes to the element terminals (see Blue Pages: *Electrical testers*).

Proctor Silex elements can be replaced from either side; on the Toastmaster, you must remove both side panels. Order the replacement element from the manufacturer, specifying the model number and the position (upper or lower) of the element.

To replace a Proctor Silex heating element, remove one of the side panels. (CAUTION The elements are then loose, so don't tip the oven.) Grasp the glass tube protruding through a hole in the chassis, and pull the tube and the element out. Slip in the replacement element tube. Be sure all the elements are correctly positioned in the terminal cups before replacing the side panel.

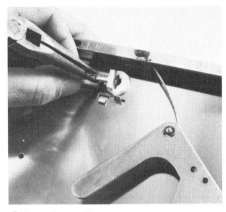

1 To replace a Toastmaster heating element, first remove both side panels. On the left side, follow the element lead to its push-on connector and detach it. Using needle-nose pliers, straighten the tab terminal on the end of the element so that the element will pass through the chassis when you remove it from the other side.

2 Detach the lead from the element terminal on the right side of the chassis, and remove the screw from the square element protector plate as shown at right. Straighten the two tabs that hold the element protector and remove it.

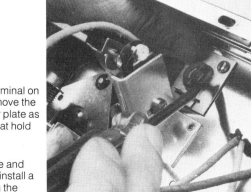

3 Grasp the element from the right side and pull it from the chassis (far right). To install a new element, reverse the steps, bending the tabs back into place.

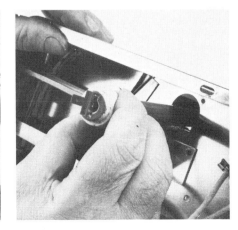

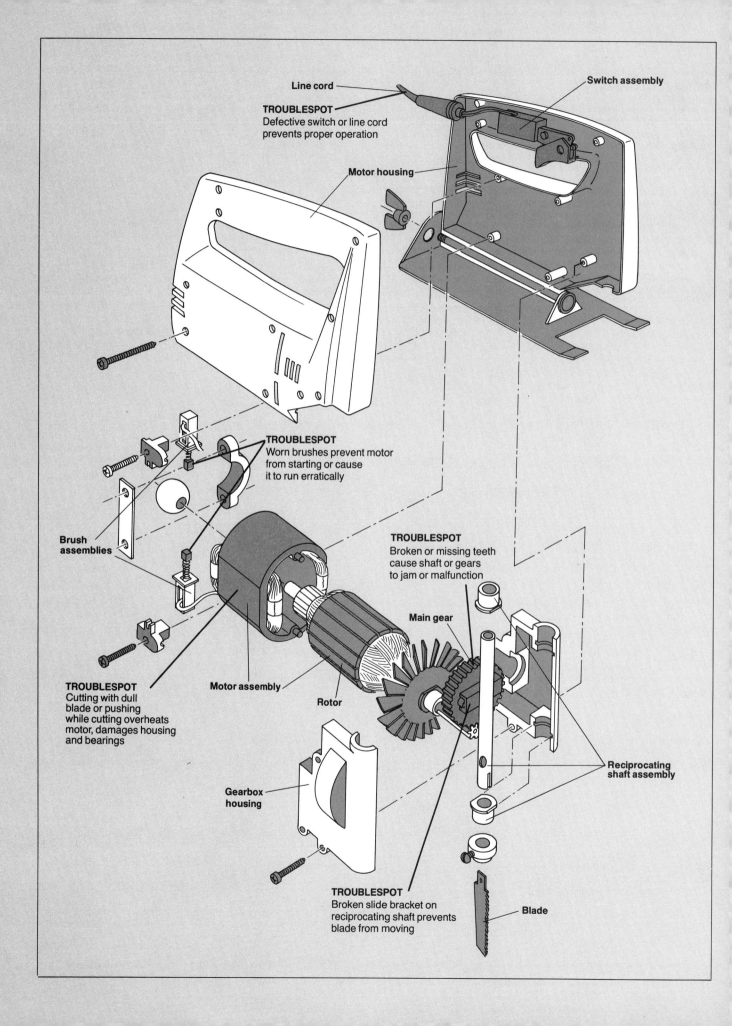

Line cord

Switch assembly

TROUBLESPOT
Defective switch or line cord
prevents proper operation

Motor housing

TROUBLESPOT
Worn brushes prevent motor
from starting or cause
it to run erratically

Brush
assemblies

TROUBLESPOT
Broken or missing teeth
cause shaft or gears
to jam or malfunction

Main gear

TROUBLESPOT
Cutting with dull
blade or pushing
while cutting overheats
motor, damages housing
and bearings

Motor assembly

Rotor

Reciprocating
shaft assembly

Gearbox
housing

TROUBLESPOT
Broken slide bracket on
reciprocating shaft prevents
blade from moving

Blade

Power Tools
Saber saws

There are always sawing jobs to be done around the house, and the saber saw is ideal for those small jobs that usually can't be done easily with a handsaw. A saber saw is relatively light, and can perform a wide range of tasks, since it can be fitted with a number of different blades for different purposes. Maintaining a saber saw is not difficult, and repairs for common problems are quite straightforward. Power saws frequently cause trouble when sawdust or other debris of use hasn't been cleaned away. At least once a year—more if the saw is used often—you should disassemble and clean it. Use a mild soap or wax cleaner to clean the housing. Then check the gear assembly, relubricate it, and check the brushes. Be certain that the soap you use has no detergents —they could damage plastic parts. This basic maintenance will prolong the life and increase the efficiency of your saw.

If your saw doesn't start at all, you will have to check the line cord and the switch for continuity. If the motor starts up and then cuts out as the saw is jiggled, it generally means that the line cord or switch may be defective. Repair or replace it. Never carry a heavy appliance like a power saw or a drill by the line cord. This could break the wire in the cord, or the cord could be loosened.

If the motor shows excessive sparking or smoking, or if it sputters on and off, check the brushes for wear. If the brushes are making a proper connection with the commutator and the motor still sputters, check the line cord, switch, and bearings.

If the motor hums, but does not turn, check the reciprocating shaft. Turn the gears to see if they are jammed or have broken teeth. The shaft and gears can be replaced separately, as needed.

Occasionally, put a few drops of oil in the oiling hole or on the lubricating pad. (Check the manufacturer's instruction manual for location and frequency of lubrication.) Remember to use sharp blades at all times. A dull blade cuts slowly, and thus you will be tempted to force the machine along by putting pressure on it. This can overload the motor and cause it to burn out. In addition, dull blades may become stuck and stall the motor, possibly damaging it. Saber saw blades are so inexpensive that sharpening is not practical. Always have an ample supply of blades on hand for your job. Replace the blade if it shows signs of sticking, cutting slowly, or burning the wood, and be sure you use the right blade for the job.

The instructions for examining the line cord and switch, checking the shaft and gears, and checking the brushes are demonstrated here on two recent-model makes of power saw: the McGraw-Edison saber saw and the Black & Decker variable speed jig saw.

Getting inside

If your unit is dead or if the motor sparks excessively, or if it hums and does not turn, you will have to open the housing to check the electrical connections, the motor, and the gears. Always unplug the saw before taking it apart. The saw generally has a rear housing, a motor housing containing the motor, and a front housing, which may hold the gears and to which the blade assembly and guard plate are secured. You should open the saw periodically for cleaning and relubricating.

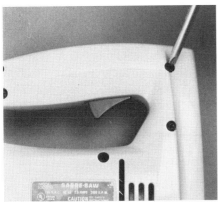

1 **To get inside the McGraw-Edison,** remove the ten screws on the side of the housing. Remember the placement of the screws; they are of different lengths.

2 Separate the housing to expose the insides of the machine. You can now clean and lubricate or make repairs.

To get inside the Black & Decker, remove the screws along the handle and side of the unit. Lift off the top side of the housing, exposing the line cord and the switch assembly.

Replacing the cord and switch

The line cord and switch are the first parts you should check if the machine is dead or if the motor stops and starts. First examine the cord for visible evidence of damage. Then open the housing and do continuity tests on the line cord and the switch (see Blue Pages: *Electrical testers*). Before you do any tests, check all the connections to make sure they are tight.

NOTE: Some models of the McGraw-Edison saw have a safety lock on the switch to prevent the machine from being turned on accidentally. Be sure to replace it with a duplicate. Many suppliers stock only the locking switch, but you can use a locking switch to replace a regular switch (below, center).

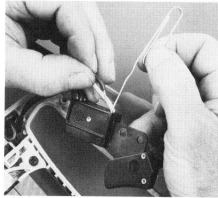

1 **To check the switch on the McGraw-Edison,** remove the screw holding the switch in place.

2 Label the leads and, using a straightened paper clip, push in on the spring holding the cord leads, and pull the wires loose, one at a time. Then test the line cord for continuity. Replace the line cord if it is defective.

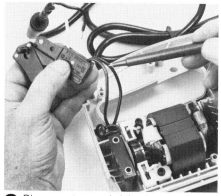

3 Disconnect one switch lead and do a continuity check on the switch. Next, check the motor for continuity. If either the switch or the motor is defective, replace it.

To install a locking safety switch as a replacement for a nonlocking switch, simply snip off the unnecessary lock with side cutters.

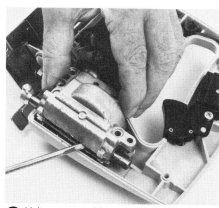

To replace the switch on the Black & Decker, first check the switch shaft for damage. If it's broken, replace the switch. The switch itself is a solid-state instrument, and so cannot be checked for continuity. If the line cord tests OK, and there is nothing wrong with the motor (see page 262), the switch is defective. Replace it.

Replacing the reciprocating shaft and gears

If the saw blade doesn't work when it's under normal pressure or if the saw is making too much noise, the problem may be with the reciprocating shaft bearings or the gears. This may also be the problem if the motor hums, but doesn't move the blade. In this case, you can assume that the line cord and switch are OK, and proceed directly to checking the shaft and gears.

1 **To get at the McGraw-Edison reciprocating shaft and gears,** open the gearbox housing by removing the screws in its top.

2 Using a screwdriver, pry open the housing covering the gearbox.

3 Separate the gearbox housing to expose the reciprocating shaft and gear assembly below.

4 Lift out the reciprocating shaft with its bearings. The shaft should be well lubricated.

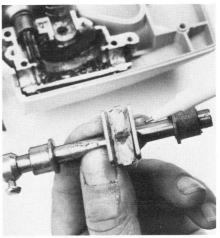

5 Check the slide bracket on the shaft (indicated here) for damage. It is not uncommon for this bracket to be broken, bent, or pulled away from the shaft. If it is damaged, the whole shaft as well as its bearings must be replaced.

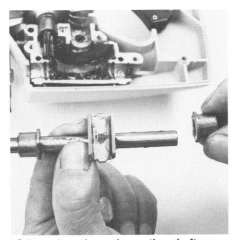

1 **To replace the reciprocating shaft,** you should first remove the top bearing, since this is not part of a replacement shaft.

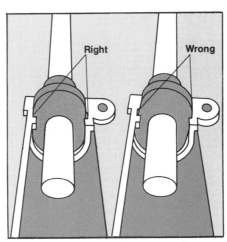

2 When you put in the new shaft, make sure that you install it so that the bearing ridges fall into their respective retainers. Otherwise, the gearbox housing won't fit properly and the shaft won't turn.

Check the main gear for broken teeth or damage if the reciprocating shaft is OK. Try rotating the gears to see if they turn. Be careful of the collar on the pinion shaft, on the side of the main gear. It can fall off as you inspect the gear. If the gear is defective, replace it.

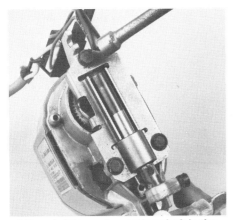

1 **To get at the reciprocating shaft in the Black & Decker,** remove the three hex nuts from the shaft assembly with a nut driver.

2 Remove the shaft assembly from the gearbox housing. Inspect the shaft and its bracket as shown above for the McGraw-Edison saw. If the bracket is damaged, replace the shaft assembly as a unit.

3 Using a pair of needle-nose pliers, pull out the main gear and inspect the teeth for wear or damage. If the gear is defective, replace it.

Checking the brushes

The brushes on the motors in these tools are small pieces of carbon held in contact with the commutator by spring pressure. Brushes on power tools used only for light hobby work may last the life of the tool. If the tool receives heavy and prolonged use, however, the brushes may have to be replaced every year to maintain proper contact.

On some models, you have to get inside to replace the brushes; on others there are brush retaining caps on the outside housings. By removing these, you can replace the brush and spring assemblies.

1 To replace the brushes in the McGraw-Edison saw, first remove the screw holding one of the brush assemblies in place.

2 Take out the brush assembly, holding the brush in with one finger. Remove the brush and examine it for wear. If the brush's length is worn down equal to its width, replace it. Then repeat with the second brush assembly. (Always replace *both* brushes.)

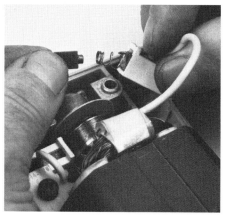

3 To install a new brush, first insert the spring. Push it back with a screwdriver. Insert the eyelet of the lead from the field coil; it goes in sideways, then is turned to face forward. Insert the new brush and fasten the brush assembly back in position.

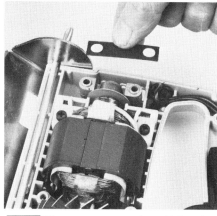

CAUTION Whenever you open the unit's housing, be careful of the bearing restrainer. It is set loosely on pins and can fall out unnoticed. Be sure the bearing restrainer is in place before you reassemble the unit.

1 To replace the brushes in the Black & Decker saw, remove the three screws at the back of the unit's housing. Lift the housing off.

2 Remove the brush assemblies from the motor housing and inspect the brushes for wear. If they are worn, replace them. Remember, always replace both brushes.

To inspect the Black & Decker's motor for obvious damage, remove the plastic plate that covers the motor. If the motor is faulty, the unit will have to be returned to the manufacturer for a new motor.

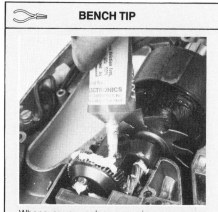

BENCH TIP

Whenever you replace gears in a power saw, clean away all the old grease and dirt. Use a solvent like kerosene. Then insert the new gear and lubricate according to the manufacturer's instructions.

Drills

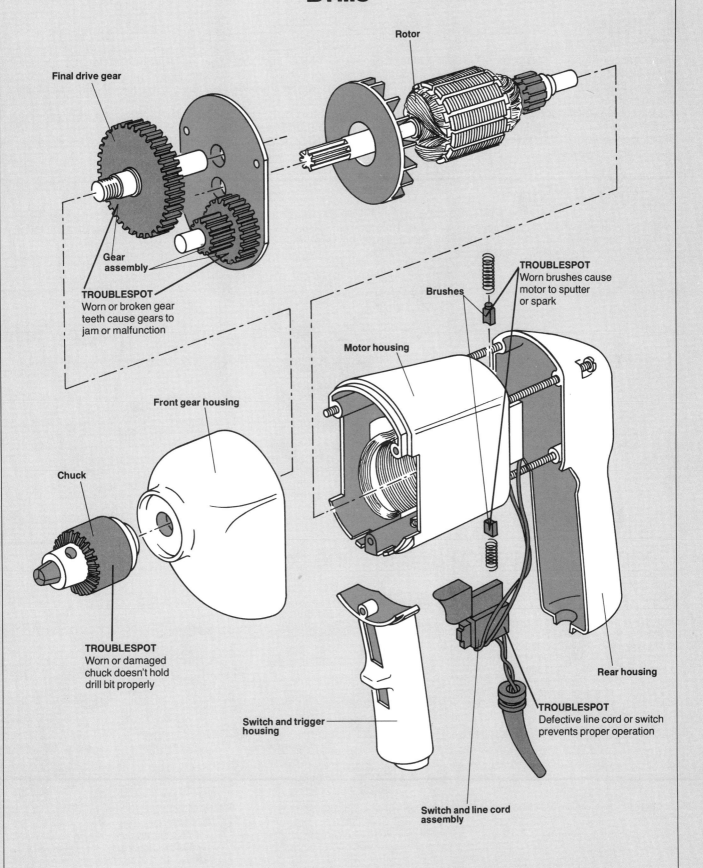

Final drive gear

Rotor

Gear assembly

TROUBLESPOT
Worn or broken gear teeth cause gears to jam or malfunction

Brushes

TROUBLESPOT
Worn brushes cause motor to sputter or spark

Motor housing

Front gear housing

Chuck

TROUBLESPOT
Worn or damaged chuck doesn't hold drill bit properly

Rear housing

TROUBLESPOT
Defective line cord or switch prevents proper operation

Switch and trigger housing

Switch and line cord assembly

POWER TOOLS
Drills

Power drills are highly popular tools for the do-it-yourselfer. One of the main problems connected with power drills comes from forcing them to work by using too much pressure on them. This overloads the motor and causes it to overheat. As with saber saws, it is essential to let the tool work at its own pace and not to apply excessive pressure. Also, it is vitally important to use bits that are sharp and are the proper size for your drill. Don't ever use bits that are too large for your drill.

If the motor doesn't run at all, first make continuity checks on the cord and on the switch (see Blue Pages: *Electrical testers*). If the line cord and switch test OK and the unit still doesn't operate, check the brushes and the motor. If the motor hums but doesn't rotate, or if it makes an excessive amount of noise, check the gears

The instructions for checking continuity and checking the gears and brushes are demonstrated here on a recent-model Black & Decker ⅜-inch variable speed drill.

Getting inside

You can get inside the Black & Decker power drill without removing the chuck, but if the problem is a damaged final drive gear (see page 265), you will have to remove the chuck to replace the gear. Remove the chuck

before taking the drill apart or you will have to reassemble the drill, remove the chuck, and disassemble again.

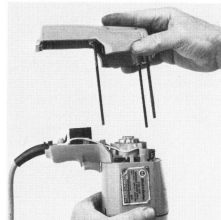

1 To get inside the Black & Decker drill, remove the four screws at the back of the drill housing.

2 Lift off the rear housing to expose the line cord and the switch.

Checking the switch and the line cord

If the drill doesn't run at all, or if it starts and stops, the problem may be a defective switch or line cord. The leads from the line cord to the switch and from the switch to the motor are housed in the drill handle.

Do a continuity test on the line cord and the motor. Some drills, like the one shown at right, have a solid-state switch that can't be tested for continuity. If the cord and motor test OK, replace the switch (see Appliance Repair Basics: *How to test a motor*, and Blue Pages: *Electrical testers*).

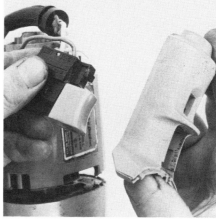

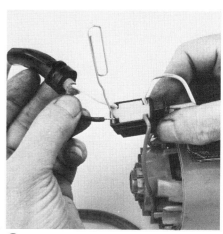

1 To get at the switch, first remove the drill housing (above). Then lift the switch out of the drill handle. You can now work on the line cord and the switch assembly.

2 The leads in the switch are held in place by locking tabs. Use a straightened paper clip to release the tabs while pulling on the leads, one at a time. Some drills, such as this one, have a solid-state switch, which can't be tested for continuity.

Checking the gears and brushes

If the motor is excessively noisy or if it starts and stops, or if it hums but doesn't rotate, the problem may be defective gears. If the drill fails to start and the line cord and switch test OK, or if the motor sparks excessively, you need to replace either the brushes or the motor.

If you suspect a problem with the gears, grasp the chuck tightly and try to rotate it while holding the drill with your other hand. Exert considerable force. If the chuck doesn't rotate, you have a problem with the gears. If any gear is significantly damaged, inspect the other gears closely for lesser damage.

1 **To inspect the gears and brushes,** pry off the front gear housing with a screwdriver.

2 Remove the gear plate (right) to expose the gear assembly (left). To remove or replace any gears, you must first unscrew the chuck (see bottom of page). This frees the gears so you can take them out.

3 Remove the small intermediate gear first. Inspect it for worn or broken teeth.

4 Remove the main gear and inspect it. If either gear is damaged, replace it with an exact duplicate.

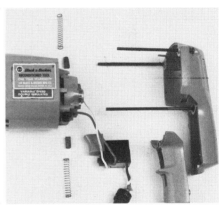

To inspect the brushes, remove the brush assemblies, lift out the brushes, and see if they are worn. If one brush is worn, you still must replace both brushes.

Removing the chuck

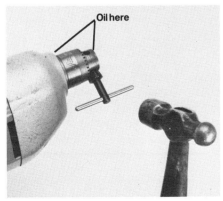

Oil here

1 **To remove the chuck,** insert the chuck key as if to tighten a bit. Rest the drill on a table so the key is parallel with the table. Strike the key sharply with a hammer, causing it to turn counterclockwise. The chuck can now be unscrewed. (It may be necessary to use penetrating oil to loosen it.)

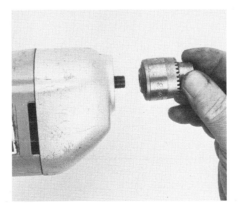

2 Unscrew the chuck and remove it. Replace the chuck if the jaws have become damaged, or if the mechanism for tightening the clamps is either jammed or too loose.

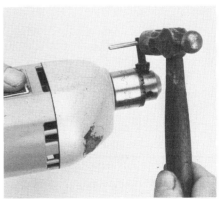

3 Screw on the chuck; tap the key lightly to seat it. Lubricate the threads and chuck and rotate the chuck back and forth in your hand to ensure that it works freely.

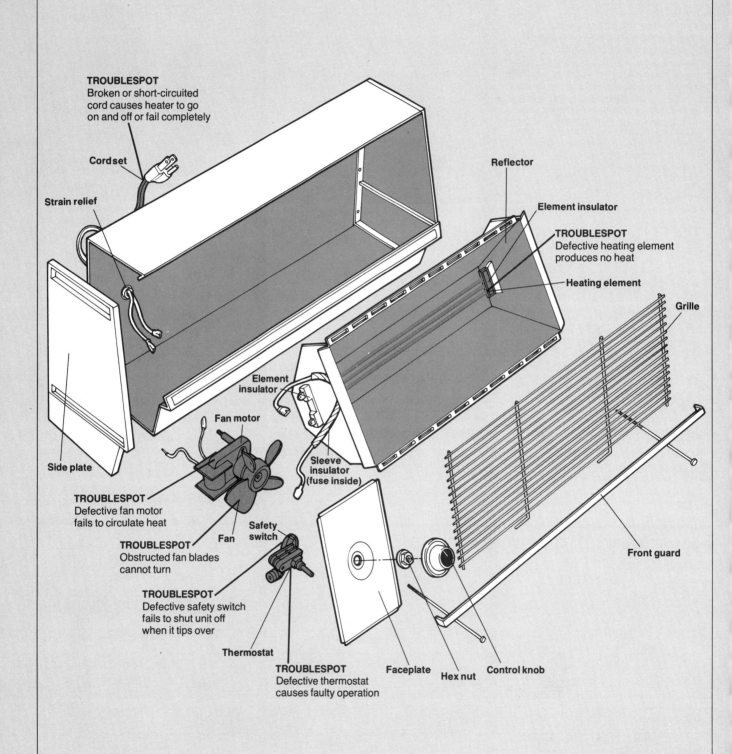

TROUBLESPOT
Broken or short-circuited cord causes heater to go on and off or fail completely

Cordset

Strain relief

Reflector

Element insulator

TROUBLESPOT
Defective heating element produces no heat

Heating element

Grille

Element insulator

Fan motor

Side plate

TROUBLESPOT
Defective fan motor fails to circulate heat

Fan

Safety switch

TROUBLESPOT
Obstructed fan blades cannot turn

Sleeve insulator (fuse inside)

TROUBLESPOT
Defective safety switch fails to shut unit off when it tips over

Thermostat

TROUBLESPOT
Defective thermostat causes faulty operation

Faceplate

Hex nut

Control knob

Front guard

Room Heaters

Room heaters supplement the home's central heating system by turning electricity directly into heat. When the heater is turned on, electric current passes through a heating element. The element's resistance to the current produces heat. It also produces light: the element glows when it is hot. Some elements are shaped like ribbons, and some like springs wound tightly around a ceramic cylinder. Behind the element is a polished metal reflector that directs the heat out into the room. Some heaters have thermostats that automatically maintain room temperature. Some have motor-driven fans to force the heat out.

If the unit fails to operate properly, follow the sequence of tests and repairs given here. First open the unit up; then check the line cord and the heater's internal fuse. Then check the temperature control switch and the safety switch (if your unit has one). Next,

make sure the heating element is in good condition. Finally, check the fan motor (if your unit has one).

TIPS FOR OPERATION EFFICIENCY

Because a room heater draws up to 1,600 watts of power, it should run on its own circuit—an iron on the same circuit at the same time, for example, will blow a fuse or trip a circuit breaker. **CAUTION** Don't use a lamp-type extension cord for a heater.

Dust accumulates in a heater, especially on the reflector. Unplug the unit and clean it with a cloth or a vacuum cleaner crevice tool.

If your heater has a fan, lubricate the motor shaft and oil ports with a couple of drops of light oil once every heating season.

Getting inside

To test the heater or make any repairs (other than replacing a broken control knob), you must open the heater up.

To get inside any heater, you may first have to remove the control knob. Most knobs simply pull off. If the one on your heater resists, look for a

setscrew to loosen. If there is no screw, pry the knob off gently with a screwdriver.

CAUTION Unplug the unit and let it cool down completely before working on it. After reassembling a room heater, always test it for ground.

To get inside the McGraw-Edison, Arvin, and Presto Lo Boy, remove all the Phillips screws around the edge of the grille. Lift off the knob, faceplate, and grille. You now have complete access to the inside.

To get inside the Knapp-Monarch and Markel, remove the screws holding the grille, and all those around the edge of the back. The Markel has an additional screw in the middle of the bottom.

To get inside the Presto Standard, remove four screws from the side plate nearest the control knob and lift the plate off. Label the leads to the thermostat and disconnect them. The control panel and the grille will now slide out.

Testing and replacing the cord

If the heater does not turn on and the fuse in the house circuit is OK, unplug the unit and open it up to check the cord for continuity (see Blue Pages: *Electrical testers*).

If the heater does not turn on and the cord is OK, the next thing to check is the heater's own safety fuse (see box, right). The fuse can be almost anywhere in the heater—to find it, follow the wiring all the way around inside the unit. In some heaters the fuse is hidden inside a fiberglass sleeve.

A simple continuity test shows whether or not the fuse is good. Some fuses melt completely when they blow. If you have this kind, you will see the problem immediately.

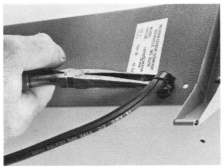

To replace a defective cord, disconnect the two cord leads inside the heater, squeeze out the strain relief on the housing, and pull the cord out. Install a new cord of the same rating, length, and insulation.

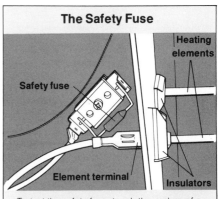

The Safety Fuse

To test the safety fuse, touch the probes of a continuity tester to the fuse terminals; no continuity means a blown fuse. To replace a fuse soldered or welded into the circuit (like the one shown), cut it out, leaving enough lead to wrap around the new fuse wires for resoldering.

Checking the temperature controls

If the unit doesn't heat up when you turn it on (and the cord and the safety fuse are OK), first check the safety switch (if your unit has one) to be sure it is not stuck in the open position (see box, right). Then check the thermostat (if your unit has one).

To check the thermostat, unplug the unit, open it up, and look at the thermostat contacts. If there are signs of burning or corrosion, clean the contacts with fine sandpaper. If the contacts don't close completely when the thermostat is set in the ON position, replace the thermostat. Instructions for replacing the thermostat in three typical models are given here.

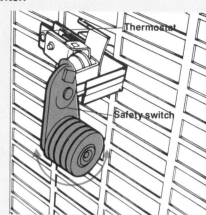

The Safety Switch

Late-model heaters have a pendulum safety switch that turns the unit off if it tips over. To test the switch, turn the unit on, wait until the elements are glowing, and tip the heater backward. If it does not shut off immediately, unplug it, let it cool, open it up, and look for the pendulum arm. Move it back and forth. If the contacts do not open when the pendulum swings, replace the switch. On most models, this switch is part of the thermostat control; the two must be replaced as a unit.

On the McGraw-Edison, Knapp-Monarch, Presto Standard, and Presto Lo Boy, with the control knob off, remove the hex nut around the shaft of the thermostat with a wrench. Label the connecting leads. Remove the connectors from the thermostat terminals, and take out the thermostat. Replace it with a duplicate.

On the Arvin, remove four screws from the thermostat assembly. Mark the connecting wires for identification. Pull off the connectors and replace the entire assembly with a duplicate part.

On the Markel, remove the knob; unscrew the Phillips screw next to the "W" on the heater faceplate at the word "WARMER." Lift the thermostat out from the rear, label the connecting wires, disconnect them, and replace the unit.

Checking the switch

If your unit has a multiple-position switch (high, low, medium heat), and the heating elements work in some positions but not in others, the fault is probably in the switch. In some models you can reach the switch to test it for continuity in all positions (see Blue Pages: *Electrical testers*). In other models, you can't reach the switch. In this case, test the heating elements. If they are bad, replace them (see next page). If they test OK, then the switch is bad and must be replaced.

To test the heating elements, disconnect one end of each element from the circuit, and test each element separately for continuity. This model has "open" elements; they look like springs wound around a cylinder. Another type of element is shown opposite, top center.

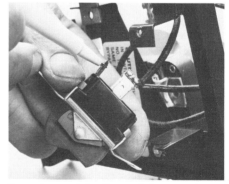

To replace a defective switch, label the push-on connectors, remove them, and unscrew the switch from its mounting. Install a duplicate switch.

Replacing the heating elements

If the heater doesn't warm up when you turn it on (and you've checked out the cord, heater fuse, and switches), the problem is in the heating elements. Unplug the unit, open it up, and disconnect the elements from the circuit. Test each element separately for continuity (as shown at bottom, *opposite*). Follow the instructions below for replacing burned-out elements (see also Appliance Repair Basics: *Types of heating element*).

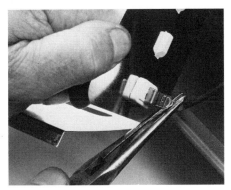

On the Presto Lo Boy, Presto Standard, and Arvin, pull off connectors from the element terminals with pliers. Make a drawing of how the heating element is strung on the insulators, remove the bad element and replace it.

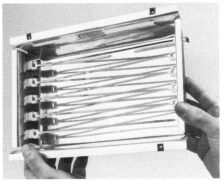

On the McGraw-Edison and Knapp-Monarch, pull off the connecting leads and lift out the reflector. The nichrome ribbon element and the reflector come as a unit. Install a duplicate.

1 **On the Markel,** remove the front guard, then remove the screw at the top center of the grille, and remove the grille by pulling it up and away from the heater.

2 From the back of the unit, remove the screw that holds the terminal of the bad element on the reflector. Release the inside element wire from the terminal and bend it so that it can be pulled through the hole in the reflector.

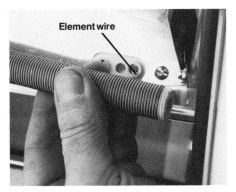

Element wire

3 From the front of the heater, bend the retaining tab away from the end of the bad element with pliers, and pull the element out. Install the new element by inserting the element wire through the reflector hole. Bend the tab down, and fasten the wire to the outside terminal.

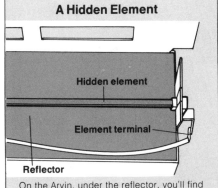

A Hidden Element

Hidden element

Element terminal

Reflector

On the Arvin, under the reflector, you'll find another element that gives the unit another 250 watts of heating power. If you don't get a noticeable change in heat when you set the switch at HIGH, this hidden element may have burned out. Give it a continuity test, and replace any bad element.

Repairing the fan

If the fan doesn't work, make sure that the blades are not obstructed by wires, and that they are not touching some part of the unit. Then check to see that the fan turns freely on its shaft. If it feels stiff, apply a little silicone lubricant. If the fan turns easily but still doesn't run, check the motor for continuity.

1 **To test the fan motor for continuity,** disconnect one lead. Now touch tester probes to the two motor leads (see Blue Pages: *Electrical testers*).

2 If the motor fails the continuity test, unscrew the motor mounting screws, pull off the connectors from the terminals, and replace the motor with a duplicate.

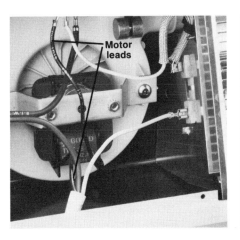

Motor leads

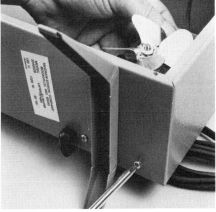

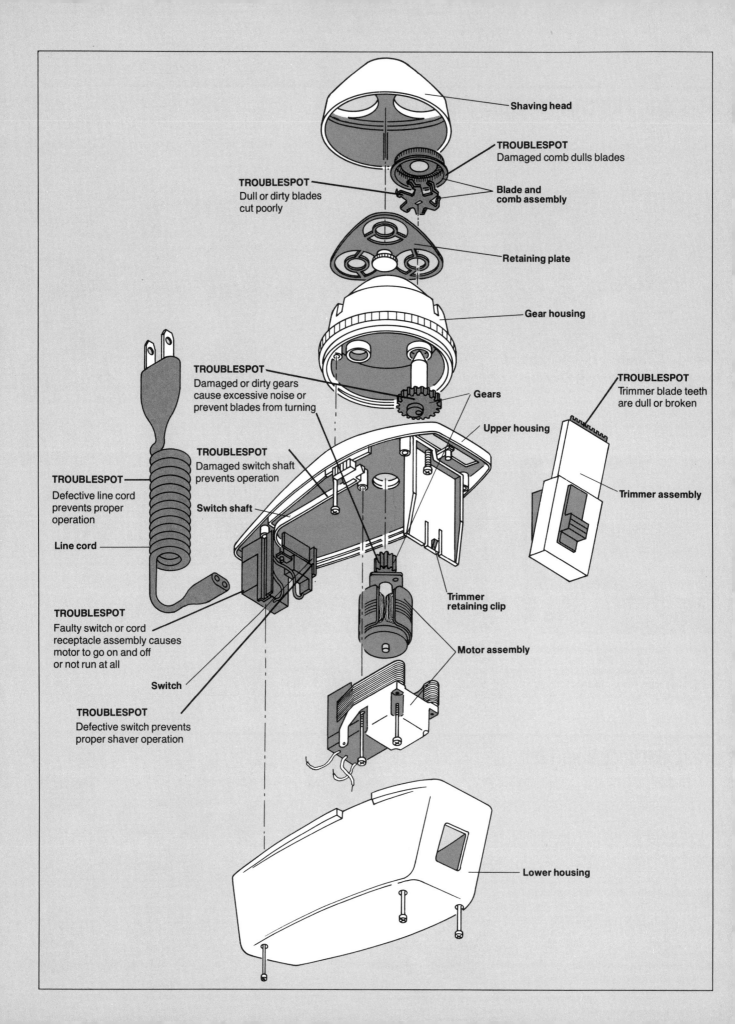

Shaving head

TROUBLESPOT
Damaged comb dulls blades

TROUBLESPOT
Dull or dirty blades
cut poorly

**Blade and
comb assembly**

Retaining plate

Gear housing

TROUBLESPOT
Damaged or dirty gears
cause excessive noise or
prevent blades from turning

Gears

TROUBLESPOT
Trimmer blade teeth
are dull or broken

Upper housing

TROUBLESPOT
Damaged switch shaft
prevents operation

Switch shaft

Trimmer assembly

TROUBLESPOT
Defective line cord
prevents proper
operation

Line cord

**Trimmer
retaining clip**

TROUBLESPOT
Faulty switch or cord
receptacle assembly causes
motor to go on and off
or not run at all

Motor assembly

Switch

TROUBLESPOT
Defective switch prevents
proper shaver operation

Lower housing

Shavers

Electric shavers differ in their cutting units (rotary or flat) and in their motors (rotary or vibrator). Rotary shavers (like the Norelco shown below) use one or more separate blades, each spinning inside a round comb. The blade and comb assemblies rest on gear shafts that float up and down to follow the contour of the face. Rotary motors are the universal type; the only repair you can make is to replace worn brushes. If the motor has other defects, you must return the shaver to the manufacturer for a new motor.

The Sunbeam shown in this section is a flat-head shaver with a universal rotary motor. This type of shaver has from three to five cutters that move back and forth in opposition to one another.

The Remington shaver shown here uses a vibrator motor. The vibrator motor drives its cutter back and forth in an oscillating manner, as the electric field changes its polarity at the 60-cycle-per-second rate of the house current. There are no repairs you can do on a vibrator motor. If it is defective, the shaver will have to be returned to the manufacturer or taken to an authorized repair shop for a new motor.

Basic maintenance—especially cleaning heads and blades—is the most important precaution you can take to keep your shaver in good working order. If your shaver doesn't work at all, you should first do a continuity check on the cord and across the terminal pins (see Blue Pages: *Electrical testers*). If these check out OK, you will have to get inside the appliance to check the switch and the motor.

Switches generally can be replaced, as can faulty cord receptacle assemblies and terminal blocks. Electric shavers are delicate instruments, however, and manufacturers tend to discourage home repair by making few replacement parts available.

Blade maintenance

If a shaver performs poorly, it may be clogged with hair or dead skin, especially if the motor runs slowly or makes an unusual noise. Constant maintenance and cleaning are essential for keeping it in good condition.

No matter what kind of cutter your shaver uses, it is apt to get nicked or become dull with use. It is necessary to check the blades on a regular basis, and replace those that have become dull or damaged.

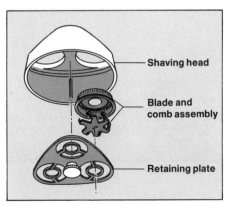

The Norelco shaver has three rotary blades, or cutters, set in combs or cutting screens. The comb and blade make up a single assembly. If the comb is bent or nicked, it may rub against the blade and dull it. You can replace any damaged comb and blade assembly, as described at right.

To get into the Norelco comb and blade assembly, twist off the shaving head and turn it upside down. Loosen the knob that holds the retaining plate. Remove the plate and lift out the comb and blade assemblies for inspection. Replace any damaged combs or dull blades. If the unit is OK, clean it with a small brush.

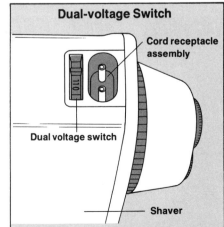

The Norelco has a dual-voltage switch (240 or 120 volts). Be sure this switch is set to correspond to the voltage you are using, otherwise, you may damage the motor.

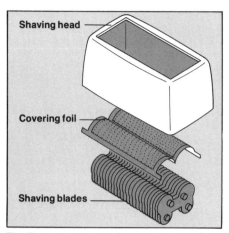

The Remington shaver has a set of round blades covered by a thin metal foil. Inspect both foil and blades for nicks or other damage, and replace defective parts. If everything is OK, clean blades, foil, and head cover with a brush.

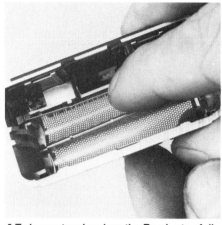

1 **To inspect and replace the Remington foil and blades,** lift off the shaving head. You can now lift out the foil. If it is damaged, replace it.

2 Lift out the blades for inspection. Replace them when they grow dull or have broken teeth or nicks.

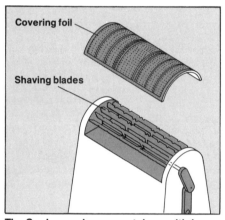

The Sunbeam shaver contains multiple oscillating blades or cutters. This model has five blades, three moving in one direction and two in the other. They are numbered 1 to 5.

1 **To check and replace blades on the Sunbeam,** pinch the shaving head of the unit and pull it off to expose the multiple cutting unit below.

2 Remove each blade separately and examine it for any signs of nicks or damage. Replace any damaged ones. Clean the remaining blades and put them back in the correct order.

Getting inside

You must get inside a shaver to check the drive gears, the switches, the cord receptacle assembly, or the motor. If the shaver doesn't run, and you have tested the cord for continuity, you know the trouble is in the switch or somewhere else inside the appliance.

1 **To get inside the Norelco shaver,** remove the three Phillips screws that hold the lower housing to the upper housing.

2 Slip off the lower housing to expose the inner workings of the shaver.

1 To get inside the Remington shaver, use a screwdriver to pry off the metal plate on the bottom of the shaver housing.

2 Carefully remove the plastic button that is under the metal plate. The button is fragile and liable to break.

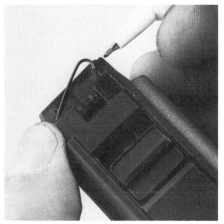

3 Remove the clip at the side of the housing. This will allow you to open the housing. Be careful; the clip is under pressure, and as you pry it up, it may fly off. Hold as shown here.

1 To get inside the Sunbeam shaver, remove the two screws on the bottom of the housing (right).

2 Pull out the whole motor assembly (far right). You can now examine the switch and cord receptacle assembly thoroughly.

To keep cutting blades like those on the Sunbeam shaver in good condition, use one of the commercial liquid cleaners on the market. Apply liquid through the comb of the shaver to the blades. Run the machine for about a minute, then take out the blades and clean them.

Checking the Norelco trimmer

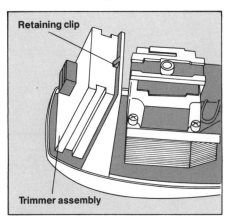

Retaining clip

Trimmer assembly

The trimmer assembly is held in place by a retaining clip. If it doesn't work, first examine the teeth. They may be broken or oscillating improperly. The trimmer may also need cleaning.

1 To remove the trimmer assembly, press down on the retaining clip with your finger.

2 Pull out the entire trimmer assembly. If it is damaged or dull, replace it. If it is OK, clean it and put it back.

Checking the switch and cord receptacle

If the line cord and the cord receptacle pins are OK, but the shaver doesn't run, check the switch and the cord receptacle assembly for continuity. In the case of Norelco, the on/off switch has a long plastic shaft that can break. The switch and the cord receptacle assembly can be replaced if they are defective. Look for any broken wires or loose connections before you start testing, and tighten or repair them.

1 **To check the switch assembly on the Norelco,** first examine the switch and its shaft on the side of the shaver (right), if the shaft is broken, you will have to replace it.

2 Check the switch assembly, which is located at the bottom of the shaver, next to the cord receptacle assembly (shown lifted out, at far right). The entire switch assembly can be pulled out and replaced if a continuity check shows it to be defective.

3 The switch shaft (right), is relatively fragile. If it is broken, it must be replaced. Fit one end into the seat, which is located in the switch at the side of the shaver.

4 Insert the small tip of the switch shaft into the hole in the switch assembly, located at the bottom of the shaver (far right). Otherwise, the shaft won't activate the switch assembly.

1 **To replace a defective Norelco cord receptacle assembly,** gently lift out the assembly with a screwdriver (right).

2 Note the position of the leads (far right) that connect the cord receptacle assembly to the on/off switch and the dual-voltage switch.

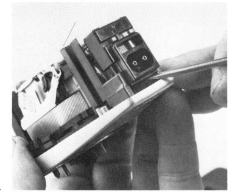 

3 Next, label and remove the wire that connects the cord receptacle assembly to the on/off switch (right).

4 Disconnect the wire (far right) that connects the cord receptacle assembly to the dual-voltage switch. Note the position of each of the wires for reassembly; it's a good idea to mark them with tape.

 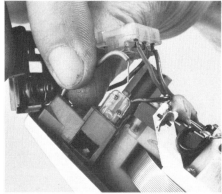

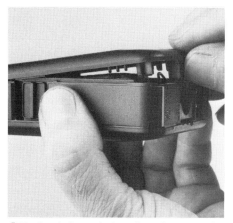

1 **To check the switch and cord receptacle on the Remington shaver,** follow the steps for opening the housing (*see Getting inside, page 273*), then pull up the side of the shaver housing. This exposes the motor, cord receptacle assembly, and switch.

2 The cord receptacle assembly, the switch, and the motor can all be replaced separately (the motor must be replaced by an authorized repair shop). The switch assembly is soldered in. Remove leads and check for continuity (see Blue Pages: *Electrical testers*). If defective, replace the switch assembly.

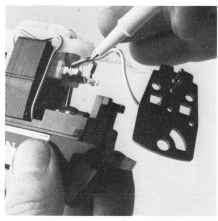

The Sunbeam cord receptacle switch assembly (if your model has one), and the board they are mounted on constitute a unit. If either the switch or the cord receptacle is defective, the whole assembly must be replaced. The board can be slipped out in some models. In other models screws must be removed first.

Checking the drive gears and brushes

On shavers that have universal motors, brushes can be checked and worn brushes replaced. The Norelco shaver has three drive gears and shafts, one for each of the three heads. These should be checked for worn or broken teeth or for misalignment if the shaver isn't cutting properly.

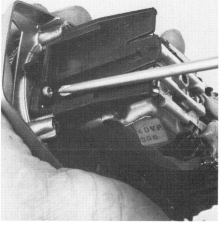

1 **To check the drive gears and brushes on the Norelco,** first remove the trimmer assembly. Next, unscrew the Phillips screw under the trimmer at the top of the motor assembly (right).

2 Remove the two Phillips screws on the side of the motor assembly, then take off the gear housing to expose the gears and three shafts (far right).

3 Check the gear drive for broken teeth or misaligned shafts (right). Each of the gear drives or shafts may be replaced separately.

On the Sunbeam shaver, check the brushes to see if they are making proper contact (far right). Brushes on universal motors tend to wear down. If the brushes are worn, replace them.

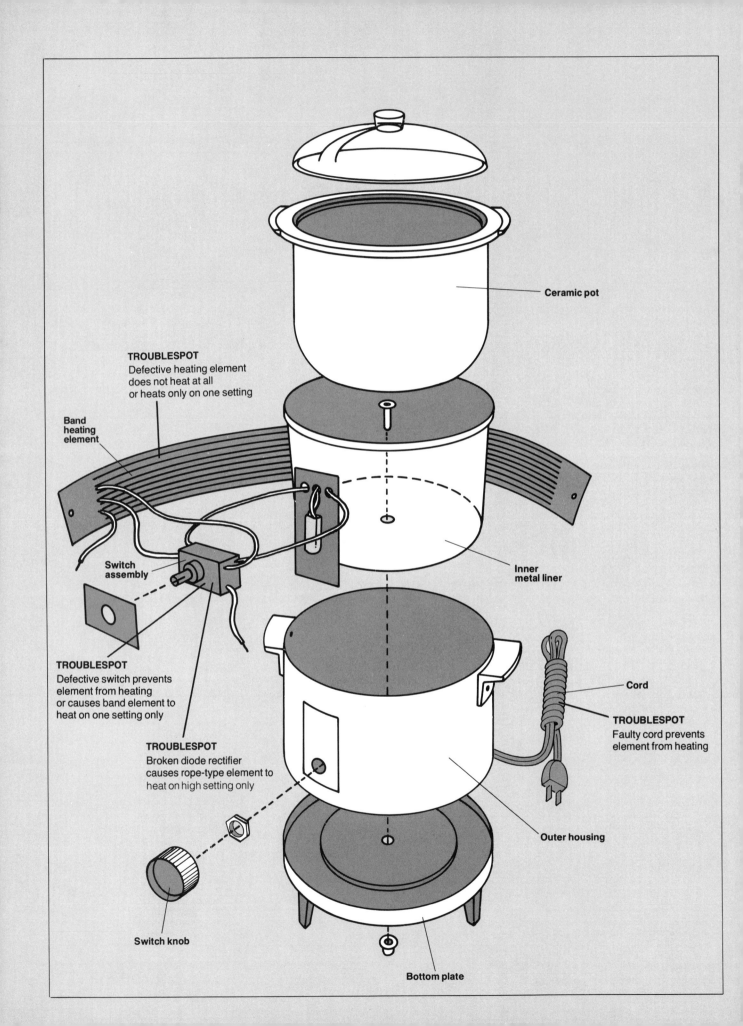

Ceramic pot

TROUBLESPOT
Defective heating element
does not heat at all
or heats only on one setting

Band
heating
element

Inner
metal liner

Switch
assembly

TROUBLESPOT
Defective switch prevents
element from heating
or causes band element to
heat on one setting only

TROUBLESPOT
Broken diode rectifier
causes rope-type element to
heat on high setting only

Cord

TROUBLESPOT
Faulty cord prevents
element from heating

Outer housing

Switch knob

Bottom plate

Slow Cookers

Slow cookers are similar in design to frying pans and some corn poppers. Basically, they consist of an inner cooking pot, a heating element, and an outer shell that protects and insulates the pot and element. Some makes and models of slow cookers are not repairable. In these slow cookers, the ceramic pot (with the heating element wrapped around it) is sealed into the outer shell. On some models, the ceramic pot is set in a metal liner—with the element wrapped around it—riveted to the outer shell.

Other slow cookers, however, are repairable. These models have the ceramic pot inside a metal liner, which fits into an outer shell that can be removed. The liner, its heating element, and the switch can be examined and replaced if defective.

Slow cookers have one of two basic styles of heating element. One is a band element consisting of two resistance wires of different wattages, set in flexible, heat-resistant material wrapped around the metal liner. The other is a rope-type element wrapped around the liner. This one is similar to the warming element in coffee makers.

The band-type element achieves high and low temperatures by switching the current from one wire to the other. The rope-type element achieves the low heat setting by changing the current with a diode. Both types use a multiposition switch with self-locking terminals. You can't repair the switches and elements themselves, but you can test or inspect them for damage. If they are defective, it's relatively easy to replace them.

The steps for repairing slow cookers are shown on two late-model units: the Hamilton Beach, which uses a band element, and the Farberware, which uses a rope-type element with a diode.

Getting inside

Unless there is a visible break in the line cord, or the switch outside the unit is clearly broken, identifying problems and making all repairs or replacements in slow cookers require you to open the appliance. This means you will have to open the unit when the element fails to heat at all, or when it heats on one level only. When you open the unit, first set aside the inner ceramic pot. It is an expensive part to replace, so be sure you put it in a safe place while you work.

1 **To get inside the Hamilton Beach,** turn over the shell and liner assembly. Pry up the speed nut at the bottom of the unit with a screwdriver. If the nut breaks, you can replace it.

2 Lift off the bottom plate. This may require you to pry a bit with a screwdriver.

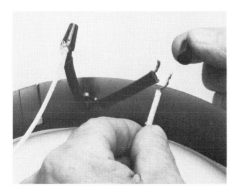

3 Disconnect the line cord. It is attached to the switch by wire nuts. Remove the wire nuts and do a continuity check on the line cord if your problem is a dead cooker (see Blue Pages: *Electrical testers*). If the cord is defective, replace it.

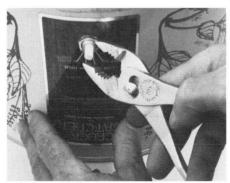

4 To get at the switch and heating element assemblies, pry off the switch knob on the outside of the unit and remove the hex nut that holds the switch.

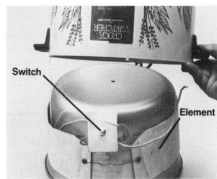

5 Push the switch out of the outer shell, then lift off the shell to expose the metal liner and the switch and element assemblies.

1 **To get inside the Farberware,** turn the unit upside down and remove the nut at the bottom of the unit. Lift off the bottom plate.

2 Use a screwdriver to gently pry off the switch knob located on the outside of the slow cooker.

3 Remove the screw that holds the switch on the outside shell and take off the shell. Disconnect the line cord by removing the wire nuts and test it for continuity if your problem is a dead cooker (see Blue Pages: *Electrical testers*).

Checking the heating element

If the unit doesn't heat at all, and the line cord is OK or it heats on one level only, check the heating element. In the Hamilton Beach, the band element can be removed from the metal liner for visual inspection and testing. In the Farberware unit, the rope-type element can be tested while it is in place.

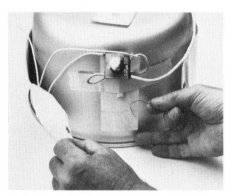

1 **To check the heating element in the Hamilton Beach,** unfasten the thin wire looped through the grommet at the end of the band element.

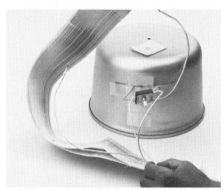

2 Remove the heat-resistant tape that attaches the band element to the liner and unwrap the element, leaving all electrical wires attached. Examine the element visually for breaks and burned areas.

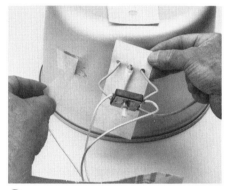

3 Remove the switch (normally held in place by heat-resistant tape) from the liner. This will prevent placing too much strain on the delicate element wires while you test. Keep track of tapes and insulators for reassembly.

4 If the element shows no signs of damage, disconnect its leads from the switch. Test the element for continuity by touching one tester probe to the common element lead (the one that connects the two element circuits) and the other probe to each of the two other element leads in turn. The element should show continuity through both leads. If either is defective, replace the element.

To examine the heating element in the Farberware, disconnect the leads from the switch and do a continuity check by touching the tester probes to the element terminals. To replace the element, bend up the soft aluminum tabs on the mounting band and pull the element free. Bend the tabs slowly and carefully, or they will break. After the new element is installed, push the tabs gently back in place.

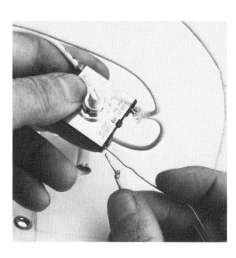

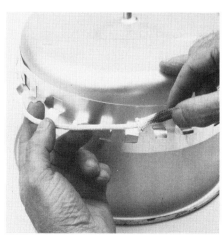

Checking the switch and diode

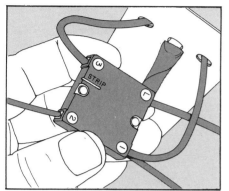

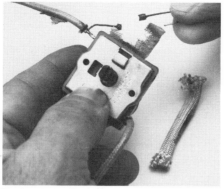

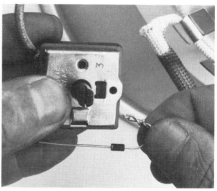

To test the switch on the Hamilton Beach for continuity, connect one tester probe to the terminal marked "L" and the other probe to each of the terminals marked "1," "2," and "3" in turn. (Use a straightened paper clip to make the connection if your clips don't fit inside the terminal sockets.) Turn the switch dial to each setting as you test its terminal. If any setting fails the test, replace the switch with a duplicate.

To check the Farberware diode (if the low-heat setting doesn't work), remove the insulating sleeve that covers the diode and inspect it for burns or breakage. Even if the diode looks all right, it may be defective. If the cord, switch, and element are OK, and the low-heat setting fails, the diode must be replaced.

To replace a defective diode, disconnect the push-in connector from the switch, and cut or unsolder the other lead. Solder the new diode back in place on the lead.

Yogurt makers and hot trays

Yogurt makers and hot trays are both simple appliances. They consist of a cord (some trays have a detachable cord), a low-wattage heating element, and a simple thermal cutoff.

Steps for opening a yogurt maker's housing are demonstrated on a late-model Salton. Remove the cover and jars before going to work. The hot tray shown here, also a Salton unit, has one innovative feature: the heating element is printed on the underside of a heavy sheet of glass. The cord and glass are one unit; if the heating element doesn't work, you need a new appliance. You can test other parts (wire connections, cord receptacle, and thermostat) and replace them if necessary.

1 To get inside the Salton yogurt maker, turn the appliance upside down. Remove the four screws in the bottom. Turn the unit right side up again (right) and lift out the plastic cup receptacle and the envelope-shaped, aluminum heat-distribution shield underneath.

2 Unfold the two sides of the shield. Lift out the insulating strip with the heating element and thermal cutoff attached (far right). The heating element assembly can be removed for replacement as a single unit. Snip out the old assembly and resolder the new one in place.

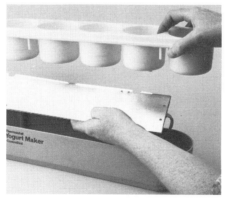

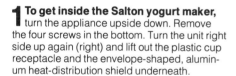

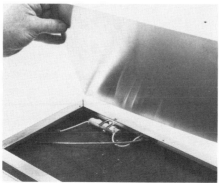

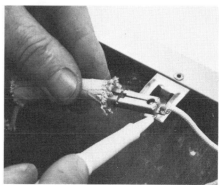

1 To get inside the Salton hot tray, turn the unit upside down and remove the six screws holding the bottom plate.

2 Lift the bottom plate to expose the back of the cord receptacle, the thermostat, and the element terminals.

3 To replace the thermostat, bend the tab to free it from its metal bracket. Slip the heat-resistant tubing off, clip off the thermostat, and resolder a new one in place.

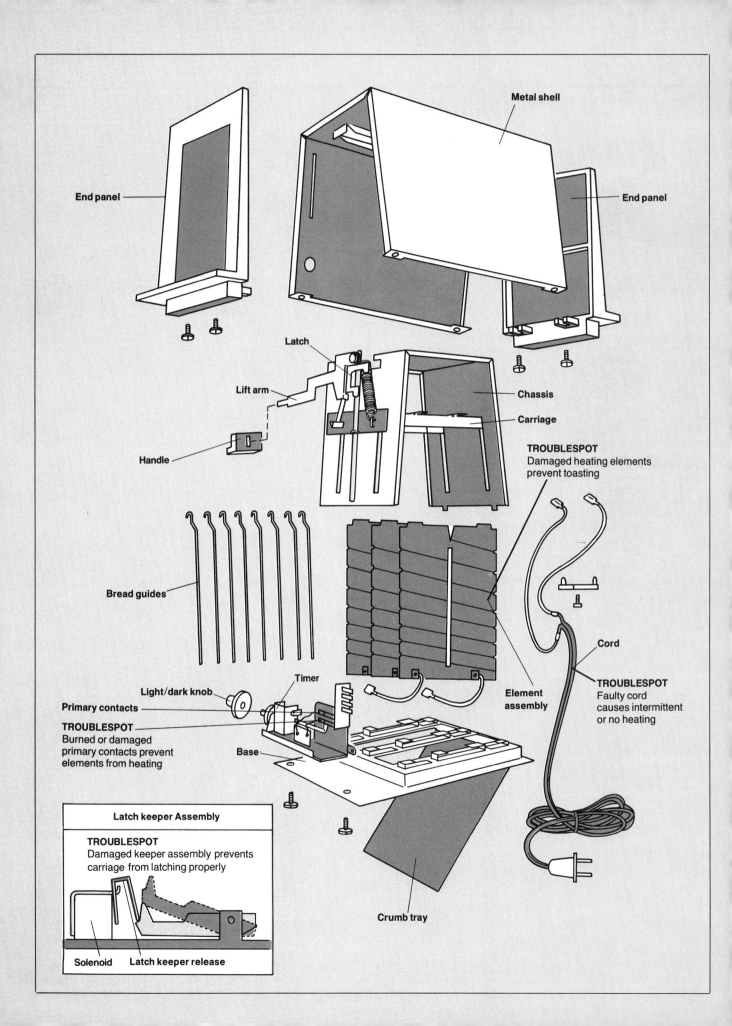

End panel

Metal shell

End panel

Latch

Lift arm

Chassis

Carriage

Handle

TROUBLESPOT
Damaged heating elements prevent toasting

Bread guides

Cord

TROUBLESPOT
Faulty cord causes intermittent or no heating

Light/dark knob

Timer

Primary contacts

Element assembly

TROUBLESPOT
Burned or damaged primary contacts prevent elements from heating

Base

Latch keeper Assembly

TROUBLESPOT
Damaged keeper assembly prevents carriage from latching properly

Solenoid   **Latch keeper release**

Crumb tray

Toasters

The apparent simplicity with which a toaster browns bread to a desired doneness and then pops up the finished slice is deceptive. For all its smallness, the mechanism of a toaster is complicated. The bread in a toaster sits on a mobile carriage, which either is depressed manually or, on some models, sinks automatically. When lowered, the carriage strikes a latch that holds it in place. This closes the primary contacts. Current is then supplied to the heating elements, which are wires wound around an insulating sheet. (The wires' resistance to the electrical current causes them to get hot.)

On older toasters, the degree of doneness is controlled by clockwork. The word "timer" still is used, but in fact the "timing" mechanism is the thermostat: doneness is governed by the degree of heat in the toaster. There are different types of thermostats: the simplest ones consist of two metal bands that are bonded together. Others have this component, and in addition are equipped with a small magnet called a solenoid. Both of these, along with those that have other modifications, operate in much the same way. When the thermostat registers the preset temperature, it activates the latch release. The bread carriage rises on its spring and turns off the current.

On some makes of toaster, various parts are riveted or soldered in place. If you have this kind, you may have to take it to the repair shop or replace it. Most toasters, however, can be taken apart at home for repair or replacement of defective parts. Directions for such repairs are given for a variety of models.

> **CAUTION** When working on a toaster, you must exercise extreme caution. Toasters draw a very high electrical current. In addition, unlike most small appliances, almost all models are encased in a metal shell, which increases the hazard of shock. Checking for ground after any repair is therefore essential (bottom of page).

MAINTENANCE

If a slice of toast or piece of muffin sticks in your toaster, never try to retrieve it with a knife or other utensil. You not only risk a short circuit or electric shock, you may also bend one of the bread guides on the carriage into the heating element. If this happens, the metal shell of the toaster will become a dangerous, shock-giving hazard the next time you use it. Instead, first unplug the appliance and wait for it to cool. Try to free the bread with your fingers. If you can't, turn the toaster upside down and shake it gently.

To clean a toaster, first unplug it. Open the crumb tray and gently clean out the inside of the appliance with a small paintbrush or soft toothbrush. *Never* use steel wool: a loose strand can cause dangerous electrical problems.

Checking for Ground

To test for ground, first unplug the toaster. Push down the carriage until it is caught and held by the latch keeper. Place one tester probe on one prong of the cord's plug and the other on the metal shell of the toaster; repeat for the other prong. If this test shows continuity, you have a short (or ground) somewhere in the toaster. (For a further discussion of ground, see Blue Pages: *Circuit faults*.) Take the appliance apart (see next page) and look for a loose wire or bent element that could be causing the short.

Two reasons for a live shell are: (1) a bread guide has knocked against the element; (2) a live wire, such as a partially stripped cord lead, is touching the shell. The bread guide can be bent away from the element with a finger. A bad cord should be replaced. NOTE: Replace the cord only with one that has the same current and temperature ratings.

After doing these repairs or any others, be sure to check the toaster again for ground. It may be grounded in more than one place.

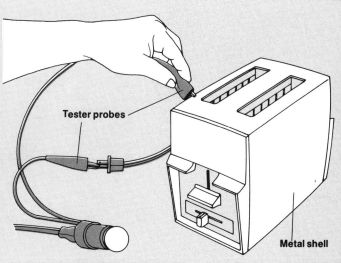

Tester probes

Metal shell

Getting inside

Any repairs on a toaster, except replacing a detachable cord, require opening the toaster. This generally necessitates removing the end panels, and then the metal shell. Unplug the toaster before starting to work.

For most toasters, one of the steps to getting inside is gently bending the metal shell to remove it and expose the working parts on the chassis. Don't be afraid to use force (within reason); if the shell gets bent, it can be bent back into proper shape when it is replaced, and it will hold its shape when screwed back together.

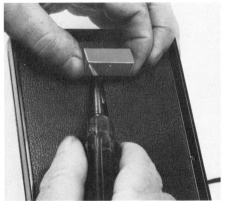

1 **To open the General Electric two-slice toaster,** first pry the handle off of the lift arm. Use a screwdriver if necessary. Then remove the light/dark indicator knob (it will pull straight out).

2 Turn the toaster upside down. With a ¼-inch nut driver, remove the hex screws from the end panels at either end of the appliance.

3 With one hand, hold the end panel from which you removed the carriage handle. Push down on the metal part of the base. This will disengage the metal tab that holds the panel and base together. Pull the panel until you can free the prongs that attach the base to the panel. Lift off the panel. Now remove the other end panel.

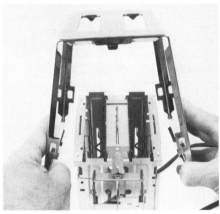

4 Turn the toaster right side up. Gently spread the shell apart and lift it from the chassis. (The lift arm extension hanging from the carriage assembly is now free and may fall off.)

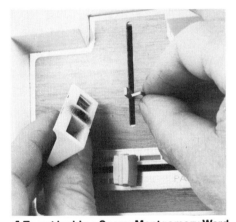

1 **To get inside a Sears, Montgomery Ward, J.C. Penney or Proctor Silex toaster,** first pry the knob off the lift arm. Do this carefully: the knob is held to the arm by a metal nib (shown here in the right hand). The nib and knob are fragile and may break.

2 Next, remove the light/dark indicator arm: turn the toaster upside down and open the crumb tray; loosen the Phillips screw that holds the indicator arm in place. Pull out the arm by means of the knob.

3 To free the shell and the end panels, first remove the four screws from the corners of the base. Pull the end panels away from the metal shell, until the prongs holding them together disengage. Lift off the panels. The shell is now free, and it can be removed from the chassis.

1 **To get inside the Toastmaster two-slice model,** first pull off the knob at the end of the lift arm. Then pull off the light/dark knob. (If it does not come off easily, gently loosen it with a screwdriver.)

2 Turn the toaster upside down and remove the slotted hex screws that attach the end panels to the shell. Pull the panels off.

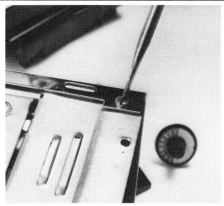

3 To remove the shell, loosen the four screws that attach it to the chassis. Holding the shell and the chassis together, turn the toaster right side up.

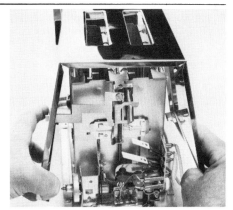

4 Pull the sides of the shell apart until they clear the chassis, the lift arm, and the light/dark arm. Lift off the shell. Since the shell holds the bread guides in place, they now will be loose. Tape them in place or note their position and remove them. Remember to put them back when you reassemble the toaster.

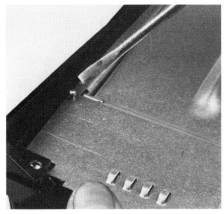

1 **To get inside a Toastmaster four-slice model,** turn it upside down and take out the four screws that hold the crumb tray and base plate to the chassis. Remove these parts.

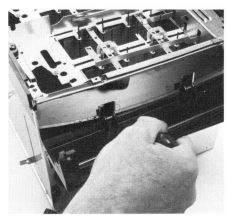

2 Remove the screws, front and back, from the plastic legs and set the legs aside. Then remove the screws from the plastic strips along the sides of the base. Take off the strips.

3 To remove the shell, first look to see if there are any tabs holding it to the chassis. If there are, maneuver the shell around them. Turn the toaster right side up and lift off the shell; there is little clearance over the chassis, so go slowly.

Line cord problems

If the toaster doesn't work at all, unplug it and first test the line cord for continuity (see Blue Pages: *Electrical testers*). Do not try to repair a defective cord. Instead, replace it with one of the same current rating and size. If the cord on your toaster is attached with crimp-on connectors, use new solderless connectors to attach a new cord of sufficient current rating and size.

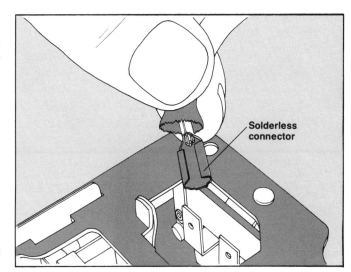

Solderless connector

To replace the cord on most toasters, pull off the solderless connectors and attach the new cord. On some models, the cord is held in place by a plastic guard or strain relief. You will have to remove this before you can take out the cord. ⟊ Pinch it with pliers and it will come out easily.

Primary contacts

If the cord is in good condition but the element fails to heat up when the carriage is depressed, you should check the primary contact points. Locking the carriage into toasting position closes contacts that send current to the elements. If the contacts are bent, try bending them gently back into position. If they are burned, try cleaning them. If the contacts are broken, or can't be bent into shape or properly cleaned, the toaster will have to go to the repair shop. In some cases, it may be cheaper to buy a new toaster.

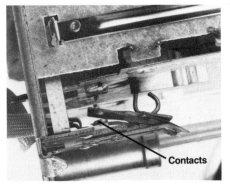

To inspect the contacts, push down the carriage and check that the contacts touch each other. If, as shown here, they do not, bend them gently with your finger until they do. If there is any buildup of carbon or burned crumbs, clean it off gently.

The primary contacts on some models have a fiber cover that makes visual inspection difficult. Slit the cover with a razor blade and fold it back. With the carriage locked down, test the contacts for continuity as shown (see Blue Pages: *Electrical testers*).

Timer assembly problems

If the carriage fails to rise or pops up as soon as it is depressed, first check the latch, latch keeper, and latch release (the parts that hold the carriage in place during the toasting process and then free it). If any are bent, straighten them; replace damaged ones if you can on your model. Most often, however, these symptoms are caused by a faulty timer mechanism. How to repair it depends on what make your toaster is, and on whether the mechanism is a simple two-band thermostat or a more sophisticated one, like the Toastmaster (opposite).

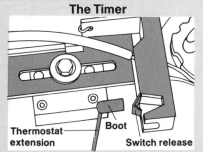

The Timer

Thermostat extension   Boot   Switch release

Toasters made by Proctor Silex, Montgomery Ward, Sears, and J.C. Penney all have a timing mechanism consisting of three separate components: the basic bimetallic thermostat that bends under heat; an extension with a tip shaped something like a boot; and an electro-magnet called a solenoid. As the band bends, the boot moves forward. When the desired temperature is reached, it kicks the switch release. This release sends current to the solenoid. The activated magnet then pulls the latch keeper away from the latch on the carriage. On toasters like these you can check to see if the timer is working simply by looking: set the toaster on end, open the crumb tray, depress the carriage, and plug in the toaster. As it heats you can see the boot move toward the release, and there should be a blue spark as contact is made. If this doesn't happen, take the toaster to a repair shop or replace it.

1 **If the carriage does not go up or down,** first check that the latch (indicated here) is clean. Remove any buildup of burned crumbs or carbon with a plastic scouring pad. If the latch is bent, straighten it.

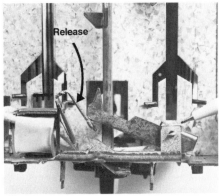

2 Check also that the latch keeper release—the inverted-V-shaped piece shown here—is clean. It must dangle free and be able to swing back and forth.

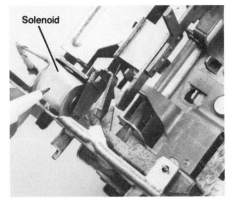

If the carriage on a Proctor Silex, Sears, Montgomery Ward, or J. C. Penney toaster still does not work, inspect the solenoid. If there is a carbon buildup the part is probably burned out. Take it to a repair shop or replace it.

To check the timer assembly on a General Electric toaster, depress the carriage and make sure that the latch catches and holds it in place. Clean any crumbs off the shaft within the spring. If the latch doesn't catch, take the toaster to a repair shop or replace it.

Toastmaster Timers

On all Toastmaster models, there is one timer unit that comprises the primary contacts, the thermostat, and the latch. (Toastmasters do not have solenoids.) If the unit is clean but still does not work, replace the timer unit, following the directions given at right for your model.

On Toastmaster two-slice models, there are two screws holding the timer to the chassis. Remove them. Label the leads, disconnect them, and lift out the defective timing unit.

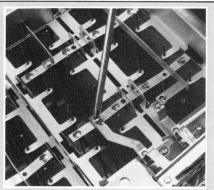

On Toastmaster four-slice models, label and disconnect the leads. Then turn the machine upside down and remove the three screws that secure the timer to the chassis. Turn the appliance right side up and lift out the timer for replacement.

Heating element problems

If all the other parts of the toaster are in working order but one or more of the heating elements does not get hot, the element itself is defective and you will have to replace the entire element assembly (see Appliance Repair Basics: *Types of heating elements*). This can be done at home, unless the heating elements are riveted or welded to the chassis; in that case you must take the toaster to a repair shop.

1 To replace the heating element assembly, take your toaster apart and remove all the bread guides from the chassis. (Note how they are positioned for later replacement.) Turn the toaster upside down and remove the crumb tray.

2 With pliers, straighten the metal tabs that hold the chassis to the base. The tabs are fragile, so do this gently.

3 Turn the toaster right side up and pry one side of the chassis loose. Lift the chassis off the base.

4 Lift the heating element assembly out of the chassis base. The leads will already have been disconnected when you disconnected the timer assembly. Even if only one of the heating elements is defective, the entire heating element assembly must be replaced.

Slots

5 When installing a replacement heating element assembly, be sure to set it correctly in the slots provided for it in the chassis base.

6 On the Toastmaster four-slice model, you must also remove the baffle that is positioned between the middle elements. After you have installed the new element assembly, replace the baffle.

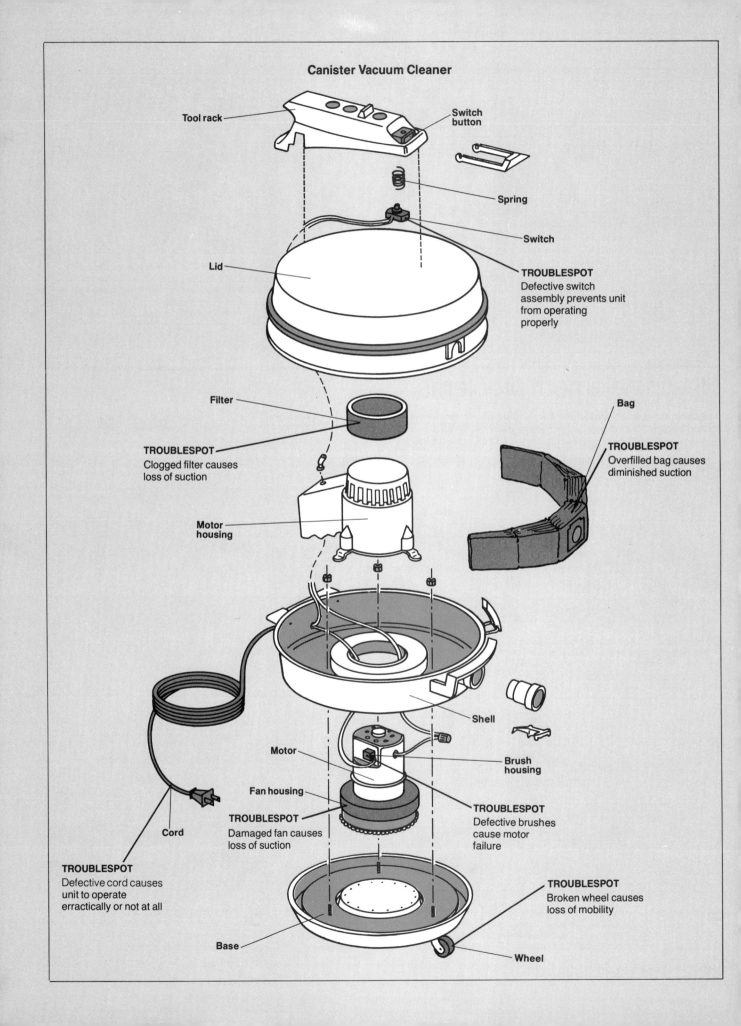

Canister Vacuum Cleaner

Tool rack

Switch button

Spring

Switch

TROUBLESPOT
Defective switch assembly prevents unit from operating properly

Lid

Filter

TROUBLESPOT
Clogged filter causes loss of suction

Bag

TROUBLESPOT
Overfilled bag causes diminished suction

Motor housing

Shell

Motor

Brush housing

Fan housing

TROUBLESPOT
Defective brushes cause motor failure

TROUBLESPOT
Damaged fan causes loss of suction

Cord

TROUBLESPOT
Defective cord causes unit to operate erractically or not at all

TROUBLESPOT
Broken wheel causes loss of mobility

Base

Wheel

Vacuum Cleaners
Canister

All vacuum cleaners work in the same basic way. A universal motor drives a fan (sometimes two fans) that sucks in air, dust, and debris. A porous bag traps the dust, while the air is expelled through the pores of the bag and out of the machine.

There are two basic types of vacuum cleaners: canisters (like the one diagramed on the opposite page) and uprights. In addition to the obvious difference in design, there are also many mechanical differences between the two varieties. Because of these differences, the description of how to repair vacuum cleaners is divided into sections. How to go about checking and repairing typical canisters is shown on the following pages. (Tank-type vacuums, the canisters made by Electrolux, are unique in design and are covered on pages 292 and 293.) Uprights are covered fully on pages 294 through 299.

Of the two types, the canister is more maneuverable. The fan, bag, and motor are contained in a housing that rests on wheels and is pulled around the floor. A flexible hose connects the canister to a rigid wand that can be fitted with a variety of specialized cleaning nozzles. (Some models have a suction nozzle equipped with an additional motor; see page 290.)

Both canisters and uprights, however, require similar maintenance practices (right). In addition, the steps to be followed in repairing the hose are the same for both types (see below). The hose is an integral part of the canister, and is an optional extra on some uprights. The procedure for replacing damaged wheels also applies to both uprights and canisters (see next page).

> **CAUTION** After making any repairs to your vacuum cleaner, always test it to make sure that it is properly grounded. (See Blue Pages: *Testing for Ground*.)

MAINTENANCE

The dirt that vacuum cleaners are designed specifically to clean up is, itself, the most common cause of damage to the machine. Check the nozzle regularly and remove any buildup of dust and debris. *Never* use your cleaner to pick up small, hard objects such as pebbles or bobby pins. If they strike the fan, which is very possible, they can cause serious damage to your machine (see page 291).

A dust bag that is overloaded will impair suction. For this reason, never use a replaceable dust bag more than once. However thoroughly you shake a paper bag clean, the pores remain blocked, preventing proper operation. If there is a filter between the bag and the fan/motor assembly, it should be changed at regular intervals; otherwise, you risk a burned-out motor.

Although canister models are designed to be pulled around the floor behind you as you clean, try not to yank the unit in such a way as to strain the cord or hose.

Clearing a blocked hose

Loss of suction is a common malfunction of vacuum cleaners. If this happens, the first thing to check on any model is the nozzle. Remove any buildup of lint and dust; then check the hose. If it is blocked, follow the directions below.

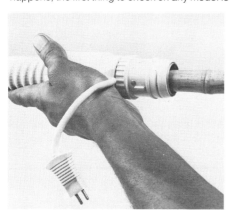

1 **If you have an obstruction in the flexible hose and cannot shake it out,** use a pole or broomstick to push it toward the rigid elbow that connects the hose to the wand. On some models the hose can be inserted into the exhaust port to clear a blockage.

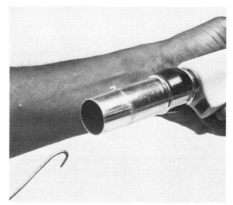

2 Straighten out a wire coat hanger and bend the end into a hook. Tape the end of the hook and use it to fish out the blockage from the hose.

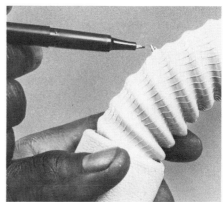

If a sharp object, such as a bobby pin, pierces the hose and acts as a dust catcher, use your fingers or pliers to pull it out through the wall of the hose. This will create a small hole, which you can cover with vinyl tape.

Wheel problems

All uprights and most canisters are equipped with wheels. Like any moving parts, they are subject to breakage. On most models, a broken wheel can be replaced individually. Wheels are not difficult to remove. On several models of uprights and canisters, you must remove some or all of the wheels to get inside the housing.

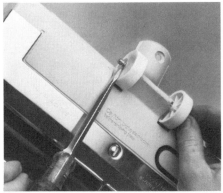

To remove a wheel secured by a cap over the end of the axle, use a screwdriver to pry off the cap. On the model shown you take off the wheel and pull out the axle and the other wheel.

To remove a wheel fastened to the axle with a clip, pull off the clip with a pair of needle-nose pliers. On some models, there is a rubber guard to protect furniture; you will have to push the guard out of the way before you can pull out the axle.

Getting inside

To deal with a problem cord, motor, or fan, you will have to get inside the motor housing. The directions given here show how to open up the motor housing on canister vacuum cleaners made by Hoover, Panasonic, and Eureka. If you own a different model, read all of these steps and then adapt the procedure to the model most like your own. You also must open up the motor housing to get at the switch assembly, unless you own a Hoover, which has a separate switch housing (see opposite page).

CAUTION Always unplug your vacuum cleaner before you take off the motor housing.

To get inside the Hoover Celebrity, open the lid and take out the bag. Remove the screws that attach the motor housing to the shell. Lift off the housing.

To get inside the Panasonic, take off the cover to the bag compartment. Open the tool compartment cover and gently spread its sides apart, until you can lift it off the chassis. Then unscrew the four Phillips screws that secure the upper motor housing to the base of the machine. Take off the housing.

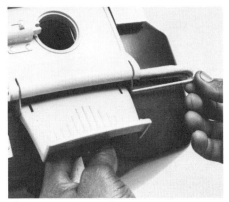

1 **To get inside the Eureka,** first remove the hinge pin from the bracket of the foot pedal. (If the pin is fitted too tightly to pull out by hand, tap it out gently with a hammer and nail.)

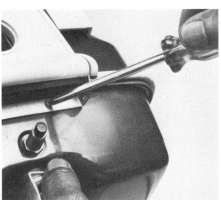

2 Remove the foot pedal and undo the two screws that secure the bracket to the housing. This also releases the bag-retainer bracket, which is located inside the housing.

3 Remove the two screws from the lower housing to release the motor, motor-mounting plate, and the cord-winder assembly. (These screws are located over each of the rear wheels.)

Electrical problems

Testing the cord

The cord on canister models is subject to considerable stress when the unit is pulled around the room. If your vacuum cleaner doesn't run at all, or runs in fits and starts, check the cord first—it is the most likely cause of the problem. Damage occurs most often either near the plug or at the point where the cord enters the machine. Another place to check for a problem is between the switch and the motor.

To test the cord, unplug the unit and lift up the lid. Remove the motor housing (see *Getting inside,* opposite), disconnect one cord lead, and test the cord for continuity (see Blue Pages: *Electrical testers*). Testing the cord on models equipped with a cord-winder is demonstrated at right. (These pictures are of the Eureka, but the same directions apply to other models.)

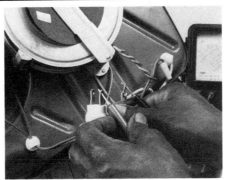

1 To test the cord on a cord-winder, first unplug the vacuum and turn the motor-mount plate upside down. Detach the leads that run between the cord-winder and the switch, and the cord-winder and the motor. Test for continuity as shown here.

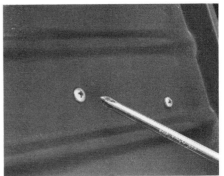

2 If the cord is bad, you will have to put in an entirely new cord-winder unit. Turn the motor-mount plate to its upright position and remove the three screws that secure the cord-winder to the plate. Take out the unit and replace it. If the cord is good, but the winder isn't, you can use the cord without the winder.

Replacing the switch

If the cord is OK and your vacuum cleaner still doesn't run, you may have a problem with the switch. Test it first for continuity (see Blue Pages: *Electrical testers*), opening up the machine as described on the opposite page. If you have a Hoover Celebrity, which has a separate switch housing, follow the directions below. If you have a Eureka, follow the directions for getting inside, and remove the switch by unscrewing the hex nut that holds it to the housing.

Another problem common to vacuum cleaners is a motor that starts but doesn't stop. This may be caused by a defective switch, which must be replaced. Or, the springs that are part of the switch mechanism may be at fault. Such springs are designed to return a foot or manual switch button to an UP position; they occasionally break and must be replaced.

1 To replace a faulty switch on a Panasonic, first undo the two screws that hold the switch assembly to the motor housing. (This also frees the switch cover and springs on the other side of the housing.) Pull out the assembly. Label the switch leads and cut them at the plastic crimp-on connectors. Put in a new switch, using wire nuts.

2 If either spring in this model's switch mechanism is defective, unscrew the switch assembly as described at left. Pull the switch cover away from the motor mount, as shown here. Replace the springs or, if it is damaged, the whole switch cover.

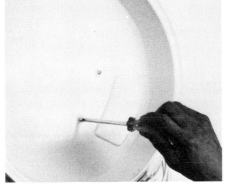

1 To test and replace the switch on a Hoover Celebrity, first open the canister and take out the three screws on the underside of the lid. This releases the tool rack atop the lid.

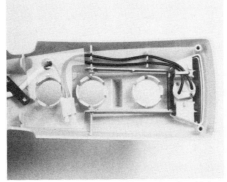

2 Close the lid and lift off the tool rack, which also serves as the switch housing. Disconnect the switch leads and test the switch for continuity (see Blue Pages: *Electrical testers*). If the switch is defective, replace it with a duplicate.

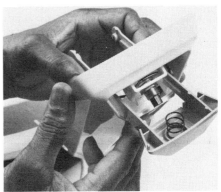

3 Unhook the switch button assembly from the tool rack. (This also frees the spring.) Remove the nut on the switch button and push out the switch assembly. Cut the leads at the crimp-on connectors; attach the new switch with wire nuts.

Working on the motor

If the motor on your vacuum cleaner doesn't run and the cord and switch are OK, examine the brushes on the motor for excessive or uneven wear (see Appliance Repair Basics: *Universal motors*). If the brushes are worn out, you can replace them unless you have a Panasonic. If the brushes on a Panasonic are faulty, you will have to replace the entire motor and fan assembly. If the motor on any vacuum cleaner is obviously burned out, it must be replaced.

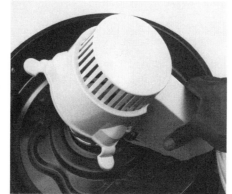

1 To replace the brushes or the entire motor of a Hoover Celebrity, first remove the two screws that hold the motor housing over the motor. They are located on either side of the protruding plastic arm where the power cord enters the motor housing. Take off the housing.

2 With a nut driver, remove the three nuts that secure the large motor and base assembly to the large, circular shell.

3 Lift off the shell and set it aside. The motor now stands free, attached only by its leads.

4 Remove each brush assembly—a single screw holds each in place—and examine the brushes and attached springs for damage. Replace them if they're defective. To remove the motor, label the leads for later identification and cut them. Use wire nuts to reconnect the leads.

To get at the brushes on the Eureka, remove the motor housing (see *Getting inside*, page 288). Loosen the two brush retaining screws, located on either side of the motor, and lift out the brush assemblies. To replace the motor, remove the four screws; label and disconnect the leads. Newer Eurekas use Torx screws (Torx drivers are available at auto supply stores).

Motorized Nozzles

An option on some canister vacuum cleaners is a nozzle equipped with a motor of its own. This motor is connected by a short fan belt to a rotary brush in the mouth of the nozzle. It's a device designed especially for cleaning carpets. The small motor spins the brush, while the main motor in the cleaner sucks up the dust and dirt.

Such nozzle brushes are subjected to hard work, and as a result the bristles tend to wear down. On some motorized nozzles there is a special NEW and OLD button, which allows the user to adjust the length of the bristles. Even with such an adjustment, however, the brush should be checked occasionally to make sure that the bristles extend beyond the mouth of the nozzle. (An ordinary straight-edge ruler works well for this test.) If they do not, replace the bristles (a feature on some models) or the whole brush.

Another problem you may face is a rotary brush that runs in fits and starts, or doesn't run at all. In this case, you may have either a worn or broken belt, or jammed side bearings on the brush unit. To check, remove the

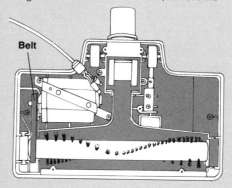

Belt

brush. Inspect the belt for wear and replace it if necessary. If there is nap or debris in the bearings, pull it out.

If the actual motor in the nozzle doesn't run, check its individual power cord for continuity (On some models, this runs out of the main housing and through the connecting hose.) If the cord is defective, you will probably have to replace the whole hose, as the cord usually can't be detached from it. If the cord is OK, the problem could be a burned-out motor. Unplug the hose cord from the nozzle receptacle. Check the motor for continuity by attaching VOM probes to the terminal pins. If the motor is defective, remove the nozzle base plate and take out the brush. Remove the screws that secure the motor housing cover, if your model has one, and take it off. Lift out the motor. Put in a new motor and reassemble the nozzle.

Fans

Common problems

The pictures at right demonstrate how important it is to avoid sucking small, hard objects into your vacuum cleaner. However harmless it may seem, a tiny pebble or nail can cause serious damage if it gets inside your machine. If you see one on the carpet you are cleaning, pick it up by hand. Otherwise it may be picked up and blown, with a great deal of force, through the wall of the dust bag and into the blade of the fan. If you inadvertently pick up such an object and it does hit the fan, you will hear a loud clanging noise. Turn off the vacuum cleaner immediately. Loss of suction and a motor that runs more noisily than usual also are warning signs that you have developing fan problems. Open up the vacuum cleaner and correct the problem before it is too late (far right).

The blades on this fan were sheared by a tiny ball bearing that was sucked through the wall of the dust bag. The damage occurred in just the few seconds between the first clang as the object hit the fan and turning off the machine.

The nub of metal on the left is all that remained of a fan that originally looked like the one on the right. The user vacuumed up a small nail. In this case, the machine was allowed to run for several minutes after the nail hit the fan with a clang. Not only was the fan ruined, but the motor burned out.

Cleaning and replacing the fan

When the fan is slightly damaged or something is stuck inside, suction is reduced and there is a louder-than-usual motor whirr. Turn off the vacuum cleaner immediately, then make sure the nozzle, tubes, and hose are clear of obstructions. Then check the fan. Some canisters have two fans with separate housings, in which case you must check them both. You can gain access to the fan(s) of most models for cleaning, but if the part is damaged, you may have to replace the entire motor assembly. Check with the manufacturer to find out if replacement fans are available.

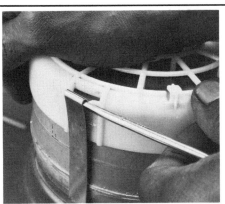

The Eureka has two fans. To clean them, use a screwdriver to pry off the side filter clips, as shown. Lift off the housing and the attached sponge filter. Wash or replace the filter as necessary and wipe the fans clean.

1 **To replace either Eureka fan,** first undo the hex nut in the middle of the fan housing (the nut holds the end of the motor armature shaft). Grip the nut with an offset wrench, insert an Allen wrench into the armature shaft slot, and unscrew the hex nut.

2 Insert a hefty flat-blade screwdriver between the parts of the housing, about an inch from the bottom of the fan housing. Pry all around the housing as shown, until you can lift off the upper portion, freeing the upper housing. The lower fan can now be removed from the lower housing.

3 Pull off the spacer washer that sits between the two fans and set it aside. Lift out the lower fan, and remove any debris or objects from between the blades. Inspect for damage.

4 To remove the fan from the upper housing, use a mallet and screwdriver, as shown. Clean out the upper fan. If either fan is damaged, you must order a new fan/motor assembly or take the unit to a repair shop. Otherwise, reassemble the fans and housing. Remember to put back a fresh sponge filter before attaching the filter clips.

Tank-type vacuum cleaner

Although tank-type vacuum cleaners are just a variation of the common canister design and their mechanical principles are the same, the component parts are arranged quite differently, as shown in the drawing at right. This means that the steps to follow when making repairs or putting in replacements are unique to these models. How to solve particular problems you might have are demonstrated here on an Electrolux. (If you have problems with suction, first check the nozzle and hose and clear them of any obstruction, as described on page 287.)

In addition to having an unusually powerful motor, Electrolux also has a very strong cord-winder. This can result in damage to the plug itself when it is snapped against the housing of the cleaner, or a bad connection between the plug and the cord. Either can be corrected simply, without opening up the machine. If you have problems with the on/off switch, the cord-winder, or the motor-fan assembly, however, you will have to get inside your cleaner.

CAUTION Always check for ground after working on a vacuum cleaner (see Blue Pages: *Testing for ground*).

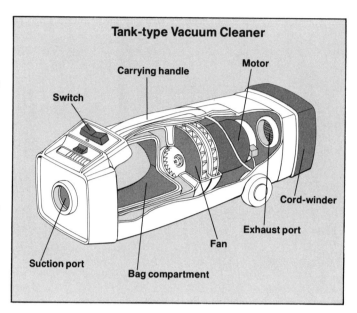

Tank-type Vacuum Cleaner

Carrying handle — Motor — Switch — Cord-winder — Exhaust port — Fan — Bag compartment — Suction port

Getting inside

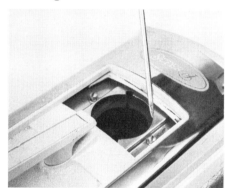

1 **To get inside the Electrolux,** slide back the cover over the exhaust port. (It is located in front of the decal.) Remove the screws on either side of the port.

2 Open the door to the bag compartment at the front of the tank. Remove the screw in front of the on/off switch.

3 Grip the model's carrying handle and lift off the upper housing.

Replacing the switch

1 **To get at the switch** if the unit is running erratically or not at all, first take off the upper housing. You can now lift away the on/off button.

2 Remove the two Phillips screws underneath the on/off button. This will free the switch assembly.

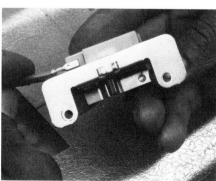

3 Pull the switch assembly out of the chassis. Test the switch for continuity (see Blue Pages: *Electrical testers*). If it is defective, detach the leads. Mark them for repositioning, and then put in a replacement.

Replacing the cord-winder

If your Electrolux doesn't run or if it operates in fits and starts and the switch is not defective, check the cord for continuity (see Blue Pages: *Electrical* *testers*). To do this on some Electrolux models, you first have to take off the cord-winder.

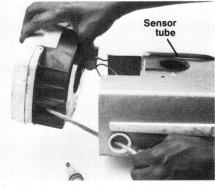

1 **To remove the cord-winder,** first remove the screws that hold it in place—there are two on top of the housing at the exhaust port, and another in the corresponding position underneath the vacuum cleaner. Then disconnect the sensor tube (see the box at the bottom of the page).

2 Grip the cord-winder and work it off the main housing until you can fit your thumb between the housing and the cord-winder, as shown here. Push the cord-winder unit out, while you pull on the cord to create a little slack. To free the cord-winder completely, slip the plug through the cord port.

3 Now you can test the cord for continuity. If either the cord or the cord-winder is defective, replace the entire cord-winder assembly.

Motor and fan problems

If you have checked the switch and cord and the vacuum cleaner still doesn't work at all, you may have a defective motor. If this is the case, you will have to take the whole appliance to a repair shop.

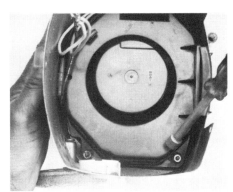

1 **To get at the motor and fan assembly,** first take off the cord-winder as described at the top of this page. Then remove the four hex nuts from the motor mount, as shown here.

2 Reach into the top exhaust port and push the motor assembly out of the back of the housing until you can grip it securely. Then pull it out completely.

3 Take the rubber gasket off the exhaust port. Label and detach the leads that run from the motor to the on/off switch. Remove the motor assembly and examine the brushes for damage or excessive wear. If either brush is damaged or is shorter than it is wide, both brushes must be replaced. ⟳ At this time, clean off any dust that you see on the motor. A paintbrush works well.

Suction Sensor Mechanism

As the Electrolux sucks up air and dust into the dust bag, it also creates a vacuum in a plastic tube, called a sensor tube, leading to the bag compartment door. A diaphragm senses the reduction of suction when the vacuum bag is full. This releases the catch that secures the bag compartment door; the door pops open and trips a switch that turns off the vacuum. If the door opens prematurely, you should clean out the sensor tube with a stiff wire.

Upright Vacuum Cleaner

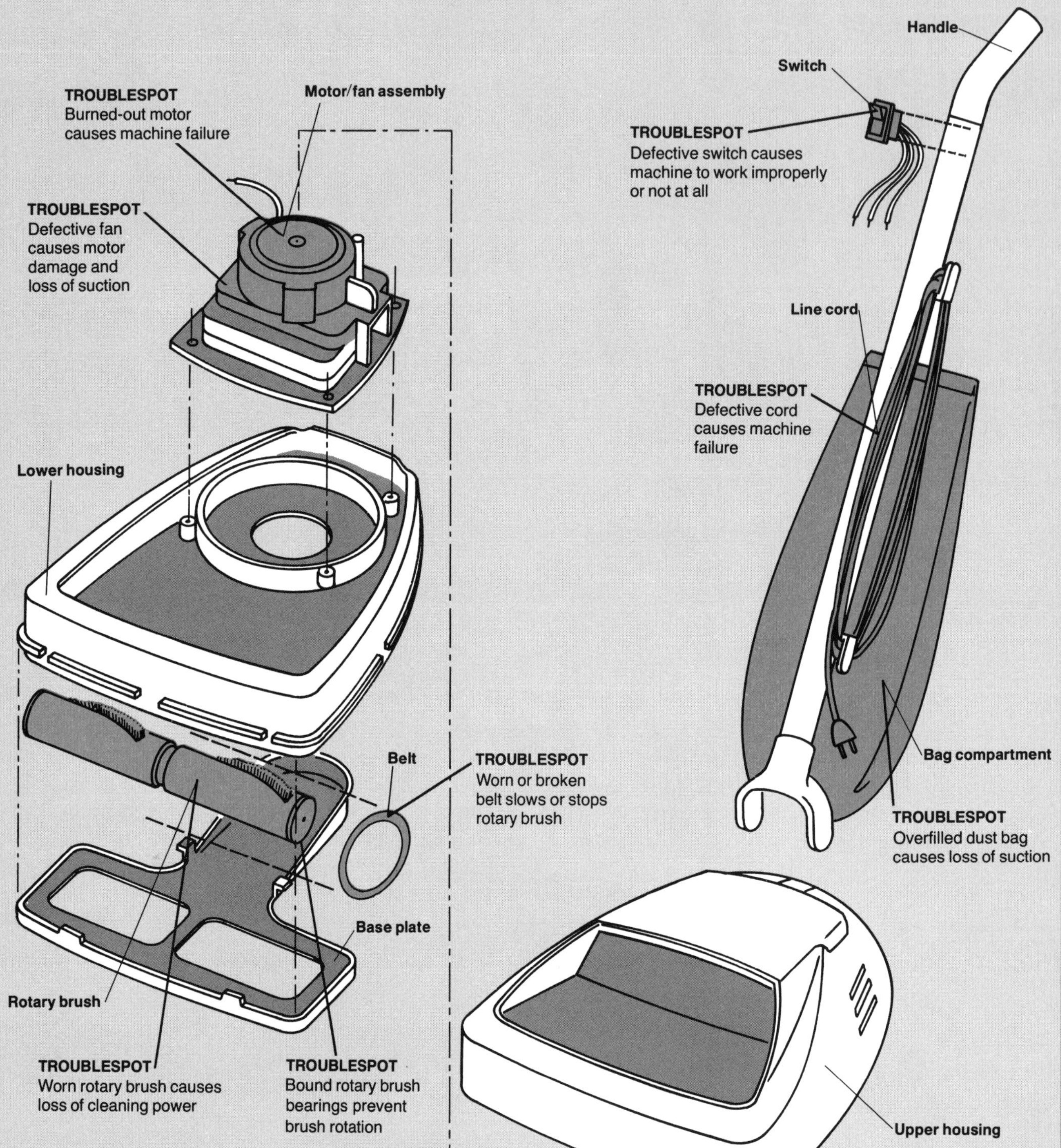

TROUBLESPOT
Burned-out motor
causes machine failure

Motor/fan assembly

Handle

Switch

TROUBLESPOT
Defective switch causes
machine to work improperly
or not at all

TROUBLESPOT
Defective fan
causes motor
damage and
loss of suction

Lower housing

Line cord

TROUBLESPOT
Defective cord
causes machine
failure

Belt

TROUBLESPOT
Worn or broken
belt slows or stops
rotary brush

Bag compartment

Base plate

TROUBLESPOT
Overfilled dust bag
causes loss of suction

Rotary brush

TROUBLESPOT
Worn rotary brush causes
loss of cleaning power

TROUBLESPOT
Bound rotary brush
bearings prevent
brush rotation

Upper housing

VACUUM CLEANERS
Upright

Upright and canister vacuum cleaners differ not only in appearance, but also in several mechanical details. Chief among these is that a revolving belt-driven brush in the nozzle is a standard feature on uprights; it is only an optional extra on canisters, and then only on some models. The fan on uprights is located approximately in the middle of the machine, between the nozzle and the dust bag; thus it *pulls* up dirt and air to a midpoint and then *pushes* it into the porous dust bag, where the dust is trapped and the air driven out. These two features account for the extra cleaning power of uprights over most canisters . Uprights, however, are one unit and are therefore heavier and less easy to maneuver than

canister vacuum cleaners, where the cleaning nozzle and hose are separate from the body and motor. The hose and nozzle can also be found as an optional extra on some uprights.

Both types of machine call for the same maintenance practices, which are described on page 287; the procedure for replacing a wheel is the same for both types (page 288). If you have a hose blockage, which is a common problem, follow the instructions on page 287.

CAUTION If you make repairs or put in new parts, always be sure to check that your vacuum cleaner is properly grounded (see Blue Pages: *Testing for Ground*.)

Replacing the belt

If your cleaner is not picking up dirt and dust efficiently, first check the nozzle and remove any buildup of dust and other debris. If you are using a hose attachment, determine whether it is clogged (see page 287). You should also check the condition of the brush, and replace it if necessary (see *Motorized nozzles*, page 290). If none of these is the problem, the rubber belt that drives the revolving brush in the nozzle may be at fault and you should check it for wear or damage. (Another good clue to the fact that you may have a faulty belt is a motor that runs more noisily than usual.)

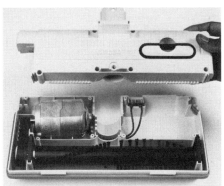

To gain access to the brush and belt, unscrew the base plate on the nozzle. If you own a Panasonic or a J.C. Penney, lift up the brush; the belt will fall off the pulley at the end of the brush. Then take the belt off the motor shaft. If the belt is stretched or damaged, replace it.

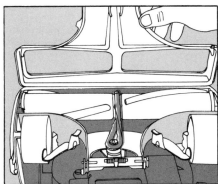

On some makes, the belt pulley is in the middle of the brush. First slip the belt off the armature. Then lift up the brush and slip the belt off. Be sure to put the new belt on so that is is twisted in the same way as the old one. Some uprights have a spare belt in a storage groove inside the machine, as shown at left.

Replacing the cord

If your cleaner doesn't run at all or works in fits and starts, you should first test the line cord for continuity (see Blue Pages: *Electrical testers*). If it is faulty, you will have to replace it. If your model has its on/off switch on the handle, check the line cord separately on either side of the switch for a

break in the circuit. Sometimes you can do this without taking the machine apart. If the switch on your model is on the base you will have to get inside to test it (see next page).

To replace a defective cord between the handle switch and the electric outlet, unscrew the switch plate and turn it over. Use a screwdriver to pry out the metal clip. This releases the clamp that holds the cord in place. Cut one cord lead at the crimp-on connector and detach the second from the switch terminal. Take out the defective cord and replace it.

To replace a defective cord between the handle switch and the motor, remove the screw that attaches the handle to the base. You can now see the receptacle where the cord from the motor plugs in. Remove the lead from the switch and from the line cord. Use a screwdriver to pry the receptacle out of the handle, as shown here. Replace the defective cord.

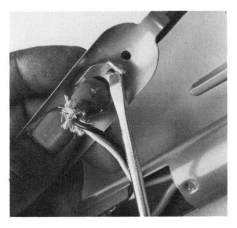

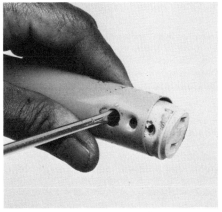

Getting inside

If your problem is not external and is not with the belt or rotary brush (located inside the base plate), you will have to open up the housing of your vacuum cleaner to check for a faulty switch (if the switch is in the base) or faulty internal wiring and also for a defective or damaged fan or motor assembly. Although the procedure is different for various makes, getting inside an upright is a relatively easy task. If you own a new Eureka, however, one step in particular can be a problem: the job requires a Torx driver, which you will have to get at an auto supply store. (See the Eureka instructions in *Working on the motor*, page 290). The instructions given here for the Oreck show how to get at the brush and belt; to get at the Oreck motor and fan, see *Fan and motor problems*, page 298.

1 To remove the Eureka belt and rotary brush, release the handle and bag compartment from their locked upright position, and lay the vacuum cleaner down with the handle and the inverted base flat on the floor. Free the base plate by pushing outward on the retaining clamps. Then you can remove the rotary brushes and/or the belt. If you are replacing the belt, be sure to set it in the groove in the base assembly, as shown.

2 Examine the brush for signs of wear. Some models can be adjusted to work with old or worn brushes. The model shown has a guide on the end of the roller to indicate when the brush is worn out. (Follow the manufacturer's directions.) If the brush still works inefficiently, or if your machine does not have this option, replace the brush.

To gain access to the Eureka motor and fan assembly, use needle-nose pliers to remove the spring behind each of the front wheels and beneath the foot pedal. Return the cleaner to an upright position. The housing may be attached to the base by a Torx screw in the middle of the "dial-a-nap" knob. Unscrew it and take off the housing, using a Torx driver (obtainable at any auto supply store).

To release the base plate on the Hoover convertible, first remove the screw that holds the handle and remove the attached bag compartment. Turn the base of the unit upside down. As shown here, push outward with your thumbs on the clamps that secure the plate. Lift the plate off.

To remove the Hoover rotary brush, slip the brush out. If the bristles are worn you can replace them or replace the whole brush. If you put in a new belt, make sure you position it correctly—across the middle of the brush and over the pulley on the armature, as shown here.

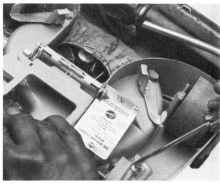

To gain access to the Hoover fan and motor assembly, first take off the belt. (The rotary brush can stay in postion.) Remove the two screws that hold the upper housing in place. Turn the unit right side up and lift off the upper housing to expose the fan and motor assembly.

To get at the Oreck brush or belt, first press the foot pedal to release the handle from its upright position and lay the vacuum down with the base plate facing up. Remove the screws that hold the base plate to the housing and lift it off.

To get at the motor and fan assembly on the Bissel, Panasonic, and J.C. Penney, remove the screws in the motor housing just below the bag compartment and lift off the housing. (If you first remove the handle and nozzle you will have easier access to the screws.) On the Panasonic you must open the bag compartment to reach the screws.

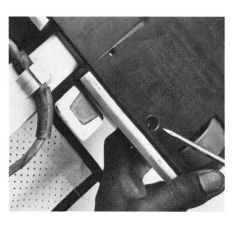

Replacing the switch

If your vacuum cleaner doesn't run and the line cord is OK, you may have a problem with the switch. Test it for continuity (see Blue Pages: *Electrical testers*). If it is defective, you will have to replace it. On some models, the switch is located on the handle of the vacuum; on others, it is operated by a foot pedal. Both types have the same basic mechanism.

1 To replace the foot switch on the Oreck, first remove the base plate. Remove the two screws that hold the switch and switch button in place.

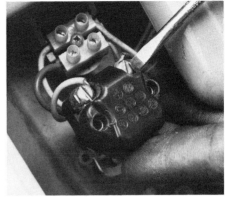

2 Pull out the switch assembly and remove the two screws that secure the leads. Label and detach the two leads that run to the terminal block above the switch, as shown here. Remove the switch and replace it.

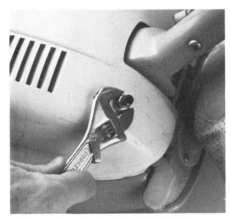

1 To replace the foot switch on the Eureka, first remove the hex nut that secures the switch button to the upper housing.

2 Pull the switch free and label the leads for later identification. Remove the wire nuts from the leads and replace the switch.

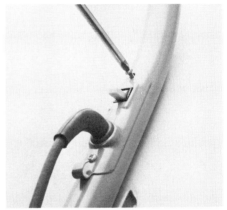

To replace the on/off switch in the handle of the Hoover convertible, remove the two screws that attach the switch plate to the handle. Lift off the switch plate. Lift out the switch and pull off the leads. Install a new switch.

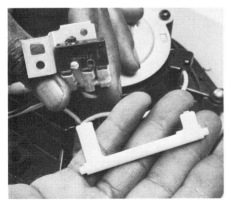

To replace the overdrive switch on the Hoover convertible (used for the hose attachment), take off the upper housing (see opposite page). The overdrive switch and the white switch lever (shown here) will now both be free. Label and detach the switch leads, and replace the switch. Put back the white switch lever.

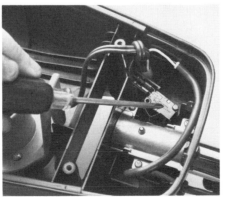

1 To replace the switch on the Bissel, Panasonic, and J.C. Penney, first take off the bag compartment door, then remove the bag. Remove the screws that secure the upper cover. (On the Panasonic, shown here, another screw holds the switch itself in place; remove this screw.)

2 Label the switch leads first and then remove them. Install a new switch.

Fan and motor problems

Fan damage is fairly common on upright vacuum cleaners because of their design. Any hard object that is sucked up is likely to hit the fan immediately. Therefore, extra caution must be taken to avoid picking up a pebble, bobby pin, or any similar object. The first warning that you have picked up an item that can cause damage is often a loud clang as it hits the spinning fan. If this occurs, switch off the machine immediately. If you don't, you may possibly end up with not only a damaged fan but a burned-out motor. Two other indications of fan problems are reduced suction and a motor that runs more noisily than usual. If the fan on your machine is damaged, don't try to repair it. It should be replaced according to the instructions given below.

If your machine doesn't work at all, the motor itself possibly is defective. On models made by Bissel, Panasonic, and J.C. Penney, you can open up the machine and inspect the brushes (see Appliance Repair Basics: *Universal motors*), and replace them if necessary. You cannot get at the brushes on an Oreck.

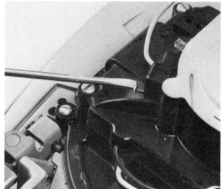

1 **To get at the fan and motor assembly on a Hoover convertible,** turn the cleaner upside down and remove the two upper housing screws as shown on page 296. Turn the unit right side up and remove the four screws that secure the plastic motor mount. In this photo, a white pen points to one of these screws.

2 Remove the brushes by taking out the screw on each of the two mounts. Take out the brushes and the attached springs. Inspect the brushes for damage or excessive wear, and replace both if either is defective.

3 To remove the fan, lift out the motor assembly and turn it over. This exposes the fan. Hold the fan with one hand and turn the hub-retaining nut clockwise, using an adjustable wrench. Remove the nut and lift off the fan.

4 Remove the two washers from the armature shaft and save them. Turn the motor upright and remove the four screws as shown. This separates the two sections of the motor housing. Next, remove the three screws that hold the metal plate on top of the housing.

5 Hold onto the armature shaft with pliers and unscrew the small cooling fan at the opposite end of the motor assembly by hand. Lift off the upper section of the motor housing, then pull out the motor.

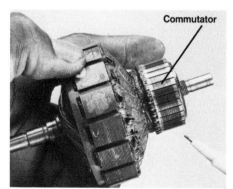

Commutator

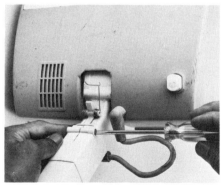

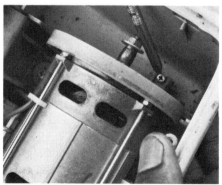

6 Clean off any carbon buildup on the commutator with fine emery cloth. Test for continuity (see Blue Pages: *Electrical testers*); you will need a VOM. If the commutator is defective, you will have to replace the whole armature and bearings. If it is OK but the motor still doesn't run, take it to a repair shop (see Appliance Repair Basics: *How to Test a Universal Motor*).

1 **To get at the fan and motor on an Oreck,** first remove the screw that attaches the handle to the base. Remove the handle. (This frees the cord from the handle.)

2 Open the lid of the base and remove the screw that secures the motor mount. Remove the motor. (You can lift it out easily by the white plastic fan housing.)

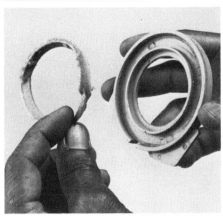

3 Once the motor is removed, you can see a felt washer on either side of the motor. If either is worn or damaged, replace both.

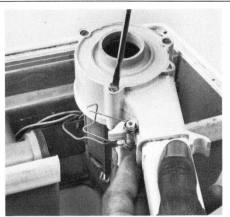

4 To remove the fan housing, take out the three screws that attach it to the motor. Lift off the housing and replace it if it is damaged.

5 To remove the fan, use a wrench or pliers to remove the nut on the fan hub by turning it as you hold the fan stationary with your other hand.

6 With the handle of a screwdriver, tap on the shaft that was covered by the nut, forcing it into the motor housing until the fan comes free. If the fan is damaged, replace it. If the motor is defective, remove the leads and install a new motor.

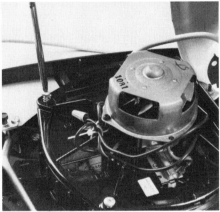

1 **To get at the motor and fan assembly on the Eureka,** first lift the lid over the base and tape it to the unit's handle to keep it out of your way. Remove the four screws that hold the motor mount to the base.

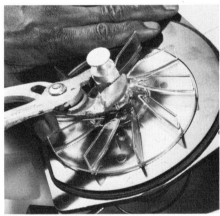

2 Lift the motor and fan assembly out of the base and turn the assembly over. Use a wrench or pliers to turn the nut counterclockwise on the fan hub as you hold onto the fan with your other hand. Remove the nut and washer and lift out the fan. If it is damaged, replace it.

3 To release the brushes, use a screwdriver to gently pry away the tabs that hold them in place. Do not bend them again until you are ready for the final motor reassembly. These tabs are delicate and break easily. Pull out the brushes and springs and examine the brushes for damage or excessive wear.

4 To gain access to the commutator, turn the motor right side up. Remove the two screws that attach the motor housing to the motor mount and lift off the housing.

5 With the housing removed, you will be able to remove the commutator. Test it for continuity (see Appliance Repair Basics: *How to Test a Universal Motor*). If it is defective you will have to take out the armature and replace it and its bearings.

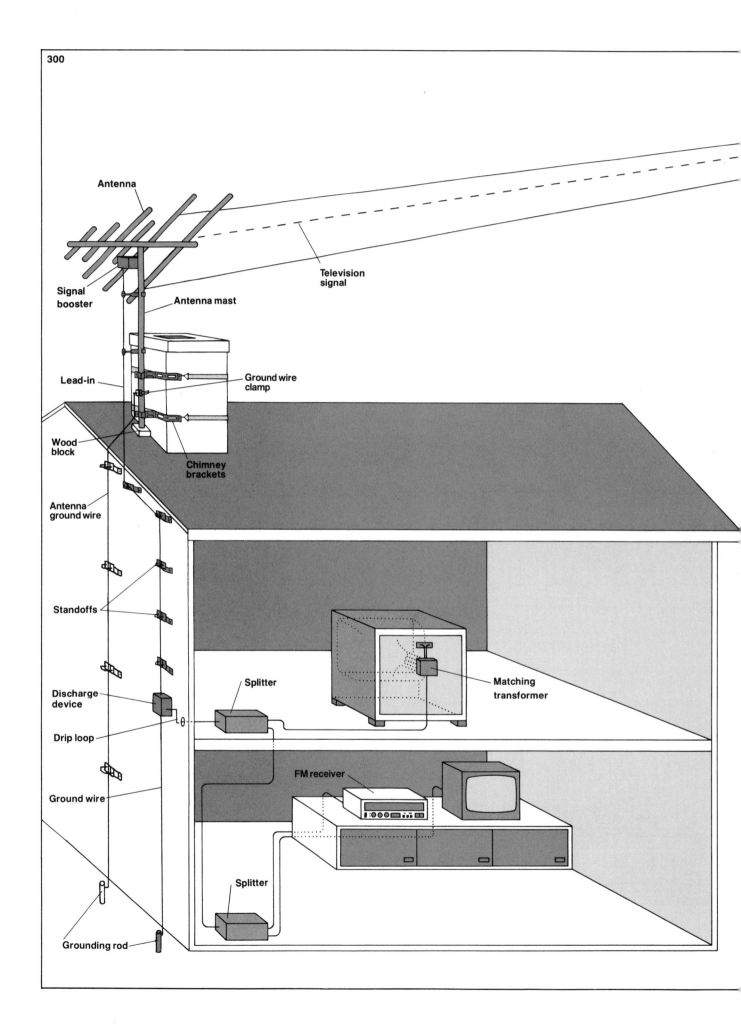

Antenna

Signal booster

Antenna mast

Lead-in

Ground wire clamp

Wood block

Chimney brackets

Antenna ground wire

Standoffs

Discharge device

Drip loop

Ground wire

Grounding rod

Television signal

Splitter

Matching transformer

FM receiver

Splitter

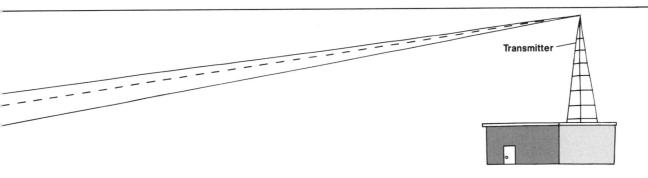

Television Sets

Because television sets—especially color sets—are very complex and often require expensive equipment for testing and repair, servicing them at home is not recommended. However, there is a lot you can do to improve the performance of your TV without ever going inside the set itself. The single most effective thing you can do is to improve the reception. The quality of the signal from the antenna to your set is absolutely crucial to the quality of the picture and sound. Maintenance of your antenna system and improvements to it will pay large dividends in better reception. Of course, hooking up to a cable system, if one is available, eliminates the need for an antenna.

In addition, all manufacturers equip their sets with several different kinds of controls. Some are designed to compensate for aging components, while others are used to combat certain types of outside interference that weaken the set's audio or video reception. If you know how to use these controls properly, you'll improve your set's performance.

Most of the information here applies to color TV sets. However, except where dealing specifically with problems relating to color, the information is applicable to black and white sets also.

The basic parts of the receiver

The broadcast television signal received on your antenna is processed in your television set by a series of components that separate picture (video) from sound (audio) and reproduce both.

The tuner

When you select a channel, a circuit peculiar to that channel (frequency) is connected to the antenna terminals on the back of the set. The channel circuit is designed to resonate only at the frequency of the selected channel carrier. This circuit then responds to all the variations in that one channel signal. A replica of the transmitted TV signal is reproduced in the tuner. The tuner amplifies the reproduced signal and then converts the channel carrier frequency, which may be anywhere between 55 and 886 megahertz (MHz), to a frequency of 41 MHz. Regardless of the channel selected, from this point on, the signal carrier frequency is 41 MHz. This frequency is known as the intermediate frequency, or IF.

The IF amplifier

Because of the carrier frequency conversion that takes place in the tuner, the IF amplifier can be designed to amplify only one frequency—41 MHz—which makes for efficient operation. The IF amplifier boosts the 41-MHz signal, which still carries picture and sound information.

Video detector

After much increase in signal strength in the IF amplifier, the signal is stripped of the program information it carried from the station. The video detector removes the picture and the sound of the original scene: the audio portion is directed to the television receiver's amplifier and loud-speaker, and the video to synchronization circuits, the picture tube, and the color block.

The color block

A portion of the complete picture (video) signal is fed to the color block. There, the light-intensity signals and the synchronization signals are filtered out leaving only the color signals. The color signals are amplified and sent to the appropriate electron gun in the picture tube.

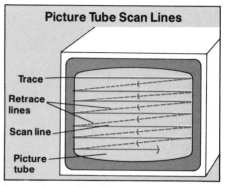

Picture Tube Scan Lines

Trace
Retrace lines
Scan line
Picture tube

Synchronization

Before a picture can appear, the screen must be scanned, or filled with light. The process begins in the electron gun at the narrow end (neck) of the picture tube. There, a hot filament, an electron-emitting electrode, "boils off" electrons directed toward the screen. Other electrodes accelerate the electrons toward the screen and focus them into a small, compact stream.

At the screen end of the tube, a highly positive electrical charge pulls the negative electrons (opposite charges attract) until they strike the inside of the screen. The inner surface of the screen is coated with a powdery white phosphor that glows when struck by the electrons. A point of light now glows on the face of the picture tube.

To paint the screen with light, the electron beam sweeps horizontally and vertically, in the same motion that the eye uses to read a page: from left to right in a straight line and then from top to bottom. This scan is repeated sixty times each second.

The scanning motion is accomplished by two sets of electromagnetic coils that surround the neck of the picture tube. One affects the vertical movement of the beam, while the other operates the horizontal plane. As electrons move through the tube, the magnetic field produced by these coils of wire—known as deflection coils—attracts and repels the beam so that it scans the entire screen.

In the United States TV system, the standard scanning pattern for the beam of electrons creates 525 horizontal lines per picture (regardless of picture size), which can be seen when the screen is viewed at close range. Not all horizontal lines are painted on each vertical scan, however. Actually only half the picture—262.5 alternate lines—are painted on each vertical scan.

Black and white picture tube

To create the lights and darks of the original televised image, the electron beam moving through the picture tube is not only deflected but also modulated. The beam is modulated in accordance with the amplitude modulation of the signal transmitted by the TV station. This means the intensity of the beam varies as it passes through electrically charged cylinders in the neck of the tube that make up the electron gun. When the gun produces a weak beam, little or no light appears on the screen and you see a black area. When the gun strengthens the beam, you see brightness. This combination, scanning and modulation, re-creates the original picture transmitted by the TV station.

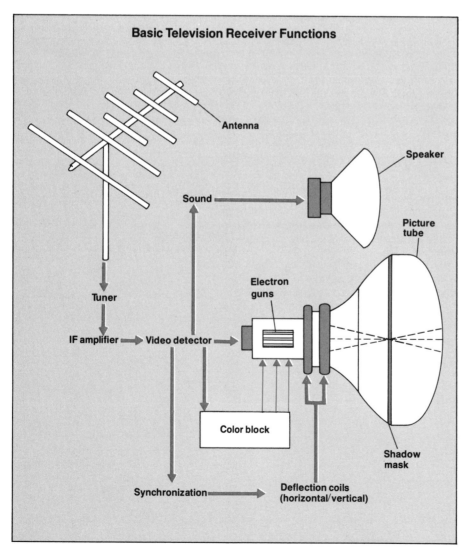

Basic Television Receiver Functions

Antenna
Speaker
Sound
Picture tube
Tuner
Electron guns
IF amplifier → Video detector
Color block
Shadow mask
Synchronization
Deflection coils (horizontal/vertical)

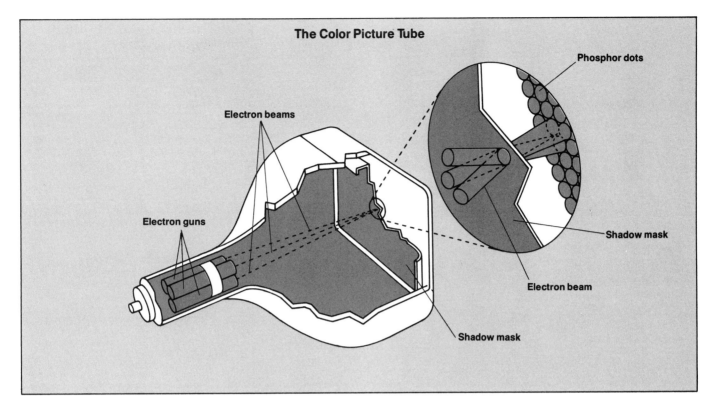

The Color Picture Tube

Phosphor dots

Electron beams

Electron guns

Shadow mask

Electron beam

Shadow mask

Color picture tube

Color picture tubes differ from black and white picture tubes in several ways. One important difference is that a color tube develops not one, but three electron beams and divides the screen into thousands of groups of three dots. (The black and white screen has a uniform coating.) Each dot is a phospor (similar to the material in a black and white screen), but it can glow in one of

three colors—red, blue, or green—when struck by an electron beam.

In the color tube, three electron guns create the three separate beams of electrons, thus keeping apart the color signals sent by the station. An instant before the beams illuminate their color dots, they pass through a shadow mask containing more than 300,000 holes—one hole for each of the phosphor-dot trios. The mask

prevents the three beams from sweeping across the screen and indiscriminately striking every color dot. It does this by shadowing two of the three phosphor dots of each trio. This way, the beams are aligned with their appropriate colors. By mixing red, blue, and green for a desired hue, a TV set produces colors that glow in different intensities of red, blue, and green to produce thousands of other hues.

Selecting the best TV antenna system

The right TV antenna for you is determined by three things: (1) the type of programming available in your area (are there many channels of VHF and UHF, VHF only, UHF only, or only a few channels?); (2) the location of the transmitting stations (are they all in the same general direction, or are they in different directions?); (3) the distance to the transmitting antenna (is your home in the city, the suburbs, a rural area?).

Areas where many TV channels—both VHF and UHF—are available are best served by one of the so-called broad-band antennas, which are designed to provide good reception across the full range of TV channels. These antennas must be aimed at the transmitter.

If the TV programs you want to watch are coming from several different directions, you should consider installing an antenna rotor. The rotor consists of a mast-mounted motor unit that can be controlled from a remote unit. The remote unit contains an adjustable dial marked with compass directions. The remote unit is located on or near your TV set. When you turn the dial, the motor moves the antenna a corresponding amount, until it points in the transmitter's direction. You simply tune your TV set to the desired channel and then adjust the dial to rotate the antenna for the best picture.

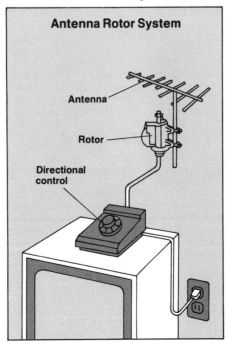

Antenna Rotor System

Antenna

Rotor

Directional control

Antenna location

TV antennas are usually mounted with supports strapped to a chimney or brackets attached to a side wall. When selecting an antenna location, take into account the requirements of the National Electrical Code and local building codes, the guidelines for a good antenna system, and the location and structure of the building.

The National Electrical Code generally specifies that TV antennas and lead-in wires be kept as far away as practical from power lines, particularly where they enter the building.

Antenna conductors and lead-in conductors must not cross over electric light or power lead-ins. In addition, they should be placed so that accidental contact is unlikely. Outdoors, the minimum distance allowed between antenna conductors and conductors for 120/240 volts is 2 feet. If both antenna and power conductors are securely anchored (so that no significant movement is possible), the clearance between them can be as little as 4 inches. Indoors, the clearance between antenna and power conductors must be 2 inches or more.

The guidelines for a good antenna system are: (1) the antenna should be mounted as high as

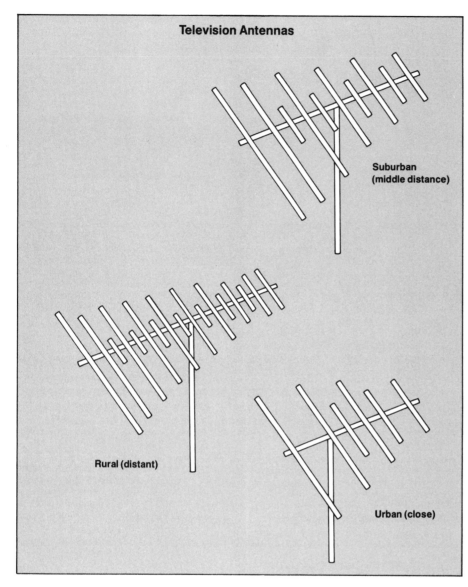

Television Antennas

Suburban
(middle distance)

Rural (distant)

Urban (close)

Grounding the antenna for safety

The National Electrical Code and most local building codes require that the antenna mast be grounded and a discharge path be provided for the antenna lead-in. The antenna mast is grounded by a grounding wire attached to the mast, then connected to a grounding rod or a metal cold-water pipe.

The antenna lead-in must be provided with a discharge path to ground (lightning arrester) for sudden high-voltage surges. Such surges can occur, for example, during lightning storms or when a high-power line breaks loose in a storm and touches the antenna. The antenna lead-in cannot be directly grounded. Such a connection would greatly weaken or completely eliminate the TV signal.

Instead, a direct grounding path is provided as close as possible to the lead-in insulation. If a high-voltage surge occurs, it will cause an arc-over from the lead-in conductor to the adjacent grounding path. The arc-over effectively grounds the surge. The device that provides the discharge path should be located as close as possible to a ground rod or other good ground and should be installed outside, before the antenna lead enters the building.

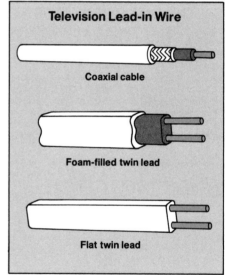

Television Lead-in Wire

Coaxial cable

Foam-filled twin lead

Flat twin lead

Antenna lead-in

The wire that carries the TV signal from the antenna to the TV set is an important element in the TV system. The right lead-in, properly installed, can keep the signal level high and reduce or eliminate interference. The most common form of TV wire is known as twin lead. This wire consists of two conductors in a plastic or foam insulation. The insulation is designed to maintain a fixed distance between the two leads.

Both of these types of twin lead are susceptible to electrical interference, which may seriously downgrade TV reception, particularly in heavily populated areas.

In areas where interference may be a problem, a special shielded type of twin lead can be used. In shielded twin leads, the two conductors are encased in plastic foam, wrapped with foil, and then covered with a plastic outer cover. A shielded twin lead may be used indoors or out.

practical; (2) the antenna should be placed so that the conductor from antenna to receiver is as short as possible; and (3) the antenna and lead-in wire should be kept as far as possible from sources of interference.

Since it's unlikely that all these conditions can be met in one installation, a compromise must be found. For example, the highest mounting point on the house may be the farthest point from the receiver. In this case, the distance from the transmitting station to the house could be a deciding factor. The main source of interference with TV signals is any device that radiates electromagnetic energy. Such devices include X-ray and diathermy equipment, some amateur or citizens band radio equipment (particularly if not properly maintained), unshielded internal combustion engines (tractors, power-generating equipment, or electric motor appliances), or high-voltage transmission lines.

When interference from any of these sources is frequent or constant, an antenna location should be as far as possible from that source. Most TV antennas are highly directional—they pick up signals most efficiently when they are pointed at the transmitter. This characteristic can be used to reduce interference; choose a location for the antenna that puts the source of

interference at right angles to the antenna's strongest pickup direction.

The location and structure of the building can also affect antenna location. Buildings in city or suburban areas close to transmitting stations usually have good reception from almost any antenna location. In these areas the antenna can be located wherever it is convenient. Buildings in rural areas far from transmitting stations need as much antenna height as possible for good reception. Antenna height should be a prime consideration when the building is a long distance from the transmitter.

It has been noted that for close-in locations, the antenna can be located wherever convenient. In some cases this can include attic mounting. VHF (channels 2 through 13) TV antennas provide good reception from attic locations in strong signal areas. Where UHF (channels 14 to 83) TV reception is important, however, attic locations are unsatisfactory.

When you consider installing or relocating an antenna, keep in mind that mounting antennas on the wall is difficult in buildings of brick or masonry construction. Use a chimney mount, if at all possible. In wood-frame buildings, either type of mounting can be used. The general procedure for each type of mount is given below.

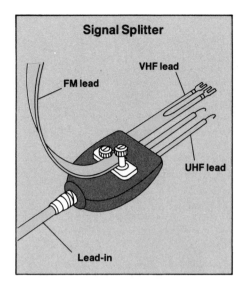

Signal Splitter

VHF lead

FM lead

UHF lead

Lead-in

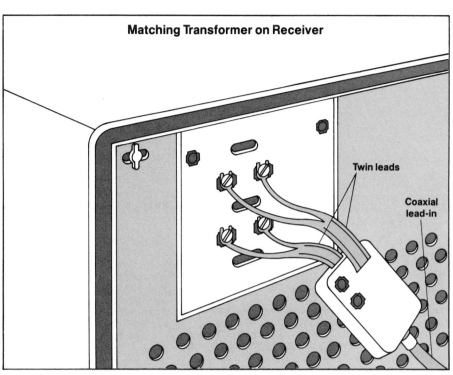

Matching Transformer on Receiver

Twin leads

Coaxial lead-in

All three types of twin lead are often referred to as 300-ohm wire. Some brands have this designation molded in the plastic. In this case, "300-ohm" does not refer to resistance, but to a characteristic of the wire called impedance that matches it to the input of the TV receiver for maximum signal strength.

A third type of lead-in is coaxial cable. This wire consists of a solid-center conductor surrounded by insulating material such as plastic or foam. The second conductor is a braided metal sleeve that covers the plastic or foam. An outer plastic cover protects and seals the wire. The braided metal sleeve acts as a shield to prevent interference from getting to the center conductor.

Installation of this type of lead-in involves a bit more work than those previously described, but you should consider it if local sources of interference are a problem. It is weatherproof and more durable than twin lead. Coaxial cable has a characteristic electrical impedance of 75 ohms and is often referred to as 75-ohm lead. If you are considering coaxial lead-in, take a look at the back of your TV set. In addition to screw terminals for standard twin lead, many sets also have a round jack marked "75 ohms." If your set doesn't have a 75-ohm input, you must use a matching transformer to connect coaxial lead-in to the set. Another matching transformer must be used to connect the coaxial lead-in to the antenna. Pin plugs must be installed on each end of the coaxial lead-in. Installation of matching transformers and pin plugs is described later in this section.

Signal boosters

When long lead-in runs are unavoidable and signal strength is low, you may need a signal booster, or preamplifier.

Preamplifiers are available for mounting directly on the TV antenna mast. These units have the advantage of amplifying the signal before any loss can occur on the lead-in run.

Where the problem is not a long lead-in but a low-level signal, an indoor booster may improve performance. If you want to have two or more TV sets or a combination of TV and FM receivers operating from the same antenna, boosters can be used to connect them.

Installation instructions for preamplifiers, boosters, and multiple-set couplers are

supplied with the units. If at all possible, purchase these units on a trial basis or with a money-back warranty. A booster or a preamplifier increases the signal it receives. That is, the undesirable part of the picture—snow caused by a weak signal, or interference—will also be amplified by the unit. You can only decide how much a booster or preamplifier will improve your television reception by trying it in your home.

Splitters

A splitter basically separates the various signal bands (frequencies) that are received by an antenna. If you own a combination UHF/VHF television and you have a UHF/VHF antenna, you can split the incoming signal from your lead-in antenna cable at the back of your television set to give you both UHF and VHF. The same is possible if you own an FM radio or tuner and your antenna covers FM frequencies. You can split the FM signal from your television lead-in cable and direct it to your tuner.

Splitters come in a variety of frequency combinations, such as UHF/VHF or FM/UHF/VHF, and also are available for different types of television lead-in cables, such as 300-ohm flat cable and 75-ohm coaxial cable.

A problem arises, however, when you split signals. For each splitter and television or radio used, you lose a proportionate amount of the signal strength received by your television antenna. To compensate for this loss, it may be necessary to install a television antenna booster (antenna signal amplifier) to boost the signal to the desired level.

Installing matching transformers

When coaxial lead-in is used, special devices are required to make the electrical connection at the antenna and the receiver. These devices are called matching transformers. An antenna or receiver designed for 300-ohm twin lead won't

work well with 75-ohm coaxial lead unless this matching transformer is installed. The transformer for the receiver connection is a small rectangular box with one or two lengths of twin lead at one end and a coaxial connector at the other. Connect the twin lead to the appropriate screw terminals on the antenna or the receiver. One length of twin lead is marked VHF and the other UHF. Connect them to the appropriate terminals on the receiver. After plugs have been added as described below, attach the coaxial lead to the coaxial connector.

The matching transformer for the antenna connection is usually a circular device with a coaxial terminal on one end and a length of twin lead on the other. Connect the twin lead to the screw terminal on the antenna. Connect the coaxial lead-in connector to the coaxial terminal on the device. Because these matching transformers are exposed to the weather, you must seal the device after making the electrical connection. Directions for making the weathertight seal are provided with the device.

Summary

Here are a few tips for determining what your requirements for a television antenna system are:

1. Check with a local professional antenna installer as to the type and range of antennas for your equipment needs. A good antenna prevents—and cures—a lot of ills.

2. Fifty-two-ohm coaxial cable is more efficient than 300-ohm cable. Most new television and stereo receivers have a direct connection for 75-ohm coaxial cable.

3. Choose a booster that will best complement any splitter you plan to use.

4. Generally, an antenna rotor is an option; it is not always needed. In some locations, however, you can't do without it.

Antenna installation

A word of caution

Roofs are unfamiliar territory for most of us. Climbing ladders and stringing antenna wire is not something we do every day. Working anywhere in the vicinity of electric power lines, particularly when using metal ladders, requires constant vigilance.

These facts add up to one thing: be careful. Many injuries and deaths happen to nonprofessional people doing antenna work. Plan your job with care. Don't rush. Work only in clear, dry weather. Stay as far as possible from electric power lines. Wear shoes with nonslip soles. Have someone around who can provide assistance if you need it.

Antenna mounts

Television antennas come in a wide range of sizes. In close-in locations, simple, fairly light antennas are OK, and obtain good reception. Remote locations require more elaborate, and therefore heavier, antennas. The weight of the antenna must be considered when you plan the installation. Keep in mind that in addition to the weight of the antenna, high winds and ice will put a strain on the antenna mount.

Chimney mounts. This is an easy and effective way to mount an antenna. If the structure is old, inspect the chimney carefully to be sure it can stand the antenna load. If mortar is loose or has fallen out in many areas, the chimney should be repaired by a mason before an antenna is mounted on it.

The chimney mount consists of metal straps that encircle the chimney and hold mounting brackets for the antenna. The mounting brackets are designed to fit on the corners of the chimney. The corner location keeps the bracket from shifting when it is subjected to high winds.

Assemble the eyebolt with the strap attached to the bracket. Secure the eyebolt with a few turns of the eyebolt mounting nut.

Select the chimney corner on which you wish to mount the antenna. Hold the bracket in place and loop the strap around the chimney. Locate the bracket about a foot above the roof. Slip a retaining clip over the free end of the strap, and feed the strap through the second eyebolt; pull it tight. Feed the free end of the strap back through the retaining clip, and hammer down the end of the retaining clip to hold the strap. Cut off the extra strap and tighten the nuts on the eyebolts to secure the bracket firmly to the chimney.

Use the same procedure to install another corner bracket higher up on the chimney. As a general rule, the distance between the straps should be at least one-third the length of the antenna mounting mast.

The mast is held in place by U-bolts mounted on the corner brackets. Slide the mast through both U-bolts. Tighten the nuts on the U-bolts to secure the mast to the bracket. NOTE: Do not let the antenna mast rest directly on the roof or chimney flashing; this may cause leaks in the roof. Set the foot of the mast on a block of wood in which you've drilled an indentation to hold the mast.

Wall mounts. Wall mounting is done by fastening brackets to the exterior wall of the house and then securing the mast by tightening U-bolts in the bracket, as in the chimney mount. The wall-mount brackets come in various sizes.

When the mounting location has been chosen, mark a plumb line on the wall so that the mast will be straight. Center the bracket with a level and mark the mounting holes. Use a small drill bit (⅛ inch in diameter) to check the mounting location. If the drill penetrates the wall easily, the area is clear. At that point, use a bolt, nut, and washer to secure the bracket. Use a larger drill bit (usually ¼ inch) to drill a bolt hole. Feed the bolt through the bracket and into the wall. Have a helper—working in the attic or crawl space behind the wall—put a washer and nut on the bolt and tighten it securely. If the drill does not penetrate readily, it means there is a stud behind the mounting hole. Use a lagscrew to secure the bracket to the wall. The lagscrew can be fastened in place from the outside with a socket or

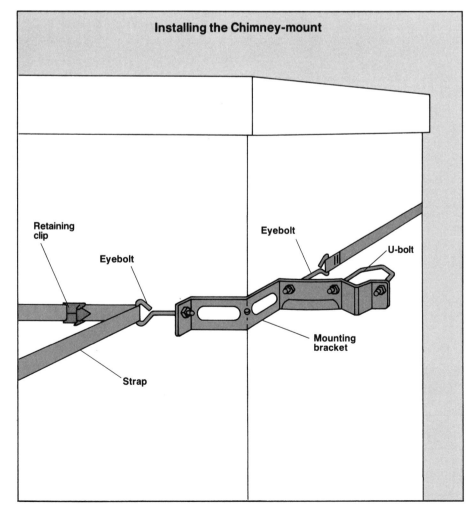

Installing the Chimney-mount

Retaining clip

Eyebolt

Strap

Eyebolt

U-bolt

Mounting bracket

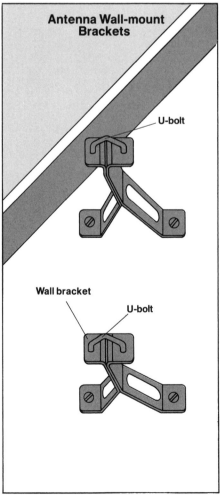

Antenna Wall-mount Brackets

U-bolt

Wall bracket

U-bolt

box wrench. Repeat the procedure for the second bracket. As noted for the chimney mount, the space between the brackets should be at least one-third the length of the antenna mast. When the brackets are in place, secure the mast to the brackets with U-bolts.

The antenna lead can be secured to the building with standoffs that can be screwed into the side wall. Do not screw standoff insulators into your roof—they will cause leaks. Remember to keep the mast-grounding wire separate from the antenna lead. Secure each wire at least once every 4 feet. At the point where wires enter the building, always allow enough slack for a drip loop. Be sure to caulk all openings.

Antenna grounding and discharge devices

Ground the antenna mast by installing a grounding clamp on the mast and then attaching a grounding wire (No. 10 copper or aluminum wire) to the clamp. The grounding wire is then brought down to ground level and connected to a grounding rod or metal cold-water pipe. The grounding rod should be copper or copper-coated. Do not bring the grounding wire inside the building.

There are two types of discharge devices, one for coaxial lead-in and the other for flat twin lead. The coaxial discharge block requires that the coaxial lead-in be cut, and pin-type connectors installed on each end of the cut cable. The grounding block is mounted on the wall of the building. The two connectors are screwed into the mating terminals on the grounding block. The grounding wire or grounding rod is then

inserted into an opening on the grounding block. A setscrew on the grounding block secures the wire or rod and assures a good ground connection.

The discharge devices for flat twin lead don't require the lead to be cut. The device is attached to the wall near the point where the antenna lead enters the building. A cover is removed from the device and the antenna lead is pushed into a channel running through the device. The cover is then replaced and a grounding wire is attached to the discharge unit. A screw terminal is provided for the gounding connection.

Installing plugs on coaxial cable

The coaxial lead-in is connected to the matching transformers (or, as noted previously, directly to the TV set) by pin plugs installed on the lead-in. The pin plugs connect to pin jacks at the antenna and receiver ends of the lead-in.

To install a pin plug, first use a wire stripper to remove about ¾ inch of the outer cable covering to expose the braided shield. Loosen the braid and fold it back over the outer covering of the cable. Trim the braid to about ¼ inch. Remove about ⅜ inch of the inner insulation with a wire stripper. Remove the collar from the connector. Slide the collar over the end of the cable, past the folded braid. The tapered end of the connector is designed to slip under the braid. Push it into the cable end until the tapered part of the connector is covered by the outer insulation and the folded braid is against the back of the connector. Slide the collar up to the back of the connector and crimp it with pliers to secure it to the cable.

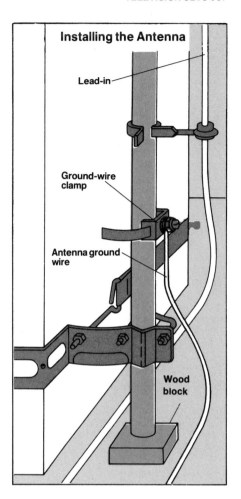

Installing the Antenna

Lead-in

Ground-wire clamp

Antenna ground wire

Wood block

Service controls

The service controls described below are the most common ones found on black and white and color sets. The items listed first are common to both; controls and adjustments specifically related to color are listed separately. Descriptions of special controls and front-panel operating controls can usually be found in the instruction manual that comes with your set.

Some sets may not have one or more of the external adjustments given here. Manufacturers try to make newer models more and more automatic. Some functions that once required manual adjustment may now be taken care of automatically in current models. Other adjustments can be made only internally on some models. In this case, the job should be left to a qualified serviceman.

Before you make any change in the setting of a rear control, mark the position of the control so you can return it to the original position if adjustment does not solve the problem. Control positions can be marked with a pencil or ballpoint pen on the back in line with the screw slot.

To keep track of the amount of adjustment, wrap a piece of plastic tape (3 or 4 inches) around the shank of the screwdriver and stick the tape ends together so they act as a pointer. For knurled knob adjustments, use a felt-tip pen to put a dot of color on the knob. Mark the back of the set at this same point. In most cases, only a one-eighth to one-quarter turn will be

needed. Turn the control slowly to allow the TV time to react to the new setting.

Because of the complexity of many TV circuits, external controls and adjustments may interact. That is, some adjustments require that two controls be adjusted alternately to obtain the desired result. Controls likely to interact are noted below.

Whenever possible, adjustments for overall picture quality—image sharpness, contrast, and color rendition—should be made during a live program originating locally (a local news program for example). Making the adjustments on a live local program eliminates picture peculiarities that may be caused by tape, film, or network programming.

Automatic gain control (AGC)

Gain refers to the amount of amplification that the incoming signal receives in the tuner and IF amplifier section of the receiver. Too much gain on strong signals can overdrive some circuits and damage parts of the set. To prevent this, an automatic gain-control circuit is built into the set. This circuit reduces the gain of the IF amplifier when strong signals are being received, and allows maximum gain on weak signals. The adjustment sets the upper limit to suit the strongest signal in your area.

To set the automatic gain control (AGC), first

select the channel in your area with the strongest signal. To find out which channel is strongest, set the contrast control to "minimum" (least contrast), then turn the selector to each available channel. Fine-tune if necessary. The channel that provides the best picture with a minimum contrast setting is the strongest signal.

With the strongest signal selected and contrast still at minimum, turn the AGC slowly clockwise. Turn until the picture distorts or breaks up, then turn back just enough to obtain a normal picture. If the AGC is set at its maximum position and the picture in the strong signal channel is satisfactory, no adjustment is required.

Automatic gain control delay

This adjustment sets a signal level at which the AGC circuit will be locked out to prevent reducing weak signals. To adjust this control, tune to a fairly strong channel on which some snow is visible. Adjust for the least amount of snow. If the control has no effect, return it to the original setting.

Horizontal hold

The horizontal hold varies the frequency with which the horizontal lines are painted on the television screen. Turning the horizontal control increases or decreases the horizontal scan rate, so that it is synchronized with the transmitted scan rate.

Vertical hold

This is normally a front-panel control; it varies the frequency with which complete pictures are painted on the screen. Turning the vertical hold varies the vertical scan rate so that it is synchronized with the transmitted scan rate.

Vertical size

The vertical size control adjusts the height of the picture. Adjustment should be set so that the picture extends slightly above and below the edges of the screen. Interaction may occur between this control and both vertical hold and vertical linearity.

Vertical linearity

This control adjusts the rate at which the horizontal lines are painted on the screen.
If the rate isn't uniform, part of the picture will appear either stretched or compressed. Make this adjustment on a picture whose general proportions are familiar to you. For example, it is easier to spot and correct stretching or compression on a head-and-shoulder close-up than on a full-length or distance shot.

Focus

The focus adjusts the size of the electron beam, which paints the picture on the face of the tube. The finer the beam, the sharper the focus. However, focus control is a matter of personal preference, and some viewers find a slightly soft focus pleasanter to look at.

Video peaking

Video peaking has somewhat the same effect on the picture as the focus control, but the action is different. Video peaking eliminates a type of high-frequency interference that appears as dot movement or busyness in picture detail. Eliminating this busyness, however, also reduces some picture detail. Adjustment of the control is a matter of preference.

Circuit breaker

Most sets are protected by a circuit breaker that turns off power to the set if an overload condition (a short) occurs. A knob or button on the back of the set allows the breaker to be reset. The circuit breaker control is usually red. Some overload conditions are temporary. Resetting the circuit breaker in these cases will restore normal operation. If the breaker turns off power as soon as it's reset or shortly thereafter, the condition is not temporary. A serviceman should be called in to correct the problem.

Color controls

Color killer. This control provides clear reception of black and white transmission on color sets by eliminating traces of color that might otherwise appear. To adjust, set the channel selector to an unused channel, then adjust the color controls on the front of the set for maximum color. Turn the color killer control fully counterclockwise. Snow will appear on the screen. Turn the color killer control clockwise to the point where the snow disappears. Now check the color picture on all channels. If color is missing on any channel, turn the color killer a bit farther clockwise until the channel has normal color.

Screen and drive controls. Screen controls set the operating level of each of the electron beams in the picture tube. Proper adjustment of these controls, known as the gray-scale tracking adjustment, will produce a color picture with good color balance in background and low-brightness areas. Also, when black and white transmission is being received, the picture will have proper gray tones.

Drive controls are ordinarily set as part of the gray-scale tracking adjustment. When the drive controls are properly adjusted, the colors in the brighter areas of the picture are balanced. If one color tends to dominate the picture, a slight counterclockwise adjustment of the appropriate control should correct the problem.

Some sets have three drive controls, others have two. On sets that have two controls, the red drive if fixed when the television set is assembled. Two controls allow blue and green to be adjusted to the red level.

When both controls are correctly adjusted, you will have the brightest color picture possible while still maintaining good black and white reception.

Service switch. Many sets have a two-position switch on the back of the set to simplify service adjustments. The two positions are marked NORMAL and SERVICE. The SERVICE position is used to make the gray-scale tracking adjustment described below. At all other times the switch should be in the NORMAL position. Some service switches also have a RASTER position for adjustments performed by a serviceman.

The procedures to use with and without the service switch are given below.

Adjusting color on sets with a service switch

1. Tune the set to a channel that has a strong signal. Turn off any front-panel automatic picture control. Adjust the brightness and contrast controls manually for a normal picture.

2. Turn all three screen controls fully counterclockwise. Turn all the drive controls (there may be either two or three) fully clockwise.

3. Set the service switch to the SERVICE position.

4. Turn the red screen control clockwise until a single red line is barely visible on the screen.

5. Turn the green screen control clockwise until a green line is visible on the screen. (If the green line coincides with the red line, a single yellow line will be visible.)

6. Turn the blue screen control clockwise until a blue line is just visible on the screen. (If this line coincides with the others, a single white line will be visible.)

7. Set the service switch to NORMAL. Turn the front-panel color control down (fully counterclockwise) to get a black and white picture.

8. The black and white picture should be completely free of color. If any color is visible in bright areas of the picture, adjust the appropriate drive control to remove it. (It is normal on many color tubes for the overall black and white picture to have a faint bluish or greenish cast.)

9. Turn the contrast and brightness controls over their full range. If the adjustment is correct, no color will appear in the picture.

Adjusting color on sets without a service switch

1. Tune the set to a strong signal channel. Turn down the contrast control, and set the brightness control for a slightly dim picture.

2. Turn off any front-panel automatic picture control and turn down the color.

3. Turn all three screen controls fully counterclockwise.

4. Turn the red screen control slowly clockwise until the picture appears slightly reddish.

5. Turn the green screen control clockwise until a lemon-yellow tinge appears in the picture.

6. Turn the blue screen control clockwise until the picture appears white or gray. (The other screen controls may have to be readjusted a bit.) Now adjust the drive controls.

7. Set the brightness and contrast control for a normal picture.

8. Turn down the color and tune in a black and white program.

9. Turn all drive controls fully counterclockwise.

10. Turn the red drive control clockwise until a slightly pink cast appears in the bright areas of the picture. NOTE: If your set has only two drive controls (blue and green), the pinkish cast should appear after step 9 has been completed.

11. Turn the green drive control clockwise until there is a slightly orange tinge in the bright areas.

12. Turn the blue drive control clockwise until a bluish-green cast appears in the bright area.

13. Adjust the blue and green drive controls—going back and forth between the two—until the picture highlights turn white. There should be no trace of color in the black and white picture. To check that the drive and screen controls have been set correctly, rotate the brightness control through its entire range. No color should appear in the picture while this is being done.

14. Turn the color control up again, and turn on any front-panel automatic picture control.

Typical picture problems

The remedies given here for some typical picture problems usually involve a check or an adjustment at the back of the set. Be sure to check the front-panel operating controls first. A complete loss of color on a set that had previously been operating properly could easily have been caused by a small child turning the color control to "minimum."

Television Sets Troubleshooting Chart
Internal Problems

	WHAT'S WRONG	REASONS WHY	WHAT TO DO
	There is vertical shrinkage (top and bottom).	Vertical size adjustment required	Make vertical size adjustment.
		Low line voltage	If other electrical devices in the house are not working properly, notify utility company of possible line voltage problem.
	Picture is distorted or shrinkage has occurred at top.	Incorrectly set vertical controls	Adjust vertical size and linearity controls.
	Picture shrinkage occurs at sides.	Incorrectly set horizontal controls	Adjust horizontal hold; if this is not effective, internal adjustment must be made by a serviceman.
	Picture breaks into black and white lines.	Incorrectly set horizontal hold	Adjust horizontal hold.
	Vertical roll occurs.	Incorrectly set vertical hold	Adjust vertical hold.
	Color is poor or there is color in black and white picture.	Incorrectly set color screen and drive controls	Adjust gray-scale tracking and drive controls.

	WHAT'S WRONG	REASONS WHY	WHAT TO DO
	Blotches of color remain stationary on screen.	Magnetized picture tube	Most sets have built-in demagnetizers. Turn set on for 60 seconds, then off for one-half hour; repeat this cycle three or four times. If color blotch is still present, have tube demagnetized by a serviceman.
	Snow occurs on all channels.	Weak signals reaching set	Check and replace defective antenna lead-in wire. Make sure antenna connections at back of set are tight. Examine antenna for broken elements and loose connections. Also check any preamplifiers, splitters, matching transformers for loose connections. Install high gain (fringe area) antenna.
	One color dominates picture.	Incorrectly set color screen and drive controls	Readjust screen and drive controls.
		If green dominates, picture tube possibly worn out	Replace picture tube or install a picture tube booster.

Television Sets Troubleshooting Chart
External Problems

	WHAT'S WRONG	REASONS WHY	WHAT TO DO
	There is hash (short horizontal lines) in picture.	Interference from auto, truck, or tractor ignition system	Reroute antenna away from source; use shielded antenna lead.
	Herringbone pattern is superimposed on picture.	Interference from diathermy equipment or two-way radio	Relocate antenna as far as possible from source; install a filter trap at antenna terminals on set.
	There are dark diagonal lines.	Interference from CB or similar radio	Install a filter trap at antenna terminals on set.
	There are white horizontal lines.	Set tuner amplifying a second channel signal, as well as the tuned one	Problem usually occurs when second signal is stronger than signal tuned to; use a more directional antenna (or rotor) to reduce strength at second signal.

Appendix

Basic Appliance Tools

A small selection of the right tools will make a tremendous difference in the speed, ease, and professional results of your appliance repairs and maintenance. The tools shown on these pages are a basic selection that will serve most appliance repair requirements.

Always buy quality tools; a cheap tool is no bargain. A poorly-made tool can let you down when you need it most, and can damage expensive appliances. Look for drop-forged tools rather than cast-iron ones—a drop-forged hammer will outlast a cast-iron one, and will not chip so easily. Look for strong handles and precise machining; a screwdriver with a flimsy handle and an ill-fitting blade may break off or strip screws.

Quality tools deserve quality maintenance. Clean tools thoroughly every time you use them. To prevent metal parts from rusting, wipe them with a cloth impregnated with a few drops of light oil. Protect sharp cutting edges by taking care not to bang them against other tools. Follow the manufacturer's instructions for maintaining power tools.

The insides of most appliances are somewhat delicate, so it is important to use tools of the right size. For example, an oversized screwdriver can slip off a screw as you twist, and damage or scratch the appliance's surface. Also, many appliances have rough or sharp edges inside. If you use too large a wrench to turn a nut and the wrench slips, you can get a nasty cut or scratch.

A volt-ohm meter (VOM) is used to test continuity and measure resistance (from 1 ohm to infinity), voltage (from 1/10 volt to 1,000 volts AC or DC), and current (only in the milliamp range).

A VOM's test leads and jacks are color-coded—the black lead is inserted in the black jack and the red lead in the red jack. When the metal probes or clips at the ends of the leads touch the items being tested, the meter indicates continuity or other circuit measurements. Many VOMs have insulated clips that are safer to use when making power-on tests.

A jumper lead is used to complete a circuit between two points that are normally not connected (such as the two prongs on an ordinary plug) when a test for continuity is being conducted.

A voltage tester is an insulated device consisting of a neon lamp and two probes. It indicates the presence or absence of voltage but does not measure the amount. When the probes touch the item being tested, the neon lamp lights if there is voltage; no voltage, no light.

A continuity tester merely indicates the presence or absence of continuity—whether or not a circuit is open. There are many types of continuity tester. The tester shown here is an electrician's flashlight with two clips. The jack plugs into the back of the flashlight and the flashlight switch is set at ON. The light goes on only if the tested circuit has continuity (or if the two probes touch each other). Without the tester leads, the flashlight works like an ordinary flashlight. Note the alligator clips at the ends of the probes.

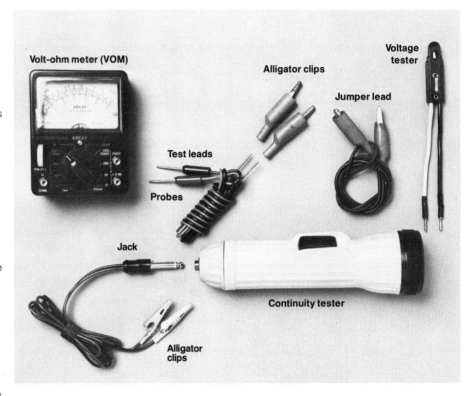

Volt-ohm meter (VOM)
Alligator clips
Voltage tester
Jumper lead
Test leads
Probes
Jack
Continuity tester
Alligator clips

Round-nose pliers are used to make loops in wires to be wrapped around screw terminals.

Flat-nose pliers are handy for removing small nuts or retrieving parts from shallow and easy-to-reach locations.

Diagonal cutters are used to cut wires and to cut off damaged or excess wire after a splice or a new connection is made.

Needle-nose, or long-nose, pliers are useful for getting into deeply recessed or other hard-to-reach places.

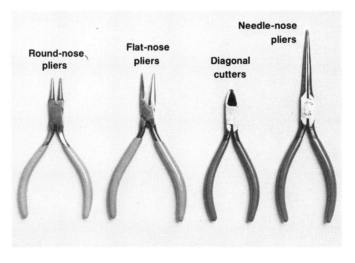

Round-nose pliers
Flat-nose pliers
Diagonal cutters
Needle-nose pliers

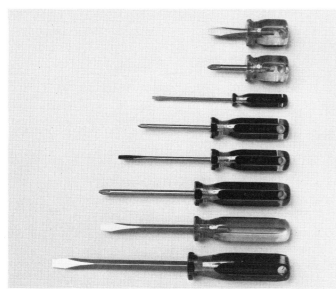

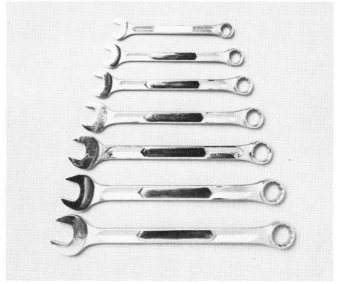

Screwdrivers are probably the most useful tools for appliance work. Shown here at the top are a flat-blade and a Phillips screwdriver, both with stubby shanks. They are called stubbies, and are used when space is too cramped for a driver with a longer shank. The next four screwdrivers (two flat-blade and two Phillips) have medium-length shanks and blades of increasing size; these are for larger screws. The bottom two screwdrivers have larger blades for very large screws (the bottom one has a thicker shank, for greater strength). The shank of a high-quality screwdriver is embedded deep in the handle, so that handle and shank cannot easily become loosened. Rubber-cushioned handles help prevent calluses and painful blisters.

Open-end wrenches, available in various sizes, are used to tighten or remove nuts and bolts. High-quality open-end wrenches are made of chrome vanadium steel machined to fine tolerances so that their openings provide a good fit around a nut. The openings on the wrenches are offset—set at an angle to the handle—to provide flexibility in tight spaces.

The box wrench at the opposite end of the tool can loosen nuts that are particularly tight. It surrounds the nut, providing turning force on all sides. Finely machined wrenches have a better fit, lessening chances that the wrench may slip—which could damage the appliance or injure your hand.

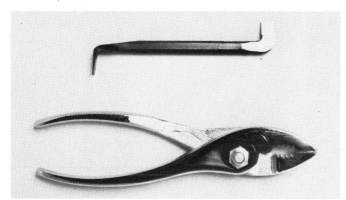

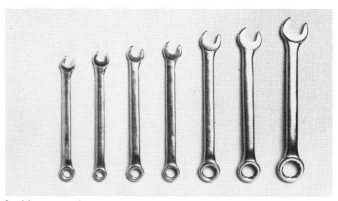

An offset screwdriver (top) is used to reach such inaccessible screws as those under the overhanging part of an appliance.

Ordinary pliers (bottom) have jaws that adjust to two positions. The jaws have a flat surface and a curved, serrated surface, for gripping both flat and curved objects.

Ignition wrenches are similar to open-end wrenches but smaller and lighter in construction; they are used on small nuts and bolts and in tight areas, where hexagonal nuts are often located. The box end can be used for very tight nuts or bolts.

Jeweler's screwdriver sets (right), for use on tiny screws, contain both Phillips and flat-blade screwdrivers, usually in five different sizes. The detachable shafts are interchangeable, fitting into one handle.

Allen wrenches (far right) are used on screws with recessed hexagonal heads. In effect, they are L-shaped keys, with hexagonal shafts, that fit into a recessed screw and also provide leverage. A basic set comprises eight sizes.

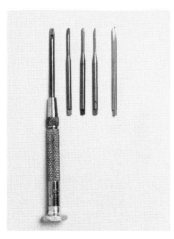

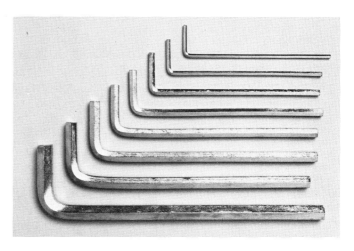

A socket wrench fits down over a nut or bolt to tighten, loosen or adjust it, exerting force on all sides, much like a box wrench (see page 313). The set of sockets (middle) fits nuts and bolts of different sizes, but each one has a ¼-inch drive socket in its bottom end. To work, sockets are attached to a nut driver with a ¼-inch drive (bottom), or to a ratchet handle with a ¼-inch drive (top). The ratchet can be set to turn the nut or bolt in one direction, and slip on the return swing. Working with a ratchet handle is often the fastest and easiest way to use socket wrenches. Other sockets and tools are shown at the top of the opposite page.

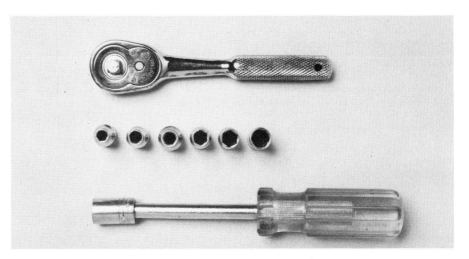

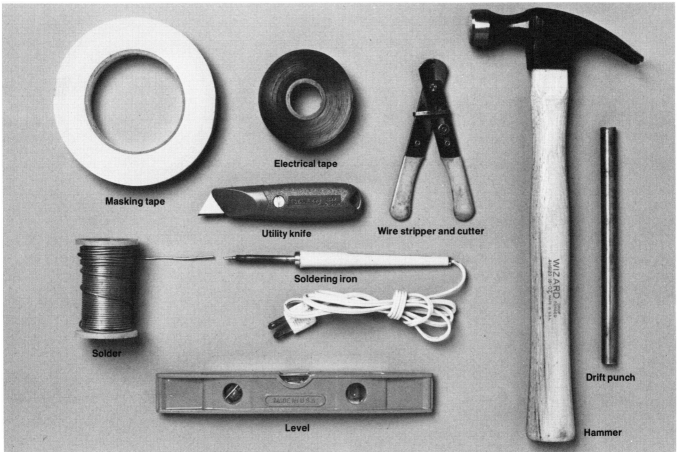

Masking tape

Electrical tape

Utility knife

Wire stripper and cutter

Solder

Soldering iron

Level

Drift punch

Hammer

Anyone repairing appliances at home should have on hand, in addition to the tools discussed, a number of ordinary basic tools and materials.

Masking tape is best for holding things in place and for labeling wire leads.

Electrical tape is used for taping wires together and insulating them, and for repairing cords.

Wire strippers and cutters are invaluable; they can be used for many sizes and types of wire, such as stranded or braided. An adjustable screw sets the blade opening so that a large number of identical wires can be cut or stripped rapidly. Most strippers have a spring that pops the cutter's handles open after each cut.

Hammers belong in every household. A high-quality claw hammer (shown here) with a solid handle (hickory, fiberglass, or tubular steel) and a drop-forged head is the best choice.

A drift punch is a brass rod used to separate or remove jammed steel components, such as the flywheel from the motor shaft of a garbage disposer. Since brass is softer than steel, the rod gives when it is hammered against the steel part and the latter is not damaged. (Often, a block of wood can be used for this purpose instead.)

A utility knife with a sharp blade has a number of uses in do-it-yourself repair. A knife with a retractable blade is safe and also keeps its edge when stored with other tools.

A soldering iron and solder are necessary for many electrical repairs. Shown here is a pencil-type soldering iron with an electrically heated tip, and a roll of electrical solder. Use only electrical rosin-core solder—not plumber's acid-core solder, which is corrosive on electrical connections.

A level comes in handy when, for example, you are installing an air conditioner. It is important that the unit tilt properly, so the water runs out the window rather than into the room. The level registers the tilt of the appliance instantly.

A set of sockets with a ⅜-inch drive (bottom right) is available to fit nuts and bolts from ¼-inch to 1 inch in diameter. The size increases in increments of 1/16 inch. Like the smaller sockets on the opposite page, these can be used with a nut driver (opposite, third from the top) or a ratchet handle, shown opposite without a socket, and middle, right with a socket attached. To reach recessed nuts or bolts, sockets can also be use with an extension (top) that is attached at right angles to the ratchet handle. The extension fits over the driver on the handle, while the socket fits over the small end of the extension. Socket sets can also be driven by breaker bars, T-bars, torque wrenches and impact wrenches.

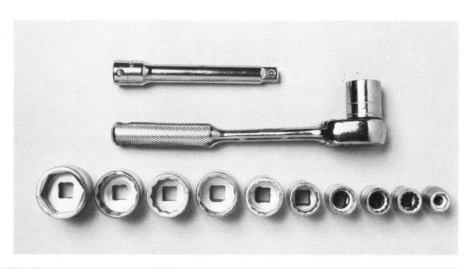

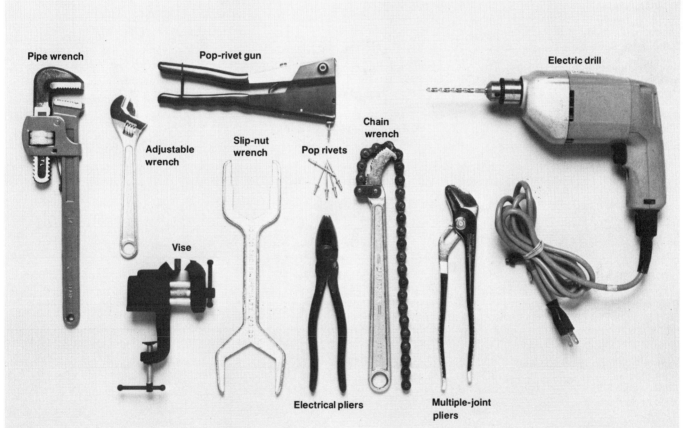

A pipe wrench is for fairly large jobs where considerable force must be applied to loosen and remove a fastener. (The wrench's toothed jaws can damage bright or soft metal.)

An adjustable wrench is an open-end wrench with smooth jaws. It is used for small jobs and is extremely useful and adaptable for appliance repair.

The pop-rivet gun and pop rivets are used where rivets must be replaced (see *Working with rivets,* page 193). Pop-riveting is much simpler than solid riveting and can be done when only one side of the work is accessible.

An electric drill is versatile. Bits are specialized for use on many materials such as wood, masonry, and metal, and they are available in a wide range of sizes. A power drill is necessary for drilling out rivets that hold defective appliance components. Power drills also have accessories for polishing, sanding, and grinding.

Multiple-joint pliers are for larger nuts and bolts. The number of span adjustments varies from tool to tool; five adjustments should be enough for

home repairs. Handles also vary in length. The longer the handle, the better the leverage; a 10-inch handle is usually adequate for home use.

The chain wrench and its companion, the strap wrench (not shown), are used when jobs are too large for an adjustable wrench. The chain (for hard surfaces) or the strap (for soft surfaces) is tightened around the piece to be removed, and the handle provides the leverage to turn the piece.

Electrical pliers have insulated handles that protect you from shock. They have a built-in diagonal cutter for wire cutting, and the jaws in front are flat for gripping flat surfaces. They are ideal for twisting wires together.

A slip-nut wrench is used to remove large nuts, like those on garbage disposers and plumbing traps.

The vise is useful for holding an appliance or component steady when you need both hands free—for example, when removing the spring-loaded leads from a switch or the brushes from an electric motor. A good vise should have jaws about 4 inches wide that open to at least 4 to 6 inches. The one shown here clamps onto any table or workbench.

Parts Suppliers

Some parts on appliances—like line cords, wire nuts, heat-sensitive fuses, strain reliefs, and diodes—can be replaced with parts meeting the same specifications, without regard to manufacturer. The best sources for these nonduplicate parts are local electronics stores, hardware stores, and repair shops.

Other parts—like housings, mounts, some switches, and bearings and gears, to name just a few—must be replaced with exact duplicates obtained from the manufacturer of the appliance or a supplier of those parts. When you order duplicate parts, look on the instruction booklet or warranty card of the appliance to find the address of the manufacturer or nearest authorized service center. To identify the part exactly, always send as much specific information about it as possible: include the make, model, and serial number of the appliance, a description of the part, and any name, number, or code letters on the part itself. If the part serves a cosmetic function, be sure to specify color.

The suppliers listed below stock parts—by brand—for most of the appliances covered in this book.

Large appliances

Appliance Parts Co.
15040 Oxnard St.
Van Nuys, Calif. 91411
Tel. 213-787-9220

Ray Jones Appliance Parts Co.
376 So. Broadway
Denver, Col.
Tel. 303-777-1222

Harris Appliance Parts Co.
51-29 Montgomery St.
Savannah, Ga. 31405
Tel. 912-352-2757

Automatic Appliance Parts Corp.
7757 West Lawrence Ave.
Norridge, Ill. 60656
Tel. 312-453-8384

M.G.M.S. Associates, Inc.
22 Water St.
Cambridge, Mass. 02141
Tel. 617-868-8360

Appliance Parts, Inc.
Box 1188
Minneapolis, Minn. 55440
Tel. 612-335-0931

St. Louis Appliance Parts, Inc.
2913 South Jefferson
St. Louis, Mo. 63118
Tel. 314-776-1445

Jacoby Appliance Parts Co.
269 Main St.
Hackensack, N.J. 07601
Tel. 201-489-6444

American Electric Washer Co.
1834 East 55th St.
Cleveland, Ohio 44103
Tel. 216-431-4400

W.L. May Co.
1120 Southeast Madison St.
Portland, Ore. 97214
Tel. 503-231-9398

Pearsol Appliance Co.
3127 Main St.
Dallas, Tex. 75226
Tel. 214-741-4638

Small appliances

California Electric Service, Inc.
1681 McGaw Ave.
Irvine, Calif. 92714
Tel. 714-545-5536

Woodall Electric Service Co.
1024 Monroe Drive, N.E.
Atlanta, Ga. 30306
Tel. 404-873-2236

Midwest Electrical Appliance Service
183 North York Rd.
Elmhurst, Ill. 60125
Tel. 312-279-8000

Allen Appliance Service
1300 East Central
Wichita, Kans. 67214
Tel. 316-262-7228

General Parts and Supply Co.
720 East Lake St.
Minneapolis, Minn. 55407
Tel. 612-827-5581

Electra-Craft, Inc.
348 West 42nd St.
New York, N.Y. 10036
Tel. 212-563-2885

DeMers Authorized Service
300 East Long St.
Columbus, Ohio 43215
Tel. 614-221-2321

Marshall Electrical Co.
200 Broad St.
Providence, R.I. 02903
Tel. 401-331-1953

Pearsol Appliance Co.
3127 Main St.
Dallas, Tex. 75226
Tel. 214-741-4638

Appliance Service Center
615 S. Second East
Salt Lake City, Utah 84111
Tel. 801-328-9703

Ajax Electric Co.
747 Fawcett
Tacoma, Wash. 98402
Tel. 206-383-3446

Index